"Children's Voices

Learn, Earn

& Become Famous!

Eleanor J. Marks

2017 Holocaust Essay Contest

Volume I

Sponsored by Bernard Marks

Sacramento, California

Printed in the United States of America
I Street Press
Sacramento Public Library Authority
828 I Street
Sacramento, CA 95814

Marks, Bernard, Editor
    "Children's Voices" Learn, earn & become famous! / Eleanor J. Marks Holocaust Essay Contest

Volume 1 ISBN: 978-1-945526-90-9
Volume 2 ISBN: 978-1-945526-91-6

1. Holocaust, Jewish (1939-1945). 2. Jews – Persecution – Germany. 3. Jews – Persecution – Poland. I. "Children's Voices". II. Eleanor J. Marks Holocaust Essay Contest, 2016. III. Bernard Marks.

ISSN: 2377-2565

Cover design by: Bernard Marks, Abbie Blackman and Gerald F. Ward
Text interior design by: Gerald F. Ward

Cover Pictures on Volume One: Blake Swenson, Savannah Risley, Page Kaufman, Samantha Bacon, Kate Gallager, Harris Prunier, Elyna Webber, Rionnan Stewart, Tom Zhang Franco, Anel Garcia, Lauren Buckmaster, Jeda Grey, Maria Eldrett-Wittenm, Anna Maagdenbergm Isabel Dixon, Ian Folkenstorm, Santiago Chang

Cover Pictures on Volume Two: Justin Cool, Spenser Wells, Gabriela Ocazones, Rena Wang, Dylan Wood, YongFen Lei (Sallay), Hanna Briggs, Dayita Biswa, Emily Shimada, Emely Seybold, Michelle Abarca, Lauren Rodenberg, Zola Grey, Sarah Becker, Luis Garbay, Madison Bennet-Wells, Sarah Cloninger, Adtya Rajavelu

www.ejmholocaustproject.com

1 2 3 4 5 6 7 8 9 10

2017 Eleanor J. Marks Holocaust Writing Project

History:

The essay-writing project began in 2008 at Congregation B'nai Israel, Sacramento, California with only four entries. In 2012 the project was opened to 6th-12th grade for public, religious and private schools in California as well as European schools. In 2014 undergraduate students from colleges and universities all over the world were eligible to participate. Over the past seven years the writing project grew to over 700 entries in 2017 alone.

Purpose:

The Eleanor J. Marks Worldwide Holocaust Essay Writing Project honors her memory by promoting remembrance and study of the Holocaust. It is also intended to enhance education in the schools through the annual essay-writing project.

The annual scholarship awards are given to winning students in each participating school:

One award of $150.00 to a student 6th –12th grades in each school

One award of $75.00 for runner-up in each school,

One award $150.00 for undergraduate college/university student.

Special awards of $50.00 selected by the Founder, Bernard Marks

Over sixty (60) judges evaluated the essays and determined the award recipients in each school.

Eleanor J. Marks Holocaust Essay Writing Project

Established 2008

Eleanor (Ellie) Marks (1931-2008) was the wife of Bernard (Bernie) Marks. These essays are dedicated to her memory.

Goals & Rules:

The goal of this annual writing project is for students to understand what the Holocaust means and why we say "Never Again."

The annual project commences no later than November 1 of each year. Essays are due no later than February 28 of the following year and must be submitted electronically as a Microsoft Word® document to **< hagibor52@gmail.com >**

To accomplish this task in a timely manner, the Judging Committee for 2017 consisted 60 plus community members. (See Judges names starting on page 564.)

Presentation of awards will be made during the Yom HaShoah (Day of Remembrance) Community event on April 23, 2017.

Awards:

1) $150.00 to one student from each school from grade 6 –12th , grade
2) $75.00 to one the runner up in each school grades 6 – 12th grade
3) $150 to the selected undergraduate essayist from a College/University
4) Special awards of $50.00 are selected by the Founder of the Eleanor J. Marks Holocaust Project.

PREFACE

How do you honor the victims of the Holocaust? The answer for Bernie Marks is to not let their spirit or memory fade. He does this by sharing their courageous stories with each new generation. His amazing personal story of survival, orchestrated by his father, illustrates how Bernie was able to endure the horrific death camps of the Nazi regime. This treasure of a man now gives first-hand accounts of the shocking truth behind genocide in an effort to ensure that these atrocities never happen again.

Obviously, as time goes on, the remaining survivors of the Holocaust become more rare. The value of Bernie's personal stories is irreplaceable and the youth understand this truth. When a slight man in his 80's can single-handedly engage 450 eighth graders, you know his message is riveting and very well received. After an assembly with Bernie, you will find a multitude of students lining up to simply shake his hand, ask additional questions, and/or take a picture. The students' "rock-star" treatment of Bernie validates the impact his message has on all in attendance.

Bernie Marks also continues to spread the truth of the Holocaust through an essay writing project that honors the memory of his late wife Eleanor J. Marks. This project allows students an opportunity to write an essay about Holocaust victims and the story behind their bravery and struggle to survive. As students research and compose their tributes to these everyday heroes, their awareness grows. At the same time, those who read their essays will understand that it takes purposeful action to prevent similar events. Bernie's message is clear that we must do all that we can to prevent the Holocaust and other events of genocide around the globe from happening again or continuing to take place.

Ron Rammer
Principal
Robert L. McCaffrey Middle School
Galt, California

INTRODUCTION

Near the end of my three-year-long graduate school experience, I was required to take a comprehensive examination on everything I had learned about German history. I recall stepping into the testing room with so little clue as to what would be asked of me. When I opened my blue book, the question that I saw was shorter than I expected: "Germany was the birthplace to the science, literature, and music that would help define culture and progress in the modern era. If this is so, how did Germany also become the birthplace of the Holocaust, an event that came to define so many of the horrors of the modern era?"

The answer was, and is, not an easy one. Simply put, while we think we know what we stand for as a society, humanity can be a fleeting thing. As a culture that prided itself on a nationalized pension plan, the speed of its automobiles, and the splendor of its medieval architecture, so much of Germany's sense of right and wrong faded overnight. Far from placing the west and its traditional bloc of democracies into the shoes of Interwar Germany, the simple take away should be that, as Americans, our own humanity and sensibilities for decency are just as susceptible to the wicked caprices of extremism and racial arrogance that affected Germany in 1933.

It is for this reason that cultivating a strong sense of humanity at the earliest of ages is imperative for a healthy democracy. And while learning from the past is engaging the past, this robust collection of essays provides a window into the bravery and sacrifice of those who stood willing to resist. To resist an ailing moral paradigm takes the strength of holding fast to one's own convictions, while thousands of voices are attempting to convince you otherwise.

What's more, with 70 years having passed between the Holocaust and today, the very act of writing enables tomorrow's leaders to explore the horrors of a broken society, giving them both a context for vigilance and a primer for understanding the earliest of warning signs.

Finally, this compilation showcases the talents and insights of some of today's finest young writers. The essays are written with a passion and dedication that should make the reader feel as if the future is in the hands of those who are willing to learn from the past and guard the sanctity of our collective future.

James C. Scott MA, MLS
Information Services Librarian

9e concours annuel de rédaction
SUR LE THÈME DE L'HOLOCAUSTE
à la mémoire de
ELEANOR J. MARKS

Pour encourager la commémoration, sensibiliser les étudiants à l'Holocauste et approfondir ce sujet.

"THÈME" 2017:
Heroes polonaise du HOLOCAUSTE
1939 — 1945
visitez: yadvashem.org

Faites des recherches sur le thème proposé, rédigez une rédaction et gagnez un prix.

Ce concours est ouvert aux étudiants de tous les établissements scolaires privés, publics, religieux et universitaires.

La rédaction doit être envoyée jusqu'au 28 février 2017.

N'hésitez pas à nous contacter par e-mail si vous avez des questions: haqbior52@gmail.com.

PRIX EN ESPECES!
Les prix suivants sont attribués à chaque établissement scolaire ayant participé:

- Premier prix pour les classes de niveau secondaire: 150$
- Deuxième prix pour les classes de niveau secondaire: 75$
- Prix pour les étudiants universitaires: 150$

Les gagnants seront publiés dans le journal mensuel "The Voice of Sacramento" et seront également annoncés lors de la cérémonie commémorative du Yom HaShoah, dédiée à la communauté de Sacramento. De plus, toutes les rédactions seront publiées dans un livre intitulé: *Les Voix des Enfants: Volume V.*

REGLEMENTS:

- Niveau secondaire- rédaction de 2000 à 3000 mots.
- Niveau universitaire: rédaction de 3000 à 5000 mots.
- Les rédactions doivent avoir une page titre contenant les informations suivantes: *En haut à droite:* nom, adresse, numéro de téléphone, adresse e-mail et le nom de l'établissement scolaire.
  En haut à gauche: une photo de l'élève qui a rédigé la rédaction.
- **Les rédactions doivant êtres rédigées avec un double interlignage en caractère 12.**
- **Les rédactions doivant êtres transmises au format Microsoft Word jusqu'au 28 février 2016 à l'adresse suivante: hagibor52@gmail.com (version électronique uniquement).**

Les récompenses seront remises le dimanche 1 Mai 2016 durant la cérémonie commemorative du Yom HaShoah, dédiée à la communauté de Sacramento.

„9. jährlich stattfindender Eleanor J. Marks Holocaust Essay Wettbewerb„

„Ehrt und erinnert an Eleanor J. Marks, fördert das Gedenken, die Sensibilisierung, die Auseinandersetzung mit dem Holocaust und fördert die pädagogische Erfahrung"
Website: ejmholocaustproject.com

Thema 2017:
„Polnische Helden des Holocaust"
1939 – 1945
Informationen unter: yadvashem.org
Wähle Helden, die von yadvashem.org aufgeführt sind!

Offen für Schüler, der Klassen 6 – 12 an kirchlichen, öffentlichen und privaten Schulen.	**PREISGELD!** Preisgeld in jeder Kategorie und für jede Schule:
	1. Preis: 150€ - ein Schüler der 6. – 8. Klassen 1. Preis: 150€ - ein Schüler der 9. – 12. Klassen
Einsende-schluss: 28. Februar 2018	2. Preis: 75€ - ein Schüler der 6. – 8. Klassen 2. Preis: 75€ - ein Schüler der 9.-- 12. Klassen
	Alle Einträge werden in einem speziellen Buch "Children´s Voices: " publiziert.
Fragen elektronisch an: hagibor52@gmail.com **oder persönlich an die zuständige Lehrkraft**	**REGELN:** Klasse 6 – 8: 850 – 1500 Wörter pro Essay Klasse 9 – 12: 2000 – 3000 Wörter pro Essay
	Einsendungen müssen in der oberen, rechten Ecke den Namen, Adresse, Telefonnummer, Email, den Namen eines Erziehungsberechtigten und den Namen der Schule beinhalten
	Essays müssen in Schriftgröße12 in Microsoft Word getippt werden. Einsendungen per Email bis zum Einsendeschluss an: hagibor52@gmail.com

Table of Contents

Shalom School 432

Sutter Middle School 452

Katherine L. Albiani Middle School, Elk Grove, CA

Harpreet Sidhu has been teaching for 20 years. She currently teaches middle school at Katherine L. Albiani Middle School in the Elk Grove Unified School District. Mrs. Sidhu is honored to serve as an advisor to the students at her school to participate in this powerfully engaging educational opportunity.

Megan Wojan, a 7th grade middle school teacher in the Elk Grove Unified School District, finds it deeply rewarding to educate her students on the historical truths of the Holocaust. Through participation in the Eleanor J Marks essay contest, her students have developed a deeper understanding of the importance of social equality, dignity, and respect. She hopes that her students will continue to educate future generations allowing us to 'never forget' the victims, survivors, and heroes of the Holocaust.

Justin Pereira has taught for the Elk Grove Unified school District for 13 years at the middle school level. As a 7th grade Social Science teacher, his students have been deeply moved by the events of the Holocaust and have developed a great level of empathy for the victims and survivors. He is privileged to help his students remember and honor the heroes of the Holocaust through the Eleanor J Marks Essay Contest

Irena Sendler

Aashish Kumar

 The holocaust caused huge trauma and loss to the world and the families. It all started when World War II broke out. When the people had lost all of their confidence in their government, the Germans came and took the city of Poland. In 1934, over 8 million Jews were alive but after the massacre of the holocaust only 1 person out of 5 people survived. The Germans were so brutal that they even went around and killed the disabled and the others in many different ways such as gas chambers or through starvation in the ghettos. Hitler was the leader of the Nazis, and he put certain rules that mostly applied to the Jews like they weren't allowed to hold a position in a public office and they didn't have the same rights as those of German citizens. Many Jews even tried to move to other countries for their own protection. Some countries wouldn't let the Jews in because they didn't want the Nazis to be there. Hitler even ordered all the Jews under Germany's control to be transported back to the cities in Poland. Out of these people, there were many brave survivors who fought through this horrible period of depression. One of them was Irena Sendler. She was a social worker, 29 years old at the time, and employed at the Welfare Department of the Warsaw municipality. After the Germans arrived in the city, her whole life was never the same.

Irena Sendler's story started when the Germans came to the city of Poland and started to make rules against the Jews. All the Jews had to wear a Star of David on their chest to show who they were. Many people were neglected and stayed away from Jews because they were taught that Jews were not good people to have. Irena helped the Jews because of that, but the Germans made the oppression even worse. The ghettos were closed off in November 1940. About 400,000 people were sent to those places and were treated very cruelly. They only got a small portion of food each day, but their condition became worse with epidemics and diseases spreading throughout the ghetto. Even though Irena wasn't a Jew herself, she still felt bad for the Jews inside the ghettos. Irena tried to help the dying Jews by getting a permit to go inside the ghetto from the municipality. Once she got inside the ghetto, she sneaked Jews out of the ghetto, put them into another part of the city and hid them away from the Germans. There was a great danger with her doing this because she could be arrested, put in a ghetto, or even be killed for helping the Jews escape. After a while, a new company was established called Council for Aid to Jews, and Irena was one of its main leaders. Even though thousands of Jews had been killed, they could still help the rest of the survivors who were struggling to hide. About 4 months later, Irena was designated as head director of Zegota's Department of Care for Jewish Children. She gave all the surviving children fake names and sent them to orphanages in Warsaw. On 20 October 1943, she was arrested but luckily she hid the evidence of the children's coded address with the Zegota. She was sentenced to death but underground activists bribed them to release her. Even after she was released, she continued to help Jews in secret. Since she was in danger and hiding, she wasn't able to attend her own mother's funeral.

Unfortunately, on May 12, 2008, Irena Sendler died due to an illness that increasingly got worse. She was credited with saving the lives of 2500 Jewish children in the Warsaw ghetto. They even planted a tree in honor of her in front of the entrance to the *Avenue of the Righteous Among the Nations.*

The Holocaust was a horrible time and so many Jews died in the process. There were many strong and brave people who helped the Jews escape and flea to other places risking their lives for someone else. I've learned that certain people shouldn't be targeted just because of their race or religion. Everyone should be treated the same. Learning about Irena Sendler has taught me to be more sensitive about how I talk to people, and I make sure that I don't offend them with anything I say. "Never again", a phrase used by the survivors of the Holocaust, means the Holocaust should never happen again. That phrase means a lot because it shows how much trauma and depression they've gone through that they don't even want to see it happen again. Some things we can do to prevent this from ever happening again are to not offend people because of what they worship and to make others feel equal to yourself, not different. We can also try to live a nonviolent lifestyle and not spread rumors about certain people's religion or life. After an event like the Holocaust, it is really important to remember the phrase "Never Again."

Works Cited

"Irena Sendler." *United States Holocaust Memorial Museum*. United States Holocaust Memorial Museum, n.d. Web. 11 Dec. 2016.

Marks, Eleanor. "Holocaust Speech." Holocaust. Kams, Elk Grove. 10 Nov. 2016. Speech.

Wojan, Megan. "Intro to The Holocaust." Intro to The Holocuast. Kams, Elk Grove. 4 Nov. 2016. Lecture.

""Women of Valor"" *Irena Sendler - Stories of Women Who Rescued Jews During the Holocaust - Righteous Among the Nations - Yad Vashem*. N.p., n.d. Web. 11 Dec. 2016.

Wincenti Tosza

Abhijith Tamatam

During the horrid days of the Holocaust, many people such as Jews, homosexuals, and the disabled were held captive in terrible camps which they were starved and abused. These innocent people were usually taken to these death camps in wagons with no ventilation and were provided without food, water, nor a toilet. When they finally did reach the camps, most of the captives were found dead due the harsh conditions. The few that did survive were separated from their families, shaved, and undressed so they would be exposed to the harsh climates and disease. Thanks to this, out of thousands of people, only about twenty people survived. At this time, all Germans were not bad people. There were thousands of people in Germany and Poland who fought for the Jews and the disabled. These people were later known as the Righteous among the Nations.

Among the Righteous was a man named Wincenti Tosza who helped a Jew named Stanislaw Hojda who escaped the nearby Plaszow Concentration Camp. Wincenti Tosza was a Catholic police officer who unwillingly had to serve the Germans after the Nazis came into power. Wincenti later moved to Radziszow, the village of his wife, Aniela's family due to his unhappiness with the Germans. Before the horrible war, Wincenti and Stanislaw had been acquainted because Stanislaw had been a furrier and sold the police officers' wives goods such as furs. Tosza had been generous enough to provide Stanislaw with food, clothing to wear, water, a home to live in, books, newspapers, and much more as if Stanislaw was part of his own family. Wincenti Tosza sheltered Stanislaw Hojda in his garret on top of his house for twenty-two months and one day. If there were any rude German soldiers or officers in the area looking for Jews that were left behind or ones that escaped, Wincenti and his son Tadek Tosza, then eleven at the time would hide Stanislaw Hojda so he wouldn't be found and taken away. Wincenti and Tadek made a brilliant plan to keep Stanislaw from being found by the Germans. First of all, Tadek would warn them of them of the impending danger. Then, both the father and son would hide Hojda under a fairly sized pile of hay and then they both poured piles on top of Hojda and the hay so the Germans' dogs would get confused and not smell Hojda in the pile of hay but would move on and sniff in some other place on the Tosza property. Thanks to this method, Hojda and the Tosza's were able to fool the confused Germans and their dogs which were breed to sniff out humans out of their hiding spots. After, nearly two years went on like this, and everyone in the Tosza family was wondering when the war would stop and who would be defeated. When Germany had finally been defeated, and Hitler was dead, the Tosza family cheered and wept in happiness as though they thought this day would ever come. The Tosza family was not the only people living in the household that were happy though. Stanislaw Hojda was also was very overjoyed to hear the great news. Even though Stanislaw was sad about leaving the Tosza family behind, he wanted to see if his own family was alive and if they were, he wanted to know where they were. Even after the Holocaust was long gone, new memories and friends were and are being made.

From learning about the Holocaust, one can experience things that they never though were possible or exist. My experience of the Holocaust taught me many things and I reacted to these things with different emotions. First of all, I learned that the Holocaust was a sad time for many people, especially the ones that lost dear family members and wanted them to be back in their home. This time must have also brought back anger and people must have wanted revenge for what had happened to them, their families, and their friends. In addition, the impact that learning about this person had on my life was a big one and really gave me a different view on how I see things now. Wincnti and his family risked their lives to save someone who they did not know too well. That is and will forever remain a great act of bravery that everyone should do if they find someone in danger or in need. In one way or another this makes me feel proud of someone I have never met nor seen. Along with this, I have learned that the Holocaust was a dreadful thing and the impact it had on people was huge. From this experience I learned that Jews lives were constantly in danger because of the German soldiers and officers hunting them down. The people that tried to protect the Jews were also in danger for supporting the innocent Jews. Many of the Jews lost their homes and the few that did survive had to start from scratch and make a new living. The Holocaust should never again happen and I will do all within my power to stop this from happening to anyone or anything. I will make sure that all the new leaders are kind and just but if they are not, I will do all I can so people will not want them to be their next leader. Equally important, we can take quite a few steps to make sure that something like this will never happen again. I could start a program to show people what will happen if bad leaders are chosen. I will also show people to learn from the past and never to ignore it. As one can see, something like the Holocaust should never happen again if we want this would to be a safe and better place.

WORK CITED

"National Archives |." *National Archives and Records Administration*. National Archives and Records Administration, n.d. Web. 12 Dec. 2016.

"91 Interesting Facts about the Holocaust | FactRetriever.com." *FactRetriever.com*. N.p., n.d. Web. 12 Dec. 2016.

Yad Vashem. N.p., n.d. Web. 12 Dec. 2016

Bani, Zofia

Abran Ramirez

 The holocaust was a very devastating event in our world history where over six million people were killed. The holocaust started with Adolf Hitler and his political party the National Socialist German Workers (The Nazi Party) in the early 1930's. The Nazis came to power in 1933 and believed that Germans were a "master race". Adolf Hitler was the leader of the Nazi party that spread the propaganda to a hopeless Germany. In the 1930's Germany was hopeless because millions of people were unemployed and they had lost faith in what they thought was a weak government. That's when Adolf Hitler came supposedly to help the German government and it's people. Nazi propaganda included films, art paintings, and books that stated that Germans were stronger, superior, and more attractive than any other race. After Adolf Hitler started to make Laws against Jews, Jewish people began to leave Germany. With these Laws Adolf Hitler started to label Jews with big yellow stars. Then they were put in ghettos so they would starve or die from diseases. Adolf Hitler didn't think the jewish people were dying fast enough so he put Jews in concentration camps or harsh slave-labor prisons. Concentration camps were built to kill the weakest Jews first including children and Women. In concentration camps 6,000 people could and would be killed a day. The one third that survived concentration

camps either escaped Germany or got help from very brave and caring people that risked their lives like Bania, Zofia.

Zofia Was born in 1907 and died in 12/06/1991. Zofia was Catholic and helped the married couple Israel and Franciszka hide from the Nazi. Zofia was a poor farmer and sometimes Frainie would help her out by giving her supplies and other food. After a while they got to know each other and became very good friends. One day Frainie had asked Zofia if they could stay in her house to hide from the Nazi. Zofia said she needed to think about it. After hearing more rumors about the Nazi's Israel decided to build an underground basement under his store. Frania and Israel had hid in the basement till October of 1942 because the Germans started to round up the Jews of Pinczow and send them away to Treblinka an extermination camp. After the roundup was over Franina and Israel needed somewhere else to stay because they would soon be caught in their basement. They were thinking of going to Russia but could not because Frania was eight months pregnant. Then they heard the news that Zofia was looking for them back in Pinczow. To get to Zofia's place they had hired a man that they trusted to take them the Zofia's house in a wagon.

Frania and Israel weren't welcomed by Zofia's husband Ludwig as much as Zofia welcomed them. Israel and France were worried that Ludwig would betrayed them so they gave him money to stay quiet. Frania and Israel first lived in the barn attached to the house and then moved in the main room with Zofia, Ludwig, and their son Maniek. The house was very safe because the closest neighbor was a half of kilometre away and they had bought a watch dog that barked when someone approached the house. At some times they would hide in the cellar for extra safety.

The dog did a very good job at protecting the house. He warned Israel and Frania that Germans soldiers were approaching the house. Israel and Frania managed to slip into the cellar. They would have to stay there the whole night because the German soldiers were planning to stay the night. Maniek had his bed moved in front of the cellar to keep the German soldiers from noticing.

Maniek played an important role in saving Israel and Frania lives. He was a young boy but understood what was going on. The night the German soldiers came Israel had a really bad cough so Maciek pretended to be sick the whole night. He was coughing and crying very loudly the whole night in order to overpower Israel's coughing.

Zofia kept Frania and Israel in her house until 1945 when the Red Army liberated the area. Frania and Israel moved to Canada after the war. Frania and Israel came back to Poland to visit Zofia with their son Saul Rubinek.

While writing this project i have learned that the Holocaust was a very important event in world history. The lost lives of millions of innocent people by an extreme ruler was an unbelievable tragedy, that should not have happened. It should teach us the importance of treating everyone with respect understanding and equality, No matter what your race or religion. The risk Zofia took for Israel and Frania did not only change their lives but their children's, grandchildren's, and the people's lives that read her story. Never Again will this happen in history as long as we treat each other with respect, kindness, and if we open our minds to accepting other race's, religion, and people with other points of views. We can prevent history from repeating itself by voting for leaders that believe in uniting our country instead of separating our country with extreme beliefs and laws.

Works Cited

"United States Holocaust Memorial Museum." United States Holocaust Memorial Museum. United States Holocaust Memorial Museum, n.d. Web. 7 Dec. 2016.

Wogan, Megan. "The Holocaust." The Holocaust. California, Elk Grove. 11 Nov. 2016. Lecture.

"Yad VAshem." Yad Vashem. N.p., 2016. Web. Nov.-Dec. 2016.

Julia Pępiak

Adam Mahmoud

Germany was suffering great economic hardship during the late 1920's and 1930's. The Germans had been defeated in World War I, and had been forced to pay a great amount of money to the Allies. As a result, Germany encountered terrible economic hardship with many people being unemployed. Led by Adolf Hitler, the German Nazis blamed the Jews for the hard times they were experiencing. His intolerant policies eventually led to a sophisticated plan to annihilate the Jewish people.

Julia Pępiak made the ultimate sacrifice by risking her and her children's lives at the time when the Nazis controlled Germany. Julia gave up everything she had to protect the lives of other people who were in danger. This was a very noble thing for Julia to do, especially because she didn't even have the same beliefs as the people she was helping. Julia dedicated herself to the security and protection of mother and daughter, Salomea and Bronia Hellmann.

In 1941, the Germans had occupied the Lwów ghetto in Poland. Despite being Roman Catholic, Julia found it in her heart to save Salomea and Bronia Hellmann who were Jewish and were under persecution by the anti-Semitic Nazis.

Because of threats being made to their Jewish race, Salomea and her daughter Bronia fled from Lwów and went into hiding in Belzec. Belzec was the birth town of Salomea. While arriving in Belzec, they went to Julia Pepiak, an old friend and neighbor, seeking not only shelter, but also safety. Julia disregarded her family's safety for Salomea and Bronia. Julia prepared a hiding place for Bronia in her barn, and protected and cared for her. However, despite precautions Julia took to ensure Bronia's safety, rumors quickly started spreading that Julia was hiding a Jewish person. This was a huge threat to Julia. At times, she even had to move Bronia to a pit in her wheat field. These rumors went to such a far extent that two SS men, who were serving in the nearby death camp, were stationed in Julia's home. However, when the dangers were clear, Julia would move Bronia back into the barn. This situation repeated itself many times. Bronia remained in Julia's security and protection until the area they were in was liberated by the Red Army. The Red Army freed the area of Belzec in July of 1944.

In the course of time in which Bronia had been living with Julia, Bronia's mother, Salomea, had been caught by the Nazis. She was taken and transferred to many concentration camps, but she was able to survive. Salomea managed to stay alive long enough for the Red Army to liberate her. Julia was able to return Bronia back to Salomea. After the war was over and everything had settled down a little bit, both Salomea and Bronia emigrated to Israel. Julia Pępiak had finally completed her near impossible mission of protecting Bronia throughout much of the Holocaust.

In my opinion, Julia Pepiak, along with the many other people that did what she did during the Holocaust, are brave, noble heroes. Julia put her family in extreme danger to help protect the lives of other people. I learned that going out of your way to help people can often be better than focusing on your own self interests. Also, it is not always good to go along with the flow of society. Just because many other people are doing something doesn't mean it is the right thing. If so, it is always good to do what you believe is right to benefit not only yourself, but other people as well. Julia Pępiak went against the society and did what she thought was right by protecting Jewish people, such as Salomea and Bronia Hellmann.

Learning about Julia Pępiak impacted my life by making me realize everything I take for granite. For example, Julia had to hide Bronia in a barn and constantly move her to a pit in a wheat field. Bronia had no home for about three years. Not only did Bronia live in these terrible housing conditions, but she was also away from her mom during this time. This makes me realize how I take my home and the people that help me through hard times for granite.

The Holocaust is something that should happen "Never Again." We can do many things in our everyday lives in order to make sure that nothing like this ever happens again. For example, we can show kindness and respect to each other so that no conflict erupts between people. The Holocaust was a tragic event, but people like Julia Pępiak minimized the damage done to society.

Works Cited

"Belzec: The Forgotten Camp." *Aishcom*. N.p., n.d. Web. 11 Dec. 2016.

Jrose. "Summaries." *Summaries, Arts, Monash University*. N.p., n.d. Web. 11 Dec. 2016.

"Saving Jews: Polish Righteous." *Saving Jews: Polish Righteous*. N.p., n.d. Web. 11 Dec. 2016.

"Saving the Jews." *Google Books*. N.p., n.d. Web. 11 Dec. 2016.

Yad Vashem - Request Rejected. N.p., n.d. Web. 11 Dec. 2016.

Krzyk Zofia

Adam Wanlin

In the early 1900s after WW1 Germany was in a great depression. They didn't know what to do, so they, for no reason, blamed it on the Jews. The Germans were harsh and cruel to the Jews for no reason. When the Germans started taking the Jews to extermination camps and ghettos, there were outstanding people who tried to stop it. They would hide the Jews in their attic or their basement or even change their identity to save them. In fact many gave their own lives to save their friends. One of those people was a women named Zofia Krzyk. She was just an average woman who was a grocery seller and farmer. But what she did was so outstanding and powerful. Because of all the things that happened then even though people that saved lives just couldn't do it all. Because of the death count and inhumanity against a race was so bad, that is why survivors say one simple quote that means so much, "never again". These two simple words are what survivors us to tell young people and future generations to never make the same mistake. But Zofia Krzyk showed us how helping people can mean an even bigger deal and that it can even be lifesaving.

Now, back to the topic of Zofia Krzyk. She was born on the first of March, 1925. She was born in Poland in a Christian family. She was a farmer and a grocery seller, kind and young, she didn't stand out very much. But, when the holocaust started, she would stand out more than anybody else. She hid 22 people and did whatever she could to protect them. She supplied them with food, water, shelter, and protection. The place she stayed in during the war was Nowe Brzesko, Miechow, Kielce, Poland. The names for all of the people she saved are still all known. She saved these 22 people, she saved the Strosberg family, people of the last name Akerman, Weissman, Two people by the name of Rozali, Rosa, Rozia, Beker, Friada, Fredzia, Alfrida, Frishman, Maria, Kornreikh, Hana, Hanka, Anna, and finally Roman. Her bravery actually got her name to be listed on to the Wall of honor in New Orleans. She is also one of more than 6,000 Poland righteous and is located on the same wall of honor with them. Only a few people were able to make it on to the wall of honor. Zofia had a brother, Wladislaw Skora. Zofia and her brother, Wladislaw, hid and supplied the Strosberg family at their home between November 1942 until they were liberated. Later in 1944, the father, Shalom, and his brother were able to join them. They all survived through much hardships. Zofia Krzyk was recognized as Righteous Among the Nations by Yad Vashem in the year 2001. She and her brother were both very important by hiding and protecting these people. He was also a farmer and he actually did some of the more dangerous work compared to his sister. He did the same supplying goods and hiding the people. But, he also did illegal transfer and arranging shelter. He actually rescued the same people as his sister but for some reason he was short by one. His sister saved 22 and he only saved 21. But he wasn't the only person who helped. Her father (unknown) and Shalom helped her in saving the large group of people. The main people that the Skora family saved is the four Strosberg sisters who were in much danger because they were Jewish. The four sisters were just a few Jewish friends that were in desperate help because they were being discriminated and they were scared for their lives. Because of Zofia's kind heart, these four young girls got to live, survive, and thrive after the war.

Because of the discrimination against Jews was so bad, somebody had to stand up. This simple Polish woman decided to take that stand. She was brave kindhearted and put so much effort into saving these people. Her bravery saved 22 people and she worked so hard to keep them safe. Her brother Wladislaw also fought hard in trying to protect these young girls even if he had to take risks like illegal transfer and hiding fugitives. She did the same, even if more, she cared for them like a family in need. She thought that everyone should equal rights and that Jews shouldn't be blamed on. She thought that they should have blamed themselves, the Germans, for being so selfish and not blaming the Jews just for being a witness. The young, the smart the brave young girl that decided to help a few people, changed the lives of many. And because of her bravery and determination, she reminds us of how we should always be good to people. She showed us how we are able to stop a horrible thing. But because of the horrible things that other people did, it reminds us of how we should say the two strong words that will hold our nation and many other too from a crisis like this to never happen again. Just two words to keep the world in peace, and those strong two words are,"never again". In all, this one woman helped many people and kept us full of hope and to make sure this never happens again.

Josef Balwierz
Aidan Eller

 The Nazi's were a political party that were in charge in Germany in the 1930's and early 1940s and started World War II by invading Poland in 1938. The Nazi party was led by a man named Adolf Hitler. Besides wanting to take over the world, Hitler wanted to make a master human race by getting rid of people he felt were less pure than Germans. This led to the Holocaust occurring during WWII. The Holocaust was a horrible event where millions of Jewish people, as well as gypsies, homosexuals, and communists were killed by the German Army. Many families were separated from each other, husbands and wives were taken apart and children were taken from their parents. The Jewish people had their belongings stolen from them, and they were forced to work in labor camps without proper food or warm clothes. Some Jewish people were experimented on by Nazi scientists. Six million Jewish people were murdered by the German Army by being shot, hanged, or put in gas chambers at concentration camps. Others were starved to death or died from infections from no medical treatment. Many people saw this happening to the Jewish families and did not do anything to help them. The person I am writing about did do something about it and saved a Jewish family.

Jozef Balwierz was born in Poland, January 1, 1919. Jozef was not Jewish but he felt a strong passion to help the Jewish people, especially the people he worked with. Jozef worked in a factory in Lwow that belonged to a Jewish family by the name of Liebeskind. The Liebeskind Family included Shmuel, his wife Zofia and their two daughters, Rita and

Irena. The year was 1941, and World War II was at a peak. That same year, the German Army reached Lwów and the Liebeskind family was sent to a ghetto to live with many other Jewish families. Unfortunately, the father of the Liedeskind family, Shmuel, was killed later in 1941.

In 1942, Zofia and her two daughters managed to escape from the ghetto and travelled to Krakow, where they were successful in reaching Jozef Balwierz, their old employee from the factory. Jozef offered them shelter at his house and said he would help them in any way he could. Josef knew that if he was caught helping the Leisbeskind family, or any other Jewish people, then he would be killed and the rest of the Liesbeskind family would be sent back to the ghetto or killed. Jozef decided to help them anyways. Jozef also helped their family members, Elka Bardech, (later changed to Idle) the daughter's cousin. Elka later was able to find a job stable as a housekeeper with a German family. When the war worsened and it was unsafe in Krakow, Jozef and the remaining Liebeskind family moved to Austria and Jozef later married Irena, the daughter of Shumuel and Zofia Liebeskind. Later in life when people asked Josef why he risked helping the Liebeskind family and others, Jozef said that he felt that it was his duty as a human being to help the Jewish family. He also said that he did not expect or want a reward for his action to save the Jewish family. On August 6, 2007, Josef was recognized by Yad Vashem as Righteous Among the Nations.

While reading about the Holocaust and Josef Balwierz, I learned that some people will face danger or death for themselves so they can help the people they care about. I also learned that war is horrible, and the Nazi's were evil people and treated the Jewish people horribly. The impact on my life was that I realized how important it is to me to stand up for those I care about, and that in a place where I was threatened, I would hope I would do the same as Josef did. I also learned that if a lot more people would have helped instead of staying silent to save themselves, a lot more Jewish families could have been saved. I understand the Holocaust was wrong and that people should stop hating other people based on what they believe in. I also know that many families were separated and that a lot of those families did not survive or never saw their parents or brothers and sisters again. "Never Again" means that this should never happen again and is very wrong. Many things can be done to help stop the Holocaust from being repeated. One step is that we all look at each other equally as humans, and no one is better than another. Another step is to make sure to stick up or stand up for people that are being bullied, or when we see someone like Hitler and the Nazi's starting to come to power, that the world come together against them.

The Holocaust was one of the saddest and evil events in the world's history. The above story is likely what happened to most Jewish families during the Holocaust and this is why we shouldn't forget what happened.

Maria Eckhardt

Ajay Kalotia

In the 1930s, Germany hit a depression and many people lost their jobs and money. This depression made many things unorganized and this gave an opportunity for a new leader. This new leader would become, Adolf Hitler. Adolf Hitler brought his Nazi party with him. On January 1933, the Nazis came to power. The Nazis called all Germans a master race. During the Holocaust, the Nazis killed six million Jewish citizens. Hitler established many acts to ensure that the Nazi message was communicated everywhere. Hitler established a Reich ministry of public enlightenment and propaganda. Hitler communicated his message through art, music, theater, film, books, radio, and the press. The Nazis passed many laws against the Jewish people. Jews were not allowed to hold public office, Jews were deprived their rights of German citizenship, and all Jews forced to wear yellow stars on their clothing to indicate that they were Jewish.

After many of these harsh acts, Jews started to flee Germany, but not all countries would allow more citizens. Eventually, Hitler ordered Jews to go to certain cities within Poland. In these cities, "Ghettos", all Jews were treated terribly like animals. These ghettos were very crowded. The Nazis main plan for these ghettos was for the Jews to gain disease or to starve to death. Jews formed resistance camps within the ghettos. Hitler realized that these ghettos were not killing the Jews fast enough, so the Nazis came up with their final solution. This final solution, was to start killing people one by one, all races. Hitler sent his security force to isolate Jews and shoot them into pits. Some Jews were not killed, but became saves. Hitler made the prisoners work everyday, and if they did not work fast enough they were beat or killed. In the camps, families were separated and everyone had to change their look. People got their heads shaved, arms tattooed, and wore prison uniforms. The last act to start killing Jews was from gas chambers. The prisoners were told that they were about to get ready for a shower, but in reality they were getting ready to get killed. Gas came out of the water faucets, killing 6,000 people a day. In this miserable period of the Nazi takeover, six million Jews were killed. Less than four million Jews survived the Holocaust. Some of the survivors had help from non-Jewish people who were against Nazi's. One of those helpers was Maria Eckhardt.

The person that Maria Eckhardt saved was Kalina Kleinberg. Kalina Kleinberg was hiding in Tarnopol, Poland. Maria Eckhardt and Kalina knew each other because their kids were childhood friends. Before the Nazi massacre, Maria told Kalina Kleinberg could spend the night at their house whenever she pleased. When The massacre had begun, Kalina remembered this offer, and asked if she could hide at Maria Eckhardt's house. Maria Eckhardt cared for Kalina Kleinberg and agreed to let her hide. Kalina hid behind a mirror in a bedroom in the Eckhardt household. Kalina hid at Eckhardt household until 1944 when the Red Army liberated the area. After the massacres of the Holocaust, Kalina immigrated to the United States. this act of help and care showed that Maria Eckhardt was against Hitler and the Nazis a lot. This also shows that Maria is very kind and cares a lot for Kalina.

From these tragic acts of the Holocausts, I learned that Jews were treated very poorly and that the Jewish population was cut down from the harsh Nazi's. I learned that because of depression in Germany, Jews were treated miss poorly and a new leader can change everything. The impact that Maria Eckhardt had on my life is to fight for what you think is right. Maria Eckhardt knew she was risking her life to save a Jew, but she was fighting for what she thought was right. I understand that the Holocaust was a harsh time for all Jews and that it could have been stopped. This tragic time hurts me and I hope that something like this happens in today's society. If I was in that period of time, I would have risked my life and tried to stop Hitler and the Nazi's. To prevent another tragedy like this to happen in today's society we need to make sure that we don't have a depression. We also need to make sure that a group can not just walk in and start to take over. We also need to have a military that will protect us from any invaders that try to change anything. We need to make sure that our country never gets segregated by skin tone or race. All in all the Holocaust was a very tragic massacre that affected many people's lives including mine. I hope that something like this never happens again and if it sadly does, then our country will protest ad fight back.

Works Cited

"Yadvashem.org." Yadvashem.org. N.p., n.d. Web

Jozef Marchwinski

Akal-Ustat Singh

In the year of 1910, Franciezk Marchwinski and Helena Marchwinski had a son. His name was Jozef Marchwinski. By the time Jozef was around 30 years old, Germany invaded Poland and started the Second World War. The Jews were treated poorly during this time. The Germans began with slowly taking away the rights of all Jews and forcing them to publically identifying them with stars. Soon afterward, the Germans took them away to concentration camps. Jozef saw this with his own eyes. He could not bear to see his country being treated wrongly and decided to do something about it.

He soon joined a Polish partisan company. After the Germans took Poland, Russian-Communist partisan companies started to spring up all over the country to take actions against the Germans. They hid in the Polish forests and opposed the Germans where they could. Many Jews escaping the Germans ran to the partisans in the forests to join them. Many anti-Semitic rumors began spreading through the partisan forces like a wildfire. They thought that the devil had brought the Jews to join the Germans and had come to destroy their cause. Soon, orders began to be released to move the Jews out of the 'main' Russian otriads into the Bielski otriad. The Bielski otriad was commonly used to dump Jewish people who needed protection into one group. At this point, Jozef was married to a Jewish woman, just like one of his fellow officers.

By this time, the rumors about the Jews who joined the Russian otriads had taken new heights. Many of them went as far as being used to continue the mistreatment of the Jews and in some cases, their murder. Since Jozef and one of his fellow officers had married Jewish women, their wives were moved to the Bielski otriad. When resisting and arguing against the order had no effect, Marchwinski, his wife, and the other pair moved to the Bielski otriad.

One of the reasons Jozef had some power in his otriads was because of his communist past. He was an old-time Communist who had spent time in Polish prisons. His commanding officers found his past a threat to them. In the Bielski otriad, even without official power, people expected him to take charge and lead them. His commanders pretended not to notice as bringing major attention to taking Marchwinski down could result in them being overthrown.

Jozef increased the morale and conditions in the otriad, which also gave him a lot more support. Soon, Jozef had literally and metaphorically built a new otriad. He raised prices for services done by the otriad and ensured that people got proper food and clothing. This resulted in Jozef gaining more support. He also formed a more political group with other otriad members that was very active and gained power day by day. Looking at his growing power, Jozef's commanding officers were growing restless. Tensions were quickly rising. Then, one day, the political group's spokesperson, went to talk to the commanding officer. Things got heated quickly and the commanding officer attacked the spokesperson and he was never heard from again.

Soon after the incident, around the summer of 1942, the Germans were murdering the last of the Jews in the towns of Nieswiez and Mir. Out of a combined population of a few hundred, possibly a few thousand, around 20 may have survived. There is no accurate record of the beginning populations and the surviving Jews, but the most sensible numbers have made it to the records. The few Jews that survived, managed to find the partisans and tried to join them. The only open otriad was the Bielski otriad and still there was a lot of hatred toward the Jews in the otriad. This did not stop Jozef and he welcomed them with open arms. As time passed and Jozef accepted more and more escaping Jews, people began to think of him as a 'Jew Lover' and in some extreme cases, a Jew himself.

After 3 long years, at the end of World War 2, Jozef left his partisan company and moved to Poland. He soon left for Denmark because he was always at odds with the anti-Semitic beliefs of the Polish police authorities. He was recognized as a "Righteous Among the Nations" in 1970 in Israel by his former comrades and employees. Jozef left this earth during the year of 1982.

While doing research for this essay, I learned many new facts. The first of many that even though there were many groups fighting the Germans, there were still a lot of people who hated the Jews on both sides. Another thing I learned was that Russia had special Communist groups in Poland to fight off the Germans. Another fact that I learned about the Communist partisans were that they were sent to defend Communism, keep Germany's attention from Russia, allowing the Russians to prepare, and to help the Allies undercover. Learning about Jozef has affected me in the sense that I am now more opposed to racism and segregation. I also now have knowledge of the horrifying Holocaust, which has helped me to be a supporter of Never Again (I did not know about the Holocaust until 6th grade, and even then only that the Jews were prosecuted). I now understand that the Holocaust was an act of taking out a particular race to ensure power and to show the world how bad the Jews were. Instead, it destroyed the Nazi Party's power and united most of the world to make sure that nothing like the Holocaust ever happens again. I see 'Never Again' as a community, essentially, trying to make the world a better place and to make sure that we never forget the Holocaust in order to prevent such a thing from ever happening again. A few steps we can take to prevent such events from happening again are to tell as many people about the Holocaust and promote Human Rights. The more people know about the Holocaust, the less likely it is to happen again. If we forget our history, we are dooming ourselves to repeating it again. Promoting Human Rights helps to make everyone happy with themselves, their lives, and also helps spread positive thinking and to suppress negative thinking. The Jews were prosecuted because the Germans were angry and thought very poorly of their lives that they became vengeful and looked for someone to blame. This was probably why Hitler gained support and power in Germany. The Jews ended up on the wrong side of Germany's anger and suffered the consequences. All in all, the Holocaust was a horrifying event and Jozef Marchwinski was one of the many heroes during that time that stood up for what was right.

Works Cited

"Jozef Marchwinski." Geni_family_tree. Geni.com, 07 Nov. 2014. Web. 01 Dec. 2016.

"Names of Righteous by Country." Names of Righteous by Country. Yad Vashem, 1 Jan. 2016. Web. 23 Nov. 2016.

Nigro, Alessandro. "Jozef Marchwinski." Jozef Marchwinski. Blogger, 01 Jan. 1970. Web. 20 Nov. 2016.

Tec, By Nechama. "Defiance." Google Books. Oxford University Press, 1993. Web. 25 Nov. 2016.

Irena Adamowicz

Alejandro Olivarez

The holocaust was the murder and persecution of six million Jewish people all started by a man named Adolf Hitler. Adolf had rose to power and taken advantage of his country's economic depression and weak government to get into a high position of leadership and invade and capture other countries to take them under German rule like Poland Austria and more. He began to isolate Jewish citizens into ghettos and small slums. Jewish people would flee to countries not under German leadership and form resistances in the ghettos. The soon Adolf's solution was to send Jews to concentration camps to die of many reasons and extermination. 63% of Jews in Europe were killed and in Poland 91% were killed. The 4 million who did survive were forever changed.

Irena Adamowicz was a righteous and brave woman who was most notable for helping activist get across the border of Lithuania in to Palestine and aided in helping underground Jewish resistance communicate. She was born on May 11th 1910 in Warsaw, Poland and died August 12th 1963 in Warsaw, Poland. Irena was a non-Jew and of Roman Catholic Polish descent and was also a girl scout. Irena was one of the leader of the Polish scout movement during world war II, she also was one of the first few who established contact with Jewish scouting. Also Irena had become a member of the home army after the invasion of Poland. Irena earned her degree in social working at the university of Warsaw. She had continued her job as a child home inspector through world war II and it let her visit the Warsaw ghetto with some acquaintances such as Cywia Lubetkin, Izaak Cukierman and Josef Kapłan. Irena had also kept some of her close friends of Jewish heritage in her small apartment during the war. Irena had a strong connection with children and teens in a Jewish Zionist movement in the ghetto called Hashomer Hazair its central mission was to escape to Palestine and form a Jewish homeland there she would illegally sneak news into the movement while being their courier. She had traveled to the ghetto of Vilnius to undergo two important missions she informed the local Zionist about the mass killing of Jews in the government. When there Irena meet Abba Kovner a famous Israeli poet and Abraham suckewer another poet. After Irena snuck into the ghettos in Kaunas, Šiauliaiand Bialystok in Lithuania where she communicated with the Zionist. In 1942 she along with other brought back sad and terrifying news to Hashomer Hazair that the Nazis in Vilnius had slaughtered thousands of Jewish occupants from the cities ghetto near the town of ponar it had changed the whole mission of the Hashomer Hazair from moving to Palestine to self-defense which was the first time a movement thought about taking up arms against the Nazis. Irena had carried out many other missions from a lot more ghettos like in kovno and siauliai and helped Jewish organizations and the secret Poland militia communicate and she did most of this disguised as a German nun. After world war II Irena stayed in contact with some of the surviving Zionist members. She had also went on to become the translator of the repatriation office in Frankfurt then went back to her old job of working as a child home inspector. Then she became a worker at the National library in Warsaw and lived the rest of her life peacefully in Poland. On the 14th of January in 1985 Irena Adamowicz was recognized as the righteousness among the nations by Yad Vashem for helping movements across Europe saving people and overall being a brave and righteous hero.

I have learned a lot from researching about Irena Adamowicz, first i have learned that just being someone who helped, hid and or aided the Jews did so even though they knew that if they were to get caught themselves and their family would not survive. I also learned that fewer than 4 million Jews survived that's less than the population of Los Angeles which is a city compared to the continent of Europe. The impact of learning about Irena had on my life is just a lesson but it's is a powerful one it is to help people out with anything because if she knowingly risked her life for people she barely knew anything about Ican help my friend if they are going through something or if they simply drop a pen. I understand that millions upon millions of people across generations were affected by the holocaust not just in Europe but in North America and West Asia. We can make sure this happens Never Again by taking steps to tell people about different cultures and people so we won't get influenced that one type of person is bad by someone who has a personal experience with them.

Websites and books information has been gathered from
https://sprawiedliwi.org.pl/en/stories-of-rescue/story-rescue-adamowicz-irena
http://www.yadvashem.org/odot_pdf/Microsoft%20Word%20-%205717.pdf
The Hitler Youth: Marching Toward Madness

Tekla Kolodziej

Alex Steensland

In history, there have been many instances of power being used incorrectly. These stories usually end in tragedy. However, with horrible stories, great heroes emerge. In recent history, less than one-hundred years ago, one of the worst tragedies occurred. But, with it came many heroes. This story is of Tekla Kolodziej.

In January of 1933, a horrible man came to power in Germany. Not by election, but appointment by the Nazi party. His name was Adolf Hitler. Hitler blamed the Jews of Germany for its loss in World War One, for Germany's economic depression, and for most of the country's other faults. In his belief that the Aryan race was the most superior, Hitler and the Nazis tried to wipe out the Jewish race. In doing so, they murdered six million Jews. When Hitler was first in office, he started an office party for propaganda, successfully teaching that Jews were inferior to Aryans. The Nazi party also passed laws such as ones that did not allow Jews to hold office did not have any German rights, and that they were forced to wear the Star of David as identification. As a result of Nazi oppression, Jews fled to France, Latin America, Britain, and the United States. Before all of the Jews could escape, however, Hitler decided that there weren't enough Jews leaving. In turn, Hitler rounded up innocent Jews and put them in ghettos like animals. Life in the ghettos was much worse than horrible. There were stone walls with barbed wire on top. The Jews were starved and diseased on purpose, though they tried to live normally. After a while, Jewish resistances were formed to escape ghettos. Even after a lot of Jews had died, Hitler hadn't gotten enough. He turned to genocide, or planned killings of the Jews. Hitler's Special Forces, the S.S., also rounded up and murdered Jews that they found. Other Jews, that were capable, worked in concentration camps for seven days a week. In the camps, it was unsanitary in every way thinkable, everything was taken including their hair, and they were tattooed for identification. They ate only soup, scraps of bread, and potato peelings, and losing fifty pounds a week. Still, this wasn't enough. Jews were sent to mass extermination areas, where they were killed with cyanide gas. Six thousand Jews were killed a day. At the end of the Holocaust, in Poland alone, ninety-one percent of the Jews were killed.

Tekla Kolodziej was unstoppable. She was and had been a loyal caretaker and nanny for the Morgensterns, a Jewish family in Drohobycz, Poland. The city was then transferred to new rule, by the Soviets, but Tekla stayed with the Morgensterns. After a few years, in 1941, the Germans retook Drohobycz, but Tekla stayed in contact with her friends, who were sent to a concentration camp. When the Morgensterns needed help, Tekla helped them and a few other Jews by providing them with food and shelter. In 1942, Germans and nationalist Ukrainians murdered many of the ghetto's Jews. After hearing the news, Tekla helped Mr. Morgenstern to escape the ghetto. She then escorted Mr. Morgenstern to her apartment on the Aryan side of the city. Once informers found out about the Jew in Tekla's apartment, they alerted German authorities. Sadly, the Germans found Mr. Morgenstern and shot him. They sent Tekla to a camp outside of Kraków, from which she soon escaped. After she returned to Drohobycz, she sent food to Mosze and Leon Morgenstern, the children she had been caring for since their birth. In 1943, the Morgenstern brothers escaped from a camp near Drohobycz and found refuge in Tekla's apartment. When the Red Army freed the area from German rule in 1944, Mosze and Leon left Tekla's apartment and went to a refugee camp. After the liberation, Tekla and her sister, Julia Roj, looked after the refugees. Mosze and Leon went to Israel and Germany after the war, but still had contact with Tekla and Julia. In 1976, Tekla passed away, more than just a housekeeper. She was aware of the danger of helping Jews, let alone a whole family. Tekla was truly unstoppable, providing help for those in need, even after being taken away from them, escaping a concentration camp for more than just herself, and not stopping, even after the war was over.

Tekla's story taught me that you are not contained to your daily life. Everyone can be a hero when the time is right. She impacted my life because of the way she acted. She showed me how to stand up for others, and didn't just tell me to. The Holocaust impacted the world by showing that when people work together, they can stop bad things from happening. This lesson can be used on a much smaller scale, too. It can be used in school campuses and workplaces. To stop something big from happening, however, we must take this lesson into account wherever we are, daily life or not. We must also control bad things or people from getting started in the first place. "Never Again"

Works Cited

Vashem, Yad. "Tekla Kolodziej." Yad Vashem. Yad Vashem, 1 Jan. 2016. Web. 20 Nov. 2016.

Wojan, Megan. "Introduction to Holocaust." Introduction to Holocaust Lecture. Albiani, Elk Grove. 4 Nov. 2016. Web.

Maria Belszan

Alex Yen-Calhoun

The Holocaust was a tragic part of history that took place in Germany and other European countries at the hands of the Nazi party during World War II. The Nazi party was led by a cruel man named Adolf Hitler. The Nazi party tried to round up all the Jewish people and put them in ghettos and concentration camps. The Nazis also put people from other places and religions in ghettos because the Nazis believed that they alone were the dominant race and that others were inferior. The Nazis killed 63% of the Jewish population in Europe, but they killed 91% of the Jewish population in Poland. The Nazis would kill as many as 6,000 people a day. They used extermination camps equipped with gas chambers. When people were put in the concentration camps, the Nazis confiscated all of their possessions, shaved their heads, tattooed numbers on their arms, made them wear prison uniforms, and many did many other horrible things to them. The men, women, and children were separated because of the Nazis. The prisoners were kept in horrible and unsanitary living quarters so that disease spread and lice infested in the barracks. Also, some of the prisoners were used for inhumane medical experiments. The hero that I chose was Maria Belszan. She was a Catholic woman who helped Jews during the Holocaust. Maria was born on February 2, 1895 and died on March 30, 1980. Maria survived World War II's events and lived to tell her story.

Maria was a rescuer who helped two young Jewish doctors by the names of Stanislaw and Barbara Wiczyk. The young couple lived in the city of Lwów, Poland. In June of 1941, the Germans came to the town and the massacre of Jews began. The couple tried to use fake Christian identities to escape the Nazis, but their plan failed. Then, a senior Ukrainian doctor saw the distress that the couple was in, so he sent a letter to the couple telling them to travel elsewhere where their Jewish identities were unknown. Stanislaw travelled alone to the town of Łuck, in search of a safe new place to live and work. When he got there, he lived with a Polish family, and by chance he met a middle-aged house-wife named Maria Belszan. When the doctor was told to try seeking employment in the county town of Włodzimierz Wołyński, Maria decided to help him. She was from that town and was planning to travel there anyway, so she could help the young doctor. Along the way, Maria earned the trust of Stanislaw and he revealed his true identity to Maria. He told her that he was Jewish, and was looking for a safe place to settle and to send for his wife. Maria had already suspected that Stanislaw was Jewish and that he needed great help. Maria was a devout Catholic and the wife of a Polish soldier that was exiled in Siberia. When the young doctor asked Maria Belszan her motivation to help him, her reply was that her religion commanded her to "help people in need without reference to creed." Maria took Stanislaw under her protection and he was hired as a doctor in a nearby town called Uscilug. Maria introduced Stanislaw as her relative. She also helped him to bring his wife from Lwów.

Maria provided Stanislaw's wife with a forged identity document and created around them a circle of loyal influential friends, who were able to protect them from any suspicions. Maria was a brave woman who knew that if she was caught trying to hide the two young Jewish doctors, she would be killed. Maria sheltered them and treated them like family. To me, Maria Belszan was a hero and was an excellent human being. She gained the trust of the doctor and when he told her that he was Jewish, she wasn't shocked or scared. She would have helped him no matter what his ethnicity was or what his background was. She was an outstanding human and her actions required a lot of courage. Some people would have turned the doctor in and asked for a reward, but she didn't. Instead, she welcomed them like family and treated them as equals, not criminals. She even provided them with forged identity documents.

What I learned is that there was a tragic event that took place in Europe. It was the Holocaust and this tragedy was led by a cruel man named, Adolf Hitler. This man was leading a party called the Nazis. When I read my hero's story, my life was changed when I realized that some people had to hide in fear or use false identities in order to survive. If they were caught, they would be taken away to extermination camps, concentration camps, or a ghettos. I came to realize that we are extremely fortunate to live in a country where things like ethnicity and religion are protected.

Holocaust survivors use the motto, "Never Again." They use this motto because they don't want another horrific thing like the Holocaust take place on the earth ever again. During the Holocaust, about six million Jewish people died and fewer than four million Jewish people survived. The motto is a reminder to us that we should fight to prevent history from repeating itself. There are some steps that could be taken so that something like this never happens again. One step is to always have checks and balances on power. No one person or group should have complete control of a country or region. Another step is to make sure that your leader, monarch, or president is a decent person who wants to help the world, not to put it into darkness. In conclusion, the Holocaust was a tragic event that occurred during World War II, but there were many heroes that bravely aided people who were targeted by the Nazi party.

Works Cited

Marks, Bernard. "Bernard Marks Survivor Presentation." Holocaust Survivor Presentation. Katherine Albiani Middle School, Elk Grove. 9 Nov. 2016. Lecture.

"Rescuer Story." Yad Vashem – Righteous Among the Nations. N.p., n.d. Web. 30 Nov. 2016.

Wogan, Megan. "Introduction to Holocaust." Class Lecture. Katherine Albiani Middle School, Elk Grove. 4 Nov. 2016. Lecture.

Alfred Wolf

Alexa Deissroth

Alfred Wolf was born in Eberbach, Germany in 1915. He died in 2004 at the age of 88 years old. Alfred Wolf was the only Jewish child at the grade school he attended. He often led his Christian classmates to a synagogue to discuss Jewish beliefs and customs. Rabbi Alfred Wolf pioneered Jewish summer camps and the interfaith movement on the West Coast. Throughout his life, he strove for his self-described goal "to serve as a catalyst in bringing people together, despite personal and ideological differences." An avid hiker and swimmer, Wolf opened his temple's Camp Hess Kramer in Malibu in 1952, which became the prototype for the American Jewish youth camping movement. Wolf served as rabbi at Wilshire Boulevard Temple, the oldest Reform congregation in Los Angeles, for 36 years, from 1949 to 1985. After his retirement, he started a new career as founding director of the Skirball Institute on American Values, sponsored by the American Jewish Committee. As founding president of the Inter-Religious Council of Southern California, Wolf brought together the region's Jewish, Christian, Muslim, Hindu and Buddhist leaders. During the 1984 Olympic Games, he and the council organized inter-religious services and lobbied for placement of a mosque at the Olympic venue. He started his religious studies at Berlin's Institute for Jewish Studies in 1935 and said he owed his life to accepting an offer to become an exchange student at the Hebrew Union College-Jewish Institute of Religion (HUC-JIR) in Cincinnati. Wolf's first job on the West Coast was as regional director of the Union of American Hebrew Congregations. During his three-year tenure, he established Reform congregations in 12 Southern California communities, among them Temple Isaiah and Leo Baeck Temple in West Los Angeles and Temple Beth Hillel in North Hollywood. In an interview with The Jewish Journal a decade ago, he described this feat as "the most unlikely accomplishment of my life." In 1965, Wolf was president of L.A. County Commission on Human Relations during the devastating Watts riots, and always felt that the loss of life and property could have been averted if the city's police chief had accepted the commission's earlier recommendations. In 1993, he co-chaired the first Nationwide Conference for Catholic, Jewish and Protestant Seminaries. Wolf taught at USC, HUC-JIR, Chapman College, Loyola University and Cal State L.A. and was the co-author of two books.

Rabbi Lawrence Goldmark of Temple Beth Ohr of La Mirada served as Wolf's rabbinical colleague at Wilshire Boulevard Temple during the 1970s, under the legendary Rabbi Edgar F. Magnin. Although overshadowed in the community by Magnin, informally known as "The Chief Rabbi of California," Wolf was fiercely loyal to his senior rabbi and declined many offers to become the spiritual leader at other congregations, Goldmark said. "Rabbi Wolf was an intensely creative person and he convinced a skeptical Rabbi Magnin to establish Camp Hess Kramer and the Gindling Hilltop Center," Goldmark recalled. A handy craftsman, Wolf personally helped build the camp's amphitheater. Wolf is survived by his wife of 64 years, Miriam; sons, Dan and David; and four grandchildren. A daughter, Judy Wolf Lee, died of cancer in 1987. Her services were held Wednesday at Wilshire Boulevard Temple.

During Wolf's time in Germany he had to surrender his passport and could not leave Germany, but he reached out to the American consulate and was able to get his passport back. He felt a sense of incarceration without a wall, and felt he was shunned from his country under Hitler's rule of Germany. He was able to get his parents and grandmother out of Germany on United States visas, and two days later the American consulates closed and no other Jew was allowed to leave Germany. Luckily they were able to get out of the country, because the United States enter the war and most if not all the remaining Jews of Wolf's home town died at the hands of the Nazis.

I have learned about the life of Alfred Wolf. I have learned when he was born, where he was raised, and when he died. I have learned the accomplishments he made, learned about his family, and learned about his life in the Holocaust. I understand the Holocaust was a terrible tragedy and a horrible act of hate. It was a dictator named Adolf Hitler who didn't like a certain group of people, for some reason, and decided to kill them all. The Holocaust wiped out almost an entire population of Jews all because Hitler said so. Jews were tortured, starved, worked to death, and just flat out killed under the rule of Hitler because he didn't like the Jews. "Never Again" is a saying Jews all over the world use to help prevent another event like the Holocaust from ever happening again. To make sure something as tragic and horrifying as the Holocaust never happens again, people today have to do simple things to prevent this. People could make sure there is no prejudice, hate, and discrimination against people with different beliefs or skin colors. People could make sure no group is rising against a certain belief or race. Simple measures can be taken to make sure a terrible event such as the Holocaust happens "Never Again".

Works Cited

02, August. "Alfred Wolf, 88; Noted Rabbi Started Jewish Youth Camps." Los Angeles Times. Los Angeles Times, 02 Aug. 2004. Web. 14 Dec. 2016.

"Rabbi Alfred Wolf | Articles." Jewish Journal. N.p., n.d. Web. 14 Dec. 2016.

"From Democracy to Dictatorship." Facing History and Ourselves. N.p., n.d. Web. 14 Dec. 2016.

"Rabbi Alfred Wolf Honored for Lifetime of Service." Rabbi Alfred Wolf Honored for Lifetime Of Service. N.p., n.d. Web. 14 Dec. 2016.

Http://www.jta.org/author/admin. "Obituary Rabbi Alfred Wolf Dies at Age of 88; Pioneer of Camps and Interfaith Dialogue." Jewish Telegraphic Agency. N.p., 04 Aug. 2004. Web. 14 Dec. 2016.

EasyBib. Chegg, n.d. Web. 14 Dec. 2016.

Teresa Prekerowa

Alexis Dodson

The Holocaust was a very dark time of Germany, not only for the Jews (the most targeted religion) but also for many other people. It was a time when Adolf Hitler and his recruited army took over Germany in January of 1933. Their mission was to wipe out any race that they thought might be powerful enough to stop them. They targeted several different groups such as the most affected- the Jewish society. They almost succeeded in demolishing the Jews massacring around six million helpless people. Luckily, there were brave Germans willing to help such as Mrs. Teresa Prekerowa (Dobrska). Teresa was born on December 31, 1921 in Warsaw. She grew up as a faithful Catholic with her mother, father, three brothers and her sister. Two brothers were executed during the German war making her two parents extremely cautious of what might happen next. The loss of her brothers pushed her to save many innocent lives. Prior to the Holocaust war, Teresa was a historian, always interested in the past. It wasn't until later that Mrs. Prekerowa learned that her knowledge of the past and her Catholic heart would save many innocent lives.

Teresa met Alina Wolman in 1940. The two young women became very close friends, which to Alina's use would come to hand. When the Wolman family was imprisoned in the Warsaw ghetto, Teresa smuggled them food, keeping them alive. Soon Mrs. Prekerowa had convinced her friend Alina to attempt to escape from the ghetto over to the Aryan part of the city. There, Teresa set her up with a job and a place to live. Alina could not have been more fortunate to have a friend like Teresa. When the large deportations began at the Warsaw ghetto, Mrs. Prekerowa worked and succeeded to smuggle out the rest of Alina's family. Throughout the war, the two stayed in touch and when the Wolman family needed her help, Teresa came to aid them. This was not the only honorable thing that Teresa Prekerowa did to earn the title of "righteous" on March 4 of 1985. For example, one day Teresa found an abandoned Jewish baby crying on her front step. She instantly reached for the child and brought him inside her parent's home. There, she nurtured and cared for the young child and once she had dressed him and taught him to behave as a Polish child should, she brought him to her covenant. Later she married a man named Mieczyslaw Preker. They then moved into a Skolimow estate near the Warsaw. This was also the spot that she hid a Jewish man named Jan Zieliński for eight months during the year of 1943. Teresa Prekerowa did many memorable life-saving things that she should be remembered for.

"Never Again." This is the quote used to describe the Holocaust. It is the expression that represents what a tragedy the Hitler Army created and inflicted on the Jewish population. Of the Jewish population in Europe 63% of them were massacred during the Holocaust. In Poland, 91% of the Jews were murdered throughout the Germanic war. Those who survived the Holocaust were changed forever. Those of the four million surviving Jews lost many family members to the six million Jews who were massacred during the Holocaust of 1933-1939. Through this experience I learned many things to help me and the future.

Learning about Teresa Prekerowa has allowed me to see everything different. I now realize how fortunate I am that I have a family who loves me and cares for me, a nice house, clothes to wear everyday, and the ability to do the leisurely activities that I love. I am so lucky for the freedom that I have as an American. The Holocaust was a very depressing and dark time for many people around the world. It changed many people's lives, whether through the death of a family member, or having those awful things happen to them and never being able to forget them. Or the students just like me who are now realizing how fortunate we are to have the things that we usually take for granted.

One valuable lesson that I learned was to never judge a person based off of what someone believes in. The judging of a group of people is what started the beginning of the Holocaust. This caused the hatred directed at the Jews. If the country started all judging others for what they believe in, then we would have a horrible catastrophe every day. People need to stop thinking of everyone around them and start believing that everyone is equal. This is one step that we as a country can take to avoid another disaster like this happening again. Another thing we could to do avert another crisis like this repeating itself would be to not go into a weak point as a country. In the 1930s, Germany went into an economic depression, causing the lack of confidence which developed into a weak government. In January of 1933, Adolf Hitler became the new leader of Germany. The unsteadiness of Germany and they're people allowed the war to begin. By staying a strong country with a solid government, people in favor of their leader, and the belief of equality throughout a country, we can avoid another version of the Holocaust from happening again.

Cited Sources

"Rescuers Defying the Nazis." Google Books. N.p., n.d. Web. 05 Dec. 2016.
Yad Vashem - Request Rejected. N.p., n.d. Web. 05 Dec. 2016
Wojan, Megan. "Holocaust Background." Classroom, Elk Grove. 4 Nov. 2016. Lecture.

Maria, Andzelm

Alexis Quihuiz

Over six million Jews were killed during an event known as the Holocaust. Young children were mostly targeted during the Holocaust. This was because the Nazis thought they were a bigger threat. They were thought to be a bigger threat because they would be able to start a new generation of Jews. The Holocaust was a extermination of Jews lead by Adolf Hitler in the year 1933. During the Holocaust many people were bystanders and let the Nazis take the Jews away to internment camps but some people stood up and helped the Jews, like Maria Andzelm

Maria was a thirteen year old Catholic girl during the Holocaust. Even though she was only thirteen she knew what was right and she wanted to help the Jews. So she did, the Andzelm's shared everything they had with Jews that appeared at their door her and her family also hid two Jewish men one named Moses and the other named Srulik. Her family hid the two in a pit under a cowshed and pigsty. The pit had boards to cover it so no one especially a Nazi could tell that there was anyone underground. Everyday Maria went out to give them food and books to read. Since the Jews hiding spot was under a cow shed, the cows would pee on their heads but the Jews weren't about to complain they were very grateful for the protection the Andzelm's family were giving them. In the dead of night everyday the Jews would sneak into the house to take a shower. The Nazi soldiers had there suspicions and occasionally showed up at the Andzelm's household, but they still continued to hide the Jews. One day as Maria was on her way back from getting books for Moses and Srulik a Nazi solider was following her, he commanded her to turn around and all the Nazi did was slap her in the face then walk away. When she returned home her parents told her that all adults were to report to the church. Instead of going her parents hid with Moses and Srulik. One day Maria went to go visit a friend and randomly a bomb went off. Maria and her friend quickly ran to her Maria's Aunts house and hid in the barn. All of Maria's family was there except her father, one of their neighbors saw her father trying to get the two Jews out of there barn and he was shot. Fear for their lives due to the fact their neighbors figured out that the Andzelm's hid two Jews, the Andzelm family besides Stefan (Maria's father who was killed when he was shot) went into hiding and Moses was able to hide them this time. Moses and Srulik were able to escape and live. Moses was able to live till the end of the Holocaust, sadly Srulik did not.

A couple years later Maria got married at age 16 to Moses. Since they both knew they weren't safe in Poland the newly wed couple left the country. Together they had two kids, Rosalie and Helene. They were married for 52 years until Moses died of a heart disease.

Completing this holocaust essay contest I have learned lots of things about the Holocaust. I have learned that the Nazis didn't just target Jews but they targeted disabled people and mostly kids. They targeted people Adolf Hitler thought unfit to be a German. Another thing I leaned is that the Holocaust lasted about twelve years. It lasted about twelve years when it really didn't need to. The Holocaust was an event in history that should have never happened and will "Never Again" happen. I believe the Holocaust lasted so long and started to begin with because there was very many bystanders that just watched the horrible event take place. Many people were scared to say anything to stand up for the Jews so they just stayed quiet. Maria Andelm had a major impact on my life. I am very impressed on how someone has enough bravery and courage to stand up to a group of people so powerful, so capable of murder. It makes me want to help everyone that needs help. I believe I look at the world differently. What I mean by this is I don't judge people just by what they look like or how they act. I connect not judging people to Maria Andelm because she didn't judge the Jews. She didn't listen to what Adolf Hitler and his followers said about them. She did what she knew what was right, she stuck up for the Jews and hid them endangering herself in the process. Not just Maria Andelm had an impact on my life, so did the Holocaust. The Holocaust had an impact on my life because it frightens me to think that someone would commit this...hate crime. It frightens me to think what people in this century would be capable of. I know as a country we will take all the needed measures to ensure this event in history Never Again happens. We will make sure not to elect potential maniacs. Overall I know this will Never Again happen…..Never Again.

Works Cited

"91 Facts about the Holocaust FactRetriever.com." FactRetriever.com. RETRIEVER LLC, 2016. Web. 11 Dec. 2016.

"91 Interesting Facts about the Holocaust | FactRetriever.com." FactRetriever.com. Fact Reciever LLc, n.d. Web. 11 Dec. 2016.

Beavers, Bryce. "Bryce Beavers." Threelakesgrade8 - Bryce Beavers. Bryce Beavers, 2016. Web. 11 Dec. 2016.

"Introduction to the Holocaust." United States Holocaust Memorial Museum. United States Holocaust Memorial Museum, 27 Nov. 2016. Web. 11 Dec. 2016.

"The Righteous." Yad Vashem - Request Rejected. Yad Vashem., 14 Nov. 2016. Web. 12 Dec. 2016.

Irena Adamowicz

Alexis Ragsdale

 The Holocaust began in 1933 when Adolf Hitler gained power in Germany and it ended in 1945 when the Nazis were defeated by the Allied powers. During the holocaust Over 1.1 million children died. Of the nine million Jews who lived in Europe before the Holocaust, an estimate of 2/3 were murdered. Millions of others, including those who were disabled, political and religious opponents to Hitler Jehovah's Witnesses, homosexuals, and Romanies were also murdered.

Irena Adamowicz was one of the few people who helped the Jews during the Holocaust. Irena was born in 1910 and died in 1963. She was born in Warsaw, Adamowicz. Irena was not a Jew in fact she was a religious catholic. She also earned her social work degree at the University of Warsaw before world war . She later became one of the leaders of the Polish scout movement when she was only a senior girl scout. In 1930 she developed an attachment to the Ha-Shomer ha-Tsa'ir Jewish Zionist Youth Movement. In this movement she took part in in its social work and educational activities. In the summer of 1942 Adamowicz carrying out dangerous missions for the Jewish underground organizations in the Kovno, Warsaw, Bialystok, Vilna, and Siauliai ghettos. Through her delivering the massages she became a source of both vital information and moral encouragement, such as her inspirational presence in Kovno Ghetto in July 1942. She carried important messages between all of the different ghettos. She also helped establish contact between the Home Army and Jewish underground organizations. After the war, she stayed in close contact with the very few surviving members of the Zionist pioneer movements who she had worked with and helped. She ended up with a Jewish nickname "Di chalutzishe shikse", this means" The Pioneering one". [

Through researching this person I learned that that even in a time of hate, mistreatment, starvation, abuse there are still caring people in the world. Learning about this person impacted me and also taught me that even if doing the right thing means taking big risks, then do what you believe is right. Researching and learning more about Irena Adamowicz and the holocaust allowed me to learn about how affil this time was and how innocent people were getting killed. I believe that the holocaust is a sad and miserable time, and I believe this because during the holocaust people were getting killed by each other just because of what they believed in. I hope that never again will anything close to the holocaust ever happen again. I hope that never again will countries, governments, states, town, or small communities let something like this ever happen again. I believe that we can prevent this from happening again by not letting anyone gain so much power because most likely before we even know it something horrible has happened. I also believe that we can prevent this from happening again by never discriminate, always stick together with you family friends, and above all do what you believe is right.

Sites used

http://www.wow.com/wiki/Irena_Adamowicz
http://www.thefullwiki.org/Irena_Adamowicz
http://www.factretriever.com/holocaust-facts
http://www.digplanet.com/wiki/Irena_Adamowicz
https://sprawiedliwi.org.pl/en/stories-of-rescue/list?role=90&page=1
http://www.yadvashem.org/

Gertruda Babilinska

Allie Couchot

The Holocaust that happened from the years 1933-1945 is something that should never happen again. Millions of people were killed because of this tragic time in history. The holocaust happened because the Nazi party was elected in Germany and Adolf Hitler thought that Jews weren't a superior race. To prove that, he made all Jews shut down their stores and sew stars of David on their clothes. After that things got worse and all Jews were moved into ghettos. There, pretty much everybody had disease and it spread like a wildfire killing thousands of people. After that, people were put into labor camps to either work of be killed if they weren't working hard enough. Millions of people were killed because they weren't given enough food to continue to be strong and work. But, through all of these very hard times, some heroes hid Jewish people in their homes so they wouldn't have to go to the ghettos or the labor camps.

One of these heroes was, Gertruda Babilinska. She was born in Danzig in 1902 and lived with her five sisters and two brothers. For fifteen years, she worked for a rich Jewish family with the name of Stolowitzky, taking care of the daughter and son. The Jewish father was taken to Auschwitz and when the daughter died in the ghetto, Mrs. Stolowitzky, thought she and her son would be safer in Warsaw, so Gerturda left Danzig and went with them. Then, the three of them heard it was better in Vilna, so they left Warsaw and went there. In Vilna the German soldiers gave the children candy with poison in it to kill them faster. When Mrs. Stolowitzky became sick and died, the Catholic woman, Gertruda became the "mother" of Mickey Stolowitzky, a Jewish child. Mickey got sick and the only Jewish doctor was in the ghetto so Gertruda had to take him to a German doctor. She lied that she was Mickey's older sister, and after several visits Mickey got better. When she tried to pay the doctor he said, "No, you have helped me feel like a man" because he knew that the boy was Jewish. Once the war ended, she knew she had to get Mickey to Israel because there was no other way she could raise him to be Jewish. During the war, Mickey had gone to church with her, he learned about Catholic prayers and became an altar boy, but he was still Jewish, not Catholic. They left on the first boat to Israel, called the Exodus. When they arrived in Israel, he became a Jewish patriot. Before she died, Mickey's Mom said his relatives would help them in Israel, but all they did was make Mickey and Gertruda's lives worse. Gertruda says she will never forgive them for what they did to her; they gave her a small room with no water and no toilet. They paid for Mickey to go to school for half of a year and he cried every day when he came home. They also said if Gertruda stayed in Israel and didn't go back to Poland, they wouldn't pay for Mickey to go to school. But Mickey said, "I don't want to be a son of your family. I want to stay with my mother forever. Where she will go, I will go." Gertruda went to work as a maid to pay for Mickey to go to school and for eighteen years she lived in the same room, with no water, no toilet and Mickey's awful relatives.

All in all, the Holocaust was a time in history that should never happen again. From learning about Gertruda Babilinska, I have learned that even though the Holocaust wasn't affecting her because she wasn't Jewish, she still helped a Jewish family. She helped Mickey get out of Germany after the war and helped him go to school in Israel. Some steps that can be taken to help prevent something like the Holocaust from ever happening again is, to respect other people and their beliefs and to always be kind to everyone, even if you don't have the same religious beliefs, political beliefs, etc.

All in all, the Holocaust was a time in history that should never happen again. From learning about Gertruda Babilinska, I have learned that even though the Holocaust wasn't affecting her because she wasn't Jewish, she still helped the Jewish family and helped Mickey get out of Germany after the war and helped him go to school in Israel. Something like the Holocaust to never happen again is, to respect other people and their beliefs and to just always be kind to everyone, even if you don't have the same religious beliefs, political beliefs, etc.

The Holocaust that happened from the years 1933-1945 is something that should never happen again. Millions of people were killed because of this tragic time in history. The holocaust happened because the Nazi party was elected in Germany and Adolf Hitler thought that Jews weren't a superior race. To prove that, he made all Jews shut down their stores and sew star of Davids on their clothes. After that things got worse and all Jews were moved into ghettos. There, pretty much everybody had disease and it spread like a wildfire killing thousands of people. After that, people were put into laboring camps to either work of be killed if they weren't working hard enough. Millions of people were killed because they weren't given enough food to continue to be strong and work. But, through all of these very hard times, some heroes hid Jewish people in their homes so they wouldn't have to go to the ghettos or the laboring camps.

Work Cited

"Rescuers: Gertruda Babilinska." PBS. PBS, n.d. Web. 11 Dec. 2016.

Bawół Sisters

Allison M. Chu

The Holocaust was a very painful time for everyone in Europe. The Holocaust began around the 30th of January in 1933 and ended around May 8th of 1945 (12 years and 3 months). When the Nazi party came of power, Adolf Hitler took charge and began blaming the Jews for every problem occurring in Europe. The Nazis would take the Jews and isolate them into another small part of town where no one can get in or out. The Nazis wanted to get rid of all of the Jews in the world, starting with Europe. There was over 6 million people killed with 24% of it being, the highest, from Poland. Even though Hitler's plan to get others away from Jews mostly succeeded, some Polish decided to help the Jews. Upon the list of heroes were the Bawół sisters, Irena Bawół-Mielecka and Felicja Tewel-Bartczak née Bawół. Irena was born on October 21st of 1921 and was a nurse in training in Warsaw. Felicja was born on October 27th of 1913 and was a medical doctor in Dębica. The Bawół sisters lived as Roman Catholics who had good hearts and hardworking hands.

The Bawół sisters did everything they could to help set the Jews free of internment camps and ghettos. As many as they saved, one of their survivors was Sabina Friedman née Poper. Felicja housed many Jews in her apartment in Dębica. Sabina described Felicja's apartments as "A Rescue Factory," quoted from Sabrina. There was warmth, food, and safety for most of who stayed, but wouldn't be in a position to stay too long. Felicja was still working her normal job as a medical doctor while also providing for refugees. Felicja fed Sabina and gave her sleep and comfort right after Sabina escaped from a traumatizing place. After staying at Felicja's apartment for a while, Sabrina started to feel unsafe since Felicja was married to a Jewish attorney, Maurycy Tewel, and Felicja's father was a Polish Army officer. So, Felicja sent Sabina to Janina Starakowa née Kołosiwska in Lublin where she took Sabina to Irena in Warsaw. Felicja also hid and assisted Maria Blumenthal and Nachman, her son, and Wiatr, a tailor. All who escaped and got her address from friends who won't take risks.

In Warsaw, Irena was studying nursing in a nursing school and sharing an apartment with her roommate. When Sabina got to her apartment, Irena hid Sabina in her closet for a couple of days along with bringing her food and water daily. Irena did her a favor of obtaining an identity card ("Kennkarte") and got an apartment for Sabina to stay in. But, when the landlord suspected her identity, Irena had to find another apartment, along with a job for Sabina to live on. Sabina moved out on the night Irena knew her roommate was on duty so that they will have time to plan. From the plan, Sabina started work at a German hospital, keeping her profile low as she went around the city. Irena didn't rescue as many Jews as her sister, Felicja, but she also rescued another Jewish women from Dębica and helped her the same way as she did with Sabina. Irena hid her, got her forged documents, and made another life for her.

Sabina and Irena became close friends, but when Sabina's fiancé escaped from the prisoners' camp he went out to join her. Once the war was over, Sabina immigrated to Israel and didn't see the sisters when she left. In 1943 of October, Felicja's husband was arrested and perished at Auschwitz. Later on in the 1900s, Irena got married and became Mrs. Mielecka and Felicja got remarried and became Mrs. Bartczak. Irena and Felicja's whereabouts and deaths after the war are not known, but on September 25 of 1989, Irena Bawół-Mielecka and Felicja Tewel-Bartczak née Bawół got recognized as righteous heroes. The Bawół sisters made a big difference in many Jewish lives sacrificing themselves for the innocent lives being taken away.

The Holocaust was a meaningful event in life teaching everyone a lesson about isolating one religion or race. The meaning of the Holocaust is "sacrifice by fire". The Nazis were sacrificing Jewish lives to something that won't help in the future. At the end of the Holocaust, it reunited the world into working together like the Bawół sisters did to save Sabina Friedman née Poper. I learned that the Bawół sisters did everything they could to save as many lives as possible. The sisters stayed strong throughout the whole journey of deaths, torture, investigations, and with their whole life on the line according to how they help each survivor. The fact that neither Irena nor Felicja got caught caring for Jews tells me that they were cautious when hiding and forging documents and identities. This story got me thinking that I should be grateful about my protection and I should fight for what I want in life that will make a difference in the world. To make sure this won't happen again, we as citizens of the United States should know this better than anyone that sticking together to band something out for good is the number one thing that is need to succeed as a group. To conclude, "Never Again" shall this situation or anything similar happen again anywhere in the world, planets, or galaxy.

Works Cited

Aleksiun, Natalia, Dr. "The Bawół Family." *Story of Rescue - The Bawół Family | Polscy Sprawiedliwi*. Polish Righteous, Aug. 2014. Web. 4 Dec. 2016.

"Introduction to the Holocaust." *United States Holocaust Memorial Museum*. United States Holocaust Memorial Museum, n.d. Web. 5 Dec. 2016.

"Mielecka Irena." *Yad Vashem - Request Rejected*. Yad Vashem, n.d. Web. 4 Dec. 2016.

"Saving Jews: Polish Righteous." *Saving Jews: Polish Righteous*. N.p., n.d. Web. 4 Dec. 2016.

"Tewel Felicja." *Yad Vashem - Request Rejected*. Yad Vashem, n.d. Web. 4 Dec. 2016.
Wojan, Megan. "Introduction to the Holocaust." Class Lecture. KAMS, Elk Grove. 4
Nov. 2016. Lecture.

Wladyslawa Cygler

Alyson Lawler

The holocaust was a horrific and shameful period in history that left many friends and families scarred and unforgetful. A group of German soldiers called the Nazis believed that the German race was the "superior" race. The Nazis was lead by a cruel man named Adolf Hitler who was born in 1889. The Jewish population in Europe was over an astounding nine million Jews in 1933 and decreased over Hitler's reign after killing over six million Jews. The Nazis viewed Jewish people as a danger to their belief in Germans being the "superior" race and German authorities targeted gypsies and the disabled. After the majority of the population was unemployed in Germany, the Great Depression took place. Hitler saw this ordeal as an offer for a political opportunity. In 1932, Adolf Hitler ran against an 84 year old man named Paul von Hindenburg for presidency. After Hitler winning 36% of the final vote, Paul died leaving Hitler with power. He gained full control over the legislative and executive branches and started to pass his own laws. On July 14, 1933 Hitler's Nazi party was declared only legal political party in Germany. From 1933 to the start of war in 1939, Hitler instituted hundreds of laws and regulations that restricted and excluded Jews in the society.

Raizel Noy of Otwok, was a Jewish victim in the horrendous time in history of Hitler and his wrong doing of the Holocaust. Thanks to Hitler's horrible actions, persuasive sayings, and dictatorship, Raizel had to suffer the tremendous consequences just like millions and millions of other Jews living in this time period of the mid 1900's. Raizel suffered a major portion of her adult life as a other mainly based on the way she looked and followed her religion eventually saved by Wladyslawa Cygler. Raizel, the woman who was saved had gave birth to her daughter in 1939 after the German occupation began. In August 1942, the noy was determined to escape from the ghetto with the young daughter of hers during the mass deportation of Jews. Maks noy, Raizel's husband, worked in a labor camp in the nearby town of Karczew. This camp was focused on German contact company at the time. Raizel and her daughter wandered around the area with an empty feeling of no hope of finding shelter. It was very depressing and hard for her, because naturally all parents want what is best for their kids and Raizel could not do that for her daughter, Ruth. Because she looked a certain way, she was faced with intense tension in fear of the lurking dangers that her and her family would face from society. Raizel looked Jewish, and so did her family members including her daughter. This woman was aware that her survival chance was very low and starting to dwindle, she decided to spare no more effort and use all her energy to protect her daughter Ruth. Noy made contact with a catholic nun who taught at an orphanage and pleaded for him to save and keep and protect his daughter. He consulted with the mother superior and agreed to spare and save and take in the young girl to protect her. Ruth was left in the convent corridor that night. When she began to cry and sob all alone in the dark, the nuns would come out and bring her inside to comfort her young self. The girl was placed with the polish children and the nuns cared for her with all they had. The sisters of the church performed the act of rescue as a human duty for the church beliefs. These nuns devoted their lives to the children they took in and took care of and also practicing their beliefs and carrying out their religious duties as church leaders and orphanage caregivers. They felt that not saving this girl would be against their beliefs and their religious duties. They endangered their lives for this girl. It was a very human act and kind thing to do to save Ruth and care for her even though she is not their responsibility. If they never saved Ruth, nobody would know what would have happened to her. Ruth's father eventually escaped from the labor camp and him and his wife found shelter in an apartment that they had rented. Although the woman knew that they were Jews, she had prepared a hide out for them anyways. This was also a very human act, for she did not have to do this for them at all. Even though she knew it could have hurt her in the long run and threatened her life, she went to extremes to protect these people. This hideout was prepared for in case of danger. This shelter would help save them from suspicious neighbors. These neighbors would suspect that they were a threat, with them being jewish. The only person who knew their address was nun of the church. Eventually they brought their child back to them from the orphanage and returned her to her parents. After the war they immigrated to the united states and still continued to stay in touch with the nuns.

This story has made me appreciate my life more. I feel more lucky and blessed to be able to be who I am without fear of being murdered or persecuted. I am also lucky to be able to practice whatever religion I want without much social disapproval. This story has really opened my mind, heart, and soul to the world and how impactful one horrible person's words could be. We have to be aware of the actions we do in order for this not to happen... never again.

"Introduction to the Holocaust." United States Holocaust Memorial Museum. United States Holocaust Memorial Museum, n.d. Web. 10 Dec. 2016.

Google. N.p., n.d. Web. 12 Dec. 2016.

Irena Adamowicz

Alyson Reiff

 The holocaust was one of the worst times in the world. The holocaust was started when Adolf Hitler was elected for chancellor of Germany. Adolf Hitler wanted to get rid of Jews. He thought Germany lost world war one cause of the Jews and he thought Germans was the highest race, which the Jews were a threat to that. Because of this, he made ghettos to kill the Jews off by sickness and hunger, but he thought

they were dieing to slowly so he made them go to concentration camps or death camps. There at the concentration camps they would work all day with almost no break and little food, only the strongest would live and at the death camps they would get sent to get killed off. As if all this was not enough, gas chambers were built at concentration camps such as Auschwitz. Prisoners here were forced into those chambers and gassed to death through use of carbon monoxide or cyanide gas produced from Zyklon B pellets. Consequently thousands of people died and they were buried in mass graves without any form of ceremony befitting a human being. The Germans were teaching their kids that the Jews were weak and not as good as them. The neighboring countries tried to let Jews in but there were too many in Germany. In 1939 the U.K, US, and china defeated Germany, Italy, and japan which lasted six years and stopped the holocaust. People who have survived from it says "never again". I have chosen Adamowicz, Irena because she has a wonderful story. Adamowicz was polish and born in November 05,1910 till December 08, 1973. She was one of the survivors. She was catholic and a daughter of polish nobles, she graduated in the university of Warsaw with a degree in social work. She placed herself in the Jewish underground as a communication among the ghettos in Warsaw. In all of her adventures, she grew close and friendly relations with the Hashomer Hatzair movement and participated in its educational and social business. Until World War II, she held a leading position with the Polish Scouts in Warsaw.

For many months, she supplied arms to the ghettos. She considered that it was her duty in life, and most issuance on Jewish armed resistance in Warsaw, Vilna, and Bialystok refer to her in positive terms. Adamowicz supplied and transported information for many of the ghettos. In June 1942, Adamowicz set out for Vilna to notify the leaders of the Jewish underground about the beginning of the mass harming and killing of the Jews in the General government and to aware them of the youth movement plans. When she entered the secure ghetto in Vilna it was difficult and, after completing the mission, she was asked to deliver the awful news to the Jews of Kaunas and Siauliai, so that they would form resistance groups in Lithuania. Adamowicz agreed to handle this mission and, at danger, completed it with great care and loyalty. After the war, Adamowicz maintained her relationship with the rest of the Zionist pioneering youth movements in Poland, which were preparing Jews to move to Israel, and with her friends in the movements.

In conclusion, the holocaust is one of the memorable events in the history of man and it is important to know some of its causes and how it was carried out. This is so as to prevent such an incident occurring and placing value in the lives of all human beings as we are all equal and with equal rights. This have taught me that one person can help greatly, some people in this world aren't as nice as they seem to be and that people will kill people to get what they want. Also, that different races don't matter, we are all people. The impact this had on my life after learning about my person is that it made me look at the world differently. It also made me respect the people who have died during the holocaust and fought against it a lot more. What I understand about the holocaust is that Adolf Hitler wanted to get rid of all of the Jewish people in Germany, so he made different camps, concentration and death, to kill them off. About 6 million Jewish people were killed. World war two happened, which had stopped the holocaust and free the Jews. The impact that it gave is that it displaced many Jews and left many frightened people. The Holocaust destroyed society. This harmful massacre killed millions of people, left thousands in physical or mental pain, and affected today's society in such a negative way. People who have survived says "never again", they never want something like this ever to happen again. The steps that can be taken to make sure something never happens like this ever again is that look more into the person you choose to elect, try to stand up and speak freely, and teach younger kids about the holocaust so they know not to allow it the future.

Work cited

http://theholocaustaturningpoint.weebly.com/long-term-effects.html
http://db.yadvashem.org/righteous/search.html?language=en
http://www.history.com/topics/world-war-ii/the-holocaust
http://www.jewishvirtuallibrary.org/jsource/Holocaust/history.html
http://www.history.com/topics/world-war-ii/the-holocaust

Chmielewska, Helena (Mother Superior)

Alyssa Arcineda

 The Holocaust is when Adolf Hitler wanted to persecute all of the Jews. He manganged to kill 6 million Jews, it took them 4 and a half years. The Jews had no way to escape, the Germans made the Jews sew a gold star onto there clothing so everyone would know that they were Jews. The Jews also weren't allowed to go into some stores. Most of the Jews were dead by 1945. The Germans weren't allowed to hold a public office. The jews started to move to other countries for there safety, but countries had to say no to some due to overpopulation. Hitler made all the Jews move to cities in Poland. They had to move to ghettos which were protected by stone walls and barb wire. The Germans wanted the Jews to die from starvation. The Germans also say that they would take care of the kids and promise very happy things, but they lied they got put in gas chambers and gassed to death. There meals consisted of thick soup, potato peelings, and a scrap of bread. The Jews would lose about 50 pounds a month. The Jews are now haunted forever because of what happened ti them. My heros name is Chmielewska, Helena (Mother Superior), she helped out the jews in many ways during the holocaust.

Helena was born in 1903 and died January 5, 1997. She was a roman catholic and survived helping Jews during the holocaust. Her prefession was an orphanage director and a nun. She hid Jews during the holocaust to help them to survive. She saved kids that were Jews from having to go to ghettos or concentration camps. There was a little girl named Rozalia her mom had gotten taken by the Germans because they were Jewish. Her father stuck by her side and was trying to find someone that would help and hide his daughter. He married a 19 year old polish girl named Czesława who was able to help him. She had Rozalia with her from now on. The father asked Czesława if she would protect his daughter for him, she agreed in helping. Czesława's family included her two parents, and four adult aged kids living out of town. She begged her father, who unwillingly let her shelter Rozalia. He didn't contribute to helping her protect the little Jewish girl, but her mom helped her a lot through the process. The first step was to make Rozalia polish, they set a priest to baptize her. Her father knew that he had to do this for the safety of his daughter. He sent information about his relatives that linve in the United States, in case he didn't survive. In 1944 je was captured by the Germans and was mudered. Czesława tried to get a job and move out of her parents house, but was unable too. She didn't know what to do so she went to her family doctor and asked for some advice. His suggestion was to send Rozalia to an orpanage. The orphanage was was ran by Helena Chmielewska, Mother Superior. She knew that some of the girls were actually Jewish, but she didn't say anything and let her join them. Rozalia wasn't the only Jewish girl in the orphanage. Chmielewska was happy to raise all of the girls that were Jews in the orphanage. The Jewish children survived the Holocaust inside of the orphange. Chmielewska cared for the children with respect, love, and treasured them. She continued to chech up on them and there situations to make sure that they were okay. After the Holocaust was finished there still had a connection. Rozalia joined her family that lived in the United States and became a pediatrician. Czesława vistited Rozalia frequently and they also stayed in touch with Chmielewska. Chmielewska helped people and there families in the Holocaust by hiding Jews. She is greatly appreciated in the world.

The Holocaust taught me that there not ever be discrimination in the world. Discriminating people is mean and not right, some people that get discrimated are good and it's not fair. Everyone in the world should have there own voice and not have to change because some people don't like them. They should be able to believe and be what they want to be. The impact that Chmielewska had on my life was that you should always try to help people that are in trouble. You shouldn't be a bystandard and let someone get pushed around you should help and say something about it. Holocaust survivors say "Never Again" because this should never happen in the world. Everyone is equal and has rights to be who they want without someone saying they can't and not letting them do what other people can. The steps that can be taken so this never happens again is that people can't let it happen. We have to stand up for whoever is getting discriminated. We have to help and take action instead of letting it happen and watching. The Holocaust was a terrible time in history and should never happen again.

Work Cited

"About the Holocaust." About the Holocaust. N.p., n.d. Web. 08 Dec. 2016.

"The Righteous Among The Nations." Yad Vashem - Request Rejected. N.p., n.d. Web. 08 Dec. 2016.

Wojan, Megan. "Introduction to Holocaust." Social Science 7 Honors Class Lecture. KAMS, Elk Grove. 11 Nov. 2016. Lecture.

Irena Sendler

An Le

 The Holocaust. The Sacrifice by Fire. Memories of piles of dead corpses, cries for loved ones, and above all, death. When the National Socialist German Workers party (NAZI) and Adolf Hitler as their leader came to power in 1933, he gave hope that Germany would come out of their depression. That was until non-Germans found out that he believed that Germans were the dominating master race. Hitler blamed Germany's hardships on the Jews. It all began with German children not being able to go to the same school as Jewish children to Germans not being able to go to Jewish shops. Aftertime, laws were being passed against Jews. For instance, in 1933 Jews were not allowed to hold public office and in 1935 the Nuremberg Laws deprived Jews of their rights as German citizens. Thereafter, Jews were forced to wear yellow stars of David to identify themselves from Germans. As the days passed, violence increased and Jews were fleeing left and right. The Nazi party had been pleas ed with the decrease in Jews, but there were still plenty more. The Germans had wanted the extermination of the Jews. Jews in countries that were under German control were all ordered in ghettos, overcrowded neighborhoods meant to starve the Jews to their death or cause them to perish of disease. Adolf Hitler was still unpleased with the amount of Jews still in Germany so called upon the "Final Solution" for eliminating the Jews and took them from their ghettos and moved them into concentration camps to be killed. This was known as genocide.

Life in the concentration camps were even worse than today's prisons. Families were separated to make captives lose all hope. No matter your gender or age, your head was shaved, arms tattooed a number you were called by, and forced to wear a prison uniforms. They all stayed in contaminated, disease ridden, and lice infested barracks. Some Jews were even taken as lab rats to be tested on inhumane medical experiments. The extermination areas were armed with gas chambers disguised as "communal showers" that killed masses at a time. It was a treacherous time.

Irena Sendler had was a 29 year old Christian when Germany invaded Poland. She had been a senior administrator in the Warsaw Social Welfare Department. This company had previously distributed canteens containing items needed for survival to the elderly, the poor, and orphans. For example, there were food, financial aid, and other services assisting them with their survival. After Irena found out about the discrimination of the Jews, the canteens sent to Jews were put under fake Christian names to prevent inquiry. Irena also added clothing, medicine, and money since Jews had been deprived of their rights as German citizens. These acts of goodwill is only the beginning of actions to help the Jews. But of course, the Germans saw these small revolutions and in 1942, the Nazis rounded up hundreds of thousands of Jews into a 16-block space known as the Warsaw Ghetto. The small area surrounded by tall, looming barbed wire only gave the Jews the hope of certain death from disease or starvation. This all but a thorn on Irena's path to helping the Jews. It was just another reason to help the Jews obtain equality.

Most of Irena's work had been inspired by her father, one of the first Polish Socialists. She joined the Zegota, the Council for Aid to Jews, organized by the Polish underground resistance movement. Irena joined as one of the first recruits and directed the attempts to rescue Jewish children. Entering the ghettos legally would prove to be a difficult task. Irena managed to obtain a pass from Warsaw's Epidemic Control Department and visited the ghettos frequently to bring food, medicines, and clothing to the prisoners. Despite her actions, 5,000 people were dying a month and Irena had to execute a mission she would have never thought of doing. Leaving the ghettos with the Jewish children.

Irena's plan started out as sneaking children out with an ambulance to mechanics carrying a baby in their toolbox. Surprisingly, sneaking the children out wasn't the hardest part. Convincing the parents to part with their children was. Agitated and tormented parents were always asking questions in worry of their children but most frequently the question," Can you guarantee that they will live?" Sendler only guaranteed that the children would die if they stayed. Irena says," In my dreams, I still hear the cries when they left their parents." She would then send the children to orphanages, religious establishments or convents, and homes. It was difficult sometimes taking in some Jewish children because that was over the fear if the Nazis ever found out. In total, Irena and her team saved 2,500 Jewish children. All of those names had been written in coded form revealing their true identity, put in a jar, and buried beneath an apple tree in a neighbor's backyard. This was all put towards the dream that she could someday dig up the jar after the war and reunite families. But this dream was cut short on October 20, 1943 when the Nazis became aware of Irena's deeds and arrested her. Irena was then imprisoned and abused by the Gestapo. She was the only one who knew the names and addresses of the families protecting and hiding the Jewish children. Irena's spirit being so strong, did not let anyone break her will, resulting to the Gestapo breaking her legs and feet. Young Sendler had withstood torture, staying loyal to her allies and the Jewish children in hiding. When she was finally sentenced to death, she was saved at the last second by the Zegota. The Zegota had bribed one of the Germans to pause the execution and freed Sendler. Though she was freed, she was pursued by the Gestapo for the rest of the War. After the war had passed, Irena dug up her jar of names to track down the 2,500 children saved thanks to her. She received many thankful calls from the children she saved after years of sacrifice for the war. Sadly, due to the long months of trying to reunite families all over Europe, Irena Sendler missed her own mother's funeral. Though Irena does not to think of herself as a hero, she always looking out for others and never has failed to inspire our humanity.

Irena Sendler was a loyal and courageous woman, always putting others before herself. I've learned that bravery and loyalty is always the best path to take, no matter the risks and consequences. You don't always have to cower in fear of ones of higher power. The ones less power usually have more heart. Irena has enforced ignorance is the worst that could be bestowed on a society during times like this. The view of my life has changed from the Holocaust. Ignorance, discrimination, and acceptance all were the cause of the Holocaust. The Germans ignored the fact that Jews were being publicly humiliated and called out. They didn't see the wrong in blaming the Jews and saw them as less than their own kind. They accepted the fact that around 166 Jews were being murdered every single day in the camps. They hid in their homes like cowards waiting for change, not wanting to cause change. Never again will mankind bestow equals so much hatred for being a different religion. Never again will we see ourselves higher than others. Never again will we be so ignorant of the changes of our world. We can prevent another Holocaust from happening again by always communicating with others and getting along with them. We can expand our roots and explore other cultures to see our commons. But never again will our discrimination kill part of our humanity.

Works Cited

"Irena Sendler." Irena Sendler | Jewish Virtual Library. Jewish Virtual Library, n.d. Web. 11 Dec. 2016.

"Irena Sendler." Irena Sendler. Louis Bülow, n.d. Web. 11 Dec. 2016.

"The World Holocaust Remembrance Center." Yad Vashem. N.p., n.d. Web. 11 Dec. 2016.

Wojan, Megan. "Introduction to the Holocaust Essay." Class Lecture. KAMS, Elk Grove. 8 Nov. 2016. Lecture.

Irena Adamovicz

Andrew Hutcheson

For my holocaust essay I have chosen a female that goes by the name of Irena Adamowicz. Irena was born on May 11, 1910 and sadly died on the 12 of August in 1973. But before she died she had a very important role in giving communication and hope. After World War 2 she still stayed close to some of the survivors of the Holocaust.

Irena Adamowicz was a Polish born scout leader and resistance worker during World War 2 Irena Adamowicz was born in Warsaw, to a Polish family. In her life she held a degree in social work from the University of Warsaw which was before World War 2 started. As a leader of the Polish scout movement (Harcerz Polski) coordinating its activities as a Senior Girl Scout. Irena Adamowicz Was a Roman Catholic at the time provided counseling and education not only for the Catholic Scouts, but also the Jewish youth movement called Hashomer Hatzair in the 1930's. While doing this she also worked with Arie Wilner. Irena Adamowicz followed the Nazi German invasion of Poland and became a member of the underground Home Array (Armia Krajowa) as a clandestine courier. Her job was to deliver messages and provide aid and moral support for Jewish ghettos in several cities. In 1985, Irena Adamowicz was given the title, Righteous Among the Nations by Yad Vashem in Jerusalem for her stand against the Holocaust. Since she worked for both, Polish and Jewish befor he attack of Poland, and her close contact with Jewish zionist movement, Irena Adamowicz went on a dangerous trip across Poland and Lithuania to establish contact between clandestine organizations in the ghettos of Warsaw,

Wilno(now Vilnius), Bialystok, Kovno (now Kaunas), and Shave. Her visits became an important source of information and moral encouragement. She earned a Jewish nickname "Di chalutz she shikse", the Pioneering Gentile.

While writing this essay I learned that anyone can make a difference no matter your religion, race, or gender. Irena Adamowicz helped realize that sometimes you need to go out of your safe zone and yy to make a difference in someone else's life and try to change their perspective on others. I understand that the Jews, and helping hands like Irena Adamowicz were trying their hardest to survive during such a horrible time period but still did not succeed in saving everyone due to the terrifying Nazi army. Now this is why the entire world needs to never ever give too much power and use all their power to make sure no one does. People also just need to start accepting their past mistake and not try to frame anyone for what they did wrong. I am proud to say the famous words "Never Again".

Works Cited

"Irena Adamowicz | Wikiwand." Wikiwand. N.p. n.d. Web. 11 Dec. 2016

Revolvy, LLC. ""Irena+Adamowicz" on Revolvy.com." All Revolvy Quizzes. Https://www.revolvy.com/main/index.php?s=Irena%20Adamowicz, n.d. Web. 13 Dec. 2016.

""Women of Valor"" Irena Sendler - Stories of Women Who Rescued Jews During the Holocaust - Righteous Among the Nations - Yad Vashem. N.p., n.d. Web. 13 Dec. 2016.

The Life of Zofia Yamaika

Andrew Quihuiz

Throughout the dark days of the Holocaust, there were many young women who played an important role in the rescue and survival of their fellow Jews. There were indeed "Women of Valor." Some worked with the Partisans and the Resistance and some fought back as individuals to save the lives of hundreds of children and adults. Their memory and courage during endless days of despair will forever shine as rays of light in a world that had lost its humanity. Zofia Yamaika, who was born in 1925 into a prominent family in Warsaw, Poland, played a vital role in the rescue of Jews.

Before armed resistance became a reality, Zofia became a leader of the children's group that would meet in her father's house. They took in children, fed them, and cared for their needs. They also owned a free soup kitchen along with cultural, educational and recreational activities.

After her parents were arrested by the Nazis and deported to the Treblinka concentration camp in 1942, she became involved in active resistance. She managed to escape the ghetto and was determined to stay with and support the partisans. In high school, she had joined a student group called Spartacus. Zofia was so athletic that she was designated by the Spartacus group to participate in a special training course for resistance fighters. Once they finished their training, they would form into small resistance groups to fight off the Germans.In a short time, she became the leader of an underground unit of five. Zofia and some of the partisans managed to help a small group of Jews escape from the ghetto. However, while waiting for a Polish courier to take them to the forest, Zofia and her Jewish comrades were betrayed by the courier and were caught in a Nazi raid in Biala-Podlaska. The Nazis marched their captives to an open area and put them aboard cattle car transports headed for Treblinka.Miracle of miracles, Zofia jumped from a moving train and managed to escape from the cattle car she was imprisoned in. Eventually, she made her way back to Warsaw, alone and without identification papers.

A Polish underground worker, Eva Pewinska, obtained forged Aryan papers for Zofia and assisted her in maintaining a false identity as a Catholic. Zofia managed to get a job working for an illegal newspaper published by the Gwardia Ludowa, which was the Polish underground that operated in an area annexed by the Nazis. However, that did not last long. Betrayed by Polish spies, she and the others were arrested in a Gestapo raid and imprisoned in the Pawiak prison for three months.As far as the Nazis were concerned, she was not Jewish. She stuck firmly to her story, and her Jewish identity was not discovered. Even though she was looked upon as a Christian, she was unable to return to her previous associates after her release for fear of getting caught in a trap. She found herself alone and helpless. A fortunate meeting with another Jewish girl, living as a Christian Pole, led to Zofia's leaving of Warsaw and joining another Polish partisan group operating in the vicinity of Radom.   Zofia's job with the new group of partisans was to be the liaison with other partisan groups who had organized reconnaissance missions in which they participated in sabotaging the German forces as often as possible. In the course of their attacks on the Nazis, the partisans managed to capture a number of Nazi spies and agents who were trying to infiltrate the partisan group. Zofia was assigned to a special squad that liquidated Polish spies and Nazi agents. In a short time, she was decorated for bravery by the General Staff.In February, 1942, the Germans retaliated against the partisans for a raid in which they had attacked the German police, enabling Poles, who had been rounded up for slave labor, to flee.The partisans were vastly outnumbered and were forced to retreat. Zofia and two Poles volunteered to stay behind to cover the retreat. Zofia took up her position where the Nazis were expected to attack and manned the machine gun. She and the two Jews held their ground and fought until they were overwhelmed. However, they did ensure the safety of the rest of the partisans who were able to escape. Zofia's heroism was recognized even by the Germans. After she was killed by machine gun fire, the Germans ordered the peasants to bury her properly, "with respect."Later, she received a military burial, and, in 1963, was posthumously awarded the Virtuti Militari, one of the Polish government's highest military awards.

I learned that the Holocaust was a very brutal "war" between the Germans and the Jews. This feud contained of unthinkable acts from the Nazi's. Without a doubt it is unbearable what the Germans did to the Jews. The impact of learning about Zofia's life made me feel thoughts and emotions of sadness and sorrow. I understand that the Holocaust was a terrible event that will never be forgotten and will never happen again. The steps that we can take to assure that "never again" will this happen is to have a clear mind and not judge anyone or get jealous.The Holocaust was a very evil act by the Germans and we should all pledge " Never Again".

Works Cited

N.p., n.d. Web.
"Our Jerusalem.com -." Our Jerusalem.com -. N.p., n.d. Web. 13 Dec. 2016.
"POLAND." Blackfriars 25.292 (1944): 241-43. Web.
"Sofia Yamaika." Sofia Yamaika in the Mural La Lucha Continua in SF. N.p., n.d.
http://www.yadvashem.org/yv/pdf-drupal/poland.pdf
Web. 13 Dec. 2016.

Heroes of the Holocaust: Krystyna Adolph

Andrew Saska

Krystyna Adolph was a righteous person for a reason. She saved two innocent Jewish twins from the wrath of the National Socialist German Workers' party, or the Nazis, for short.

Krystyna Adolph was a survivor of the Holocaust and a righteous one. She was a Polish woman who taught in a high school. She was Catholic, so she would not be hunted by the Nazis, unless she helped a Jewish person or persons during the Holocaust. She did exactly that. She helped two twin sisters survive the Holocaust.

Krystyna Adolph was a high school teacher at Czartoryski High School in Vilna, Lithuania before World War II broke out. Twin sisters Monica and Lydia Aran (Jewish) were students in her high school class. When World War II broke out, Krystyna, widowed at the time, was left to support herself and her young daughter on her small farm. The Arans lived in Vilna, not far from her farm, and Krystyna lived in a small village, named Ignalio, near Troki, about thirty miles from Vilna.

When the Germans were about to occupy Vilna, Krystyna sent a messenger to Vilna to tell the Aran sisters that they were welcome to stay at her farm for as long as they wanted to if they were ever in danger. When the Nazis established the Vilna Ghetto in September 6, 1941, the Aran sisters knew they were in trouble. They took up Krystyna's offer and went over to her farm. They received a warm welcome and the sisters spent three years at the farm. Even when the Nazis occupied Krystyna's village, they stayed at the farm. They were being passed off as Krystyna's relatives who fled from hard farm labor. The only people who knew the Aran twins real identities were Krystyna and her late husband's father and sister.

Krystyna not only helped the Aran sisters, but she also helped the twin's mother, too. Krystyna obtained false identity papers for their mother so she could live on the Aryan (German religion) side of the area and be safe. Krystyna knew she was taking a great risk. That idea was magnified when she heard that the Germans burned down a house in a neighboring village, with the family inside, when they found a Jewish family hiding inside.

The Aran twins survived the war and moved to Israel where they stayed in contact with Krystyna.

This story moved me. It taught me that I should always help someone out in a tough situation, or just whenever I can. I will help people every day, if I can. That's a result of learning the kindness of Krystyna Adolph.

While I was researching Krystyna, I learned some things about the Holocaust. I learned that there were more ghettos and concentration camps than I thought. I learned that there were, on average, about ten per country. I also learned that the Holocaust was called something different by people who spoke Hebrew, so mostly Jewish people. They called the Holocaust the Shoah, which means catastrophe. I would say that it is a good word to use because the Holocaust was a catastrophe.

I understand that the Holocaust was a mass execution of Jewish people and anyone who was brave enough to help them. The Holocaust was a persecution and genocide of millions of innocent Jewish people. It was nothing more than an execution of people just because they were of a different religion than the German religion, Aryan. About ten million innocent Jewish people, and the people who helped them, were brutally slaughtered. Ten million people were slaughtered from the year 1933 to 1945, when the United States of America dropped a nuclear bomb called "Little Boy" on Hiroshima, Japan, thus ending the war.

Krystyna Adolph made an impact in some people's lives. She saved three innocent people (Monica and Lydia Aran, and their mother) from the horror of the concentration camps. She saved them from being executed by the Nazis. She was their hero, and she deserves all the recognition she can get. This is actually one of the reasons why I picked Krystyna, because she saved three lives.

We can stop this from happening again. We have to learn from our mistakes in the past, and fix any that we come across. We need to have a more secure society, with laws that keep us safe and are beneficial for the people that our society is built of. We need to be vigilant, but we also need to be wary of impending threats. We need to have more security so if disasters do happen, we will be ready.

I will say two words and two words only. Never again. These two words have the power to change the world. If you use these two words, you could stop someone in their tracks. If you use these words, you could change someone's mind about doing something horrible. So, use these words whenever you can. They will remind people of what happened and it will stop people from doing the same.

Therefore, we must learn from our mistakes and try to prevent them so they will never happen again. Never again.

Works Cited

"Adolph Krystyna." Yad Vashem - Request Rejected. Yad Vashem. The World Holocaust Remembrance Center, n.d. Web. 17 Nov. 2016.

The Righteous Among the Nations." Yad Vashem - Request Rejected. Yad Vashem. The World Holocaust Remembrance Center, n.d. Web. 05 Dec. 2016.

Gilbert, Martin. "The Righteous." Google Books. Google Books, n.d. Web. 06 Dec. 2016.

Rudolf Weigl

Andrew W. Westfall

 The Holocaust was, undoubtedly, one of the worst times in history, because it was the mass persecution of an entire race of people. A holocaust is a mass destruction, slaughter, and death by fire. In the year 1932, the Nazi party, led by Adolf Hitler, came to power in Germany. His belief was that the Germans were a "master race" called the Aryans and that all other people, especially the other Jews and all people who were not Aryans were inferior and were considered a threat to their "perfect" race. In the year 1939, the German government began to make laws against Jews, prohibiting them from holding public office and other positions of power. Eventually, violence broke out when the Germans began persecuting them, like breaking windows in Jewish business districts. Later, the Jews were moved from their homes and isolated into ghettos. The ghettos were overcrowded, overpopulated, unhealthy, had barely any food and water to feed the Jews, and the ghettos were a breeding ground for diseases of all kinds.

Luckily, there were some Germans who did not believe what Hitler had to say about the Jews and decided to help them. These people are called "the righteous" by the Jews. The righteous man who saved Jews during the Holocaust that I chose for this essay, was a man named Dr. Rudolf S. Weigl. Dr. Weigl was a Catholic biologist of German ethnicity. He was born in 1883, in Prerau, Moravia, when it was still a part of the Austro-Hungarian Empire. Dr. Weigl died on August 11, 1957, in Zakopane, Poland. Dr. Weigl was also nominated 75 times for a Nobel Prize. He is considered a righteous person because he rescued 4 Jewish people: Paula Meisel, Henryk Meisel, Felicja Mikolajczyk Meisel, and Bronislaw Knaster Lilienfeld.

When Dr. Weigl was a little boy, he lost his father in a bicycle accident. His mother remarried to a Polish teacher and they moved to Jaslo, Poland. Later, his family moved to Lviv, Poland where he graduated from the university there.

Dr. Rudolf Weigl was a Polish biologist who graduated from the biology department at the University of Jan Kazimierz and was the inventor of the first effective typhus vaccine. Typhus is a potentially fatal disease that is transmitted by lice. He founded the Weigl Institute in Lviv, Poland, where he and many other scientists conducted medical research for a possible vaccine for typhus. There, during the Holocaust, he harbored and protected the four Jews by employing them as lice feeders in his laboratory. A lice feeder is someone who is clean and sterile, then they put little cages filled with lice on their body. The lice feeders would then allow the lice to suck their own blood. There was no chance at all of the Jews being contaminated due to the fact that they were sterile. He then invented a technique for making the vaccine that involved dissected lice guts.

During the German occupation of Poland, the Nazi's attempted to turn Dr. Weigl's institute into a production plant that made typhus vaccines. They were afraid of the typhus epidemic spreading throughout Germany and did not want their soldiers to die from the fatal disease. In an effort to thwart the Nazi's efforts, Dr. Weigl successfully smuggled his good, strong typhus vaccines into the Jewish ghettos and instead sent weak, useless typhus vaccines to the Nazi's. This act saved countless Jewish lives. Due to the weak vaccines that were still being sent by Dr. Weigl's lab, the Nazi's continued to catch typhus and die from it, however the ghettos became much more healthier than they had ever been because of the strong vaccines. During the German occupation of Lviv, Poland, he continued to smuggle more Jews from the ghettos into his laboratory by employing them as lice feeders. In the year 1944, the Institute was shut down by the Soviet Union.

If Dr. Weigl had not chosen to save Jewish people from the concentration camps, then one of the many people that he saved, Henryk Meisel, would not have been able to study medicine in Vienna, because he would be dead. Henryk would not have gone on to be appointed as the director of the institute for bacteriological and experimental medicine in Warsaw, Poland.

After reading about Dr. Weigl's life and learning what he did to save Jews during the Holocaust, I learned that he risked being sentenced to the death penalty for harboring Jews, and that he was a very brave man because of his humanitarian decisions. The impact on my life that Dr. Weigl made has been that I have learned what courage really is. Courage is when you risk your life, your family, and everything you love, for something that you feel is right even though you might die from doing the act. I understand now, reading about what the Holocaust really was, I never want something like it to happen again. In order to make sure that something like the Holocaust never happens again, we need to understand each other better, and learn that all people, whether they are German, Jewish, have black skin or white skin, all need to understand that everybody is equal. No man is greater than another man.

Works Cited:

"11 Feb 1943 in Auschwitz #Holocaust 5 Employees, from the Weigl..." RENA'S PROMISE. Admin, 14 Feb. 2013. Web. 10 Dec. 2016. <http://www.heatherdune.com/renaspromise/2013/02/14/11-feb-1943-in-auschwitz-holocaust-5-employees-from-the-weigl-institute-were-registered-in-auschwitz-with-their-wives-and-their-children/>.

www.yadvashem.org/yv/pdf-drupal/poland.pdf

Revolvy, LLC "Rudolf+Weigl" on Revolvy.com." All Revolvy Quizzes. Jan.-Feb. Web. 10 Dec. 2016. <http://www.revolvy.com/main/index.php?s=Rudolf%2BWeigl&item_type=topic>.

Allen, Arthur "How Scientists Created A Typhus Vaccine In A 'Fantastic Laboratory'" NPR. NPR, 22 Feb. 2014. Web. 10 Dec. 2016. <http://www.npr.org/2014/07/22/333734201/how-scientists-created-a-typhus-vaccine-in-a-fantastic-laboratory>.

Natalia Tomczak

Angela Tomasello

The Holocaust during 1933 was a traumatic time for many Jews trying to flee the Nazi regime. As many as 1.5 million children who were from Poland, Soviet Union, or Romania perished along with over 1 million Jewish children. Many children lived in poor conditions and what the Nazis referred to as the ghettos of Germany. Starvation, disabilities, inadequate clothing were some of the reasons children died during this portion of Jewish history. The official date of the Holocaust began January 30, 1933,

Adolf Hitler was elected as chancellor of Germany with the Nazi party.

Prior to Adolf Hitler's inauguration he had attempted to over throw the Bavarian government in 1923 and was imprisoned as a result. During his time in prison he began to develop his belief that the Aryan brotherhood were a superior race, which had despised Jews and their lifestyle. January 30th 1933 became the beginning of an era that almost completely wiped out all Jews. His ultimate plan was to first embarrass Jews and created laws that claimed Jews could not keep their own businesses and property, Hitler had his Nazis keep Jews away from public events, he had burned their religious books, kept Jews from running in office, and had them wear a yellow stars of David everywhere they went so they could be embarrassed in public.

Among other drastic decisions Hitler had conducted he had moved Jews to Poland in ghettos and kept them from their families in complete isolation, he was determined to make Jews weak mentally and physically. Hitler had made them do hard labor, gave them little food, and had all Jews, including children, watch them hang potential spies, and he slowly killed women and children under ten. Hitler's final conclusion was to put Jews in extermination camps and he had killed 91% of Jews in Poland using methods such as gas chambers which had potentially killed a massive amount of Jews almost decimating their existence. This unfortunate event was a reality for many Jews not ending until May 8, 1945. Although there were many killed some did survive to tell their story which in many cases can be inspirational and open others eyes to realize how truly disgusting this time was in Poland.

During this horrible time, there were many people in Poland who were willing to risk their lives in attempts to save Jews lives, we call these amazing people Heroes of Poland. Natalia Tomczak is one of many Polish heroes and survivors living to tell their stories in hopes that this type of event never takes place again. She was born on 1909 and was raised as a catholic. Her husband was in an army and was taken prisoner before the ghettos were created and she was left alone with her son in Warsaw, Poland. One day a women named Anna Mozes asked Natalia to help her and her four year old son, Martin, escape the dreadful ghetto. Luckily, Natalia had immediately said yes and was able to take Anna and Martin into her home. It took a while, but she was able to gather documents that stated Martin was her son and Anna was her sister who was married to a Polish officer. Fortunately, nobody had found out about this during the Holocaust. When the horrid Holocaust was over Anna had married a man and moved to Israel with him and Martin. Anna and Martin still talked to Natalia until she died in 2007.

After reading Natalia's story on how she was able to rescue Jews, it has given me a new perspective on how much I should appreciate how things are today. Today, we have media, and we can figure out everything about someone, when during the Holocaust, nobody could've known anything else about Hitler except for his idea of a superior race. Natalia's story, and every other Holocaust survivor's story, has inspired me, and shown me what happens when people, and myself, believe in propaganda. These stories have taught to look over the propaganda, and see the truth behind it first.

Natalia, Anna, Martin, Natalia's son, and every other Holocaust survivor able to tell their stories have mentioned the words, "never again." Never again, is a way Holocaust survivors and others raise awareness to what could happen if we fall for propaganda. To never let people have to suffer like the Jews did, to never let us be tricked easily by propaganda, and to have us think of ways that could prevent something as devastating as the Holocaust from ever happening again.

Some ways that could help raise awareness to the Holocaust is by making more websites and videos reminding people what will happen when we believe in something too good to be true. Many kids have access to the internet, so they can stumble upon a Holocaust website or video. This way, kids can learn about this time and start thinking of their own ways to make sure this never happens again. Also, kids can go on websites and learn propaganda at a young age which will prepare them for when they're an adult and can vote for their country, and be reminded to not vote for propaganda and do their research.

With websites and videos, we can change many people's perspectives, and have others realize that something like the Holocaust has potential to happen again, and we need to think of ways to prevent this from ever being a problem. Hopefully, people will get inspired and think of their own ways to prevent such problems from occurring, and let the words "never again" stay true.

Works Cited

Wojan, Megan. "Introduction to the Holocaust." Elk Grove, Rancho Cordova. 4 Nov. 2016. Lecture.

Yad Vashem - Request Rejected. N.p., n.d. Web. 11 Dec. 2016.

"The Definition of Adolf Hitler." Dictionary.com. N.p., 2012. Web. 11 Dec. 2016.

United States Holocaust Memorial Museum. United States Holocaust Memorial Museum, n.d. Web. 11 Dec. 2016.

Holocaust Essay

Angelica Slivinskiy

Imagine German soldiers knocking telling you to open up the door, getting impatient during the Holocaust (that had started in 1941 and finally ended in 1945) and you were hiding a few Jews in your home. You prepared yourself by hiding them so that they won't be found and taken to concentration camps because after all, they are your closest friends. You too would be taken to the camps because you helped hide them (because back then, if you helped a Jew, your punishment could be death). Well that's exactly what happened to a brave and courageous Zofia Bania (1907-1991) who helped her friends that were Jews stay alive during a scary time for Jews.

Zofia Bania was a poor farmer in the village of Wolchy and happened to be a regular customer in Israel and Frania Rubinek's store that sold basic goods to farmers. After a while, Zofia and Frania became very close friends. When the Germans started to take the Jews into custody in October 1942, they knew they had to hide so, Zofia decided to help, even if it risked her life. Israel build a bunker under the store and stayed there wife with his until after the Germans stopped the roundups. Then they fled to a nearby town but couldn't go to Russia for safety like many others have because Frania was eight months pregnant. When the two were deciding what to do, they heard good news that Zofia was looking for them and they were happy that she still wanted to care for them and make sure that they are alive and okay. Israel hired a trustworthy man to take them to Zofia's house. When they arrived to the one roomed home, they were welcomed with open arms by Zofia but her husband Ludwig didn't wanted them to be there but, the Rubinek's tried to please him and they paid him for his silence because they worried that he would turn them in. In December 1942, in that house, Frania was going into labor but the baby died at birth.

SInce it was half of kilometer from the nearest neighbor, it was a pretty safe place for them to hide. They also had a guard dog that would bark very loudly when someone came close to the house. In one event, the dog's barked helped notify Zofia and her guests that the German soldiers were near by. Zofia immediately had them go and hid in the cellar as the soldiers came up to Zofia and said that they would spend a night at their house. She put her six year old son Maniek's bed right in front of the entrance so the soldiers didn't suspect anything or see the refuges. At that time Israel was suffering from a bad cough that was easily heard. Maniek, despite his young age, was smart enough to make up a plan on the spot and pretended to be sick and cry loudly so the German soldiers did not think that it was really a sick Jew coughing but that it was the little "sick" and tired boy. Zofia hid the Rubinek's until the area liberated by the Red Army in January 1945. Later the two moved to Canada then traveled to Poland in 1980 with her son Saul Rubinek, who was a filmmaker and recorded his visit in a documentary called So Many Miricles, went to see Zofia and thank her for risking her life to save theirs.

In my understanding, the Holocaust was a tough disgraceful, disgusting and cruel time for the Jews and the one's who were brave enough and had enough courage to stand up for them. This has encouraged me to stand up for people and for what I believe what is right even if I'm the only one who believes. The Holocaust had a huge impact on the happy Jews who were tortured and are devastated. We as people can stand together for what is right, for all people. Black or white. Boy or girl. Religious or non-religious. We as people can defeat negativity if we really tried and if we all try so that this horrific and shameful event doesn't ever happen again. So that signs on the cardboard that were held by the hopeful Jews would be true, the cardboard signs that read "never again". So that this happens "never again".

Works Cited

"Why Is the Phrase "Never Again" Associated with the Holocaust?" Etymology - Why Is the Phrase "Never Again" Associated with the Holocaust? - English Language & Usage Stack Exchange. N.p., n.d. Web. 13 Dec. 2016.

Yad Vashem - Request Rejected. N.p., n.d. Web. 13 Dec. 2016.

This has encouraged me to stand up for people and for what I believe what is right even if I'm the only one who believes. The Holocaust had a huge impact on the happy Jews who were tortured and are devastated. We as people can stand together for what are right, for all people.

Irena Sendler

Angelina San Miguel

Adolf Hitler's promise for change and a chance for hope had many people fooled. Instead of change and uniting people he tore apart friends, families, and neighbors. He made people believe Germans were superior and Jews, Gypsies, and the handicapped were lesser people. During the holocaust many men, women, and children died. Over one million Jewish children died, tens of thousands of Gypsy children died, and thousands of handicapped children died. In total one and a half million children were murdered during the holocaust. Irena Sendler saved many Jewish children from ghettos and families that may have died without her help.

Irena was born in 1910, in Poland. When the Nazi's took control of Germany, she didn't believe Hitler actually wanted change and didn't believe that he provided hope for economic growth. She knew, before most people, Hitler's real plan. She was given permission by the Germans to go into ghettos and control the spread of typhus and other diseases so they wouldn't spread outside the ghettos. She even wore a Star of David, and she told the Germans it was to make her unnoticed among the Jewish. Irena would smuggle children and infants out of the ghettos. The hardest part of sneaking children out of the ghetto was getting permission from their parents. Some parents didn't want their kids to leave because they were afraid they would never see them again, or they were afraid they were going to lose their heritage. Irena would respect their decision, but when she would return the next day the children and their families were sent to concentration camps. She put small infants and children in the bottom of her tool box, and the larger children in a burlap sack at the bottom to cover them up. She had trained a dog to bark on her command to cover up the crying of the children. After the kids were taken out of the camps, she kept them in the back of her ambulance under blankets, in tool boxes, in sacks, and even in caskets while she was driving them to safety. She would then give the children new identities, and give them to non Jewish families, Roman Catholic churches, and orphanages. When she had a new child she would say "I have clothing for the convent," which was code for "I have a new child." She made sure to keep the children's real names in a glass jar under a tree far away from her home. She also worked in an underground network to sneak Jews out of Germany. While working underground she made fake documents for over 3,000 families to help them escape Germany. She was caught, arrested, and tortured. She disobeyed the German soldiers many times. One time was when Irena and a few others cut holes in the German soldiers' underwear while doing their laundry. Irena and the others were caught, put in a single file line, and every other person was shot and killed. After one last torture session, before she was going to be executed, both her arms and legs were broken. After that last torture session while she was conscious, and to her surprise, her friends from the underground network bribed a German soldier. He left her in the woods to be rescued, and marked her off as executed. This is one of the many times Irena escaped death. After the war was finally over she tried to find the parents of the children she saved. Most of their parents were killed in concentration camps. She was able to reunite a few families that survived the war. In 2007 she was nominated for the Nobel Peace Prize. She unfortunately lost to a man named Al Gore who won for a slideshow on climate change. Irena Sendler died on May 12, 2008, in Warsaw Poland of pneumonia. Irena was born in Warsaw, died in Warsaw, changed thousands of lives in Warsaw, and declared war on Hitler in Warsaw.

Irena Sendler was a truly inspiring woman. After reading about the holocaust, how people were treated, and how many brave people risked their lives to save people they even didn't know, I learned so much. I learned that you should always stand up for what you believe in, and small actions can have a big impact on people. After reading about Irena Sendler, she inspired me to always do what's right. She showed me that we are all equal, and all people should be treated the same regardless of race, religious beliefs, or physical appearance. I understand that the Holocaust had an impact on many people's lives. I know many innocent people were killed for nothing more than their religious beliefs. Even small actions such as not making fun of others for their looks, beliefs, and religion can prevent something like the holocaust happening again. The holocaust was based on hate on one group of people, and if we can learn that all people are equal, and stop discriminating that will prevent anything like the holocaust ever happening again. The holocaust should have never happened in the first place, but I, along with many others, hope and pray that never again will anyone have to suffer the way many did.

Works Cited

@moralheroes. "Irena Sendler - Moral Heroes." Moral Heroes. N.p., 14 Dec. 2015. Web. 11 Dec. 2016.

"POLAND." Blackfriars 25.292 (1944): 241-43. Web. 6 Dec. 2016.

Stromme, Lizzie. "Irena Sendler: The Holocaust Heroine Who Saved 2500 Jewish Children from Nazi Evil." Express.co.uk. N.p., 13 Sept. 2016. Web. 11 Dec. 2016.

Zofia Bania

Angelique Le

Zofia Bania was a poor farmer who lived in a small house with her husband and son. Zofia was born in 1907 and died in June 13, 1991. Zofia would go to a shop that sold basic goods for farmers. When she couldn't pay, the owner of the store would give her food and other things on credit. The owner and Zofia became great friends. Unfortunately, the couple who owned the store was Jews and would soon be hunted done. This is the tale of how Zofia saved the couple from the Germans.

Israel and Franciszka (Frania) Rubinek was a married couple in the town Pińczów which was already under German occupation. The couple opened a small shop which sold basic goods to local farmers. One of their customers was Zofia Bania, a poor farmer who lived in the nearby village of Włochy. At times when Zofia couldn't pay, Frania would give her food and other things on credit. Frania and Zofia got to know each other very well and became friends. Once, Frania asked Zofia, when the need arose, that she and Israel could hide from the Germans in Zofia's house. Zofia said that she would need some time to think about it. In the meantime, after hearing rumors about the fate of Jews living elsewhere, Israel decided to build a bunker under the store.

In October of 1942, the Germans started to round up the Jews in Pińczów and send them to Treblinka. Israel and Frania hid in their bunker until the roundups were over and then fled to a nearby town. They could not continue onto Russia like other Jews because Frania was eight months pregnant. Eventually news came to them that Zofia was looking for them back in Pińczów. So they hired a man they trusted to take them to Zofia's house in his wagon.

Zofia lived in a small, one room house with her husband, Ludwig, and six year old son, Maniek. When Israel and Frania arrived, Zofia came out to greet them warmly. However, Ludwig did not accept Israel and Frania in the home. Frania assured Ludwig that she would not betray her friends. Instead, the Rubineks thought that Ludwig was going to betray them. So the gave him money for his silence and tried their best to appease him.

At first, they stayed in the hayloft of the barn, which was attached to the house. It was there that Frania went into labor with only Israel and Zofia to care for her. The baby died

50

at birth and Frania fell seriously ill for three months. After that, the Rubineks moved into the main house where they shared one room with Zofia, Ludwig, and Maniek.

The house was on the outskirts of Wlochy, which made it relatively safe. Ludwig bought a guard dog, as an extra precaution, that would bark loudly if someone were to approach their house. On such occasions, Israel and Frania would hide in a tiny cellar that was used to hold potatoes. On time, towards the end of the war, German soldiers came in and declared that they intend to stay the night. Luckily, Israel and Frania were able to slip into the cellar, thanks to the watchdog, before the German soldiers arrived. Zofia placed a bed for Maniek directly over the entrance of the cellar so the German soldiers wouldn't notice it. The situation was still very dangerous because Israel was suffering from a cough. Maniek was well aware of the situation and thought that it was his duty to be responsible for the safety of the Rubineks. Maniek pretended to be sick all night, pretending to cough loudly and crying, thus saving the couple's life.

The Rubineks stayed with Zofia until the area was liberated by the Red Army in January 1945. After the war was over, the couple immigrated to Canada. In 1986, they traveled to Poland along with their son, filmmaker Paul Rubinek, to visit Zofia and Maniek.

I learned that the holocaust was a result of needing to blame someone after World War I ended. After World War I ended, Germany was blamed for what happened and had to pay for all the damage that occurred. Germany fell into a great depression. When Hitler came into power, he told everyone that the Jews were the cause of their depression and if they wanted someone to blame, blame the Jews. The German people were influenced by Hitler's words and discriminated the Jews. Zofia was a brave person. Even though she knew that she would be hated for saving the cause of their depression, she chose to do what felt right to her. And that was to save her dear friend Frania and Israel. Never Again should this happen. Discriminating one race of innocent people for the problem that you caused. We should first off never let a dispute like this happen ever again. Then we should take precautionary measure to ensure that genocide like the holocaust never happens again. Never Again.

Works Cited Page:
"The Righteous Among The Nations." Yad Vashem. N.p., 2016. Web. 30 Nov. 2016.
"Zofia Bania." Yad Vashem. N.p., 2016. Web. 30 Nov. 2016.

ANIELA MARIA ELZBIETA WORONIECKA

Anjli Tejpal

Often in the life of a 7th grader, a tear comes to your eyes when you think about doing homework. It's not often, when an assignment causes you to feel appreciative, makes you cry, and feel blessed to have acceptance of the rich diversity we have in our society today. This is exactly how I felt after understanding what other individuals had to go through during the persecution of the Jewish race. Having researched this topic, and the thousands of individuals who were part of the efforts to save the Jewish race truly helped me delve into this topic and although I wanted to research more than just one person, I am honored to have had the opportunity to write about one such wonderful person.

The Holocaust was described as the systematic, state-sponsored persecution and murder of six million Jews by the Nazi regime and its collaborators. Holocaust is a word of Greek origin meaning "sacrifice by fire." The Nazis, who came to power in Germany in January 1933, believed that Germans were "racially superior" and that the Jews, deemed "inferior," were an alien threat to the so-called German racial community. I am humbled by the opportunity to write this essay about a horrible time in our history from the prospective of a wonderful and positive person, Aniela Maria Elzbieta Woroniecka (I will refer to her as Aniela throughout the essay). As I read through the various literature surrounding the Holocaust I realized that there were many individuals who played an integral role in not only hiding and feeding Jewish people, but also putting their life on the line to ensure safety and health. I chose to focus on Aniela. Aniela was an individual classified as a holocaust rescuer. Specifically, she helped a family of 3 survive through the troubled times during this horrible phase in world history. Her efforts did not stop there. She helped countless individuals survive.

Aniela was born May 5th, 1898 and died July 7th, 1978. Living in Czartoryska from childhood, Aniela obtained the title of duchess. Aniela was one of the few individuals who was dedicated to helping persecuted Jews from the very beginning of the war. She shared food, clothing and provided medical help. During the wartime era, helping Jews was an offense punishable by death, and Aniela risked her life and home to provide Jewish refugees with temporary shelter in a special hiding place within her home. Her home was in Warsaw and she not only let refugees utilize her home, she also actively sought out other places of refuge where refugees could stay.

One of the survivors who was saved by Anelia, was Dr. Edward Reicher and his family. The Survivor wrote in his memoirs: 'Aniela Woroniecka was an angel in a human body. This woman was not even a bit demanding. She led her life sacrificing herself for others. She needed nothing for herself. She was the kindest human being I have ever met in my life'. In commemoration of the 70th anniversary of the creation of the polish council to aid Jews. Anelia was among those honored and received the "The Righteous Among The Nations Award". Part of what made Aniela's actions so special was that she had to fight against her family's wishes. Unfortunately, they were not in favor of helping persecuted Jews.

This is one of those times where I pray the words "History Repeats Itself", does not come true. A truly devastating experience that humans had to live thru, and the wonderful individuals who risked there homes, families, and above all their lives to save persecuted Jews. I understand now the impact that the Holocaust had on other individuals who were not Jewish. That is truly one of the biggest lessons I learned as I wrote this essay. Further, Anelia has become one of my hero's. She showed me that fighting for what you believe in leaves you fulfilled at a higher level and only god can understand the emotional impact of these actions. Moving forward I will remember Anelia's sacrifices and in my own way, see what I can do to have a positive influence on not only my life but those around me. One of the hardest questions I asked myself was, "how can such a catastrophe be prevented in the future". There were a few thoughts that came to mind. Specifically, No country should ever be allowed to have a sole dictator capable of making such ludicrous decisions. Secondly, the international community (i.e. United Nations), should intervene immediately as a united coalition. By standing together against a tyrannical opponent, there would be no chance for an event of this magnitude to occur again. Lastly, nations have agreed to meet and discuss global issues on a regular basis. Humanity and humane actions should be a standing agenda topic. This will help curtail any topic that veers in this direction, and bring international attention to it immediately. Finally, I feel empowered after learning about the difference one person can make. I will do my best to positively influence those around me to better our society and help to my part in erasing adversity.

Title: ''Ż Ż E G O
Authors: Ewa Rudnik, The Director Of The Righteous Department, Emba[...]
http://cmbassies.gov.il/warsaw/Departments/Sprawiedliwych/Documents/2012-12-04_ENG.pdf
https://www.myheritage.com/names/aniela_woroniecka -

Krystyna Adolph

Annie Carmichael

A horrible happening in history. "Why?" we all ask ourselves. There is no answer, as to why a man would destroy another race of people through genocide. Though we do not like to admit it, we could have done something more. Something. We will always remember and dwell on the lost lives of our loved ones. But, we will always celebrate survivors as well. All of them. But, without the help from others, they might not be alive today. One huge helper of sisters in Poland, with a story I find very intriguing, is Krystyna Adolf, a Holocaust hero.

Before the Holocaust, World War II, and Adolf Hitler becoming a German ruler, Krystyna was a teacher. She taught at Czartoryski High School in Vilna, Poland. Two Jewish, female, twins in her class, that she grew very close to, were named Monika and Lidia Gluskin. When the war occurred, she had to support her daughter and herself on a tiny farm in Ignalio, a small village closeby Troki. Troki was a village under Polish rule. Soon after the war broke out, Krystyna found out that the Germans were rounding up all of the Jews in Vilna, where she taught, and where Monika and Lidia were. She immediately wrote and sent a letter to the sisters, offering to care for and shelter them on her farm, instead of having them stay in the Vilna ghetto. This meant taking on a lot. She could barely support her and her daughter nevertheless support two more girls. But, she knew it was the right thing to do. When the Germans put up the Vilna ghetto, the twins took-up her invitation. Monika and Lidia fled to her farm, arriving with a warm welcome. They became family, and were able to stay in hiding for three years, as the war went on. Over those long years, the "family" worked together to do housework, take care of animals, chop firewood, and tend to the gardens and fields. Krystyna also allowed other neighbors and relatives into her home. Even though all residents were trusted, she always kept the Monika and Lidia Gluskin's true identities a very well kept secret. If the identities were ever released to the public, both families would be in very serious trouble. The nasty Germans would stop at nothing to make sure they were found and killed. The were such awful people that they make sure that they would suffer in their death. They would not make it quick and easy because they wanted the victim to understand that what they did was somehow "wrong". Only Krystyna's sister-in-law and father-in-law knew the Monika and Lidia's true identities. Krystyna's sister-in-law even created false documents on the girls' identities to try to fool the German soldiers. She forged signatures to insure Monika and Lidia's safety from the crazed Germans. Krystyna Adolf also created false documentation for the girl's mother. Very luckily, no one was ever caught. But, the thought of being caught was always on everyone in the household's mind, especially after watching a house being burned down, with the family still inside, because of illegal hiding. If one member of the 'family' everyone in the house would be blamed, and killed. That is how crazy the Germans were when it came to the harmless Jews. After the war, when and everyone and everything was safe, Krystyna accepted no remuneration (money or other objects in payment for actions) for her actions. She felt as if it was her job, not her decision to help out others, supported by her Catholic beliefs. The Gluskin sisters moved and settled in Israel. They kept in touch with Krystyna for many years.

This story has had a huge impact on my life. I have learned so much from this one story. I have learned to be such a nice, well-rounded human being. Krystyna has such an amazingly inspiring story. She was so considerate to others, which is something today's society can learn from. Though I have highlighted Krystyna in this article, all Holocaust heroes were an extreme help in stopping Hitler from accomplishing his absurd mission. All others who hid, or forged papers, or did anything else to get Jews out of the horrible situation should be honored always and forever. Their courage is extremely admirable. I think everyone should look into a Holocaust story, whether it be survivor, hero, or lost loved one. Anyone can learn from anyone else's story, and make this world a better place. I think everyone can learn something from this story. I believe that nothing even remotely close to a Holocaust should never again happen. To make sure of this, I think people everywhere should listen and hear about the inspiring and sad stories of the Holocausts. Not even just this one Holocaust, but the Holocausts that are very unfortunately happening everywhere. The Holocaust is a very dark time in our world's history. We should learn from that so we make sure that it does not ever happen again. Never. Again.

Work Cited

http://www.yadvashem.org

Ferdynand Arczyński

Annie Zhang

The Holocaust was a mass genocide of 6 million Jews that resided in Europe, as well as many other persecuted groups. This started in Germany, where Jews were already disrespected and looked down upon. This was mainly due to a newspaper that published comics that made the Jewish seem lesser than the Germans. Then, Hitler started taking control of Germany. Soon after Adolf Hitler was announced chancellor of Germany in 1921, the Nazis were formed. By 1934, Hitler had power over the whole of Germany. The Nazis started making concentration camps to contain the Jews, forcing them to ghettos and shipping them into extermination camps where they were gassed to death. The ghettos where tiny cramped spaces that were much too small to fit the Jews. With such terrible living conditions, most Jews died of hunger, overcrowding, and exhaustion before even reaching the camps. By the end of the Holocaust, over seventy percent of the Jewish population in Europe was dead. Only a few escaped the wrath of the Nazis. However, many courageous souls decided to stand up to the Nazis, and risk their lives to help the Jewish, even though over 700 Poles had already been slaughtered by the Germans for concealing Jews in their houses. They knew the risks and were willing to go through many lengths to save them. Ferdynand Arczyński was one such man determined to help his Jewish neighbors.

Ferdynand was a member of Zegota, which was the code name for the Council to aid the Jews. Going by the code name "Marek", he became the head of legalization and treasurer of the Zegota. The Zegota was an underground organization in Poland dedicated to rescue as many Jews as possible. Founded in the October of 1942 by Henryk Wolinski, there wasn't a more dedicated organization in all of Europe. Instead of hiding the Jews in people's homes and risking death, Zegota tried to aid the Jews a different way, by providing them with the essentials to survive. This was a difficult task, seeing as the Jews weren't easy to reach. They still Ferdynand helped provide food, medicine, shelter, money, and fake documents. This was a huge risk because it was against the law to help the Jewish and was punishable by death. Zegota also helped orphaned Jewish kids find a family. As the head and treasurer of this organization, Arczyński worked tirelessly to create hundreds and hundreds of fake IDs each day, in addition to giving places to live, cash, and medical help.

Arczyński had also participated in the Silesian Uprisings, three uprisings whose main purpose was to make Upper Silesia its own country, but it was currently under German rule. The first uprising was caused when German guards murdered ten Silesian citizens at a mine in Mysłowice in 1919. Many of the Silesian miners started protesting, causing an estimated 140,000 people to revolt against Germany. However, the German army immediately killed the uprising, and hanged or shot over 2,500 Poles as a punishment. In 1920, violence broke out again in Germany, as a result of Italy, Britain, and France taking sides. In a newspaper, they printed an announcement, saying that Warsaw fell to the Red Army in an attempt to stop the fighting. This however was a lie, and the violence continued. The very next year, it was rumored that Britain and Italy would prevail, and Germany would keep control over Silesia, therefore, another uprising was planned. At first, the rebels had much success and took over a large part of upper Silesia. However, they lost most of the land that they got. Soon, the last uprising was over and it was up to the League of Nations to decide. Poland only received a third of the land, but they gained a lot more in mines and other natural resources. Germany lost three-fourths of their mines to Poland.

I have learned many things from doing this assignment and researching for my person. Ferdynand was very brave, and so were the others who risked or lost their lives to help save the Jews. They stood against the Nazis, and had the courage to save the victims. The Holocaust was a terrible and cruel mass murderer of so many, and we must all take measures to prevent such a genocide from happening again. One of the main causes of this massacre were racial/religious injustice, the Germans thinking that they were superior, and the Jews inferior to them, therefore thinking that they should be eliminated. In the modern day, I think that even though there are these problems, that it has gotten much better. Another reason the influence of press and their leader, Hitler. If not for the press printing out so many terrible things about the Jews, I think that the Holocaust might not have happened. Hitler also played a big part in the destruction of over one third of the entire world's population of Jews, commanding the entire genocide. So many innocent people were slaughtered in this massacre, and those who survived work to tell us about the Holocaust, so we may never repeat this terrible event again. Never Again.

Citations

"Ferdynand Arczyński | Wikiwand." Wikiwand. N.p., n.d. Web. 14 Dec. 2016.

Leszczyńska, Magdalena. "Arczynski Marek Ferdynand." Story of Rescue - Arczynski Marek Ferdynand | Polscy Sprawiedliwi. Magdalena Leszczyńska, Nov. 2010. Web. 14 Dec. 2016.

Levine, Jason. "Jewish Resistance:Konrad Żegota Committee." The Żegota | Jewish Virtual Library. American-Israeli Cooperative Enterprise, 2016. Web. 14 Dec. 2016.

History.com Staff. "The Holocaust." History.com. A&E Television Networks, 2009. Web. 14 Dec. 2016.

"The Holocaust: An Introductory History." An Introductory History of the Holocaust | Jewish Virtual Library. N.p., n.d. Web. 14 Dec. 2016.

Levine, Jason. "Adolf Hitler." Adolf Hitler | Jewish Virtual Library. American-Israeli Cooperative Enterprise, 2016. Web. 14 Dec. 2016.

"Silesian Uprisings of 1919, 1920, and 1921 | Article about Silesian Uprisings of 1919, 1920, and 1921 by The Free Dictionary." The Free Dictionary. Farlex, n.d. Web. 14 Dec. 2016.

King, James M. "Blackwell Reference Online." Silesian Uprisings : The International Encyclopedia of Revolution and Protest : Blackwell Reference Online. N.p., n.d. Web. 14 Dec. 2016.

"World War 2: Zegota - Council for Aid to Jews." World War 2: Zegota - Council for Aid to Jews. N.p., n.d. Web. 14 Dec. 2016.

Malgorzata Wolska

Anthony Vivaldi

The Holocaust was a tragic period in world history. It all started when the economy of Germany was going down. Some Germans blamed the Jews for this. The Nazis criticized and were cruel to the Jews. Millions were killed in gas chambers and were burned to get rid of the bodies. Adolf Hitler, the leader of the Nazis, led the charge. He had the idea of eliminating every Jew. Hitler was very anti-semitic toward Jews. They lived in ghettos. He was responsible for six million Jews being annihilated. A brave woman helped many Jews. Her name was Malgorzata Wolska and her life is the story of survival.

Malgorzata Wolska lived with her family on Grójecka Street in Warsaw, Poland. They owned the property. It was a two-story building with a greenhouse and a well-tended garden. The greenhouse was taken care by her son, Mieczyslaw, he was a gardener. The others living with Malgorzata were her sisters, Halina and Wanda and her nephew, Janusz. They were a strong Jewish family who worked hard.

This family risked their lives to provide shelter to hide the Jews from the Nazis. In 1942, Malgorzata's brother Mieczyslaw built a hideout under the greenhouse. He had the help of his sisters. When finished, they hid over 30 Jews. Dr. Emanuel Ringelblum was a well-known historian and social activist. He and his wife Judyta and son Uri were among the first to go in hiding. They called the hideout Krysia. The hideout had one large room; it was only five by seven meters. The room had bunk beds, tables and benches. It had a very small kitchen that connected to the chimney of a Jewish neighbor. They had a little bit of light and water. To get to the bathroom, they had to go through the kitchen. They kept the entrance to Krysia camouflaged on the outside so the Nazis wouldn't find them. Once the hideout was completely finished, there were jobs that needed to be done. The family was in charge of making food and bringing it to the hideout, supplying pure drinking water, and getting rid of trash. Once all Jews were in the hideout, they created a committee to divide up the jobs, such as cleaning, and guarding the entrance. Even with the committee,

Malgorzata's family was still in charge, and did the job of communicating and shopping for meat. They also shopped for supplies that they needed and other items that were important.

While they were in hiding, everyday life still went on. They read newspapers, they gave language lessons, and the group stayed up late talking. Dr. Ringleblum continued his work writing about the Polish-Jewish relations during the German occupation. He was able to keep contact with the Jewish National Committee while he was in hiding. His writings later became a well-known published dissertation.

The dreaded day came on March 7, 1944, after two years of hiding. Fear and sorrow filled their eyes as they looked out the window of their home to see the worst thing possible. It was the Nazi's and Blue Police. They took Malgorzata's brother Mieczyslaw and walked him to the garden. They found the Jews hiding in the Krysia. All the Jews came out with their hands up. Her sister Wanda screamed that they should hide. The three ladies quickly hid. The blue police smashed and burned the Krysia. All the Jews that were hiding with Malgorzata family were murdered. She watched her brother get badly beaten before being executed. About 40 people were killed, including Mieczyslaw, her brother and Janusz, her nephew. Malgorzata and her sisters Halina and Wanda were the only ones out of the group who survived. The blue police guards stayed and watched their house three more days. When Malgorzata and her sisters returned to their home it was in shambles. None of their neighbors or acquaintances would speak to them out of fear. She had risked everything to help them, and now they were dead and she was back home.

In 1989, the Medal of the Righteous Among the Nations was awarded to Małgorzata Wolska, and her family members Mieczysław Wolski, Halina Wolska, Wanda Wolska, and Janusz Wolski. In 1990, a memorial plaque was placed on the wall of the former hideout on Grójecka Street, which is now called Kysria Bunker.

I learned some important lessons. People don't always do things because they want to, or because it is easy. Learning about Malgorzata Wolska made an impact on how I look at things. It made me realize that when I think homework is hard, it doesn't compare to a lady tending to over nearly 40 people to keep them alive. She didn't help hide the Jews because she had to; she did it because she wanted to help them survive. She took a big risk to hide people. I don't take many risks. Sometimes people have to stand up for what is right and not stand down for what is wrong. I understand that the Holocaust happened for all the wrong reasons. People should not be cruel. They can all have different ideas, but should not kill or harm those who don't agree with them. "Never Again" means exactly that, the Holocaust was horrible and should never be forgotten or repeated in any way. Steps can be taken to make sure it doesn't happen again, our government should protect all people. Our schools should keep educating all students about the Holocaust so it never happens again.

Works Cited

Wojan, Megan. Social Science 7 Honors Introduction to Holocaust. KAMS, Elk Grove. 4 Nov. 2016. Lecture.

"Flowers at 77 Grójecka Street" - Virtual Shtetl. N.p., n.d. Web. 10 Dec. 2016.

Yad Vashem – Malgorzata Wolska and her children N.p., n.d. Web. 3 Dec. 2016.

Krystyna Adolph

Arushi Jain

 Holocaust is one of the experiences that people would or never want to have because it was a one of a distressed and a disturbing situation that Jewish people ever forcefully experienced. One of the Jewish Holocaust person and survivors was Krystyna Adolph. She and her twin sister were born in 1921, in Vilnius or Vilna, the capital of Lithuania, just one year after it was abducted by the Poles. Krystyna and her twin had given names which were Meena and Liah. Although, she and her sister didn't like the names so they did, later on, changed them to Monica and Lydia. Those were the names under which Krystyna Adolph and her twin sister had lived during the Nazi occupation. The city Vilnius had changed hands several times, but its group that is higher to the rest in terms of ability or qualities and most of its population had always been Polish. However, from the 15th century on it was an important center of Polish culture, experiences, and learning.

Krystyna's parents seemed unconcerned in their ancestry, though she noticed that her mother's family came from Dwinsk (Dinaburg) in Latvia, her father is from Slonim in Belorussia. Her mother's father had been a wealthy wholesaler, trading in architecture materials. In her earliest memories, her grandfather was already retired although she and her sister honorably visited their grandparents from time to time, but there was no warmth or closeness in their relationships. As for her paternal and overprotective grandfather, who worked for the Jewish association as administrator of the Vilna Jewish cemetery. Adolph Krystyna and her sister did like, their grandfather, but theirs favorite was Grandmother. Their grandmother was a short, round, and a warm-natured woman. After, their grandfather's death, their grandmother came to stay with Adolph and her family.

Krystyna and her sister grew up in significant circumstances. She grew in a middle class, a civil family with no interest in Jewish culture. Her father, who had changed his first name from Solomon to Severin, was one of the few Vilna Jews classifying themselves as "Poles of the faith," in the useless ambition of becoming combined into Polish community. Moreover, Adolph Krystyna mother, Liuba who was an approved, but a non-practicing surgical nurse. The only time Adolph Krystyna remember being in a Jewish religious surroundings was on national holidays when Jewish students in the public schools were marched to a Jewish assembly for an official business while Christian girls and boys celebrated a memorable mass in the church.

Krystyna's father handled a strong thin wooden board factory in the limited establishment of Waka Murowana, which lay in hardwood rich religion about 25 miles west of Vilna. Aside from the industrialized combination and a bridge over a dam utilizing the waters of the Waka river, the settlement consisted of only one real house. That was the manager's headquarters where Adolph Krystyna's family lived. Their house(the manager's house) was made with an irregular way in which wooden building on a hill was surrounded by a garden. Krystyna and her family also kept an apartment in the town, where meanwhile the school year they and their mother often stayed on weekdays. But Waka was their real home.

Though Krystyna's parents in Vilna, had their own company consisted almost exclusively of Jews, members like themselves of the small Polish-Jewish league who were only partly understood to Polish culture and society. Especially who was educated in Russian schools, Krystyna's mother and father both spoke Polish to her and her sister at home and Russian hardly between themselves. Therefore, they made a great attempt to manage the right relations in order to get both she and her sister into the city's most inspiring and respectable school for girls, itself because of a relevant step towards confirmed government-run section to the university with its number of requirements for Jews.

Before the war, Krystyna taught at the Czartoryski High School in Vilna, and the twin sisters Monica and Lidia Gluskin were students in her class. Only when the war broke out, she was forced to support herself and her young daughter on their small farm in Ignalio, a village near Troki, about thirty kilometers from Vilna. When the Germans being used by someone in Vilna in 1941, Krystyna sent a specialized messenger to the Gluskin sisters and provided to shelter them at her farm should they be in danger. When the Vilna ghetto was well-established, Monika and Lidia took up the request, and fled to the farm, and were given pleasant welcome. The Jewish twins spent the next three years at the farm, helping Krystyna do the housework, take responsibility for the animals, chop firewood, and tend the vegetable garden and the farmland. Only the father and sister of Krystyna's late husband knew their real personality when they visited the farm occasionally and Krystyna's sister-in-law provided the hidden twins with fake papers.

Krystyna was fully aware that she was risking her life by sheltering Jews, especially since the Germans had burned down a house in a neighboring village with the entire family inside after discovering a Jewish family hiding there. Krystyna also helped the twins mother by achieving false identity papers for her with which she left the ghetto and survived on the Aryan side. Krystyna accepted no commission for her actions, which were suggested by her charitable and Catholic beliefs. After the war, the Gluskin sisters settled in Israel and remained in touch with Krystyna Adolf for many years. On May 14, 1984, Yad Vashem identified Krystyna Adolph as Righteous Among the Nations.

I learned that Krystyna Adolph was a special personality that people knew or didn't know lived because she was one of the smart, spirited, and strong holocaust survivors who as a Jewish did hide for few years. Moreover, she had a wonderful effect on the other people in the world because she was so brave and confidential that she never gave up, and that's why people really admired her. She actually did take a lot of risks for her family and herself, even if she was getting unsuccessful in some. However, I think people should care and learn about the major event Holocaust that happened in the history because when the Holocaust was ended people who did survive were holding the boards in their hand which said: "Never Again". If somehow the Holocaust thing ever happens again then the people should stand up and fight together through the struggle, so the Germans couldn't win the battle and try to make Jews the target again.

Works Cited

Aran, Lydia. "Krystyna's Gift." Krystyna's Gift. N.p., 1 Feb. 2004. Web. 9 Dec. 2016.

"The Righteous Among The Nations." Dutt Yad Vashem. N.p., n.d. Web. 9 Dec. 2016.

Franciszka Bil

Ashley Black

The Holocaust will never be forgotten. Many people lost their lives or lost their loved ones. This was said to be the cause from the lack of confidence in the government. Jews provided the chance for a new leader to rule their weak empire and soon the Jews wished they hadn't chosen a leader at all. Hitler established a Reich Ministry of Public Enlightenment and Propaganda to ensure that Nazi's message was successfully communicated. But when he started that Enlightenment it deprived Jews their rights of German citizenship. Soon Jews started to flee Germany for their own safety. But they got caught and each and every Jew was either sent to a concentration camp or enslaved as labored prisoners. Everyone had to shave their heads. They had to have their arms tattooed, and had to wear prison uniforms. There was even a point that Hitler thought people were dying too slow so he put poison gas in the showers and cleared out 6,000 people a day. By doing this, it wiped out 63% of Jews in Europe and 91% of Jews in Poland. When the Holocaust finally came to an end, six million Jews had innocently died. There were fewer than four million Jews that survived this horrible time. Those who survived were forever changed and will always be impacted by this time period. Franciszka Bil was a survivor and a hero. She was 70 years old when the war happened. She owned a three room apartment big enough just for her and her husband.

In 1942, Franciszka hid a 12 year old Jewish boy named Mark Wallach in her home. She knew him from his parents who they were friends with before the war. For 20 months straight he was in a separate room away from a window hidden from the outside. While he was in the room all he did was read Franciszka's poetic books. It was hard even for them to survive. They were really poor and since they were poor everyday each person got barely anything to eat. But somehow she managed to take food to Mark's dad and it was a struggle because she got beaten by S.S. men. Mark's dad somehow escaped the camp and came to Franciszka for help. And she hid him and his son together in the same hidden room. In the last weeks before the liberation, they were joined by Sidonia Wallach, the mother, because her previous hiding place was no longer safe. After the liberation, on July 27, 1944, the survivors left Lwów and later immigrated to the United States. Franciszka never saw them again and did not know what became of them. On August 15, 2004, Yad Vashem recognized Franciszka Bil as Righteous Among the Nations. Later Franciszka died a couple years before 2000.

During the Holocaust she helped one family that were really poor and helped them survive through the war. I don't know a single person who would get beaten several times just to give food to her friends. I thought she was a very kind woman who would do anything to help people in need. Since she was a devout Catholic, Franciszka spent a considerable amount of time praying and tried to get young Mark to join her in her prayers. She did informally baptize him and gave him the Christian name, of Anthony. What I learned from Franciszka, is that sometimes in your life you need to take risks for people. You never know if a simple act of kindness can save someone's life or change it for the better. Franciszka is a person who risked her life. She was a 70 year -old woman that got beaten because she hid a child and their parents to save them. I am young and strong, so I can take a couple risks in my life. I also learned that if you do something good then you get something good in return.

I understand that the Holocaust was a horrible, challenging, and a depressing time for the Jews. A lot of innocent people died during this and the way they died was really harsh and for no reason at all. I think it impacted our lives today by honoring the ones who died and it depends on how people treat other people today. Ever since that war today nobody judges on whether you're black, white, or even if you're a different race. In my opinion I think people are perfect the way they are and if someone has a problem on how someone looks or acts then there is something wrong with the person who thinks that. "Never Again" where people will have a war based on what they are. And "Never Again" where we will have to leave the country because of someone who wants to follow a law and turns into a war. What we can do to prevent this from happening again is that again we can stop judging people on how they act or what they look like. And we can treat each other nicely and not try to kill people. Lastly, and this kind of repeats it but don't try to change people, let the person they want to be, be themselves in front of other people. Or in other words, do the opposite of what happened during the Holocaust, because, if you don't then there is going to be another war similar to the Holocaust killing many innocent people.

Irena Adamowicz

Audrey Lee

 Irena Adamowicz was born on May 11, 1910 in Warsaw, Poland. She was born into a wealthy Catholic Polish family. Irena was a smart woman that had a degree in social work. She graduated from the University of Warsaw before World War II. After she graduated she became a girl scout and served as one of the leaders of the Polish Scout Movement. She provided counseling and educational services to other scouts and for the Jewish youth movement called the Hashomer Hatzair. Irena was also one of the people who establish contact with the Jewish Scouting by developing many close friends. She maintained contact with the Jewish Scouts and strengthen the relationship.

After the Germans invaded Poland, Irena then became a member of the underground "Home Army" and served as a person who provided cooperation and communication among the ghettos of Warsaw, Vilna, Bialystok, Kaunas, and Siauliai. She delivered messages, provided aid to those in need, and moral support for those in the ghettos. Irena also was meeting with the underground leaders, passing down information about the ghettos for at least a couple of months.

Due to Irena's work for helping the Jews before the invasion in Poland, she remained in contact with the Jewish Zionist movement, and was a devout Catholic. Irena was able to help with the Jewish fighting during War World ll. She was also assigned to create a channel for communication for the Jews in the ghettos so that they can remain in close contact throughout the war.

In late 1941 a meeting was held in Warsaw. The meeting was for the Jews to make secret organizations in the ghettos of Warsaw, Wilno, Bialystok, Kovono, and Shavle. Irena was sent on this dangerous mission with her group to create these organizations. Since Irena created the organizations her visits became more of a source for information and moral support. In June 1942 Irena was put to a mission to go to Vilna to inform the leaders of the Jewish Underground and tell them that there was a mass destructions of the Jews. After she finished her mission Irena then went to the ghetto of Vilna and was asked to deliver the bad news for the Jews so that they can form resistance camps. In July 1942 Irena earned a Jewish nickname called "Di chalutzishe shikse" meaning the Pioneering Gentile.

Irena went on many dangerous missions by going to ghettos. The reason why she would go to the ghettos is that she would take a group of Jews and transport them into a safer place across the Lithuanian Border. Her other mission that she did was to also travel to places like Warsaw, Vilna, Bialystok, Kaunas, and Siauliai to go and sneak into the ghettos and help the Jews escape into resistance camps so they would have more protection in the cities of Lithuania.

After War World ll Irena remained in close contact with the holocaust survivors and worked with the Polish Reputation office in Frankfurt as a translator. She quit her job to be an inspector at children's homes and she then quit that job to be an employee at the National Library of Warsaw. In 1958 Irena left for three months to travel to Israel. She went there for a long visit as a guest of the Hakibbutzs Ha'artzi movement. When Irena returned to Poland she was never again to contact her friends in Israel. Irena remained in Poland for the rest of her life. After Irena died she was named "Righteous Among the Nations" in 1985 for her brave journey throughout the Holocaust. She was also written in a book with her own history that tells of how she helped the Jews in the Holocaust through 1939 and 1945. The story was written by Bartoszewski and Lewin. The book was called "Righteous Among Nations".

The things that I learned about the Holocaust is that some of the Jews hid other Jews from getting taken away to camps, a work area called the Jewish underground who helped the helpless Jews in the ghettos, and that some of the members of the Jewish underground went on dangerous missions warning others in the ghettos that some of the Jews will be taken into extermination camps. Irena Adamowicz gave me a good learning experience by going on dangerous missions that she could have been taken or killed in to save the Jewish people from going into extermination camps. I understand that the Holocaust was a really dangerous time when it came to Jewish people and that the Jews had to go through a lot of pain and suffering by losing the people that they love and by doing tons of work at the camps. I know that people should always remember this and to never again let this ever happen to any other kind of race. The steps that can be taken to never let this happen again is that we could be more fair to any kind of people no matter what they are or where they're from.

Works Cited

"The Righteous Among The Nations." Yadvashem, http://db.yadvashem.org/righteous/family.html?language=en&itemld=4013667 Accessed 4 December 2016.

Krol, Joanna. "Story of Rescue-Adamowicz Irena." Sprawiedliwi, http://sprawiedliwi.org.pl/en/stories-of-rescue/story-rescue-adamowicz-irena. Accessed 4 December 2016.

Holocaust Hero: Michał Żytkiewicz

Katherine L. Albiani

The Holocaust was a terrible time for many. Very few had survived this horrible time in history. This happened when Adolf Hitler became the leader. He said that Germans were the master race. Hitler said that Jews were interfering with the "master race". So he needed to get rid of them. Hitler took away their rights and home. Moving almost every Jew to a ghetto. He had only kept the ones with special talents, so they could work for him. When Hitler realized the race wasn't disappearing fast enough, he took it over board. He started killing thousands. By the time the Holocaust ended six million Jews had died. Everybody knew what the Nazi were doing was wrong, but very few did anything. People just sat there and watched it happen, they willingly let it happen. These were bystanders, Michał Żytkiewicz wasn't he was an up stander.

Michał Żytkiewicz was born in the year 1896, male. He had an occupation of a painter and a building contractor. His wife, Irena, was a Jew. An old family friend of Irena, Nina, escaped the Warsaw ghetto and looked towards Żytkiewicz to help her. Near Warsaw Żytkiewicz bought a partially burnt home. He gave time, effort, and his own money to renovate the home. He had two other Jews help him make secret rooms. These Jews would later hide in the house as well. Żytkiewicz also hid many other Jews including Feliks Brodzki. He did him two times, if it weren't for Żytkiewicz Feliks would have died. Michał Żytkiewicz often visited the house and brought them food. The Jews with money payed for the food, but the ones with no money didn't pay for it. Żytkiewicz arranged fake documents, hid the Jews, and gave them shelter. Żytkiewicz ended hiding six people from the Nazis in all. Nina was very thankful for the things Michał Żytkiewicz did for her. She decided to visit him. At this time Żytkiewicz was sick with tuberculosis. He had died, on January 3, 1946, before Nina could reach him. Out of the six people Żytkiewicz helped five had survived the Holocaust. Michał Żytkiewicz worked very hard to help the Jews. He spent a lot of his time working for what he wanted. He knew what was happening and he did something. Michał Żytkiewicz did something very few would do. He risked his life to help a small amount of people. Michał Żytkiewicz was an up stander.

I learned from Michał Żytkiewicz story. I learned that many will just stand around as they see injustice, but there are people who will do something to make a change. I also learned that Michał Żytkiewicz was very hard working and what he did was risky, but it helped others. Żytkiewicz risked his life for others, but he did it for a good cause. This story had a large learning impact because it shows no matter how big a problem is one person at a time can help solve it. This doesn't only apply to this problem it can apply to many different problems. In my opinion the saying "Never Again", means to not have a have society that won't stand up to big problems like the Holocaust, and not having people be scared to help. A rabbi, part of the Jewish community, during the time of the Holocaust once said, "The most important thing I learned is that bigotry and hatred are not the most urgent problems. The most urgent, the most disgraceful, the most shameful, and the most tragic problem – is silence." If this was ever to happen again, we as a country should work together to stop it. Lots of people do hope that this kind of problem never happens again but if it did, we would need easy steps that would make it simpler to stop it. One way to help a problem like this would be for everyone to stand up not just a few. This would help because instead of having a class of people we could have school of people. Having more people will support better than just one or two people. A way to help prevent the problem is two have a system so there is no political corruption. Another way to stop a problem like this is to have no one to support this kind of topic. If there were many that watched the change happen, there had to be people who made the change happen. One of those people was Michał Żytkiewicz.

Work Cited

"The Righteous Among The Nations." Yad Vashem - Request Rejected, Yad Vashem, db.yadvashem.org/righteous/family.html?language=en&itemId=4018475.
Johnson, Lyndon Baines. "A Tribute to Eleanor Roosevelt: Address to the First Anniversary Luncheon of the Eleanor Roosevelt Memorial Fund." 9 Dec. 2016.

Anna Bloch

Austin May

The Holocaust was a very tragic time in all of our lives. The Holocaust was a time when Adolf Hitler took control of Germany and mass murdered six million Jews. The Nazis believed that the Germans were more superior to everyone else. They also believed that the Jews were "inferior". In the beginning of the Holocaust (January 1933), not many people stood up and tried to help the Jews but later there were hundreds of thousands of people trying to help free the Jews. First, Hitler took the Jews from their homes and put them in ghettos. Then, he moved them to concentration camps like Auschwitz. Then he burned and / or gassed the Jews alive. Many Jews suffered greatly.

Anna Bloch, a Roman Catholic was born on January 1st, 1875. She was a woman who risked her life to save many Holocaust victims. She was a hero. She helped many people by supplying basic goods they needed to survive. She also illegally transferred and hid Jews from Adolf Hitler's army. Not only did she do provide them with food and necessities, but she also supplied shelter for them. She would do this by hiding them in her home in the panty. Anna Bloch not only saved but also helped Holocaust victims to survive from Hitler.

Anna rescued Holocaust victims from Radwan, Dabrowa, Kraków, and Poland. If someone was in the ghetto in trouble, she'd be there trying to help. She saved many people, some including Regina Haber, Amir Chawa Amsterdam, and Zvi Henryk Amsterdam. She rescued people of all ages from kids to seniors.

In July, 1942, Anna's good friend, Sabina Solomon, nearly didn't make it out of the Krakow district ghetto. Anna hid her from the police for six months until Sabina informed her parents, who had also escaped Hitler, where she was. She then left to be with her family. In autumn, 1943, Sabina Solomon became ill and later died. Her family kept in touch with Anna, who sent them food and took care of them until the area was liberated by the Red Army in January of 1945.

Usually there were big groups (organized networks) of people saving Jews but Anna was only one person saving all those innocent Jews. Some religious rescuers were Protestant, Eastern Orthodox, and Muslims. Anna happened to be one of the Catholics who rescued, along with these groups, thousands of Jews. Some European churches let the Jews hide in their place of worship.

Jews were forced to live in ghettos in order for the Germans to have control of them. Most of the victims Anna saved came from ghettos. Ghettos were in areas of towns that a lot of Jews lived in. These areas were usually the older parts of town. Sometimes non-Jews were forced out of their homes to make room for other Jews. This was a place where Germans put Jews so they knew where they were. Ghettos had barbed-wire fences around them to keep the Jews from escaping. Another thing stopping the Jews from escaping was heavily armed guards around the barbed-wire fencing. The largest ghetto was in the polish capital, also known as Warsaw, were about half a million Jews were confined.

In the concentration camps, they were fed a little bit of stew and sometimes a slice of bread two to three times a day. Anna gave them basic foods to eat when she hid them in her home or else where.

Anna took a big risk by helping the Jews, but she still survived. If she had been caught, she could have suffered major consequences. She was recognized as a hero on May 5th, 1998, 123 years after she was born, yet no one knows when she died.

By doing this essay, I learned that the Holocaust was a horrible event. I also learned that something like the Holocaust could happen again. The Holocaust was like a case of bullying on Hitler's part. When I started learning about this I started taking everything more seriously and started helping with everything as best I could. Learning about Anna and how she risked her life to save others has made me want to be a person that helps other people that need help as well. I understand that the Holocaust isn't something that you can take lightly. It's a very serious matter and not something to be joking about. When I hear the words "never again", I think of what this must have felt like for someone who had actually experienced the Holocaust. For that reason, I will do what I can to make sure that it doesn't ever happen again. To make sure this never happens again we can make sure that a democracy is always present in our politics. There should not be just one person in control of everything, such as a dictatorship. The dictatorship of Adolf Hitler is what led to the Holocaust. We could also just be nicer in general. Another thing we could do to prevent another Holocaust is make better laws or a better law system or even a better law enforcing system.

Works Cited

"Ghettos in Poland." United States Holocaust Memorial Museum. United States Holocaust Memorial Museum, n.d. Web. 11 Dec. 2016. <http://www.ushmm.org/>.

"Introduction to the Holocaust." United States Holocaust Memorial Museum. United States Holocaust Memorial Museum, n.d. Web. 11 Dec. 2016. <http://www.ushmm.org/>.

Marks, Mr. "Mr.Marks Lecture." Mr.Marks' Speech. Katherine L. Albiani Middle School, Elk Grove. 9 Nov. 2016. Lecture.

"Rescue." United States Holocaust Memorial Museum. United States Holocaust Memorial Museum, n.d. Web. 11 Dec. 2016. <http://www.ushmm.org/>.

Vashem, Yad. "Anna Bloch." Yadvashem. N.p., n.d. Web. 11 Dec. 2016. <http://db.yadvashem.org/righteous/righteousName.html?language=en&itemId=4013977>.

Vashem, Yad. "Bloch Family." Yad Vashem - Request Rejected. N.p., n.d. Web. 11 Dec. 2016. http://db.yadvashem.org/righteous/family.html?language=en&itemId=4013977>.

Sister Gertruda Stanislaw Marciniak

Ava Lown

In 1933 a terrible event began that would lead to the murder and persecution of millions of innocent people; This event was called The Holocaust. The Holocaust targeted Jews, Homosexuals, Arabs (Other Semites), Black, Criminals, Gypsies, Handicapped People, Jehovah's Witnesses, Political "Criminals", The Slavs, Asians, Latin Americans, and Native Americans, but I'll be mainly focusing on what the Jews went through. What happened to the poor victims of this calamity had to go through such torture which included being starved, worked to death and an excessive amount of discrimination that their life must have been impossible to bear. At first, Jews had to shut down businesses, wear stars and carry ID that showed they were Jews, Jews couldn't marry Aryan's, and many other terrible things. Not long after targets were moved to places called "Ghettos", which were sealed by fences with barbed wire, they were also known for malnutrition, overcrowding and poor sanitation. Many died while in the Ghettos, unfortunately the Ghettos weren't the end of the genocide in progress. After the Ghettos, the next step was for Jews to be put in concentration camps in Poland to be starved and worked to death. While be transported to the camps Jews were separated by gender and age, children 10 and under were sent elsewhere to be gassed and killed immediately along with anyone physically or mentally handicapped or "challenged". Now, there was just one more step, the extermination. For this step the Nazi's sent Jews to extermination camps where they were gassed, burned and shot. This final "official" step was where thousands died every day. Though it was the last official step, after this, when Nazi's had to speed up the extermination process, in concentration camps Nazi's made buildings that looked like showers but were really gas chambers that sprayed a gas called Zyklon B that would kill people in 3 through 15 minutes. The worst case was in the death camp Auschwitz-Birkenau which had 4 operating gas chambers where approximately 8,000 people died every day. After prisoners were gassed or killed then other prisoners would be forced to move the bodies to crematoriums where the bodies would be burned. Finally, when allied troops began to close in during the year 1945 Nazi's began destroying crematoriums and camps. During this time Nazi's ordered death marches that reached over long distances in which approximately 250,000-375,000 prisoners died during these marches. Finally, the Soviet Army entered Auschwitz, which was the largest camp, and liberated more than 7,000 prisoners that were mainly either ill or dying. While liberating prisoners from the camps U.S. troops found thousands of rings, watches, precious stones, eyeglasses, gold fillings and clothing articles. In the end, so many people died for absolutely no reason other than for who they were, thankfully some were saved, some were harbored during those horrid times the people who risked their lives to save another were called "righteous people".

Sister Gertruda Stanislaw Marciniak was born in 1898 in Piotrow.Before the Holocaust Marciniak was a nun who started an orphanage in Grabbie before the Holocaust began. When the German occupation Marciniak was arrested before being released in 1940. After she was released Marciniak decided to go to Warsaw and then to Swider to open up an orphanage and an adjacent home for girls with tuberculosis, which in turn exploited the Germans fear of contagious diseases. During the holocaust she also hid resistance members and children rescued from a transport set to deport Warsaw's Zachodni Station. Elizabethan sisters helped Marciniak harbor Jewish children who they provided with forged birth certificates. She saved so many people by keeping them in the orphanages and risking her own life. One thing she liked to say was that, "Once a child has come to me, their fate will be my fate too." This showed just how much she was really risking when she took those children in under her wing, it showed just how much she cared that they lived. One person she had taken care of in the orphanage was named Dan Landsberg. He decide to visit the orphanage many years after the Holocaust had ended, only to find Sister Gertruda on her deathbed. While he was there Sister Gertruda told him of a time when the Nazi's had once burst into the home in search of Jewish children, since this was when Dan was still very young Sister Gertruda had been able to hide him by covering him with her habit and standing completely motionless until the German's had left. The people who sheltered the Jewish children like Sister Gertruda had were called "occupation others". Dan and his family before escaping during liquidation had been placed in the Otwock Ghetto. When his parents escaped during liquidation they smuggled Dan into the Elizabethan home where he received a birth certificate with the name Wojciech Plochowski and later placed with a Polish family where he survived the war. Sadly, almost all his relatives were killed including his father. His mother was the only person in his family who survived.

Hopefully everyone learned a good life lesson from that catastrophe. What I learned was that even though somewhere could seem strong and safe, you never know what could happen. If something terrible happens than someone like Adolf Hitler could slip into power and do something horrible. Learning about my person had such a great impact on my life because now I know that I have to try to protect people if I can and that it really can impact someone elses life or even save their life. There are no true steps to take to fully prevent something like this from happening but we can try by really being cautious about who gets power and we can also stand up against something that is wrong. Another thing we could do is make sure we know what is really going on behind the scenes. "Never Again", that is what we should strive for, "Never Again".

Works Cited

Sidhu. Sacramento: Ms. Sidhu, 15 Nov. 2016. PDF.

"NAZI Holocaust: The Targets." War and Social Upheaval: World War II -- the Holocaust Targets. N.p., 13 Feb. 2004. Web. 14 Dec. 2016.

"Teachers Who Rescued Jews During the Holocaust." Sister Gertruda Stanisława Marciniak | Teachers Who Rescued Jews During the Holocaust | "Their Fate Will Be My Fate Too..." | Yad Vashem. Yad Vashem, 2016. Web. 14 Dec. 2016.

Feliks Zolynia

Ayush Jain

Holocaust is one of the experiences that people would or never want to have because it was a one of a distressed and a disturbing situation that Jewish people ever forcefully experienced in the early 1930s. When Germans were losing in World War I, they need someone who can lead them on the safe path, and then the new leader rises, who was Adolf Hitler. Adolf Hitler was the person who does not allow Jews to hold public office, he also deprived their rights of being German citizenship, and he also forced Jews to wear yellow stars of David on the outside of their clothing to identify themselves. In addition, when Jewish people saw that they were being untreated they moved to other parts of the world. When Hitler saw that the Jewish people are moving, he thought of killing of entire Jewish people by shooting at the gunpoint or by poisonous gas, firing their houses, also some were taken to the concentration camp, where they worked 7 days a week and get beaten if they don't work. Some of the persons risked their own life to save Jewish people. One of the person from Poland, who risked their own life to save Jewish people was Feliks

Zolynia. Feliks Zolynia was born in 1905 and he was recognized on February 21, 2012. Feliks Zolynia helped the family name Sztajnberg, who lived in Janow Lubelski, consisted of five people: mother Fajga (b. 1916), father Izhak (1910), and three children—Tsivia (b. 1934), Menachem (b. 1936), and baby Frieda. When the war began, their house was soon bombed and they had to move in with Izhak's parents in Modliborzyce. Soon the Germans reached there as well, so they all moved to the safe village called Wierzchowiska.Izhak would sometimes go to town and trade in tobacco with the locals. He was captured by the Germans several times, but he always managed to escape from germans. Some Christian neighbors let them stay for a while, but after a while, the Christians could not tolerate. So they moved again and they he went on a search for help and the person who help the amily was Feliks Żołynia. Zolynia helped Izhak by letting his and his family to dig an underground hideout on his land. In meanwhile Zolynia Brought potatoes to eat and some other things to eat. In addition, one time Feliks's brothers Bolek came into the barn by accident, and then Izhak had to beg to not tell anyone and then he explained that his and Zolynia family and Feliks would be facing death. After hearing that he was so frightened and afraid that he never said a word and he even help and bought food and other supplies to Sztejnberg family. Moreover, when the liberation was approaching, Zolynia warned them that that German army was destroying every building in its wake. After 22 months, the family members can barely walk, but they were forced To run away to the forest. After the liberation, the Soviet soldiers aided them greatly and warned them against the roaming groups of armed poles, and transferred them to Lutsk, which was in Soviet territory and where they were Jews to help them. The Sztejnbergs returned to Poland in 1957 and they moved to Israel via Austria and the Czech Republic. Sztejnbergs also remained in touch with Feliks. I learned that Feliks Zolynia was a special personality that people knew or didn't know lived because he was one of the smart, spirited, and strong holocaust survivors. Moreover, he had a wonderful effect on the other people in the world because he was so brave and confidential that he never gave up, and that's why people really admired him. He actually did take a lot of risks for Sztajnbergs' family and for himself, by allowing them to dig and underground hideout,so no german can kill them. I think people should care and learn about the major event Holocaust that happened in the history because when the Holocaust was ended people who did survive were holding the boards in their hand which said: "Never Again" which probably means that they have suffered a lot and they want "never again" the Holocaust thing happen to the world. The things that I learned from Holocaust are that holocaust is racial cleansing, racial terrorism, and corrupted society, At the end of the holocaust 5 million people got killed. The consequences of Holocaust are: fears surrounded the Jewish people, it was hard for Jewish people to find a safe place, lot of people were traumatized, Jews were considered as the specific problem to the society, and it was one of the reasons that cause world war second. The steps to prevent holocaust are we need stable democracies and legal systems that make sure that criminals like the Nazis can't come to power. People have to learn not to be racist and to be immune to any such ideology that tells them there were "subhumans" or whatever word they might use and Genocide prevention should become part of domestic laws and national constitutions as well as of relevant international conventions and parts.

Works Cited

What Do You Understand by the Holocaust? Critically Analyse the Causes and Consequences of the Holocaust. - INSIGHTS." INSIGHTS. N.p., n.d. Web. 12 Dec. 2016. <http://www.insightsonindia.com/2015/01/12/1-what-do-you-understand-by-the-holocaust-critically-analyse-the-causes-and-consequences-of-the-holocaust/>.

Jojan, Wegan. Editorial. Holocaust Pptx 22 Nov. 2016: n. p. Print. "The Righteous Among The Nations." Yad Vashem - Zolynia, Feliks. n.p., n.d. Web. 12 Dec. 2016.

Scherrer, Dr Christian P. "InstaGrok." InstaGrok. n.p., 28 Jan. 2000. Web. 12 Dec. 2016.http://www.instagrok.com/results.html?query=what%2Bcan%2Bwe%2Bdo%2Bto%2Bprevent%2Bholocaust>.

Pelagia Jasinka

Bailey Tran

Pelagia Jasinka, Helped a family of two in the spring of 1943, The Names Of those two saved by Pelagia Jasinka is Helena Kanarek and her daughter Margalit. When Helena and her daughter fled from the ghetto Kielce district, They went to go find somewhere to hide and went to her non Jewish Friend Pelagia And Pelagia gladly let her daughter Margalit stay with her but soon after took Helena's daughter to Her Parents Home, The Bielas. Pelagias Father Worked as a miner, barely making any money to support his own family but still took Margalit in as his own daughter and treated her the same as his small son who grew up together. Pelagia Knew that her life wasn't great but still cared her friend Helena Because she was a friend and wanted to help her daughter to grow up. As Pelagias Parents took care for Margalit even though she had the Pelagia and her husband go to prison in Auschwitz. Before Pelagia went to prison, she had a economic situation which bankrupted her, She had made a living of selling cigarettes and alcohol .

If Pelagia Jasinka Had never took in Helenas daughter, she still would be living a normal life but she dint want her friend to die in the camps along with Helenas Daughter. Pelagia never regretted every decision she made to save her friends life. She was grateful enough to bring Helenas Daughter to her parents house and her parents also cared for the Jewish child even though the father didnt have a job to make money a lot of money for his own family, they took in Margalit. They Took after the girl like their own granddaughter and watched her grow with their grandson. Because of Pelagias Decisions, She was recognized as Righteous Among the Nations Just like the others who saved Jewish family's out there when the Holocaust, And by learning and the things The rescuers Of the Jewish family's went through to save them, We Won't Never Ever Let this happen again so other races won't suffer the same fate and as well as the rescuers to.

Leokadia Jaromirska

Bella Albani

Wife, mother, friend, gentile, hero. These were all words that have been used to describe Leokadia Jaromirska, a Polish Catholic woman who saved a Jewish infant from starvation and death on the streets of Poland. Jaromirska was living in Warsaw when the Nazi's invaded poland on September 1, 1939. Europe was facing hard times, the holocaust had begun, Hitler was leading the Nazis in an attempt to conquer the world, and World War ll had begun. One October morning in 1942 while Jaromirska was walking to work near the Warsaw Ghetto with another woman, Jaromirska heard a baby crying. When she went to investigate, she found a young girl and her 8 month old baby sister abandoned on the street. The other woman, with much persuasion from Jaromirska, took the children home with her. Later that day, when she finished her work and went to go check on the children, she found that the little girl was gone. Jaromirska asked the other woman what had happened and found out that the woman had freaked out and taken the little girl to the police station so that she would not get in trouble for helping and hiding a jew. Jaromirska did not have a child of her own, her husband had been taken to Auschwitz in 1940 as a political prisoner, so she decided to adopt the baby. It was hard for her to raise a child, for she could barely take care of herself with the meager earnings she got working at a German factory, but Jaromirska made it work. She named the child Bogusia.

Jaromirska raised the child in a barrack-like house with the help of her roommate, Irena Hamerska. Most of their neighbors knew that Bogusia was a Jew, but mostly everyone was helpful. Even the local policeman, who lived nearby, helped. His wife gave Hamerska the address to Bogusia house inside the Ghetto. The house was long abandoned by that time, but it was still a kind gesture of goodwill. When the Russians came to Poland Jaromirska was forced to evacuate, and she took little Bogusia with her. Together the two hoped from town to town searching for food and shelter. Jaromirska fought with all her might to keep her and her small child from falling into the gaping hands of starvation and death. Miraculously the two survived, and eventually the war ended. Jaromirska's husband, Bolek, returned from Auschwitz and together she, Bolek, and Bogusia returned to their ruined home in Warsaw and started to try to put their lives all back together again.

But Jaromirska's husband was not the only one who was freed from Auschwitz. Bogusia's father, Geniuk Jonisz, also left Auschwitz and set on a mission to find the two children he and his wife had abandoned on the streets of Warsaw years before. He searched all over Europe and eventually found an Italian fortuneteller who told him that a small soul was waiting for him. He traced down Jaromirska and went to her house in Poland where he identified Bogusia, who's real name was Shifra Jonisz , by her birthmark. Shifra did not want to leave Jaromirska because she had identified her as her mother, but Jonisz demanded it. The two continued to fight over custody of the girl until Jaromirska wrote a letter to the pope asking for permission to keep the girl. Less than a month later she received a letter back from the pope telling her it was her duty as a good Catholic to return the child to her father and to do so with good will and in friendship. With a heavy heart Jaromirska returned Shifra to her father and was left childless. The two Joniz then left Poland and immigrated to Israel.

Eventually, with the help of Shifra's husband in Israel, Shifra regained contact with Jaromirska. They wrote letters to each other until, in 1969, Jaromirska visited Shifra in Israel for six weeks. They planted a tree in Jaromirska's honor in the Avenue of the Righteous at Yad Vashem. The two remained in close contact with each other until, in 1979, Jaromirska passed away. Learning about the life of Leokadia Jaromirska and how she saved a Jewish child at the risk of her own life and learning about the holocaust in general has changed me as a person. Leokadia and Shifra's story has taught me two main lessons as a Catholic and as a human being. First i have learned that nothing can get in the way of love, not even an impossible search for someone you don't even know is alive, the search that Mr. Jonisz made to find his daughter. I also learned that we must listen to God in his mission for us. Leokadia Jaromirska asked God for guidance in the form of the Pope, and even though she did not like what God had to say, she followed his orders because she knew it was the right thing to do. Learning about the Holocaust has also showed me that we must stand up for what is right no matter if it doesn't suit our personal agenda. If people had stood up to Hitler when he had just began his segregation and mistreatment of Jews, none of the horrifying things that Hitler did to start the Holocaust would have happened and millions of lives, Jewish and Gentile, would have been saved. The Holocaust must never again sustain the world's history red with innocent lives. We must all say "Never Again."

Works Cited

"Jaromirska Leokadia." Polscy Sprawiedliwi. Polscy Sprawiedliwi, 2016. Web. 10 Dec. 2016.

Rychlak, Ronald J. "Hitler, the War, and the Pope, Revised and Expanded." Google Books. Web. 10 Dec. 2016.

"Warsaw." United States Holocaust Memorial Museum. United States Holocaust Memorial Museum, 2016. Web. 10 Dec. 2016.

"Leokadia Jaromirska." Yad Vashem. Yad Vashem The World Holocaust Remembrance Center, 2016. Web. 10 Dec. 2016.

Maria Fedecka

Blake Swenson (Winner)

"Everyone should remember her name and friendship in times of hostility terrible" (Abraham Sutzkever). Unfortunately, thousands and thousands of Jews were killed during the horrific events of the Holocaust, and we only have a few survivors still alive at present. However, the non-Jews, many of them Catholic, who stepped in to help others, are extremely important to the survivors we have today. One of these people who stepped up was Maria Fedecka.

Fedecka was born in Moscow in 1904, and died peacefully after 73 years of life, on December 21st, 1977 in Warsaw according to sprawiedliwi.org. Fedecka was born into a very large family, with 12 siblings. She married Stanislaw Fedecki, at an unknown date, and together they had three children.

During Fedecka's entire life, she always had a true passion of wanting to help those in need, whether it was financially, emotionally, morally, or those who were politically discriminated against. In 1941, when Germans began to be extremely harsh as they politically discriminated against Jews, beginning to send them to various camps without a good supply of food or water, hard labor, and horrible living conditions, Fedecka began to hide and save them. She welcomed them into her home with open arms. They received emotional support, food, shelter, and false paperwork allowing them to work. She was so dedicated to saving others, that she eventually had her own children leave the house with false papers, to keep them safe as Christians and make room for more Jews to take shelter with her. She did so, not knowing if she would ever see her children again, says http://db.yadvashem.org. What a sacrifice it would be to send your own children away. This is clear evidence of her true passion.

There are some great examples of how Fedecka saved and affected many Jew's lives. Many stories of these accounts are written by those Fedecka helped saved in various books, articles, and poems. A great example is a quote in an article by Erna Podhorizer. She wrote, "I would like to evoke the memory of a particularly generous woman, who defended everything that was human and progressive; her name was Maria Fedecka and she was already known before the Second World War. Maria Fedecka - a Polish woman with a kind heart - was never indifferent upon witnessing an act of constraint, violence or injustice" (Erna Podhorizer). By reading this quote, we can tell how important Fedecka was in saving many Jews, and that she always was a great member of the community she lived in. Words such as "defended everything" and "she was already known before the Second World War" stand out in showing this.

Keep in mind that according to, https://www.ushmm.org/learn/timeline-of-events/1942-1945/german-poster-announces-death-penalty-for-aiding-jews, those who took the act of hiding and/or assisting the escape of a Jew from a camp, faced the death penalty of their entire family if caught. This is probably one of the reasons why she sent her children away. We still have to think of how stressful it would be to have not only your own life at risk, but the lives of your children at risk at the same time.

According to http://www.mariafedecka.republika.pl/artykuly.htm, Erna Podhorizer also quoted, "There was such a night when he was at home pp. Fedeckich (Fedecki) they not stayed overnight Jews" (Erna Podhorizer). This quote shows us Fedecka was always doing as much as possible to comfort and save Jews. From this quote, we can understand what Fedecka would undergo to save someone. She would do anything to save a Jew's life. Erna Podhorizer even said many Jews owe her their life. An occasion of her writing this is, "Former Chairman of the Council in Vilnius Jan Druto with his family just owes her his life" (Erna Podhorizer). Reading this, we can see that she not only saved Jan Druto, but his entire family. Imagine how Jan Druto felt when Maria Fedecka gave his family a chance of survival in the Holocaust. Imagine how his children reflected on the sacrifices made by Fedecka. Maria Fedecka was a hero, a hero of Poland, to him and to his family.

Although many of the details are somewhat limited on the countless names of those who Fedecka saved, the story of Adlena Smilg is a great illustration of Fedecka stepping in. Adlena was a baby born from the parents of Adolf and Lena Smilg. She was born during 1942, in a Vilna ghetto. The parents, Adolf and Lena, made multiple attempts to save their baby from having to go through all of the extremely harsh conditions. As weeks and months went on without any luck, they worried that the baby would soon die. Fedecka stepped in to save the baby, by agreeing to take care of it. As yadvashem.org says, she, "…looked after the baby with true devotion…" (yadvashem.org). After Fedecka took great care of the baby for nearly two years, the baby was returned to her parents when the area was liberated. This baby is another example of the many lives that Fedecka truly did save.

Around 1945, after the area was liberated, and after Fedecka saved many more from deportation to the USSR and from their imprisonment, she left the town of Wilno, moving to Sopot. With friends Zdzislaw Grabski and Michal Pankiewicz, she founded The League for the Struggle Against Racism, to raise awareness of political discrimination, and to make sure that something like this would never happen again.

During this project, I learned about how horrible, unfair, and uncalled for, the Holocaust was. I learned about the incredibly difficult work and the harsh conditions people went through, with hardly any food, water, clothes, and poor living quarters. I even heard a speech from a Holocaust survivor at school, Mr. Bernard Marks. Marks spoke of how horrible life was to be a Jew during that period of time. But I also learned that those who stepped up during the Holocaust, risking their lives to save others, were an extremely important part of those who survived and the survivors we still have today. I better understand how unfair this racial discrimination was to Jews. This project has made me look at racism in the past and present differently, and has made me think about how hard it is to be discriminated against. I look at Hitler, Jews, and Germans differently. I think that all countries will forever interact and look at Germany differently than they did before the Holocaust. The world makes a better effort to avoid racial discrimination and to make sure that something like this will never happen again. To avoid this kind of event, we must look for warning signs, and we must always speak up. We all have to remember we have a voice, and that one voice is always better than none. Everyone counts. We have to be prepared to handle a disaster.A hero. Maria Fedecka truly was a hero to many victims of the Holocaust. To give of herself wholly and willingly, at a risk none of us will ever come close to realizing the magnitude of today. Never again.

Works Cited

"Google." Google. N.p., n.d. Web. 22 Nov. 2016.

History.com. A&E Television Networks, n.d. Web. 24 Nov. 2016.

Leftwich, Joseph. Abraham Sutzkever: Partisan Poet. New York: T. Yoseloff, 1971. Web. 22 Nov. 2016.

"Maria Fedecka (born Krzywiec)." Historical Records and Family Trees - MyHeritage. N.p., n.d. Web. 22 Nov. 2016.

"Maria Fedecka." Maria Fedecka. N.p., n.d. Web. 22 Nov. 2016.

Marks, Bernard. "Never Again." Holocaust Survivor. KAMS, Elk Grove. 9 Nov. 2016. Speech.

"Never Again: Heeding the Warning Signs." United States Holocaust Memorial Museum. United States Holocaust Memorial Museum, n.d. Web. 25 Nov. 2016.

Podhorizer, Erna. Maria Fedecka, the Woman Who Helped Others. N.p., n.d. Web. 22 Nov. 2016.

"Stories of Rescue | Polscy Sprawiedliwi." Stories of Rescue | Polscy Sprawiedliwi. N.p., n.d. Web. 22 Nov. 2016.

United States Holocaust Memorial Museum. United States Holocaust Memorial Museum, n.d. Web. 23 Nov. 2016.

Yad Vashem. N.p., n.d. Web. 22 Nov. 2016.

Wladyslawa Choms

Brandi La Valley

Before World War 2 started, Choms lived in a town named Drohobycz. She was born in 1891 when everyone was at peace with each other. This town was populated with Ukrainians, Jews, and Poles. In 1927 Choms became head of the municipal social welfare council. In Chom's town there were many problems with ethnic tensions, and rivalries often occurred, however such thing did not bother Chom. In her town most of the Jews were not wealthy capitalists, in a way you would say they were very poor. As time went on Choms became a very sympathetic person towards Jews, in fact she sympathized with the Zionist students who were often beat up or attacked by the Ukrainian and Polish students. They were armed with brass knuckles, clubs, and razor blades. Although she was a Polish and Roman catholic, those in the anti-semitic national Democratic Party thought of her as a traitor and as the "Jews mother".

Choms personality got her many friends, but most of her friends didn't support her beliefs. Choms husband Friedrich, a major in the polish army, wants to be crucial to her later activities. With Friedrich unable to follow the rules by his fellow officers he resigned for the military. In 1934 Choms and her husband went to visit Palestine and were very impressed on the achievements of the Zionist pioneers. On their way back to Poland, with their son, settled in a city similar to Drohobycz called Lvov is has an ethically mixed population of Jews, Poles, and Ukrainians. When World War 2 started in September 1939, the attack of the Nazi's on Poland resulted in occupation and partitioning of the country. All central and western parts of Poland were either

Transported to Germany or turned into a colony named Generalgouverment. During this time the Nazi's harshly treated both the Jews and Poles. But from the two of them the Jews were treated more harshly than the Poles were. Form September 1939 to June 1941 Lvov became part of the Ukrainian Soviet Socialist Republic. Through this rough time Jews did not need to fear of their religion because Stalin's goal was to make his power stronger rather than a social transformation. During this time and conditions Wladyslawa Choms could focus on her work making the Jewish community better. The defeat of Poland had crucially affected her life because of her son and husband leaving to fight the Nazi's. All the time throughout the war she didn't know weather to think her husband was alive or dead. Finally after the war she heard that he had survived through it all, but he was not safe. Even though her husband had survived he was taken in as a prisoner of the Germans. But she later figured out her son had escaped England, but like many other people who had escaped he had lost his life in a fight as a pilot in the Royal Air force in 1941. The Nazi's job of Lvov, which started in June 30 1941, was a tragedy for the cities population but particularly for the Jews. In the beginning many Jews were murdered by the gangs of Ukrainians. However it had gotten worse, the system of violence, carried out by the German occupations, forces all extermination of Jews. Under the government of mass murder, Choms was both defiant and practical in her resistance. She collected all she could for the Jews families including jewelry, and money from the wealthy Jews. Choms used these items to create an aid for both Jew families and individuals. Over time Choms ha developed a strong relationship and trust with the Jews and soon created a group of Polish women and men who risked their lives to fight against

The Nazi's to save as many Jews lives as they could with the risk of being eliminated at any possible moment. After the Nazi's had built something called a ghetto for Lvov and her community it became hard for them to fight against the Nazi's. But nothing could possibly stop their will to do everything they can to stop the Nazi's for doing no good. They smuggled in food quite often to those in need, and provided them with medical care, and gave them fake identifications so that they could try and move them to safer locations. On many occasions they brought whole Jewish families to safety, sometimes even away from Warsaw. With Choms a member of the Democratic Party no one doubted her sincerity and courage. As the Germans deported more and more Jews to death camps, Choms and her group did everything they could to save them and bring women, children, and even men to safety. Most Jewish infants, which were rescued were brought to safekeeping Polish families who had volunteered to keep them safe, which came the responsibility of getting caught which could lead to death. Since Choms job was so dangerous she had changed her name and address, but this did not prevent people from finding and calling her. Along her journey of saving many lives of the Jews she saves a women named Klara Chotiner-Lustig along with her small child. They appeared on her front doorstep hungry, frightened, and exhausted. Choms had taken them in and took care of them until they had regained some strength, then she soon found them a place to stay at her neighbors house. Very soon after that she had gotten forged papers stating that they could both receive legal food rations. After all of that had taken place Klara was so grateful, so she ended up joining Choms group to save more Jews like her. In November 1943, the Polish underground central command ordered Choms to leave Lvov. After all that had happened Choms had become known as the "angel of Lvov". Her countless will to save people, endangering both her and her co-workers lives, helped save hundreds of Jew lives in danger. Even after she was ordered to leave Lvov she continued to her resistance activities and survived the bloodbath of 1944. After the war had ended Choms had started working on restoring her own life again. After she had settled she had gone to look for her husband and had found him alive after surviving Nazism for several years of slave labor. Many of her Jewish friends decided to move to Israel while her husband and her decided to stay in Europe, mostly because of her husband's fragile health. After her husband's death in France in 1951, she thought about moving to Israel, in 1963 she finally made the choice to move there. Although she was not a Jew she felt as if she was respected and at home in Israel. Because of all the friendships she had made saving so many peoples lives, made it much easier to bear with the pain of losing her son and husband. In the year of 1963 Choms had received an award of the Righteous among the Nations. Sadly Choms had died the year of 1989.

Throughout my experience learning about the Holocaust has made a huge impact on my life about how she didn't only help save hundreds of Jews lives but also stayed humble and strong along the way. I learned that even though there might be very hard times in your life you need to stay strong and no matter what comes in your way you need to stay positive. The impact the Holocaust made on many people of that time must have been very hard nut what I notice about almost all of the survivors is that they stayed positive and strong throughout their journey. From all that has happened in the past we have learned that this all should "never again" happen. What we could do to prevent this from happening is to stay positive, strong, and respectful for others, and most importantly keep peace with the society.

Works Cited

Women in World History. Gale Research Inc., 2002. Web. 4 Dec. 2016. <www.encyclopedia.com>.

Helena Stypulczak

Brandon Fong

It began in 1933, but it should have never happened. The terrible, wrathful Nazis became Germany's sovereignty, and began the "sacrifice by fire." The Holocaust, a reign of excruciating pain and terror, marked the beginning of an attempt to eliminate and brutally slay the innocent Jews. Adolf Hitler, the Nazis' leader, blamed the Jews as the cause of Germany's downfall. This struck fear and anxiety into the Jews' hearts with fear and concern for their family's fate. However, the blamed Jewish people had some luck; the generous, kind-hearted people of Poland, and many other areas, were willing to risk their freedom for the tormented Jews that could end up in filthy ghettos, tortuous death camps, or in lines for inhumane deaths. However, some of the heroes, like Helena Stypulczak, sacrificed their peace and joy for those unable to fight back.

Helena Stypulczak was born in 1923 in Lwow. She grew up to be an activist in the Polish left-wing youth movement. During the forever haunting Holocaust, Helena rented out a worn down room at a manor in the country near Wola Filipowska. Here, from June of 1942 to September of 1943, Helena hid three frightened, persecuted Jewish children and a friend.

Helena found Michal Zachaczewski, a friend's son, inside the Lvov Ghetto, cowering with homesickness, hunger, and terror. He thought he might have to face the gas chambers.

At the time, he was only eight years old, yet he was stuck in the miserable place the Nazis sent the powerless Jews to die of starvation, overcrowding, and disease. Luck was on Michal's side though. Helena's kindness and generosity empowered her to prepare fake documents for Michal and his mother, who also was imprisoned. When Helena attempted to help them escape from the ghetto these documents gave them a new identity to allow them to not be sent back to the ghetto if the Gestapo searched Helena's house. Michal's luck really was true because, thanks to Helena, Michal survived the awful ordeal he was put through.

Helena Stypulczak also saved a six year old and nineteen month old infant from their fate of cyanide gassing at a concentration camp they could be sent to. The six year old, Halina Lachowicz, was in Warsaw, afraid for herself and her feeble, weak body, when Helena gave her shelter at her place in Wola Filipowska. Lidia Uzwij was only about a year and a half old when Helena, a friend of Lidia's parents, brought her home with her. She provided a much needed place of secrecy, hope, and rest for them. Warsaw was a major area where Jews were mindlessly obliterated by the cruel and unrelenting Nazis. Therefore, Helena was right in saving these youth from a slow, painful death of excruciating agony and torture.

Now, in June of 1943, Helena had developed a knack for rescuing, as we see when she saved yet another friend from the cruel punishments of Adolf Hitler. This time, Helena met Helena Tybińska in an apartment desperately needing a place to hide from the Holocaust's unforgiving conditions. She had fled the Lvov Ghetto with fear, imagining the punishment that would be inflicted upon her if she was found, but also with gratitude that she was still alive. So, once again, Helena gave a friend a place to recover from the horrors they experienced or witnessed. Helena Tybińska hid at Wola Filipowska until September of 1943.

However, Helena Stypulczak's luck was dissipating. Helena was arrested and sent to the miserable and torturous Auschwitz concentration camp. She was then transported to the women's subcamp, KZ Flossenbürg. Luckily, she survived the painful, terrible place, and was liberated in April of 1945. She was exhausted from demands of the guards, but also joyful because she was free and knew she had made a difference in multiple people's lives.

Helena's good willed spirit and courage to defy the orders of Adolf Hitler and his Nazis to single out and persecute the Jews paid off. The preservation of three children's lives and a friend from the demented, agonizing pain of the Holocaust was an act of heroism on her part. It allowed these children to feel love and compassion from a stranger, enabling them to push through the pain and grief the Holocaust caused. Furthermore, the children could now grow up and end events that jump out at them as a possible Holocausts. This is a very key component to preventing another Holocaust, because history repeats, so they can know when take the initiative to break this cycle. The motivation of kind strangers and the conscience of the remarkable human brain, helped guide these youth to being an upstander to righteousness.

Take for example Michal; at eight he would have a vivid recollection of the Holocaust, its tortures, and its persecution of the Jews. This enables him to recognize events with similar intentions to kill mass proportions of people and persecute them. So, now envision Michal multiplied by millions, the number of children that were torn away from their beloved families and put through immeasurable sorrow and agony. All these survivors create a chain with iron links that will help avoid and eradicate future Holocaust's.

Helena's courageous act to hide these terrified youth, victims of the treacherous World War II and inhumane, cruel treatments that caused it, also made her a true Holocaust Hero. She bravely rescued and hid three children that couldn't fight back by themselves. Therefore, she started three precious lives back on the path full of human dignity after they were mistreated by the Nazis. This helped to rehabilitate their injured minds; like an amateur psychiatrist.

A true hero of the Holocaust, Helena Stypulczak, hid three young, frightened children and a friend in her home in Wola Filipowska from the torturous, bloodthirsty Nazis with evil intentions on their minds; to erase the Jews from Europe. She was prepared to risk her life for them to save their human dignity and life. She was arrested and sent to a concentration camp because of this. The Holocaust's purpose was to kill, eliminate, and destroy the Jews because they were accused by Adolf Hitler to be the cause of Germany's poverty after World War I. He created inhumane ways to wrongfully destroy them. Jews were savagely killed and put through unimaginable torture. Therefore, Helena's actions and motives have really inspired and impacted me through showing that good intentions will always make the world better and safer. Even if you must make major sacrifices that risk your personal safety; you still must make a commitment to mankind because it will greatly improve and help the world.

Every person that has made it through the terrible era of the Holocaust, says, "Never Again." This means that the Holocaust, or any other event like it, will never happen again. They and their fellow Jews experienced pain, hunger, and torture beyond what any human being should ever know. It is our responsibility, as free people, raised to be righteous, to stand up for what we know is right; no matter the cost. To ensure the safety of the future, we need to take steps to engrain in people's heads that we need to fight for what we know must happen to keep this world welcoming and happy. For example, we can teach students and citizens about crimes and their effects so that they can understand that crimes have consequences; for the criminal, victim, and community. The consequences hurt everyone greatly, just like the agonizing Holocaust, where one hero stood out; Helena Stypulczak.

Works Citeed

"Helena Stypulczak." Polscy Sprawiedliwi. POLIN Museum of the History of Polish Jews, 2016. Web. 09 Dec. 2016.

"The World Holocaust Remembrance Center." Yad Vashem. Yad Vashem, 2016. Web. 17 Nov. 2016.

Wojan, Megan. "Introduction to Holocaust." Social Science 7 Honors. Katherine Albiani Middle School, Elk Grove. 4 Nov. 2016. Lecture.

Jozef Balwierz

Brandon Saelee

The holocaust made some of the worst villains, but made normal, average people heroes. Sometime during the 1930s, an economic depression completely decimated Germany's overall wealth, leading to a dishonest government to citizens. Germans could no longer trust and follow the government. This provided a new leader to come to power and lead Germany to a "better future", Adolf Hitler. Adolf Hitler was a Nazi, who believed that Aryans were the best race. Aryans were anybody who was Germanic, or Nomadic, Hitler was Germanic. Hitler and his Nazis made a great decision to exterminate all other races, but above all other ones, Jews. Some Germans and non-Aryans let Hitler kill off an entire race, but some people like Jozef Balwierz, didn't. His family saved Jews, and he was rewarded with the Righteous Among Nations award.

Around 1940 during World War II everything changed. The holocaust happened near the end of it and Adolf Hitler was part of it. Adolf and his Nazi's wanted complete dominance over the world as well as, the Aryan "master race." The "Master Race" meant invading everybody and every place. After getting control of Germany, Germany's government was not trustworthy since it had lost its wealth and became poor. Adolf rearmed Germany and got the treaties with Italy, Japan, and Soviet Russia, although later broken, he began his campaign. He began by sending Russia to invade Poland from the East on September 17, 1939, and finished it by sending his German forces on the West on April 9, 1940. They soon took over Greece and Yugoslavia and invaded Soviet Russia. During this time, ideas for the Holocaust were thought of and soon carried out. It took 5 more years for the war to end against America. After this it wasn't a pretty result. 45-60 million people died, 6 million of them were Jews. No country was ever the same after World War II and the Holocaust.

Jozef Balwierz had a decent life that he risked for Jews. He originally lived in Krakow, Poland. He got a job of destroying apartments. Through his job, he became friends with Zofia Bross and Stefan Bross. He also learned of their cousins Zofia Liebeskind, with her daughters Irena and Rita whom his family hid. Jozef went and had an average and okay life, but it every single part of it changed once he learned of the Libeskinds.

Jozef hid many Jews along his life, by providing them a place to stay in his home. Zofia Liebeskind's husband, Samuel Liebeskind died in 1941 due to Jew roundups, Hitler ordered all Jews to be grouped together in groups. Jozef's family then hid Zofia Liebeskind and her daughters Irena and Rita, by using documents to change their identities. Irena's new name was changed to Hela and Rita's new name was Misia. Jozef then hid Irena and Rita's cousin Ilka Bardaka and brother Ryszard Burdach. He also hid other Jews even though he was at risk with them. All this time, Hitler and his Nazis were still looking for them. Jozef risked his life to save random Jews whose live shouldn't have mattered to him.

Jozef's life returned to normal after being a hero. After hiding for 2 years, Zofia Liebeskind moved to Vienna to avoid oppressors and so did Irena in 1943. Jozef also moved to Vienna to be closer to Irena. While there, he worked at an oil industry at Dobermannsdorf. He then eventually got married to Irena. At this time World War II was ending and so they returned to Krakow. They fortunately found Rita and Ilka, but unfortunately without their mother Zofia Liebeskind or Ilka's brother Ryszard. They didn't survive the war. After studying, in 1958 Jozef and Irena both moved to Brazil, then eventually decided to settle down in Sao Paulo in the country. In 2007, Jozef was awarded with Righteous Among Nations. (The title Righteous Among Nations is an award given to non-Jews who risked their lives to save Jews from being killed by Hitler). As he puts it," The help I was able to provide was my own reaction against injustice and crime." He died 4 years later in 2011. Jozef lived an adventurous great life just for the cause of saving people under great force.

Jozef's story as well as others proves one point, anybody can be a hero. Balwierz decided he would stand against Hitler's heavy force and save someone, some he barely knew. These events tell us it's okay to stand up to people. That's the only way the holocaust can Never Again. Everybody has to stand up to injustice, bigger force, and sometimes, themselves. However, this cannot only be used against racism and killing off an entire race. It can be used any time someone is in trouble; or is facing against injustice. We must always stand together as well. Together, we can stand against even bigger threats. The holocaust taught humanity the greatest lesson, stand together and be a hero.

Works Cited

"Balwierz Jozef." Story of Rescue - Balwierz Jozef | Polscy Sprawiedliwi. N.p., n.d. Web. 12 Dec. 2016.

The World Holocaust Remembrance Center. "Balwierz Family." The Righteous among Nations. N.p., n.d. Web.

Perirera, Justin. "The Holocaust." Holocaust Powerpoint. Katherine L. Albiani Middle School, Sacramento. Oct. 2016. Lecture.

"Nazi Ideology." Nazi Ideology. N.p., n.d. Web. 12 Dec. 2016.

History.com Staff. "World War II History." History.com. A&E Television Networks, 2009. Web. 13 Dec. 2016.

"About the Righteous." About the Righteous. N.p., n.d. Web. 13 Dec. 2016.

Jerzy Bielecki

Brian Tauber

My survivors name is Jerzy Bielecki and he escaped from the concentration camp in Germany. He lasted about four years in the camp and eventually got angry and wanted to escape. The men and women were apart from each other one day the gates opened that separated the men from women. She caught the eye of Jerzy and they both were seventeen. Her name was Cyla they talked for a while and eventually fell in love with each other they talked of escaping but they hadn't thought of the brilliant idea before. The idea was to steal one of the guard's uniforms and a name tag and be a guard. He would take her and her friend out of there as do other guards with others. When they walked out they ran for 10 days.

They ran out of food and water, and grew weak. Cyla said for them to go on bet Jerzy couldn't leave her behind he carried her all the way. He finally found one of his close relative's houses and they stayed there for a while. Cyla left with friend and Cyla told Jerzy to meet her at a barn she had found. The barn was about 40 kilometers away from his relatives. He ran there but he had been 4 days late and she had already left Poland. She met a Jewish man that had also escaped they later got married. Jerzy got married as well to a lady they lived a very happy life he became a director for school mechanics.

Cyla wanted to meet with Jerzy so they did she was trying to make him leave his wife. Her marriage wasn't very good they yelled a lot and grew apart. He couldn't leave his wife and she got so mad that when he would send letters she wouldn't respond they never saw each other again and she still regrets that.

I learned that the Jewish people in the concentration camps lived a life unimaginable and nobody should have to go through that. They lived off a scrap of bread and a piece of potato and no meat. They grew weak and many died. The Soviet Union went into Jerzy's camp and they found about 7,000 survivors and about 1,000,000 died inside those gates. The impact on me hearing Jerzy's life story made me feel that I will do anything to prevent that from happening again.I have learned that the holocaust was terrible and should not be thought of or done ever again. Hearing Jerzy's story has inspired me to encourage this not to happen again I will stop this if it ever happens again. I will try to stop this if it ever happens again because it was the worst thing to happen again. The Holocaust has greatly impacted the population of Jewish people and the world's population. The phrase never again means a lot to me because it shows that we will prevent this from ever happening again. I know that if this or something close to this ever happens again we will defeat the cause of it and our military will stop it in its tracks. Never again shows that we are not scared to show that we care and that we will make it never happen again forever.

The steps I will take to make sure this will never happen again are to make speeches to teach people what really happened so they hopefully will never do anything like that. My next step is if it were to happen again I would show the person that is doing it what they truly are doing Jerzy's story has inspired many and will continue to as long as his name is still around I picked Jerzy Bielecki because I read his past and I thought it was very inspiring and courageous. He is very interesting and I love his story. He went through a lot to save his friend and her friend. He risked his life for 2 others and every day he is talked about for his courage, how much his friends mean to him, and because he was strong to get out of there and get others out. Never again means so much to me and a lot of people. I found never again inspiring because people aren't scared to show their courage to stand up for others. I learned that never again isn't just for the survivors of the Holocaust it is for everyone, it is a chance to show that they will stand up for what is right. This is one of my favorite sayings because it has inspired me to show that I will stand up for whatever is right. I have found inspiration that I have been looking for, for a while. Thank you for passing on your stories. I will never forget the very many deaths and that is because I have stories to pass on what happened and where it happened. Anyone that is reading this and experienced all of that I want to thank you for not being afraid to tell your stories to all of us.

Works Cited

"San Diego Jewish World." San Diego Jewish World. N.p., n.d. Web. 11 Dec. 2016.
"Www.yadveshem.com." Www.yadveshem.org. N.p., n.d. Web.

Irena Adamowicz

Brianna Swanson

The Holocaust was a period of time when Hitler and his followers, the Nazis, took over Poland and imprisoned the Jewish people. The Jews were imprisoned mainly in Germany and Poland. The Nazis believed that they were superior to the Jews and that the Jews must be exterminated. So, the Nazis imprisoned the Jews and tragically killed over six million of them. The word Holocaust literally means a sacrificial death by fire. A hero is someone who saves lives, helps others, or even just provides a bed for someone to sleep. Irena Adamowicz was a true hero of Poland. Irena was born into a noble family and was a scout leader in the Polish scout movement.

Irena was born in Warsaw in the year 1910. She worked many hard years towards a degree. Finally, in 1930 her hard work paid off and she had earned a degree in social work at the university of Warsaw. Irena helped many children in her social work including Jews and non-Jews alike. Irena provided counselling and educational services to Catholic scouts and for the Jewish youth movement Hashomer Hatzair. She was not a Jew but she saw how wrong Hitler was about in his treatment of the Jews. Irena was a Roman Catholic and a leader of the Polish Scout Movement. When World War II struck, Irena became a resistance worker because she wanted to fight for equal rights. She wanted to do something special, she wanted to help; not for the sake of being noticed but for the sake of others.

In the 1940s, Irena carried messages between ghetto camps numerous times. She did this even though she risked her own well-being. She wanted to help even if others feared the Nazis and Hitler. The Jewish Fighting Organization saw how passionate, strong, and brave she was as a resistance worker. They decided that she would be the right person to make a channel of communication between ghettos and them. Irena became quite close to some of the imprisoned Jews. She even went to ghettos trying to boost the spirits of Jews that were imprisoned by ensuring them that everything would be okay and that the Allies would win the war. Irena became a member of the Home Army as a clandestine courier. Irena also believed in the Hashomer Hatzair, a resistance club that had fought in the Warsaw ghetto uprising in 1943. Irena worked very close to another resistance worker named Izreal Chaim Wilner who later became a great friend of hers. In 1941 Irena brought terrible news to her fellow leaders and workers in their movement; the Nazis had killed thousands of Jews in cold blood. This news began to rapidly spread throughout the movement as it had been the first news of a mass killing by the Nazis. This dramatically changed their plans so a new plan was put in place for Irena to go to Lithuania. Irena sat with the leaders of AK, Stanislaw Hajduk, Mordechaj, Icchak Cukierman, Josef Kaplan, Cywia Lubetkin. AK stands for Armia Krajowa. It was the Home Army's resistance group formed in February 1942. They had discussed what would happen next and what would be their next step. As result Irena and the others decided that she would go to Lithuania. So, in the summer of 1942 Irena went on many dangerous trips to Lithuania trying to gain contact with clandestine organization in many ghetto camps. Irena went to various camps including, Warsaw, Bialystok, Vilna, Kovno, and Siauliai. She worked for the clandestine organizations establishing contact with many organizations and various people seeking any information on the Nazis. The clandestine organizations were a group of people who kept their activities a secret avoiding law enforcement. Due to the fact that Irena was very close with the Jews as well as her home country of Poland, Irena would continue going between camps many times endangering her life encouraging imprisoned Jews and gaining information. Due to this the Jews in Kovno ghetto were inspired by her and gave her the nickname of "Di chalutzishe shikse", which means the pioneering gentile. After World War II ended, Irena kept contact with some of the Jews she had worked with underground that had survived the Holocaust. Irena was a true hero who only cared for what was right. She risked her life so many times trying and succeeding in helping the Jews. Irena was born a scout leader and raised in an environment that was for equal rights. A tree was planted in Jerusalem in honor of her in 1985. She was named Righteous Among the Nations through many efforts of her close friends who had survived the Holocaust and who had fought alongside her. She had earned this title all her life, but sadly wasn't alive to see how much people noticed her accomplishments and how much people saw her bravery. I have learned so much about what it means to be a true hero, the holocaust, and Irena Adamowicz. It has been a great pleasure being able to participate in this contest although it has taken a lot of work and effort.

Never Again.

Sources

http://www.revolvy.com/main/index.php

http://www.eilatgordinlevitan.com/kovno/kovno_pages/kovno_right.html

http://www.nationalarchivesstore.org/?utm_source=google&utm_medium=cpc&utm_campaign=brand&gclid=CjwKEAiAj7TCBRCp2Z22uerj4SJACG7SBEEt2mBENJswQE77CxQtBbq9MdRRaObfC7ZX-_Hq_WoxoCRVnw_wcB

Maria Burdowa

Brisa Blomquist

Imagine that you are a Jewish citizen living in Poland in 1933. You hear through rumors that a new German leader named Adolf Hitler has now been selected for office. He promises to end worldwide depression and free Germany from its misery. Little did you know, he had another plan that would forever change the course of history. It started when the German government decided to take away the Jewish peoples' rights of German citizenship. Your entire family is suddenly forced to wear the yellow Star of David so Germans could identify you as a "Jew". You are not allowed to eat at your favorite restaurant, or sit on park benches because no "Jews" are allowed, and your supervisor fired you from your job because you are a "Jew". The Jewish people suddenly found themselves taken from their homes and forced to live under deplorable conditions in crammed ghettos, until they would be sent off to concentration camps or even to death camps. Many non-Jewish citizens had no idea what life was like in the camps. As time went on, Hitler's hatred for the "Jews" fed into his determination to destroy them. Some Jewish citizens got lucky however, and were able to escape Hitler's brutality thanks to the help from non-Jewish people that were willing to put their own lives on the line to help hide them from the Nazis. Maria Burdowa was one such person who hid two young Jewish girls named Eva (Chava, Ewa) and Marian (Moshe) Klarfeld. These two girls managed to survive through the Holocaust thanks to Maria's help.

Salia and Richard Klarfeld and their two young daughters once lived in a nice house in Lvov, Poland. Maria Burdowa, who came from the town of Jaworow, would frequently visit the house selling flowers for the holidays. Over time, the family's bond with Maria grew, and soon they were very close with one another. In April, 1942 life was becoming more dangerous for the Jewish people, so Salia and Richard asked Maria to take care of their one-year old baby Marian and their four-year old daughter, Eva. They planned to go away until things calmed down, and they offered Maria money to help with the extra expenses of taking care of the two girls. They also gave her the addresses of their relatives in America in case they didn't return. Maria devoted herself to keeping the little girls safe, and she tried to raise them as if she were their mother in her home back in Jaworow. During one of her visits back to the Klarfeld home, Maria discovered the house was empty, and the property had been requisitioned. She later learned that Mr. and Mrs. Klarfeld had been deported and taken to the Belzec extermination camp to be exterminated. Maria was now solely responsible for the lives of Eva and Marian. One of my sources from www.Yadvashem.org stated that "Maria took care of the children throughout the war-never, to their memory, displaying any anger or resentment. She was always calm, collected and kind". Maria also made sure Eva and Marian stayed healthy by having them drink lots of milk and explaining the importance of being strong and healthy. Maria had to deal with the dangers of German raids on Polish houses as they searched for Jews in hiding. Even through the frequent

German inspections, Maria had always been her kind, gentle self. After the war, the Klarfelds' American relatives could not be found, and Maria could not arrange any schooling for Eva and Marian. She took them to an orphanage where she often visited to make sure they were in good condition. Maria died in 1970 alone with no family members to support her. Eva and Marian, by now all grown up, remembered little of their time hiding in Maria's home, but knew that without her help, they may not have survived. They decided it was their job to honor Maria as their rescuer and contacted YadVashem. To honor Maria, her name was placed on YadVashem's Wall of Honor where her name still lies.

I saw Maria Burdowa as a hero in my eyes for her courage and bravery to break the Gestapo's rules and save the lives of two little girls who later came to honor her name. If she hadn't done that, Eva and Marian would likely have been killed along with their parents in the extermination camp. YadVashem and my other sources described Maria as a kind and noble woman who was willing to sacrifice herself for the lives of others. The Holocaust impacted hundreds of thousands of people, and the words "Never Again" bring an important message to ensure a horrible event like this is never repeated. In the future, I hope we can look at one another's differences as something unique and special. I think it is important to be different so we can learn from one another. The words "Never Again" hold a special place in my heart along with the heroes and Jewish people that suffered during those times. All I can do is pray that we will "Never Again" make that same mistake in our time.

Works Cited

"Maria Burdowa." Maria Burdowa. N.p., n.d. Web. 09 Dec. 2016.

Yad Vashem - Request Rejected. N.p., n.d. Web. 09 Dec. 2016.

Villanueva, Alexis. "Maria." Prezi.com. N.p., 01 Mar. 2016. Web. 10 Dec. 2016.

"Yad Vashem - Yad Vashem Magazine #46 - Page 14-15 - Created with Publitas.com." Publitas: Publish Catalogs Online. Inspire Visitors. Sell More. N.p., n.d. Web. 10 Dec. 2016.

Henryk Slawik

Brooke Albee

 Henryk Slawik was an unsung hero, who saved many lives during the holocaust. During World War II, he was a soldier, Polish politician, diplomat, and social worker. He saved 30,000 Polish refugees, of which 5,000 were Jews by issuing false documents. He never once gave up his duty to protect his people, and in the end died knowing he did everything he could to save as many of them as possible.

Slawik was born in 1894 in Timmendorf, Poland, one of 5 children. He attended secondary school at his mother's request, and was soon drafted after graduation into the army in World War I. He was captured during the war and interned but was released in 1918. Upon his return, he joined the Polish Socialist Party. In Warsaw, he took active part in the Silesian Plebiscite as one of its organizers and began working as a journalist. In 1922,

Slawik was then elected president of Worker's Youth Association and took part in setting up Worker's Universities. In 1928, Slawik married Jadwiga Purzycka and later had a daughter named Krystyna.

At the outbreak of the Polish Defense War of 1939, Slawik joined an army police battalion, where he fought with distinction. Near the border of Slovakia, Slawik's men were ordered to retreat towards the newly established Hungary border. On September 17, the Soviet Union joined the war against Poland, therefore, Slawik crossed into Hungary and was taken to a refugee camp. There he met Jozsef Antall, the Hungarian Ministry of the Interior, when he brought the needs of the refugees to Antall's attention. To właśnie z nim, już jako przewodniczący Komitetu Obywatelskiego do Spraw Uchodźców Polskich na Węgrzech (na początku 1940 roku Sławik objął to stanowisko decyzją rządu emigracyjnego), organizował pomoc dla uciekinierów z okupowanej RP. Because Slawik was fluent in German, Antall brought him to Budapest and allowed him to create the Citizen's Committee for Help which organized help for refugees from occupied Poland.

Ludzie napływali ze wszystkich stron - grupami iw rozproszeniu, cywile i żołnierze, dzieci i dorośli. People fled to Hungary and while it was considered a safe place, the government in Budapest issued racial laws and began separating Polish refugees of Jewish descent from their compatriots. Knowing what the Germans did to Jews, Slawik began issuing false documents to the refugees with Aryan sounding names confirming their Polish roots and <u>Roman Catholic</u> faith using his own signature. Slawik along with Antall then organized jobs for the POWs and displaced persons. One of Slawik's key initiatives was creating an orphanage for the Jewish orphans. To avoid suspicion, the children were visited regularly by Catholic church authorities who taught the children Hungarian rather than religion. In March 1944, the Germans took over Hungary. Slawik went underground and ordered the evacuation of all refugees under his command. All the children in the orphanage were able to escape from the Nazis, and were placed in homes with other children or sent to the countryside away from the capital. In the last intense phase of the rescue of the Polish Jews, Slawik was joined by Henryk Zimmerman, who was a Jew and a lawyer. After Zimmerman decided to flee, he tried to persuade Slawik to do the same, but he stated "I cannot. Honor will not let me. I am responsible for them."

On July 16, 1944, Slawik was arrested. There are a few stories surrounding how it happened but either way Slawik was at the top of the Nazi's list of counterintelligence and was sentenced to death. Although he was brutally tortured during the trial, he never gave up his colleagues and with all documents in his name, there was no proof. On the ride over to the Mauthausen concentration camp, Antall was able to squeeze his friends hand thanking him for saving his life. Although his burial place is unknown, prison records show that he died in August 1944 along with several other inmates. Slawik's wife miraculously survived Ravensbruck, another concentration camp and found their daughter who was hidden by the Antall family. After the war, they returned to Silesia.

After 1948, authorities finally did commemorate his deeds for humanity. On January 26, 1977, Henryk Sławik was posthumously awarded the title of <u>Righteous Among the Nations</u> by <u>Yad Vashem</u> Commemorative Authority, but only after <u>Henryk Zimmerman</u>, his wartime associate and a distinguished Israeli politician, provided evidence, did he achieve true recognition in the 1990s. Since then, a book and a video have been made in Poland about his life. But even without recognition, his legacy would still live on through the 30,000 lives he helped save.

This project has allowed me to learn that everyday citizens could be unsung heroes. Slawik wasn't a Jew but he saved thousands. I now believe that I can save lives by collecting canned food or helping at a homeless shelter. I might not be able to save 30,000 people but I can help somebody have a meal or even receive a new pair of shoes. The Nazis believed that certain races were dangerous and needed to be terminated primarily the Jews. It started with wearing yellow stars then moving them to the Ghettos and lastly concentration camps. They created machines that could kill thousands of people in a day. There were piles of hair and shoes and glasses of the people who died left as remnants. They were lucky to get 500 calories a day which left them walking skeletons. Six million innocent people died just because a certain race had too much power. "Never Again". Never Again should any race be treated as badly as those during the holocaust. No one, not even the worst criminal, should endure the pain of working everyday while weighing under 70 pounds. Steps that people could take would first to be more open minded about people's differences. Treat everyone with your highest respect because you might not know what they are going through. I strongly believe that nobody should have too much power. Even in a democracy decisions are made based on majority vote or input even though a final decision may be made by the person in charge of a whole nation. Lastly, never forget what happened. Teachers and parents should tell their children at the appropriate age about the holocaust so no one will forget this enormous tragedy. Every school should have a survivor like Bernie Marks visit and provide them with an explanation about the holocaust. Henryk Slawik saved thousands of lives and I am truly honored to write about him.

Work Cited

"Henryk Slawik." Henryk Slawik. N.p., n.d. Web. 11 Dec. 2016.

"Henryk Slawik – Alchetron. The Free Social Encyclopedia." Alchetron.com. N.p., 18 Jan 2014. Web. 11 Dec. 2016.

"Henryk Slawik – Bohater Zapomniany." FAKTY W INTERIA.PL – Najnowsze Wiadomosci Z Polski I swiata, Polityka, Fakty Dnia I Najwazniejsze Infomacje, Sawsze Aktualne Wiadomasci, N.p., 16 Sept. 2010. Web. 11 Dec. 2016.

"Henryk Slawik: Piekna, Przemilczana Postac." NOW A HISTORIA W INTERIA.PL-Archiwalne Zdjecia I Niezane Fakty Dotyzace Niepodleglosci Polski, Ciekawe Postacie, Opinie I Publicystyka Historyczna, Interesujace Wydawnictwa, Aktualnosci I Wydarzenia,. N.p., n.d. Web. 11 Dec. 2016.

"The Slawik Family." Story of Rescue - The Slawik Family | Polscy Sprawiedliwi. N.p., n.d. Web. 12 Dec. 2016.

Jerzy Bielecki

Bryan Aquino

The Holocaust was one of the most devastating events in world history that included the death of many Jews. These events happened during around world war two in parts of Germany and Poland. These events happened when Germany's new leader, Adolf Hitler, created a force, the Nazis, who's plan was to exterminate what they thought to believe non pure Germans. A lot of these people were Jews and so 91% of the Jewish population was killed. Out of the victims of the holocaust I have chosen to write about Jerzy Bielecki. Jerzy was widely known for escaping the Auschwitz concentration camp, which changed his life forever.

Jerzy was born in Słaboszów, Poland on March 28th in 1921. Jerzy lived his life as a Roman Catholic. His life changing problem occurred in 1940. At 19 years old he was accused of being part of the polish resistance after Nazi soldiers caught him trying to escape from Poland to Hungary. After these events happened they sent him to the Auschwitz concentration camp. Like all prisoners of the concentration camp he had a number tattooed onto his arm which is 243. In these concentration camps people were under going extreme suffering. People who came here were treated like prisoners while being innocent. Your chances of surviving are by working or by rarely escaping. For the next three years at the concentration camp he was able to work hard enough for his survival till he met his first love in 1943. In 1943 he met Cyla Cybulska. She was a Jewish prisoner from Lomza. Male and females were not aloud to meet in the concentration camp but Jerzy and Cyla met secretly and so then fell in love with each other. After a year together Jerzy planned and plotted a way to escape from the camp. Jerzy disguised himself as a guard after scrimmaging through out the camp warehouse and coming out with a different uniform. In addition with the uniform he had a document that made him have the ability to state that he is bringing a prisoner to do some work. But instead he came to Cyla's Barracks and took her. This became one of the most nerve-racking escapes in the history of the holocaust. After that they kept walking and walking through the forest they went Cyla came to a point of exhaustion and begged Jerzy to just leave her there. But that wasn't Jerzy's mentality. Jerzy wanted to escape not live in the dangers of a concentration camp and so it happened. Refusing this to happen he carried Cyla all the way for 10 days until they reached a village called Munikowice. This village was part of the Kielce district in which Jerzy had before lived at and because of that he had family that could take care of them. Till liberation Jerzy joined a Polish underground partisan group and Cyla stayed with a random couple in a local village. After the war Jerzy stayed in Poland and had a family there while on the other hand Cyla moved to the United States and lived in Brooklyn, New York. The reason they new met up shortly after the war is because they Cyla thought that Jerzy was dead and Jerzy thought that Cyla was dead. Jerzy met up with Cyla a while later after her polish cleaning woman heard a similar story on Polish television and wanted to track down Jerzy.

Jerzy met up with her 15 ore times until she died in 2005. In addition to these events Jerzy had a great accomplishments during the post war. One of these is that he was inducted on to the list of being Righteous Among the Nation. 6 years after the death of Cyla Jerzy died on October 20, 2011.

It was so then that Jerzy has not just fell in love with someone, but he saved someone. If it was not for Jerzy's plan to escape Cyla, she would probably be another dead victim of the Holocaust and is why Cyla is so thankful for Jerzy to be in her life. I have learned a few things through his story. I found out that love is a powerful aspect of life. It was for that of their relationship they kept Jerzy stayed strong to keep each other alive through a hard journey to get to the nearest place of place that has people. Bonds are also important because without loving people in your life you wouldn't be happy. People tend to become depressed and sad when they are not around of other people or at least not fond of other people. With loving people in your life you would be supported through hardships and get to be able to get help when you are having a difficulty. If Jerzy was not there to pick Cyla up during her point of exhaustion then she would be dead. This shows that saying "two is better than one." Jerzy's family had to help the duo get food. Cyla would have never track down Jerzy if she didn't have her cleaning woman. We don't want people to have hardships in our generation and let people know that events like this should never again happen in history.

Work Cited

Hevesi, Dennis. "Jerzy Bielecki Dies at 90; Fell in Love in a Nazi Camp." Nytimes.com. N.p., n.d. Web.

JLedger. "Jerzy Bielecki, Saved Jewish Girl from Auschwitz." Jewishledger.com. N.p., n.d. Web

"The Righteous Among Nation Department." Yadvashem.org. N.p., n.d. Web.

Stefan Dobrzanski

Bryce Davis

"I'm not going to do anything more. Never Again? Well not so much, They don't let you" (A.A Mine). The holocaust was an economic depression that had hit Germany hard, Germans lacking confidence in their government. They tried to provide the chance of a new leader, Adolf Hitler. Many Nazis came to power in Germany in January of 1933. Many of those Nazis believed Aryans were a master race. Adolf Hitler established a reich ministry of public enlightment and propaganda. Stefan was born in the year of 1910 and died on December 14, 1999. Stefan was one of many people survived this tragic incident that will "Never Again" happen. Stefan was one of many people in his family he had two sons, and eight brothers. Stefan was as part of the military and served many of his lifetime years. Many of Stefan's family members had escaped including his sister and her personal daughter escaped from the warsaw ghetto. Them both were told where to go and finally arrived to the apartment complex. The both of them went to Stefan's house, he hid both of them, he did not expect anything in return as well.

Them both stayed with Stefan until the spring of 1944, when Boguslawa moved with Maria and Jan Krasen who lived in Laskowa, a remote village in the Beskidy Mountains. This disaster will never again happen to these young people who had escaped a ghetto where they could have died. Also, the Krusnas were guided by humantarian motives, which overrode considerations of personal safety or economic hardship. On December 4, 1983, Stefan and some of his family members were recognized righteous among the nations. Even when them both moved to Poznan, the Krusnas continued looking after Boguslawa. In december 1945, his mother, who toward the end of the war,she had been working in Germany under an assumed identity, as well as that the identity had returned to reclaim her daughter. Stefan did not have a clue that the daughter would never be reclaimed and stayed at Stefan's house without being caught or found. Stefan saved the life of many people but one of favorites that he had saved the life of was Jadwiga Heskin, she also escaped from the warsaw ghetto but she had been caught and Stefan helped her keep up to him and his family. As well as that he was safe and afterall himself was a safe man. He was taken to a local place with shelters where he lived happy ever after. Also Stefan saved many people's lives by taking them and making them follow him, many people from the warsaw ghetto escaped at the time Stefan did and most of them escaped and some of them did not and they had to side track and try to escape by themselves. As well as that Stefan had many citizens sacrifice their lives in s great so he can use the strategy of distracting the guards and escaping. He traveled with a large herd of people which almost all had survived and where taken to local shelters to live and not be in such a horrible place. This tragic time and event will never again happen unless those horrible people come and start it. Next,many citizens tried to do what Stefan had done but some of the next chances were unsuccessful and many and almost all of them died because they did not use the strategy correctly. Although his strategyu many people think it will always work again but in thois situation under high-security, they did not escape.

I learned that during the Holocaust, many of the citizens were killed and it was so a harsh that many people were not able to handle it, they tried to escape but many died. Stean affected my life because: First, it made me very sad that many of these people who were living a great life until this happened were under death contention. Also, many people were under high-security, when they tried to escape many of them were caught and killed.Although they were under high-security, many people were put into showers which were actually gas chambers that killed people instantly. Also, people people were put into concentration camps and ghettos. I understand that it could be a hard time on Earth but people need to take risks and try to escape and not be under so much death contention. This tragic time will never again happen and hopefully many of those horrible people will never again come back and try to kill many people unexpected. Steps that can be taken to secure this time on Earth is to have a strong military that are surrounding the borders and as well as have a strong security system. Although they had a military, they need to upgrade it and have a technology source to have a source of communication. Also have military troops in many large populated cities. This tragic time will never again happen. Another step they could take is to have cameras all around to make sure unrecognized people let anywhere near the citizens either the city or country. That is why this tragic time of events will never again happen.

Work Cited

"YadVasHem." N.p., n.d. Web.

"Stalony-dobrzanski/biografia." N.p., n.d. Web.

ALFRED WŁADYSŁAW ŻBIK

Bryce Madsen

It was January, 1933 when the Nazis came to power in Germany. The government decided that the Nazi party would take full control of the country to reestablish it to its former glory. Under the leadership of their leader Hitler the Germans began to despise, hate, and criticize the Jews. It started subtle like Jews being shown pitiful and weak in front of great strong Germans and Jews being discriminated and forced to wash sidewalks. But as time went on, it grew worse and worse. Like it was not appreciated to shop at Jews businesses and live with, and marry Jews. Not many people decided to help because it would make them to, be treated unfairly by the government and possibly be killed. But there were a select few who decided to stand against the tyranny of Hitler even with the consequences in place by the government. One of these people was Alfred Wladyslaw Żbik and his wonderful loving family.

Alfred housed, fed, hid and helped escape 2 people named Edward and Krystyna and the Kern family. Edward and Krystyna were in a small concentration camp located in the Krakow neighborhood of Grzegorzki. Edward was in the camp one evening when he saw a truck come in carrying scary, heavily armed SS men. He realized the camp was about to be liquidated so he ran to were Krystyna usually worked and convinced her to attempt and escape. Others joined in with them as they ran for the exit being shot as they went slowly dying one by one until they had stopped completely either dead or barley alive. Edward and Krystyna very luckily found themselves not dead but under a pile of dead bodies when the shooting subsided finally. They rested then under the cover of night they crawled their way out of the bodies and to the camp perimeter cutting the barbed wire with a knife Edward had found on one of the dead Jews. Then they ran swiftly and efficiently to the Vistula to wash of the human blood from their dead friends back at the camp. They made their way soon after to the Zbik's. Edward knew the Zbik's from Alfred Zbik who he knew from school. At the time Alfred was in Warsaw but his family still let them stay for the time being, clothing, feeding, and providing a place to hide. They also provided fake I.D's to them so they could walk around freely in town. Later Alfred an AK activist, returned from Warsaw. Then he used his underground connections to secure documents for Edward and Krystyna. Those documents allowed them to move to Germany 2 months later. Were they were soon liberated by the American army. Edward and Krystyna soon got married together and moved to Canada later to live long and happily in the protection of their home.

Alfred helped the Kern family in a very close way. He organized secret documents through his connection in the underground again and gave them to the Kern family. Zygmunt Kern got a job in nearby Krakow next to the ghetto there so the family moved there with him. The family soon all got jobs were they could work. Earning a good living and surviving through the documents in their names on a day to day basis. They waited out the war there slowly. When the war finally ended Zygmunt Kern moved to Canada were he met Edward who he knew from his days at school back in Poland and were surprised that they both were saved by Alfred. They both together appreciated what Alfred had done for them and how much he had risked. A quote from Edward said, "The help given to us by the Żbik family came from the bottom of the heart. They never asked for anything in return; no money could ever repay their goodness, love and unselfish help." Then Alfred said in a testimony," "How could we not have helped them, knowing that it would have been the same as giving them a death sentence," This shows the love that Alfred and his family had for a family and 2 people even though they didn't even know them that well.

In conclusion, let's stop judging people by the religion, race, or color. People like Alfred and his family are heroes for what they did and the example they created. I wish everyone in the world could be like this. If so then everyone would be caring enough to give up something of their own to help another person out. Plus people could walk around freely and it would have helped through ruff times in American history like back when the African american population was in slavery. It would also make life easier for everyone not having to worry about being treated unfairly. "Never again" should a thing like the holocaust happen again.

Works Cited

Marks, Bernard. "Yadvashem.org." Yadvas Hem. N.p., n.d. Web.

Wojan, Megan. "Introduction to the Holocaust." Holocaust. Kams, Elk Grove. 4 Nov. 2016. Lecture.

Ryszard Degorski

Calvin Mansel

Ryszard Degorski (1904-1982) played a great part in hiding Stefania Bergson just a few days before the Warsaw ghetto uprising, and led a very interesting war life. Ryszard was an officer in the Polish Army 8th regiment heavy artillery before the ghettoes were put into place by Adolf Hitler. Ryszard Degorski was born on October 4, 1904 in Gradowo, Poland, to parents Constantine and

Stefania. He was married to Jadwiga Degorski. The main heroic deed of Ryszard's is a pretty astonishing one, and it gave him the title of Righteous Among the Nations, a distinction reserved for heroes who risked their own lives in order to preserve those facing the Holocaust. The setting: Warsaw Ghetto, April 1943. Stefania Bergson successfully absconded the boundaries of the Warsaw Ghetto. But, she was robbed by blackmailers in the Aryan side. Then, having no money, she went to Janina Fraczak, who was the doorkeeper at the apartment she used to live in. The caretaker welcomed her, but she realized that since the apartment was patronized often by other tenants, it was not logical to stow Stefania away there. So, Janina stowed Stefania in the basement of the building, where all of the coal was stored. Janina realized, however, that it was not a long term solution, so she turned to Ryszard Degorski, her brother-in-law. Ryszard was an officer in the polish army and underground member. Ryszard forged the necessary documents to get her to a summer apartment he rented for her in Milanowek, about 35 kilometers away. He provided her with clothes and food, as well as kept her company and assuaged suspicions until the Red Army liberated the area.

Ryszard was also a Captain Major under the code name "Birch" in the V circuit (Mokotow) of the Warsaw district home army, second region of the infamous Warsaw Ghetto Uprising. The uprising lasted from April 19, 1942, to May 16, 1943, between the Jews and the Nazis. The Nazis started deporting the last surviving members of the Warsaw ghetto to Treblinka, where they were being exterminated. When news of this mass murder reached Warsaw, young people who heard it formed the Z.O.B, or zydowska organizacja bojowa, which means Jewish Fighting Organization. They shot at Nazis deporting more Jews, and that was the start of Nazi resistance. The resistance fighters used guns smuggled into the ghetto. The uprising, however, did not officially start until April 19, 1942, when resistance went out to fight Nazi troops. The fighters survived for about a month, but in the end Ryszard, as well as the freedom fighters who weren't shot on sight, sadly enough, were taken out of Warsaw. He probably went to a labor camp, considering the fact that he survived the war and lived until 1982. He died on June 3, 1982, and is buried in Koszalin cemetery, Kociernzyna, Pomorskie, Poland.

Obviously this hideous atrocity took the lives of millions and is the worst genocide the world has ever seen, but we now realize that the Holocaust actually helped us in some ways as nations. I'm not saying that it is good that all those Jews died, because that was a horrible event, but because of the Holocaust, the United Nations was founded. We now have a non-elitist group of nations that takes measures against genocide and makes sure all countries have equal rights for their citizens. I learned that if power of an official is unlimited, the official may use that power in unjust ways, as Hitler did. Researching Ryszard taught me that it is important to stand up to what is right, even if it is against the law.

Even now, however, genocide is a global problem. There are threats like ISIS who go around blowing themselves up and shooting at crowds to kill people who are not Muslim. That is technically a form of genocide. There are so many things we could do to make sure that "Never Again" is achieved. We could make sure that all countries are aware if something like the Holocaust is happening in a country not connected to the United Nations, and that at least some, if not all, countries take action. We can also ensure that every nation has a suitable army program. But above all, we have to pass this story down, because pretty soon, all of the holocaust survivors will no longer be with us. If we don't tell the story, we are doomed to repeat its mistakes with the same consequences. We must not have another holocaust! Can you imagine walking down the street and seeing a man so starved he is LITERALLY skin and bone? These people did! These brave survivors lived through the worst period in world history, so the least we can do is honor them by telling stories of these horrid true events so that they and their ancestors never have to see these things again. We must honor Ryszard, honor all the survivors, for what they overcame. They saw so much bloodshed, so much death, so much cruelty, and yet they overcame. Out of so many, so few. It pained them to talk about this, but they did! Why? Because they needed to prevent it from happening again, and we do as well.

Works Cited

"Google Maps." Google Maps. Google, n.d. Web. 11 Dec. 2016.

Google. "Ryszard+degorski - Google Search." Ryszard+degorski - Google Search. Google, n.d. Web. 11 Dec. 2016.

Google. "Warsaw+uprising - Google Search." Warsaw+uprising - Google Search. Google, n.d. Web. 11 Dec. 2016.

"Obwd V MOKOTW." Obwd V MOKOTW. N.p., n.d. Web. 11 Dec. 2016.

"Powstańcze Biogramy - Ryszard Degórski." Powstańcze Biogramy - Ryszard Degórski. Warsaw Uprising Museum, n.d. Web. 11 Dec. 2016.

"The Righteous among Nations." Yad Vashem - Request Rejected. Yad Vashem the World Holocaust Remembrance Center, n.d. Web. 11 Dec. 2016.

"Ryszard Degorski." Global, Find A Grave Index for Burials at Sea and Other Select Burial Locations, 1300s-Current - Ancestry.com. Findagrave.com, n.d. Web. 11 Dec. 2016.

United States Holocaust Memorial Museum. "The Warsaw Ghetto Uprising." United States Holocaust Memorial Museum. United States Holocaust Memorial Museum, n.d. Web. 11 Dec. 2016.

The Holocaust Contest Essay

Carlo Sumpo

With a harsh and traumatic time comes with great heroes who will be honored with great remembrance. The Holocaust was the persecution and murder of over six million Jews. This traumatizing event began in January 1933, when Adolf Hitler and the Nazis came to power. Adolf Hitler first made laws against Jews (Not allowed holding office, forced to where yellow stars of David on their clothing, etc.). Then Hitler transferred all Jews that he could find then put them into ghettos around Europe where many Jews died out because of the horrid living conditions in each ghetto. Most ghettos were located in Poland, but there were some ghettos located around Poland as well. After Hitler put the Jews into ghettos, he then decided to put the Jews into concentration camps were the genocide, a systematic mass killing, began. In each camp, Jews had their possessions taken, heads shaved, arms tattooed, and where forced to wear prison-like uniforms. Families where separated because they were put in to gender and age groups. Life in these camps where certainly unpleasant because it was unsanitary, which made disease and famine linger around the camp and lice infected the barracks. The only way to survive concentration camps is to have tons of trade and physical skill. The Nazis in the camps did inhumane experiments to the Jews as well as killing them in large clusters. Camps were equipped with gas chambers, where the Jews were tricked into going into the chamber, where they were gassed and died. This was not the only way Jews died, Jews were also sent to extermination camps were they were shot once they got to the camp. But, with this horrid and trauma experience, the Holocaust, came great heroes who saved many Jews from there dark future, an example of one of these heroes was Janina Zilow. Janina was born on January 1st, 1901 and died November 2nd, 1957. Janina was a Polish female who believed in god as a nanny. She saved Jews in her home land, Poland, where most Jews were sent.

Janina lived in Poland where she went to Warszawa, Lublin, and to Lwow on her journey to save the two girls from their imminent death in camps. These three places served a cause into helping Janina rescue the two girls Elizabeth, and Lili. Lili was born 1929 in Lodz and Elizabeth born 1936. When they tried to flee from the Nazis, they ended up in a large ghetto in Warsaw. This is where Janina rescued them and helped them escape from the Nazis. Janina was only able to rescue the two girls, Elizabeth and Lili. The escape to Lwow was not smooth at all, but successful, but they managed to get to Lwow. But it was tough to live because of hiding the two Jewish children.

At this time, Janina got Lili documents to work, once she got the work documents, she got a job in Warsaw then volunteered to work in Germany. Because the fact that her Jewish looks caused danger, she worked with Americans to blend in, so that she wouldn't be noticed as a Jew. She worked in the town of Lage from November 1943, when the war is about to end, but then she was about to be denounced by Polish workers, so then she had to hide in a nearby forest where so managed to survive. Lili then became a DP for Bergen Belsen, where she immigrated to England then to US in 1947. Meanwhile, Janina and Elizabeth where hiding in Lublin, until the war ended. After it ended, Janina vowed to deliver Elizabeth to her family in Los Angeles. They first went to Sweden then to Cuba, before reuniting Elizabeth and her paternal grandfather as well as obtaining visas. Sadly, Janina died in New York, November 2nd, 1957, at the age of 56. Elizabeth later named her daughter Nina after her rescuer, Janina Zilow.

From learning about the Holocaust, I have learned that every terrible event also includes many heroic people to save people in need of help or guidance, in this case Janina Zilow. Even though this is only one person, she had made a big impact on us as well as the other heroic people who will be remembered as righteous people. I have learned from Janina that it only takes so little to make something so big. Janina was only one person who made a huge impact by changing our perspective on our lives, to teach us what to do and not do. The Holocaust changed and impacted our lives as well. The Holocaust has not only changed the life of Holocaust survivors, but teaching us how to prevent and control bad situations. I think a way of which we can prevent bad events (911, The Holocaust, etc.) is to make peace with other countries and keep an eye out on them to ensure safety of life on earth. We can also improve the security of our country and to other countries that need it. As many Jewish, Holocaust survivors said, Never Again.

Work Cited

Vashem, Yad. "Zilow, Janina." Yadvashem. Yadvashem, 12 Dec. 2016. Web. 12 Dec. 2016.

Bib, Easy. "Easybib." EasyBib. Chegg, 12 Dec. 2016. Web. 12 Dec. 2016.

Stefan Konopka

Cassandra Dawn Blevins

The Holocaust was the genocide of six million Jewish people during World War II. Adolf Hitler, Chancellor of Germany and head of the Nazi Party, believed that the Aryan race was superior to all others. He believed that the Jews were an inferior race, and they were cause for political corruption in Germany. It all began with rules that forced all Jewish people to be separated from the the rest of the general population. Jews were forced into ghettos: small, cramped, dirty areas of the city, which were generally used as holding areas. People were then systematically put on trains and taken to concentration camps, where they were forced into slave labor until disease, starvation eventually killed many of them. Over time, as the Nazis began to conquer new areas of Europe, new ghettos and concentration camps were set up. Death squads began to execute Jews and others in mass shootings. Later in the war, the Nazis began to turn concentration camps in to extermination camps. The purpose of these camps was to kill as many people as possible, in as efficient a manner as possible. Estimates vary widely on how many concentration camps there were. According to the the German Ministry of Justice, about 1,200 camps were run in countries occupied by Nazi Germany. The Jewish Virtual Library believes there were about 15,000 concentrations camps. There were six death camps: Auschwitz-Birkenau, Belzec, Chelmno, Majdanek, Sobibor, and Treblinka. These were all located in Poland. A death camp is a special kind of concentration camp that was designed for systematic murder. The Nazi's packed the Jews in gas chambers where they used poisonous gas to kill them. After their death, the bodies were cremated.

Stefan Konopka lived with his wife and kids in Warsaw before the war. He fought with other Polish people against the Germans in September and October of 1939. After the fighting ended, he moved back with his family to Warsaw. He later joined the Polish Home Army. He worked as a supervisor engineer at a repair and construction company. In this position, he had the ability to arrange official certificates for members of underground organizations and hide Jews who needed help. The Konopka's welcomed into their home, other Jews and members of underground organizations. He also began to start demolition works in the area of the destroyed Warsaw ghetto. Stefan also helped people escape its ruins. After the destruction of the Warsaw ghetto in May 1943, he and his family moved to

Twarda 16. In early 1943, Stefan helped over 300 Jewish fugitives, including Leon Krotowski. He arranged forged documents for him, under the name of Antoni Piotr Krajewski. Leon became registered as a resident in the house, as a brother of Stefan's wife. To provide extra security, he built a double wall in one of the rooms, creating a refuge if the Nazis came. Leon was treated like family at the Konopka's. He even went with the family to church every Sunday, and was not afraid of being caught by the Nazi's. Even when the Nazis conducted searches of the house or during a few dangerous situations, Stefan never stopped providing protection for other Jews. After being arrested once by the German Schutzpolizei, he still provided aid to other Jews in need of help.

Stefan was released from jail after paying bride. Leon stayed with the Konopka's until the outbreak of the Warsaw Uprising. He and Stefan got to the village of Antoniew, where Mr. Dąbrowski, the owner of a farm, let them stay there. On October 14, 1944, Stefan and Leon were arrested and taken to the Sochaczew camp. After a few weeks, they were able to escape, and went back to the farm in Antoniew. On December 25, the two were again arrested while on the way to church, but they escaped and hide until the end of the German occupation. Both Leon and Stefan survived the war, and afterwards, Leon stayed in Poland and occasionally contacted the Konopka's. Later on, Stefan tried to save the lives of Lipszyc Ludwik and his son, who were held captive in the Lublin camp. Ludwik denied the offer to leave the camp, even though Konopka set up a forged transfer for he and his family to Warsaw. Cwibak Jerz was hiding at Stefan's house until the uprising in Warsaw on August 1, 1944. Leszczyńska Irena gave birth to a baby in the village of Antoniew-Żdżary, while Stefan delivered the baby.

I learned from Stefan Konopka's rescue story that, during this time, these special people had extremely kind hearts, and would do anything for someone who needed help. It didn't matter that they may complete strangers. I also learned that if you are determined enough, you can do almost anything you set your mind to, like surviving the Holocaust in Poland during World War II. Stefan Konopka's story has impacted my life by giving me a great appreciation for the hardships and courage of the Jews who survived the Holocaust. I understand that the Holocaust was a devastating and unfair thing that happened to the Jews, who had done nothing wrong. It had an impact on world by ending the lives of millions of people who would have all made contributions to mankind. So this never happens again, parents and teachers should teach children about the Holocaust and its devastating impact on an entire race.

Works Cited

"Digital Collections." Digital Collections - Yad Vashem. Yad Vashem, n.d. Web. 12 Dec. 2016.

Grądzka-Rejak, Martyna. "Stefan Konopka." Story of Rescue - Konopka Stefan | Polscy Sprawiedliwi. POLIN, Nov. 2015. Web. 12 Dec. 2016.

History.com Staff. "The Holocaust." History.com. A&E Television Networks, 2009. Web. 12 Dec. 2016.

Skatrix.com, Programming:. "A Brief Holocaust Summary." Holocaust Summary. Maya Productions, 2013. Web. 12 Dec. 2016.

Rudolf Stefan Weigl

Catherine Bui

Rudolf Stefan Wiegl was a brave man who had been born on 1883 in Prerov, Moravia. Although he wasn't born in Poland, he is recognized by Poland for working to save many Jews that had lived in Poland and risked his life to save the others that had been captured during the Holocaust. He has come up with an ingenious plan to stump the Nazis and save the lives of hundreds of Jews.

During the Holocaust, hundreds of thousands of Jews had contracted illnesses and died. Weigl would soon come up with a vaccine to save thousands of Jews from the Typhus epidemic that had taken over in the Holocaust. Both prisoners in the concentration camps and the Nazi had contracted the disease from lice and the Nazi troops had turned to Weigl and his vaccine to fight the epidemic to continue fighting. Now Weigl had his chance to help defeat the armies and save thousands of Jews in need of a cure for the fast-spreading epidemic that would soon take the lives of millions and cause millions more to suffer.

Rudolf Weigl and his partner, Ludwick Fleck, had managed to create a vaccine for Typhus that is no longer in use today as it was a dangerous vaccine to create. By dissecting and using body parts from the lice that carried the disease at the time after allowing them to feed on human flesh. Weigl had managed to create a weaker and stronger version of the vaccine, giving the weaker vaccine to the Nazi troops to delay their healing while giving the stronger vaccine to Jews in the concentration camps to keep them alive and aid the suffering Jews in the concentration camps as they went through the ordeal.

Dr. Weigl had saved about 30,000 Jews that suffered from typhus during the Holocaust by using various techniques to smuggle in the stronger vaccine to them. The main way he had managed to smuggle the vaccine to the imprisoned Jews was by lying to his boss and telling him that he needed to experiment on the suffering Jews in the camps to make sure the vaccine worked. Weigl had managed to continue to sneak the vaccine into the ghettos and concentration camps of the Holocaust throughout the entire war and avoid being caught.

After the war, Weigl had held a high and prominent position at a university in Krakow, his association with the Nazis in the war had greatly damaged his reputation. His partner had been arrested by the Nazis in 1943 and was forced to work in labs at concentration camps under their direct supervision, leaving Weigl to work on his own for the rest of the Nazi reign. While Weigl continued to help Jews in concentration camps, his partner working directly under the Nazis. He himself was still helping them in some way by giving them the weaker vaccine for typhus mentioned earlier, even though his main intention was to save the Jews, had affected the way the public looked at him. Rudolf Weigl would soon be forgotten by the Europeans after the war ended and die without anyone acknowledging his death or accomplishments for decades after his passing until he was recognized by righteous among the nations in 2003.

Weigl's extremely dangerous way of creating his vaccine for typhus during the Holocaust would soon be replaced by more modern medicines that were made in labs and save his subjects that he had used to feed the lice and create the vaccine from having to deal with the excruciating pain of having hundreds of tiny lice sucking and biting at their legs for hours to prepare the vaccine. Although his vaccine is now irrelevant to our daily lives as we now have lab made injections, it had made history as he saved thousands of lives and created a starting point for our vaccines and medicines today used to treat typhus. He has had a book written about him, his name honored and recognized by his country, and saved the lives of those suffering during the war, making him a true hero.

Rudolf Stefan weigl may be long forgotten by now as it has been more than half a century after his death, he will still be able to inspire many of those who learn about him. He had made the choice to risk his life and save others that suffered and had played a great role in history. His scientific breakthrough had created a new foundation for medicines that play a huge role in our lives today. But most importantly, he had helped in the Holocaust, not to get rid of lives, but to save them .

Most people that wanted to help in the Holocaust were too scared. They didn't want to risk their own lives while trying to save another's. But Rudolf Weigl was a man who had the courage and the bravery to do something right. Even though he damaged his reputation by associating himself with Nazi's to do so, it was all worth saving so many lives that suffered pain and loss due to one greedy man who wanted power and money.

The Holocaust had ruined the lives of so many people that had been forced to go through it and took the lives of many, many more. It was an act of disgrace that was caused by a man named Adolf Hitler, who was filled with anger, greed, and hatred. Something like this should never again happen and be repeated in history. Telling others about the story of the Holocaust can prevent this from happening by teaching the world that this was a cruel act, not a good willed favor to the world. I have learned from the brave man that went by the name of Rudolf Stefan Weigl is that standing up against wrong can do more than what you'd expect and to never be afraid to risk your life to save another, as long as the life you save is not going to do wrong.

Franciszek Pasz

Caullin Moore

The Jewish people have been scarred for generations. Now, these scars have now become the looking through which the survivors and their children's view the world, Through squinted eyes, the survivors share everything they have gone through, experiences they had gone through during the Holocaust. These new views on the world show how the survivors live, interact, and raise a family socially and in other ways. Some survivors like Franciszek pasz are scarred so deeply they can not escape the past feelings and images of terror; they call this Survivor Syndrome. A Survivor is one who has encountered, been exposed to, or witnessed death, and has himself of herself remained alive. The symptoms affected not only survivors, but their families as well. The symptoms included an inability to work, and even at times to talk. The Jewish people fear that it may happen again. This later led to the death of jewish survivor Franciszek pasz; born: Sep. 21, 1885, death:age 61 Dec. 29, 1946 (http://www.findagrave.com/cgi-bin/fg.cgi?page=gr&GRid=17489948) (http://www.dictionary.com/browse/survivor-syndrome) Franciszek experienced these symptoms, but at the time, he was just a child, he was also a worker, surrounded by the tortured souls of his own kind. Imagine everyday waking up to cries of children getting taken away from their parents, then all of a sudden you're getting dragged away from everything, Then the next day you get shaved, they take your shoes,you're working hard, people dropping like flies all around you, then finally after a long day of hard work you get a small bowl of soup not even enough to satisfy you. (http://www.   theholocaustexplained.org/ks3/the-camps/daily-life/processing-and-routines/#.WFCgrHeZOt8) These are all the troubles Franciszek pasz had to go through as a child. Him and millions of other people even had thoughts of death, nightmares, panic attacks, and various other symptoms. Had no wanting for life anymore. Some survivor or even civilians remember feeling helpless at times of need, "why didn't I resist" or "how could I have saved someone." The survivor can not escape the feeling of debt to the lost and feels guilty. Some survivors have been known to feel worse about the Holocaust then the actual suspect. To deal with the guilt there are many support groups/therapies that are opening doors wide for the Jewish people to come and be set free from the guilt. many survivors have shut themselves out from the world and have lived lives lonely, depressed, and guilty, because the guilt is too much for any one person to carry. This guilt is a direct cause of the Holocaust and because of it, the Jewish people will never be the same. Franciszek and other survivors are always on guard watching out for another Holocaust to happen. Some survivors may not take the hand of someone there to help, in fear it may be a Nazi trick and a sign of weakness. The ridicule the survivors suffered made them paranoid and unable to place trust in any one. They feel as if tainted by the Holocaust they no longer belong. Likewise, they feel feared and hated by others, they feel distrust in all human relationships and feel everything around them is fake. (http://peterfelix. tripod.com/home/Ho.pdf) After the holocaust Hundreds of thousands of people that were lost and had no place to go, no money, no identity, and no one to trust but each other, just lost souls not knowing where and what to do. (https://www.ushmm.org/wlc/en/article.php?ModuleId=10005139) The Jewish people had to fight for their "promised" land and give away a lot to get it. They can no longer interact with the rest of the free world as they did before. In addition, they will always remember the terrible things that have happened on one of the worst days on earth, that as well as the paranoia and feel full of terrible images from their past. As a result, Franciszek pasz was forever scarred for this huge execution, genocide. This Should "Never again" Happen, That starts with you, make a change. All of this can teach you that there will always be twisted people out there, planning something, but you need to make a change in this society, make a difference, if you don't and nobody sticks up then people like Adolf Hitler will create a different type of holocaust, maybe with a different race, different culture, or even different countries/states.

"Never Again." this should change your look on the holocaust as it did with me Caullin Moore, Because this changed my outlook on this I have a lot more respect for victims and so should you. Just remember, try to think of what they went through, Think before you whine about you hitting your toe on a bed because they probably hit their toes 100 times when they were at work.

The Holocaust

Caydence Tatlow

The Holocaust was a horrific time when many innocent lives of many Jewish people. During the Holocaust it was not only Jewish lives taken, people of different nationalities, homosexuals, slaves, and many other people that had done nothing wrong to deserve such horrible torture. In Poland, the Jewish population dropped significantly after the Holocaust. Before the Holocaust, Poland's Jewish population started at around 3,300,000 Jews, after the Holocaust the Jewish population dropped significantly to around 300,000. That is about 3,000,000 lives taken. An estimated 91% of the Jewish population in Poland suffered tragic deaths. All together the Holocaust ended up killing about six million Jews also including the other people of the world that were considered not normal or people that were getting in the way of the Nazis. Most of the Jewish population, and others that were considered to be aliens, were sent to concentration camps to most likely be killed. Some of the people in the concentration camps were able to survive and were rescued before they almost starved to death. Before they were sent to concentration camps they were all gathered together and sent to live in terrible, small communities that were crammed with the maximum amount of Jews or "aliens" called ghettos. The little amount that survived after they went to ghettos and concentration camps either survived the concentration camps or were rescued by heroes that allowed them into their homes to hide from the Nazis and escape the horrible death that they may have had to encounter if they had been taken into the ghettos and concentration camps. Even though allowing the "aliens" or Jews into their homes put them at risk of death also preventing more deaths from the people that were so close to them like friends or neighbors was worth the risk.

One of these courageous heroes was Krystyna Adolph. Krystyna Adolph lived in Ignalina, Święciany, Wilno, Poland during the time of the war. She was also rescued in Ignalina, Swieciany, Wilno, Poland. In Ignalina, she lived on a farm and she was a widow. Krystyna was Polish and she was a Catholic. During the war she was forced to support and care for herself and her young daughter by herself. She also had to take care of the old father of her late husband. Before the war broke out, Krystyna was a teacher at Czartoryski High School in Vilna. Krystyna knew the Gluskin sisters, twins from Vilna. They were living in Vilna when the war happened. Soon after the Nazis invaded and took over Vilna, Krystyna invited the Jewish twins to come stay with her at her farm in Ignalina. The Gluskin sister, to avoid getting captured and sent to ghettos, accepted the invitation. They soon arrived to her farm and were let in with a warm welcoming. After they started living with Krystyna on her farm, they ended up staying at Krystyna's farm for around three years. Because of all of the deaths happening in the concentration camps, if either of the Gluskin sisters, or any other Jews, were found and identified as Jews, they would be taken to a concentration camp to most likely be greeted by death. While the Gluskin sisters stayed with Krystyna at her farm, they found things to do to keep them busy and entertained since they could rarely go out because of the risk that the Nazis portrayed. Some of the things they did while on the farm were housework, farm work, tending the crops and animals, and helping with her daughter. The Gluskin sisters did not see many people, but sometimes they got to greet some of the neighbors or some of Krystyna's friends. Even though they got to meet some people, rarely, the only people who knew their true identities were Krystyna and Krystyna's late husband. Because of Krystyna's bravery she prevented two deaths of innocent Jews even though she knew the risk. During this horrible time in history it was people like Krystyna that protected most of the Jews that were survivors of the Holocaust. Krystyna's date of recognition by the Righteousness Amoung the Nation was May 14, 1984.

The Holocaust was not just a horrific time of the past, it was a teaching moment that we must never forget. The Holocaust affected the population of innocent Jews, it also has greatly impacted our society today. The holocaust has taught us a lot about discrimination. It has taught us that we cannot kill innocent people just because they are different than them. There are also many other horrifying events that happened in the past that we must learn from like Pearl Harbor and 9/11. If we do not learn from these mistakes then history may repeat itself and one of these tragic events could be replicated. The Holocaust has affected us like no other horrible event in history ever has. Today we have been taught not to discriminate others the way the Nazis did. We need to make sure that this "NEVER AGAIN" happens. The Holocaust could affect in any time, past present or future.

Works Cited

@Commentary. "Krystyna's Gift-A Memoir - Commentary Magazine." Commentary Magazine. N.p., 01 Feb. 2004. Web. 05 Dec. 2016

"Introduction to the Holocaust." United States Holocaust Memorial Museum. United States Holocaust Memorial Museum, n.d. Web. 06 Dec. 2016.

"The History Place - Holocaust Timeline: Statistics of the Holocaust." The History Place - Holocaust Timeline: Statistics of the Holocaust. N.p., n.d. Web. 05 Dec. 2016.

"The Holocaust - United to End Genocide." United to End Genocide. N.p., n.d. Web. 05 Dec. 2016.

Yad Vashem - Request Rejected. N.p., n.d. Web. 15 Nov. 2016.

Zofia Bania

Chad Breslin

In the year 1941, there was a couple, Israel and Franciszka (Frania) Rubinek, that owned a shop in Pinczow during the time of the Germans controlling the city. The shop sold basic goods to local farmers. One of the local farmers they sold to was Zofia Bania, a poor farmer from a village nearby called Wlochy. At certain times in her life, she couldn't pay for food, so Frania would give her the food and other necessities for free. Eventually Zofia and Frania got to know each other and became good friends. One time Frania asked Zofia, if needed, an opportunity to hide in her house with Israel. Zofia needed some time to think about it. Israel decided to build a bunker under her store after hearing rumors about what was happening with the other Jews. In October of 1942, the German invaders were starting to round up the Jewish people of Pinczow and send them all to Treblinka. Israel and Frania hid in the bunker they built that was under their store until the roundups were over. The two later fled to a nearby town. Even though many other Jewish people did, they could not continue to Russia because Frania was pregnant for eight months at the time. The Rubineks were trying to decide what to do next, but then they heard that Zofia was looking for them in Pinczow. So, the couple hired a man to take the two back to Pinczow in his wagon.

Zofia and her family, her husband named Ludwig and her six-year-old son named Maniek, lived in a small, one room house. When the Rubineks arrived Zofia greeted them with great welcome. Her husband was not as welcoming and was very difficult because he was anti-semite so he did not accept the Rubineks into his home. Despite her husband's disapproval, Zofia insisted that the two stay with them because it was her repayment for all they have done. The Rubineks were always worried that Ludwig would betray them, so they bribed him for his silence and cooperation. At first Israel and Frania stayed in the hayloft of a barn that was attached to Zofia's small house. In that barn, on December in 1942, Frania went into labor with Israel and Zofia at her said to care for her. During its birth, the baby sadly died, and after that Frania became terribly ill for three months. After that, Zofia allowed the couple to move into the main house. The couple now shared the one small room with Zofia and her family.

The house that Zofia lived in in was on the far part of Wlochy, about half a kilometer from their nearest neighbor, which actually made it somewhat safe. An extra precaution that Ludwig made, was purchasing a guard dog that would bark incredibly loud if an intruder approached their house. If someone were to approach, Israel and Frania would hide in a cellar that Zofia would use to store potatoes. When the war was close to ending, their was a close call, when German soldiers came to the house to stay the night. Thankfully, the dog began barking to warn the Rubineks and allowed them to escape to the cellar. Zofia created a bed for her son, Maniek, on the only entrance to the cellar, hiding it from the soldiers. With all the luck that has been given to the Rubineks, Israel had been suffering from a nasty cough. Maniek, even though he was six-years-old, understood the situation and like his mother felt as if it was necessary to protect the Rubineks. So, he spent the entire night pretending to be sick, by coughing and crying to block out the sound of Israel's coughing from under the cellar, which saved their lives from the soldiers.

The Rubineks were staying with Zofia and her family, in her house, until the area was liberated by the Red Army in January of 1945. After the war, the couple moved to Canada. In 1986, the Rubineks went back to Poland with their son to visit Zofia and her family.

In this essay, I learned that helping someone, pays off. If you help someone, they may help you in return. In this situation, the Rubineks were helping out Zofia by giving her goods and many other necessities, and in return Zofia saved their lives by letting them hide in their barn and in their house. The impact I had on learning about this was that this let me know that if I can, I should help someone out. So that way they would help me out, just like I did to them. I understand that the Holocaust was probably one of the worst things that ever happened in the history of the world. The impact was probably one of the most devastating things, in lives lost, for really no good reason. I understand the this should happen never again ever in anyone's lifetime. A couple steps that should take place so that this never happens again is:

1.Settle our differences in the world and have one universal peace treaty that connects all countries, cultures, and religions.

2.Strengthen the United Nations who is already trying to keep this from never happening again and keeping everything peaceful.

3.Have everyone show kindness to each other with each others differences respected.

Work Cited

"Digital Collections." Digital Collections - Yad Vashem. N.p., n.d. Web. 03 Dec. 2016.

Stasia Drygasiewicz

Charles O'Bear

The Holocaust was a massive genocide by the Germans on the Jews. In the 1930's, a depression hit Germany and their government became weak. This weakness provided an opportunity for a new leader, Adolf Hitler, to come to power. Hitler and the Nazis used the Jews as a scapegoat for Germany's biggest problems. Hitler blamed the Jews for Germany's economic depression and their loss in World War I. The concept of anti-semitism was not new, but Hitler took it to a whole new level. Hitler and his followers believed that Germans were the superior race and that all power should be theirs. On the opposite end of the spectrum were the Jews, the inferior race who needed to be contained and controlled. The Nazi party came into power in 1933. The Nazis started depriving Jews of their rights right after Hitler became their leader. The Nazis were humiliating the Jews by shaving their heads and beards while taking pictures of them. And this was just the beginning. Because the Jews were being targeted, they began leaving the country to escape this type of ridicule. Therefore, Hitler ordered that the Jews in all countries under German control must be relocated to cities in Poland and be housed in ghettos. If the Jews were not taken to the ghettos, they were interned in concentration camps. Once most of the Jews were put in ghettos and concentration camps, Hitler decided to commit genocide. He killed six million Jews by shooting them, working them to death, putting them in gas chambers, or starving them. Sixty-three percent of Jews were killed in Europe, and ninety-one percent in Poland were killed. My holocaust hero is Stasia Drygasiewicz, she was a Polish Catholic woman who hid and gave Jews a home during the holocaust.

Before the war, Stasia, or Stanislawa, Drygasiewicz worked in Warsaw for a Jewish family, the Caitungs. The Caitung family consisted of Marge, her husband Seweryn, and their son Ryszard, who was born in 1938. Stasia looked after Marge and Seweryn's young son. The parents were scared for the well-being of their only son, so they wanted him to leave the ghetto with the help of Stasia. However, Stasia didn't want to be away from her employers. Although initially hesitant, Stasia eventually agreed to leave the ghetto and take Ryszard with her. With the help of her employers and family, Stasia made a plan to save Ryszard. At first, she took him to her sister Anielia's apartment in the Praga quarters of Warsaw. It was very nerve-wracking to Stasia to stay in Warsaw so she decided to pack up Ryszard and move. Stasia moved to the country and worked for a Polish Officer. Luckily Ryszard was fair-haired and blue eyed and so it was easier for her to convince people he was her nephew. She told people that Ryszard was the son of her sister, who was working in Germany as a forced laborer. People seemed to buy her explanation of the boy, but it was still very dangerous to be transporting a Jewish child around German territory. In fact, she moved to seventeen different places to avoid suspicion.

Before the Warsaw Ghetto Uprising of 1943, Marge and Seweryn escaped with Anielia's help and the help of Marge's three sisters, Frania, Stefa, and Maria. They hid with Anielia and her friend, Maria Jakubowska, who also lived in Praga. They all hid in the cellar under the kitchen and they all survived. Seweryn wrote in his testimony that, "Maria was a poor woman. When we ran out of money, she went to work to earn enough to get us food." Marge missed Ryszard so much, she forged documents using a deceased Polish woman's identification allowing her to travel by train and visit him. It was important to find a place for Marge to stay closer to Stasia and Ryszard. Eventually, Anielia took Marge to her friends, Mr. and Mrs. Zawadzki, who lived in Puntelnik, close to where Stasia was hiding Ryszard. Anielia told them that Marge was her cousin's wife and they agreed to let her stay. From the Zawadzki's house, Marge could walk to the church nearby and she could visit with Stasia and Ryszard.

During Stasia's time with Ryszard, she moved often and got many other jobs and took Ryszard everywhere to avoid being detected by the Nazis. Seweryn emphasized that all who helped rescue his family were motivated by religious convictions. After Warsaw was liberated, Ryszard was reunited with his parents and his whole family moved to the United States of America.

I have learned many things about the holocaust and why it happened. I learned how one person was able to convince a civilized democracy to kill millions of people based on his ideas of superiority and inferiority. In addition, I learned that average citizens followed orders without question and ordinary men and women tended to follow along. Lastly, I saw how ordinary citizens became heroes, like Stasia Drygasiewicz and her family. These heroes risked their lives and made great sacrifices in order to save those who were persecuted because of their race and religion. The research I did on my chosen holocaust hero of Poland has impacted my life on many levels. It has showed me that an average citizen can make a difference on global issues. Stasia and her family had the courage to risk their lives to save others. The holocaust was a horrible tragedy that killed six million Jews and impacted the lives of many others. It is important for us as a society to take steps to make sure this happens "never again". Even though it may be uncomfortable to talk and learn about the Holocaust, we need to resist the temptation to forget what happened. We need to remember so that we do not sit by and allow it to happen again. We cannot stand by silently while other people are suffering, and we should accept the moral challenge to do more in our own lives as we confront injustice and hatred.

Works Cited

"The Holocaust: A Learning Site for Students." United States Holocaust Memorial Museum. Web. 8 Dec. 2016. <https://www.ushmm.org>.

"The Righteous Among The Nations." Yad Vashem: The World Holocaust Remembrance Center. Web. 4 Dec. 2016. <http://www.yadvashem.org/>.

"Saving Jews: Polish Righteous." Saving Jews: Polish Righteous. Web. 10 Dec. 2016. <http://savingjews.org/>.

Stichting, Anne Frank. "Anne Frank Museum Amsterdam - the Official Anne Frank House Website." Anne Frank House. Web. 3 Dec. 2016. <http://www.annefrank.org/>.

"Why We Remember the Holocaust." United States Holocaust Memorial Museum. United States Holocaust Memorial Museum. Web. 11 Dec. 2016. <https://www.ushmm.org/remember/days-of-remembrance>.

Wojan, Megan. "Intro to Holocaust 2016." Class Lecture. KAMS, Elk Grove. 30 Nov. 2016. Lecture.

Irena Sendler

Charlie Harris

 For my project I have picked a girl named Irena Sendler out of all six thousand for the reason that she is person who is very motivational. For my essay I will be talking about how cool and meaning full she was. Being Born on February 15,1910, in Warsaw wasn't such a good time or place to live, especially with Hitler rising with the power that he had yet Irena still managed to do amazing things. She did a bunch of inspirational stuff that they even had a movie made out of her life and all of her accomplishments.

Just one of her amazing accomplishments is managing to save two thousand five hundred people from the Warsaw Ghetto. All of this information about her rescuing so many people almost went missing along with many other rescuers from that time for sixty years. When people finally found all of the missing information they thought it was a mistake and crazy that one person could possibly save over two thousand lives. At the height of just 4'11" she was determined as a fearless resistance leader. Having the courage to carry out children while they're still alive past guards who were armed and not afraid to kill was exactly what Irena had. The question everybody was asking was were did she find such great courage? "My parents taught me", Irena wrote back," that if a man is drowning it is irrelevant what his religion or nationality. One must help him." Not only was she brave enough, but also the fact that she was smart enough to get people out of the concentration camps. She managed to do this by having fake documents made for the families that had escaped so the guards who'd not know, she also smuggled children directly out of the Warsaw Ghetto with the help of about twenty five social workers, and she even told the guards that she was examining the Jew's of diseases but really looking for more Jew's to sneak out. She also had five main ways of getting kids out of the camps. "1- using an ambulance a child could be taken out hidden under the stretcher. 2- escapes through the courthouse. 3- a child could be taken out using the sewer pipes or other under ground passages. 4- a trolley could carry out children hiding in a sack, in a trunk, a suitcase or something similar. 5- if a child could pretend to be sick or was actually very ill, it could be legally removed using an ambulance. Irena did use a dog on occasions, but very few times out of the many rescues." Once these kids got away from the camps, "Irena hid the children in orphanages, convents, schools, hospitals, and private homes, she provided each child with a new identity." This is just the tip of the iceberg with all of the amazing things that she did for the Jew's.

With all of Irena's hard work in saving peoples lives she still had time too have a normal life and have an education. She did however get suspended from a polish university, but only because she was standing up for a Ghetto bench system at the schools. After school she had a son and a daughter, who Janka, still lives in Warsaw, Poland and in 1999 her son Adam passed away. After helping all of those innocent kids from dying, she did however get caught and arrested from by Gestapo, which is a secret German state police, she was even sentenced to death but was rescued and saved for by Zegota. She even got a new name from the company so she could continue working for them, and helping people. "Irena was Senior Administrator in the Warsaw Social Welfare Department." They used a thing called canteens (a thing that provided almost everything needed for homeless people such as food, aid, money, and even orphanage service) which Irena's company gave to Jew's under the christen name so people would not get suspicious. They even told the Guards and people who saw who they were giving the food to that the families had serious diseases like typhus and tuberculosis. When the war had finally ended Irena's first marriage ended up as a divorce. She got married again and had the three children that I had mentioned in the first part of this paragraph, but I did not however mention the third child, Andrzej, who had died as an orphan. After her current husband died she remarried her old husband but there connection that they had did not last too long for they got divorced yet again. Even with all of the hard and well know work that she had done she still was able to keep a normal life.

Just imagine doing all of the amazing things that Irena has been able to accomplish, well I've told you a lot about this person and how she contributed to the Warsaw Ghetto camp, but there's one thing I haven't talked about. Her skill in being a nurse. Irena was a member of the Zegota, which is an organization, were people help and aided any Jew's or Jewish families. She had a special permit from working, as nurses to enter the Warsaw Ghetto, her along with other courageous girls were able to save thousands of people. When she became older she worked for a new company called the Ministries of Education and Health, were she still gets do what she loves which is helping people, she gets too organizes files and other things for kids, orphans, families, and elderly shelters. Through all of the stuff that Irena Sendler did I don't think anybody could ever thank her enough.

While I was doing this essay I have learned numerous thing such as how much people sacrifice to help people and risk their life for others. I have also learned about how sad World War Two was and that people should not have to go through all of this just because they have a certain religion. Irena Sendler showed me that no matter what the risk you should always sacrifice if you truly believe in what you fighting for. I have understood that the Holocaust was a terrible event that took place in Germany. Hitler Aldoh was an evil man who wanted to get rid of all the Jew's in order to make the perfect human race, so he gathered all of the Jews and torched them with little food and little water eventually killing six million. Too make sure that nobody has to go through this horrible torture again people have to make sacrifices before we even start to get close to this ever happening. Most important of all we need to have free speech so people know what is going on and can stop it before it ever happens again.

Works Cited

Biography.com Editors. "Irena Sendler." Biography.com. A&E Networks Television, 21 Mar. 2016. Web. 11 Dec. 2016. <http://www.biography.com/people/irena-sendler-031616>.

"Irena Sendler (1910-2008)." United States Holocaust Memorial Museum. United States Holocaust Memorial Museum, n.d. Web. 11 Dec. 2016. <http://www.ushmm.org/information/press/in-memoriam/irena-sendler-1910-2008>.

"Irena Sendler." Irena Sendler. The Holocaust: Crimes, Heroes and Villains, n.d. Web. 11 Dec. 2016. <http://www.auschwitz.dk/sendler.htm>.

Kroll, Chana. "Irena Sendler - Rescuer of the Children of Warsaw." The Jewish Woman. Chabad.org, n.d. Web. 11 Dec. 2016. <http://www.chabad.org/theJewishWoman/article_cdo/aid/939081/jewish/Irena-Sendler.htm>.

Life in a Jar Project. "Facts about Irena." Life in a Jar: The Irena Sendler Project. Life in a Jar Project, n.d. Web. 11 Dec. 2016. <www.irendasendler.org/facts-about-irena/>.

TheFamousPeople.com Editors. "Irena Sendler Biography." The Famous People. N.p., n.d. Web. 11 Dec. 2016. <www.famouspeople.com/profiles/irena-sendler-6152.php>.

Josef Fink and Lucyna Fink

Chase Cook

 Josef and Lucyna Fink can be introduced as a very brave and heroic couple, who acted selflessly to protect the lives of six Jewish acquaintances during the German invasion of Poland, in World War II. Not only did the Finks risk their own safety and the security of their family by helping their Jewish friends, but they also did what they could to make them feel as though they were not a burden during this time, even though they had to rely on the Finks for every aspect of their survival. The Finks took many risky steps, over an almost two year period, to not only rescue their friends from a German occupied area, but to also hide them and to ensure they would go undetected by the Germans. This couple went above and beyond for their friends, during one of the most horrific times in history.

Under the Finks' protection, a married couple named Chana and Szepel Grynberg survived the Holocaust, with their two children Sara and Yitzhak. Their mutual friends Pinchas and Shoshana Rafalowicz, who were married without children, also survived. These families had come to know each other prior to the invasion of Germany. They all met each other when Josef and Lucyna Fink would frequent shops that were run by the Grynbergs and Raflowiczs in Sokolow Podlaski, which is in the Eastern part of Poland. Josef Fink was the director of a school that he and his wife ran, in a nearby village. The Finks lived on a property in that nearby village, which contained the school, a barn, and some farmland. They also had two young children, Maria and Waclaw, that lived with them.

In 1940, the Germans established a guarded area (ghetto) in Sokolow Podlaski, where they controlled the Jews that lived there, and they also brought in Jews from Kalisz, a town near the center of Poland. At that time, the Grynbergs were forced by the Germans to give up their apartment due to the area being too over-crowded with all of the additional Jewish people forced there by the Germans. They had to go live with the Raflowiczs, along with many other members of each of their families, where it became extremely crowded. They all lived together within this new German occupied area, with guards at the entrance gates, but the borders where not entirely secure. The villagers were allowed to go in through the entrance of the ghetto, to purchase goods from the Jewish shop owners.

There came a time in 1942, that the Germans had eliminated the Jewish population in another similar Ghetto in the town of Siedlce and when the news was heard, it was assumed all of the Jewish people in the ghetto in Sokolow Podlaski would also suffer the same ending. Josef Fink risked his life, at that time, by entering the German secured area to rescue his friends, but was only able to leave with Sara Grynberg, who was 12 years old at the time. Josef ended up returning her to her family in the Ghetto shortly thereafter, again risking his life, because she missed them too much. The Grynberg and Rafalowicz families did end up leaving the ghetto not too much later, to dig potatoes on a nearby farm. In the meantime, the ghetto in Sokolow was also eliminated by the Germans and that's when the Grynbergs had to ask the Finks to take them and the Raflowiczs into hiding.

The Finks agreed and the Grynbergs and Raflowiczs lived in a handmade bunker, under the Fink's barn. This was a tiny space, only a couple meters wide, at best. The entrance was hidden inside the barn and camouflaged to keep them safe. For almost two years, Chana, Szepel, Sara, Yitzhak, and their friends Pinchas and Shoshana, would live in that bunker. They not only endured very cold winters, but had to depend on the Finks to bring them food and supplies to survive. The Finks continued to run the school on that very same property and it was very difficult to leave the bunker, for fear that the school children would see them. This means that they would rarely go out of the bunker, and usually under the cover of night. The Finks would encourage them to stay busy, to make sure they felt productive, whether it was sewing or another job. The Finks also provided books and underground news for them to read. The Finks had to support their own children, plus these two other families that were in hiding.

Toward the end of the two years, it became even more difficult for the Finks to hide their six Jewish friends. The Germans decided to take over the school and they specifically used the barn to house their horses. For six straight days, it was nearly impossible to get food or supplies down to the bunker, which was also lacking in oxygen, as well. Luckily, it was at this time that the German soldiers ended up fleeing the area due to the threat of incoming Soviet troops. Unfortunately, it was still not safe for the Finks to reveal that they had been helping to hide their Jewish friends. Other Jewish people had been murdered or robbed when they had come out of hiding and they couldn't risk this happening. They were able to sneak out, over several nights, and return to the old apartment that had been previously occupied by the Grynberg Grandparents, who were no longer there. All six of them continued to live in that apartment. They had then realized the tragic loss of their other family members, as well as most of the other Jews in the area, and they didn't feel safe enough to stay there long-term.

Once Poland was completely liberated, the two families moved to the Lodz area, in central Poland. Sara continued her education and graduated. Eventually, they all moved to Israel in 1950. The surviving family members of the Grynbergs, Raflowiczs and Finks all remained friends. They continued to stay in contact with each other. The Fink children and Grynberg children were especially close.

From this story, I have learned that true friends will help you when you need them the most. This has impacted me because I realized that the friendship between the Finks and the Grynbergs was strengthened through a time of horrible tragedy. Even though the Finks knew what horrible things were said about Jews they didn't care, they helped them when they needed them the most. But sadly, this didn't happen for most of the Holocaust victims. Most of them were brutally killed in a sick, inhumane way. From this horrible event, we all learned that it should have never happened, and will hopefully never happen again. We can prevent this in the future by promoting worldwide equality and respect towards each other.

Works Cited

"Kalisz - The Oldest Town in Poland! Welcome to Its Website!" Kalisz - The Oldest Town in Poland! Welcome to Its Website! N.p., n.d. Web. 10 Dec. 2016. <http://www.kalisz.info/english>.

Mahler, R., B. Wasiutynski, S. Bronsztejn, M. Gelbert, and P. Granatstein. "Sokolow Podlaski." Encyclopaedia Judaica. Encyclopedia.com, n.d. Web. 10 Dec. 2016. <http://www.encyclopedia.com/religion/encyclopedias-almanacs-transcripts-and-maps/sokolow-podlaski>.

Rytlow, Jadwiga, and Sarah Glicksman. "Rodzina Finków." Relacja Sary Glicksman | Polscy Sprawiedliwi. Polin, Nov. 2010. Web. 08 Dec. 2016. <https://sprawiedliwi.org.pl/pl/historie-pomocy/relacja-sary-glicksman>.

Staff, History.com. "Germans Invade Poland." History.com. A&E Television Networks, 2010. Web. 10 Dec. 2016. <http://www.history.com/this-day-in-history/germans-invade-poland>.

United States Holocaust Memorial Museum. "Lodz." United States Holocaust Memorial Museum. United States Holocaust Memorial Museum, n.d. Web. 10 Dec. 2016. <https://www.ushmm.org/wlc/en/article.php?ModuleId=100050

Edward Chadzynski

Chester Madison III

The Holocaust is an event that should "Never Again" happen. The Holocaust started in 1930 with an economic depression that had hit Germany hard. The German citizens were lacking assurance in their unsteady government. Then, Adolf Hitler became leader of Germany and provided the chance for a rise. In January of 1933, the Nazis came to power in Germany. The Nazis believed Aryans was the master race. Adolf Hitler arranged Jews in all countries under Germany's authority to be moved into particulars cities in Poland. Then some Jews arranged resistance organizations within ghettos. There were extermination camps built with gas chambers and could kill as many six thousand people in a day. Most of the extermination camps were built in Poland. The percentage of the Jewish population that was killed in Europe was 63% and the percentage of the Jewish population that was killed in Poland was 91%. Also there was a total of six million Jews that died and fewer than four million Jews survived. For the ones who survived the holocaust, their lives changed forever. As a result of the Holocaust there were persecution and murders of six million Jews. The name of my rescuer is Edward Chadzynski.

Mr. Chadzynski was born on January 10, 1907. Mr. Chadzynski's nationality was Polish, his religion was catholic and he worked as a lawyer. Mr. Chadzynski mode was to hiding, illegal transfers, arranging shelter, providing forged documents, supplying basic goods, and providing false documents. In 1926 Mr. Chadzynski was recognized as a

Righteous Commemorated with the Wall of honor. Mr. Chadzynski worked in the public records department for the Warsaw city administration during the war. This meant Mr. Chadzynski position could give Jews false documents. Also Mr. Chadzynski was an activist in the Polish resistance movements. One of Mr. Chadzynski missions was to organize false documents for underground activities. Mr. Chadzynski used his work connections from work to help people who were in need of hiding places. Mr. Chadzynski was asked a question from Felicia Stern if he could save her four-year-old son in March 1943. Mrs. Stern got Mr. Chadzynski's telephone number because she had a friend from work who had Mr. Chadzynski's telephone number. Mrs. Stern called Mr. Chadzynski even though she did not know him directly. The next day, Mr. Chadzynski companionless sister, Janina Zaremba, arrived in Mrs. Stern's workplace to meet her. Mr. Chadzynski met with Mrs. Stern the following day and informed her how to get her four-year-old son out of the ghetto and turn him over to Mr.Chadzynski. When Mrs. Stern spoke to Mr.Chadzynski she didn't have enough money or any prized possessions to cover the costs of keeping the child, Mr. Chadzynski replied and said, "We are talking of a child's life, not of money." Mr. Chadzynski thought she didn't look Jewish herself, so she should move to the Aryan side. Then Mr. Chadzynski snuck into the ghetto and smuggled Mrs. Stern's son out of the ghetto and settled him in Mrs. Zaremba's apartment where her and her two children lived. Mr. Chadzynski had also provided him the Aryan documents. In the meantime, Mr. Chadzynski made plans for Mrs. Stern to stay with his aunt originally. However, after Mrs. Stern obtained a kennkarte, she relocated to the apartment of Jadwiga Patronska which was Mr. Chadzynski's cousin. Originally, Mr. Chadzynski could afford the costs of keeping Mrs. Stern and her son. However, Mrs. Stern earned enough money from working to add towards their living cost. When the war was over, Mrs. Stern and her son migrated to Israel. Mrs. Stern stayed in contact with Mr. Chadzynski and his siblings until the outbreak of the Six-Day War in 1967. Also during the war Mr. Chadzynski helped Maciej Daniel. Mr Chadzynski helped Mr. Daniel find an apartment and obtain false documents. "Many times after the liberation I turned to him and proposed some sort of compensation for what he had done for me. He rejected such offers as a principle. A modest, quiet hero of the times," noted Mr. Daniel in his testimony.

When Mr. Chadzynski helped get Mrs. Stern's child out of the ghetto this showed he was not thinking for himself but for Mrs. Stern son. Mr. Chadzynski would provide false documents which meant he was risking his own life. Mr Chadzynski was going give money to Mrs. Stern. This showed Mr. Chadzynski is willing to give up money to help other people. Mr Chadzynski even had family members help Mrs. Stern, showing that Mr. Chadzynski's family is willing to help other people too. Mr. Chadzynski found an apartment for Mr. Daniel. This shows that Mr. Chadzynski went out of his time to find an apartment for Mr. Daniel. Mr. Chadzynski showed that he cared about getting a child before figuring out who would pay the keeping of a child. This shows that Mr. Chadzynski cares more about people than money.

What I learned from this is that you can help somebody and what you did can change their lives for the better. Also I learned that no matter what somebody looks like you should treat them with the same respect as anyone else. I have learned you should do what is not just best for but what is best for everyone else. The impact Mr. Chadzynski had on me was that you should always help others when they are in trouble. Also the impact that Mr. Chadzynski had on me was you should sacrifice your your time to help somebody that's in trouble. I understand the Holocaust and its impact was an important event that should "Never Again" happen. The holocaust's impact was important because I learned you can't trust everybody. The steps that can be taken so this never happens can start with treating everyone respect and kindness. Also we should not judge people by their religion or the way they do things. In conclusion, by helping one person, can change their life forever.

Works Cited

Madison, Chester. "Museums." Museums. N.p., n.d. Web. 12 Dec. 2016.

Wojan, Megan. Introduction to Holocaust. KAMS, Elk Grove. 4 Nov. 2016. Lecture.

HENRYK SLAWIK

Christine Bao

In 1933, disaster struck and there were complications in Germany with their economic dilemmas. Germany was suffering from economic depression after the war, and needed help from someone. A populous amount believed they needed a new leader and president, and so election day came. The old German president, Paul von Hindenburg, re-won, but many were rooting and favoring the Nazis giving Hitler a chance of fame. After a bit, Adolf Hitler was given a chance and was nominated as chancellor, but he wanted more than to be a chancellor. Hitler wanted to become the president and leader. Hitler believed that the Germans were the most superior compared to others, and Jews were their problem for their bad government. Hitler gave hope to all the troubled Germans, starting the Holocaust, also known as the mass murderer. The Holocaust lasted for 12 years throughout 1933-1945. In those 12 years, over 6 million Jews were killed, including some not Jews, from concentration camps, beatings, hangings, gas chambers, shootings, burnings, etc. The small, yet large portion of non Jewish people that were killed, died usually being a hero. Why were they sent away and killed? Some people who had the courage, risked their lives and attempted, and sometimes succeeded, in helping out the Jews to escape death from concentration camps.

Henryk Slawik, a member of the Citizen's Committee for Help for Polish Refugees and Polish activist, was one of many heroes from Poland that helped many. The committee that helped Henryk save many, included of Antall and Henryk Zvi ZImmerman. Henryk saved and rescued many lives of Polish refugees and Jewish orphans from the Nazis. When Poland was defeated, many refugees left and relocated in Hungary. There were many Polish Ghettos being constructed and Jewish families coming to Hungary for a place to settle in. Henryk was considered a prisoner for getting caught crossing the border, and later on met Antall. Slawik eventually escaped being a prisoner and later on, created a group with Antall.

Antall and Henryk introduced and created the Committee to Aid Polish Refugees group including Jews. Later on, many more people joined and became a part of the group. After the committee and the Holocaust began, Henryk Slawik and the committee began creating and providing fake passports for the refugees. The priests provided the Jews with fake birth certificates and false Aryan documentation also. When Hitler shifted into Hungary, Henryk constructed an orphanage for the Jewish children. Although this orphanage was for Jewish children, Henryk disguised it to hide them, calling it the School for Children of Polish Officers. Many children and teachers came regularly to give the school a more Christian and Polish look so nobody would notice. In 1944, Germany started to invade Hungary even more, slowly one by one. Henryk had no choice, but to tell his refugees and orphans to escape and evacuate Hungary. Even though Henryk knew the dangers and the chances of death or torture, Henryk still moved on to save many people and orphans. Luckily, all of Henryk's orphans including him, escaped in time, and Henryk decided to appoint a new leader. Later on sadly, on March 19, 1944 Henryk wasn't able to leave and escape in time, and was caught and captured helping some escape. Even though he was threatened and tortured for his associates' names Henryk never told the Gestapo who they were even if would be killed. Henryk was arrested and thrown into Mauthausen concentration camp, for that reasoning. On August 1944, Henryk was unfortunately shot and killed in the concentration camp that he spent this time in. Henryk was considered a hero for his act of bravery, and was commonly named and described as the "Polish Wallenberg." Henryk succeeded in helping and assisting over 30,000 people including Polish refugees and Jews in Hungary. From risking his life, Henryk Slawik saved about 30,000 lives of the innocent people.

Henryk Slawik has impacted many lives from his story including my life. He has impacted my life with his amazing and extraordinary acts of kindness to the people in danger with him endangering himself. Although he died while saving various people, those people and us will always remember what he did for them. Henryk Slawik has taught me that despite the fact that it may be hard, it is possible if you can believe in yourself. Many things were hard and difficult during the Holocaust, but Henryk was able to push through and save 30,000 lives. The Holocaust was one of the worst, impacting wars that happened killing over 6 million innocent lives. No one especially children, should have to experience something as cruel and sickening as the Holocaust. For this to never happen again, we must not rate and rank each other treating each other equally with an organized government. We should treat one another like we would want to be treated, and not like what you wouldn't want to be treated. Since Hitler believed Germans were the best and hated Jews, that resulted in this tragedy. This event to this day should never repeat itself. "Never again" should this disaster occur and happen again.

Works Cited:

"Adolf Hitler Becomes President of Germany." History.com. A&E Television Networks, n.d. Web. 4 Dec. 2016.

"Henryk Slawik." Henryk Slawik. N.p., n.d. Web. 2 Dec. 2016.

History.com Staff. "The Holocaust." History.com. A&E Television Networks, 2009. Web. 4 Dec. 2016.

"POLAND." Blackfriars 25.292 (1944): 241-43. Web. 2 Dec. 2016.

@PolishEmbassyUS. "7 Polish Heroes The World Should Know Of On The 75th Anniversary Of WWII." BuzzFeed. N.p., n.d. Web. 2 Dec. 2016.

Yad Vashem - Request Rejected. N.p., n.d. Web. 2 Dec. 2016.

Antoni Fularski

Christopher Morley

 Throughout history, people have made some terrible, devastating mistakes. They have destroyed things, started wars, or even killed people for illegitimate reasons. But through these crises, unexpected heroes have emerged and helped those who were persecuted or injured as a result of these mistakes. One of the worst of these horrible mistakes actually happened quite recently, in the 1930s and early 1940s. This mistake was the Holocaust. The people who made this horrible mistake were a group of Germans, who were known as the Nazi party. They tried to commit genocide on the Jewish race and others that they considered political opponents and racially inferior. World War I had recently devastated Europe, and the allied nations blamed Germany for starting the war and causing much damage. Germany's territory was reduced by 13% and they were also forced to pay heavy reparations to the Allies. Germany was soon in a terrible economic depression. Severe inflation left currency worthless. In 1929, when the worldwide depression hit, the banking system collapsed and by 1930 unemployment skyrocketed to 22%. Adolf Hitler, the future Nazi leader, was quickly gathering followers. His ideas included territorial expansion and elimination of European Jews as well as other groups of people that he thought to be inferior to the German race, and he wanted revenge for what the Allies had done to weaken Germany. The Nazi party organized their ranks, recruited people, and even published a newspaper to spread their massage to people. They gained broad support. However, they didn't have to win an election to gain power in Germany. The old war hero, President Paul von Hindenburg, invited Hitler to serve as chancellor. Once they had power in Germany, they started at once to separate the groups that they thought to be racially inferior. They forbid marriages between Germans and Jews. Other groups such as Slavs, Blacks and Roma (also known as Gypsies) were also labeled racially inferior. The German government gradually excluded these groups from many rights that German citizens enjoyed. The goal of the German government was to encourage Germans to see the German Jews as dangerous outsiders living in their midst. They soon arrested all Jews and forced them to live in ghettos, which were isolated areas with cheaply made, sub-standard components, where they lived imprisoned behind barbed wire and brick walls. Living conditions were terrible in the ghettos because of the lack of food and terrible overcrowding, as well as a lack of sanitation

that caused diseases to spread quickly throughout these ghettos. Soon, as the Germans started to invade neighboring countries, they started using a more efficient way to keep the Jews and other groups out of the way. Concentration and extermination camps were built all over Europe, and the Germans found more efficient ways to kill off these groups of people. The mass murder of the Jews had begun.

Through the German extermination of the Jews, many unexpected heroes stepped forward to help them. They started to sneak food and medicine into the ghettos and concentration and extermination camps, and in some rare cases they were even able to sneak people out. But in most cases, they were able to hide people from the Germans during the time when they were trying to arrest all the Jews to take them to the ghettos and camps. More people were killed in Poland than anywhere else, and there were also more people that helped the persecuted people in Poland as well. These people didn't help the Jews for fame or for a reward, but because they recognized that they were human beings, and they didn't deserve to be slaughtered more than anybody else. One of these brave heroes who helped the Jews during the time they were being persecuted was named Antoni Fularski. During the German occupation, he helped his Jewish friends that were in the Warsaw ghetto by bringing them food and medicine, as well as keeping their spirits up. In 1942, he hid Symcha Korngold's three children, who were smuggled out of the ghetto by their father. The children stayed with Fularski for a short time, until he arranged for them to move in with acquaintances. Eventually, Korngold also fled from the ghetto and met with Fularski, who provided him with "Aryan" documents and arranged a hiding place for him outside the city. Korngold's sister also fled from the ghetto with a group of fighters during the Warsaw Ghetto Uprising, and Fularski arranged accommodation for her in a nearby village. Fularski also helped Eta Bernstein and her sister, Roza Lampert, who had both managed to escape from the ghetto. He quickly found places for them to stay near Warsaw. Ultimately, Antoni Fularski helped seven Jews escape from the Germans: Pola Adres, Eta Bernstein, Symcha Korngold, Arje Korngold, Amnuel Korngold, Jafa Korngold, and Roza Lampert. After the war, these survivors immigrated to Israel. By helping the Jewish refugees, Fularski realized that it was his duty to help fight the common enemy. Antoni Fularski was recognized as Righteous Among the Nations in 1966. He was one of the unexpected heroes that stepped forward, risking his life, and helped the persecuted people because he believed that they didn't deserve any more than anybody else to be killed.

When the German concentration camps were liberated by the allies, they found piles of corpses, human bones, and human ashes, as well as other proof of Nazi mass murder. They also found many survivors suffering from diseases and starvation. Many Jewish survivors feared to return to their former homes because of the antisemitism, or distrust and hatred of Jews, that the Nazi party had encouraged in Europe. Some who returned to their homes feared for their lives. In postwar Poland, there were many violent anti-Jewish riots, some of which even resulted in the death of more Jewish people. In the largest of these riots, Polish rioters killed 42 Jews and beat many others. There were few possibilities for immigration, and many homeless Holocaust survivors migrated westward to other European territories liberated by the allies. There, they were housed in refugee centers and displaced person camps administered by the United Nations Relief and Rehabilitation Administration and the occupying armies of the United States, Great Britain, and France. Although Germany had been defeated and their concentration and extermination camps liberated by the allies, most of Europe still didn't trust the Jewish Holocaust survivors.

I have learned a lot about the Holocaust and its impact on the Jews by completing this essay. I learned how Hitler gained followers and approval of the persecution of the Jews, and how the Jews were slaughtered by the Germans in the most efficient and terribly cruel ways possible. I also learned how important it can be to step forward to help people, even if you probably won't get a reward for your good deeds. I now truly understand how horrible the Holocaust really was and the impact it had on Europe as a whole. Many families lost their loved ones and millions of Jews were killed because the Nazis tried to commit genocide on them. We need to remember this horrible mistake so that we remember to never do something so terrible again. Never again should we ever try to commit genocide on an entire race of people.

Works Cited

"Righteous Among the Nations-Antoni Fularski." Yad Vashem - Request Rejected. Yad Vashem, n.d. Web. 13 Dec. 2016.

"The Path to Nazi Genocide Full Film." United States Holocaust Memorial Museum. United States Holocaust Memorial Museum, n.d. Web. 13 Dec. 2016.

"The Aftermath of the Holocaust." United States Holocaust Memorial Museum. United States Holocaust Memorial Museum, n.d. Web. 13 Dec. 2016.

Jozef Krzymowski

Christopher Powers

The holocaust was very horrible time for the Jews during the 20th century. Hitler rose to power in Germany giving the German hope that he would lead them out of the economic depression that the country had fallen into. He ordered a mass killing of Jews because he thought that they were a threat. My hero Jozef, Krzymowski helped protect some of the Jews from being in the hand of the Nazi's.

In the summer of 1942 there were operations to kill Jews in the towns around Lubin. A girl named Chaja Gutterman from Slawatycze, out now she was looking for the light, of nowhere, appeared at the front door of Mrs. and Mr. Kryzmowski home in the village of Kolonia Lizna and asked if she could come in for shelter. She was barefoot, exhausted, and unkempt, she had made a difficult and long journey from escaping the killing site in Lomazy where in August most of the Jews from Slawatycze were slaughtered and killed. She said "God saved me from the Germans' bullets, now do with me what you will. You can kill me or hand me over to the Germans- I am in your hands." Mariana, Jozef"s wife, had known her since a little girl. When Chaja and her sister were orphaned, Chaja's mom looked after them, now she was looking comfort, for the light. The Kyrzmowski's had three children in the house ages from four to nine in the house already and being a farming family, they were afraid of the risk they would have with Chaja with them, but their compassion for her overcame their fears so they took her in.

In the house they assigned her a hiding spot above the baking stove in the kitchen and she hid there for two years, until liberation in the summer of 1944. It wasn't easy being hidden in one situation someone had reported that the Kyrzmowski family had been hiding a Jewish woman and the Nazi's searched the home. Jozef managed to escape, but Mariana was seized and was interrogated. The Nazi threatened to execute her if she didn't reveal where they were hiding the woman.

Since he helped a woman that was jewish escape the grasps of the Nazi's he is a hero. He may have save only one, but one is the start to the many Jews that were saved at the time during Hitler's reign.

I feel that this hero is recognized as a hero because he saved a life but he did more than just save a life. He showed what it is to care for another no matter what religion you are and that is what matters most. A hero isn't someone who will save your religion or skin color a true hero could care less about that a hero would only care about your safety and well being. That is why Jozef is recognized as a hero, that is why he is in the Yad Vashem Righteous category. Because he is a true hero and true heroes deserve to be recognized and remembered. This is what I feel about my hero and why I chose him. Because he, his wife, and even his children kept quiet about having the woman in the house. His entire family should be recognized as heroes because his entire family kept her in their home and no matter how many threats they got from that Nazi's they still chose to do it because it was the right thing to do.

We really don't know if she would've survived in whatever internment camp the Nazi's were going to put her into, but hiding her in secret and risking his entire family's lives increased her chances of living. The actions he chose to do to help people stay alive at the risk of his own life, even his wife and his children's lives is worthy of being recognized as a hero.

There were people who were trying to help the Jews during the holocaust like my hero we still today need to make sure something like this never happens again. No matter what color somebody is, no matter what religion they are, we still need to make sure we don't have another holocaust. The holocaust was genocide and tore apart the lives of children and young adults at the time and in this world today we cannot afford another one or we'll end up breaking another war out.

My hero is one of the many people who supported this and didn't stay silent and took action to try and help those who were about to be under Hitler's wrong doings. Today we need to not stay silent and break out of a shell of fear that others won't like what you are doing and do what you do because that's what we live life for.

We have museums about the Holocaust, we still remember those who were lost in the Holocaust and still we should make sure something like this should never happen to humanity or any type of religion or race again.

Yad Vashem. Yad Vashem, 12 Apr. 2016. Web. 24 Nov. 2016.

Irena Sendler

Cindy Hua

 The Holocaust, meaning "sacrifice by fire", was a deadly war between the Germans and the Jews, taking away the lives of about six million Jews. This unforgettable event lasted for 12 years, beginning in 1933 when Adolf Hitler came to power, and finally ending in 1945. Although this was only between the Jews and the Germans, many non-Jews have risked their lives during the Holocaust to save the Jews. These non-Jews were honored with the name "Righteous Among The Nations". One very important Righteous Among The Nations was Irena Sendler.

Irena Sendler was born on February 15, 1910, in Warsaw, Poland. Her father, Dr. Stanisław Krzyżanowski, was a physician and her mother's name was Janina. Irena was born in Warsaw, but she grew up in the town of Otwock, Poland. In 1917, her father died from typhus that was contracted from his patients. Jewish community leaders offered her mother to help pay for Irena's education. She later studied Polish literature at Warsaw University, but was suspended for three years because of her public protest of the ghetto-bench system. Irena had a daughter, Janina, and two sons, Andrzej and Adam. However, Andrzej died in infancy and Adam died in 1999.

Beginning in 1939, Irena started helping Jews by offering them food and shelter. She created over 3,000 fake documents to help Jewish families. Once the Warsaw Ghetto was built in 1940, Irena could no longer help isolated Jews but instead started saving the orphan children. She led the Children's Division of Zegota, a Polish underground group to help Jews. As a Polish social worker, Irena used her papers to enter the Warsaw Ghetto. The old courthouse on the edge of the Warsaw Ghetto was one of the main routes that Irena used to smuggle children out. Of course, Irena and her small group of mostly women had used many techniques to smuggle the children out, but they had five main ways of escape. One, they would use an ambulance and carry a child hidden under the stretcher. Two, they escaped through the courthouse. Three, they could use the sewer pipes or other secret underground passages to take the children out. Four, they hid a child in a sack or trunk and carried it on a trolley. And five, a child could pretend to be very sick or ill, and they could legally be taken out. She wrote down the names of the children on cigarette paper, sealed them in a bottle, and buried the bottles in a garden. Elzbieta Ficowska was only one of the children who Irena saved. She was smuggled out of the ghetto in a toolbox when she was just five months old. In total, Irena rescued about 2,500 Jewish children.

Finally on October 20, 1943, Irena Sendler was arrested by German soldiers. She was held at Piawiak prison, where she was constantly questioned and tortured. Irena received a death sentence and was to be shot. Secretly, her group Zegota tried to bribe the executioner, who later helped her escape. The Germans proudly announced her execution with posters put up all over the city. During the remaining years of the war, Irena lived hidden. She survived, and after the war, Irena dug up the bottles with the names of the children and handed them to Jewish representatives for attempts to reunite them with their families. Sadly, most of them died in concentration camps.

Irena Sendler is still remembered as a hero today. In 1965, she received the Yad Vashem medal for the Righteous Among The Nations. Irena was awarded with Poland's highest honor, the Order of the White Eagle, in 2003. She had also been nominated for the Nobel peace prize in 2007, but she eventually lost to Al Gore. It was on May 12, 2008, when Irena finally died of pneumonia at the age of 98 in Warsaw, Poland.

The reason why I chose to write about Irena Sendler is because she inspires me and other girls around the world. Although she was a woman, she still worked hard to save the Jewish children from the Nazis. One thing that I learned about her was that she was nominated for the Nobel peace prize in 2007, but she lost. After learning about Irena, it led me to think that anything is possible for girls as long as they set their minds on it. The Holocaust left a huge impact on the world today. The survivors were frightened and shaken up from suffering and the war. They would have these painful memories for the rest of their lives. The phrase "Never Again" was created to say that an event like the Holocaust would never repeat itself in history. This phrase was directed to the whole world to make sure that no one else would suffer because of their religion, the same way that Jews did. To stop an event like the Holocaust from happening again, everyone needs to learn to accept each other's races. Although people may have a different religion, they are the same as other people in the world. We are the only way to stop an event like the Holocaust from happening again, and we can do that by treating others with respect instead of discrimination.

"Works Cited"

"Irena Sendler." The Telegraph. Telegraph Media Group. 12 May 2008. Web. 19 Nov. 2016.

"33 Facts You Should Know About the Holocaust." About.com Education. N.p. 09 May 2016. Web. 15 Nov. 2016.

"Facts about Irena - Life in a Jar." Life in a Jar. N.p. Web. 15 Nov. 2016.

Connolly, Kate. "I'm No Hero, Says Woman Who Saved 2,500 Ghetto Children." The Guardian. Guardian News and Media, 15 Mar. 2007. Web. 17 Nov. 2016.

Mikkelson, David. "Irena Sendler." Snopes. Snopes. 05 June 2015. Web. 19 Nov. 2016.

Harding, Louette. "Irena Sendler: A Holocaust Heroine." Mail Online. Associated Newspapers, 01 Aug. 2008. Web. 20 Nov. 2016.

"Irena Sendler Obituary on Legacy.com." Legacy.com. N.p., n.d. Web. 19 Nov. 2016.

John Damski

Codin Cheng

John Damski, a survivor and rescuer of the Holocaust, was born in Germany in 1914. He died in 1997. John had two brothers, one sister, and was born to Polish parents. They moved to Solec-Kujawski, Poland when Damski was five, four years after World War I. In school, he excelled in track and field and once came second in the Polish National Championship Triple Jump Event.

He spoke German fluently. The skill to speak German was very helpful and saved his life multiple times during the war such as getting him to escape prisons, trick German authorities and officials, and to get jobs. Throughout the war, he rescued and hid Jews and found ways give them fake identities as non-Jews. On September 1, 1939, he was serving in the Polish army, in the Battalion for the Defense of the Seashore at Gdynia. He was taken as a prisoner of war when the Germans had invaded Gdynia. As he was being taken to the prisoner of war camp, he managed to escape. He got a job at the power and water company, when one day, Germans had come and said to Damski that he should declare himself as a German but he refused. The Germans then told him to leave the town within 24 hours. Refusing to leave, Damski was put in an area they called General Government, led by Hans Frank. Hans Frank was a German lawyer working for the Nazi party, later then became Hitler's personal lawyer. Damski escaped the General Government in December 1939 with two of his friends. The Germans had caught him once again and sent him to another prison where every night 6 to 7 people were killed in a truck by toxic gases that were put inside. The prisoners who either lived through the toxics or was never killed in another way, was sent to Auschwitz Birkenau. But Damski was not taken with them. Auschwitz Birkenau is a German concentration and extermination camp. It was made with fortified walls, barbed wire, platforms, barracks, gallows, gas chambers and cremation ovens. Eventually Damski was the only one left in the prison and a German soldier told him there were no files of "John Damski" so then he was released. The soldier let him go but told Damski to leave the town immediately. He finally found his missing brother at a place where Damski attempted to go to every time he had escaped from the prisons and camps.

They moved to a town called Zamosc, Poland. He found a job at a chief electrician in a German airfield where 6 airfields were to be built. He heard a lot of information about the Germans' next invasion. His boss asked him to find more electricians to work in the factory so the job could be done faster. He traveled to the Warsaw Ghetto to find electricians. He took no more than ten people from the ghetto, who were also Jews. He would take several trips to the ghetto and when he tells the workers that he would go back to the ghetto for more people, they would ask to go with him so they could see their families. Every trip, he took 4 or 5 people with him. Damski was able to save a couple hundred Jews by putting them to work, which was similar to what Oskar Schindler had done. To save the Jews, Damski had to withstand 2 Nazi prisons.

In October 1941 in Zamosc, a girl named Sara Rozen, from Lvov, Ukraine, had moved to Damski's neighborhood. She came to Zamosc illegally so one day the Gestapo came to look for her. Damski wanted to see what happened as the Gestapo came to Sara's apartment, so he went to a bench that was outside where he could see through their window. Sara had jumped out onto Damski's lap. They ran to hide from the Gestapo. Damski had give Sara's family fake identities and Christine Paderewska was her new name.

They moved to Czestochowa, Poland after hiding in Zamosc. When they came there, everyone thought that they were married. They moved again to Warsaw because the Gestapo figured out where Christine was. There was an Uprising which is the Germans invading Warsaw. Damski and Christine survived after many difficulties. They hid in a basement of their apartment during the Uprising and their apartment was on fire. They tried putting it out with water but it failed. They hid in a hole in their basement for three days. The fourth day a German ordered all the remaining people to get out to show themselves. All the people were taken to the basement of the opera house. Every man was called up and the Germans shot every one of them. Christine took off the coat she wore and covered Damski with it and sat on him to hide him in the basement from getting killed in the first floor. The fifth day Christine and John saw a S.S. man pass by who assumed that John was Polish. He apologized after John spoke in German to prove he wasn't Polish and asked what John was doing in Warsaw. They went with an S.S. man, who was drunk, to Bielany, a village in Poland, the next day. Christine and Damski left the S.S. man and moved to Ozarow themselves. A man in a car from the previous town Damski was at and worked for the man, arrived at Bielany. The man needed someone to organize the fruit and vegetable operation, so he asked John. They hired 119 people for the operation and sold four thousand tons of vegetables. There was never such a wholesale business in Poland. It was a great success for them. The Russians had come to Ozarow in January 1945. They had survived the Holocaust and it was over.

When typing this essay, I learned that the holocaust was a time of war and death. To stop this from happening again, we could past the story on to later and next generations, treat each other equally, especially a country to another, and to not think of one race superior or higher than another because each race is different. Learning about John Damski made me understand that people can be cruel so I would make this so that it would never happen again. Learning about John also made me realize that I should not take things and people for granted and to respect and appreciate everything that I have.

Works Cited

Scholastic Inc. "We Remember Anne Frank-- Stories of Courage." We Remember Anne Frank--Stories of Courage. Scholastic Inc., n.d. Web. 11 Dec. 2016.
    < http://teacher.scholastic.com/frank/stories.htm >.
Philemon, Chrys. "John Damski." Prezi.com. Prezi Inc., 05 Feb. 2014. Web. 11 Dec. 2016. < https://prezi.com/vlny0rvnxaaw/john-damski/ >.
Ronner, Jessica. "John Damski." Prezi.com. Prezi Inc., 31 Jan. 2014. Web. 11 Dec. 2016.
    < https://prezi.com/7ztv2cepn5gk/john-damski/ >.

Humboldt Education. "John Damski Story, Part 1." John Damski Story, Part 1. Humboldt Education, n.d. Web. 11 Dec. 2016.
    < http://www2.humboldt.edu/rescuers/book/damski/johndstory1.html >.

Humboldt Education. "John Damski Story, Part 2." John Damski Story, Part 2. Humboldt Education, n.d. Web. 11 Dec. 2016.
    < http://www2.humboldt.edu/rescuers/book/damski/johndstory2.html >.

Humboldt Education. "John Damski Story, Part 3." John Damski Story, Part 3. Humboldt Education, n.d. Web. 11 Dec. 2016.
    < http://www2.humboldt.edu/rescuers/book/damski/johndstory3.html >.

Humboldt Education. "John Damski Story, Part 4." John Damski Story, Part 4. Humboldt Education, n.d. Web. 11 Dec. 2016.
    < http://www2.humboldt.edu/rescuers/book/damski/johndstory4.html >.

Humboldt Education. "John Damski Story, Part 5." John Damski Story, Part 5. Humboldt Education, n.d. Web. 12 Dec. 2016.
    < http://www2.humboldt.edu/rescuers/book/damski/johndstory5.html >.

Humboldt Education. "John Damski Story, Part 6." John Damski Story, Part 6. Humboldt Education, n.d. Web. 12 Dec. 2016.
    < http://www2.humboldt.edu/rescuers/book/damski/johndstory6.html >.

Humboldt Education. "John Damski Story, Part 7." John Damski Story, Part 7. Humboldt Education, n.d. Web. 12 Dec. 2016.
    < http://www2.humboldt.edu/rescuers/book/damski/johndstory7.html >.

Centre, UNESCO World Heritage. "Auschwitz Birkenau German Nazi Concentration and Extermination Camp (1940-1945)." UNESCO World Heritage Centre. United Nations, n.d. Web. 11 Dec. 2016. < http://whc.unesco.org/en/list/31 >.

The Life of Piotr Budnik

Cole Hanna

A hero is a person who is admired for courage, outstanding achievements, or noble qualities. An example of a hero during World War II is a man named Piotr Budnik. Piotr Budnik was a Polish Roman Catholic who was born in 1916. He was a farmer who grew up in a cottage with his elderly parents in the village of Kaczanowka (Tarnopol district, modern-day Ternopil, Ukraine). As the Germans began to occupy Kaczanowka, many of the local jews including Piotr's neighbors and long-time friends, the Hellraichs, were sent to the Tarnopol ghetto. In 1942, the Germans began liquidating the ghetto and deporting the remaining Jews to the Belzec dealth camp. Piotr remembered his long-time friends and decided to risk his life by going into the ghetto in order to save the three Hellraich children (Adela, Ester, and Zeev). Budnik's courageous act of saving the Hellraich children from the Tarnopol ghetto is one of the many reasons why he is now remembered as a hero of World War II.

In addition to risking his life to save the Hellraich children from the ghetto, Piotr also housed them in the outhouse of his farm. Not only was Piotr hiding the Hellraich children from the Germans, he was also hiding them from the knowledge of his own family. He sold extra produce from his farm to help provide for the three children. Piotr was constantly trying to find different hiding spots for the kids and made sure that they always had enough food and water. After two of the kids contracted typhus and the risk of discovery increased, Piotr dug a bunker in a distant field and transferred them there to keep them safe. Even when he himself had contracted typhus, he would continue to bring them food during the night because he knew that they were his responsibility. This routine of finding new hiding spots almost every other day and providing food for the children carried on for at least eighteen months. It was an enormous feat for Piotr Budnik to rescue and single-handedly care for the Hellraichs while keeping it secret from both the Germans and his own family.

During World War II, the Nazis created hundreds of ghettos which were sections of a city in which all Jews were required to live. The Hellraichs, Piotr's neighbors, were sent to the Tarnopol Ghetto. The Tarnopol Ghetto was a Jewish World War II ghetto that was first created in 1941 in the city of Tarnopol (now Ternopil, Ukraine). In Tarnopol, Jews made up forty-four percent of the city's population which made it the largest Jewish community in the area. In July 1941, a few days after the German army conquered the city of Tarnopol, about 2,000 Jews were killed. Two months later in September of 1941, the Germans announced that they were creating a designated Jewish ghetto in Tarnopol around the Old Square and the Market Square Minor. Twelve to thirteen thousand Jews were soon put into the ghetto and were given minimal food and lived under very harsh rules, including receiving the death penalty for leaving the ghetto illegally. The conditions of the ghettos were appalling. They were filthy, extremely overcrowded and had poor sanitation. Disease spread quickly through the ghettos. Those who did not die from disease, often starved to death due to the short supply of food. In the winter of 1941-1942, the ghetto's condition became so bad and the mortality rate was so high that the Judenrat (an administrative agency imposed by Nazi Germany during World War II) had to begin burying corpses in mass graves for sanitation concerns. In August of 1942, around 3,000-4,000 Jews were gathered and put into cattle cars for two days without water. While this was going on, another cattle train arrived with Jews from two other ghettos. The two trains were connected and sent to Belzec death camp, where a total of 6,700 Jews would be exterminated. On November 10, 1942 another 2,500 Jews from the Tarnopol Ghetto were put onto trains and sent to extermination camps in Belzec. The population of the Tarnopol ghetto decreased by a significant amount and was later partly turned into a labour camp. Although many terrible things went on in this ghetto, it brought out the good in many Polish people who lived in Tarnopol. Many of these people risked their lives to save the lives of others. Their motivation was solely because it was the humane thing to do and could not understand how a civilized person could harm or kill another person. Piotr Budnik is a shining example of one of these people.

There are many things that define a hero, including noble qualities, important achievements, and courageous acts. Piotr and all of the other rescuers performed many brave acts motivated solely for the purpose of helping these people and standing up for what they believed was right. Piotr risked his life by entering the Tarnopol Ghetto to rescue his neighbors, the Hellraichs. He prepared multiple hiding places to keep them safe and to avoid their persecution from the German army. In addition, he provided daily care for them under very difficult circumstances. Piotr Budnik's courageous acts are why he is now known as a hero of World War II.

Work Cited

."Righteous Database." Yadvashem.org. Web. 27 Feb. 2017.

"Tarnopol Ghetto" revolvy.com. Web. 26 February.2017.

HENRYK SLAWIK

Colin Craven

During the Holocaust in the 1930s and 1940s, millions of Jews cried out for help, needing someone to make a difference in their life, as they suffered persecution, humiliation, torture, and slaughtered because of their religion at the hands of their own government. Offering help or showing compassion to a Jew would put anyone and their family in danger. Jews were horrified and alone, praying that somehow to be rescued. Sadly, most people were too scared for their own safety, but one man did not consider the risk to himself, and stood up because it was the right thing to do. Henryk Slawik was a selfless man who stood up to the Nazis and helped these frightened Jews escape to a new life.

Slawik was born in 1894 in Szeroka, Poland. Straight out of secondary school, he enlisted into the Polish military to serve his country. When his military days were over, he moved to Silesia, where he joined the police force to serve his community. There, he was a member of the right-wing faction of the Polish Socialist Party and edited the Socialist Newspaper. During this time, the political climate was changing, and more anger and hatred were heating up in his home country and in Germany. Jews feared for their lives, and others were unsure about the direction their country was going in. This eventually led to the Holocaust, the most brutal, evil event in modern history.

Leading up to the Holocaust, the right radicalized system of government secured control this execute this mass operation. Starting in 1930, when an economic depression hit Germany, Germans lacked confidence in their weak government. It was this uncertainty that allowed the rise of the Nazi party. In January 1933, the Nazis came to power with the rise of the notorious Adolf Hitler. Hitler and the Nazis believed the Aryan race was the "master race" and nobody else deserved to live. They mostly used the Jewish people as a scapegoat for all of Germany's economic problems and failure in the first World War. In order to get rid of their "problem", the Nazis masterminded the persecution and killing of 6 million Jews.

The Holocaust was a systematic approach to annihilate the world of all Jews. To ensure the Nazi message was successfully communicated, Hitler first established the Reich Ministry of Public Enlightenment and Propaganda. Anti-Jewish messages saturated advertisements, music, and even children's books. Then, Jews were prevented from holding public office, and later from holding citizenship. Finally all Jews were identified by requiring them to wear a yellow six pointed star of David patch on their clothing. This is when German Jews began to flee their country, and Slawik comes into the picture.

Around 1939, Slawik joined a mobilized police battalion that was part of the Krakow Army, a militia fighting against the Nazis. When his crew crossed from a German-run Austrian border to Hungary, he was placed into a refugee camp. Because of his fluency in German, he was taken out of the camp by a man named Jozef Antall, who was a member of the Hungarian Ministries of Internal Affairs. Antall took Slawik to Budapest, a city in Hungary flooded with Jewish refugees. In Budapest, Slawik, along with Jozef Antall and a man named Zvi Henryk Zimmerman, created the Citizen's Committee Help for Polish Refugees. This committee provided forged passports and identification papers for refugees, giving them protection while hiding in plain sight. Here, he and Countess Erzebet Szapary and Jan Kollataj-Srzednicki, the leaders of the Polish Red Cross in Hungary, located Jewish refugees in camps. He gathered 76 children and led them 30 kilometers to the city of Vac, where they passed as Catholic school children. While at these camps, Slawik also issued thousands of documents certifying those refugees were Christian. He established a boarding school for the children he gathered to hide from the Nazis, other children were placed in a Catholic orphanage. At this time, Jews in this area felt safe.

Meanwhile, Hitler's genocide was in full force, Jews were moved into ghettos, isolated from society. The majority of German and Polish Jews were either in concentration or extermination camps, where they did slave labor until they died or were executed. Those who were not killed by natural causes were either shot, or put into gas chambers, slaughtering up to 6,000 people in a day. All these murders were not enough to satisfy Hitler and the Nazis, they wanted more death, more suffering. Hitler then sent his military to Hungary to round up the refugees and slaughter the Jews.

On March 19, 1944, the Slawik's boarding school came under threat. Posing as someone else and relying on false documentation was no longer enough to protect Swalik's refugees. Shortly before the school became a target, Slawik ordered all refugees in Hungary to evacuate. Because of this heroic action, Slawik was appointed leader of the Polish Resistance, a resistance movement fighting against the Nazis. But on this fateful day, Slawik was not thinking of his new appointment, his mind was on the thousands of refugees escaping to safety. Once they fled, Slawik's mission was completed. Slawik was not so lucky and was arrested by German forces. He was tortured by the Gestapo, the German police force that punished anyone who opposed the Nazis. Even after hours of torture, Slawik never gave up any of his associates. He was sent to the Mauthausen Concentration Camp, where, in August of 1944, he was executed. Swalik saved a total of 30,000 refugees, all of whom survived.

Slawik was a selfless man. He enrolled into the military to serve the people of his country; he became a police officer to ensure his community's safety; and he stood up for his beliefs publicly by editing the Socialist Newspaper. Given an opportunity to make the world a better place, he helped people. During the most atrocious slaughter in modern history, Slawik did not shy away. As the war raged on, he was not silent, he stood up for what he knew was right. From him, I learned even in the toughest, darkest times, there is still good, there is still hope. Slawik was that hope to many individuals. Slawik amazed me on how he could save so many lives, not to be a hero, but because it was the right thing to do. He inspired me to always stick up for what is right, no matter how much it may hurt.

During that time in history, Jewish families faced an uncertain future and the prospect of incredible pain and torture, after laws were passed to alienate them from society. I've read about the pain, I've learned about the suffering, but now I understand that Jewish men, women, and children must have undergone unimaginable for people to feel that their government was going sideways even before the genocide began.

After the Holocaust, survivors started a simple movement to educate people and share their stories to ensure nothing like this happens again. This movement was headlined by two basic words: "Never Again." Of course we never want this to happen again; killing in this magnitude is horrible. But, this was not just a killing, it was a systematic approach to wipe out all Jews. Instead of accepting their mistakes and building for a better country, the German government blamed all of their problems on one group of people because of their race and religion. Six million Jews, 63% of the Jewish population in Europe, 93% of the Jews in Poland, all perished because of their ethnic backgrounds. There is no reason for this to ever happen again.

To prevent another genocide, society must take a thoughtful approach. First, it must admit and accept mistakes. If the Germans accepted their mistakes for their failure in the first World War, and the economic collapse, they could take action to correct them. Second, it must listen to the opinions of all people before making decisions. Jews weren't allowed to serve in the government, so their voice was not heard. Finally, it must simply stick up for what is right. Inside each of us has a conscience that knows right from wrong. I am certain many Germans heard this voice when the Nazis were voted into power, but ignored it.

Henryk Slawik was an amazing selfless man, who risked his life and stood up to the Nazis, helping defenseless Jews escape to a new life.

Works Cited

Davolt, Nathan, Austin Hansen, and Jacob Hansen. "Henryk Slawik." Henryk Slawik. Nathan Davolt, Austin Hansen, and Jacob Hansen, n.d. Web. 14 Dec. 2016.

"Portrait of Henryk Slawik." United States Holocaust Memorial Museum. United States Holocaust Memorial Museum, 7 Jan. 2002. Web. 14 Dec. 2016.

"The Righteous Among The Nations." The Righteous Among The Nations. Yad Vashem, 2016. Web. 14 Dec. 2016.

Holocaust Essay: Sabcia Saaroni

Colin Singh

Have you ever wanted to change your name or be someone else? For most survivors of the Holocaust this was not an option, it was survival. Most people had to change their name multiple times in order to survive, like my survivor. My report is on Holocaust survivor Sabcia Saaroni, born as Sabcia Fishman. Sabcia was the youngest of four children and was only 13 when World War II began. Her home, Lubin Poland, was bombed on the first day and her family hid in their apartment cellar for three weeks. Sabcia said that she was two different people during the war: a 14 year old that was younger than she really was; and a 14 year old being forced to grow-up, and she was both for the whole war.

Sabcia lived with Polish farmers outside Lubin for about two years, but then the Nazis came. Sabcia and her family hid in the fields and when they returned many other families were dead. Luckily, there was another family there that survived too and they had four children as well, one of which was Sabcia's friend.

Sabcia was lucky and had "Good Looks" meaning she did not look Jewish which helped her obtain a job in a canning factory in Hamburg, Germany. She had to get a new birth certificate but it said she was 22 when Sabcia was only 16. She took a risky move and acquired new documents to fit her age. Her new name was Lidia Wornik.

The bombings returned and then came the "Firestorm" It was a continuous, rapid bombing that looked like it was raining fire. Everything was blown up or burning, 42,000 civilians were killed and 37,000 were wounded. Sabcia somehow managed to survive.

She decided to leave her job in Hamburg because the city was now in chaos. She and her friend from the factory, Zosia, were running away and later found a German village, where they were able to do farm work for the summer. In the fall, police came to arrest Sabcia, when they asked her name she said Lidia Wornik, and one of the officers said that she was Sabcia Fishman. She denied it and was taken to the local Gestapo station and detained for two days. There she was questioned and created a new story about her identity. In the end, she was allowed to leave but was told they would check to confirm her story. This provided Sabcia and Zosia time to run away.

Sabcia came back to Hamburg and returned to work at the canning factory, but knew that if the police had come once they would come again, so she decided to leave again. Thankfully, a Jewish woman at the factory provided her with money and an address. She boarded a train to Gotha but when she arrived she could not find the address. She made an almost fatal mistake by asking an officer for directions. Because she did not have any documents she was arrested again. The officer would not believe her story and kept her in a cell for three days where she could not sit or eat. She wanted to die. She told the officer that she was Jewish, hoping he would kill her, instead they put her back in the cells and she would later take a train to a concentration camp.

Sabcia was able to regain her will to live when she heard rumors that the German military was retreating on all fronts. She escaped by leaving at the peak morning hour, while they were putting the prisoners on trains, she slipped out and no one noticed. They were calling the men on board first so she had time before the police officers noticed. She boarded a train going in the opposite direction. Luckily, there was only one other person on board, but, it was a military man in a brown uniform. All she had to do was make sure her train left before the prisoner's train but they had already found out she was missing, police were looking in all the carriages. Luckily, the train departed and she eventually got off in a town called Grossrohrsdorf, near Dresden.

Sabcia was fortunate to obtain a job in a nearby bakery. She made it past the police check and worked there for months. Sadly, the fire-bombings came back and killed another 25,000 people. Sabcia and the other bakers watched in horror as Dresden was bombed. Thankfully, the war would be over soon.

Germany surrendered and Sabcia went back to Lubin, all of the people she knew did not want her around, all because she was Jewish. The good news was that both of her brothers were alive, one of which she had not seen since she was ten. Sabcia eventually moved to Palestine, where she was reunited with her brother. She currently lives in Australia and is a well-known sculptor.

I have learned that no one should ever have to go through anything close to this no one should have to suffer like this, just because of their religion or nationality. This has taught me you should never discriminate someone over what they believe in or where they come from. Learning about Sabcia taught me that everyone who survived the Holocaust must have been very strong, brave, and incredibly lucky. I understand that the Holocaust is one of the worst parts of human history and this should never happen again even though it has. Never again, no one should ever be hurt, tortured or killed for what they believe in. Everyone should be able to accept everyone else's religion and nationality.

Works Cited

Makler, Irris. "Pickled Cabbage." Food Is Love. Food Is Love, 17 Jan. 2016. Web. 12 Dec. 2016.

"Names of Righteous by Country." Names of Righteous by Country. N.p., n.d. Web. 11 Dec. 2016.

United States Holocaust Memorial Museum. United States Holocaust Memorial Museum, n.d. Web. 11 Dec. 2016.

Franciszek Jankowski

Collin Coppola

 The Holocaust, the mass slaughter or reckless destruction in life and murder of approximately six million Jews by the Nazis and their collaborators. The period at which the world was in danger, the head leader Adolf Hitler, planned to kill as many Jews as possible. People do not realize the loyalty and respect that came from the righteous and brave up standers that stood against Hitler, and what Poland did for the Jews is unbearable to think about. As much help as the Polish people attempted to save the poor Jews, many people suffered. Many of the Poles suffered risking their lives for the Jews. About 3 million poles suffered during the Holocaust, but that's why we shall remember them in honor for what they did. Out of the rare thousands that were awarded Righteous among the Nations of the World a man named Franciszek Jankowski stood out. This man wanted world peace, no more war. This is one of the most honored metals that doesn't just get passed out to anybody randomly, it's for people that risked their lives and their future for someone else in order to assist in world peace among our nations.

Died 1956, born 1904 raised in Nakło nad Notecią, the man Franciszek Jankowski, was the man in honor. It all starts from where and when you grow up. This man did a lot as a kid. In his early life in Germany at which he participated in the life of the Polish community, Westphalian. As Mr. Jankowski got older he grew more and more engaged in writing, where he wrote articles magazines, and poems. His kindness toward the young ages was known from his writings. His pieces were filled with enchanting fairy tales. This indeed, impressed the young and so he began writing more fairy tales. He also was interested in writing stories about the daily news, or being a reporter. Because of his wonderful writings, he advanced in loyalty of those who were fans of him. He established a puppet show with a group of teachers and kindergartners. He helped many high rated schools, helping in writing or readings, or even acting. On the 10th anniversary of Polish education in Germany, he created his version of "ABC Polish little ones in Germany." He was also an employee of the publishing department of the Union of Poles in Germany. Before 1939, he published numerous articles, poems and short stories (mainly for children and youth in Germany).

Franciszek got tired of writing the same things, so he wanted to learn about war. He then got interested in war. He wrote after his studies in poems and articles. His pre-war poems and prose texts are scattered, often published under the "Little Pole in Germany" and "Young Pole in Germany." After 1935, he published in the "Word of Warmia and Mazury" and "Western Poland." Franciszek was also director of the Polish school in Sadłukach Powiśle (Germany). After receiving an exception from the Germans for the right to teach, he was forced to move to Berlin where he worked in the editorial "Little Pole in Germany." He ran in this newspaper column, which was known as "Uncle Frank" which kept Polish children from the areas of Germany. In the years 1937-1939 he worked as a teacher of foreign languages in Polish school in Bytom which helped him to communicate to many of the people around him either in Germany or his home in Poland. Shortly before war broke out, for fear of arrest, he fled to Poland. During the war he worked to continue as a teacher of foreign languages. In 1949, he immigrated to Germany, where he again worked in the Polish organizations after clearing his name of being noticed. Now that you know about Franciszek Jankowski, you shall be informed what he did. This is something to remember for our history, because what he did was out of the greatness of his heart.

On June 21, 1945, in Warsaw ten people were awarded "Righteous among the Nations of the World" medals. The medals are given to individuals and families who risked their own lives to rescue Jews during World War II. Polish President Lech Kaczyński attended the ceremony and said that he had demonstrated "supreme valor." There are many reasons why he was awarded out of the ten people that were chosen that day. He and his family all got awarded this medal because of how many either Polish-Jews or just Jews were saved by them. He was a huge part in the act of being an up stander to fight against Adolf Hitler. To inform you, Poland was occupied by the Nazis from 1939 to 1945 and no Polish collaboration government was ever formed during that period. The Polish Government in Exile was the first to reveal the existence of Nazi concentration camps and repetitive extermination of the Jews by the Germans. It is not known how many Jews were helped by Franciszek but at one point in 1943 it had 2,500 Jewish children under its care in Warsaw alone. In that moment he began to help families survive or escape without getting exterminated. The government in exile also provided special assistance, including funds, arms, and other supplies. They supplied this to Jewish resistance organizations. The recipients that were honored with a medal, were Julia Dąbrowska and her mother Gabriela Elżanowska; Władysława Fiks; Franciszek Jankowski; Karol Koźmiński, whose family rescued 21 Jews and whose son was sent to Auschwitz as a result, many families and people survived. The exact number of Holocaust survivors is unknown still, but we believe the amount of Polish Jews escaped was about 300,000. When the ghettos were closed from the outside, unhealthy or severely injured people kept alive off whatever was left in the town either food or shelter. Escaping into Aryan was attempted by some 100,000 Jews, and the risk of them being turned in by the Poles was very small. The question asking the real chances of survival once the Holocaust began is unknown, but people still wonder since of all the power that Hitler had over the Jews, it's amazing of how many Jews survived. The Germans made it extremely hard to escape the ghettos just before to the death camps. They didn't want any Jews escaping because there hatred for them was high. Thick and tough walls were rebuilt containing fewer gates, including policemen that ordered the whole concentration camp. The relations between Poles and Jews during World War II presented one of the strongest alliances in the history of the Holocaust. A good 10 percent of the Poland's Jews survived the genocide, but unfortunately about sixty percent of the Jews that were in the concentration camps died and yet, Poland accounts for the majority of rescuers contained the title of "Righteous Among the Nations. "Franciszek and his family were one of the most famous people who risked their lives to save the poor Jews. The Poles today are honored by Yad Vashem all around the world. "The Righteous among the Nations of the World medal is the highest honor that can be given to people who are not citizens of Israel.

Over 20 thousand of the medals have been awarded, with Poles receiving over 6 thousand, more than any other group. Franciszek Jankowski might not be the only person that was awarded with the medal, but what he did for one person is more than a mouthful than many people can take in today.

Franciszek made sure that "Never Again" shall this occur in our history of the world. The Holocaust affected many people in World War II but what can we do today to never again let this happen? Well...The word Genocide, the attempted extermination of a certain race. Nothing is more sickening than the idea of somebody trying to exterminate some group. For this to happen was a surprise to many people. In order to prevent another horrific event like the holocaust, would be universal effort, and so that we can one day live in peace, without fear of persecution based on our race or religion. We shall not live on Earth with fear of a massive extermination of population, so what we do is to join forces and communicate with each other worldwide. Over my studies and information that I have learned, the Holocaust to me shows that people can show how much power they have by killing a race, but the people who watch others die without standing up against the power, will suffer in compared to the people like Franciszek Jankowski, who made a purpose in life only by his decision. To make this world a better place, as it today. With the help of people joining together to destroy the terrible Holocaust, we in our history have learned to never let this happen again.

Teodor Pajewski

Daisy Bajwa

 The Holocaust was a tragic event in history that we shall never forget, but we also know that it shall never again happen. The word Holocaust is from the Greek origin meaning 'sacrifice by fire' and it was the slaughter of six million Jews by the Nazis lead by Adolf Hitler. This event can be classified as a mass murder or genocide. Under the rule of Hitler, after he came into power in 1933, all Jews had to wear the Star of David on their clothing to indicate that they were Jewish. Although many people perished during the Holocaust, some individuals risked their lives to help the suffering Jews and their families in danger. These people were called the righteous basically meaning even if they were not Jewish, they still helped hide and protect the Jews. One man, Teodor Pajewski, went out of his way to help these Jews and people called him crazy for doing it. Teodor Pajewski was an "underground officer" or a railway man. He wasn't some rich person with tons of money or a famous king of some sort, all he was was a railway man yet he made such a big difference in these Jews' lives. Pajewski and his family had been known to help the Jews but Pajewski himself had been more famously known to hide Emanuel Ringelblum, the Jewish community leader. Unfortunately for the Jews who couldn't be saved had to go to concentration camps where they worked hard as laborers until they eventually perished or were pulled into groups and slaughtered in the most terrible ways, one of which involved Jews being rounded up and being told that they were

showering when really, they were being gassed. This killed approximately 6,000 people each day. Prisoners at the camp had to have their possessions taken away, shave their heads, have their arms tattooed and then were separated into groups of men, women, and children.

Pajewski was able to take Ringelblum to Warsaw after his rescue from the Trawniki camp in July 1943. He even hid a Jewish refugee family in the cellar of his apartment-like building. Pajewski's family, who lived on the countryside, also concealed Jews in their household. While in hiding, Ringelblum wrote a description of Pajewski's bold stunts of concealing Jews, and Ringelblum was right about Pajewski's actions. They were extremely risky and could get him killed. Mieczyslaw Wolski and Mieczyslaw Marczak's family, hid Ringelblum in a bunker, called "Krysia" with over 30 people. They were discovered and killed but Pajewski had taken Ringelblum and a family of Jews in his hidden basement. Pajewski supplied the Jews that he was protecting with money and food so that they wouldn't go into poverty but one of the most amazing and kindest things that Pajewski did for the Jews in hiding was keeping them in touch with their family and friends. Pajewski didn't make these Jews feel like they were refugees in danger, he made them feel like they belonged and they could truly be free and safe and at the same time, he was searching for new places to hide other refugees and other areas to keep them safe in case they had to abruptly move or find another place to hide in case there were any searches in the buildings they were hiding in which was very common. Pajewski forwarded money and rescued Jewish prisoners. One man, a caretaker, in Pajewski's building, suspected he was hiding Jews and continually harassed him because of it. After a while of doing this, the caretaker in Pajewski's building ordered a search of Pajewski's room with some residents of the building but thankfully found nothing of the Jews since Pajewski kept them so well protected. Later, the caretaker reported that he was sure Pajewski was concealing Jews so the Germans came and arrested him. They sent him to a POW camp where he eventually passed away on February 18, 1953 at age 77.

I have learned so much after researching Pajewski's story and not just about him. I learned that there were so many people with kind hearts that risked their lives protecting Jews. Learning about Pajewski has definitely opened my eyes about the world around us and how taking bold actions everyday can change the future of another individual's life. The Holocaust was something that we will never forget but we all must ensure that it will be something that never occurs again. "Never Again" is something survivors of the Holocaust say and to make sure this never happens again, we can take small steps in life like simply helping a friend who is being bullied. Just as I stated, you don't have to have power or some cool reputation, all you need is courage like Pajewski and stand up for those in need. To make a difference, we have to help others to make certain this is something that shall never again occur. All it takes is a smile to a stranger, a "back off" to a bully. Speak up for yourself and for your friends to make sure we don't repeat the past.

Works Cited Page

"Teodor Pajewski." Polish Genealogy/Genealogia Polska. N.p., n.d. Web. 10 Dec. 2016

Wojan, Megan. "Introduction to the Holocaust." Introducing the Holocaust. Katherine L. Albiani Middle School, Elk Grove. 4 Nov. 2016. Lecture

"United States Holocaust Memorial Museum." Www.ushmm.org. United States Holocaust Memorial Museum, n.d. Web. 8 Dec. 2016.

"The Righteous Among the Nations." Http://www.yadvashem.org/. N.p., n.d. Web. 8 Dec. 2016.

"Saving Jews: Polish Righteous." Http://www.savingjews.org/righteous/pv.htm. Saving Jews: Polish Righteous, n.d. Web. 7 Dec. 2016.

Irena Adamowicz

Danica Hsieh

Irena Adamowicz was a Holocaust survivor, and a daughter of Polish nobles. She was also a Polish Non-Jew scout leader of the movement and a Resistance worker during World War II. Before the astonishing war, Adamowicz was a graduate that held a degree in social work at the University of Warsaw, and provided help for the Jew and refugees from the Warsaw Ghetto. She was born on the Russian Empire on May 11, 1910 and passed away on August 12, 1973.

Adamowicz and was a religious Catholic. During the 1930s, she developed an attachment to the Ha-Shomer ha-Tsa'ir Jewish Zionist Youth Movement, and took part in the educational and social work activities. During the summer of 1942, Adamowicz went on a brave trip across Poland and Lithuania to establish contact between underground organizations in the ghettos of Warsaw. Her visits became a basis of both vital evidence and moral inspiration, such as her stirring presence in Kovno Ghetto in July 1942. She had risked her life by carrying out risky missions for the Jewish underground organizations in the Warsaw, Bialystok, Vilna, Kovno, and Siauliai ghettos. She became a member of the underground Home Army, also well known as the Armia Krajowa, as an underground courier. Adamowicz carried both important communications between the diverse ghettos and increased the moral and aid support of the Jewish ghettos in several distant cities confined in them. Until the outbreak of World War II, she held a leading role with the Polish Scouts in Warsaw. Throughout the years, she developed close and friendly relationships with the Hashomer Hatzair undertaking and participated in its educational and social originalities. During the work, she not only maintained contact with the Jewish youth movements, but strengthened the relationship. She also helped to establish contact between the Jewish underground organizations and the Home Army, also known as the Polish underground militia. After the war, she remained in close contact with the survivors of the Holocaust, with whom she had worked with and aided in the Jewish underground. Thanks to their efforts, she was named "Righteous" among the Nations in 1985 as well as a Jewish nickname of "Di chalutzishe shikse," the Pioneering Gentile.

The Holocaust started in 1941, after the German invasion of the Soviet Union, when the Germans instituted the orderly process of killing all Jews under their influence by gassing and shooting them. After the invasion of Poland in 1939, the Germans established ghettos in several Polish cities, where Jews were confined. The living condition in the ghettos was overcrowding, horrendous, and diseased. The Germans deported Jews to these ghettos. In 1933, when Hitler rose to power, he began employing simple discrimination laws against Jews and others who were lower to create his Master Race. He convinced his followers of this issue with the Jewish Question, as it was known, and get away with murdering millions of people. In 1944, the Allies were advancing on the Germans. Finally, they began taking over their camps. In July 1944, Maidanek, a camp in Poland, was liberated by the Soviets. This was followed by many more liberations and takeovers as the Americans and other Allies slowly removed Hitler from power. In January 1945, Auschwitz camp was liberated. The liberation of this camp was a major milestone in the end of the Holocaust.

As survivors and children began aging, the terrifying flashbacks return to their minds. The Holocaust not only affected all the survivors and harmless souls that died, but the Holocaust impacted our world. The Holocaust just gives an example of how prejudice our society can be. The Holocaust today still affects us by the government cracking down. Today, most countries don't accept dictators to take over. They did this because of the Holocaust. They don't want any reoccurrence of this horrific massacre that stole the innocent lives of Jewish people. Students are taught from day one to "treat others the way you would want to be treated." The Holocaust has affected our society like no other war or battle has. The Holocaust has and will affect us whether it was in the past, present, or future.

In conclusion, I have learned that Irena Adamowicz was a true survivor of the Holocaust. She was one of those "tough survivors" that is willing to survive a long way without passing out or getting severely sick. I have also learned that the Holocaust destroyed society. This shocking, upsetting Genocide killed millions of people, left thousands in physical or mental pain, and affected today's society in such a negative way. People were killed dishonorably and those who luckily got away will be devastated for the rest of their lives. These survivors still face the long-term effects from the holocaust. One cannot stop genocide unless the rest of humanity is united against it. We will continue to have Holocausts, though they will be on a smaller scale simply because the news will break out almost instantly. Hopefully, we will not have to wait for millions to die before action is taken. The future may come to an end, or it shall stay. I am unable to predict someone's future, but it will all depend. All we can do is hope for the best.

Works Cited

http://www.yadvashem.org/odot_pdf/Microsoft%20Word%20-%205717.pdf

.., __, and Shoah Resource Center, The International School For Holocaust Studi. Adamowicz, Irena (n.d.): n. pag. Print. https://www.revolvy.com/main/index.php?s=Irena%20Adamowicz

Revolvy, LLC. ""Irena+Adamowicz" on Revolvy.com." All Revolvy Quizzes. N.p., n.d. Web. 05 Dec. 2016. http://isurvived.org/TOC-II.html

"Part II - Heroes and Heroines of the Holocaust." Part II - Heroes and Heroines of the Holocaust. N.p., n.d. Web. 05 Dec. 2016. http://www.sixmillioncrucifixions.com/How_did_the_Holocaust_start.html

"How Did the Holocaust Start?" How Did the Holocaust Start? N.p., n.d. Web. 05 Dec. 2016. http://www.hitlerschildren.com/article/634-how-did-the-holocaust-end

Skatrix.com, Programming:. "How Did the Holocaust End?" How Did the Holocaust End? N.p., n.d. Web. 05 Dec. 2016. http://theholocaustaturningpoint.weebly.com/long-term-effects.html

"Long Term Effects." The Holocaust: A 20th Century Turning Point. N.p., n.d. Web. 05 Dec. 2016. https://www.quora.com/Genocide-How-can-humanity-make-sure-something-like-The-Holocaust-never-happens-again

N.p., n.d. Web.

http://www.digplanet.com/wiki/Irena_Adamowicz

"Irena Adamowicz." Learn and Talk about Irena Adamowicz, People from Warsaw, Polish Righteous Among the Nations, Polish Scouts and Guides, Polish Nobility. N.p., n.d. Web. 05 Dec. 2016.

http://www.wow.com/wiki/Irena_Adamowicz

"Irena Adamowicz." Irena Adamowicz - WOW.com. N.p., n.d. Web. 05 Dec. 2016.

http://db.yadvashem.org/righteous/righteousName.html?language=en&itemId=401366
7

Yad Vashem - Request Rejected. N.p., n.d. Web. 05 Dec. 2016. http://savingjews.org/righteous/av.htm

"Saving Jews: Polish Righteous." Saving Jews: Polish Righteous. N.p., n.d. Web. 05 Dec. 2016. http://www.thefullwiki.org/Irena_Adamowicz

"The Full Wiki." Irena Adamowicz : Wikis (The Full Wiki). N.p., n.d. Web. 05 Dec. 2016. http://db.yadvashem.org/righteous/family.html?language=en&itemId=4013667

Yad Vashem - Request Rejected. N.p., n.d. Web. 05 Dec. 2016.

Irena Sendler

Daniel Fernandez

 During the Holocaust about a third of the Jewish population were killed in Europe, the rest of the Jewish people were either in different countries, or in hiding assisted by some of the few brave people who dare to put their lives in danger in order to help them. Many different people from various countries helped the Jews during these horrific times. For instance, a twenty nine year old Polish girl named Irena Sendler was one of these people who helped the Jews escape during the holocaust. Irena Sendler managed to save two thousand five hundred Jewish children with her colleagues, and four hundred Jewish children personally in the Warsaw Ghetto during the Holocaust.

Irena Sendler was born in February 15, 1910 in Otwock. The town of Otwock is about fifteen miles southeast of Warsaw. Both of Irena's parents were part of the socialist party and her father was a doctor who died of Typhus when Irena was only a child. Like her father, Irena wanted to work in the medical field and help people with their illnesses and injuries.

When Irena was old enough to get a job, she became a nurse and was working as a social worker at the same time. In 1931, Irena married Mieczysław Sendler, and after the wedding they both moved to Warsaw before World War Two abruptly started in the 1930's in Europe.

In 1940, the Nazis were forcing the four hundred thousand Jewish people living in Warsaw to go in a small locked ghetto area where they were killed by the thousands, by disease or by starving to death. Since Irena was a social worker she was allowed to enter the ghetto to aid the residents regularly. Irena soon joined the Żegota, which is a council to aid the Jewish population. Irena and her colleagues were putting their themselves in danger by setting out to save Jewish children from death in the holding areas or from getting deported to concentration camps.

The Żegota first started saving the Jewish children by saving the Jewish orphans. Some Żegota members saved the orphans by putting them in coffins or potato sacks and smuggling them outside of the ghetto. Other people loaded them in ambulances and drove them elsewhere. They also used other more risky ways to escape by using the underground tunnels in Warsaw. Some of the Jew children also used the Catholic church to change their identity by adopting new religion in order to save themselves from the Nazi. Irena helped the children with the new identities by placing them in convents or having them live with non- Jewish families.

When the problem with the ghetto's Jewish children became dire, Irena started to go far beyond helping orphans, and started to ask the parents of Jewish children to let her get them out of Warsaw's ghetto and get to safety. Irena knew she couldn't promise them that the children would survive, but she offered them chance at getting away from the Nazis. If the families did nothing they will be killed regardless. Irena Sendler kept very detailed records of the rescued children in a jar, so she can reunite them with their family after the war. Most parents of the children didn't make it and the kids never saw their parents again.

On October 24 of 1943, the Nazis had arrested Irena Sendler for aiding the Jewish children and sent her to the Pawiak Prison. In the prison they tortured her so she can give up the names and information of the her colleagues in Żegota who assisted her with the escaping of the Jew children. When she refused to reveal any information she was sentenced to death. The Żegota members bribed the Germans, so they overturned her sentence and released Irena in February 1944. Irena Sendler had continued her work in saving children in Warsaw until the war had ended in 1945. Irena and her associates had saved about two thousand and five hundred Jewish children in the Warsaw ghetto. Irena personally saved four hundred children in the Warsaw ghetto.

After the war ended, Irena had gotten a divorce and later married another man named Stefan Zgrzembski. They both had three children together, a daughter named Janka, and her two sons, Adam and Andrzej. Unfortunately Andrzej had died when he was a infant. Later her husband Stefan died and Irena remarried Mieczysław, but their marriage didn't last long and again they divorced for the second time.

In 1965, a memorial organization named Yad Vashem, had named Irena Sendler Righteous Among Nations for her extraordinary and brave work in saving the children of the Warsaw ghetto from the Nazis who had invaded in 1939.

In 2003, Poland also honored Irena with the Honor of the White Eagle for her work in the Warsaw Ghetto.

In 2008, Sendler had been nominated for the Nobel Peace Prize, but unfortunately she did not win. Irena Sendler then died in May 12 2008, at the age of ninety-eight in Warsaw.

In conclusion of what I learned from the story of Irena Sendler, I now understand that it takes bravery, courage, and strength to stand for your beliefs, in this case Irena stood up for the children of Warsaw and saved many children with the help of her colleges. The impact of researching Irena's life had on me was that it taught me a lesson that I have to stand up for what I believe in no matter what the consequences are. She put her own life and freedom at risk and she proceeded regardless of what could happen to her to save the children's lives. The Holocaust was so devastating to the world and to the Jewish community because of the mass killings of the Jews. The overall population of the Jewish community dwindle and even impacts the world today. Now we have memorials for victims. We also have ceremonies to remember the heroes of the holocaust, such as Irena Sendler. We know how prejudice can make people act in horrific ways. Prejudice about a person's color, religion, or race can lead to a mass genocide like the holocaust. The world can avoid an event like the Holocaust by teaching people how to respect another person's culture and accept diversity in race and religion so a mass genocide like the Holocaust will never happen again.

Works Cited

"Facts about Irena - Life in a Jar." Life in a Jar. N.p., n.d. Web. 10 Dec. 2016.

@FACTSlides. "34 Facts about The Holocaust ←FACTSlides→." Holocaust Facts: 34 Facts about The Holocaust ←FACTSlides→. FACTSlides.com, 28 Nov. 2016. Web. 10 Dec. 2016.

"Irena Sendler." Biography.com. A&E Networks Television, 21 Mar. 2016. Web. 10 Dec. 2016.

"Long Term Effects." The Holocaust: A 20th Century Turning Point. N.p., n.d. Web. 10 Dec. 2016.

Jerzy Bielecki

Darius Coxum

Adolf Hitler is responsible for the tragic event called the Holocaust. Hitler was a bad and powerful man who hated Jews because he thought he was superior to them. He began to slowly separate them from society and put them in concentration camps. The concentration camps separated families while they were each tortured and killed. The Nazis (Hitler's soldiers) hunted and captured and killed them, transported them and tortured them. Some Jews escaped and made a resistance to fight Hitler and free the the rest of the Jews.Jerzy Bielecki is one of the few 6000 survivors to escape a concentration camp called Auschwitz with his newly found love.

Jerzy Bielecki (a.k.a Jurek) was born in Slaboszow, Poland, on March 28, 1921 and died when he was 90. While making an attempt at escaping Nazi occupied Poland to Hungary, Bielecki was captured by Nazi troops and accused of assisting the Polish Resistance force on June 19. He was transported to Auschwitz where the number "243" was tattooed on his arm. Bielecki was forced to work in a grain warehouse. One day a line of women were herded through the door. As they passed, Bielecki saw a dark haired women wink at him and it was Cyla Cybulska. Cyla and her family were put in a train and shipped to Auschwitz but only Cyla survived. Cyla and her family were put in a train and shipped to Auschwitz but only Cyla survived. She was assigned to repair the grain sacks. Over the next 8 months, even though they only talked a small amount of time each day, they fell in love. Shortly after, Bielecki began to plan their escape. With the help of a friend in the uniform warehouse, Bielecki began to piece together a uniform and stole a pass to transport prisoners. Bielecki led Cyla out of her barrack onto a path along a gate where a sleepy guard let them pass. They walked all night and during the day they hid in the fields from the Nazi troops for 10 days. After the 10 days they reached a relative of Bielecki's house. Even after all they been through Bielecki found a hiding place in a polish family for Cyla and joined the Polish underground. After saying one last goodbye Bielecki left. For the next 39 years they did not see each other and believed that the other died. Cyla married another survivor of the Holocaust, David Zacharowicz and started a jewelry store in Brooklyn. Bielecki had a family and was a director for a school of car mechanics. Cyla was talking to the women who cleaned for her, telling them about the escape she made with Jerzy. One of the women claimed she saw Jerzy on TV. Cyla looked into it and found out Jerzy's phone number and address. In 1883 Bielecki and Cyla met with each other for the first time in about 40 years. By that time David had already passed away. Cyla called and set up a meeting. As soon as she stepped off the plane Jerzy gave her 39 roses for each year that they were apart. After that they met about 15 more times and became great friends for the rest of their lives.

The Holocaust has taught me many things. One is that the most tragic problem during the Holocaust was not hate or racism, but silence. Many people knew what Hitler was doing was wrong but they said nothing about it. The Holocaust could have been stopped earlier if more people who knew it was wrong said something and stood up to fight against Hitler. There are things we can do so events like the Holocaust will never happen again. We can speak up to protect people that don't get treated correctly because of their ethnicity. People who think they are better than someone else because of their ethnicity is not the right thing to do, but not saying anything is even worse. By not saying anything is like supporting the racism because you don't care enough to speak up and help someone. People who speak up to help are helping to prevent another horrible event like the Holocaust and make sure it will happen never again.

Works Cited

http://www.nytimes.com/2011/10/24/world/europe/jerzy-bielecki-dies-at-90-fell-in-love-in-a-nazi-camp.htmlHevesi, Dennis. "Jerzy Bielecki Dies at 90; Fell in Love in a Nazi Camp." The New York Times. The New York Times, 23 Oct. 2011. Web. 06 Dec. 2016.

Press, The Associated. "Former Inmate Recalls Daring, Romantic Escape from Auschwitz."Haaretz.com. N.p., 20 July 2010. Web. 10 Dec. 2016.

"Jerzy Bielecki, Who Saved Jewish Girlfriend in Auschwitz, Dies at 90." The Washington Post. W P Company, n.d. W

"Jeb. 10 Dec. 2016.

Vashem, Yad. "The Stories of Six Righteous Among the Nations in Auschwitz." Jerzy Bielecki | The Stories of Six Righteous Among the Nations in Auschwitz | Yad Vashem. The World Holocaust Remembrance Center, 2016. Web. 13 Dec. 2016.

Jerzy Bielecki

Dathan Nguyen

The Holocaust is one of the largest genocides in history. It should never be forgotten or repeated. There were many innocent and good-hearted people who were forced to suffer Adolf Hitler's wrath due to their beliefs or ethnicity. Luckily, there were men and women who stood their ground for what was right and helped the victims of the Holocaust.

Jerzy Bielecki was of the few able to escape the Nazi internment and extermination camps. He saved his girlfriend's life with both a cunning plan and a will to be free.

In June 1940, Bielecki, with five friends and the intention to fight with the Polish Armed Forces in France, was falsely convicted of helping the Polish resistance while making an attempted escape from Nazi-occupied Poland to Hungary. The Roman Catholic was tattooed number "243", and was part of the first group sent to the notorious Auschwitz. Bielecki cycled around many jobs and was eventually permanently assigned the occupation of a laborer in a grain warehouse in the camp.

In his years in the camp, Bielecki witnessed and experienced many harsh painful moments. One day, Bielecki saw a group of about 25 men pulling a huge roller. At noon, a man who had been pushing all day with no rest stumbled and fell to his knees. The man was whipped a few times, but he couldn't any move longer. The one and a half ton roller was still moving and his legs were eventually flattened along with the earth. Bielecki was used to witnessing death, maltreatment, and beatings, but this event opened his eyes to the reality that this could be him if he wasn't careful.

On one occasion, Bielecki attempted to escape work due to an injury. He was caught by a Schutzstaffel (S.S.) guard. Their punishment for him was swift and brutal. Bielecki was sentenced to the infamous hanging. A S.S. officer led him to the dark attic of a building, then ordered him to stand on a stool. He tied his hands together with a chain and hooked the chain to a hook on the beams above. Then, without any warning, the S.S. guard aggressively kicked the stool from under Bielecki. Bielecki could feel his arms being pulled apart slowly from his shoulders. It was over 100 degrees Fahrenheit in August and Bielecki had to hang there for an hour.

One day in the storehouse, the door opened and a few girls rushed in. A pretty brunette caught Bilecki's eyes.

In Fall 1943, Cyla Cybulska and her family were sent from Lomza ghetto in northern Poland to Auschwitz. Her parents and sister were immediately killed in gas chambers, whereas she was sent with her brothers to work. The number "29558" was tattooed on her arm. By September, she was the only one in her family who was still alive, and she was assigned the job of repairing grain sacks.

In the Nazi camp, inmates of opposite gender were forbidden to meet. However, Cybulska and Bielecki still met in private. Although they were only able to exchange a few words each day, their love blossomed, and Bielecki became more and more determined to escape with Cybulska.

Their first plan for escape was aborted in early 1944 due to unknown reasons, but Bielecki was determined to be free with Cybulska. From a fellow Polish inmate working at a uniform warehouse, Bielecki was able to slowly piece together a S.S. uniform. Bilecki was also acquire a stolen pass, but was in the name of Storm Trooper Helmush Stehler, who was well known amongst the guards. With a pencil and eraser, Bielecki was able to change the name to Steiner. But another dilemma presented itself. The pass was green, and the camp commandant often changed the color of the pass from time to time, so Bilecki had to wait until the color was green again.

On July 21, 1944, the passes were green and the time was perfect. Dressed as Helmuth Steiner, Bielecki entered the laundry barrack where Cybulska was working for the day and demanded custody of Cybulska from her overseer in fluent German. With every step, the pair was trembling and anxious. Jerzy recalls feeling the part on his back where he was expecting to be shot. When they got to the side gate of the camp, Bielecki held up his arm, shouted "Heil Hitler," and gave the pass to the drowsy guard. The guard stared at the pass and then to Bielecki quizzically. Then in slurred speech, miraculously said , "Ja," which means "Yes," and opened the gate.

Hiding and dozing during the day, and walking through the night, Cybulska soon was very tired. She insisted Bilecki on leaving her, but he refused. Bilecki even carried her whenever he could. After nine nights of walking, they arrived. Word had been spread throughout the area that the prisoners had escaped. It was still very dangerous, so the two decided the best way is to go their separate ways.

Bilecki took Cybuska to a nearby farm while Bielecki stayed with a friend and joined a guerrilla unit of Poland's Home Army. After the war, Bielecki walked 40 kilometers to the farmhouse Cybulska was hiding at but was four days too late. Due to their religions, Bielecki was told that Cybulska had left for Sweden and perished in a hospital. Cybuska was told that Bielecki was killed in a raid.

Thirty-nine years later, Cybuska was telling her escape story to her Polish cleaning lady in the United States. The cleaning lady said that she had heard a story similar to that on television.

Cybuska was eventually able to track down Bilecki's phone number. They soon met at Krakow Airport, where Bielecki presented Cybulska with a bouquet of 39 roses. One for each year spent apart.

The Holocaust was a painful moment for many people. Families were torn

Works Cited

"The Stories of Six Righteous Among the Nations in Auschwitz." Jerzy Bielecki | The Stories of Six Righteous Among the Nations in Auschwitz | Yad Vashem. N.p., n.d. Web. 10 Dec. 2016.

Duell, Mark. "Extraordinary Story of the Brave Auschwitz Prisoner Who Escaped with His Girlfriend by Dressing as an S.S. Officer... before Reuniting Four Decades Later." Daily Mail Online. Associated Newspapers, 24 Oct. 2011. Web. 10 Dec. 2016.

Hevesi, Dennis. "Jerzy Bielecki Dies at 90; Fell in Love in a Nazi Camp." The New York Times. The New York Times, 23 Oct. 2011. Web. 10 Dec. 2016.

"Jerzy Bielecki, Who Saved Jewish Girlfriend in Auschwitz, Dies at 90." The Washington Post. WP Company, n.d. Web. 10 Dec. 2016.

Prisoner in Auschwitz Holocaust Testimonies WW2History.com. N.p., n.d. Web. 10Dec. 2016.

Press, The Associated. "Former Inmate Recalls Daring, Romantic Escape from Auschwitz."Haaretz.com. N.p., 20 July 2010. Web. 10 Dec. 2016.

"An Auschwitz Love Story." San Diego Jewish World. N.p., n.d. Web. 10 Dec. 2016.

Gertruda Babilinska

Diego Medrado Garmatz

Gertruda Babilinska was a true hero of Poland, amongst the thousands of righteous people who risked their lives to save Jews and other undermined races from the terrors of the Holocaust. The Holocaust began in 1938 and was a result of the rise of Adolf Hitler and his corrupt campaign to destroy all races that did not fit Hitler's spectrum of superiority in the Aryan race. The Holocaust claimed the lives of millions of Jews, but fortunately there were heroes who did all they could to rebel against the onslaughts and the Nazi invaders. Babilinska was one such hero Born in 1902 Starogard, Poland she was the eldest of eight children. While working as a nanny, she later on put her life on the line rescuing Jews. Even after her death on January 1st, 1995, Gertruda Babilinska is still a Polish hero to remember today.

Gertruda Babilinska's rescues started in 1939 when Nazi Germans invaded. Gertruda was working as a nanny to the Stolowicki family when the Nazis were taking over Warsaw. While all the traitorous servants and workers left the Stolowickis to perish, Gertruda still remained loyal to them, ensuring that they would survive. Gertruda, Lidia Stolowicki, and her three-year old son Michael Stolowicki fled from Warsaw in an attempt to reach Vilna, where they could hopefully go abroad. Although their getaway car broke down and the roads were constantly being bombarded by bombs the three escapees managed to reach Vilna by a horse-drawn cart.

Shortly upon reaching Vilna, Babilinska and the Stolowickis became stranded along with other Jewish refugees, with barely any money to survive. Sadly, Lidia Stolowickis died due to being unable to cope with illness and poor conditions in April, 1941. Before dying from stroke, Lidia asked for Babilinska to take care of her five-year-old boy and to take him to the Land of Israel if the war ever ended. Living in Vilna soon became more difficult because the Soviet Union was attacked by the Nazis, and they occupied the town. The Nazis began to kill a number of Jews and turn the town into a ghetto in September, while Gertruda used her resourcefulness to obtain fraud papers and a baptismal birth certificate to convince the Nazi soldiers that Michael was her nephew. This kept both of them out of the ghetto and enabled them to live like local Germans.

As times turned for worse, Gertruda used her knowledge of the German language to write petitions to the authorities to complain about the conditions in the town. In turn she received dairy products, some eggs, and meat to get by. Both Gertruda and Michael lived in constant danger and had to endure hazardous situations. Nazi Germans where constantly making raids in the refugees' apartments, checking for any clues of rebellion or escaped Jews. Meanwhile, Gertruda went her way to help all she could, from taking care of fellow acquaintances' in the ghetto, to getting Michael to a Jewish doctor living in the area when Michael went ill. Gertruda did all she could to help Jews in need, ensuring that they would survive until the war ended.

Finally, on May 8, 1945, World War II ended after the Allies beat the Nazis and Adolf Hitler died, along with his inhumane campaign. Shortly after the war ended, there was still one promise that Gertruda refused to break, which was getting Michael to the Land of Israel. Before going on the journey, Gertruda traveled to her family's home in Warsaw to say goodbye to them. While they used persuasion to get Gertruda to stay, she refused, sticking to her promise. After saying her farewell, Gertruda left to join a group of surviving Jewish refugees leaving the country, to get away from all the lingering destruction, death, and despair that hung in the air. Unfortunately, immigration to British-controlled Palestine was restricted, so Gertruda and Michael set out to a DP (displaced persons' camp) in Germany, where they would stay until a passage would be opened for the refugees to embark on a boat that would take them to Israel illegally. Even with the reassurances of a Jewish defense force, the Hagana, that Michael would be safe with them and he would reach Israel, Gertruda remained by his side, refusing to part with the young boy.

In 1947 the boat, 'Exodus' left France to get to Israel. It contained Holocaust survivors including Gertruda and 11-year-old Michael. While the boat wasn't noticed initially, the Exodus was eventually intercepted by British warships and the distraught passengers were forcibly put on the warships then sailing back to Europe. The passengers however, refused to disembark once in the French harbor. The ship then went to port in Germany, where the disgruntled refugees had to live in another displaced persons' camp. Gertruda still refused to give up even with major setbacks. She and Michael were eventually able to set foot on Israel soil in 1948. Although Gertruda completed Lidia's request, she continued on raising Michael as a son while making a living by cleaning houses and living in a room of a house. Gertruda had helped many other Jews over the years during World War II, but fulfilling her promise to see to it that Michael live in Israel, a distant country may have been the most memorable one of all.

In conclusion, I learned that Gertruda was a true hero of Poland, helping the helpless when they needed it by providing essentials, such as food and water, and fulfilling a promise of a mother who wanted her child to be able to reach and live peacefully in the Land of Israel. I also learned how difficult it must have been to help others and at the same time help them stay hidden from the Nazis. This story about Gertruda Babilinska impacted me, because it is difficult to stay true to one's word and fulfill a promise to make sure that someone will stay safe and survive under such difficult circumstances. Gertruda was undaunted never forgetting her important promise. She took many risks in hope that she would make it come true. The story also showed me that it is hard to do right when it seems that there is no hope left such as in the Holocaust-one of the worst mass genocidal massacres in human history. I understand that the Holocaust impacted the world as an inhumane, racist campaign to slaughter all other races that were cruelly labeled 'inferior.' The Holocaust killed millions of innocent lives at the hands of a dictator and a terrible powerful army. Never again. Never again should we repeat the past. Never again should we let another twisted mind brainwash others into slaughtering all that do not fit their idea of "perfection". Never again should we have to hear, see, or breathe another Holocaust. Never again should anyone kill to exterminate a group or groups of people. Even small steps to ensure that this never happens again in our lives or in the future will change the lives of many others. Step number one is to educate others about the Holocaust. If we can educate people on how bad the Holocaust was, they can spread the word so that everyone is aware that there should not be another slaughter, and we will save lives. Step ones is to stand up for others who are being tormented. It doesn't matter if you are just a kid. Stand up for others so that the bully will back down and the bullying will stop quickly rather than leaving it to escalate. Step three is to deactivate the threat as fast as possible. In the Holocaust, no one stopped the threat until it was at its height. For example, if you alert others that a small fire is started on a house, firefighters, or other friends can put it out quickly. But if you wait, the fire will turn into an inferno and the house will burn down by the time you get support. With these important steps, we can ensure that another Holocaust will never happen.

Works Cited

"Gertruda Babilińska." Yadvashem. Yad Vashem The World Holocaust Center, n.d. Web. 06 Dec.

2016. < http://www.yadvashem.org/righteous/stories/babilinska >.

John Damski

Diego Valencia

As a kid, John Damski always did well in sports. He decided to join the local gymnastics team. There, he had the first incident with a Jew (his friend, the family of Dauman). One day a guy from the district organization came to their practice and made a big deal about Jews being in their group. The man seemed furious with the fact Jews were in the group. The oldest of the three Dalman brothers stood up and told him that the Jews were just as good as the Poles when it came to patriotism. A day or two passed and the whole organization fell apart because Jews were in the group. Eventually, everyone in the organization basically dropped out.

John Damski's next encounter with a Jew was in 1935. John Damski, at the time was at training camp. A guy named Israelowicz (the former state champion of the 100m run) was in the camp. According to John Damski, Israelowicz was the first Jew to show him what anti-Semitism (racism to the Jews) was all about. One day, John Damski and Israelwicz were walking through the streets and they saw a poster of this girl name Joan Crawford. This poster was promoting travel to the U.S. to see her in a film. Israelwicz started complaining about other Jews and himself couldn't go to a foreign ministry and get a passport. This is when John Damski realized that Jews were treated differently.

John Damski's next encounter after that with a Jew was when he was a grown man. One day, he ran into an old school friend and his girlfriend at a night club. They started to have a couple drinks, then all of the sudden John's friend's girlfriend saw a Jew and said, "To hell with the Jews!" John was ashamed, especially because he knew those two girls. His school friend then, slapped his girlfriend in the face. He was mad that someone could say such a thing in public when it's not even their business to worry about.

These three encounter with the Jews showed John Damski that anti-Semitism was a big problem. John Damski hated this fact that it was a real problem. John Damski wanted it to stop.

On September 1, 1939, the Germans invaded. Unfortunately, John Damaski was in the army. He was taken as POW (prisoner of war). On the way to the camp, John Damski managed to escape. It wasn't a big deal for him to escape, logically escaping a night would be easier because you can hardly see when it's dark. He returned back to Gdynia, and found a job working for an electrical type company. Later, some Germans came and said that since John Damski was born in Germany and spoke German almost as excellent as Polish, he may as well be a German. John Damski didn't think about it twice and said no, he knew he would never do it. John Damski knew he wasn't German, he accepted himself as 100% polish. The Germans, then had kicked him out of town and said he had town twenty four hours to evacuate the city. This basically happened to all the Polish people in the surrounding area.

Early in December, 1939. John Damski and two friends tried to travel to Hungary, and eventually move to France. December 9th John Damaski was really close were really close to the Hungarian border. Then, German soldiers caught them, and delivered them to the Gestapo. The German soldiers made his friend and John Damski undress completely. As they were naked the Gestapo made all sorts of insinuating remarks, threatening to shoot them, etc. Then they sent him and his friend to a jail at Sanok near the Ukraine. He basically went to jail for no reason. The only people who were in the cell were political prisoners, doctors, lawyers, and professionals. All the men totaled to be about three hundred forty-five men altogether. The living conditions for them were horrid. They had forty-five people in a cell that should only be used for about seven people. There was basically no room at all for them, they basically had to sleep on their sides. The toilet was just a bucket. They were never allowed to go out. Fleas, flies, gnats, spiders, etc. were also there in their cell.

On June 14th the middle of the night, the cell men had heard trucks. John Damski looked outside through a small opening and saw trucks. The trucks were gathering prisoners and loading them into the trucks. A few seconds later, everyone knew what was happening. Before you knew it everyone started to pray. It didn't matter if they didn't believe in a God beforehand, they just prayed. They were hoping not to get shot like the other unlucky people, they wanted to live.

Later, everyone was transferred to Auschwitz, but John. Then, a man came and told John Damski something, with a puzzled look on his face. He told him, that he had no record of him. John told him that he was arrested at the local railroad station, but he was looking for a job at the battery factory. He then told the officer he was German, at first he didn't believe John Damski. Suddenly, he used a German expression and the officer was impressed. He then was given permission to leave the jail cell, but the officer wanted him to leave town.

August 9th, John Damski was released from the Prison. He was only 97 pounds when he left! Later, he wanted to go to Lublin to find his brother Zygmunt, but he couldn't afford a train ticket. John Damski was then kind of sneaky and boarded the train without a ticket. Unfortunately, the train only traveled 100 miles so he had to walk to the next station and keep boarding the train without a ticket. Finally, he got to Lublin and his brother. His brother and John decided to make a plan and move to Zamosc, because it was a small and quiet town.

Eventually, John Damski found a job with the Germans building an aircraft field as an electrician. Sometime later, his boss said that he had to go to Berlin for two weeks. John Damski then, had an Idea about looking into the Zamosc Jewish labor camp. There were a couple hundred Jews there. He found the supervisor and told him that he needed a fellow electrician to work with him. He found this guy named Feignbaum, he eventually became his chief assistant. He brought him to the aircraft and people started complaining that he was there.

Days, later his boss told him he needed more electricians, so John suggested that he would go to Warsaw Ghetto. Then when John was going to leave, Jews came up to him and asked him for the lift so they can see their friends.

Once John got into Warsaw, he was surprised, he thought it was like a whole other world of life. John then walked a little ways and saw a guy lying on the sidewalk with his hand sticking out. John Damski thought he must have been at least 60. The man then asked him for a piece of bread, right when he said that John Damski felt bad for him.

After they found the guys they needed, they wanted to leave right away. They got into the truck and asked if everyone was ready. He looked back at the Jews to look for a sign, but he noticed something weird, he saw about ten Jews hiding underneath a canvas. John had to make a quick decision and decided that he should smuggle the Jews. They drove for a while and was past the Warsaw, so John Damski dropped the Jews off.

When John came back home to Zamosc, he and his brother were renting a small room in a two family house. The Rozen family were the people allowed John to live there. Later on he met their daughter Helen. In 1941 Helen's sister (now to be Christine) came from Lvov to be with her mom and dad. With the walls very thin, John Damski became in love when he first heard her voice.

Eventually, John Damski and Christine had a thing for each other. Christine and John had to go through all sorts of trouble, but later they got "married". Once they got married they started saving lots of Jews. If you were a Jew, you were told to find John Damski.

Now, John Damski is a hero. He will always be known for saving Jews during the war. He will always be remebed for his actions and what he has done. We also must remember that it can never happen again, no one would need go through all the trouble saving all these people. No one wants to see people going through death again.

Never Again

Works Cited Page
I would like to thank the follow site for giving me the resources to write this essay:
"John Damski Story, Part 1-7." John Damski Story, Part 1-7. N.p., n.d. Web. 14 Dec. 2016.

Gertruda Babilinska

Dominic Carrasco

Gertruda was born Starograd, near Gdansk in 1902. Her family consisted of ten people, her mom, her dad, five sisters, two brothers, and herself. Gertruda was the eldest of all her siblings. Gertruda's father worked at the post office. Her family was very religious and Gertruda was raised Catholic. At the age of nineteen she began working as a nanny in Warsaw. The family decided to move to Palestine and offered Gertruda to stay with them, but she decided to stay in Poland. She then began to work for a rich, Jewish family called the Stolowitzky. Gertruda lived in the family's mansion taking care of their baby daughter. Later on the daughter died and Gertruda stayed to look after Mrs.Stolowitzky because she was devastated that her daughter had died. In 1936 the couple had a son, Mickey, and Gertruda became his nanny. In 1939 danger struck, the Holocaust began.

Mr.Stolowitzky was taken to Auschwitz. Mrs.Stolowitzky was scared of what would happen later on and decided to move to Vilna, because she heard it was safer over there. Before they left to go to Vilna Mrs.Stolowitzky made Gertruda promise that if anything happened to her she take Mickey to Israel after the war. They began their journey to Vilna by car, eventually the car broke down and they continued by horse-drawn cart. The roads were being bombed and everyone was frightened, Gertruda took charge they eventually reached Vilna. With the little money they all had they rented an apartment. The mother of Mickey began to become ill and in April 1941 she died and was buried in the Jewish cemetery. Now it was just Gertruda and Mickey. At this point Mickey was five years old. Along with themselves there were many other Jewish people there in Vilna. The Nazis would give poisonous candy out on the streets to kids.

At this time Gertruda needed to teach Mickey to not take anything from strangers. The Germans attacked the Soviet Union two months later. Shortly after, the killing of the Jews began to take place.

In September the ghetto was established and Gertruda had Mickey registered as her nephew to hide him from the Germans. Their situation started to become worse and they had to move to a smaller apartment. Gertruda used her knowledge of German to write petitions on behalf of the local people. In returns for thee petitions she received eggs, dairy products and poultry. The Germans were in the habit of conducting raids on the apartmants in Warsaw. From where Gertruda and Mickkey lived they could see the ghetto and were a witness of the grouping

of the Jews. Mickey eventually fell sick and Gertruda took him to see a doctor inside of the ghetto. She was scared to take Mickey to this doctor because Mickey was a Jewish boy and the doctor was German. Mickey went to the doctor several times and eventually began to feel better. Gertruda asked the doctor what she owed him and he told her that she owed him nothing because she made him feel like a man. It was clear now that the doctor knew that Mickey was a Jewish boy. When the war ended Gertruda kept her promise to Mrs.Stolowitzky and together Mickey and Gertruda began their journey to Israel.

They got on the first ship to Israel, the Exodus. The ship was very crowded and they could not dock in Palestine. Gertruda worked as a made and looked after Mickey. She lived in a small room and made living cleaning houses. Gertruda kept her promise to Mrs.Stolowitzky and is know as the nanny that kept her promise.

I learned many things while doing this essay. I learned that you should always keep your promises and that sometimes you need to put others lives before your own. Gertruda kept her promise to Mrs.Stolowitzky by taking Mickey to Israel after the war was done. She put Mickey's life before her own by taking care of him throughout the entire war. If she was caught protecting Mickey she would have been killed because Mickey is Jewish. Learning about this person made me realize that I am so lucky to liv in a time where this wasn't happening. This was a terrible time to live in and this was one of the worst events to happen around the world. The Holocaust was the time of the Nazis and the time when Adolf Hitler killed between five and six million Jews. Some Jews were killed at concentration camps and others were killed by gas chambers. The Holocaust impacted many people's lives and many people were tortured by this event. Everybody at concentration camps weighed about fifty pounds and the weakest people were killed and the strong people were kept alive and were forced to do hard labor to survive. This was a terrible time to live and is definitely one of the worst events to ever happen throughout the world. "Never Again". To make sure this never happens we should choose carefully who we choose to be leader. We could also make better and safer choices within our country.

Works Cited

"KVIE Public Television." KVIE. N.p., 04 Dec. 2016. Web. 04 Dec. 2016. N.p., n.d. Web.

Zytkiewicz, Michal

Draven Her

In the year 1930, a huge decrease in money hit Germany and caused tone of people to go homeless or lose their jobs. This was right after World War I and the German's confidence dropped dramatically after their lost. This meant that they need a new leader which was Adolf Hitler. He formed a organization called the Nazis which took over a lot of power in January 1993. The Nazis believed that the Germanic race were the only master race. But to the Nazis, they thought that the Jewish people were an inferior threat and started a Holocaust to exterminate all of the Jew race. Now, Zytkiewicz Michal saved many Jewish people during this time. He was born in Poland in the year of 1896 to the year 1946. He was a painter and a building contract worker before the war. He had one wife Irena who was also a Jew and had no kids. Michal saved people by hiding them into hideouts and was able to save 5 out of 6 people after all.

Michal saved people by hiding them inside small bunkers or known as hideouts to keep them away from the Nazis. Hideouts during this time were very risky, because if you were caught saving people who escaped or were inside these camps, you were sent to the same place where they were at. Michal was able to get away with this and was successful in saving many people. Michal's first hideout was in a warehouse which was burnt in the year 1939 while Michal invested a lot of money to rebuild it and it eventually turned into a hideout for Jews. His wife Irena and Michal brought many Jews to safety in these hideouts and it eventually paid off by saving Nina Bonio'wka, Izabella Bonio'wka, Leon Rappaport, Henryk Bonio'wka, and Feliks Brodzki.

Michal traveled to many places during the Holocaust on foot and unarmed to save many people. One place Michal traveled was to Czestochowa where he actually lived before the war and this was where he did all of his hard work. Secondly, he went to Dwikozy where he found Nina Bonio'wka by having Irena his wife, looking for her who was in need of help. Next, Michal traveled to Burak'ow Maly to hide Nina after she was betrayed by the many people who lived there in Dwikozy. Fourth, he went back to Dwikozy where he was able to save Feliks Brodzki who would have died if it wasn't for Michal. Michal traveled back to Burak'ow Maly where he saved a few other Jews and sent them safely back to the hideout. Michal then returned to Dwikozy where Halina and Mieczyslaw Szaszkiewicz who were the House sole inhabitants who took care of the hideout people but Michal didn't worry about them, and he still got up and took care of the endangered Jews. After a Liberation in 1944 Nina, wanted to thank Michal for all of the things he did for her but as she was traveling to him, he was already infected tuberculosis and died knowing that he did something good for many people. Michal was able to save many people and was successful in doing so during the Holocaust.

In the history of the Holocaust, Michal is someone who should be honored by everyone.

Michal saved 6 people at this horrible time. Saving 6 people is hard work because you would have to be super secretive and put safety measures everywhere. After saving them, Michal would go to the hideout and give those people some food so that they would feel like it was home to them. Some of them even paid if they had money and those who didn't, didn't. The people who were held captive did not have a home anymore because it was either burnt down or torn down by the Germans. The Jews that were brought to the hideout were lucky enough to survive because Adolf Hitler was executing all of the Jew race. But Michal still hid the Jews and risked his life for the people of Poland. He was also a Jew and wanted to help the other Jews who were trying to escape. Michal didn't want any fame or glory, but he does deserve respect for saving at least a few people. After the Holocaust ended Michal died in 1946 by dying to a disease, but Michal did a good deed to the people who he saved and ended in him dying.

After all, I learned that the Holocaust is a horrible event to talk about from the people who still survived today. I could not imagine what it would be like to lose my family and sisters and brother and all of my belongings. This person had a huge impact on me because it made me change about how I feel about people who go through hard times in their lives such as losing a family member. I understand that the people who talk about this that survived it are true heroes such as Michal. I now understand why the people who survived the Holocaust now say "Never Again." In the future this can be prevented by stopping bullying and just in general being nice to people can stop this from happening again. The Holocaust should "Never again" happen again in the history of the future.

Works Cited Page

Hem, Yad Vas. "Zytkiewicz, Michal." Yadvashem. Yadvashem, n.d. Web.

Wojan. "Intro To Holocaust." Intro To Holocaust. Elk Grove, Sacarmento. 20 Nov. 2016. Lecture.

Jozef Balwierz

Dylan Barrett

The Holocaust was one of the single worst events in history. It was created by Hitler and the Nazis army and lasted for 12 years. The Holocaust lasted from 1/30/1933 to 5/8/1945. While millions of people died, there were also so many people who risked their own lives to help others. During this time period the Nazis murdered over 6 million Jewish people and over 400,000 more non Jewish people. By 1945 the Germans killed 2 out of every 3 Jewish people in the camps. To achieve this they set up a ghetto and concentration camps. The Nazis main concentration camps were Auschwitz, Belzec, and Dachau. In the Holocaust timeline there were several hundred camps. In 1945, after the war ended, Anglo-American and Soviet troops entered the concentration camps and discovered piles of corpses, bones, and human ashes. Soldiers also found thousands of Jewish and non-Jewish survivors suffering from starvation and disease. There they were housed in hundreds of refugee centers in Germany. The United Nations Relief and Rehabilitation Administration (and the occupying armies of the United States, Great Britain, and France) administered these camps. In December 1945, President Harry Truman issued a directive that loosened quota restrictions on immigration to the US of persons displaced by the Nazi regime. Under this directive, more than 41,000 displaced persons immigrated to the United States. Approximately 28,000 were Jewish people. Other Jewish refugees in Europe emigrated as displaced persons or refugees to Canada, Australia, New Zealand, western Europe, Mexico, South America, and South Africa.

Jozef Balwierz was a hero thanks to his kindness toward others and his his willingness to put his life on the line for others during the Holocaust. He was born 01/01/1919 and his nationality was Polish. Before the Holocaust, Josef worked in a factory that belonged to the Liebeskind family in Lwow. During the Holocaust, Shmuel Liebeskind, his wife Zofia, and two daughters, Rita and Irena, were taken to the ghetto. Unfortunately Shmuel Liebeskind was killed while in the ghetto. The good thing was that in 1942 Shmuel's wife and two daughters escaped the ghetto. When Josef found this out, he found them and brought them back to his house, helping them any way he could. The place were he was hiding and where he stayed during the Holocaust was in Prokocim, Krakow, Poland. The way he rescued people was by hiding them. He rescued many people including Rita and Irena's cousin Idel Bardach. She stayed with them for 3 weeks before finding a job as a house keeper for a German family. When the situation got worse Josef and the Liebeskinds went to work in Austria. Then, after the war, they returned to Poland and Josef married Irena Liebeskind. They later moved to Brazil. When asked why he saved and helped people he said it was a merely human duty. He didn't do it for an award nor did he expect one. While he did survive the Holocaust, he died in 1945. At the Wall of Honor in Sao Paulo, Brazil., Jozef was honored for his sacrifice on 06/08/2007 There he is honored as a hero for helping the families of those people he saved and a hero to the people he saved. During the Holocaust he wrote a book called OD Krakowa Do Brazi.

With the end of World War 2 and collapse of the Nazi regime, survivors of the Holocaust, which totaled over 200,00, faced the daunting task of rebuilding their lives. Camps were built for displaced people who couldn't return to their homes because of the threats of danger from some anti-Semitic people who were still in the country. These camps remained in existence until 1957 when all of the people in the camps had been re-homed. With little in the way of financial resources and few, if any, surviving family members, most eventually emigrated from Europe to start their lives back again. Between 1945 and 1952, more than 80,000 Holocaust survivors immigrated to the United States. Beginning in 1953, the German Government chose to acknowledge the German people's responsibilities for the crimes they committed by making payments to individual Jews and to the Jewish people. Some names of survivors from the Holocaust are Thomas Buergenthal, Aron and Lisa Derman, Regina Gelb, Blanka Roshschild, and Norman Salsitz.

Throughout my research for this essay I have learned many things. Not only have I learned about the Holocaust but also about Jozef Balwierz and the sacrifices he made. Three main things that I have learned about are how many people made choices that had helped people, people that made choices to hurt people and families, and then finally a lot of people just stood around living normal lives not caring what was happening to other people. People like Jozef risked their own lives to try to help people that were in danger and suffering. Those are the type of people that I look up to. Some people, the Nazis army, were trying to find people just so they could either make them work hard and torture them or just kill them. Those are the type of people that make me think that the world is very sad. The people that just stand there like nothing is happening I don't get mad at. They probably didn't want to risk getting killed themselves. I don't like to say this but if I were in their shoes I would probably do the same. The impact the Holocaust has had on us is that we can change the world so this doesn't have to happen again. I understand that the Holocaust was a horrible thing and its impact was huge. The steps that we can do to have this never happen again are simple. Don't let the government have to much power and have people respect each other regardless of the color of their skin, their religious beliefs or how they choose to live their lives. I hope that this will never happen again and the world will not let something this huge happen again.

Works Cited

Hazikaron, Har. "Names of Righteous by Country." Digital Collections - Yad Vashem. Webmaster@yadvashem.org.il, 1 Jan. 2016. Web. 11 Dec. 2016.

History.com, Staff. "The Holocaust." History.com. A&E Television Networks, 2009. Web. 11 Dec. 2016.

"The Holocaust: An Introductory History." An Introductory History of the Holocaust. Ed. Jason Levine. American-Israeli Cooperative Enterprise, 2016. Web. 11 Dec. 2016.

Karp, Pam. "Jozef Balwierz." Geni_family_tree. Geni.com, 21 Jan. 2016. Web. 11 Dec. 2016.

Adamek, Malgorzata

Dylan Forbeck

 The Holocaust was a horrible time for not only Jewish people all over the World. In the 1930's, an economic depression struck Germany after they had lost WW2. This provided a chance for a new leader that would later be known as Adolf Hitler. Hitler started a political propaganda. Jews were not allowed to hold public offices like businesses along the streets. He also deprived Jews of their citizenship in 1933. The Jews were forced to wear a golden star to be identified. Later as the ruling got worse for the Jews, they fled Germany in safety. Hitler ordered all Jews under German control to be moved to ghetto's. Once in those ghetto's they formed resistance groups to try to make an attack on the guards and other high ranked authority's. When genocide came around , a system of killing of entire people, the Jewish community began to decrease fast. This went for all races, inferior had to be eliminated because they could overrun Germany some day. When the mass killing began the German soldiers rounded up everybody in the ghettos and were shot or were taken to concentration camps to be killed or were enslaved laborers. Hitler wanted to speed up the elimination of Jews. In the camps, the people had been tattooed, had their possessions confiscated, inhumane science experiments, and men, women, and children were separated. The Final stage was when the extermination camps were built and equipped with gas chambers to kill faster. Most of the extermination camps were built in Poland and could kill as much as 6,000 people a day. 63% of the Jewish community in Europe was killed. 91% of the Jews in Poland were killed during the ruling of Hitler's Regime.

Malgorzata opened the gates to 17 members of the Illegal Jewish Zionist pioneer underground movement. When she realized that all these killing is ghettos and concentration camps were to exterminate and get rid of all Jewish and non-German people, she had to act fast. Years later she made underground movements to try and stop these all so wrong killings. She said not to be like sheep and be slaughtered but to fight back against Hitler's Regime. By the end of december of 1941 the pioneers decided to leave the safety of the convents and go back to the ghetto to establish a movement group. The first move to this movement was to get weapons. A nun named Borkowska was the first person to sneak in weapons (grenades) even though she has promised not to use violence, she had to or else she and everyone in the group would also die without weapons to fight back. In 1943 a suspicious Natzi of her mounted, the Germans had Borkowska arrested because of smuggling grenades into the ghetto. Even though she was arrested she took one for the team and got multiple weapons into the camp before arrested. Borkowska's help will never be forgotten by the Zionist pioneers who had immigrated to Israel after the war, but in only 1984 was contact with her reestablished. By the time she was old and 84 she was living in a small apartment in Warsaw.

Under Hitler's rule I learned many things in the story I read about Adamek, Malgorzata. One major thing I learned is to not treat someone differently because of their color, religion, believes, or personality. Everybody should be treated equally and that was not the case in the 1930's. In the 1930's horrible things happened that are farther more than bullying. It was a racist ruler who didn't care about anybody else but his kind which was the Germans. I have learned not to go with the majority vote that I don't even agree with but to stand up for what is right. That is what Adamek, Malgorzata did in the camp to save 16 lives. If more people stood up for what is right and we're not scared this would have been stopped very quickly and not last over 10 years. The impact that this person had on my life is that one person can make a change and not many people think that because either they are insecure or scared to make the change. This also taught me to work with others even if you don't know who they are but what they are trying to conquer. The words "Never Forget" mean to not forgot this tragic time in history and not to make this same mistake Hitler and the Germans did in the 1930's. If this happens again today I think it will be ended a lot qucker because of the fact that this has already happened and more and more people will stand up to what is wrong and not go 10 years with people in horrible conditions. The step that I can do if this happens again is to use my kind words at first and not use violence. If that doesnt work then I will go to violence but that is on extreme measures. If this happens today all of the countries will stop it because they relized the damage that was ahppenign to the world during this horrible time.

Bando- Stupnicka, Anna

Dylan Lam

The Holocaust was a very important time in history not just for the jews but for everyone. The Holocaust all started in 1933 when Adolf Hitler became leader. Jews were gathered to "Ghettos" and there were many few people that helped the Jews. After that most Jews were taken to internment camps like Auschwitz to camp Omen. There many jews were being killed. The Nazis killed about two-thirds of all Jews living in Europe. There were approximately 9 million people living in Europe that got killed in the time of World War 2. It was hard to live while Jewish people all around you were being killed by Hitler and The Horrible Nazi. "Heil Hitler!", the army said as they killed Jews "Heil Hitler!". When Hitler first became leader one of the first things Hitler did was making Jews wear Yellow stars that said "Jude". Hitler also targeted the disabled, Gypsies, and the homosexual. The Nazi killed all of those people and to be suprised that Hitler couldlive with himself while killing millions of people. All of this horror was just because a few Jews made fun of him. Because he became leader he thought he could do anything he wanted like torture and kill all Jews. Ever since that day there are only a few survivors left from the holocaust to tell all of us about the horrifying moments they went through.

Going deeper into the Holocaust people were wondering if some Jews fought back when all of this happened. Not Exactly. Many Jew revolted and there was a special "organization" or revolution that occurred called the Resistance. The Resistance was not a fighting in violence kind of thing but a fight back to not following the rules and keep religiously believing in what the Jews believed in without the Nazi knowing. A quarter of the resistance is abut fightin back with violently agianst the Nazi with few of the guns and resourses they had.

There were few people that stood up to Hitler against his time of terror and one of those people was a young 12 year old girl named Anna Bando-Stupnicka.

Anna Bando-Stupnicka was a 12 year old girl that loved in Warsaw loved to give back by going to the store with her mom and buying food and books for the Jews in the Ghettos. By the age of 12 Anna was a big hero by smuggling a Jew named Liliana so she won't be killed. The Jew got smuggled Liliana by disguising her with Anna's school uniform so that allowed Liliana to pass as a christian. After that Liliana was considered her "cousin" for the next four years. Anna being at a very young age wanted to risk her life of being caught by the Nazi to help Jews keep their lives.

There were many other people that Anna helped like Ryszard Grynberg and Mikolaj Borenstein. Ryszard Grynberg was the son of re-war acquaintances, who stayed in Anna's apartment until the finally got him "aryan" documents. Mikolaj Borenstein was a Jewish Doctor and wound up in the Ghettos. Mikolaj bathed, slept, and ate at Anna's apartment. One day Anna and her mother got a Kennkarte or an identity document so Mikolaj and The 11 year old Liliana to emigrate to France.

All of this ended in 1945 when Allied forces invaded germany and Adolf Hitler knew he was defeated. Adolf Hitler commied suicide instead of being tortured like most of the Nazis.

This horrifying moment in history has left many few people still injured and has heft stories to tell and pictures to see of this time of our world being ruined my the disliked Adolf Hitler.

In Irena Gut Opdyke's Hands

Elena Waechter

In ancient times, the word holocaust meant the sacrifice of an animal to God by fire. Today, holocaust has a different meaning because of the events that took place in Germany before and during World War II. The Holocaust was a horrible event in world history. It was a mass killing of the Jewish people and many other persecuted groups. The German political group called the Nazis, led by Adolf Hitler, organized and carried out the Holocaust during which large numbers of ordinary people turned against those who they felt were inferior. However, many other people also felt that this was wrong and vowed to help the Jews. These righteous individuals risked their own lives to save the Jews during the Holocaust. In Poland, there were many people who were righteous and helped the Jews. Among these was Irena Gut Opdyke.

Irena was born in Poland in 1921. Her family was Catholic. She had always wanted to be a nurse and help people. In 1939, when she was eighteen years old, she succeeded. She finished nursing school in central Poland, and joined the Polish army as a nurse. Then, when Russia invaded Poland that same year, she and other nurses were captured by Russian soldiers. Three of the soldiers attacked her and left her in the snow to die. However, she was found and brought to a Russian hospital where she recovered. She was later able to return to Poland, which was now occupied by Germany.

She began working in a German munitions factory to supply the troops. The factory was full of fumes. One day, the fumes in the factory caused her to faint next to a German Major. Irena looked like she could be German because she had blue eyes and blond hair. However, when he asked her if she was German, she said no. The Major liked her honesty so he gave her a new job cooking for and serving German soldiers. One day, after completing an errand for the major, she saw a Jewish neighborhood called a ghetto. She said, " There were all kinds of people, pregnant women, children screaming,"Mama, Mama!" Then I saw a woman with an infant in her arms. With one movement of his hand, the SS man pulled the baby away and threw it to the ground...I could not understand. But later on I realized that God gave us free will to be good or bad. So I asked God for forgiveness and said if the the opportunity arrived I would help these people." That day she made a promise to herself and God that she would help the Jewish people.

The Major she was serving soon transferred to a different Polish town. He had taken her with him. There she met and befriended twelve Jewish people who were working in the laundry room. One night while serving dinner to the Major, she overheard a German officer say that they would raid the barracks. A few days later, she heard them making plans to kill an entire ghetto in Ternapol, and she knew her friends would all be killed. She knew that she had to do something. About three days later, a miracle happened. The Major called her and told her, " I have a villa and I want you to be my housekeeper." She smiled and accepted the offer. She would hide her friends there. They would stay in the attic when the major was downstairs and in the cellar when he was upstairs.They had only one problem. One of the couples, the Hallers, was expecting a baby soon. The baby would make too much noise. They said they would give up the baby, but Irena refused to let them. She would make sure that the baby remained with them. When the Major left the villa, she would lock the door to insure that her friends would not be found. One day, she forgot and the Major walked in on them. He was shaking. He went to his library to his phone. Irena ran after him. He was screaming at her, saying," I trusted you. How could you do this behind my back?" She started crying, kissing his hands and holding his knees, saying, "They are my friends." He left saying he would return with his decision. Irena ran to her friends. She said if she did not return in three days she was either dead or arrested and they would have to run. They were hiding in the cellar where the Major would not find them. They were ready to leave. He returned three hours later and said he would keep her secret but only if she was his, willingly. She said, " It was not easy, but it was a small price to pay for so many lives." This went on for several months until the Germans started losing the war. Then the Russians came and they were free. On May 4, 1944, a little boy was born, born free. His name was Roman Haller.

Irena then went to live in a displaced persons camp with many Jews and other people who were left homeless after the war. A delegation from the United Nations came there and an American, William Opdyke, interviewed her. He said that the United States would love to have her as a citizen. She accepted and lived at first in New York working alone for five years. She went to the U.N. one day to have lunch in the cafeteria and there she started talking to a man she soon recognized as William Opdyke. They fell in love and were married six weeks after their lunch. Two years after their marriage they had a little girl.

Even after the war was over, Irena never told of the horrors she had experienced and what she had done for her Jewish friends. It was not until the early seventies, when a newspaper article came out suggesting that the Holocaust had never happened, that she decided to speak out about her experiences. From then on, she gave speeches all over the country about the Holocaust. She made her final speeches at age eighty-two. She died in 2003 a proud and happy woman.

Irena taught me that the Holocaust was a terrible incident in human history that destroyed millions of lives. About six million Jews were killed. Millions of other non-Jews were killed as well. Yet, hearing about Irena's story gives us hope. It tells us that one person can have an amazing impact if she puts others before herself. We must teach each other to respect one another and must continue to remember the Holocaust to ensure that we never let it happen again. Irena Gut Opdyke said it best when she said, "Hate is easy, it takes real courage to love. We have an opportunity everyday to show love---give it out freely. One person can make a difference."

Works Cited

"Holocaust - Non-Jewish Holocaust Victims." Holocaust - Non-Jewish Victims of the Holocaust - Pictures - Stories. N.p., n.d. Web. 23 Nov. 2016.

"Irene Opdyke | ,." Irene Opdyke | ,. N.p., n.d. Web. 23 Nov. 2016.

Opdyke, Irene Gut, and Jennifer Armstrong. In My Hands: Memories of a Holocaust Rescuer. New York: Knopf, 1999. Print.

"Rescuers: Irene Opdyke." PBS. PBS, n.d. Web. 12 Dec. 2016.

Dr. Miron Lisikiewicz

Elinor Washington

 The Holocaust was one of the largest genocides of all time. More than six million people were murdered. A whole population was extinguished and almost completely wiped out. So much blood was shed because of one reason. Everyone who was not of the Aryan race was considered an inferior. The most persecuted race was the Jews, and Adolf Hitler would stop at nothing to diminish their population to a small amount, even willing to make the Jewish population extinct.

Dr. Miron Lisikiewicz is a hero. He was a Catholic man, who was Polish. Although he only saved two lives, those of Rena Dworecka and Sala Friedman, every life saved counts. Miron Lisikiewicz was the district doctor in Krosno, Lwow in Poland. Krosno was a small town with beautiful buildings, and lovely rivers in southeastern Poland. Strong laws were enforced that restricted Jews from living in this town, until they were changed by the Austrian Empire. Jews then began to populate the small town, and find jobs. Miron lived and worked in this town, which is not far from the Lesko ghetto. Ghettos were crowded with over-population. At this time, Jews populating the Lesko ghetto, were being deported to a labor camp. Miron was an intelligent man, and was aware of the risks that came with helping Jews. He could lose his job, or be put in jail for harboring Jews. Even with consequences that he could await, Miron wanted to help two woman that were his colleagues once. He heard about the deportations occurring, and sent his assistant to rescue Rena Dworecka and Sala Friedman from the cemetery, where they begged for salvation. Miron hid these two Jews in his attic from August of 1942, to July of 1944. During this time he sheltered the woman, brought food to them, and cared for their needs. In 1944, the Red Army liberated those from the Lesko ghetto, and town of Krosno. Miron extended his generosity to Rena and Sala, as they lived with him for many more years as he cared for the refugees. Out of all that live in the Lesko ghetto, only four survived the holocaust, two of the survivors were Sala Friedman and Rena Dworecka.

Today, Dr. Miron Lisikiewicz is honored for his courageousness, selflessness, and bravery with a tree and a plaque with his name on it. Dr, Lisikiewicz brave actions teach us a valuable lesson, that we should always do the right thing and help others, even if the outcome does not turn out in our favor. Miron's action were valiant and he should forever be remembered for the courage that he showed. His actions may seem small, for he only saved two lives, but in reality he risked everything. Not only could Dr. Lisiskiewicz lost his job, but he could have been sent jail, and even killed for harboring two Jews that were supposed have been killed at a labor camp. Every live saved mattered. Out of all the citizens that lived on the Lesko ghetto for a short period of time, only four people (including the two woman that Miron saved) survived out of the several hundred that populated that ghetto. The other deceased could have died at labor camps, or been sent straight to extermination camps. Dr. Miron Lisikiewicz is a brave, daring man who is responsible for saving the lives of two innocent women, who did nothing wrong.

From my research, I learned that kindness isn't always the easiest thing to do, but it's the right thing to do. Miron could have sat back and just let innocent people die, but he showed kindness, and it saved two lives. This shows that we must always show bravery and kindness, even if it is hard. My life has been greatly impacted and changed from learning about Dr. Lisikiewicz. I now know, and realize, how grateful I should be that people who are my nationality and heritage are not persecuted like Jewish people were. I also feel very grateful that I live in a time where there is not war, and I don't have to live in fear of being persecuted by any group. I now understand the huge impact the Holocaust had on people, and that many individuals and groups were constantly living in fear of being killed and tortured till death. I'm glad that I have spent time learning about the event that had a huge impact on history, and our world today. I wish that more people could have survived, that more lives could have been spared, and that more people could have helped victims of the Holocaust. I myself even wished that could have helped these innocent people who did nothing wrong, and change their horrible fate. I feel very thankful and blessed knowing that I live in a time where no one is going to hurt me just because of my race. We must have knowledge that diversity is good, and race does not define one as superior or inferior. It is very important that people now, and in the future are educated about what happened, so that history does not repeat itself, and something as horrible as this never happens again. Ever.

Works Cited

"Lisikiewicz Miron." Yad Vashem . N.p., n.d. Web. 13 Dec. 2016.

"Jews in Krosno." Krosno, Poland (Pages 7-27). N.p., n.d. Web. 13 Dec. 2016.

Irena Sendler

Elizabeth Romero

Today, if someone hears the word "Holocaust" they think of the genocide of six million Jews (and members of other persecuted groups, such as Gypsies and homosexuals), but it was originally a word created by the Greeks: "holos" meaning "whole" and "kaustos" meaning "burned." But the word, "burned" is sadly, partially accurate when describing the Holocaust we know as well, since the six million Jews were tortured, beaten, killed, and then their dead bodies were burned. This horrific genocide occurred from January 30, 1933 to May 8, 1945 in Germany and in countries in Europe that have an alliance with Germany. This horror was started when Adolf Hitler, a veteran from World War One, with many others, blamed the Jews for their country's defeat in 1918 in the First World War. From there, Hitler joined the National German Workers' Party, which later became the National Socialist German Workers' Party (NSDAP). Later, Hitler was imprisoned for treason for his role in the Beer Hall Putsch in 1923.

After his decade of imprisonment, he started to gain power. On January 20, 1933, he was named chancellor of Germany and when the President of Germany, Paul von Hindenburg died in 1934, Hitler declared himself as the "Fuhrer," making himself Germany's supreme ruler. However, when Hitler was in prison, he had predicted that the war would result in the massacre of Jews, and he became obsessed that Germany should only house "pure" or only "perfect full blood" Germans.

Well, not everyone agreed with that cruelty that happened to the Jews, including Irena Sendler, a Polish Catholic social worker and nurse born on February 15, 1910 in Otwock, Poland. She was a member of the Zegota, a secret organization set up by the Polish government to rescue Polish Jews. Irena, brave and courageous, organized a group of members to save children in the Warsaw Ghetto, which was an extermination camp as well. She devised a plan that was long and elaborate to save the children and at the same time, keep her sources and identity secure.

As the administrator in the Welfare Department, she used her power and the belief of disease spreading, to be permitted to enter the ghetto. From there, her team smuggled young children out in toolboxes, coffins, ambulances, and gunny sacks. They also were constantly sneaking the older children to an old church inside the ghetto, make them appear as Catholics, pass through security, and they were out. They would go to Irena's friend's house, the Piotrowski residence or Maria Kukulaska's house to rest before going to live with an adopted family until World War Two ended. Even though her life was always in danger, she continued to go to the ghetto every day and save children for eighteen months.

Irena Sendler was always careful to save the names of each child and their parents in hope to reunite families after the war. The names were put in glass bottles to preserve and were buried safely in Irena's friend's backyard, under an apple tree.

As good her intentions were, the Germans began suspecting Irena for freeing Jews. On October 1943, she was arrested and taken to the Gestapo headquarters, the headquarters of the Nazi's feared police force. Beating her to say the headquarters of the rebels and the children's location, she refused to budge and it resulted in her legs and feet broken. On her way to be executed, members of the Zegota bribed a guard to leave her in the woods and she was taken to safety.

She was a tremendous loss to the world, dying on May 12, 2008 in Warsaw, Poland. She was a very humble lady, never calling herself a hero and she even believes she didn't do much. She became a mother to the children she saved, since mostly every child's parents didn't survive. She, with every other righteous person in the world, knows that what Hitler did wasn't right. Irena Sendler herself said this, "The term 'hero' irritates me greatly. The opposite is true. I continue to have pangs of conscience that I did so little." She also said, "I was brought up to believe that a person must be rescued when drowning, regardless of religion and nationality." That statement is important, since mostly everyone during her time was always discriminating due to skin color, race, religion, and much more.

On top of it all, you would assume that she's some tall, buff woman. Honestly, she wasn't that tall, only four feet and eleven inches tall, perfectly being the example that everyone can totally make a difference. Her bravery was honored when she was nominated for the Nobel Peace Prize in 2007, the Order of the White Eagle, the most honored award in Poland, and many other awards. She is remembered, as well as every other righteous person that ever lived, because she was the living example that what Adolf Hitler did was unjust, and it should never happen again.

There are still acts of discrimination going around the world today. Follow Irena Sendler's example, stop the insulting, rude, racial jokes. One mean comment about nationality can lead to massive bullying and even wars if it's between two important military or political leaders. Irena Sendler was well educated, going to school as a child and attending the University of Warsaw and was the administrator in the Welfare Department. She threw away a safe, happy life to save innocent children. That's why we remember, honor, and respect these righteous people; they risked their lives to save the lives of others. We must remember this so it never happens again, so our world can slowly lead to peace.

Works Cited

History.com Staff. "The Holocaust." History.com. A&E Television Networks, 2009. Web. 11 Dec. 2016.

"Introduction to the Holocaust." United States Holocaust Memorial Museum. United States Holocaust Memorial Museum, n.d. Web. 11 Dec. 2016.

Connolly, Kate. "I'm No Hero, Says Woman Who Saved 2,500 Ghetto Children." The Guardian. Guardian News and Media, 15 Mar. 2007. Web. 11 Dec. 2016.

"Life in a Jar - The Courageous Story of Irena Sendler." Life in a Jar. N.p., n.d. Web. 12 Dec. 2016.

Kroll, Chana. "Irena Sendler - Rescuer of the Children of Warsaw." Rescuer of the Children of Warsaw - Dealing with Challenge. N.p., n.d. Web. 12 Dec. 2016

Wladyslaw Olizar

Ellen Flores

 The murder of six million Jews took place during the Holocaust. The Holocaust was a time period in Germany that was led by Adolf Hitler. Hitler wished to wipe out an entire population of Jews because the Nazis believed that the Aryans were the "master race." The Nazis came into power on January 1933. The Holocaust murdered six million Jews.

Wladyslaw was born in 1908 and died in 1982. Jadwiga Wladyslaw's wife, was born in 1911 and died in 2000. Wladyslaw was the son of Kazimiera Jawornicki, a hotel owner who later died upon the arrival of a Jew named Irena E. Jadwiga had a sister named Alexandra who married the engineer, Stanislaw Zaryn. Irena was warned that the end of the Jews was near. She fled to St. Mary's Family because they were giving work to Jews. Mother Matylda Getter made Irena into a maid to work for the estate of Szeligi II near Warsaw. Both Wladyslaw and Jadwiga and Alexandra and Stanislaw had children who some were in their teen years. Both of the couples knew that Irena was Jewish and treated her very well. They found out later that Irena's maid wok was to hard for her, so they turned her into the governess for Alexandra's children. Wladyslaw found a farm for Irena's husband since he did not work for the estate. Halina Pesko, the housekeeper of the Jewish couple, cared for them. A delegation asked for Wladyslaw to remove Irena from working in the hotel because they felt that since there was a Jew their own safety was compromised. Wladyslaw said no and the delegation did not bother him again. Irena, Wladyslaw and Jadwiga, and Alexandra and Stanislaw had to leave the estate on January 20, 1944 because of the agricultural reform in Poland. Irena and the Olizar's kept each other company by using letters and gifts, since they didn't see each other often. On January 29, 1998, Yad Vashem recognized them as "Righteous by Country," but only Jadwiga was able to go to the ceremony representing Irena, Wladyslaw, and Alexandra. Jadwiga was ill and in her 80s when they did the ceremony honoring them on January 14, 1999.

I learned that some people did try and help some Jews. Wladyslaw offered a Jew to work at his estate even though everyone's lives would be at risk. I can understand that Wladyslaw and Jadwiga tried to show kindness and fight for the Jews and their rights. I can understand that the Holocaust was about getting rid of the Jews to make sure only Germans existed in Germany. The fact that it required to kill and impact so many innocent people and families is what made this wrong.

People still tried to fight, but others kept quiet. I can only imagine what some of the Jews felt when their friends and neighbors knew that this was wrong, but didn't say anything, didn't do anything about it. Having people you really care about sell you out like that can hurt in an unexplained way that maybe most people did not understand. Those feelings were probably anger, betrayal, and sadness as they watched everyone they cared about turn their backs and walk away. The people that they were happy with slowly disappear into despair. I can only imagine how so many people felt when that happened to them. There are some people though, that did not abandon a friend in need, that gave them a place that they could call home. To show someone that they are being cared for and loved. That is what Wladyslaw and Jadwiga did to Irena when she needed it. Let someone believe what they want to believe in peace. We try our best to make sure that it will never happen again. Sometimes we succeed, but sometimes we fail. The times that we fail, we need to get back up and fight again, we need to make sure that we will never have something this horrible happen again. Let everyone do what they believe in, in peace. If people believe that there is only one God, let them. If people dream to be want they want to be, whether it's an astronaut, a dancer, a singer, whatever they dream in being, let them believe. Let that person believe in what they want to, don't shoot them down, be the one to let them fly. Don't be the one staying quiet like so many people did during the Holocaust, be the one to say something or help others. You may think that it will not do anything, that it won't make a difference, but it will do something to the person you helped, it will make a difference to that person. If you could help people that need it, every day, you are making a difference to those people every day. You may think that helping one person, out of millions, doesn't do anything, but it does help that one person. You can't help everyone, but you can help everyone you see that need it the most.

Works Cited

http://www.savingjews.org/righteous/ov.htm
http://www.yadvashem.org/righteous/statistics

Irena Gut Opdyke

Emi Brennan

 Irena Gut Opdyke, also called Irene, was a Jew who survived the Holocaust and witnessed its horrors. She was born in 1918 to Catholic parents named Maria Gut and Wladyslaw Gut. Irene had four sisters and their names were Jania, Marysia, Bronia, and Wladzia, while her parents were Maria Gut and Wladyslaw Gut. Irene's mother had a very strong influence on her.

Irene always wanted to be a nurse and help people. So, in 1939, when Irene was eighteen years old, she attended nursing school, which was two hundred miles from her home. Then, like other nurses, Irene joined the Polish Army.

When Irene was only a teenager, the Nazis attacked Poland. After joining the Polish Army, she was captured by the Germans and was forced to serve as a slave laborer. Three German soldiers assaulted Irene, and the next moment she was on a truck headed to a Russian hospital. She began working in a munitions and armaments factory. Unfortunately, Irene fell ill because of the toxic fumes in the factory and fainted at the feet of a German major. The German major, Major Eduard Rugemer, empathized with Irene and decided to give her a better job. He also thought Irene was German with her blonde hair and blue eyes and asked Irene if she was. Irene responded honestly and told him she was not German. Because of Irene's illness and honesty, German major Eduard Rugemer transferred Irene to a hotel serving Nazis. The hotel was located next to the Glinice ghetto in Radom.

One day while Irene was running an errand, she found herself in the ghetto. Irene saw a mother with an infant in her arms, but the German officer pulled the infant away and threw it to the ground. The mother of the baby was grief-stricken. Irene couldn't understand why the German officer would kill an innocent baby. This was one of the many horrors Irene had to witness.

Later, Irene watched the Nazis unleash attack dogs on the Jews and heard much gunfire. When she watched this happen, Irene was about to yell, but a German officer's hand was clamped over her mouth. He threatened her not to scream and make herself heard. Ever since this incident, she saved leftovers from the kitchen in boxes for the Jews whenever she could, knowing that they needed the extra food to keep them alive. The German officers made sure everyone knew that the consequences for helping Jews were life-threatening, but this didn't stop Irene.

Soon, Major Rugemer was moved to Lwow and Irene was forced to accompany him. Irene met a Jewish lady named Helen Weinbaum and they immediately became close friends. Helen's husband, Henry, worked at a nearby camp. The German officers moved Henry Weinbaum, so Irene, Helen and Irene's sister, Janina, followed. They saw horrors that would imprint in their minds forever. German officers were everywhere killing many women, children, and elderly Jews. There was one incident that stood out. A German officer tossed an infant in the air and shot it. He then turned and shot the crying mother. The prisoners fortunate enough to survive the raid were marched out of the village.

Then, the German major was transferred to Ternopol along with Irene. She resumed her work in the kitchen and met twelve Jewish people in the hotel laundry room. Irene immediately became friends and saved extra food for them to eat and blankets to keep warm.

When Irene was serving dinner to the German soldiers and officers, she heard them discussing a raid happening in the ghetto. Irene wanted people to be safe and got the word out, so the majority of the Jews were able to escape. Irene went on to rescue and smuggle Jews, once helping six Jews escape by driving them deep into a forest and letting them go.

One day, Irene overheard German officers making plans to kill all of the Jews in the Ternopol ghetto. She was very worried because she knew that her friends doing laundry would be killed. Fortunately, a couple days later, Major Rugemer promoted Irene to be his personal housekeeper. Irene decided that she would hide her Jewish friends in the villa. She hid her friends in the attic when the major was downstairs and in the cellar when he was upstairs. After eight months, Major Rugemer finally found out that Irene had hid her friends in his villa. Since it was his villa that they were hiding in, he didn't turn Irene and the Jews in. As long as Irene would be his mistress, Major Rugemer would assist the Jews. So, Irene became his mistress, and as a result, twelve Jews were saved. She saved Henry Weinbaum, Moses Steiner, Marian Wilner, Joseph Weiss, Klara Bauer, Abraham Klinger, Herman Morks, Pola Morks, Mozes Lipszyc, Natan Morks, Gina Morks, and another Jew with the last name Wilner (whose first name is unknown). Irene later became a United States citizen and married.

From researching Irena Gut Opdyke, I learned how tragic the holocaust was and how it tore many families apart in the process. The Jews were a race like any other, but Adolf Hitler wanted all Jews killed in his quest for ethnic cleansing. There were fake showers where, instead of water, poisonous gas poured from the showerhead burning the Jews. The media was taken over by the government and horrible things were published. It is difficult to understand the benefit of killing an entire race. Learning about Irena Gut Opdyke had a big impact on my life. I now know that many life-threatening things can happen and that I shouldn't take life for granted. With the time given, I should try to make the most out of life and make the world a better place so that this doesn't happen again. The Holocaust killed millions of Jews. How could someone even think of trying to wipe out a whole race? Well, Adolf Hitler did just that and Jews died from starvation, disease, exhaustion from working, or because the Nazis burnt, shot, or killed them in other ways. I hope that the world has learned from his mistake and this doesn't happen ever again. History shows that we often repeat dreadful events. During the period of the Holocaust, the United States forced the Japanese into concentration camps for a crime based solely on race. To ensure something like the Holocaust never happens again, we need to encourage and help people learn about the Holocaust, so they are aware of the horrors and consequences of having such a dreadful event take place. We can do this by having assemblies at schools, conferences, or showing the public what the Holocaust did in other ways. Education fosters understanding of our world and helps to build a sense of identity and unity.

Works Cited

"A Holocaust Rescuer: Irene Gut Opdyke Timeline." Timetoast. N.p., n.d. Web. 11 Dec. 2016.

"Irene Gut Opdyke: She Hid Polish Jews Inside a German Officers' Villa." Teenage Nurse Rescue Jews During the Holocaust. N.p., n.d. Web. 11 Dec. 2016.

"Rescuers: Irene Opdyke." PBS. PBS, n.d. Web. 11 Dec. 2016.

21, May. "Irene Opdyke, 85; Hid Jews in Poland During the Holocaust." Los Angeles Times. Los Angeles Times, 21 May 2003. Web. 11 Dec. 2016.

"The Righteous Among The Nations." Yad Vashem - Request Rejected. N.p., n.d. Web. 11 Dec. 2016.

Krystyna Adolph

Emily Bigley

The Holocaust is one of the most devastating examples of racism ever shown. The Holocaust took place in Germany from 1933-1945 under the reign of Adolf Hitler. He tried with all his powers to wipe out all Jews and anybody who wasn't full German, because he felt the ruling class of Jews was responsible for World War 1 which caused over 100,000 German soldiers to die. He also felt the Jewish were to blame for the depression in Germany as they controlled the merchandise market and were not affected by the depression as they were wealthy. This was one reason he was able to gain so many supporters to take down the Jews. He destroyed many families and took away many lives, by sending in Nazis, members of the SS Army, to eliminate all Jews. The Nazis would take any known Jews to ghettos, camps, or simply take them out the fields and shoot them. Millions of Jews were separated from their loved ones, taken to different camps where they were barely fed and later died. They would also steal valuables from the Jews when raiding their homes and businesses. In spite of Hitler, many Germans did illegal acts to keep some of the Jews safe. The most famous German who helped over 1,000 Jews was Oskar Schindler. However, there were many more that helped save the Jews, one of those was a woman named Krystyna Adolph.

Before the war, Krystyna had become a widow and was raising her three year old daughter and caring for her father- in-law. Krystyna was a high school teacher at Czartoryski High School in Vilna. In her class, she had two, Jewish twin sisters by the name of Monika and Lidia Gluskin. Once the war was about to break out, Krystyna wrote them a letter saying that if they wish to stay with her and be safe, she will open her home up to them. When the war was just about to kick off, the twins took Krystyna up on the offer and they were welcomed with open arms. For the three years they lived with Krystyna, the girls did housework, took care of the animals, chopped firewood, and took care of the vegetables and fields. Krystyna's sister-in-law and father-in-law were the only ones who knew that they were Jewish. Krystyna would introduce the twins to her neighbors as relatives who left from forced labor. Krystyna's sister-in-law helped her out by providing Monika and Lidia forged papers. Krystyna was aware that she was putting her own life in danger by breaking two rules: providing forged papers and hiding Jews. She had just witnessed the Germans burning down a house with the family still in there after they had found out that there was a Jewish family hiding in the house. Krystyna also helped Monika and Lidia's mother by providing forged papers for her as well. The twins' mother was living in a ghetto and was able to flee and avoid the Nazis. She survived and made it to the Aryan side. The twins survived the Holocaust thanks to Krystyna. They later moved to Israel and kept in touch with their hero, Krystyna. On May 14th, 1984, she was given the "Righteous Among the Nations" Award where her name is now on the Yad Vashem, a memorial to the victims of the Holocaust.

From doing research, taking notes, and listening to a Holocaust survivor, I have learned a lot. I learned that 6,000,000 million Jews were killed during the Holocaust. Also, Germans would place the Jews in horrible places: camps, ghettos, showers with genocide, and ovens. Many Germans were forced to make a hard decision, follow the law of Adolf Hitler to turn their backs on all Jews or put their lives at risk to help. Many stayed true to Hitler and turned their backs on Jews, while many didn't. I was surprised to learn how many people put their lives and their family's lives in danger by hiding Jews and protecting them from the Germans. Krystyna Adolph impacted my life because she is courageous for saving other's lives while putting hers in danger along with it. This makes me wonder if I am strong enough to stand up for what is right. In today's society, we are faced with a major social issue of racism. While I have not yet personally been mistreated because of my race, I hope that I can keep an open mind to the feelings of others who are. Krystyna Adolph's actions make me wonder if I have the courage to put everything, my life, my home, my family, on the line to save those who are being mistreated in this world. Many people today are fearful because of the president elect, Donald Trump, and feel that he is racist and won't protect them. As a society, we have to come together and stand up for what is right. Luckily today, no one man has absolute power and the United States Government has checks and balances which would prevent a tragedy like the Holocaust from ever occurring here in America. As I think about the impact of the Holocaust, if it were ever to happen in America, it would kill every person living in the following states: Wyoming (563,600), Vermont (626,042), Alaska (738,432), North Dakota (756,927), South Dakota (858,469), and Delaware (945,934). When I hear that six million Jews died, it sounds like a lot. However, when I put the numbers to the seven states in America, the impact becomes more real. The contributions to the world that these six million Jews might have had, we will never know. One of those people could have been the first scientist to find a cure for cancer. To think that this all occurred because of someone's race is ridiculous.

Something like this should never happen again. We should never again take people's lives because of their race.

Works Cited

Holocaust. Yad Vashem, n.d. Web. Nov.-Dec. 2016.
Yad Vashem - Request Rejected. Yad Vashem, n.d. Web. 1 Dec. 2016.

Wojan, Megan. "Intro to Holocaust." Holocaust. KAMS, Elk Grove. 4 Nov. 2016. Lecture.
"Enchantedlearing.com." Enchantedlearing.com. N.p., n.d. Web. 11 Dec. 2016.
"War History Fans." War History Fans. N.p., n.d. Web. 11 Dec. 2016.

Olucia Somienek

Emily Eng

In the early 1930's, economic depression hit Germany hard causing them to lack confidence in their weak government. Adolf Hitler, from the Nazi party, saw this as a chance for the rise of a new leader. He saw Aryans, the German race, as the "master race." Hitler first started by making Jews stand out, like wearing the yellow star of David. He wanted them to stand out, and soon enough, people were hated on just because they were Jewish. In January 1933, the Nazis came to power in Germany and started to begin his plan of eliminating Jews. The Holocaust involved the murder of six million Jews and fewer than four million survived. The Holocaust, or "sacrifice by fire," ended in 1945 when World War II was finally over. Those who survived this horrible event were changed forever because their closest family or friends could be dead. A hero who saved a Jewish family, Olucia Somienek, was in her 20s and lived in Poland. She was the housekeeper for the Zweig family, who lived in Ottynia, Poland. Isak and Elke Zweig had four daughters, Bronia, Sala, Chana, and Loncia. Olucia lived nearby in a village with her mother. She had helped one of them to escape this horrible tragedy.

Germans arrived in Ottynia in 1941, and mass executions quickly began. They tried to take the head of the Zweig family, Isak, but he was in hiding. Instead Germans took Elke, Bronia, Sala, and Chana. Loncia was quickly pushed under her bed by her mother and was not taken. Everyone in the Zweig family perished, but soon after, Olucia discovered Loncia and took her home and protected her. News spread and raids occurred in Olucia's house. People constantly searched for the rumored Jewish child. She constantly hid Loncia, once in a doghouse with a dog, another time in a garbage bin, and a third time in a mattress. However, not once was Loncia ever found. Olucia took care of her for about two years and soon Loncia went with her cousin and put her in an orphanage. This was a way to get Loncia adopted in the United States.

This shows that Olucia was a caring and loyal person because she had known the Zweig family for a while. She risked her own life by hiding Loncia from harm. Even though threats and rumors were spreading quickly, she kept Loncia and hid her from raids. People would tell about the presence of a Jewish child in Olucia's house and she as often raided. But, she did whatever she could to prevent the little girl to be found. Olucia was able to protect Loncia until the Holocaust was over, and Loncia eventually was adopted by Harry and Pauline Bernhotlz. They were actually distant relatives of her father. However, Loncia finally figured out what had happened to her until she was an adult. Olucia was like a mother to Loncia and took care of her for many years and protected her from any harm.

Even though she was just the Zweig family's housekeeper, Olucia proved that she was a faithful member of their family for her acts of bravery. She did everything she could to protect Loncia from the dangers of the Germans.

The Holocaust was a terrible event and should happen, "Never Again." This quote explains how this was such a tragic action and should never happen again. The Holocaust was a disastrous event in history, so survivors say "Never Again." This genocide contained the persecution of about six million faultless Jews. In addition, 91% of the Jewish population in Poland was killed. The survivors would be changed forever. Learning about Olucia has really showed me about how brave some people are. They would risk their own lives to protect others that are special to them. She was a loyal and courageous hero and deserves recognition for her brave actions of saving some Jews. The Holocaust was truly a devastating time in history and killed many innocent Jews. We should try to prevent something like this from even happening again by doing simple acts. Our society should learn not to single out people because of their appearance, race, or beliefs. This would ensure that something like this would happen never again. People should be appreciated for who they are, not what the look like. We shouldn't discriminate against somebody because of their appearance. It is their personality and character that is important and unique. Inequality is still a major problem in our world, and not one person should be better than everyone else. In addition, we could do acts of kindness to others. Showing kindness could make someone's day and ensure that something like the Holocaust doesn't occur. These acts would assure that nothing alike this horrible disaster would ever occur, "Never Again."

Works Cited

Wojan, Megan. "Introduction to the Holocaust." Social Science 7 Honors Class Lecture. Katherine L. Albiani Middle School, Elk Grove. 4 Nov. 2016. Lecture.

Yad Vashem - The World Holocaust Remembrance Center. N.p., n.d. Web. Dec. 2016.

Stephania Hingler

Ethan Burns

The Holocaust was a very horrendous event for the whole world. Over 6 million Jewish lives were lost during this time from 1933-1945. Adolf Hitler and his men wanted to take over the world and they didn't quite do that. Instead, he killed 6 million Jews by either shooting them, starving them, or even gas poisoning them. This event in time was also very important; it changed our lives and how we live today. Today, we learn about this event in school for a reason, "Never Again." Many of these people who were killed are heroes in some eyes. One of these heroes was Stephania Hingler, who helped hide Ziegfried Rappaport and his wife Lidia. There were countless of these innocent heroes who helped others during this event. Those people were either killed or escaped and tell us the story of how they did it to this day.

I have learned many things from this person and how she influenced the people that know about her that helping just a little can maybe save someone's life. I've also learned many personal things about Stephania and who she was and did before the Holocaust struck. She was a retired opera singer and was about 60 years old when she was taken into the Holocaust. During the Holocaust, I've learned even more about her and her amazing actions. She helped hide and cover Ziegfried Rappaport and his wife Lidia for about two years. During that time, she had a feeling and concern about her neighbor knowing what she was doing. To help that concern, she asked her other neighbor, Kazimierz Peirz for help. These two will go down in history as very brave people and whoever learns about them will know that some people risked their lives, took the time out of their day to help others in need. The last thing I learned was why she did it. Wouldn't you also think why some random woman would want to protect a random family from bloodthirsty killers in concentration camps? She did it because she cared for others. This is important to this day because people nowadays don't care as much as few others do. People now only care about themselves or people they know.

Some people nowadays don't know how significant the Holocaust was. Some people are so clueless about it that they use it as jokes. The Holocaust was not a joke! Adolf Hitler and his men killed 6 MILLION people. Do you know how much people that is? That is equivalent to the Pope's gathering in the Philippines, and about as much as World Youth Day in 1995. This is also important by the tremendous ways of how Adolf and his men killed these people. Killing people is one really bad thing, but how they killed them is just insane. The ways they killed them were truly horrendous and the ways they did it were starving them, mass open air shootings, extermination camps, heavy labor, overcrowded in ghettos in Poland, disease, and death marches. People don't know how disgusting and cruel these things were. You may wonder where the bodies are today, well, most of them were cremated (burnt to ash) which adds to the point on how sick and twisted the Nazis were. The biggest impact the Holocaust had on everyone's lives was simply the amount of people killed in that short of a time. 12 years isn't that long of a time, but one person and his own nation doing it single handedly is insane. To conclude, the impact the Holocaust had was very big because it teaches us that stuff like this will never happen again.

There could be many ways to secure that something like this never happens again. One way to stop this from happening is to stop worldwide racism. Racism is pretty much the main factor that the Nazis killed all the Jews. It was because they were Jewish! The way we can stop racism today is to report racist things posted on social media. One of the main drama spreaders today is social media and reporting racist things can stop people from seeing racism. Another useful way to end racism is to teach it in schools. Most kids go to school, learn stuff, and grow up to be successful knowing that stuff. From then they pass on their knowledge. Starting with school, teachers can help educate children to end racism and one day it will never exist as like another Holocaust will never exist. One last way to spread the word "Never Again" about the Holocaust is to make Holocaust awareness sites and organizations and spread them worldwide. The way to do this is make websites to make sure there's never another Holocaust. You can also do this by making organizations with people and survivors to go around and spread the word. This is important because it is another big factor in getting the word around, "Never Again".

In restatement, the Holocaust was a very horrific moment in history. Many horrible events took place during that time and we will always remember. It is good to learn about the Holocaust because of one very big saying, "Never Again". Stephania Hingler was also a very important person during this time because of her heroic actions she did.

Adam Rysiewicz

Ethan Ho

 Any individual can make a difference in the world, but only if he has the courage to stand up for himself and others. Adam Rysiewicz is an example of one such individual. This twenty-six-year-old man who died from an enemy bullet straight through the heart believed that differences in race, creed, religion, etc. should not matter. Adam was born on February 24, 1918 in Wilczyskach, Poland. His father was a farmer who had several positions in the local town government, while his mother was a peasant from a family that owned a sawmill. Adam was a highly intelligent child and displayed leadership abilities as early as high school, graduating in 1936.

Upon graduating from high school, Adam attended Jagiellonian University to study law. It was here that he learned about the ideology of the Polish Socialist Party (PPS) and joined the Union of Independent Socialist Youth. From there he became the first insulting epithet, named Red Lynx. Adam was young and idealistic, and loved all people; race, class, color and creed meant nothing to him. In September 1939, Adam went to Lions. During his several weeks stay in this town, Adam witnessed detentions, deportations, rapes and murders carried out by the NKVD, a law enforcement agency for the Soviet Union. Adam was forever changed by this, and he wanted no more of communism.

Rysiewicz returned to Krakow in November 1939 and immediately sought out many of his closest friends to help him create Krakow PPS. He and his friends worked hard to make sure that they had people working to stop the evil in their world, and they got the word out through the newspapers. Their group also began recruiting others into the organization, and it grew larger and larger. The PPS soon began moving around to try to provide more assistance to the Jews and Adam was stationed near Auschwitz, a major concentration camp in Poland.

Upon the arrest of Joseph Cryankiewicz, one of the key members of the Regional Committee of the Workers' PPS (OKR-PPS), in April 1941, Adam was appointed secretary of the OKR-PPS. He also became the Secretary of the Municipal Committee of the Worker's PPS in Cracow. Because of his high position, Adam was able to organize the escape of Jews from the camps and ghettos and provide them with false documents. The Jews were hidden in the PPS hideouts and they were provided with food, medical care, and financial assistance. This cost the secret organization quite a bit, but the price they paid was worth the many lives they saved.

One of the least known methods of saving Jews was to organize road metastasis fugitives from the ghettos in Hungary. This proved to work very well, because it allowed many fugitives to escape and keep their lives. Although it was unorthodox, the tactic worked well enough to save hundreds of Jewish people, and success usually makes the unorthodox acceptable.

Soon, however, the rescues slowed in frequency, as the rescuers were being hunted down. The Nazis were angered by the rebellion in Poland, and so they began to arrest Jewish people and Polish people with new intensity, arresting people for standing up for others, being Jewish, and hiding Jews. Adam was working day and night, traveling everywhere, living in the same place for only a short time, before moving on, to avoid being tracked. The young man knew that if he was to save any more Jews and Poles, he would have to stay hidden first.

On June 22, 1944, Adam made another attempt to free Cyrankiewicz, a former member of PPS from a concentration camp. Adam had already failed several times trying to free his close companion, and felt that he must continue until he did. Adam was not aware that Cyrankiewicz was promised entry into China. Adam and his two friends, Richard Krogulski and Wladyslaw Denikiewicz, arrived at the camp, only to find out that Cyrankiewicz was no longer at the camp. The trio headed back on June 24, and were joined by a young man, Joseph Kornas. As they were about to cross the border, the four men were seen by a group of guards, who were as startled by seeing the other men as Adam was seeing them. Adam reached for the pistol concealed in his pocket, but it was too late to do anything. The squad of guards shot at Adam and his friends, killing him, Joseph, and Richard immediately. Wladyslaw escaped, and told the organization about the loss of their commander.

In conclusion, Adam was a young man who died from an enemy bullet, standing up for what he believed in. I learned that it is very important to stand up for what you believe is the right thing to do. Adam did just that, giving his life to help the Jews of Poland. The Holocaust was the cause of this, and if the Holocaust had never happened, millions would still be alive. To make sure that this happens NEVER AGAIN, we have to learn from the past and set aside our disputes that came from our differences. Only then can we stop making the same mistakes over and over again.

Works Cited

(john@spartacus-educational.com), John Simkin. "Spartacus Educational." Spartacus Educational. Spartacus Educational. Web. 11 Dec. 2016.

"Święty Z laickiego Kalendarza [Adam Rysiewicz]." Lewicowo.pl. Web. 11 Dec. 2016.

Buza, Tadeusz

Ethan Le

 The Holocaust was a terribly horrific event that humanity should be ashamed of and that did sadly happen in our history. Hopefully, nothing like this awful event will ever happen again in our world. In the early 1930's, economic depression hit Germany so they elected Adolf Hitler to strengthen their weak government. It turned out that Hitler was the wrong person for the job since he initiated bad things against the Jews. Hitler created a terrible organization named the Nazis and he began a genocide of Jews. The Germans thought of themselves as the pure race and that Jews were imperfect and because of that were to be shunned out of society. At first the Germans started by in a way, brainwashing the children by sending messages in arts, books, films, etc. that Jews were inferior and Germans were the master race. Later, several laws were forced upon Jews like losing their rights of German citizenship and having to wear the yellow stars of David. Then, since countries around Germany couldn't contain all the Jew refugees that were escaping Germany the remaining Jews were sent to ghettos which were inhospitable. Finally, this mission of the Germans led to genocide at mass extermination camps where sadly many people died, some other non-Aryan races and people who helped Jews were also sent to these camps. There were gas chambers created to kill Jews faster and in addition, the Germans tricked those who were selected and told them that is was a shower. After Jews were killed their bodies were burned in furnaces. One Poland rescuer of Jews was named Tadeusz Buza. Tadeusz was born in 1911 and he was a Second Lieutenant of the Polish army. He was Catholic and had the professions of a bus driver and tram conductor.

After Tadeusz had escaped from the Gross-Rosen and Bergen-Belsen camps in the end of 1939 he became a tram conductor for Warsaw. He continued in the German occupation and in the meantime he secretly joined a Polish underground movement-Armia Krajowa. This movement would try their best to help the Jews and they would put their effort into stopping the German forces because they knew that what the Germans were doing was wrong. While Tadeusz would pass by the Warsaw ghetto on a tram he would smuggle food to the poor Jews living in the ghetto. These Jews needed the supplies to help them live in the harsh and difficult conditions of the Warsaw ghetto, which was overpopulated and unsanitary.

Tadeusz was sent to work as a bus driver in 1941 before the Nazi-Soviet war in the eastern parts of Poland which were under the control of the Russians. During his trips, Tadeusz gave letters and parcels from Jews in the Warsaw ghetto to their relatives in towns called Lwów, Radziwiłłów, Brody and Zdołbunów. Since that the Warsaw uprising was such a dangerous task Tadeusz helped some Jews in the ghetto escape through the sewers and into the Aryan side to save them. He also saved a Jew named Schachter Leon who was a resident of Stanisławów. Schachter escaped from that ghetto to the Lwów ghetto and then to Warsaw all by using a forged identity.

Tadeusz then sheltered Schachter for about a month in his apartment until he had obtained an Aryan Kennkarte for Schachter. Aryan Kennkarte were actually pretty tough to forge and the penalty for doing so is a big deal. Germans would check the files of people if they became suspicious to ensure that they had a true Aryan Kennkarte. Soon the neighbors became suspicious of Schachter's identity so Tadeusz transferred him to a friend's apartment, further away. Tadeusz still continued to help Schachter until the war was over.

I've learned from Tadeusz story that helping others is really important and is the right thing to do even if it's something that could be dangerous, at least you are helping someone in need. His story has impacted on me that this Holocaust was just terrible and loved ones would try to transport letters to their loved ones knowing that soon they might be slaughtered by the Germans which is just horrible to think about. I understand that this tore apart families and friends which is not right. I know that never again should this happen since it's a disgrace in our history and it was just terrible that people would do that to other people. Why would we discriminate against each other? It's wrong to do so and I can't believe that people can be that cruel. Never again should this happen that is for sure, however, sadly there still are people in this world who abuse others like Hitler did. We must keep the peace and not repeat something like the Holocaust. I can let people know about the Holocaust and how terrible it was and spread the word. At school I can talk to my friends and others about it and hopefully it will spread. That way we could stop something like the Holocaust before it starts.

Works Cited

Wojan, Megan. "Introduction to Holocaust." Lecture. Katherine Albiani Middle School, Elk Grove. 4 Nov. 2016. Lecture.

Unkown. "Righteous Among The Nations." Yad Vashem. Yad Vashem, n.d. Web. 4 Nov. 2016.

Holocaust Essay

Ethan Prevatt

The Holocaust is something that should happen never again. Something where you kill off a certain people just because of their race is not okay. When I learned about it, I was not only shocked but horrified. Things like warfare are scary enough, but when they kill children and break apart families, that has gone too far. People were sent to concentration camps where they were worked hard until they died of starvation or were shot. The Jews were also gassed in fake public showers. Jews were not only persecuted but were humiliated and most of their businesses were shut down.

We got through this only by helping the jews. Many people helped the Jews, but the most were in Poland. About 6,620 people from Poland helped Jews, but 26,120 people helped in total. People from Hungary, Greece, and even people from the U.S.A. helped. There are many stories including a couple who dug their own "grave" with their fingernails and lied there for eighteen months total. A couple would change their chamber pot (which was like a toilet without plumbing) and help them bath once a week. They would also give them food and water every day. But the couple I chose is the Gardzinski couple.

The Gardzinski couple lived in a village called Borowe close to Mogilnica Grojecka, Chelm prov. Klementyna (wife) and Eugeniusz (husband) were both teachers. This couple helped many Jews including many young children. They first took in two children of Klementyna's sister, whose father, Zygmunt Jaffe, was Jewish and kept the two kids until the end of the occupation. They also housed a nine year old girl, Eugenia Erlich until she became independent. For two years, they cared for the two year old Danuta Gorny, whose father claimed her after the war. From 1944 until the end they took in Stanislaw and Josef Zalewski. They all survived and traveled to different countries.

There are many facts that the Holocaust brings, and some are very sad. Over 1.1 million children were killed and children were targeted by the Nazis because they would grow up to be a new generation of parenting Jews who would have survived the Holocaust. Most of the children would be suffocated on the stuffy cattle cars with no ventilation and any who survived were taken to gas chambers immediately. More than 33,000 Jews were killed in two days in September of 1941 when the German soldiers asked them to get undressed and stand at the edge of the Babi Yar Ravine. Then, they shot the Jews and when the last ones were killed, the Nazis pushed down the ravine walls, burying the Jews forever in that rocky tomb. On November 9, 1938, Kristallnacht, night of broken glass, occurred. The Nazis destroyed over 1,000 synagogues and 7,000 businesses. Approximately 6 million Jews were killed during the Holocaust. The word Holocaust comes from the Greek roots holo -"whole"and kaustos-"burnt"which was an animal sacrifice when when you would burn the whole animal. When the Jews were transported, they had to travel in cattle wagons that had no food, water, a toilet, or ventilation. Millions of others, not just Jews were murdered also. The disabled and political and religious leaders that were against Hitler were killed. Romanies, Jehovah's witnesses, and homosexuals were also murdered.

The concentration camps were very bad places. The Jews were forced to work until they died of starvation, frostbite, or getting overwhelmed. Many Jews were gassed in gassing chambers. The gas would start at the floor and then travel up, leaving Jews to trample each other. When all the air was out, you could see that the stronger ones were on the top of the pile. There wasn't very much food at these concentration camps. You would have about 500 calories a day which is about the equivalent to one part of the bun of a hamburger bun. If you were lucky and first in line, you could get a potato. Kids about 12 or 13 years old would weigh about 45 pounds, which is less than the average weight of a 6 year old. Many kids were killed in concentration camps, due to starvation. Families and siblings were separated into different segments of the camps,or sent to completely different plants altogether.

Hitler was born in Austria in 1889. He served in the German army in World War 1. Hitler blamed the Jews for the country's defeat in 1918 like many anti-semites in Germany. On January 20, 1933 Hitler was named chancellor of Germany and after President Paul von

Hindenburg's death in 1934, he anointed himself as "fuhrer" making himself supreme ruler of Germany.

As we know, history such as the Holocaust shouldn't be repeated. When mass killings happen for no reason, people raise awareness to fight back. The words never again exactly describe the Holocaust. If you ask any survivor, you will know why this should never happen again, as genocides are very terrible. The Holocaust was very scary to many people and should never be repeated.

Works Cited

History.com Staff. "The Holocaust." History.com. A&E Television Networks, 2009. Web. 12 Dec. 2016.

Marks, Bernard. "Mr. Marks Survivor Presentation." Mr. Marks Survivor Presentation. Kams, Elk Grove. 4 Nov. 2016. Lecture.

"91 Interesting Facts about the Holocaust | FactRetriever.com." FactRetriever.com. N.p., n.d. Web. 12 Dec. 2016.

"Saving Jews: Polish Righteous." Saving Jews: Polish Righteous. N.p., n.d. Web. 11 Dec. 2016.

"Yad Vashem." Yad Vashem. N.p., n.d. Web. 12 Dec. 2016.

Maria Polkowska

Ethan Tianco

The Holocaust is one of the most disastrous events in the history of humankind, but a minority of the people out of the many that died, had chosen to endanger their own lives to save others. The Holocaust was mainly between the Germans and the Jewish religion. The Germans thought that the Jews were a threat to their people, and they thought that they must be rid of them. The Germans could've have chosen a less violent way to express their feelings towards Jews, but they chose the most cruel, violent choice, to torture, beat, and violently execute the Jewish religion. The Holocaust means sacrificed by fire, or whole and burned. It all started in 1933, when the Nazi political party chose their leader, Adolf Hitler. To Hitler, the Jews were an alien threat, just for this specific reason, he slaughtered and murdered approximately six million Jews. Jews were killed in many varieties of ways, sickness, infection, execution, concentration camps, and more. Jews weren't the only targeted group, homosexuals, and other persecuted groups were included. There was also multiple stages of this mass murder, but each stage moving forward had increased in cruelty and pain. All of this torture and beating of a people just because he had an opinion, and didn't like them. A courageous, righteous human, Maria Polkowska. She had helped a defenseless child that had been sent to her by the unknown.

On Christmas Eve of 1942, Maria had discovered a "present" in rags on her front steps. She was surprised to find a baby girl, about one year old. She immediately recognized that the girl was the daughter of Abraham Hofman, a Jewish tailor from Wawolnica, from the Pulawy county, in the Lubin district. A letter explained all of this, it had told Maria that if Abraham Hofman didn't survive through the Holocaust that she were to be the caretaker of his daughter. Even though that she knew she was better off without a child, especially a Jewish one during this time, she chose to take her in. People knew that she had the Jewish child so people demanded that she turn the child over or the Germans would be informed. She remained brave and denied the threats. She ended up caring for the Jewish child for the next three years, and eventually figured out that the parents of Barbara didn't survive. After the war Barbara's relatives found her and Maria handed her to the aunt, who then adopted Barbara. After Barbara grew up she left Poland, married, she lived in England. Barbara had never forgotten what Polkowska had done for her, because if it wasn't for her she would have lived a painful and most likely short life.

Polkowska has taught me that even though helping a person in need may make life harder for yourself, but most people would want to live knowing that they helped a person who truly needed it and that they greatly appreciated it. Polkowska also taught me that never expect a reward, because after she had finished taking care of the child and the aunt took Barbara into her hands, she just continued on with her life never thinking for a second or was waiting for a special reward. Maria's reward was one of the most satisfying feelings that could possibly be felt, being appreciated. Maria impacted me because she taught me that you should help anyone who trusts you with something important or because everyone should be a good human being and care for all. I understand that the Holocaust will have an ever-lasting effect to the religious world and the whole world in general. The Jewish and other religions that support them may have a permanent with Germans, but it depends on the personalities of their people. The people pf the German community even to today should always feel a mistake in their actions, regardless if they had a part in the disaster. I believe that even though that there may be a grudge for many years to come, there still should be the occasional group of people that forget the past, what is done is done, now it is time to start a new era. The motto of survivors, "Never Again" shouldn't just be for this specific disastrous event, but I wish that it was rarely used because then that would mean that there isn't a lot of disastrous events in the world. Steps we can take to make sure that an event like this never happens again is to being accepting of the fact that all people will have different beliefs and may not be the same. If we were all the same we wouldn't be "human". Another way to prevent another disastrous event being similar to this is to hold no grudges, and be smart and think about the consequences of the action. In conclusion, the Holocaust was and is one of the most disastrous events in human history and preventing another disaster like this may sound like an easy task, but it is easier said than done.

Works Cited

"The Righteous Among Nations." Yad Vashem. The World Holocaust Remembrance Center, 2016. Web. 12 Dec. 2016.

Jerzy Bielecki

Ethan Williams

 In January 1933, a member of the Nazi party by the name of Adolf Hitler rose to political power and began what is now known as the Holocaust, an event that cost the lives of over six million Jews, homosexuals, and other persecuted groups. Hitler saw these groups of people as inferior and dangerous to the purity of the Aryan race and so he came up with a "final solution." Hitler's "final solution" was compiled into stages. The first of which was to establish ghettos in Poland, which were blocked off from the rest of the world, where Jews were to be kept in. The ghettos in Poland were cramped with little food. Once the Nazis saw that the ghettos were getting too crowded, he sent the Jews to concentration and death camps in March of 1933. The most infamous of these camps was the Auschwitz concentration camp. Over 1.1 million prisoners in Auschwitz were killed, but in all the chaos, a detainee in Auschwitz named Jerzy Bielecki managed to save himself and his love, Cyla Cybulska, from being burned.

Jerzy Bielecki was born in Slaboszow Poland, 1921. Alone, Jerzy Bielecki was brought into Auschwitz at the age of 18 in 1940, after he was caught by the Nazis trying to flee from Poland to Hungary. At Auschwitz, he had various, rigorous jobs until he escaped. During his four years at Auschwitz, he fell in love with a Jewish woman named Cyla Cybulska, whose family was killed shortly after she arrived in Auschwitz. The two spoke briefly every day, as men and women in Auschwitz were forbidden to converse since the Nazis wanted to exterminate the Jews as fast as possible, and they couldn't have Jews repopulating.

In 1944, Jerzy thought of a way to escape the inescapable fortress that was Auschwitz. He informed Cyla about his plan and at first she was skeptical, but since it was almost time for her to head to the gas chamber, there was no other choice. For this plan, Jerzy needed an SS uniform, forged documents, food, clothing for Cyla, and probably the most important thing he needed was luck. Since there were only a few escapees out of the million detainees that were held at Auschwitz, he needed a lot of luck. Once Jerzy gathered everything he needed, he put on his stolen SS uniform and walked nervously to the laundry room where Cyla worked. He went to the SS woman in charge of monitoring Cyla's workplace and told her that he was going to take Cyla for interrogation. She allowed Jerzy to take Cyla and they walked out of the laundry room without drawing too much attention.

Outside the laundry room, Jerzy and Cyla were stopped by another SS guard. To pass, Jerzy pulled out his forged documents that allowed him and Cyla to pass the guard station to a nearby work farm. The two escapees, determined to live, walked out of Auschwitz and ran to freedom. They were, however, still in danger of being killed. Since they both still had tattoos on their arms, they could be easily identified and captured by the Nazis, which would lead to immediate death. Jerzy and Cyla ran and ran until Cyla almost gave up. She told Jerzy to leave her, but he wouldn't. Instead, Jerzy carried Cyla to the home of one of his relatives. It took them ten nights, resting during the day, to finally reach safety. They stayed at Jerzy's relative's house for a few days until Jerzy managed to find Cyla a permanent place to hide with a willing Polish family. Eventually, the two lost contact with each other and both of them came to the conclusion that the other was killed.

Jerzy however, was very much alive and he had married and stayed in Poland, while Cyla, who was also still alive, flew to the United States and married there. In 1983, 39 years later, Cyla and Jerzy, now a widower, found each other again only by sheer luck. The two survivors would meet again 15 more times, until Cyla Cybulsky died in 2005 peacefully. Jerzy would go on to hold several interviews with the press and would publish a book, He Who Saves One Life, that would lead to the release of the film adaptation of his and Cyla's story, called Remembrance, directed by Anna Justice and released in 2011. In 1985, Yad Vashem recognized Jerzy Bielecki as righteous among nations, which was long overdue.

Reading Jerzy Bielecki's story taught me that human morality and human kindness always perseveres over the prejudiced and hateful. He has taught me to be selfless when he risked his own life to save Cyla's. Their story moved me in a way that no other story I've ever read had: it was so dramatic and sad, but in the end it was all okay. I wish I could say the same for all of the other victims of the Holocaust, but I can't. The Holocaust destroyed families, lives, and children who have had to live through this hell for no other reason than Hitler said so. Hitler deliberately started World War II and the Holocaust, just to see the world burn. Never again should this amount of life be lost by the hand of one person. Never again should one person be able to dictate who was inferior and then have the audacity to say that they were doing a good thing for the human race. In order to prevent another Adolf Hitler, we have to make sure that a man like Adolf Hitler does not gain a foothold in politics. People can't afford to give power and the ability to start another world war, another genocide to a man filled with greed and hate.

Works Cited

"Auschwitz." United States Holocaust Memorial Museum. United States Holocaust Memorial Museum, n.d. Web. 11 Dec. 2016.

"The "Final Solution"" United States Holocaust Memorial Museum. United States Holocaust Memorial Museum, n.d. Web. 11 Dec. 2016.

Hevesi, Dennis. "Jerzy Bielecki Dies at 90; Fell in Love in a Nazi Camp." The New York Times. The New York Times, 23 Oct. 2011. Web. 11 Dec. 2016.

History.com Staff. "The Holocaust." History.com. A&E Television Networks, 2009. Web. 11 Dec. 2016.

"Jerzy Bielecki: A Story of Moral Courage." Keene. Keene.adu, 2016. Web. 11 Dec. 2016.

"Jerzy Bielecki Obituary on Legacy.com." Legacy.com. Legacy.com, n.d. Web. 12 Dec. 2016.

"Jerzy Bielecki, Saved Jewish Girl from Auschwitz." Connecticut Jewish Ledger. Connecticut Jewish Ledger, 26 Oct. 2011. Web. 11 Dec. 2016.

"Jerzy Bielecki, Who Saved Jewish Girlfriend in Auschwitz, Dies at 90." The Washington Post. Associated Press, 24 Oct. 2011. Web. 11 Dec. 2016.

Press, The Associated. "Former Inmate Recalls Daring, Romantic Escape from Auschwitz." Haaretz.com. Haaretz, 20 July 2010. Web. 11 Dec. 2016.

"Remembrance." Rotten Tomatoes. Rotten Tomatoes, n.d. Web. 11 Dec. 2016.

"The Righteous among Nations." Yad Vashem. Yad Vashem, n.d. Web. 11 Dec. 2016.

Spier, Joe. "An Auschwitz Love Story." San Diego Jewish World. San Diego Jewish World, 15 May 2015. Web. 11 Dec. 2016.

Www.auschwitz.org. "AUSCHWITZ-BIRKENAU." News / Museum / Auschwitz-Birkenau. Auschwitz-Birkenau, n.d. Web. 11 Dec. 2016.

Franciszka Abramowicz

Evan Brown

The Holocaust was a very rough time in our world's history. Many very bad people did things that an average human would never even start to think about doing. Many Jewish and non-Jewish men and women tragically died either as being a victim of the Holocaust, or trying to save the people who were victims. Many people did the right thing and tried very hard to save people of Jewish religion. One person in particular who saved a jew from being taken away and maybe slaughtered, was Franciszka Abramowicz. Franciszka was born in 1899 in Poland. Mrs. Abramowicz knew that what the Germans were doing during the Holocaust was wrong. She knew that she had to do something about it. Although she didn't know exactly what to do to help the Jewish men and women, she would do everything he could to try.

Franciszka went beyond her abilities to save the Jewish community. She hid a Jewish man named Sneder Dyszel, she supplied him with food, water, and other necessities, and she transferred him to a much safer place in the hopes that he would escape Poland and escape the Holocaust. It is truly amazing that a human being would put their own lives in death's arms just to save people in need. I don't know how Franciszka accomplished all of these great things but she did, and because she did, she saved the life of a wonderful, innocent young man. Mrs. Abramowicz was living in a small town in Poland, living a completely normal life. Well that is, before the Germans came. Franciszka was a Roman Catholic woman but she still felt bad for the Jews. One of her neighbors, Sneder Dyszel, was a Jewish man with no family, and was living all alone. When the news spread that the Germans were coming and looking for Jews, not only was he scared for his own life, but Franciszka was also scared for Sneder's life. She was a good friend to Sneder so she knew she had to help him. Mrs. Abramowicz decided that she would let Sneder live in her house in her cellar until the Germans were gone and the coast was completely clear. In Franciszka's cellar, Sneder Dyszel lived in there for about two weeks. Eventually one of Franciszka's neighbors, Mr. and Mrs. Sonowski, a Catholic couple who were completely against people of Jewish religion, noticed that Franciszka had been providing Mr. Dyszel with shelter and food and water. Since they were against the Jews, they immediately reported the woman to the Gestapo. When the Gestapo (German Police) came, they searched up and down Franciszka's house only to find that there was no sign of any Jew or person besides Mrs. Abramowicz living there. It turns out, right when they found out that they were being reported, Sneder went out into the forest to hide from the Gestapo. The Gestapo came back randomly to Franciszka's house and they continued to find no sign of the Jewish man that had been living there. While in the forest, Sneder continued to receive a lot of help from Franciszka. She still provided him with food and water and other items that he would need to be in the forest alone. A few days later, Franciszka saw that the coast was clear and that the immediate danger had passé. She invited Sneder back into her cellar and he continued to live in the cellar with the help of Franciszka. Days past and weeks past, then months past and Sneder was still living in the cellar or Franciszka's beautiful home. They knew that there was a chance that the Jewish-seeking Germans were out of sight, they two people did not want to take any risks that might end up getting them both caught and murdered. So, they waited a few more days until they heard good news. They heard that the Soviet Union was moving in close to their town. When the Soviet Union arrived and liberated their whole town, Sneder was able to leave Franciszka's cellar and flee to Argentina in 1947. That was the last time Franciszka Abramowicz ever saw her friend.

Franciszka's incredible story has taught me the most amazing things in the most heartwarming ways. I learned about how your own neighbors can betray your trust. I learned some people, (Nazis), can be so cruel to other human beings. But most importantly, I learned that human beings can do some of the most amazing things, just out of kindness. No, Franciszka didn't have to help her neighbor. She could have reported him to the Gestapo and watch him die. Not only did she not do that, but also she provided him with shelter, food, water, and all the other necessities that Sneder would need to survive. It warms my heart to hear such an incredible story like this one of a human showing such love and kindness towards a person in need. Although this makes me happy, this also makes me sad because of the fact that people on this planet would treat other people like they are completely irrelevant and treat them like they are not suppose to be on this earth. The Holocaust shows me that people are capable of not only mistreating others, but slaughtering over six million other people just because they don't like them or they think they are inferior to their race. It is completely disgusting. I know that there are things that need to be done to make sure things like this never happen again. An obvious one being, we need more people like Franciszka in this world. The type of people who will not only protect the lives of other people, but people who will put their own lives at risk in order to save either a complete stranger, or even just a family member. Imagine, if the whole world was filled with people like that, crime and things like the holocaust wouldn't stand a chance against humanity. Things would be just about perfect. Also, one of the main things we need to do to stop this from ever happening again is if everybody on this earth is aware of what happened during the Holocaust. If everybody is aware of what happened, people will know what we did wrong and how to not make those mistakes anymore. I dream, that people will change over time, that people will never redo these horrible, tragic mistakes ever again, and I dream that people will begin to rise up and stand up for one another, no matter how intense the situation. I dream, of the phrase, "Never Again".

Works Cited

"The Righteous Among The Nations." The Righteous Among The Nations. N.p., n.d. Web. 04 Dec. 2016.

"Abramowicz Franciszka." Story of Rescue - Abramowicz Franciszka | Polscy Sprawiedliwi. N.p., n.d. Web. 04 Dec. 2016

"The Righteous Among The Nations." The Righteous Among The Nations. N.p., n.d. Web. 04 Dec. 2016.

Edmund Holka

Evan Hays

Holocaust was originally used to describe a sacrificial offering burned on a alter The Holocaust was a tragic event that started in 1933 caused by the Nazis. The leader of the Nazis was a German man named Adolf Hitler. Adolf Hitler wanted to rid the world of the jewish religion. Adolf Hitler was elected the leader of Germany in 1932. Hitler slowly made the Germans dislike the jewish religion by blaming them for problems. Eventually most of the Germans hated Jews. First he made the Jewish wear stars on their clothing so it was easier for people to recognize them. Next he banned Jewish people from going to certain schools. He started to convince the community that the Jews should be sent to ghettos. The community agreed so the Jews were sent away. After going to ghettos, Adolf Hitler took them to concentration camps where he separated families. Then he started by lying to them saying that the children would go to special schools where they could learn and play. Instead of doing what he said, he started to murder them. He then put the adults who could work into work camps. Those who couldn't were also killed. The adults worked for most of the day and got very little to eat. If you became unable to work, he would kill you. He continued to use this method of starving, gassing, and burning to kill over 6 million people of the Jewish religion and even some gypsies and homosexuals. Fortunately, some Jews were able to escape these camps with the help of individuals like Edmund Holka.

Edmund Holka, a savior to many Jews, was born on January 1st, 1890. He was a wool trader in Poland until he was thrown from his home in 1939 when the German Reich took over the city of Gniezno. He then created a plant with some jewish fundings. The plant was used to treat clothing provided by a German company. Many Jewish in the Warsaw ghetto worked there as employees. After the ghetto was destroyed some of the Jewish employees took on Polish identities to continue working at the plant. Edmund mostly knew who was Jewish and helped them out the best he could. One of his employees, named Roman Polirztok, was taken with his family to Treblinka. Edmund saved him by convincing the German Officer in charge that Roman was an essential worker in the factory. He then found a place for Roman's wife and son to hide. They survived while Roman went back to the ghetto and was rounded up to his death. He also helped Jerzy Lando, an escaped Jew, by hiring him for decent wage and treating him like part of his family.

I learned that whatever job you have you can make an impact on the world. Whether you have a multimillion dollar company or you are a wool merchant you can do something to change the world. I also learned that if you see something wrong try to fix it, don't just stand by and watch. You can also do something to hide a person if they are being targeted or are going to be. I learned from Edmund to never give up when it seems like all hope is lost. When Roman and his family were taken Edmund could've just given up, But he didn't. He persuaded a officer to let them free and hide Romans family and they survived. I also have learned to be fair. Edmund saw that Jerzy was a Jew and could've hired him for low wage and take advantage over him, but he hired him for normal wage and treated him like family. The holocaust was more than a tragedy it was a disaster. It caused so much fear in so many people to this day, it scarred people for life, but it also was an awaking. It awoke us to the possibility of this happening. We can never again let that happen. Let a single person kill millions, force people out their homes just to destroy them, cause the entire Earth to be at war. If we ever see this start to happen again we need to swiftly end it and all followers of this idea.

Work Cited

History.com Staff. "The Holocaust." History.com. A&E Television Networks, 2009. Web. 12 Dec. 2016.

Vashem, Yad. "Holka Edmund (1890 - 1972) Personal Information." The Righteous Among The Nations. The World Holocaust Remembrance Center, n.d. Web. 12 Dec. 2016.

Vashem, Yad. The Righteous Among The Nations. The World Holocaust Remembrance Center, n.d. Web. 12 Dec. 2016.

"The History Place - Holocaust Timeline." The History Place - Holocaust Timeline. N.p., n.d. Web. 12 Dec. 2016.

"Introduction to the Holocaust." United States Holocaust Memorial Museum. United States Holocaust Memorial Museum, n.d. Web. 12 Dec. 2016.

Zofia Bania

Fataba-Miatta Koilor

Meaning sacrifice by fire, the Holocaust killed as many as six million Jews and five million Non-Jewish people, people that weren't like Adolf Hitler. In the 1930s, economic depression had hit Germany vigorously leading German citizens to think Adolf Hitler and his Nazi Part was the last result in solving their problems. Nazis believed that Aryans were a "master race" and any other races, such as Jews, were enemies. The beginning of the Holocaust started with a ministry that was anti-Jewish propaganda, which was also used in schools. Soon afterwards, laws were made against Jews, such as they were forced to wear the yellow star of David to identify themselves. As Jews began to escape Germany, Hitler thought this was the solution to the problem until other countries

wouldn't take any more Jews. Small ghettos with barbed wire and stone were then established where Jews were left to starve and to get infected with many diseases. But in fact, Jews tried to have "normal" lives and did not die, forming resistant groups in the ghettos. Jews were rounded up by SS (elite security forces) and were taken to some of the biggest concentration camps located in Poland to speed up the total elimination of Jews. In the camps, it was unsanitary and people were treated as inhumane medical experiments. These camps were where many loved ones were separated from families and lost their lives from labor and starvation.

Zofia Bania was born in 1907 and became a poor farmer. Unable to pay for food, Mrs. Bania would go to a small shop and get food from Frania Rubinek, a Jew, for free. They became close friends so when the Germans started rounding up Jews in October 1942, Frania and Israel Rubinek turned to Zofia, who responded, ¨Maybe. ¨ Waiting for Zofia´s answer they soon fled to a nearby town, waiting to go to Russia, but Frania was eight months pregnant. They received a message explaining that Zofia was searching, so they traveled back in a wagon of a trusted man the Rubineks hired. Zofiaś small one story house was soon to be shared among her husband and son, and the Rubineks and their future child. Zofia's husband, Ludwig, didn't want to accept The Rubineks in his home, but they continued trying their best to please him, giving him money for his silence. When Frania Rubinek gave birth in December of 1942, the baby died leaving her ill for six months. She was cared for by her husband and Zofia, who then shared the one story house with the family.

Ludwig bought a guard dog for the safety of the Rubineks. Because of the dog's warning, Frania and her husband were able to enter a cellar just as German soldiers burst through the house, stating they would be spending the night. A bed for Zofia's son was placed on top of the cellar door to avert the soldiers from noticing. The Rubineks still were not safe enough because Frania's husband had a terrible cough which could be heard in the small house. Zofia's son was just so devoted to the Rubineks as his mother, so he spent the whole night pretending to be sick, coughing, and crying loudly. Zofia's son's courage kept the Rubineks from being discovered by the German soldiers. The Rubineks managed to immigrate to Canada after the war and soon traveled back to Poland to visit Zofia and her family. Sadly, Zofia Bania died in 1991.

The Holocaust ended in May 8,1945 lasting a long staggering 12 years. 91% of the Jewish population in Poland was killed, whereas 63% of the Jewish population was killed in Europe. 11 million people died leaving only 7,650 living prisoners and 14,000 pounds of human hair. Many Jews that survived, such as Frania and Israel Rubinek, survived with help from non-Jewish people who were against Nazis. These people risked their lives by hiding or helping Jews escape, which is honor and glory.

Zofia Bania's bravery taught me that even though there might be bad people in this world, there would always be a small portion of good. Although Zofia wasn't able to save every Jew out there, she still meant a lot to Frania and Israel Rubineks and that means a lot to us today. This taught me that no one should be singled out by religion or how they look. The Holocaust was brutal and it impacted me in a way of emotion. "Never Again" was the motto of the Jewish Defense League and first appeared on signs in April, 1945.

The Holocaust should never repeat itself again. This act of wickedness didn't happen overnight, but can also be prevented in many ways. The Holocaust should never be forgotten, and needs one big step to prevent anything like this from ever happening again. Our generation is the generation to make a difference with all the wars that have gone on, and all the segregation. We can start with honesty and move on from there. Every religion has something in common which should be told and stated. "Never Again" was once stated, and I believe we should continue standing by it. "I swore never to be silent whenever and wherever human beings endure suffering and humiliation. We must take sides. Neutrality helps the oppressor, never the victim. Silence encourages the tormentor, never the tormented."

— Elie Wiesel This quote should be taken to heart, and not just read through.

Work Cited

Wojan, Megan. "Intro to Holocaust." Megan Wojan, 30 Nov. 2016. Web. 12 Dec. 2016.
"Quotes About Holocaust (335 Quotes)." (335 Quotes). N.p., n.d. Web. 12 Dec. 2016.
"Bania Family." Yad Vashem. N.p., n.d. Web. 12 Dec. 2016.

Heroes of Poland

Fox Jordan

There were many heroes of the Holocaust. Many were from Poland. I am writing about this Polish hero and his family, Stefan. Stefan and his family lived in Zimodry. A priest from a town called Stara Wilejka asked his wife, Teofila, to take care of an orphan Jewish girl, named Czertok, who was from a place called Wilno. She recently escaped from a ghetto and had no place to go. Then she asked the priest for help and ended up at the Szwajkajzer household were everyone took care of her. To prove that she was a part of the family, they received a document proving she was a relative. And to avoid forced labor, they got a forged document saying she was already working. But in 1942 she was detained due to an informer. Zbignew, her "relative," went to the police in an attempt to release her. Before this happened to her, she fled to Wanda (Zbignew's sister).

Wanda was a teacher with a room with a peasant family who lived 10 kilometers away from Kurzenic where the rest of her family resided. Wanda then contacted Czeslawa through the Jewish pharmacist who had joined the partisans. Czeslawa then went back to her foster parent's home only to find that they had been deported. She then went to Zimodry were she met up with Teofila who, as you remember, was the foster parent of Czeslawa. They then went their separate ways in agreement to come back to Poland. Then, in 1948, they met up in Warsaw, and discovered that Czeslawa had been recently married. They were then reunited as a family until 1969 when again they parted as to Czeslawa had left to Israel. In 1983 Yad Vashem recognized the family as "Righteous Among the Nations."(http://db.yadvashem.org/).

I learned that the Holocaust affected many people besides Jews. Other people such as gypsies were also prosecuted. I learned that this took place during WW II and continues to happen even when we interfere and try to stop it. The Holocaust also affected caretakers of the Jewish refugees (some were German). I learned that one of the main causes of the Holocaust was Adolf Hitler and that he blamed the Jewish people for all the Germans' problems. And he claimed that they were a disgrace to god and that people needed to stop buying things from them. They became racist and unjust. The people helping the Jews could be prosecuted and killed. This meant that taking care of a Jewish person was very risky and could cause great harm. The Holocaust started out as blaming Jews for all of their problems. When Hitler started calling the Jews out it began as discrimination and unfairness. Then it became calling them out and mass discrimination. Then they were forced into ghettos. Then concentration camps to try and kill them by starvation. Then it became extermination camps with gas chambers and other methods of extermination like firing squads This person has taught me a lot about the Holocaust and why we can't let it happen again. If it does happen there will always be people to help the people affected. If it negatively affects some, people will go against it even if they positively benefit from it. And to dispose of the bodies they burned them. I also learned that it was Adolf Hitler that had built up this uprising. The Holocaust impacted many people and severely impacted those who were closely tied to it, like some cousins and family members

The meaning of "Never Again" is to never let something like this ever happen again. This is a motto of sorts for Holocaust survivors who have been through this terrible event and who understand the importance of making sure an event like this never happens again. Some things we can do to make sure this never happens again are to be kind to those who are different than us and respect their differences and religion. We can also make sure that the people around us respect others. We need to respect race and take responsibility for our own mistakes. We need to stop these things from happening and be careful about those who we place in power. When something like this does happen, we need to do all that we can to help those we are able to. We have to rise up when we can see this happening and fight for those who have done no wrong. We need to bring others together to stop this before it can start and learn from our mistakes. We have to learn from past experiences and learn when things get out of control. All of us must take our knowledge of the past and present to shield ourselves and protect others. We should learn from those who have experienced these horrible things and pass on this knowledge we have gained to the generations ahead of us and be sure they learn why it is important to make sure this doesn't happen and what can happen if it does. There could be chaos and destruction especially with the weapons we have now. We have to learn that it could cause us trouble and make sure that we protect ourselves and those we love and cherish. All of us should learn from the Holocaust and make sure that we do all in our power to make sure something like this never happens again.

Works Cited

History.com Staff. "The Holocaust." History.com. A&E Television Networks, 2009. Web. 2 Dec. 2016.

Yad Vashem. N.p., n.d. Web. 16 Nov. 2016.
<http://db.yadvashem.org/righteous/family.html?language=en&itemId=4039812>.

Maria Andezelm

Gabby Cortez

The Holocaust was a horrible time in our history. An economic depression hit Germany hard in the 1930's. All Jewish people were deprived of all their rights, and they were forced to wear the yellow star of David to be recognized. They were not allowed to be in certain businesses or places, and eventually were taken away from their homes and placed in concentration camps. The concentration camps were horrible because they separated all family. They were forced to live in unsanitary barracks, and were given barely given enough food to survive. 91% of Jews in Poland were killed. After they were taken from their homes, the Jewish people began to flee. There were some people of other religions who were open to helping the Jews. For example, Maria Andzelm and her family took in two Jewish boys.

Maria lived in Janowiec, Poland on a farm with her family where she worked. She had two younger brothers, Jan and Stanislaw. At the age of 16 she was married to Moses, one of the Jewish boys. They had two kids, Rosalie and Helene. She and Moses were married for 52 years until he died of a heart disease. She was a petite thirteen year old when her best friend, Rivka, left to a concentration camp because she was a Jew. Maria and her family were Christians that had the hearts to not discriminate and help the Jews. The Germans occupied their whole land and took most of their possessions. They were very poor themselves, but they took the chance to help other people on the streets.

 Maria and her family began to help Jewish people when a Jewish woman on the verge of leaving with a baby came to their doorsteps. It was against the law of the Nazis to help the Jewish in any kind of way, but they did not care. They gave the woman and her baby milk and food, and sent them on their way. After the woman, more and more came. They could not buy a lot of food and supplies to help them because they were worried the Nazis would suspect them. Her brother wondered why they kept giving food away. When Maria was sleeping she could hear the voices of the people they were helping, but just went back to sleep.

In 1942, finally Maria's father one day told the family what they did to help and that they were going to be hiding two Jewish boys, Moses and Srulik. To hide the two boys secretively, they dug a little box under a cowshed and pigsty with boards on top of it, they did this for two years. Sometimes the cows and pigs would pee through the boards onto their heads, but they didn't mind because it was better than being in the possession of the Nazis. Maria and her younger brothers helped anyway they could. They went down there sometimes, fed them three times a day, brought them books to read, brought stuff for their hygiene needs, and brought them out for fresh air once in awhile. One day she was off to her friend's house when, all of a sudden, a bomb went off. Maria and her friend quickly ran to her aunt's house in fear, but had to leave after three days because it was to risky. They decided to go to the house of a woman across the lake. All of her family was there, except their dad. He was shot saving the two Jewish boys during the bombs. Since all the neighbors knew now that they were hiding the Jews, they had to leave home for fear of attacks. The rest of her family moved to the United States to help a widow with her farm. They moved to an apartment, paid by Moses. After the Holocaust was over, Maria and Moses moved to the United States, because it was still not completely safe in Poland, and they opened up a cigar store. Maria Andzelm is a bold, brave, and risk-taking girl. She and her family helped save many Jews, during this horrible time in our history, from being discriminated and maybe even killed. They took a big risk, because if they were caught doing the right thing they would have been killed as well as the Jewish boys they were helping. Since she helped and saved Jews, she is a Polish Holocaust hero.

These people did the right thing. Even though they weren't in the situation themselves, they didn't just stand by and let it happen. They helped in any way they could, which made them great heroes. I don't know what I would have done if I was in the situation of the Jewish people or even if I was a different religion. They were punished wrongly for being themselves. I'm so glad that I live in a later day and in a different age where we don't discriminate against ethnicity, religion, and color. We really have come a long way from that horrible time in history. Even though I would have been frightened, I would have done the same as Maria did and try to help as many Jews as possible. I hope this "Never Again" happens in our history and I will try to make sure of that. I have great respect for Maria and others who helped the Jewish people during that time.

Works Cited

"Maria Anzelm." Heroes of the Holocaust. N.p., n.d. Web. 09 Dec. 2016.

Yad Vashem - Request Rejected. N.p., n.d. Web. 09 Dec. 2016.

Megan, Wojian, "Introduction to Holocaust" (lecture) Nov.4,2016

Stanislaw Betiuk

Gabriel Jones Jr

 The Holocaust was a brutal genocide, which was ordered by Adolf Hitler to exterminate all the Jews in the country of Germany. All races except for Germans were brutally executed and were separated from their parents and loved ones. Stanislaw Betiuk was born on August 5th, 1917 in Poland and he and his family were part of the Catholic religion. He was also a male farmer and has survived the whole Holocaust and lived to tell his story. He rescued Jews by illegal transfer. He hid them in his barn under the floorboards, supplying basic goods, and providing false evidence to the Germans. He was recognized on February 16, 1984 and he has a tree in his honor.

Stanislaw Betiuk was a resident of the village of Strupin, near the location of the Lublin voivodeship. He was a business acquaintance for the Handelsman family in the nearby town of Chelm, who had provided him with a great orchard. In the beginning of November 1942, before the last liquidation of the Chelm ghetto, Betiuk went to see the Handelsman family. He was always visiting them, providing the family with basic needs, such as foods and items to clean themselves with. When he was visiting the family on November 24, 1942 he had offered protection for the two daughters of the family and the parents agreed. At this time Fajga Handelsman was 19 years old and Brucha Handelsman was 17 years old and Brucha was a housekeeper for a German doctor's house. The doctor had advised her to take shelter in a Polish acquaintance's house and hide for a while. After the parents agreed, Betiuk had secretly taken the sisters to his farm the generous family had given him. He had then prepared a bunker for them underneath the cowshed, covering the entrance with large planks of wood covered with straw. Every day, he would sneak during the night to give the sisters food, water and trips to the restroom. In due course, rumors had spread about Betiuk keeping and hiding Jews at his house and farm. When the village elder received these rumors, he had informed the German police and he was then arrested and interrogated. During his interrogation, he was severely beaten, but he did not betray the sisters and continued telling the police he did not know about any Jews hiding. After the German police conducted a search, they could not find the hidden bunker or the sisters and they let Betiuk go. He had taken care of and supported the sisters until the Red Army liberated the area in July of 1944. Betiuk had asked for nothing in return and acted purely out of the friendship of the sisters' parents.

After the war, Betiuk had married Brucha, who had converted to Christianity. During this time, he and the sisters had learned that the parents had died at the concentration camp in Treblinka, Warsaw. Brucha's sister, Zlota Helena immigrated to Israel with her husband and lived there. She had kept in contact with her brother-in-law and former protector. She had also hosted him in her house when he had visited Israel in January of 1967. On the 16th of February 1984, Yad Vashem had recognized Betiuk as a Righteous Among the Nations and had given him a very special tree in his honor.

I had learned how so many people had risked their lives to help the falling race of the Jews in Poland and many other places around the world. I also learned that the survivors of the Holocaust came up with the saying, "Never Again." In addition, I had learned that many of the protectors had died while trying to save or hide the Jews in their homes, barns, and many other places. Learning about my person really made me feel proud that they were doing something heroic like this. But, also hearing about how many people were killed through the years of the Holocaust made me very sad and angry someone would do that to another race. I understand that the Holocaust was a very sad part in the German history and people who had died will never see their loved ones again. The impact took a big role because most of the Jewish population was exterminated and it took a while to let the number of Jewish people rise up again.

"Never Again" means that something like the Holocaust should never happen in history again in any country. What "Never Again" means to me is that we should all be equal and something like this should not happen ever again. We could first erase all of the racism in our world and countries and all of the hate towards any race or people. Everyone should be equal and treated the same as the other people in the country or community. In conclusion, I know some people won't change, but if this does happen there would be less chance for another Holocaust or genocide in our history.

Works Cited Page

"Stanislaw Betiuk." Yadvashim. Yadvashim. 2016. Web. 13 Nov. 2016.

Wojan, Megan. "Introduction To Holocaust." Social Science 7 Honors Introduction To Holocaust. KAMS, Elk Grove. 4 Nov. 2016. Lecture.

Gertruda Babilinska

Gabriella Glaser

Gertruda Babilinska was one of the many "saviors" for some Jews in the time of the Holocaust. She was born North of Poland, near Danzig, in 1902. She was one of eight children in her family. For a long part of her life she took care of children who were part of a very wealthy Jewish family, the Stolowitskys. When the Nazis came through Poland they took Mr. Stolowitzky to Auschwitz, away from his family. After the father was taken away, Mrs. Stolowitzky, her family and Gertruda moved to many places. She first took them to Warsaw and then to Vilna. They got an apartment in Vilna, right outside the ghetto, but they could never stop thinking about the Nazis and if they would come. Soon enough the Germans attacked the Soviet Union and remained in Vilna. Mrs. Stolowitzky made Gertruda promise to take care of her daughter, Mickey, before she died. When the Germans moved into France they always had to be aware of what was going on. She was terrorized when the killing of Jews began abruptly and the ghettos were formed. Mrs. Stolowitzky was unable to survive with the harsh conditions that they were living under and she died in April 1941.

Gertruda was not going let anything happen to Mickey, so she had to act fast. Gertruda managed to get false papers and a baptismal certificate for Mickey to be considered her nephew. When Mickey became ill she had searched for a doctor, but all she found were non-Jewish doctors. She then ventured into the ghetto to hopefully find a doctor. She remembered what Mrs. Stolowitzky had told her, that if she made it to the Land of Israel she could locate her cousins and they would take care of Mickey and she could go back to Europe. She knew she could not raise a boy to be a Jew when she was a Catholic woman. After the war ended is when they tried to leave. All transportation out of Europe at this time was very crowded. They finally got a ride on a boat to Israel, the Exodus. When they arrived and Mickey stepped off the boat he became a Jewish patriot. She began to look for the mother's relatives and, according to PBS.gov, "I would never forgive them for what they did to me. They gave me a tiny room upstairs with no water or toilet. They would only pay for a half of a year for school for Mickey." The relatives wanted to adopt Mickey from Gertruda and send Gertruda back to Poland. She was told that if she stayed in Israel they would not pay for school for Mickey, but Gertruda wouldn't give in that easily. Mickey refused to stay with the relatives and he would go wherever Gertruda went. So she got a job as a maid to make sure they stayed in Israel with a roof over their heads and food to eat. When Mickey finished school he worked for Copel Towers arranging tours. He then got to move to Miami to work, but Gertruda and Mickey's relationship hadn't reached the end quite yet. He would always visit her in Israel many times a year and he stills visits her to this day.

Gertruda along with many other rescuers demonstrated a few qualities that made them rescuers. Not only did they house and feed the Jewish people, but they had the courage to see beyond the facts that they are Jews, but they saw that they are people who didn't deserve this kind of treatment. From this essay I learned that just because someone is different than you, even in the slightest way you shouldn't treat them differently than you would treat someone else. Segregation is not right. Our lives would probably be just a little better if we chose to accept people for who they are inside not what they look like. Being mean is not why the world was created and it's not why our world is still spinning on its axis. Our beautiful Earth is still turning because of those people who decided to not make more enemies, but help others in need. Learning about Gertruda Babilinska was a great experience to me while I was young so I didn't have to grow up living a life of being rude to people who are not the same as me. She chose to help the Stolowitzkys because she knew that they didn't deserve this treatment for having their own beliefs and stayed with Mickey because she saw a future in a young girl needed a role model. The Holocaust should have never taken place because one man thought it was right to harm people, physically and mentally, because he had power over others that were different than what he thought was right. "Never Again" should never happen again and what was done to these people was not just and should never reoccur. To make sure this never happens again everyone should be treated equally and respected for their beliefs. A person's culture, looks and beliefs shouldn't matter to who they are on the inside. I chose Gertruda Babilinska because she was a hero in disguise to a family in need of saving just so their child could live the life he deserved when this war was all over.

Works Cited

"Rescuers: Gertruda Babilinska." PBS. PBS, n.d. Web. 07 Dec. 2016.

"About the Righteous." About the Righteous. N.p., n.d. Web. 07 Dec. 2016.

"Gertruda Babilińska." Gertruda Babilińska. N.p., n.d. Web. 07 Dec. 2016.

" ." The Remarkable Story of Gertruda Babilińska - Virtual Shtetl. N.p., n.d. Web. 07 Dec. 2016.

Antonina Bak Essay

Grace Ahumada

To begin with, the Holocaust was the scariest and saddest thing that I have heard and learned about in my life. The Holocaust started when Hitler formed a military and called it the Nazi Army and that is when the Germans begin to hate the Jews. For example, the Jews were forced to wear a star so the Germans could tell that they were Jews, and Jews were not allowed to go to the stores because the sign said "No Jews Allowed." But, there were numerous people that were righteous. The one person I pick was Antonina Bak.

The righteous person was Antonina Bak that stands out to me. Anotnina Bak was a female who was born on March 31, 1909 and was an expert in farming. She was raised in Poland and her religion was Catholic. Also, she lived from 1909 and died on an unknown date. In summary, I picked Antonina Bak as a righteous person.

Antonina Bak was righteous by helping three brothers who escaped the camps. Antonina helped them by hiding them in her yard where she worked. She would bring them loaves of bread up to 8-10 of them. Their recused place was in Poland, Jurowce and more. Therefore, Antonina was righteous by helping the three brothers in hiding from the ghettos.

In conclusion, Antonina Bak was a righteous person in helping the three brothers in escaping the ghettos. Antonina sadly past away but she will always be the righteous that stood out to me. I learned that the Holocaust was all started by a German named Hilter. In my opinion I hope the Holocaust will never again happen. Treating each other equally is a step that would happen never again.

Work cited

Vashem, Vad " Names of Righteous by country." Names of righteous by country. Yad Vashem The world Holocaust remembrance center, 1 Jan. 2016. Web. 12.dec 2016.

The Gawlak Family, Heroes During the Holocaust

Grace McGee

The word "Holocaust" was, in the past, used to describe a sacrificial burning. Now the word has taken on the horrendous new meaning: it represents the genocide massacre of six million Jews by the German government, led by Adolf Hitler. Adolph Hitler was obsessed with the idea of a place of "racial purity" where "pure" races like Germans were in control and the weak or handicapped didn't live. He deemed all the Jewish "impure" and he blamed the Jews for Germany's defeat that it had at the end of World War I, in the year 1918. Unfortunately, there is even some evidence to suggest that the Jews were still treated badly long before the Holocaust happened, even dating back to ancient times. During the rule of the ancient Roman Empire, the Romans destroyed a Jewish temple of worship in Jerusalem and then forced the Jews to leave Palestine to live scattered elsewhere. Survival often required a great deal of bravery from individual Jews, as well as the bravery of kind people.

Luckily, there were some people brave enough to help the Jewish people, even in horribly dangerous times. The Gawlak family was just one of the many such families who helped the Jews during the Holocaust. They aided a woman named Ola Schary to survive the Holocaust. Also, with great patience, and after many months, assisted reuniting her with the rest of the surviving members of her family.

The German army forced more than a thousand Jews from their homes and into ghettos. A Ghetto is an area in a city, usually a slum, where Jews were concentrated and forced to live. In the year 1943, Ola and her husband hurriedly escaped the ghetto in Warsaw to the other side of the city. Jacob, her husband, was killed during the escape attempt. Ola obtained some fake identity papers from a woman named Helena, who was Catholic, and got hired as a housekeeper for a Polish family. But months later, Helena was fired because the family she was currently working for feared she was Jewish. The family didn't want to put themselves at risk by harboring a Jewish person during the Holocaust. A person caught harboring a Jew could be shot to death by a German soldier.

Later, Ola found a newspaper that said the Gawlak family needed a housekeeper, so she set out immediately to apply for the position. The Gawlak family hired her as a housekeeper and nanny of their 3-year-old daughter, Ewa. Ewa and her mother, Aurelia, both liked her, but they suspected she was Jewish. In summer 1944, Ola told the Gawlaks that she was Jewish because there was talk of Germans at the Warsaw ghetto. Soon afterward, they took Ola and left, but at the transit camp in Pruszkow she fell ill. She had to go to the hospital and Aurelia gave Ola a substantial amount of money so that Ola would be taken care of after recovering from her illness. Ola was very lucky to have found a job with the Gawlak family just in time.

Ola was very lucky she survived, as were a few of her family members. Ola's mother and father were killed in the war but her brother, Joseph, had luckily escaped and survived. Her sister, Sabine, survived and made a new life in Canada. Ola went to Canada to see her sister and she then married Zelman Schary whom she met in Canada and they both moved to New York. In 1987, they moved to Israel and she told her story to her brother and daughter, Helen. She wished to repay the Gawlak family for their kindness, so Helen published an article in a paper to tell her mother's story and to publically thank the kind actions of the Gawak family. Ewa and Helen now stay in contact with each other.

Ola couldn't have survived if not for the Gawlak's generosity and bravery. They were willing to risk themselves and their 3-year-old daughter in order to save her life. When she had no one, she was helped, saved by a kind and caring family. They knew she was Jewish, but they didn't care and treated her just the same when she told them. I have learned that it's not hard to come by heroes, and they can be just the same as everyone else on the outside, but have a hero's heart on the inside. Learning about this kind family has had a big impact on my life. I now try to be more generous and forgiving of others. I also try not to hold long-term grudges, for example if some kid stole my juice box from my lunch in first grade. I understand that the Holocaust was something much bigger than simple teasing; this was mortal cruelty. The world got a message from this event, to never let genocide, especially this big, happen. "Never Again" is what we all desire. We can learn from our mistakes using historical events so nothing this gruesome ever happens again. By completing this essay kids can learn about the holocaust and its impact. It gets kids more aware of the past so that this new generation can have the wisdom to cease each and every undertaking like the Holocaust.

Works Cited Page

History.com Staff. "The Holocaust." History.com. A&E Television Networks, 2009. Web. 12 Dec. 2016.

Righteous Among the Nations Ceremony. Yad Vashem, n.d. Web. 12 Dec. 2016.

The Righteous Among the Nations. Yad Vashem, n.d. Web. 12 Dec. 2016.

Irena Sendler

Grace Smith

 Ever since the Holocaust, the world has come to a great change. The word "Holocaust" comes from the Greek words "holos" (meaning whole) and "kaustos" (meaning burned). The Holocaust refers to the time period from January 30, 1933, when Adolf Hitler became the chief minister of Germany, to May 8, 1945, when the war in Europe finally ended. By the end of this the Germans had killed nearly two out of every three European Jews as part of Adolf Hitler's "final solution." One point five million children were murdered. That is terrorizing and heartbreaking which is why so many people should remember the Holocaust. This is a big event that people should be aware of for the rest of their lives.

Yet there were acts of human decency and courageousness during the Holocaust and one of the people that did just that was Irena Sendler. A remarkable woman defied the Nazis and saved two thousand five hundred Jewish children by smuggling them out of the Warsaw Ghetto. As a health worker, she sneaked the children out between 1942 and 1943 to safe hiding places and found non-Jewish families to adopt them.

When the city's Jews were imprisoned behind a ghetto wall without food or medicine, Irena Sendler went to closest friends and colleagues, mostly young women, some barely out of school. Together, they smuggled aid in and smuggled Jewish orphans out of the ghetto by hiding infants on trams and garbage wagons and leading older children out through secret passageways and the city's sewers. Identification papers and Catholic birth certificates were forged and signed by high ranking officials in the Social Services Department and priests so that children could be taken from safe houses in Warsaw to orphanages and convents in the surrounding countryside.

The memory of the Holocaust is what shapes and teaches us to be better. I think we should always remember the Holocaust because this was an event that people were persecuted for being something that they couldn't change and it wasn't really something that was up to them along with their fault. This event is what happens when hatred and discrimination get way out of control. People shouldn't ever hate or discriminate against someone for being something they can't change about their own self. The Holocaust was an event that shows us what happens when we stop seeing people as people, when we fail to see a person as a unique individual. The Holocaust was a historical tragedy that affected the whole of the globe. I believe that intolerance of history isn't only disrespectful, but I think that future generations should be made aware of all major events in history such as the Holocaust so that important lessons regarding things such as human nature and acceptance can be learned. This is so as to avoid major historical tragedies ever happening again.

I learned a lot from the Holocaust. I learned that a lot of people suffered from this event and a lot of people risked their lives to help others during this event. From learning about this event makes me more aware about life and what people have done because they didn't like other people. It really shocks me that people didn't like other people for who they were so they just decided to end their lives. They were completely innocent and they didn't do anything to harm them. Learning about Irena Sendler has had an impact on my life. From her risking her own life to help the lives of children and make sure they were safe and sound is completely courageous and outstanding. She has made an impact on my life because her actions are completely inspiring. They inspire me to want to grow up and be like her because, not only do I want to help people now because of her actions, I want to live like her: courageous and passionate.

We can make sure that an event like the Holocaust never happens again by making sure hatred and discrimination of other people don't happen as well. As society grows more and more, people stop seeing each other as their own unique selves. People hate on other people and people discriminate against other people. People don't see other people for someone that they are on the inside, they see other people for someone they are on the outside. By making sure we don't do that, we can be kind to everyone and love everyone the exact same. Yes, some others will choose to show hatred for some people for being somebody that they have no control of whatsoever. But, to make sure that an event like the Holocaust never ever happens again, we can choose to be kind to one another and adore one another for who they are on the inside not outside. We can choose to show equality for everyone and not single anybody out for their differences. We should always be kind to one another no matter how different they are from us. That's what I think we could do to make sure an event like the Holocaust never happens and never even is thought of.

Helena Bereska

Gracie Bailey

The Holocaust slowly happened over a long period of time. The Holocaust happened in Germany, in 1933 until about 1945. The Holocaust was led by a guy named Adolf Hitler, and his army, known as the Nazis. Hitler believed that all Jews were bad. He believed that Jews were bad because of his experience with Jews in the past. In the past, they had wronged Hitler, so Hitler decided to get revenge by getting people on his side, then by proceeding to lock away the Jews. Eventually, the Holocaust led to about 6 million, about 1.5 million being children, Jewish lives lost. Not only were there a lot of Jewish lives lost, but over 5,000 Jewish communities as well. While in the concentration camps, the Jews would only get a piece of bread for free if you were a kid. If you were an adult, you would have to pay for it. Not only that, but for a bowl of soup, which was simply hot water, you would pay for that, too. If a Jewish person did something bad, the Nazis would have a list of punishments and how many times that certain Jew had gotten in trouble. For example, if you tried to take some food back to your bed so you can eat it later, and got caught, the Nazis would whip you until you bled.

The Holocaust may have been a terrible event in history, but there were some good people during the Holocaust. On May 17th, in 1973, a Polish, Catholic woman, by the name of Helena Bereska, was recognized as Righteous Among the Nations. Helena Bereska, with great determination and courage, helped a young Jewish family survive during the tragic Holocaust. Without her, this family would have lost their beloved child as soon as they were put into a concentration camp, since their child was an infant. This small-town hero of Poland single-handedly saved an infant, helpless, and discriminated baby.

It all started in 1938, when Israel Kerners escaped to the Soviet Union-occupied zone, leaving his wife and daughter, named Beata Kerners, behind. Helena was employed by the Kerners as a domestic helper, or a person who cleans around the house, almost like a maid. Helena refused to leave the distraught wife and child alone, so she offered shelter at her brother's house. After a while, Helena's brother got suspicious of his new house guests being Jewish, so eventually he kicked them out. Helena, the child, and the wife, were forced to seek a new place to stay together in.

With time and determination, Helena found a place to live in Krakow, near Wieliczka. After a few years there, in 1941 Helena traveled to Warsaw so that she could bring the husband, Israel, back to the wife and daughter. When they got back, they were incarcerated into the Wieliczka ghetto. But still, despite the consequences, Helena would not leave the family's side.

Unfortunately, in liquidation of the ghetto, Israel and the wife, passed away suddenly. Beata and Helena escaped and reached a village called Krakow. They stayed in that village until they were liberated by the Red Army. After the liberation, Helena and Berta returned to the place they called home for many years, Krakow. Beata stayed with Helena until 1950. In 1950, Beata got traced by a long-lost aunt who brought Beata to Israel.

In brief, Helena Bereska was a spectacular and amazing survivor of the effects of the Holocaust, who would not just stand by to watch something horrid and painful happen to the ones around her or the ones she loves. Helena has taught me so much about being an up stander, and she also taught me to help those around me in need and protection. Helena has also encouraged and inspired me to give back so I can help people in need who have helped me before, such as helping my mom when she asks me to do things like the dishes and help clean, which is nothing compared to the pain and misery the Jews were subjected to. I understand the Holocaust has affected how our world thinks about new leaders. The Holocaust was a huge event that happened in history that has greatly affected and changed the way we think and judge our leaders. To remember the Holocaust's tragic and sad events, the survivors and heroes such as Helena created a simple but meaningful phrase, "Never Again." "Never Again" is used as a phrase to spread awareness and remembrance among people about the Holocaust. So this never happens again, we could stand up for what we believe in and rise against something we think is wrong. We could also be aware of what is happening in other countries. In conclusion, the Holocaust should forever be remembered as a tragic and sad event that has happened many years ago.

Works Cited

"The Righteous Among The Nations." The Righteous Among The Nations. N.p., n.d. Web. 12 Dec. 2016.

"An Introductory History on Holocaust." Jewish Virtual Library. N.p., n.d. Web. 13 Dec. 2016.

Władysław Bartoszewski

Grace O'Brien

In 1933, the population of Jews was over 9 million. By 1945, German Nazis killed two-thirds of the Jews. They also killed off the disabled and mentally ill. Victims were murdered, put into extermination camps or ghettos, or died of starvation or disease. This terrible time when Nazis invaded the Jews is called the Holocaust.

During this frightening time, many people risked their lives and went out of their way to save others from death. These people are called The Righteous Among the Nations. The Righteous hid Jews on the rescuers' property (or their own), provided false papers and identities, helped Jews escape, and rescued children. Righteous people have been recognized from over 40 countries. A Righteous One from Poland, named Wladyslaw Bartoszewski, was a very influential and inspiring role model during and after the Holocaust.

Władysław Bartoszewski was born on February 19, 1922 in Warsaw, Poland. He attended private Catholic schools and grew up with his mother and father. His mother was an accountant and his father a banker. When he was seventeen years old, Germans invaded Warsaw. He participated in the defense of Warsaw with the Polish Red Cross and was sent to Auschwitz as a prisoner in September of 1940. From this battle, about 18,000 citizens were killed and about 140,000 were captured. Bartoszewski was released in April 1941, thanks to the Polish Red Cross. He wrote reports on the violations of the Nazis as a journalist upon coming back to Warsaw. Wladyslaw joined the Polish Home Army (or the AK) in 1942.

Władysław Bartoszewski was a leader of ŻEGOTA, which was a codename for The Council of the Aid of Jews. This council was formed in December 1942. ŻEGOTA saved tens of thousands of Jews by illegally giving money, false identities, food, water, shelter, and protection, especially during the Warsaw Ghetto Uprising. The Council for the Aid of the Jewish also rescued many Jews from camps, deportation trains, and ghettos. Members of ZEGOTA also risked their lives by rescuing many Jewish children and provided homes for them.

He was also a participant of the Delegatura, and he took part in the Warsaw Uprising from August 1 to October 2 in 1944. After the Polish government arrested him, he spent about eight years in prison before the court addressed him as being falsely accused as a spy for Germany. After being released, he became a lecturer for Catholic churches and wrote many books about the German occupation of Poland and the fate of Jews. In 1965, Wladyslaw Bartoszewski became a Righteous Among the Nations after being recognized by Yad Vashem. This title made him one of the first non-Jews recognized by the State of Israel. After his last marriage to Antonina Mijal ended due to divorce, he got remarried to Zofia Bartoszewski. He was confined again in the 1980s after breaking martial laws while overpowering communism with Solidarity. From 1990-1995, Bartoszewski was Poland's ambassador to Austria. He was also Poland's Minister of Foreign Affairs. Also in 1990, Wladyslaw was voted Chairman of the International Council of the Auschwitz- Birkenau State Museum. Bartoszewski was the Secretary of State in the Office of the Chairman of the Council of Ministers. Władysław Bartoszewski was the last survivor of ZEGOTA before dying of a heart attack on April 24, 2015 in his hometown Warsaw in Poland. At 93 years old, Wladyslaw's death was a depressing day.

While researching and writing about Wladyslaw Bartoszewski, I have learned many things about the Holocaust and the Righteous. In multiple countries, numerous rebellions took place in order to stop the Germans and their camps. Many people, including Wladyslaw, risked their lives to rescue others and left a huge impact on us and our world today. These people set a great example and we should do good, just like they did in times of danger and risks of life and death. Today, we know the true dangers and cruelty of murdering the innocent, taking people hostage just for their beliefs, and the responsibility of standing up and protecting others. Nobody should ever judge an individual based on their beliefs. We should show respect to those who stood up and fought back against the Nazis and risked their lives to save others. Writing about the Holocaust has made me realize that we need to be brave in times of trouble.

"May Holocaust Remembrance be not only an act of remembrance, but a remembrance to act," states Holocaust Studies. "Never again will we be silent or indifferent in the face of evil." We should always stand up for what is right, and never encourage anyone to do the wrong thing. Like Wladyslaw, we need to be a voice and speak for what is fair. His great accomplishments have changed the world, and we should always remember everything that the Righteous have done for us. Researching Bartoszewski was a great opportunity and I have learned many important lessons. The Holocaust was a terrible time for millions of people, but it has taught us a lot and has greatly impacted our world today.

Works Cited

"About the Righteous." About the Righteous. N.p., n.d. Web. 11 Dec. 2016 <http://www.yadvashem.org/righteous/about-the-righteous>.

"Bartoszewski, Wladyslaw - The Jewish Foundation for the Righteous." The Jewish Foundation for the Righteous. N.p., n.d. Web. 11 Dec. 2016. <https://jfr.org/rescuer-stories/bartoszewski-wladyslaw/>.

The Great Survivor." The Economist. The Economist Newspaper, 09 May 2015. Web. 11 Dec. 2016. <http://www.economist.com/news/obituary/21650524-wladyslaw-bartoszewski-polish-statesman-died-april-24th-aged-93-great-survivor>.

"Introduction to the Holocaust." United States Holocaust Memorial Museum. United States Holocaust Memorial Museum, n.d. Web. 11 Dec. 2016. <https://www.ushmm.org/wlc/en/article.php?ModuleId=10005143>.

United States Holocaust Memorial Museum. United States Holocaust Memorial Museum, n.d. Web. 11 Dec. 2016. <https://www.ushmm.org/information/press/in-memoriam/wladyslaw-bartoszewski>.

Natalia Abramowicz
Gurnoor Sohal

The Holocaust is a gut wrenching reality. It led to discrimination and social exclusion that was primarily based upon nationality. It was a time where the world stood divided. Hitler was central in shaping the message of the Nazi Party, which blamed all of their current social and economic problems in Germany on specific groups such as Jews, intellectuals, and capitalists. Poland was one of Hitler's first targets for annihilation during the Holocaust. His armed forces invaded Poland on September 1, 1939 with a clear-cut mission of intimidating people emotionally and physically through the use of inflammatory rhetoric. One such victim affected was Natalia Abramowicz.

Abramowicz was born on February 10, 1897 and survived while being a camp inmate in Ravensbruck Concentration Camp. Ravensbruck was an all-women concentration camp that housed gypsies, Jews, and communists as mentioned earlier. Life under Hitler's armed forces in these concentration camps was unhygienic, ruthless, and inhumane. In Ravensbruck, women underwent tormenting medical experiments such as leg amputations, faced a plague of lice because of the poor living conditions, and were provided with a scarce amount of toilets that had absolutely no privacy. Eventually, the camp was liberated by the Soviets on April 29, 1945. To date, an estimated 50,000 women died at Ravensbruck from

May of 1939 to April of 1945. Although, Natalia Abramowicz was destined for a concentration camp and eventually managed to survive, her story starts much earlier.

Abramowicz actually provided her house as a safe haven to six individuals, two of them being children, for a total of nine months. She did this purely from her altruistic and kind nature. The Gestapo raided Natalia's apartment while the people she provided her home to had escaped. Just like that, Natalia and many others like her were torn from a world of freedom and thrown into one which operated as a killing machine that wiped out innocent lives in a fashion that gave little importance to actual human beings who had futures ahead of them, who had families to take care of, who had to live and embrace life. Natalia was arrested and deported to Ravensbruck where she remained until the Soviets liberated the concentration camp. Ultimately, she died on January 1, 1979.

To give further insight into what life in Ravensbruck concentration camp was like, the prisoners were divided into sections each with a distinctive figure. Prisoners of war such as the Soviets wore red triangles. Gypsies wore black triangles. "Criminals" that broke Nazi laws wore green triangles. Jews wore yellow triangles and within these triangles was a letter that exemplified the prisoner's nationality. Some of these prisoners were pregnant upon their arrival and, oftentimes, newborns and children were murdered by Nazi nurses and doctors. This shows how unempathetic and manipulated Hitler's forces were. Later on, when the liberation happened, many of the war criminals were doctors and nurses who participated in these experiments and were often sentenced to death. The Nazis also utilized women slave labor to win the war. This trickled down to the expansion of the concentration camp and as a result products such as explosives, ammunitions, weapons, and aircraft supplies were made. Though these women knew that these supplies would be going to Hitler's regime, they could not do anything about it because the consequence was always death even for the pettiest crimes.

In February of 1945, a gas chamber was constructed known as the "Mittweida," which was a Nazi code name. By April of 1945, about 2,300 women were brutally killed in this gas chamber. The majority murdered were Hungarian, Polish, Russian, and Jewish. Women prisoners who worked as scribes counted an estimated 6,000 deaths in its entirety. It was almost impossible to resist this treatment since the Nazi soldiers were armed with weaponry and surrounded each of the four corners of Ravensbruck Concentration Camp. However, some of the prisoners engaged in "resistance" through modes of preparing imaginary meals, sharing recipes, and speaking their own languages. There was even a secret newspaper when the concentration camp initially started. These activities helped women prisoners to survive and provided them with a little sense of motivation and worth.

Modern society, at least in democratic nations, most likely prevents directed injustice towards a specified race. I learned that social exclusion will not bring anything positive into this world. Instead, it is vital to understand each individual's beliefs and practices as long as they are humanitarian and progressive. Natalia Abramowicz shows me that even in times of difficulty, one should not be silenced when another is suffering. The best way to make history not repeat itself is by way of educating children early on, since they are the responsible for the future. Educating children by ways of reading autobiographies, books, and documentaries is truly what is effective. This will bring awareness to the youth, to the middle aged, and to the elderly. The Holocaust is one of the tragic events that never leaves the memory of a nation. I sincerely hope that a calamity like this never happens again. Such tragedies often bring people closer than ever before to reinforce peace, and our nations alike should be equal than ever before.

Works Cited

"Ravensbrück Concentration Camp: History & Overview." Jewish Virtual Library. American-Israeli Cooperative Enterprise, n.d. Web. 11 Dec. 2016.

"The Righteous Among the Nations." Yad Vashem. The World Holocaust Remembrance Center, 2016. Web. 11 Dec. 2016.

Maria Andzelm

Hailey Hernandez

The Holocaust was a sad and tragic time for Jewish people and many more. In the 1930s, depression had hit Germany and there was a lack of confidence in Germany's weak government. With these problems it provided Germany with a new leader and that leader was Adolf Hitler. When Adolf Hitler became the new leader he established a Reich Ministry of public enlightenment. To ensure that the Nazi's message was communicated, the Ministry communicated it through art, music, theater, films, books, radio, and education materials. In the month of January 1933, Nazis had power. Since the Nazis now had power they passed rules, like in the year 1933, they passed the law that Jews were not allowed to hold public office, and in the year 1935, another law was passed that all Jews were deprived of their rights of German citizenship. It was not only the laws though, they also made Jews wear yellow stars of David outside their clothes to identify themselves. Ever since the Nazis passed those laws, Jews were worried about themselves and their family, so they started to flee Germany. After that, Hitler ordered that all Jews in all countries be moved into certain cities in Poland.

When the Nazis were deporting the Jews into the cities, they treated them like animals getting herded into small ghettos. The ghettos were sealed off with stone walls and barbed wire and the Jews tried to live life as normal as possible. Also in the ghettos there was barely any food, so most Jews died in the ghettos. Since all of the Jews didn't die in the ghettos, Hitler had a final solution, which was genocide, the systematic killing of all people. To Hitler, all races inferior had to be eliminated and Jews were one race. Since the Genocide did not work as fast as he wanted it to, Hitler went to rounding up Jews then shooting them and sending them to concentration camps or slave labor where their possessions were taken away, heads were shaved, arms tattooed with numbers or codes, and they had to wear prison uniforms. In the camps men, women, and children were split up based on their trade skills and physical strength. Certain extermination camps were installed with gas chambers and they kill about 60,000 people a day. These extermination camps were mostly found in Poland. Later, Nazis built crematoriums, or ovens, to burn the dead Jews bodies. In the Holocaust, less than 4 million Jews survived and the ones who did, their lives were forever changed in a way that is not describable by words.

The person that I want to talk about that helped Jews during the Holocaust is Maria Andzelm and her family. Maria was Catholic and lived and worked on a farm. Her parents were Stefan and Waleria Andzelm. The Germans occupied their town and took their stuff. They were already poor, but they still helped people on the street. When Maria's best friend was deported, she wanted to do something to help, but she couldn't do anything because she was just a kid and what can a kid do? One day her father called her into a room and told her an important secret that they were going to hide a Jew and that Jew was Moses.

Before Maria Andzelm and her family saved Moses he was in a labor camp nearby Opole. After that, he escaped and went across the Vistula River in Janowiec. There was no ghetto, so he rented an apartment in the home of Stefan Andzelm's mother. It was 1942, the Jews from Janowiec were being deported, but as soon as they were, Moses escaped from transport and found shelter in the home of Stefan and Waleria Andzelm. If they were found hiding Jews, they would be killed. So to hide the Jewish man, Moses and Marias father, Stefan, built a little box underground for him. For the next two years Moses hid in the underground box and Maria fed him three times a day and brought him books to read. Also Maria and her brothers, Jan and Stanislaw, helped the Jewish man as best as they could by meeting his hygienic needs and taking him out from time to time for fresh air or just to walk. Before the war ended, there was an attack and Maria and her friend rushed to their cellar. They stayed in there for two days when someone came to the cellar. Maria asked what happened to her family. The man said her father was shot saving two Jews and the rest of her family moved to a farm to help a widow. After that, Maria and her family moved into a house that was being paid for by Moses. Later Maria married Moses and they did not feel safe in Poland anymore so they moved to the United States of America and opened a cigar store. After they opened the store, Moses died of a heart disease.

The story of Maria Andzelm and her family have taught me many things, but the best one is taking a risk to help other people even though you might get caught. It taught me this by Maria and her family helping Moses and Maria's dad, Stefan, trying to help two Jewish men, but getting shot in the process. This story had a great impact on my life greatly. It had a great impact on my life by learning the greatness in someone and that someone was Maria Andzelm. I say that because she helped Moses when he needed it greatly and took care of him even though her and her family might get caught. The words that I would like to use for this amazing story is "Never Again." I say these words because "Never Again" will this tragic and heartbreaking thing that happened, what Adolf Hitler did to Jewish kids, to Jewish women, and to Jewish men. We can make sure this will never happen by sticking up for people that get treated like that and to speak up.

Work Cited

Yadvashem.org

4holocaustheroes.weebly.com

Wojan, Megan. "Holocaust." Holocaust   Speech. Kams, Elk Grove.4 Nov. 2016.
Lecture

Władysław Kowalski

Hailey San Filippo

 Wladyslaw Kowalski's significant impact to the Jewish people played a major role in the Holocaust's remembrance. He saved about 50 Jewish refugees from certain death in Poland. This was done without concern for his own safety. After being approached by a young seventeen-year-old boy, Bruno Boral, he decided to make it his life's mission to save Jews. His objective was to save innocent people from being persecuted for no other reason than being Jewish.

Kowalski was born in Kiev, Poland on September 25, 1895 and died on February 3, 1971 in Jerusalem. Raised in Kiev, he studied at St. Petersburg and, in 1915, received a degree in agronomic engineering. During World War I, he enlisted in the Polish brigade to fight for Poland's independence, and at the same time his parents were murdered by the Bolsheviks. Later, he joined the Polish army and retired as a Colonel in 1935. Kowalski took a job in Warsaw, Poland and worked for the Dutch electronics firm Philips. After Poland was invaded by Nazi Germany, Kowalski was commanded to defend Warsaw and refused to ever give up. As a result he was taken to the prisoner-of-war camp for Polish Officers. Because he was an agent for Philips he was given early parole.

In 1940 he was approached by a 17-year-old boy, Bruno Boral, begging for food. Kowalski decided to give the boy shelter along with food and a safe haven. This is what led to Kowalski's new path in life. After Boral he rescued a Jewish lawyer and his two siblings. Kowalski was able to move about the ghettos because of his job with Philips. He was able to bring medical supplies and weapons back to the underground. Because of all of his help bringing supplies and weapons to the underground, it gave the fighters hope, in 1943, when they took on the Nazis. Kowalski continued with his rescues and, not long after, saved Leah Butcholtz, her son and 19 others, removing them from the ghettos. For a long time, Kowalski was watched by the Gestapo and arrested numerous times but never let the Jewish people down. Toward the end of the war, in January 1945, Kowalski hid in a homemade bunker with 49 Jewish refugees, soon to be liberated by the Soviet Troops along with the surviving Jews from the camps and those who were still in hiding. Knowing that any rabbi caught doing any ceremony would be persecuted was the only thing holding Kowalski back from converting to Judaism.

After the war, the survivors immigrated to many different parts of the world. Kowalski and Leah Butcholtz, who was soon after his wife, along with her son, immigrated to Israel where Kowalski was treated like a hero. As the face of a hero, Kowalski traveled around the country doing a variation of different jobs. After a time, because he was away from home very much, his marriage fell apart. As time went by, he moved to Jerusalem and was hired to work in the documentation department. No one knew of his life story for a long time. In 1961, Kowalski attended a conference with immigrants in Tel Aviv. At that time he shared, "I did not do anything special for the Jews, and I do not consider myself a hero. I only did my duty as a human being toward people who were persecuted and tortured. I did not do this only because they are Jewish, but rather I helped every persecuted person without regard to race or origin." Two years later, on February 3, Kowalski died in Jerusalem at the age of 75. Before he died he requested to be buried alongside the Jewish people. The rabbinate struggled to find Kowalski a Jewish cemetery not prohibited to Christians. His body lay resting in the Tel Aviv morgue for five days straight. Then Yad Vashem and Chief Rabbi Yedidya Frenkel of Tel Aviv found and arranged a burial site at the Kibbutz Yad Mordecai in southern Israel. This cemetery was named after Mordecai Anielewiz who was a commander of the Jewish Combat Organization during the Warsaw Ghetto Uprising. Later on, it was official on February 10, 1971, that Kowalski had been accepted and was buried alongside the Jewish people that he dedicated his life to. Imprinted on his tombstone was the Righteous Among The Nations Medal that he had earlier received from Yad Vashem. Kowalski received the medal because he devoted his life to helping the innocents. Also along with the medal is a quote saying, "He risked his life to save Jews during the period of the Holocaust and the heroism." According to jta.org, "Vered Bar-Semech, a Yad Mordechai native and the director of the kibbutz's museum, hopes to locate Kowalski's daughter, stepson, granddaughter and any other descendants. Meeting them, she hopes, will enable her to learn more about Kowalski's life. Bar-Semech would like to include the Kowalskis in programs run here for visiting students and soldiers or collect from them personal items and documents to exhibit in the museum. Miriam Vardi, Kowalski's daughter, wrote a letter to Bar-Semech's father, Artek Wieneman, saying, 'To our unforgettable father, from his wife Lea, children Miriam and Michael and granddaughter Ruti.' Vardi wished for this to be put on a wreath to adorn her father's grave."

While researching Wladyslaw Kowalski's life story, I learned that people were persecuted for no other reason than their religious beliefs of Judaism. I learned that there are some out there who would sacrifice their life to save others. Also, that integrity, courage, and bravery can save as many lives as 50 people or more. I learned that just one person can make a difference to so many people. This research impacts my life because it reminds me how fragile life is and what it means to have freedom and a democracy where we all have rights and protection under the law. "Never Again" should we allow this type of massacre to happen again without coming to their defense. "Never Again" should this happen to any race or religion, because, at the end, it affects every living person on Earth. A group from various countries should form an alliance to investigate any accusations regarding abuses to any human being.

Works Cited

Bartop, Paul R. "Resisting the Holocaust." Google Books. ABC-CLIO, 6 June 2016. Web. 06 Dec. 2016.

Http://www.jta.org/author/admin. "Seeking Kin: Kibbutz Searches for Descendants of Holocaust Hero Buried in Its Cemetery." Jewish Telegraphic Agency. N.p., 15 Dec. 2015. Web. 07 Dec. 2016.

"The Righteous Among The Nations." Yad Vashem. Yad Vashem, n.d. Web. 07 Dec. 2016.

Helena Matacz

Hailey Truong

"Never shall I forget the little faces of children, whose bodies turned into wreaths of smoke beneath a silent blue sky," as Elie Wiesel, a Holocaust survivor, once said. It was January 1933, when Nazis came to power in Germany with their leader Adolf Hitler. The man believed in a "master race," so he decided to try to wipe out the Jewish population because they weren't his ideal thought of a perfect race. Hitler spread the word and, soon enough, laws were being passed that Jews could not hold public office, could not go into certain stores, could not sit on specific benches, and all because they were one thing: Jewish. He deprived Jews of their rights as German citizens and he made them wear yellow stars of David to identify who was who. Jews began to flee Germany for their own safety. Eventually, Hitler came to a "final solution" and attempted to kill off an entire race. He rounded them up and then shot until there was nothing left in them, or he took them to concentration camps and made them work until they died. Once they were in the concentration camps, their possessions were confiscated, heads were shaved, arms were tattooed, they were given prison uniforms, all were separated, and survived based on trade/physical skills. Fewer than four million Jews survived and those who did survive were forever changed. The Holocaust was the persecution and murder of six million Jews and this was the story of one hero who saved some Jews' lives: Helena Matacz.

Helena Matacz lived nearby Ewa Wasserman-Feldsztejn and her child. Ewa and her husband had been living in the Warsaw Ghetto in 1942 and had a son, Stefan, while down in the ghetto. Her husband had managed to sneak them all out of the ghetto and went to an acquaintance's home. Her husband left to go to Hotel Polski for safety and it turned out to be a trap, so he was taken to Auschwitz and later killed. Now, Ewa was all alone with her child, but soon Helena found them and decided to take care of both of them for herself.

She knew that if she were to be caught, she would be killed. However, this didn't stop Helena from helping. She had already had been hiding a family that was Jewish, so Helena knew what to do. The fact that hiding Jews was against the law, it simply made Helena work harder to keep them safe and, to do that, Ewa needed a disguise. Helena was a religious Catholic, so to let Ewa pass as being Polish, she taught her the correct behavior in church and in society. She worked and worked. Helena took care of Ewa and her son as if they were children of her own. She fed them and gave them protection.

Years passed and as Stefan grew older, got married, and had a child of his own, he decided to move to the Baniocha village for their safety. Ewa, Helena, and Helena's sons all decided it was best for them, so they moved out. After the war, Ewa dreamed of seeing her rescuers once again, for if it wasn't for them, they would not have been here to this day.

Overall, I've learned that an act of kindness can go a far way. Helena didn't have to do go through all the trouble to protect someone and risk her own life for someone else, but she did. She broke the law for an act of kindness. This shows how much she cares about the lives of those who are being mistreated and how much she'll go to help others in need. This story has inspired me to spread more kindness because nobody ever knows what's going on in that person's life and they may need a little act of kindness to brighten up their life. Never Again are we to make the mistake of killing off an entire people because of what they believe in and what their faith is. Never Again are we to try to make the "perfect race" because our differences are what make everybody unique. Our uniqueness is why we are all so special in our own way. If we kill off the differences, then what is there left? This will never again happen because we have witnessed the trauma and the fear people have had because of this event. Fear is our worst enemy, and fear is what keeps us worried, stressed, anxious, or sad. To make sure this never happens again, we honor our differences and show each other what's so special about each and every single one of us. Looks and appearances should not affect the way people eat, sit, dress, or work. Our individuality is what makes us unified and stronger. "The opposite of love is not hate, it's indifference," said Elie Wiesel, a Holocaust survivor.

Works Cited

"Heroes of Poland." Yad Vashem. N.p., n.d. Web. 04 Nov. 2016

Wojan, Megan. "Holocaust Guidelines." N.p., n.d. Web. 04 Nov. 2016.

Sendler, Irena

Hala Ahmed

The Holocaust was the killing of six million Jews in Germany lead by the Nazis. The leader of the Nazis was Adolf Hitler. The Holocaust started off by the Nazis bullying the Jews that then got into a more serious matter. They would take rights away from Jews, such as sitting on benches and going to stores only for Christians. They also started writing books that made Jews look like terrible human beings and Christians were better then them. They started teaching kids at young ages that Jews were horrible. They didn't let Jews and Christians go to the same school. Then Hitler started to round up all the Jews and they were sent to ghettos with very poor hygiene and little to no food. Concentration camps were even worse than ghettos. They were killed or were forced to work physical labor until they were too weak to continue. They would kill Jews by putting them into gas chambers and making them think that they were going to take a shower. Then they would burn the dead bodies to make room for the next group. The Nazis also had a different way to kill children. They would say that the children were going to go to a school since education was very important. So the kids would go on to the bus thinking that it was a normal bus but it actually had something wrong with it. They bent the gas tube so that it would be inside the bus and the driver would drive around for a while until all the kids died. 6,000 plus people saw what the Nazis were doing was wrong so they tried to help the Jews escape from the Nazis. One of these people was a woman named Irena Sendler.

Ms. Sendler was a 29-year old who worked as a social worker in Warsaw the capital of Poland. She took advantage of her job and tried to help the Jews but, when the ghettos were closed off, her plan demolished. When the Council for Aid of the Jews was established she became one of their most important activists. She noticed that the ghettos were very unsanitary and had many diseases killing the Jews. She managed to get a permit to enter the ghettos and inspect the diseases. Once Ms. Sendler managed to get into the ghetto, she contacted the Jews and told them she could smuggle their kids and infants underneath her toolbox in order to get them out of the ghetto. She also had a burlap sack in the back of her truck for the larger kids. She had a dog trained to bark so the guards couldn't hear the noises of the kids and infants. When she took the children she found a hiding spot for them and gave them food to survive. She was successful in smuggling out 2,500 kids and infants. The Nazis discovered her and they broke both her legs and arms and beat her. The Nazis tried to locate all the Jews she rescued but she wrote down all the names of the people she rescued and put it in a glass jar underneath a tree in her backyard.

After the war she tried to find the children's family so they could reunite but most of them got gassed. She became the leader of Zegota's Department for the Care of Jewish Children after the ghetto was completely demolished in 1943. She sent all the children whose family didn't survive to Rodzina Marii Orphanage in Warsaw. In 1943, Ms. Sendler was arrested and sentenced to death in the Pawiak Prison. Underground activists bribed officials to release her and they were successful.

I learned that the Holocaust all started from just an act of bullying. Just one small "joke" that you might think is funny is most likely not funny to the other person. Bullying grows and grows if you don't stop it from the beginning. That's what happened in the Holocaust. No one stood up for another because they were too afraid of what their consequence was going to be. Irena Sendler showed me that she was brave enough to actually rescue 2500 and more Jews. She took advantage of her work position to forge "Aryan" documents and smuggle 2500 kids and infants out of one ghetto. She inspired me to stand up for another person so the situation doesn't grow into a war. I understand that the Holocaust was a discrimination against Jews. Hitler believed that Jews were threatening Christianity with their beliefs so he wanted to exterminate them. In most people's eyes during that time he was a hero, but he was actually a villain. Many people say the phrase "Never Again" and I say it with them.

Works Cited

"Introduction to the Holocaust." United States Holocaust Memorial Museum. United States Holocaust Memorial Museum, n.d. Web. 13 Dec. 2016.

"The Righteous Among the Nations." Yad Vashem. N.p., n.d. Web. 12 Dec. 2016.

@snopes. "Irena Sendler." Snopes. Snopes, 05 June 2015. Web. 13 Dec. 2016.

Irena Mielecka

Hannah Bates

The Holocaust is considered to be one of the most painful times in history. The Holocaust was a genocide, started by Adolf Hitler, that killed nearly 6 million Jews. Jews were seen as inferior and as a threat to Hitler. With the help of some brave heroes, fewer than 4 million Jews survived the Holocaust. Among these heroes was Irena Bawol (later Mielecka) and her sister Felicja Tewel: two women who risked their lives to save Jewish families.

Irena and her sister were very brave females who helped hide Jews. Irena and her sister were Roman Catholic, Irena studied nursing and Felicja was a Doctor of Medicine. Irena's whole family was focused on helping the Jews during this rough time. Felicja was married to a Jewish attorney, whose house was often referred to as a "rescue factory." When the time became too risky for Felicja and her husband to take in and rescue Jews, Felicja sent them to her sister Irena, in Warsaw. Irena was in nursing school and lived in a very small apartment but used her clothes closet as a safe place until further arrangements could be made. Irena was known for providing Jews with a safe place to stay, finding jobs and producing forged documents for identification cards.

One person in particular who Felicja sent to Irena was Sabrina Poper. Irena hid her friend in her closet for several days until she was able to obtain an identity card and an apartment for Poper. While living in the apartment for a while, the landlord for the apartments started to get suspicious of Poper's identity and notified Irena about her suspicions. As Soon as Irena found out the landlord was getting suspicious she quickly found Poper a new home and job at a German Hospital. Soon Poper's fiancé escaped from a prison camp and reunited with her. Irena and Poper remained very close friends and once again Irena helped her friend through the Gestapo that raided her apartment looking for her escaped fiancé. Later, Poper immigrated to Israel. As the years passed, Irena and Sabrina lost contact, but after the war, Sabrina tried to find the sisters who saved her life. It wasn't until 1987 that they were reunited.

After Poper, Irena and Felicja continued to risk their lives rescuing Jews. Felicja's home in Debica became the address for many Jews. Even after Felicja's husband was arrested by the Gestapo and taken to Auschwitz where he later died, Felicja continued to open her home to many more Jews. In total, there were 7 Jewish families who were rescued and survived the Holocaust by these two courageous women and their families. It wasn't until September 25, 1989 that Irena and Felicja were inducted into the Righteous Wall of Honor in Yad Vashem.

History is what changes the world. Everything that has happened in history regardless of how big or small leaves a print and causes change. It took one person to have a significant negative impact on history and many individuals to conquer and stop him. The impact of the Holocaust on the world is significant and the effects of this event are still felt today. The Jews that survived were forever changed and saw the world differently because they and their loved ones were tortured and many watched as their loved ones were being tortured, and died through execution and suicide. These humans were treated like experimental animals. This view on life carried down through generations into today. Today, one cannot say the word "Jew" without thinking about the horrific suffering that they had to endure.

People like Irena and her sister are heroes. It is frightening to think that one man can cause such a movement and mass execution of human lives. This event led to a major World War that ended with Jews being freed and world hoping that something like this would "Never Again" happen. Irena and Felicja's story is an inspiring one. Despite the risks of rescuing and protecting Jews, the two sisters never for a second hesitated to help these people. Irena and Felicja treated Jews like family with respect and compassion, and gave them hope. The two sisters have reminded me how we are all human despite religion, race, or sex and deserve to be treated with dignity. I also learned that although I am one person, I can make significant change and spread the positive on to others.

In a sense, Hitler was a bully on a worldly scale and unfortunately many were brainwashed and became bullies as well. Change begins with one person and can spread in masses. In my life, the steps I can take to ensure that something as significant as the Holocaust doesn't happen again is to stand up against bullies and treat people as humans and accept the difference between us all. We are all the same inside and it's the outside stuff like religion, race, sex, and looks that make us unique. None is more dominant than the other. I embrace different, it's what makes this world a more interesting place.

Works Cited

Wojan, Megan. "Introduction of the Holocaust Essay." Class Lecture. KAMS, Elk Grove, CA. 4 Nov. 2016. Lecture.

http://db.yadvashem.org/righteous/righteousName.html?language=en&itemId=4013843

http://db.yadvashem.org/righteous/family.html?language=en&itemId=4013843

Yad Vashem - Request Rejected

http://db.yadvashem.org/rihttp://db.yadvashem.org/righteous/family.html?language=en&itemId=4013843ghteous/family.html?language=en&itemId=4013843:

Jozef, Julia, and Daughter Janina Bar

Harsimran Kaur

The Holocaust was a sad and terrible time that no Jew can ever forget. The Holocaust takes place a long time ago from 1933 to 1945. Millions of Jews suffered for the twelve years they spent with the Nazis. Not many people survived the Holocaust; most were killed or died of hunger and diseases. About six million Jewish men, women, and children were murdered during the Holocaust. Jews lived in Ghettos where life was spent terribly. Each apartment would have many families living in it, the plumbing always had problems, human waste was thrown on the roads, diseases spread, houses were very messy, there were always hunger issues, etc. Jews were only allowed to eat a tiny bit of bread and potatoes, so everyone was very thin. Some people were forced to steal food or trade money for extra food in order to stay alive. Some people were killing themselves so they wouldn't have to live this terrible life and many children were becoming orphans, living on the streets, and freezing to death.

When we think of the Holocaust, we think of the one man who started it all, the man who was the reason that this many people died in those twelve years: Adolf Hitler. Hitler became chancellor of Germany from 1933 to 1945. He slowly started to make everything different for the Jews. Jews had to carry around IDs and had to have their passport stamped with the letter "J." In 1938, Germany, Austria, and parts of Sudetenland started "anti-Jewish programs" where they vandalized Jewish homes and almost 100 Jews were murdered. In 1939, Germany invaded Poland and was responsible for killing about six million Jews, which made up two-thirds of the Jewish population in Europe.

One Christian family risked their lives to save a Jewish family during the Holocaust. Jozef, Julia, and their 19-year-old daughter, Janina Bar, allowed Joe Riesenbach, his mother, father, grandmother, and two younger sisters to stay in their home during the time of the Holocaust. The Riesenbachs promised to give everything they owned to the Bars after the war was over. The Bar's lives were in danger because, if the Nazis found out that they were helping a Jewish family survive, they would be killed. They lived together for two years and Mr. Bar built a bunker for the Jewish family to hide in if there was danger.

While the Riesenbachs lived with the Bars, they had a lot of close calls about being discovered. The first one was on one Sunday morning when the Bars went to church. The priest there said that two Jewish families were lost, so every house would be searched for Jews. When the Bars heard the news, they came home and told all the Riesenbachs to go into the secret bunker. Later, they all heard dogs barking outside and people knocked on their door. When Mr. Bar opened the door, there were four people and they all started searching the home, looking for any Jews. But Mr. Bar tried to distract them by talking about the new recipe for liquor. They started a conversation that only lasted about two minutes and then they left. While in the bunker, they made no noise because, even if a little noise was heard, they would have been exposed.

The second time the Riesenbachs had a close call was on April 1, 1944. All of the Bars were working out in the field and the Riesenbachs were in the living room. While they were stretching themselves out, they started hearing dog barks from outside and Joe Riesenbach's father peeked outside the window and saw some men with rifles in their hands coming toward the home. They didn't have enough time to go into the bunker and hide because that would have made a lot of noise and the men would have known someone was inside. They all lied down on the floor near the wall, so that the men could not see them through the window. They rung the doorbell and no one moved or made any noise because their lives were at risk and they were so scared about being exposed, that they wouldn't dare to make any noise. After standing there for a while, the men left thinking that no one was home at the time.

In 1944, the Holocaust started to end and the Jews that were still alive became free and were treated like every other race now. The Riesenbachs returned to their home because there was no reason for them to stay with the Bars anymore. Even though they all went their separate ways back home, they still stayed in touch. Now the Riesenbachs sent the Bars clothing, food, etc. Joe even requested to bring Janina Bar to Canada for her to visit and explore. She denied the request because of her age, but she sent her grandson there for fourteen months. The Riesenbachs stayed in touch with the Bars even after they returned home because, if it weren't for them, they all probably would have been dead by now.

Overall, I learned that many Jews back then suffered a lot. Never again should this happen to anyone of any race. Everyone in the world matters the same. No matter what race they are, no matter what they believe in, no matter who they are, they deserve to be treated just as well as everyone else. Jozef, Julia, and Janina Bar were great people and I respect the fact that they risked their own lives to help one Jewish family survive during the Holocaust. If it weren't for the Bars, the Riesenbachs probably would've died of diseases or hunger. This is one reason why we should all get the power to vote because there may be people who want to come into power but are going to do something like Hitler and start another Holocaust. We all look back at the Holocaust as a terrible time that should never happen again. Now we must all get together and make sure that we stop people who are going to ruin this world and bring problems. This was an experience that we should learn from and we should all make sure that we prevent our world from becoming a terrible place like the one that Hitler wanted. Are you in?

Work Cited

Knesset. "The Holocaust- Historical Overview." Knesset.gov.il. Knesset, 2005. Web. 12 Dec. 2016.

"Life in the Ghettos." United States Holocaust Memorial Museum. United States Holocaust Memorial Museum, n.d. Web. 12 Dec. 2016.

Lungen, Paul. "Canadian Jewish News - December 14, 2000." Canadian Jewish News - December 14, 2000. Canadian Jewish News, 14 Dec. 2000. Web. 12 Dec. 2016.

Riesenbach, Joe. "The Story of the Survival of the Riesenbach Family." Riesenbach Survival Story - Joe Riesenbach. Polish Publications, 17 Dec. 2000. Web. 12 Dec. 2016.

The Biography.com Website. "Adolf Hitler." Biography.com. A&E Networks Television, 26 Nov. 2016. Web. 12 Dec. 2016.

Ivan and Mariya Kut

Hayden Kell

 The 1930 economic depression hit Germany hard and the Germans lacked confidence in their weak government. Adolf Hitler, of the Nazi party, decided to run for politics and he won. The Nazis took control in January 1933 and they believed that Aryans were the master race. He persecuted Jews and didn't let them be in public office. Hitler started propaganda to ensure that the Nazi message was communicated to everyone. Jews were also deprived of their rights as citizens. The Jews were forced to wear yellow stars of David to be able identify the Jews. Jews started to flee Germany for their safety. In all countries that Germany controlled the Jews were sent to cities in Poland. The Jews formed resistances and fought back against the Germans. Jews were rounded up and taken to concentration camps or ghettos. Their possessions were confiscated and their heads were shaved and tattooed. They wore prison uniforms and the men, women, and children were separated. Families were separated. Their survival was based on their trade skills. Extermination camps were created and they had gas chambers that could kill 6,000 people per day. 63% of the European Jews were killed and 91% were killed in Poland. Fewer than 4 million Jews survived and they were changed forever. Ivan and Mariya Kut were simple farmers helping a 12-year-old boy named Rafael by providing him job. Then one day that all changed.

Ivan and his wife Mariya were just simple farmers and letting a Jewish boy help out on the farm. On June 30, 1941 Germans conquered the area and Rafael stayed the night sometimes because the Germans were not nice to the Brody Jews. On November 2, 1942, when Rafael was at home, they murdered his family. But he then lived with the rest of the Jews in a ghetto. He was one of the many gathered in one of the buildings and he was shot at. Many were killed but Rafael was wounded and passed out from loss of blood. When he woke, he walked to the Kut's home. Mariya tended to his wounds and hid him for the next two months in their home. The whole family was in charge of looking after him. Mariya in the two months fed him, clothed him and sheltered him until he decided to go to the marshlands. The Germans had put up fortifications after Rafael left the Kut's home. Rafael was posing as a Ukrainian orphan. After the war, Rafael left Soviet Ukraine. The Kuts always remembered Rafael after he left because they felt as if he became one of their own children. Rafael in 1992, renewed his contact with the Kut family. One year later, Stefanyia (the daughter of Mariya) went to visit him in Israel where he now lived. She was overjoyed to see him. The Kut family was recognized by a museum called Yad Vashem on December 22, 1992.

The Holocaust was a horrific event that hurt and killed many innocent people for a belief that the Jews were bad people and had caused the economic depressions to happen. This event should never happen again. We can learn from the past and see that the

Holocaust was a very bad event and took many lives of innocent Jewish people who were just people like me and you. This person's impact on me was that heroes aren't always people from the big cities and wear capes, but can come from small towns and wear nothing but a tunic and a skirt or pants.

"Never Again." To make sure that we do not repeat this again we can set aside our differences and try to become friends with everyone. Instead of teasing, say something nice to someone or compliment them. We must stop all the negativity and racism in the world and come together to help make the world a better place. The Jews had to fight for their rights and freedom. In the times in darkness, people like Mariya and Ivan will provide a light and restore the good back in the world. If we can all do something small we can change the world. The leaders of the world should place rules on discrimination such as racism, genocide, and enslaving people to work for you. I believe that if the Holocaust happens again we have repeated a horrible mistake and have killed many innocent people for no reason. Religion, race, hair color, eye color, and other differences that people have were all reasons that the Holocaust happened and took so many valuable lives of people that were doctors, grocery store clerks, pharmacists, police officers, business men/women, mine workers. Now I truly understand "Never Again." Never did I think that this was such a horrific event. In second and first grade, I loved learning about World War II and what happened, but it never explained the Holocaust. Although it was a major part of the war, it never explained the horrific events. Even as the years went on, I still read on the subject and still never found anything until when we started the Holocaust unit. "Never Again."

Work Cited Page

Yad Vashem - Request Rejected. N.p., 2016. Web. 12 Dec. 2016.

Wogan, Megan. "Holocaust Introdution." Elk Grove. Lecture.

Jozef Biesaga

Hayden Taylor

Jozef Biesaga was born on March 9, 1931. He was born in a town outside of Krakow. He was eight-and-a-half when the war started. When the war started, the Biesaga family owned a farm in the village of Smardzowice, north of Krakow and just south of Skala. At the wars start there were six people in the Beisaga family, Jozef, Jozef's parents, an older brother and two younger sisters.

Before the war, Jozef's family was friends with a Jewish family. When the war started Dawid, one of the members of the family, and his family and friends were captured by German forces and locked up in a building near a Jewish cemetery in Shaka. The Jews were kept locked in place for a few hours while the Germans planned to shoot them. Finally, the Germans ordered them to undress. Dawid was chosen to check the bodies and clean the place, but his wife told him to run. He ran away, naked and with only a prayer book, while the Germans were shooting at him. They all missed. Dawid headed for Jozef's house.

When he reached the Biesaga family home, he requested to hide there. Jozef's mother didn't want to help Dawid because of the risk of the Germans discovering them. On the other hand, Jozef's father, who was a strong Christian, decided that they were going to help him because that is what Christ taught. Once they decided to hide Dawid, they thought of the safest place to do it. The Biesagas created a special room for him. There was a small shed for tools next to the barn and next to the shed was a dog house, the entrance to the hiding place was in the dog house. The dog that the Biesagas had was a mean dog and everybody was afraid of him, but he knew Dawid so he wouldn't attack or bark whenever he entered or exited the hiding place. Just to be safe they had a second hiding place for emergencies. On the second floor of the barn there was a big stack of hay. The hay was prepared, in case of danger, so that in one move, Dawid could make the hay collapse and conceal him.

After Dawid's arrival, Jozef's parents set strict rules. His parents forbid them to talk about Dawid and were told if they did they would be risking the whole family's lives. Jozef's youngest sister was taught to call Dawid Kitek. Besides the Beisaga family on the farm, only Jozef's grandmother, Jozef's uncle and Jozef's cousin knew about Dawid.

Over the course of hiding Dawid, Jozef earned new responsibilities. One of these new responsibilities was to bring food to Dawid every day. Since the hiding place was twenty-five meters away from the house, Jozef had to deliver food at night. Another important duty Jozef had was to spy on the Germans. He had to check where they and the police were, in case he had to tell Dawid to run and hide in the forest. A third responsibility Jozef had was to Scout out places in the forest where strawberries and other edible plants grew. After finding a spot he would then tell Dawid in case he was in the forest so long he needed food. This task was especially challenging because there was often nothing to eat.

Most of the time Dawid's life in hiding was extremely boring. The only thing he had was the prayer book so he did a lot of praying. Dawid was a very religious man, he even fasted during Yom Kipper even though he didn't have much to begin with.

The Biesagas protected Dawid day after day, year after year, until finally the Germans were defeated. At the end of the war, Dawid had been in hiding for thirty-seven months. Before the war, Dawid was poor and had a small piece of land. He tried to give that land to Jozef's father, but he refused. He said he doesn't want a prize because God will give him one in heaven. To show thanks, Dawid would get them small presents on Christian holidays. Eventually Dawid moved to Israel where he lived until his death. Dawid stayed in touch while in Israel and once sent Jozef a pair of military boots.

The other people in the village knew something was up but didn't say anything. Everyone in the village had a strong connection and they didn't want to betray the Biesagas. Jozef's father passed in 1972 and his mother passed four years later in 1976. To Jozef, both of them were heroes. Much of Jozef's career was spent as a government transportation employee. He has a son and a daughter. He also has three grandchildren and one great-grandchild. He was inducted into the Righteous Among the Nations in 2000.

While studying Jozef, and what he did to save Dawid, I learned that there were some people that didn't see the world like the Nazis, that some people would rather risk their lives to save others. Learning about Jozef has shown me that doing the right thing can save lives. That even during hard times you should stick to what you believe in. I now understand the impact the Holocaust had on Jews and Christians and Catholics alike. The Nazis invaded lands, took the Jews from their homes, and created strict rules that Catholics and Christians were forced to follow. Never Again can we let this happen. Never Again should an event such as this occur on earth. Never Again can we let people die because of who they are. Everyone is equal and should be treated as such. We must teach equality around the world. We must show the impact this terrible event had on everyone. We must remember all of the bloodshed this event has brought upon the world. We must cherish those that have passed due to this. Never Again can another Holocaust occur, as long as the last man is still breathing.

Work Sited

Tammeus, Bill, and Jacques Cukierkorn. They Were Just People: Stories of Rescue in Poland During the Holocaust. Columbia: U of Missouri, 2009. Print.

Gertruda Babilinska

Hazel Garza

Born near Starograd, North Poland in 1902, Gertruda was the oldest of her two brothers and five sisters. Gertruda's father worked at the post office. Gertruda's gamily was a caring family who was always worrying about others more than themselves. Gertruda speaks of her mother in the same way, "We were a good religious family. The proverb in our home was 'Love your neighbor as yourself.' My mother was always concerned about everyone else. For instance, when I went into the ghetto to see Mickey I was gone for several days. When I returned home my mother opened the door, and instead of saying, 'How are you?,' she asked me, 'How is the child?'" This shows how caring of others Gertruda's family is. At nineteen, Gertruda went to the ghettos seeking work.

Gertruda's family is Catholic, though she worked babysitting for a rich Jewish family, The Stolowickis. She had worked with them for 15 years. The Stolowickis had a son and a daughter. The daughter's name was not mentioned, though the son's name is Michael (Mickey). When the Holocaust started, first the dad got taken to Auschwitz, then the daughter, only a baby, died, then the couple had Mickey. Mrs. Stolowitzsky decided that moving to Vilna would be the safest thing to do, so Gertruda moved with them. The journey was not smooth though, the car broke down part way through and they had to go by horse-drawn cart. The roads were bombed as well. Lidia, Mickey's mother, Stolowicki was terrified, so Gertruda had to take charge.

Talking to Yad Vashem, Gertruda spoke of her circumstances: "I was left alone, with a circumcised five-year-old child." To make things worse, they had to move to a smaller room.

Gertruda decided to rent an apartment. She rented an apartment there, which she stayed in for four years. She saw many things. The Nazis would give the children poison candy. Unable to handle the stress, Mickey's mother became sick and died. Mickey asked Gertruda, "I have no mother. Will you be my mother?" Of course, though this can be a big commitment, she has known him for such a long time. Though she agreed, and Mickey was happy. Mickey and Gertruda moved to the Ghettos. Mickey then got sick, and Gertruda had to take him to a German doctor, because there weren't any in the Ghettos. Trying to find a doctor that was non-Jewish was very hard. At moments things got very hard for her, "There were many difficult moments," she said in her testimony. "But I knew that my mother was praying for me." And after several visits, Mickey finally got better. Though he did not charge her, he only said to them, "No, you have helped me feel like a man." So he did know Mickey was a Jewish boy.

As soon as the war ended, Gertruda knew she needed to get Mickey to Israel where he had some relatives and could study as a Jew. They took overseas, though tempting to illegally get to Israel. He wouldn't have to study Catholic with Gertruda and could grow up to be a Jew with the rest of his family in Israel. Gertruda worked as a maid for Mickey's schooling. Mickey attended Be'er Shemin, a school especially for children from Europe, just like him. They then planned to leave Europe and start over and rebuild their lives in Israel but were turned around by British warships. They were put back in DP camps. Though the troubles never put her down. They finally arrived at the shores in Israel in 1949. They settled there in Israel, where she raised Mickey.

The boat returned to Hamburg, Germany

Gertruda and Mickey lived in the same room with no water and the job as a maid left not much money for things for Mickey. Mickey grew up to be a good Jew, and Gertruda was so proud of him. Gertruda says, "He is the most wonderful son in the world." Mickey grew up to work for Copel Tours in Israel. He arranged tours, and they moved him to Miami in 1976. Now Mickey lives in New York, and brings tours to Israel for another company. Gertruda lived in a small room, making a living cleaning houses. Gertruda stayed a devout Catholic, but kept her promise to raise Mickey as a Jew.

Gertruda Babilinska is one of many who saved a Jew in the Holocaust and kept Mickey safe through the many ups and downs. Though she could've given no concern, she chose to stand out, to be an upstander, to make a difference. She saved Mickey and tried her hardest to take care of the rest of his family though losing them to illness, or being taken to the camps. She made sure that Mickey was always safe. Gertruda now joins the few that say "Never again." We have learned from our mistakes, learning that such things cannot happen again, such pain, suffering, and loss.

Work Cited

"Gertruda Babilińska." Gertruda Babilińska. N.p., n.d. Web. 14 Dec. 2016.
"Rescuers: Gertruda Babilinska." PBS. PBS, n.d. Web. 14 Dec. 2016.

Zofia Yamaika

Hector Hernandez Jr.

Zofia Yamaika was born in 1925 in Warsaw, Poland. She was raised in a very hard-working lady place. But later on in her life she joined a club called Spartacus, a group that was against the growing fascist movement in Europe. When she was 14 years old, she stopped going to school when the Nazis banned Spartacus, but somehow Zofia found a way to revive the club. Then a year later, she and her family were part of the Jews so they had to move to Warsaw, a ghetto settled in November 1940. Through her training, she managed to smuggle a gun from Communist partisans. If Zofia wanted to join, it meant risking her parents' lives. But when they were deported in July 1942, she escaped and joined the Lion partisans near Radom. Then, some Nazis attacked her group her group in 1943. Then, Zofia was armed with a machine gun letting the Nazis come within eighteen feet before she fired. But, sadly, her position was overtaken and she was killed at the age of eighteen, but her unit managed to retreat.

Zofia Yamaika did a lot during the Holocaust. She joined a group that was against the Nazis, but to do that, she had to escape from them, which she did and joined Lion partisans. She stood eighteen feet within a Nazi before she fired, but then was killed because her position was discovered. But it takes guts to do what she did. She was one of the bravest women during that time period.

The Holocaust was a time when a German Nazi named Adolf Hitler killed six million Jewish people just because the people were Jewish. To Hitler, the Jewish were a danger to the German community. So Hitler's solution was to put the Jewish in concentration camps and hurt them just because they were Jewish. The concentration camps covered up all of Poland. The first ever concentration camp opened in March 1933, in Dachau. Six years later the German army filled half of Poland. Then the German police forced Jews out of their homes and into the ghettoes, giving their property to other German people. The ghettoes were very well protected with guards everywhere and surrounded by a very tall barbed wire fence. The concentration camps were overcrowded with people, which meant that diseases were going to spread. The disease that spread was called typhus. Then the Nazis chose seventy thousand Jewish people to mentally kill and torture in chambers or in front of everyone. But after the Holocaust ended, in 1945, the population of Jewish people in Germany dropped dramatically.

What I learned about the Holocaust is not to discriminate a person by how they look or what religion they are. Adolf Hitler killed Jewish people in Germany and placed them in concentration camps because he thought the Jews were a danger to the German community. I also learned that Hitler didn't just kill people off the streets, he placed them in concentration camps all over Poland. He also ordered the German police to go Jews' houses and take their property and give them to other Germans and then put the Jews in concentration camps. Adolf Hitler was a bad man. He killed over six million Jews in Germany in just two years. He killed them in vicious ways by putting them in gas chambers and mentally killing them. He also overcrowded the camps with Jews. So with a lot of people in a camp, a disease started to spread. The disease was called thymus. The concentration camps were not a peaceful place to live in. There were guards everywhere, a very tall barbed wire fence and not a very big place. Plus your room was not personal. You lived in a room with a lot of people. They also didn't feed you very good food or big amounts of it. They also tricked you into thinking that you were going to go eat or take a shower where really they were going to kill you. Such as putting in a gas chamber, burning you to death and even mentally killing you. It was a very terrible time, and very awful place for Jewish people to live in Germany where Adolf Hitler was being a dictator.

But, in the end, I learned that Adolf Hitler was a very bad person for putting Jewish people in concentration camps and killing them. But Zofia Yamaika inspired me to not be scared and stand up for what you think is wrong, to do right from wrong. For her, she stood up against the Nazis and Adolf Hitler. I understand that the Holocaust was a very terrible time in our world and I hope something like this will never again happen or someone like Adolf Hitler will never come into this world being a dictator. For something like this to never happen again we need to work as a community, to not discriminate, be racist, or don't judge someone by their skin tone or religion. I hope something like this will never ever happen again.

"Zofia Yamaika." United States Holocaust Memorial Museum. United States Holocaust Memorial Museum, n.d. Web. 10 Dec. 2016.

History.com Staff. "The Holocaust." History.com. A&E Television Networks, 2009. Web. 10 Dec. 2016.

Jerzy Bielecki

Helen Shibeshi

 Jerzy Bielecki was a survivor of the Holocaust and, out of love, helped another survive. Her name was Cyla Cybulska, a Jewish woman who was deported to Auschwitz with Mr. Bielecki three years after he got deported himself at age of 19. They were separated after they got rescued, thinking the other was dead for the next 39 years.

In that 39 years, Mr.Bielecki was discovered for his heroism for saving Cyla. They first met in a grain warehouse where Mr. Bielecki was forced to work. One day, several young women were brought into the warehouse that Mr. Bielecki was placed in. One of them was Cyla. Cyla came with her family: her mother, father, two brothers, and younger sister. They got deported in 1943 on a crowded train with thousands of other Polish Jews. Out of her five family members that came with her, only she would survive. During their eight months together they said very few words to each other, but were secretly in love with one another. Mr. Bielecki started to plan their escape out of Auschwitz. With the help of a friend who worked in the uniform warehouse, he put together a SS guard uniform. With a stolen pass, he forged a document stating that he had the authorization to take a prisoner to work at a nearby farm. The plan came to life on July 21, 1944 when Mr. Bielecki led Cyla out of her barrack on to a long path to a side gate where a sleepy guard let them pass. They walked for 10 days, hiding by day, walking in the fields by night. Finally, after the tenth day, they reached one of Mr. Bielecki's relative's house. Although he was very much in love with Cyla, Mr. Bielecki decided to join the Polish underground and leave Cyla to a Polish family.

During the 39 years that they were apart, Cyla migrated to America.

Mr. Bielecki was recognized for his act of bravery by the Yad Vashem Institute, in Jerusalem, in 1985. He was a Catholic man who risked his life for a Jewish woman, which wouldn't had have happen if the Nazis didn't have the false suspicion that he was a resistance fighter and haul him off to Auschwitz. Mr. Bielecki died over five years ago on October 20, 2011. Jerzy Bielecki was an extremely brave man, and will always be remembered with the righteous heroes and survivors of the Holocaust.

Work Cited

Hevesi, Dennis. "Jerzy Bielecki Dies at 90; Fell in Love in a Nazi Camp." The New York Times. The New York Times, 23 Oct. 2011. Web. 06 Dec. 2016.

Duell, Mark. "Extraordinary Story of the Brave Auschwitz Prisoner Who Escaped with His Girlfriend by Dressing as an S.S. Officer... before Reuniting Four Decades Later." Daily Mail Online. Associated Newspapers, 24 Oct. 2011. Web. 12 Dec. 2016.

Unknown, Unknown. "Jerzy Bielecki Obituary on Legacy.com." Legacy.com. Unknown, unknown. Web. 12 Dec. 2016.

Arczynski Marek Ferdynand

Henna Randhawa

The Holocaust was a very tragic event that happened in our word history. It affected the lives of many, especially the Jewish people. During this event, which began in the 1930's, Jews were treated with absolutely no respect. This all happened because Adolf Hitler came to lead Germany. He was elected by the Nazi party and he believed that Aryans or Germans were the superior race and that they had some sort of hierarchy over the Jewish people. Over the years, Hitler tried to exterminate all Jews, he sent them to concentration camps to do hard labor with little food. Then extermination camps where they would slaughter all Jewish people. Some Non-Jewish people were willing to help Jews by hiding them in their homes, creating fake identities, and helping them through underground tunnels to get to safe points. Some of these brave people had the same fate as the Jews when and if they were caught. They were shown no mercy for what they had done. And today we honor those brave men and women and have great respect for them. Arczynski Marek Ferdynand was a Polish hero who saved the lives of so many. He was born on December 8, 1900 and sadly died on February 16, 1979. Arczynski was a courageous man who used many techniques to save about 4,000 Jewish people.

Arczynski was part of the Third Silesian Uprising, also known as the Slask Uprising, before the Holocaust and after the First World War. These uprising were between the Polish and Germans. The Polish wanted to break away from German rule and not have to listen to the German government. The Polish were able to part and join the Second Polish Republic. So, Marek had already had war experience and was very smart when it came to helping others.

Ferdynand was a social and political activist. Many people new of him and he needed a place to hide in order to not be caught. His hiding place was Krakow, Poland. Arczynski was a member of the Board of Zegota which was a council aid for Jews. He was the organization's treasurer and here he was an important part in all of the lives saved. He was also part of a select group who distinguished themselves in rescuing surviving Jews in Poland. His co-workers and other activists say that many people owe their lives to him. He spread hope to all who believed in his cause.

There were many different ways you could help the Jews if you were Polish. Arczynski arranged places to live, medical help, and monthly cash to help. These were only some of the accommodations he made. Ferdynand was the head of the Legalization Department, so he forged documents like work permits, identity cards, passes, marriage certificates, etc. These contributions were such a huge part of why all these people were saved.

Arczynski lead Jews through underground tunnels and into safe zones where the Germans would not and could not attack. These journeys were very hard to make, but Marek got used to it and continued to help others. These tunnels were very deep underground. They were located underneath death camps and extermination camps. People would come and lead the Jews out. They couldn't take to many at once, but they got as many people as possible. This system of rescue was very useful and saved so many people's lives.

I thank Arczynski Marek Ferdyand for what he did to save the lives of as many Jewish people as possible. Without him, so many people would not be where they are at today. I have learned that helping people isn't about making it known and being famous for it. Helping people is something you do to help and fight for something you believe in. You do it because it helps the people who need it. It doesn't matter if people don't who you are as long as you are able to help the people in need. The Holocaust was such a tragic event and people should be very appreciative that we live in such an amazing and versatile country. I know that racism is such a horrible thing that should never even happen to anyone. Nobody deserves to be treated with disrespect and it is not kind at all. Everyone is equal and it is not fair to think that people can be treated with no humanity what so ever.

In order to make sure something like this never happens again, it starts with the small things. Don't be a bystander. Stand up for people who get bullied and try to make sure it stops. You could stand up to the bully and tell them to stop. Or you could tell an adult what is happening and try to stop it. "Never Again." We cannot let something like this occur again. This is especially true for survivors and heroes. They worked so hard to stop this in their lives and they do not want it to happen again no matter who it is. All people are the same no matter how they act. People may act out because of how they are treated and they should not have to. They deserve to be treated the same and not be scared for their lives. In conclusion, the Holocaust was such a sad time in world history and these heroes of Poland had a great contribution in saving the lives of Jews.

Work Cited

Yadvashem. N.p., n.d. Web. 2 Dec. 2016.

Wojan, Megan. "Holocaust Background." California, Elk Grove. 9 Nov. 2016. Lecture.

"Arcsynski Marek Ferdyand." Sprawiedliwi.org. N.p., n.d. Web. 11 Dec. 2016.

Gertruda Babilinska

Hillary Chu

In 1993, Adolf Hitler, the leader of the Nazi political party, became the new leader of Germany. The Nazis came to power in January 1933; they believed that Aryans were a "master race," so they started to put Jews into ghettos. Later on, when the Nazis realized that the Jews weren't dying fast enough, they sent them to concentration camps. The Nazis then took it to another level by sending Jewish people to extermination camps, which is known as the Holocaust. Over 6 million Jews were killed in this process, which lasted until 1945. Gertruda Babilinska, who was born in 1902, is one of the few rescue heroes who survived the Holocaust. She was a nanny who helped keep Michael Stolowickis alive during the Holocaust by supplying basic goods, providing forged documents, and hiding Michael.

Gertruda was originally born in Starogard, but later moved to Warsaw to find a job. She found a job taking care of two children for a Jewish family. The family decided to leave to Palestine and offered to take Gertruda with them. However, she wanted to stay in Poland and was soon engaged as nanny to the Stolowickis, a prosperous Jewish family in Warsaw. She took care of their baby daughter while living in the family's mansion. When the little girl died at a young age, Gertruda took care of Lidia Stolowickis, the little girl's mother, who was sick. In 1936, the family had another child named Michael and Gertruda became his nanny. When the Germans attacked Poland in 1939, Mr. Stolowickis, Michael's father, was in Paris and never joined his family again. Lidia Stolowickis took her 3-year-old and fled from Warsaw with Gertruda even though many of their other servants and employees turned their backs. They headed to Vilna where they had heard it was possible to go abroad from there.

During their journey, they encountered many hardships and difficulties. At first, their car broke down so they had to go by horse-drawn cart. Then, the Nazis started to bomb the roads, which terrorized Lidia and led to Gertruda taking charge. When they finally made it to Vilna, they were stranded with many other refugees with barely any necessities and money except for the little money that Gertruda was able to make. Lidia couldn't handle the harsh conditions and became very ill, had a stroke, and then in April 1941, she died.

Before she died, Lidia realized that the end of her days was coming soon, so she asked Gertruda to take care of Michael and bring him to the Land of Israel after the war.

Soon after Lidia's death, the killing of the Jews began and Gertruda stayed in her apartment with Michael. From where they lived, they could see the ghetto and were witnesses of the roundup of Jews. She managed to get him false papers, a baptismal certificate, and had him registered as her nephew. To supply food for Michael, Gertruda wrote petitions to authorities on behalf of local people to get eggs, dairy, and poultry in return. When Michael became ill, she was afraid to go to a non-Jewish doctor, so she went into the ghetto where she often went to help some of her acquaintances to find a Jewish doctor who helped treat Michael. In 1945, when the war was finally over, Gertruda kept her promise to Lidia by taking Michael to the Land of Israel. Before she left on her journey, she brought Michael to her parents' home to take leave of her family. They tried to persuade Gertruda to stay; however, she had made a promise to Michael's mother and she was going to keep her promise, so they joined the other Jewish refugees who were also leaving the country.

Michael and Gertruda stayed in a displaced-persons camp in Germany until passage was arranged for them since immigration to British-controlled Palestine was restricted. Even though the members of the Hagana assured Gertruda that they would look after the boy and make sure he reached Israel safely, she still insisted on coming with him. In 1947, they sailed on the "Exodus" toward Israel when the boat was intercepted by British war ships and passengers were forcibly put on British ships that took them back to Europe. When the passengers refused to disembark in the French harbor, the boat was returned to Hamburg where they were again put in displaced-person camps, which didn't stop Gertruda from fulfilling her promise. She made the journey again and was able to reach the shores of Israel in 1948. She settled in a small room in Israel where she raised Michael as a son and made a living by cleaning houses. Although Gertruda remained a Catholic, she raised Michael as a Jew just as she had promised.

"Never Again" is what people call a slogan, but it is more than just a slogan or quote. It is a reminder to us that we shall not let anything like the Holocaust happen ever again. Gertruda Babilinska is an amazing hero and a great example to me and others. She shows loyalty and has taught me that if I make a promise, I should keep it. I have learned that the Holocaust is a terrible tragedy that caused millions of people pain and loss. By learning about the history of the Holocaust, we can learn from our mistakes and make sure that history doesn't repeat itself, "Never again."

Works Cited

Yadvashem. "Yadvashem." Yadvashem. Yadvashem, 2016. Web. 28 Nov. 2016. <http://www.yadvashem.org/>.

Wojan, Megan. "Holocaust Notes." Holocaust. KAMS, Elk Grove. 20 Nov. 2016. Speech.

Edward Chadzynski

Hope Brazier

The Holocaust started on January 30, 1933 and ended on May 8, 1945. It was a traumatic time where over six million people who were thought to be subhuman to the Aryan race by Hitler and the Nazis were killed. In 1939, Hitler took power of Poland. He started to blame Jews for everything wrong in the world. Hitler decided to identify the Jews. He did this by making all Jews wear a yellow star that said "Jew" on it. Later, Hitler took away most of their freedom. Jews weren't allowed to go to public schools, grocery stores, sit on park benches that weren't for them, and basically couldn't really go anywhere public unless it was for them. The places set aside for Jews were not in the best shape. They were most likely dirty or not very good quality. Next, Hitler decided to round up all Jews and stick them in a ghetto. A ghetto is a restricted part of the city that is designated for certain people. In these ghettos there were many people living in a small space. Disease spread quickly and many died from disease or starvation. Some were unfortunately shot or deported to concentration camps. Some ghettos didn't last very long and others lasted for up to four years.

After the ghettos weren't in use anymore the Jews were sent to concentration camps. The first concentration camps were developed in 1933, but were not used straight away. In fact, they weren't really used at all. More and more concentration camps were established but weren't used. By 1937 only four were left, Dachau, Sachsenhausen, Buchenwald, and Lichtenburg. More concentration camps were built after these and were used more. In these concentration camps people weren't treated very well. They worked most of the day, even if they were young, and weren't fed very well. A lot of people died in these camps. Some from disease, starvation, gas chambers, or were shot as they arrived. Most people who were gassed had a mental illness or physical disability. They also used gas vans. Gas vans were trucks sealed from the outside with engine exhaust directed into the interior of the van. Both gas methods and the shootings were used to clear out large groups of people quickly. To dispose of the bodies they would burn them or use mass graves.

Many people didn't agree with Hitler. These people were courageous and strong and held their beliefs. These people helped Jews escape or hide. One such person who stuck to his beliefs was Edward Chadzynski. In Poland, when the Nazis had invaded, Edward lived in Warsaw and worked at the Registry Office of the Municipal Council. In this department, they collaborated with the Resistance Movement by preparing false documents for Jews. To do this, Edward obtained the cooperation of nearby parish churches, such as St. Mary's Church and St. Anthony's Church.

The exact number of Jews Edward helped is unknown, but there were many. In a statement by Zdzislaw Goldberg, he mentioned papers that were obtained for the eleven members in his family and other family friends. Maciej Daniel also wrote that he received

papers from Edward and so did twelve or so of his friends. In 1943, Felicia Stern went to Edward and asked him to help save her four-year-old son. The next day, Edward's sister,

Janina Zaremba, went to Felicia's workplace to meet her. Edward then met with her a day later. Edward instructed her on how to get her son out of the ghetto and turn him over to Edward. He also added that she should consider moving to the Aryan side because she didn't look Jewish. Edward entered the ghetto, smuggled the child out, and placed him in Janina Zaremba's apartment, after giving him false documents. Edward also arranged for Felicia to stay with Edward's aunt and then Felicia was moved to the apartment of Jadwiga Patronska, Edward's cousin. Felicia told Edward she couldn't pay him for this. Edward replied, "This is a child's life we are talking about." Edward covered the costs of keeping Felicia and her son alive, but Felicia began to work and saved enough money to pay their living costs.

Every year multiple high school students take part in the March of the Living. The March of the Living is a trip where teens walk from Auschwitz to Birkenau. In 2012, Felicia Stern decided to join this. She went with two other survivors and her granddaughter. She was able to teach kids about the Holocaust and why it shouldn't happen again. This trip connects kids with their grandparents by allowing them to see what it was like in the concentration camps.

Overall writing about Edward has taught me so much about the Holocaust. Learning about Edward has taught me that you should always take action if you see something wrong. The Holocaust was bullying at its most extreme. "Never Again" should this happen. In this world, if everybody is nice to each other then we can prevent this from happening again. We all need to accept each other for who we are. We should never forget this period of time. Generation after generation, we all need to learn about this so history doesn't repeat itself. "Never Again."

Works Cited

Vashem, Yad. "Edward Chadzynski Survivor Story." N.p., n.d. Web. 17 Nov. 2016

"Gassing Methods." United States Holocaust Memorial Museum. United States Holocaust
Memorial Museum, n.d. Web. 11 Dec. 2016.

"Home - Jewish Ledger." Jewish Ledger. N.p., n.d. Web. 11 Dec. 2016.

Sprawiedliwi.org. N.p., n.d. Web. 3 Nov. 2016.

Aneila Broszko

Ian Immeker

On the terrible day of January 30, in the year 1933, the Holocaust started and Jews started to get rounded up and put in the Ghetto and wait for death. The Holocaust was a sad time for most Jews because they were most likely to get put in a Ghetto and killed. Jews tried to escape and most of them made it out of Germany because of brave men and women who took in the fugitives to their home until the liberation happened. This essay is about one of those people named Aneila Broszko who risked her own life to save three fugitives named Zygmunt Warszawski and his daughters Rachel and Julia.

The fugitives escaped the liquidation of the Stanislaw Ghetto with the assistance of Aneila Broszko, who gave away her husband and daughters' identity cards. Aneila Broszko found refuge for the fugitives in a nearby relative's house but the fugitives soon had to leave because their true identities were found. Then later Aneila Broszko found a safe place and a job for Zygmunt in the village of Ciężkowice. Zygmunt was at work while Rachel and Julia lived in a local covenant. After a couple of months of this Zygmunt got found out and was taken to a concentration camp. But he survived the war. Rachel and Julia were found out and got kicked out of the covenant but not taken to the Germans. When Aneila Broszko found out she came to their aid and hid them till the end of liberation when she was freed.

At the end of the war Aneila Broszko found Zygmunt and reunited their family while she came back to find the Germans raiding her house and being accused of keeping Jews in her house and it got burned to the ground and she got arrested. While in jail the family heard about it and broke her out as thanks for saving their lives. They immigrated to America and lived their about 20 years. Later Zygument and Aneila Broszko with the girls moved back to Poland and on the trip back Zygument died of a heart attack at the remains of Aneila Broszko house. "This is where he wanted to die," said Aneila Broszko. "He told me when I saved him. He said if I was having a medical condition bring me here so I can die where you saved my life."

Aneila Broszko officially took control of Rachel and Julia two months later when it was Rachel's birthday. Aneila Broszko got a present from the girls on the anniversary of Zygument death. They gave her an heirloom of their family which now would have a price of over 1,000,000 dollars. Aneila Broszko and the girls then traveled to China where Rachel died of cancer in her sister's arms. They then traveled to America again where Aneila Broszko and Julia got the news of Julia's grandparents so they went to visit them.

When they went, the grandparents immediately recognized Julia but not Aneila Broszko because the grandparents saw Julia in Germany but left when things started to go awry. When Julia explained, the grandparents thanked her and gave her 400 dollars for her sacrifice for their family and welcomed Aneila Broszko into their home and treated her like family and five years later she had a job and set off with Julia and went to go live next door to her and eventually went to New York City and got a job as a writer for the news. Now she lives in an apartment by herself and no one knows what happened to her after that. Julia moved to California to make a life as a mother. When she got diagnosed with cancer she asked if she and Aneila Broszko could go to Poland, Germany to go die in the same place that she got saved in all those years ago. She died of cancer with Aneila Broszko just like her father did.

In conclusion I learned that Aneila Broszko only saved three peoples lives and the people she helped saved her from jail and they traveled the world losing two along the way. I learned that if you help someone they can help you, so always be nice and treat others the way you want to be treated. I understand that the Germans would stop at nothing to make sure that Jews got caught and killed. Never again shows in this because of the way the Jews and the heroes got treated and that you actually need heroes to help them. You can have all of the religions in every country as normal people who are your friends and have the government to solemnly swear to never do this again. The Holocaust ended on May 8, 1945, and Aneila Broszko was recognized as Righteous Among the Nations on October 26, 1981.

Work Cited

"Holocaust Essay," Yad Vashem - Request Rejected. Yad Vashem, n.d. Web. 8 Dec. 2016.

Gertruda Babilinska

Ilana Tran

 In 1902, Gertruda Babilinska was born in Starograd near Gdansk. She went to Warsaw seeking work when she was 19. She found a position as a nanny for a Jewish family, the Stolowickis, a very prosperous family. She lived with them for a while, taking care of their young daughter, until she had died at a young age. Then Gertruda took care of Lidia Stolowicki, the mother who was very ill.

In 1939, the Germans attacked Poland. While many of the employees and servants turned their backs on the family, Gertruda assumed responsibility for their survival and stayed loyal. When Lidia Stolowicki decided to take her son and flee from Warsaw, Gertruda went with them on the dangerous journey. Eventually, they were able to reach Vilna but were stranded there with many other Jews with very little money. Lidia fell ill and suffered from a stroke in April, 1941, when she was unable to work with the harsh conditions. Before her death, however, she asked Gertruda to take care of her son and take him to the Land of Israel after the war was over. The Germans attacked the Soviet Union two months after Lidia's death and occupied Vilna. "I was left alone, with a circumcised five-year-old child" Gertruda said to her testimony to Yad Vashem.

Soon the killing of the Jews began, and the Ghetto was established. Gertruda decided to stay in her own apartment. She demonstrated enormous resourcefulness and managed to obtain false papers for the boy and had him registered as her nephew. From where they lived, they were able to see the Ghetto and became witnesses to the roundups of Jews. Gertruda sometimes went into the Ghetto to help some of her acquaintances. On other occasions when Michael fell ill, she was too afraid to go to a non-Jewish doctor. So she went into the Ghetto to find a Jewish doctor for Michael. "There were many difficult moments, but I knew my mother was praying for me..." she said to her testimony.

When the war had finally ended, Gertruda decided to keep her promise and take Michael to the land of Israel. Before going on the journey, she took the child to her parents' home near Gdansk to take leave of her family. Even though her parents tried to persuade her to stay, she wouldn't break her promise, and she joined the Jewish refugees who were leaving the country where their homes and communities had once stood. What had used to be a peaceful society, had now become the sites of death and destruction. Since immigration to British controlled Palestine was restricted, Gertruda and the child (Michael) stayed in a DP camp (displaced persons camp) in Germany until a passage was arranged for them on one of the boats that had tried to illegally get to the Land of Israel. Although, members of the Hagana (the pre-state Jewish defense forces) kept assuring Gertruda that they would look after the boy and make sure that he would reach the Land of Israel safely, Gertruda insisted on coming with him. She even declared her willingness to throw herself into the lot with all the other clandestine immigrants.

In 1947, the boat that they were on, the Exodus, sailed from France. The boat was eventually intercepted by British war ships and the passengers, Holocaust survivors who wanted to leave Europe and rebuild their lives in Israel, were forced to get on British ships that took them back to Europe. The passengers refused to get off the ship in the French Harbor, and the boat was returned to Hamburg, in the British zone of occupied Germany. When they got there, they were put in DP camps again.

However all the hardships did not falter Gertruda's kindness and loyalty, she dauntingly did the journey all over again, finally arriving at the shores of Israel in 1948. She settled in Israel, where she raised Michael as her son. She made a small living cleaning houses and lived in a very small room. Although she remained a devout Catholic until the day that she died, she still fulfilled her promise to Michael's mother and raised him as a Jew.

I have learned that there are many different types of people; there are a lot of bad and greedy people in the world, but there are good ones too. Gertruda Babilinska is an amazing, great, and kind person who was so loyal and went on a whole journey, just to keep a promise. As I was reading Gertruda Babilinska's story, I felt so inspired to be like her. This is a story that proves that, it doesn't matter your size, looks, or if you are even human, anyone or anything can be a hero. I feel as though Gertruda's story has changed me today to see the world differently, Gertruda is my true role model. I finally understand the impact of what the Holocaust did to so many survivors. There are not many people like Gertruda in the time of the Holocaust, people that were willing to risk their life to keep a simple promise. "Never Again" should something like the Holocaust happen. If history were to repeat itself, the world wouldn't be any better. To make sure that something like this won't happen again, we should try to prevent bullying because that can form a thread of hatred which can only grow bigger. It won't be easy though. This is why Gertruda Babilinska is not only my role model, but also my hero.

Work citations

Tran, Ilana. "Gertruda Babilińska." Gertruda Babilińska. N.p., n.d. Web. 11 Dec. 2016.
Wojan, Megan. "The Holocaust Intro." KAMS, Elk Grove. 4 Nov. 2016. Lecture.

Irena Sendler

Ingrid Yee

Irena Sendler was one of the most heroic and courageous person who helped the Jews during the very depressing Holocaust. She was born in a town 15 miles east of Warsaw, Poland in 1910. She risked her life tremendously for the lives of the Jews. She changed the terrible future for many Jewish children excessively. Her father was a doctor (she was a nurse) and many of his patients were poor Jews. She came up with ingenious plan to help the poor and dying Jews that would change their lives forever. Her achievement was recognized by four young students along with their teacher in Kansas many years later in a play called Life in a Jar. She was awarded the Order of White Eagle in Warsaw, Poland's highest distinction on November 10, 2003. Her actions are still greatly honored today. Unfortunately, she passed away in 2008, at the old age of 98.

The Holocaust was a devastating period of time when the Nazis started to kill off the Jews. The Nazis were very sneaky in doing this. When they first came to Poland, they were greeted by many excited Jews. Some time later, the Nazis closed Jewish shops and took away their rights and put them in compact spaces called Ghettos. Eventually, signs were put up that said "No Jews allowed," even on benches. The Nazis said that they had to evacuate every Jew to place like paradise, but the Jews arrived at nothing like what they were told. Soon, they found out that Hitler had tricked them and that they were being sent to concentration camps to do physical labor until they died. Most of the Jews died and very few of them survived until liberation. This kind of torture should never again come to our world.

Even though she brought medicines, food, and other needs for the Jews daily to the Ghetto, Irena couldn't bear to look at 500,000 people slowly coming to death. Irena knew that the Jews would die if they stayed in the Ghetto any longer. She was already delivering clothes, food, and other items to the poor and elderly and gladly delivered these to the Jews as well.

It took a lot of bravery and tremendous effort to smuggle 2,500 Jewish children out of a Ghetto. As a worker in the Warsaw Social Welfare Department, Irena provided the needs for elders and orphans including Jews. She hid the children's' identities in a jar and buried it. They were given code names and identities to protect them from the Nazis. To prevent the Nazis from ever finding the children she gave them all Christian names. She decided to help the poor Jews who were slowly dying from horrible starvation and disease. For many years, she managed to keep her secret unrevealed and safe.

She also joined the Zegota, the Council for Aid to Jews which was a program that started to help Jewish children survive. She had to get a pass from the Warsaw Epidemic Control to visit the Ghetto daily. It was hard to see your children leave you, even if it was for a good reason. It was a terrible task to part parents from their children. Irena eventually persuaded parents to let her take their children. She could still hear the cries of families to their children years later. The parents were so worried and scared that the children wouldn't survive, but Irena told them that they would surely die in the Ghetto. She knew that they would never survive in the horrendous Ghetto.

She employed one person from each of the many centers in the Warsaw Social Welfare Department. Using body bags and potato sacks, Irena successfully brought the Jewish children to safe hiding places. She started to smuggle them with an ambulance. The children were brought to a church and were very excited. The children were overjoyed when they were free from the Ghetto. They were sent to homes and orphanages with special code names to ensure their safety. No one of the non- Jewish people ever denied taking one of the Jewish children.

Some time later, she was arrested by the Gestapo, the German police, and they broke her feet and legs. She would not reveal the secret identities of the children even if it meant death. She was sentenced to death until the Zegota arrived and persuaded the Gestapo to stop. Irena eventually escaped, but the Gestapo was still suspicious.

She went back to same apple tree and dug up the jar after the war. She planned for the 2,500 children to rejoin with their families. Unfortunately, most families were lost during the war. Many years later, her photo appeared in the newspaper and she was honored for her accomplishments. A painter called her and he told her that he recognized her. He said, "It was you who took me out of the Ghetto!" She had many calls similar to this one. Sendler didn't think of herself as a hero. She said she could have done more and did not claim credit for what she did, although she should have.

Even though she didn't claim credit for what she did, she is an amazing hero. She changed the future of freedom that everyone deserves for more than 2000 Jewish children. She sacrificed her own life for the lives of others. Irena Sendler is a hero that should never be forgotten.

Work Cited

"Home | Jewish Virtual Library." Home | Jewish Virtual Library. N.p., n.d. Web. 04 Dec. 2016. < http://www.jewishvirtuallibrary.org/ >.

Rudolf Weigl

Isaac Peter Colendres

There are many fictional heroes in our lives today, but the real heroes are the ones that risk their life to save many other people. The hero that stood out the most to me was Rudolf Weigl.

Rudolf Weigl was considered a genius. Before the war, he was a Polish biologist at a University. He was famous for creating the first vaccine against typhus. He protested against racism and violence between the Polish classmates and the Jewish classmates. Soon after the war broke out, his vaccine interested the Germans. They soon hired Rudolf to ship vaccines to the German soldiers.

The Holocaust was a genocide, which killed many innocent people because they were Jewish. The Holocaust happened in 1930s-1945 when Hitler decided upon his final solution. Hitler's final solution caused the Holocaust. The mass killings began; Jews were gathered up and shot. The men, women, and children had their valuables confiscated, their arms tattooed or marked with a special code, and were put into slave labor prisons. This sped up the elimination process. The Nazis performed horrific inhumane experiments on the Jews. Your chance of living was based on your trade and your physical attributes. Then the Nazis built extermination camps which were where the Jews were gassed and killed. Most of these camps were built in Poland and these camps could kill up to six thousand people a day. After the war, there were fewer than four million people and sixty-three percent of the Jewish population in Europe was killed.

The typhus fever was very deadly in the Warsaw Ghettos because of the unsanitary conditions and the lack of medical attention. Mr.Weigl was actually forced to create vaccines for the Germans. During the war, Rudolf would smuggle large quantities of vaccines to the Warsaw Ghettos. Since Rudolf smuggled vaccines to the Warsaw Ghettos this lead to many people being saved from the deadly typhus disease. This illegal way of transporting the vaccines could cause Weigl and the people working with him death. The vaccine that Rudolf created would help save millions of people in the future. In Weigl's institute they provided protection from arrest and deportations to concentration camps. Weigl would protect the unemployed professors and make them lice feeders. By employing them as lice feeders they would be partially immune to deportation and arrest. Weigl would use his fame and scientific connections with German biologists to protect some people from the Nazis. Weigl created "Ausweiss" or identification cards from a German Chief of the German army. These inventions somehow saved many lives.

Zofia Bania

Isaiah Singh

The Holocaust was an attempt to kill the entire Jewish population. This attempt was led by a very evil man known as Adolf Hitler. He put the Jews in Ghettos or places isolated from the real world and later put them in concentration camps, labor camps, and extermination camps, also known as death camps. These were the hardest times in Jewish history, and many people thought it was unjust. People who helped the Jews escape the Ghettos or any of the camps, were called the Righteous. One of these many people is Zofia Bania.

Zofia Bania was born and raised in Pińczów, Poland, 1913. She lived an average life. She had one sister. She was married in 1941, in her hometown Pińczów. Zofia herself had always been a poor farmer but always a great person throughout the hard times. She told Franciszka (Frania) Rubinek, a good Jewish friend who owned a nearby store, that if worse came to worse she could hideout in her home. In the meantime, Franciszka's husband,

231

Israel, decided to build a bunker underneath their small store. But eventually Franciszka and Israel took Zofia up on her offer, once the Germans started rounding up all the Jews.

News eventually got to Zofia, and she hired a man she trusted to take Franciszka and her husband to Zofia's home. Zofia lived in a small, one room home with her husband and her six-year-old son. Zofia's husband was against the Rubineks' coming to live at their home. Zofia protested that they were her friends and that she could not betray them. The couple often fought about the situation. The Rubineks' constantly did their best to appease Ludwig, Zofia's husband, and they gave him money for his silence and continued assistance. During the Rubineks' stay they lived in a hay loft in a barn connected to Zofia's house. It was in the loft in December of 1942, when Franciszka went into labor with only Zofia and Israel for her assistance. The baby died at birth. Franciszka fell seriously ill for the next three months. After that, the Rubineks moved into the main house, where they shared a small bedroom with Zofia, Ludwig, and Maniek, their son.

The house was on the outskirts of Wlochy, about a half kilometer from the nearest neighbor, which made it extra safe. Even though the house was pretty safe, Ludwig bought a guard dog as an extra precaution. The dog's purpose was to bark whenever someone came to the door.

On rare occasions, Israel and Franciszka would hide in a cellar that was used to store potatoes. Once, toward the end of the war, the Rubineks, thanks to the dog's warning, managed to slip into the cellar just as German soldiers entered the house and declared that they intended to spend the night. Zofia placed a bed for Maniek directly over the entrance to the cellar to prevent the soldiers from noticing it. But Israel was suffering from a cough, which could be easily heard in such a small space. Maniek, despite his young age, was well aware of the situation. He was devoted to the Rubineks and felt responsible for their safety. The young boy spent the entire night pretending to be sick, coughing and crying loudly in order to overcome the sound of Israel's coughing, saving the couple's lives.

The Rubineks stayed with Zofia until the land was freed by the Red Army. After the war, the couple migrated to Canada. In 1986, they traveled to Poland to visit with their son, Israel, and Maniek. On August 16, 2011, Yad Vashem recognized Zofia Bania as one of the Righteous Among the Nations.

The Holocaust was a very important time in our life. Some concepts I learned from the Holocaust are that the Germans had no right to what they did to the Jews and that the many great people who helped the escaped Jews should always be remembered. The Holocaust has definitely taught me never to take anything for granted. The Germans took everything away from the Jews because they were successful and needed someone to blame. I understand that the Holocaust was an awful time for the Jews and that something like this could have annihilated the entire Jewish population. A mass genocide of the Jews should never happen again. This experience obliterated the Jews; it took years for them to rise from poverty. Some steps that need to be taken to stop this from happening again are having many checks and balances that limit leaders' power. Another way to ensure that this can never happen again is to be certain that no rulers become so corrupt and caught up in their own lies.

Events like this can change the human race as we know it, and not for good. The last step in order to achieve less mass murders is for countries not to fight. Although none of this is likely, these are the steps the world needs to take in order to stop these horrible genocides.

Works Cited

"Zofia Bania." Geni_family_tree. N.p., 18 Nov. 2014. Web. 13 Dec. 2016.

"The Righteous Among The Nations." The Righteous Among The Nations. N.p., n.d. Web. 13 Dec. 2016.

JAN KOMSKI

Ivan Lun

 Jan was born in a Catholic family in a small Polish town called Bircza. His was a World War I veteran and had moved his family to a small manufacturing town in southeastern Poland called Brzozow after the war. After he had graduated from his secondary school and he had enrolled at the academy of fine arts in Cracow. But as time passed, the Germans started to invade in September, 1939.

Jan had escaped the German army and had hoped to join the Polish army. As he reached the Soviet border he was afraid of Soviet rules, so he returned to confront the German army and was soon arrested. He was first taken to prison then he was sent to a camp called Auschwitz in June 14, 1940. He had a fake identity paper that held the name Jan Baras. In the camp, all the prisoners were given number from 31-758 and Komski got number 564, but luckily at that time they weren't tattooed to their arms.

After two and a half years, Komski and three other comrades planned an escape. They had already forged a pass and had already stolen an SS uniform, so it is time for them put the plan into action. In the afternoon they would pass through a gate on a two wheeled cart that was drawn by two horses, with one of the inmates dressed as an SS solider pretending that he was escorting the prisoners to a different camp. Then they would pass a check point with the perfectly forged pass. They would then make their way to a village called Broszkowice where a woman would provide civilian clothes and a place to rest. The woman was named Andrzej Harat and had actually rented the apartment from an SS soldier.

The next day Komski was arrested in a round up when he was sitting on a train ready for the departure to Warsaw. Nobody recognized him because his real identity was Jan Komski. He was going to be sent to Auschwitz. While the SS soldiers loaded all the rounded up Jews, he had thought all the SS soldiers that work in Auschwitz would remember his face so he ran down the street. The guards fired shots at him and one of them had hit his ankle and he fell. The guards ran toward him and they thought about killing him on the street, but one of them said they had to do it in prison, so they beat him unconscious and brought him to an infirmary.

He was left in the infirmary and they bandaged his ankle without changing it at all, but luckily he didn't get an infection and survived. After he had healed, he was about to enter the gate when a prisoner had recognized him, but he didn't turn him in to the SS soldiers. He had instead told the prisoner who ran the office, and was part of the camp resisting movement, to have them cut the orders in order to send Komski to Auschwitz II. Then he was sent to Buchenwald concentration camp in Germany, and then to Krakow for interrogation, than to another camp called Gross Rosen and was then shipped to Sachsenburg. Lucky none of the SS soldiers in those camps had recognized him or else he would have been killed. On May 2, 1945, he was liberated from the camp called Dachau, the last camp he had been through, by U.S. troops. After the war he had immigrated to the U.S.A. and worked for the Washington Post as an illustrator for many years. He lived alert, lively, very courteous and caring of others before he passed away.

I had learned that the Holocaust affected the Jewish population because the Nazis killed more than one million Jews. I was actually surprised on why one person decided to kill all the Jews and why nobody that was following that person stood up against his acts. The Holocaust almost wiped out an entire race and changed the world forever because of one person's wrong actions. None of the Jews deserved to die but they still suffered starvation, death, and the pain of being mistreated.

There are steps to take in order to stop this from ever happening. One thing to do is that everybody must stand up to what they think is right and wrong. Another thing is that there must not be a dictator that is so powerful that he can do almost anything in this world.

Website Citations

Dunn, Michael Declan. "Jan Komski's Story." The Holocaust History - A People's and Survivor History - Remember.org. FMGNetwork, Apr. 1995. Web. 13 Dec. 2016.

"Jan Komski." United States Holocaust Memorial Museum. United States Holocaust Memorial Museum, n.d. Web. 14 Dec. 2016.

Irena Sendler

Ivy Le

The Holocaust began in the 1930's, when economic depression hit Germany. The Germans lacked assurance from their government which gave Adolf Hitler the chance to rise. The old German president, Paul von Hindenburg, reluctantly agreed to let Adolf Hitler to become chancellor due to populous amounts of people blaming the less extreme parties for Germany's economic problem. Hitler and the Nazi Party began the Holocaust after Hitler was chancellor and started blaming the Jews for the economics. The Nazis and Hitler began shooting the Jews and wanted to speed up the elimination of the Jews, so they rounded them up and sent them to extermination camps or slave-labor prisons. The Holocaust began in January 30, 1933 to May 8, 1945, which lasted for 12 years. Throughout the 12 years, over six million Jews were either killed from extermination camps, shot, gas chambers, murdered, beat to death, hanged, etc. Less than four million Jews survived the Holocaust and were forever changed. A small portion of non Jews died or survived helping the Jews escaping concentration or extermination camps became heroes. Those people had the courage to risk their lives saving the Jews from being killed or murdered. One of those heroes was Irena Sendler.

Irena Sendler's was born on February 15, 1910, as Irena Krzyzanowska in Otwock, Poland. Her father, Dr. Stanis Krzyzanowska, was a physician, and her mother was Janina. Her father died in February, 1917, which led many Jewish leaders to offering to pay for Irena's education. She studied Polish literature at Warsaw University, but was suspended for three years due to withstanding the ghetto-bench system.

In 1939, Germany began to invade Poland when Irena was a Senior Administrator in the Warsaw Social Welfare Department which operated canteens within the city. The clothing, food, money, etc were registered under made-up Christian names and Irena prevented inspections by reporting diseases such as tuberculosis and typhus. By 1942, the Nazis herded thousands of Jews inside a sixteen block area that is known as the Warsaw Ghetto, which was a very high wall that blocked the Jews from leaving the Ghetto so that they could die there. Sendler was horrified by the conditions and joined Zegota (Polish Council to Aid Jews) which was organized by the Polish underground resistance movement to rescue Jewish children and later on was in charge of Zegota. Irena was able to get into the Ghetto legally by managing to get a pass issued from Warsaw Epidemic Control Department; she used papers from one of the workers at the Contagious Disease Department. She visited the Ghetto daily to bring food, medicines, and clothing, but 5,000 people were dying from starvations and diseases, so she decided to help the children first. It was not easy for Sendler to find shelters for the children when she had to persuade the families to risk their lives. Irena smuggled about 2,500 Jewish children with temporary new identities and false documents with forged identities. Irena and her helpers made over 3,000 documents for the Jewish children who were in the Ghetto. The children were either taken out in gunnysacks, body bags, buried inside loads of goods, carried in potato sacks, placed in coffins, taken out in an ambulance under the stretcher, through the courthouses, etc. The children entered a church as Jews and exited as Christians to successfully escape the Ghetto. After that, the children were given false identities and then placed in orphanages, convents, and home. Sendler carefully wrote down the coded form and true identities in jars buried beneath an apple tree that was in a neighbor's backyard across the street from German barracks. On October 20, 1943, Irena was arrested, imprisoned, and tortured by the Gestapo, secret police of Nazis, who broke both her legs and feet. Sendler was in Pawiak Prison where she was being tortured for not saying the name and addresses of the families that were sheltering the Jewish children; she didn't want to betray her associates or any of the Jewish children. Before Sendler was sentenced to death, her Zegota members saved her at the last minute. After the day Irena escaped, posters were all over the city with the news that she was shot, but was still chased by the Gestapo. After the war, Irena dug up the jars and tried to track down the 2,500 children she saved to be with their relatives in Europe, but most of them died during the Holocaust in Treblinka concentration camps. The Jewish children all grew up and recognized her after she was awarded for her wartime work even though they only knew her by her code name, Jolanta.

In conclusion to Irena Sendler's story, I learned that Irena was a very brave woman who risked her lives to save Jewish children. She did everything in her power to save the children; from joining Zegota, asking families to keep the children safe, and making false documents with forged signature. Learning about Irena Sendler's story, I feel that people should stand up for what is right and not stay silent to be safe for their own concerns. I do not like the name of Hitler because I do not want another version of the Holocaust to happen again. Hitler and the Nazis killed many family members of the Jews. Those who had survived will always remember their parents, siblings, close relatives, or friends who had been with them. The survivors are forever changed and do not need this to happen again. I would start World Peace where everyone loves each other without being racist, judging people on who they and their disabilities. People from all over the world would join to share their stories about things that have scarred their life. People should learn to love each other no matter when they look like, beliefs, and culture. "Never Again" shall this happen; everybody should learn about the Holocaust to prevent this from happening ever again.

Works Cited

"Adolf Hitler Becomes President of Germany." History.com. A&E Television Networks, n.d. Web. 11 Dec. 2016.

"Facts about Irena - Life in a Jar." Life in a Jar. N.p., n.d. Web. 11 Dec. 2016.

"Hitler Becomes Chancellor." Hitler Becomes Chancellor - 1933 Key Stage 3 - The Holocaust Explained. N.p., n.d. Web. 11 Dec. 2016.

"Irena Sendler." Irena Sendler | Jewish Virtual Library. N.p., n.d. Web. 11 Dec. 2016.

"The Unsung Heroines." The Unsung Heroines. N.p., n.d. Web. 11 Dec. 2016.

Maria, Adamkowska

Jacey Quigley

The Holocaust was a dangerous and horrible experience for all Jews. The Holocaust started January 30, 1933 to May 8, 1945, when the war in Europe officially ended. There were six million Jews, 1.5 million being children, who were murdered. On January 30, 1933, Adolf Hitler was chancellor of Germany. In 1933, Jews were not allowed to hold public office, not allowed to be with their friends or talk to Germans. They had to wear yellow stars on their shirts to identify themselves. Hitler decided to imprison all the Jews because he thought Jews had to be eliminated. In Poland there was 3,001,000 Jews killed. Many healthy, young strong Jews were not killed. At the end of the war, between 50,000 and 100,000 Jewish survivors were living. One of them is named Maria Adamkowska.

Maria Adamkowska was a survivor of the Holocaust. Her religion was Roman Catholic and she was female. Her profession was a teacher. The place she was during the war was Warszawa, Poland. She was also rescued in Warszawa, Poland. To get rescued she was constantly hiding and arranging her shelter. She is on the Wall on Honor in Ellis Island in New York Harbor. Her date of recognition was 13/02/1968.

During the German occupation, Maria Adamkowsha lived in a two room apartment in Warsaw. One of the rooms was rented to a municipal office employee, Dr. Leon Gottesmann, who worked under an assumed name using "Aryan" documents. One day Maria learned that Leon was Jewish and that his true identity was in danger of being discovered. She offered unconditionally to shelter him in her own rooms and Gottesmann moved into the room beside her. To his astonishment he found two Jewish woman there also equipped with "Aryan" papers, who told him of Maria's kindness in caring for and protecting them. In the course of time, the fugitives were joined by two more Jewish women, one of whom, Rubinlicht by name, had a heart attack and died shortly thereafter. With great courage Maria informed the German authorities that the deceased was her aunt and contrary to the usual procedure they waived the mandatory inquest and permitted Rubinlicht's burial.

The four Jewish fugitives remained with Maria until the suppression of the Warsaw Uprising in by the Red Army in January, 1945, and Maria, who had been deported to Germany, was liberated from Buchenwald by the American army three months later. On February 13, 1963, Yad Vashem recognized Maria Adamkowska as Righteous Among the Nations. Never Again should the Holocaust happen.

I learned that the Holocaust was scary and dangerous and different because you didn't know what is coming up next because you are with untrusting of people. There could be a shooting by the time you blink. There could be an elimination right around the corner. The people were all scared because they don't know what was going to happen next. Learning about my person's story and where they are from and just about them I was just really scared for them. I can tell from what I learned that it would have been really frightening and scary. Most of all the time seemed really dangerous. It was dangerous because a person would go from not telling what was going to happen, to being taken away to a camp not knowing what to do; being taken to a concentration camp and being separated from your family and children that you deeply love and not knowing what to do. I understand the pain the people went through and didn't know how to stop it and being afraid of everything they see and nervous to go around the corner.

Never again should any of this happen, never again should these people be frightened by someone who should've been put to a stop. Never again should Hitler, or anyone like him, command and demand people to do what he says. They should have never had to be labeled in what they wore nor do all that work for free. Never again should any of this happen! Every single thing you can name that happened in the Holocaust should have never happened. Never Again. I bet everyone who lived through the Holocaust, and has survived to tell about it today, does not want to look back at when they were young and remember how terrifying it was and how scary they might have been. During the Holocaust 6,258,673 people were killed and about 3,546,211 survived. Hitler and his Nazi army killed about 6,000 people a day. Each person was probably hoping they were not going to be one of them. Never Again is associated with the Holocaust because Never Again should this happen, Never Again should they be put this way; wearing clothing that has stars on it every day, not being able to do stuff with their friends anymore, being put down by someone that shouldn't even be telling anyone what to do. The shoes Jewish people would wear were sandals. Sandals were very hard because all the work they had to do with them on and how it would affect them with their working because they couldn't do much. Jewish people went through hard times; they went through good times; they were put through lots of scary times. Never Again.

Works Cited:

Rozovsky, Lorne. "Jews and Shoes." Mitzvahs & Traditions. Lorne Rozovsky, 14 Nov. 2008. Web. 13 Dec. 2016.

NELSON, SORAYA SARHADDI. "A Holocaust Survivor, Spared From Gas Chamber By Twist Of Fate." NPR. NPR, 27 Jan. 2015. Web. 13 Dec. 2016.

Stewart, James. "How Many People Survived the Holocaust?" Yahoo! Answers. Yahoo!, 18 Apr. 2007. Web. 13 Dec. 2016.

Gertruda Babilinska

Jade Light

Gertruda was one of many rescuers that stood up for what was right during the devastating period known as the Holocaust. Gertruda saved a little boy named Mickey, who had lost his family when separating to different Jew camps. She led Mickey through tough times and would invest in his time and education. Through Gertruda's whole experience she gained a child named, Mickey.

Gertruda was born in North Poland in the year of 1902. She lived in a religious family with seven other siblings. Her father worked at the post office while her mother stayed home was concerned about everything. As Gertruda grew up she was working for a very rich, Jewish family. The Stolowitzky family hired Gertruda as their maid. While working for the family the Holocaust began and the father was taken to Auschwitz while the mother and two children traveled to Vilna because it was the safest place. Gertruda felt so attached and sorry for the family that she decided she would stay with the family in Vilna to protect them. Conditions got very bad and the mother of only the son now had told Gertruda that if anything had happened to her to save Mickey, the only son, and run away to somewhere safe. Although the community was the safest, the Nazis there were very harsh about extinguishing Jews. The Nazis tried many things to kill the Jew children; first by, handing out poisoned candy. Gertruda moved into her own apartment in Vilna to give Mickey and his mother some privacy. Mickey's mother died from a terrible sickness. Mickey walked over to Gertruda's apartment and told her that he had lost her mother and would love it if she would take her place. She had a hard time answering this because she was 40 years old and was single. Adding on to all that, the child was Jewish and she was very Catholic. Gertruda finally said that he could stay with her in her apartment and she would protect him. Right after she said that, Mickey threw his arms around Gertruda. After a month of living together, Mickey got very sick and the only doctor Gertruda knew was German. She tried to sneak him in as her younger brother but he noticed but continued to make him feel better. The war ended but Gertruda knew her job wasn't done because she needed to get Mickey to Israel because that was the only place where Mickey could pray to the Jewish religion and Gertruda could pray in a Christian church. On the way to Israel they took a ship named the Exodus but, it was very crowded and there wasn't any food. When Mickey first stepped on Israelite land Gertruda knew that that was the place for them to live for the rest of their lives. Right after getting off the ship they went directly to Mickey's relatives. His relatives wanted to adopt him and send him to a Jewish school but, Mickey protested back saying that Gertruda was his mother and he was going to go where Gertruda was going. Gertruda started to evolve around Mickey and did anything to keep Mickey in school and living. Gertruda became a maid for Mickey's relatives and was paid just enough to send Mickey to a school for Jews who had grown up in Europe. Mickey grew up to be a committed and friendly Jew who didn't break any "laws" of his religion. About 40 years later, Gertruda found a warm and cozy elderly living community to settle in with its very own Christian church. There was one thing that made the church not real to Gertruda. This fact was that the priest was a converted Jew and that made her think of all her journeys with her son. After raising Mickey, Gertruda settled in Israel while Mickey moved several times from the United States to Israel. Gertruda left a remarkable mark on the world today because she brought a little happiness in the miserable times of the Holocaust. Gertruda was so remarkable that she was awarded the Righteous medal by the Yad Vashem Institute in 1963.

While experiencing the struggles of Jewish prisoners and the righteous people of the Holocaust I have learned that all Jews were discriminated which shouldn't have happened. I learned that if it wasn't for the righteous people who saved some of the Jews that went through struggles we wouldn't be able to learn from the stories of saved Jews. This made an impact on my life because I realized that freedom doesn't come easily and that I shouldn't judge someone on how they look because you have no idea what they have or go through. I understand that the Holocaust was a deadly, scary time in history and that many Jews lost their lives for being smart and being better that another race. One way to make sure that this never happens again is to treat people the way you want to be treated. For example, if your race is hated then that isn't fair and could cause similar incidents like the Holocaust. "Never Again" will this happen if we drop technology and pay attention to the world.

Works Cited

The Remarkable Story of Gertruda Babilińska - Virtual Shtetl. N.p., n.d. Web. 11 Dec. 2016.

"Rescuers: Gertruda Babilinska." PBS. PBS, n.d. Web. 11 Dec. 2016.

Jerzy Bielecki and Tzila Cybulska

Jaden Thai

Jerzy Bielecki was a Polish social worker that was one of the few workers of the Auschwitz concentration camp able to escape with success. During the Holocaust one day, Jerzy was working on repairing grain sacks and when he looked up for just a moment he thought he saw another girl wink at him, and this girl is named Ms. Cybulska. Since both of them could only talk for a few moments a day, they now had to work together and planned for a way out. This was a story of love and courage and how powerful feeling and emotions can actually be in life.

Jerzy Bielecki can be looked upon to be an example of a daring and loving man who escaped with another person, and that was Ms. Cybulska. Before Jerzy and Ms. Cybulska met, he was a Roman Catholic who met occasionally with the underground resistance to help out the Jews in Poland. Later on, the German suspected him as a member of the Polish resistance, and he was put into hard labor in Auschwitz, with the number 243 labeled on his arm. As he met more and more with Cybulska, they began to fall in love with each other and began their plan of escape with the help of Jerzy's friend who was a uniform worker. Time passed and the plan was finished by the time the German uniform was made. One day, Jerzy took Cybulska out of her barracks while in the soldier uniform, shaking with fear and nervousness, taking her on a long path. When the sleepy guard saw both of them he stared at them as Jerzy gave him the forged pass he had made. Then, he looked at them curiously for what seemed a very long time to Jerzy and quietly answered,"Ya, danke." ("Yes, thank you") As they snuck their way through the fields in the day, they would just walk during the night time, and this process continued for 10 days and 10 nights. In the middle of their journey to freedom, they had run out of food. When Cybulska felt as though she could no longer continue, she begged Jerzy to leave her behind, but he would not and even carried her on his shoulders when he had the strength to do so.

Much in love, Jerzy still thought that he had a role in the underground too. When the two arrived at a certain village, Jerzy coincidentally found his brother. He asked for a safe place to stay and for the items needed to stay alive. Jerzy also found a safe place for Cybulska to stay while he went to join the underground resistance with his brother to stay informed about what they planned to do. As they lost contact due to many misunderstandings, they both assumed that the other was dead until 39 years later when they met up again in Poland.

I have learned that life is easier if you have somebody or something to rely on for help. By learning about Jerzy and Tzila, I feel as if my life is just fine the way it is and that maybe I should think about others more than I already do and help them if needed. As I am still young and have not had enough experience in life to judge others or make important decisions by myself, I still believe that the Holocaust was unjust and should never happen again under any circumstance. I understand that the Holocaust was basically genocide, killing one because of their race, and from that I learned that the world isn't a safe place for anyone. I also admit that if I was in the Holocaust I would only worry about myself and whether I would die that day or get to live another rough and painful day, and I would probably also think about a plan to escape without worrying about the other Holocaust victims. I feel as though "Never Again" means that the Holocaust's events should never be repeated no matter what, and that it can be interpreted to never let the Holocaust happen ever again. To make sure that the Holocaust never happens again, we have a law where if someone attacks somebody for religious purposes that they get sent to jail for what I'm guessing is a long time. We can also prevent the Holocaust from happening again by making sure that nobody judges anybody based on religion, but by their good traits and bad traits. Even though nowadays it isn't common for somebody to judge another based on religion, we should still be cautious of reality especially when something crucial to your life appears or happens. Everyone should be wary of the things happening in the world so that if they can change it for the better they can speak up before it's too late and disaster strikes. Though I can't make important changes in the world yet, I will try my best to become my ideal self in the future.

Hevesi, Dennis. "Jerzy Bielecki Dies at 90; Fell in Love in a Nazi Camp." The New York Times. The New York Times, 23 Oct. 2011. Web. 12 Dec. 2016.

Reuters. "Jewish Girl's Polish Savior from Auschwitz Dies, Age 90." Haaretz.com. N.p., 22 Oct. 2011. Web. 13 Dec. 2016.

Feliks Zolynia

Jaiden Miller

The Holocaust was a tragic persecution and murder of over six million Jews. In the 1930's, an economic depression hit Germany very hard. The Germans started to lack confidence in their weak government. This provided the chance for the rise of Adolf Hitler, who came to power in January, 1933. He then started to blame the Jews for the cause of their depression. Hitler started a government with enlightened propaganda to ensure the Nazi message was successfully communicated and the Aryans (Germans) were known as the "master race." Jews were not allowed to hold public office and were deprived from their rights of German citizenship. To easily identify the Jewish race, Jews were forced to wear yellow Stars of David.

Jews then started to flee Germany for their own safety and to get away from harsh discrimination. Hitler ordered all Jews under Germany's control to be moved into certain cities in Poland called Ghettos; there they lacked food, space, and hope. Hitler's "final solution" was genocide (planned killing) to speed up the process of Jewish extermination or all races inferior needed to be eliminated. Mass killings began; Jews were either rounded up and shot, taken to concentration camps, or killed right there on the isolated spot. In the camps all children and adults were treated equally. They got their arms tattooed with a number that became their new name. Men, woman, and children were separated even if you were family and they were used in inhumane medical experiments. Six thousand people a day were tricked and killed from gas chambers. Sixty-three percent of the Jewish population in Europe was killed and ninety-one percent of the Jewish population in Poland was killed. Fewer than four million Jews survived. Those who survived were forever changed, but they couldn't have done it without help.

Feliks Zolynia rescued and hid the Sztajnberg family, Izhak and Fajga Sztajnberg and their children Cywa, Frida and Menachem. The Sztajnberg family lived in Janow Lubelski then first relocated to Modlliborzyce to live with Izhak's parents until Germans invaded there and Izhak's parents were executed. He and his family fled to Wierzchowiska. The Sztajnbergs moved into a small apartment, but soon received no tolerance from their neighbors. They decided to seek help from Zolynia Feliks (1905-1971) who was a rescuer who could help hide the Sztajnbergs. Zolynia let them build an 80 by 180 centimeter underground pit in his barn and he always slept with them outside the pit to keep guard if anyone wandered into the barn. Twice the Sztajnbergs almost got caught, once by Zolynia's landlord and once by his brother. Zolynia's landlord heard suspicion about Zolynia hiding a Jewish family and when he finally found the Sztajnbergs hiding in the barn, Izhak made a deal with him that he would better hide the entry of his pit if he kept their secret, so he agreed because the landlord was also against Hitler's beliefs. One night Zolynia's brother, Bolek, came to visit him and during the middle of the night. When Zolynia went to fetch water, his brother accidentally wandered into the barn and saw Izhak getting his family more food, but Zolynia was able to talk some sense into his brother and to have him promise to help keep the Sztajnberg family safe because that also meant keeping his brother safe. Sometimes Bolek even brought the Sztajnberg family their daily food and supplies. Father Izhak often snuck out to trade some of their belongings for food because all Zolynia had left to feed them was remaining potato skins.

Several times Izhak was captured by Germans but he miraculously always managed to escape. Even when the liberation was approaching, the Sztajnbergs' agony was not over. Zolynia warned them that the German army was destroying every building in its way, and the pit would soon become unsafe. After 22 months in the claustrophobic pit the Sztajnberg family could barely walk, except Izhak, but they were forced to run away to the forest. After the liberation of the area, the Soviet soldiers guided and cared for them very much, warned them about the armed Poles, and transferred them to Luck (today Lutsk), which was in Soviet territory and where there was other Jews. In 1957, the Sztajnbergs returned to Poland and moved to Israel, Austria, and the Czech Republic. They kept in close touch with their rescuer, Feliks Zolynia.

Feliks Zolynia and many other rescuers understood the Jews were being mistreated and murdered and that it was wrong, so they stood up for the ones who had no voice. The Holocaust hurt tons of Jewish families and without the rescuers the chance of surviving would decrease. I learned that if something is wrong and I know its wrong you should never be a bystander, you should help. Many people during the Holocaust knew the Jews were being treated horribly but they were too scared to fight for what was right. To prevent anything like this from happening in the future you need to stand up for your peers because the Holocaust was scary; no one wants to experience anything that harsh. "Never Again" is a saying to ensure that something this heinous never happens again. For all the Holocaust victims: "Never Again." The sun always shines through a thunder cloud, there is always hope even in your darkest scariest times. Feliks saved many families including the Stzajnbergs and I know they deeply appreciated it; he was their sun and hope.

Works Cited

"The Righteous Among The Nations." The Righteous Among The Nations. N.p., n.d. Web. 09 Dec. 2016.

Wojan, Megan. "Introduction to Holocaust." Honors Social Science 7 Holocaust Lecture. KAMS, Elk Grove. 4 Nov. 2016. Lecture.

Adolf Brauner

Jake Firch

In the 1930's, an economic depression hit Germany hard, leaving Germans with little confidence in their weak government. This provided the chance for a new leader, Adolf Hitler. Hitler and his "Nazis" took power over Germany in January of 1933. The Nazis believed that the Aryans were a "master race." Hitler's goal was to exterminate over six million Jews. However, Adolf Brauner was determined to help save the Jews. Brauner worked for Hirszberg&Birenbaum firm, located in the city of Lodz. He was later appointed for the position of managing the director of the firm.

Brauner was escorting Chaskiel to the office and he realized that he was wearing the yellow Star of David. Later, they passed a synagogue, which the Nazis had set on fire. Those who were engaged in setting that fire attacked Chaskiel. Brauner used his big muscles and diplomacy in order to save the Chaskiel's live. From 1940 to 1942, Brauner helped him smuggle his family's valuables from Lodz and Warsaw Ghetto. He also smuggled them food. In September of 1942, Chaskiel's wife, Dworjanee, was sent to a concentration camp in Treblinka. Once there, she perished in the gas chamber. In 1943, Chaskiel and his son Boleslaw were killed in Lubin. Now, Chaskiel's daughter, Lusia, was the only one alive from their family. Brauner saw this and immediately knew what he had to do. Brauner gave her an Aryan name, Bogucka. She escaped from the Warsaw Ghetto and made it to the Aryan side of the city, where she pretended to be a Polish woman. She did this so that she could be sent to Germany to do work. Eventually, she, along with many others, was sent to Germany, where she stayed till the war was over. She worked as a kitchen-maid in a hotel and at the Volkswagen factory. During all that time, from 1943 till 1945, Brauner sent her packages with money, food, and letters of encouragement. After the war, Brauner returned all of the valuables that Chaskiel had left for him for safekeeping. Lusia then immigrated to Australia, where Brauner had sent her property deeds that belonged to her family.

In addition to watching over Lusia, Brauner was married to a Jewish woman and they had a son named Gerhard. While he spent so much time caring for Lusia by sending her packages, handwriting her notes of encouragement, and sending her deeds of land that her family owned, he also made time to help his own family members. This was amazing that he watched over two children that were being hunted down because of their beliefs at the same time. He risked his life. If any German found out about this and found him, he would be shot on the spot, dead in his tracks. Many people had helped save Jews but has anybody besides Brauner watched over two at a time? Brauner's son Gerhard grew up during the war, but he was never forced to go to a concentration camp. He was seven years old when the war had come to an end.

Through reading the story of Adolf Brauner, I have learned how important it is to take care of each other; that we should always make sure that our friend are feeling well, not hungry, and not being bullied. Every day I am always taking notes on how my friends are feeling, and if they are sick, how I should keep my distance so that I don't become sick as well. Adolf Brauner's story has had a tremendous impact in my busy life. It has helped me to understand how important the Holocaust was in our history. If this event occurred in our history, we would never know what a cruel man Adolf Hitler really was. All we would know was how many Jewish people were on the planet at the time. The streets of Poland would be crowded if he did not kill so many Jews. There would be nowhere for them to live because all of the hotels, shelter homes, and generous people's houses would be filled with so many of them. Not to mention how low the food level would go. All the good citizens of Poland would be starving because of how much the people ate. How if we ever let this happen again, we could be in grave danger. Nobody wants to be locked away in a camp that you were going to be killed in. Just the thought of being locked up gives me the chills. Never again will we have such a tragic event occur in our country. I hope that our leaders will keep this from happening again. I hope they will keep our country from being bombed, invaded, and from being taken over by another country. To keep this from happening, we will need our military to be strong. That means lots of love and support from our citizens is required.

Work Cited

Wojan, Megan. "In Class Lecture." Www.yadvashem.org. N.p., n.d. Web. 8 Dec. 2016.

PAWEL CHARMUSZKO

James Velasco

 The Holocaust was a horrible destruction and persecution of Jewish lives. The reason why the Holocaust started was because the Germans blamed the Jews for bringing the Black Death to them. In the history of the Holocaust, many Jews were killed by the Nazi party, a group of Germans led by a person named Adolf Hitler. The deaths of many Jews included burning of bodies, gaseous deaths, and death marches. In this harsh environment, the Jews lost all their belongings and their work. They were shaved, got diseases from unsanitariness of the camp, and tried to survive based on their survival skills. The Nazis took the gold teeth from the Jews to increase their wealth. There were piles of shoes, clothing, hair, and jewelry stacked in mountains. The gas chambers were camouflaged in shower rooms. In the gas chambers, 8,000 people were gassed to death per day. The solution in gaseous deaths of Jews was Zyklon B gas. Many families and children lost their lives from this terrible event. When the Soviet troops liberated the camps, they only found at least 7,500 alive prisoners. Unfortunately, many Jews, at least six million, did not survive the harsh punishments of the Germans. Only about 3,600,000 Jews lived through the Holocaust. Jews were separated from their families and were brought to different concentration camps, which were camps that lacked food. With the population overcrowding, many Jews died from starvation. Extermination camps were also established and many Jews were slaughtered there too.

For some people who survived it was because they may have been helped by very brave heroes who cared about them so much and risked their lives to save and escape these lucky Jews and hide them from the Nazis. Well, one of those brave heroes included a man named Pawel Charmuszko. Pawel Charmuszko was born on November 17, 1905, and was a Catholic farmer at Lososna, which was close to Grodno and is now present-day Belorussia. He chose to assist his fellow neighbors in a village at Grodno and decided to protect them. Some Belorussians wanted to hand over a family of Jews to the Germans and Charmuszko persuaded them that it was against the two principles of morality and religion. From this act, many beings benefitted from heroic actions. Charmuszko smuggled the Jews to Grodno, but most of them were transported to Warsaw. From November, 1941-April, 1942, Charmuszko helped at least 20 Jews escape from Grodno to Warsaw and out of the Soviet Zone. Some of the Jews that Charmuszko was not able to save were helped and liberated by the Red Army. During one of his escapes, he called Doctor Emanuel Ringelblum and talked about his efforts on behalf of the Jewish and Polish relationships. Among these escapes, some of the people that were saved were engineer Fajerstajn, Jacob and Helena Lipszyc, engineer Jerzy Lacher, his wife and his daughter, and engineer Berg. Almost everyone that he helped escape were able to survive and leave for Israel. His rescue method was to use forged documents, illegal transfer, and arranged shelter for the Jews. After this war, survivors who loved him considered him as a person with great compassion because he had to risk and face many dangers just to save and help the Jews escape. He was just part of this great rescue, but he was one of the heroes that really cared about the Jews being tortured. On May 28, 1968, which is 23 years from the end of the Holocaust, Pawel Charmuszko was recognized by Yad Vashem as Righteous Among the Nation. He was also honored in the Wall of Honor.

Learning about this person has impacted my life and many other human lives because it shows us that you have to help and assist other people when they are at risk and that you should care about everyone and not just about your family. It also shows us how to be better people as we grow up. In the Holocaust, the murdering of six million Jews affected the lives of many survivors that had relatives included in the slaughter. I understand that the Holocaust was a very devastating event that happened all because of the Nazi party doing acts and harsh things to the Jews that resulted in the mass slaughter of the Jewish people. On a regular day, people were do their daily routine and somewhere in the middle of that day, the Jews lives were ruined by the Nazis taking them to concentration and extermination camps just to die. They never did anything wrong, but the Germans believed they did. It was a very emotional day for the Jews. I also understand that the Holocaust will always be remembered by the people that were affected by it. The Holocaust has changed many people's lives today. Today, we as a nation should take an act to do something so that the Holocaust will "Never Again" happen. We should do what is right for our country and treat each other with respect and kindness. We should hope that our leaders should act quickly and wisely. Let's also hope that we correct our mistakes from the present to the future. Our leaders and politicians will choose what is right for us. The government should not make any big mistakes. We should have trust in our leaders on what they could do. This is why we should stop for a moment and remember the bad things that happened in the Holocaust. We should remember all the lives of families and children that were lost during the six years of the Holocaust.

Works Cited Page

Poray, Anna. "Saving Jews: Polish Righteous." Saving Jews: Polish Righteous. N.p., n.d. Web. 12 Dec. 2016. <http://www.savingjews.org/righteous/cv.htm>.

Yad Vashem. "The Righteous Among The Nations." The World Holocaust Remembrance Day. Yad Vashem, n.d. Web. 10 Dec. 2016.
<http://db.yadvashem.org/righteousName.html?language=en&itemld=4014290>.

Yad Vashem. N.p., n.d. Web. 12 Dec. 2016.
<http://db.yadvashem.org/righteous/family.html?language=en&itemld=4014290>.

Zofia Bania

Jamie Pealer

The Holocaust was something we'd never expect to happen. The Holocaust started in 1933, and ending in 1945. It first started when Adolf Hitler had been elected leader of Germany, creating a group called the Nazis in January, 1933. They came to power, wanting to eliminate all Jews. Jews' rights were taken away, such as even being able to be near a German, or being able to shop at the same stores as them. Hitler transferred Jews to concentration camps, to do loads and loads of work. Poor Jews hardly got anything to eat, which made many die of starvation. Jews were tortured and beat to death, or even being tricked to death. All Jews were taken under control by the Germans and the ones that tried to save themselves, mostly likely ended up losing their life. All this nonsense continued for 12 miserable years. All together, about six million Jews were murdered during this horrible time period. To tell Germans and Jews apart, Jews had to wear yellow stars on their clothing to identify them.

We never want this to happen ever again. So many had died, but we need to recognize the individuals who served us well. One righteous person that needs to be known was Zofia Bania. Zofia was born in 1907, and passing away in 1991. She is known as a survivor, who did good deeds and saved two of her closest friends. The two people she saved were Israel and Frania Rubinek, whom she had met through being their customer at their small local shop. Zofia tremendously helped this small family become safe and have the rest of their life to live, without being taken away from the Germans

My hero's story is one that will make you realize how rough it was to be a Jew and all the procedures you had to do just to make sure your life was in a secure place. My hero, Zofia Bania, was a hard worker and a creative thinker. I'm going to tell you the process of what Zofia, Israel, and Frania went through to carry on with their life without being caught and sent away. Frania and Israel's shop was located in a city where Germans were already looking for Jews to send away. Zofia entered their shop and her good friend Frania asked a much needed favor. She asked if it would be okay if she and Israel could hide in her house to stay protected. Zofia was confused and thought this question was totally irregular. She didn't realize the Germans were already there to attack, and they could possibly be taken away. She needed time to think about this, and meanwhile Israel did all he could and built a bunker underneath the store grounds. Over time when they were hiding in the bunker, Frania became eight months pregnant, becoming harder to move and harder to travel. It took awhile for Zofia to come up with a decision, but while Frania was pregnant, the news was that Zofia was looking for them. She had come up with an answer that had changed their lives forever. Zofia was letting them into her house, but it was going to be a very tight fit.

Zofia lived in a small, one room house, and she wasn't the only one living there. She had her husband, Ludwig, and her six year old son, Maniek. All three of them lived in that one room, now they needed to add even more room for two more people, Israel and Frania. Ludwig wasn't so sure about having even more people come into their house, but Zofia didn't mind at all. She wanted them to stay there and be safe. That was the best option for them and she did the right thing. There obviously wasn't very much room left in the house, so Israel and Frania had to live in the hayloft of the barn that was connected to the house. But that wasn't it. One night, Frania went into labor and she only had Israel and Zofia to help and care for her. Sadly the baby died at birth and the Rubineks shortly moved into the same room with Zofia, Ludwig, and Maniek. Now that the Rubineks were moved into the house, it was even more unsafe because a German could just show up and discover their hiding place. They made the executive decision to get a guard dog to make it a safer environment. This guard dog just about saved their lives. One time a German guard came up to Zofia and Ludwig's house for a check up. The guard dog instantly started barking when the stranger showed up at the door. Once Frania and Israel heard the barking sensation, they knew it was bad news. They hopped into a tiny cellar that was used to store potatoes. They were safe from the German guard. But there's always a bad side to when things are going good. Israel had a terrible cough and was very ill. They knew that if he kept coughing, they would find their hiding place. But smart Zofia thinking, she came up with a brilliant plan. They put Maniek's mattress over the cellar opening so he wouldn't be suspicious. To save them from hearing his cough, Maniek acted like he was sick and constantly started crying to cover up the noise of Israel's cough. This plan worked throughout the entire night. The Rubineks secret was safe and they weren't captured by the German's. Zofia's mission was complete. My hero helped save her friends and they continued to live a happy life ever since.

I learned so much from this story and the overall effect on the Holocaust. From this story I learned that if you have the courage, the respect, and the care to help save someone, you should reach out and help them before you could end up losing them. From the Holocaust I learned that we can't go out and just judge people because of their nationality or what they like to do. We never want to encourage anything like this again. This was one of the worst things to ever happen. Never again do we want to trace back and repeat these steps. For now on we shall live a calm life, accepting any kind of person and living in a peaceful society.

Works Cited

"Yadvashem." Yadvashem. N.p., n.d. Web. 8 Dec. 2016.

Wojan, Megan. "Introduction to Holocaust." Holocaust. KAMS, Elk Grove. 4 Nov. 2016. lecture.

Irena Sendler

Jasmine Ma

Irena Sendler was a brave woman born in a time of lost hope and despair also known as the Holocaust. Irena was born on February 15, 1910, in Warsaw, Poland. She was the daughter of Stanislaw and Janina Krzyzanowski, who were both Polish Catholics. Her father was a doctor and Socialist, but he was one of the few doctors willing to treat Jewish patients. Growing up, Irena always defended herself and others. For example, in 1923, Irena got in trouble for fist fighting with two other students. Irena got into this fight while defending the Jewish student being bullied by the two other students. In summation, Irena Sendler was a courageous woman in a time of need.

Sendler's desire to help people passed on into her adult life. During the Holocaust, Sendler risked her own life to help give food and shelter to those in need. She helped save over 2500 children from the Warsaw Ghetto, a highly concentrated ghetto in Warsaw, Poland. Irena started a children's rescue group with fellow accomplices. They came up with unthinkable, imaginative ways to help as many children as possible escape. Escaping the tall walls was not easy, but they were able to come up with ideas like putting the children in tool boxes, coffins, and through churches and cellars.

Sendler was eventually caught and arrested, in 1944, shortly followed by an interrogation. While in her time of interrogation, the interrogatories broke Irena's feet and legs, but no matter what they did she would not tell them anything about what she knew, what she planned to do in the future, or reveal any names. Because she did not budge, they sent her to be executed. On her way to execution, Irena managed to escape with the help of her friends, shortly followed by going into hiding. In the same year, Irena hid jars in the ground of her neighbor's garden filled with all of the children's names. One year later, in 1945, Irena dug up the old jars and gave the lists to the Jewish community. Irena claimed that after the war she returned to a normal life.

Two years after digging up the children's names, Irena and her original husband divorced. She remarried and had a son and a daughter. After the war, Irena received many awards of righteousness. She was even recognized by Pope John Paul II, who had sent her a letter of recognition praising her wartime effort, which was in 2003. Also, in 2007, she was nominated for the Noble Piece Prize. In 1991, Irena was made an honorary citizen of Israel. These are only a few examples of Sendler's awards. Unfortunately, Mrs. Sendler died on May 12, 2008. She died at a nursing home in Poland at an outstanding age of 98.

From the researching for facts to typing out the essay, I have learned much about Irena Sendler. I have learned that Irena was a very courageous woman ever since she was young. She was a brave and loving person, willing to put her life above anyone in the need of her help. She was there when the world needed her most; in this time the world needed people like Sendler. What she has taught me is a lesson I will never forget. Irena Sendler sacrificed her needs above others. I sit at home everyday in the comfort of my bed and my family. I drink my fresh water while I eat my delicious food on my dining table. These are all examples of things many people could not have done during the Holocaust, these are things I take for granted. I complain how after doing physical education, I am tired and dehydrated. I have no idea how actual dehydration feels and fatigue, no problem for some. Irena sent most of her life helping others, risking her existence to help others save theirs. What I have learned: Irena Sendler was a brave woman, and that I should take more consideration in the things I have in life.

The Holocaust, a living nightmare, a period of time everyone remembers, but wants to forget. The Holocaust, the time of over six million deaths, a time should never replay. But, had this event never taken place, we could have done it today. The wounds of the Holocaust are some of the deepest wounds in history, injuries that leave the world hurt and with a scar. But, with time that scar will heal and the world will make sure that the wound is never reopened, hurt, or touched. We, the people of this world, need to stand together as equals, eye to eye. We must protect our own world and not wait for the world to change, because eventually if we continue to wait we will never have a chance to change the world. I believe we can live in a world that this situation never occurs again, a world where religion, skin, or beliefs do not affect a person as a whole. This world, an ideal world, may never be accomplished if we do not try. With this world, together we can make sure there is never another Holocaust. Never again will the Holocaust, or any sort of mass murdering, takes place.

Work Cited

"Irena Sendlerowa." Who Was Irena Sendlerowa? - History's HEROES from E2BN. East of England Broadband Network, n.d. Web. 29 Nov. 2016.

"Irena Sendlerowa." Irena Sendlerowa - Timeline - History's HEROES from E2BN. England Broadband Network, n.d. Web. 29 Nov. 2016.

"Thesaurus.com - The World's Favorite Online Thesaurus!" Thesaurus.com. N.p., n.d. Web. 29 Nov. 2016.

Bazyli Bogdan

Jason Schubert

Hello my name is Jason Schubert and this is my essay on the Holocaust. The Holocaust was the mass slaughtering of Jews. The German Nazis killed them in extermination camps that had gas chambers into which they would put the Jews. The gas would kill them. The Nazis punishments were life threatening and cruel. I saw an image of an extermination camp and it had a bunch of chimneys coming out of the ground that had Jews in them. Jews were only allowed 500 calories a day. Those 500 calories were a bowl of hot water that they called soup and a piece of bread that was 50% flour and 50% dirt and hay. You had to be a certain age to be at the concentration camps and if you were below this age or a girl you went to the death camps. Other ways that the Nazis would kill the Jews was burning their little, cramped house that is underground while they're inside. Adolf Hitler was the one that lead all of this. He was responsible for all of the murders of the Jews.

The person that I found and researched was named Bazyli Bogdan and he saved about 22 Jews. He was born 12/27/1905 and died 9/18/1980. In 1992, after Germans had begun to liquidate the Jews in the vicinity of the city of Dubno in the Volhynia District, Mendrel Titelman and his wife escaped from the mass slaughter. They wandered through villages and fields for two weeks and eventually knocked on the door of Bazyli Bogdan who lived in a remote village of Panska Dolina. Bogdan was a poor farmer. He made a special hiding place for the Jews under his pigpen and also shared the little amount of food he had with them. Titelman's other family was still hiding in the forest so Titelman asked Bogdan to take in the rest of his family. Bogdan went into the forest and brought back Titelman's sister, Malcia, and a relative named Sara Winokur. Bogdan helped them with all of their needs too.

A little while later Bogdan found another group of Jews in the forest, Nachum and Rachel Titelman with their son Aszar, Batja Lewi with her daughter Szoszana, and Jona Winer. He brought them to the hideout with the rest of them. He also fed them and let them rest. A little while later, some of these people and other Jews in the area fought alongside the Polish people living in the village against the attacks from the Ukrainian ultra naturalist. Mendel Titelman and his wife stayed under Bogdan's protection together with Malcia and Sara until their liberation by the Red Army came in March, 1944. Bogdan settled in a different spot within Poland's new borders.

I learned that the Holocaust was one of the worst parts of history and that it killed billions of innocent people. It was a mass slaughter of the Jews. If you were a Jew before the mass slaughter you would have had to wear the yellow Star of David that indicated that you were a Jew. Some people and families that didn't like the Jews being killed took them in and cared for them, gave them food, pretended that they were a part of their family, and hid them from Nazis and others. If you were a Jew in this time period you were probably one of the unluckiest people around. Adolf Hitler was the one that started all of this. He was an evil man. He committed suicide by gunpoint and a cyanide pill at the same time. He did so in an underground bunker on April 30, 1945. The impact of the learning that Bazyli Bogdan had on my life is great. I feel so good that he helped save all of these Jews. I am also glad because he didn't have to, but he did anyway. It also helps my understanding of what a true good person is and how this person helped somebody or multiple people in need of help. If I was in his place I would have done the same exact thing.

The impact that the Holocaust had on me was much greater. It made me near tears when the guest speaker came in and talked about his miserable life that he had at the concentration camps. The Holocaust's impact on me is just so sad that I can't even put it into words. To make sure that this never happens again we should not be rude or act differently to people of a certain religion, race or country ever. We should also make sure that we don't allow a leader or anybody else that wants to put people in camps, make them work or die

"Bazyli Bogdan." Bazyli Bogdan. N.p., n.d. Web. 12 Dec. 2016.

Yad Vashem.-yad vashem. N.p., n.d. Web. 12 Dec. 2016.

"Adolf Hitler Commits Suicide in His Underground Bunker." History.com. A&E Television Networks, n.d. Web. 12 Dec. 2016.

Maria Assanowicz and Halina Bajraszewska

Jaspreet Kaur

 The Holocausts were a very tragic time in history where Germans, led by Adolf Hitler were eliminating Jews, because they thought Jews were more superior then them. Holocausts mean "sacrificed by fire." Some people were afraid to stand up for themselves or for other people who were Jews, but two who did along with others were Maria Assanowicz and Halina Bajraszewska and here is their story.

The story begins when two Jews named Nina and Martin Danzig. They escaped from Warsaw to the small town of Tuczyn, which was under Soviet rule. But, when the Germans conquered that land Nina was having a baby girl whose name was Edith. Nina started

working at a workshop that produced machine-knitted socks when she met Halina Bajraszewska, daughter of Maria Assanowicz, who was trying to escape hard labor. After having a conversation, it turns out that Halina and her family had been very friendly to Jews and encouraged Nina to ask her mother, who lived in Korzec, to give refuge to Edith so she could be safe from the Germans. Assanowicz agreed to take care of Edith from September, 1942, until November, 1943. Maria cared for Edith as if she was her own daughter. The Danzigs escaped from the Tuczyn Ghetto and were reunited with their daughter. The Danzigs moved back to Warsaw and helped Maria and Halina return to Poland from the Soviet Union and settle down in a new home. After their immigration to Israel the Danzigs still maintained contact with Maria and Halina and gave them financial support. In their subsequent testimony the Danzigs said that not only was their daughter Edith's life saved by Maria and her daughter Halina, but also theirs and without them, they would not be here standing at this subsequent testimony and owe all of their lives to Maria and Halina.

I think this story shows how much Maria and Halina contributed to this Jewish family, because they both could have been punished and caught by Germans and be in big trouble for helping a Jewish family. So, they basically saved the lives of this Jewish family even if their life was on the line and not many people would even dare to do that. I also think they are great heroes because they sacrificed their family and themselves for a family that wasn't theirs and I think that is very great heroism. Maria could have said no to helping Edith, and Halina could have just not mentioned her family was friendly to Jews before, but they didn't. I wholeheartedly believe they are heroes by risking everything to help someone else's family other than their own. I'd like to maybe be just like them and be a hero that wants to protect the ones who need it.

I also think that Maria and Halina were so great because what if some of their family believed in Germans and what they were saying about Jews, they would risk going against their family which is not easy. Maria could have done horrible things to Edith, but instead she gave her all the warmth and attention she'd give to her own daughter.

I learned that the Holocausts was a very sad time and that all those people who saved Jews or tried to protect them were very good people that wanted to do what was right and see what's really going on and not to follow something that wasn't right just because everyone says it is. I also learned about amazing people who protected a Jewish family even if their own lives were at stake, which I think is true heroism and bravery. Learning about this person has had a big impact in my life so in the future I will be trying to protect other people that need help and encourage others to do the same so something like the Holocausts will come "Never Again."

I understand the Holocaust was a very sad and tragic time for Jews who did nothing wrong in their life and it has a huge impact on you; you don't want this to happen again so you want to do everything you can to stop it. It makes you think there are people who need more help then you do, so you should stand up for them to ensure that this happens "Never Again." The steps that can be taken to make sure that something like this doesn't happen again is standing up for people who need as much help as possible, try to help people who need protection, and speak up for what is right. Also, when someone else is doing something that you absolutely know is bad, don't follow them. When you treat people, treat them the way you want to be treated and stay true to the people who need you to protect them, because there are people out there who need you to be there to protect them so something like the Holocausts happens "Never Again."

Works Cited

Yad Vashem - Request Rejected. N.p., n.d. Web. 13 Dec. 2016.

Maria Nowak Bozek

Jeavenjot Kaur Zenda

The Holocaust was one of the most dramatic events in Jewish history. The Holocaust took place from January 30, 1933, to May 8, 1945. The Holocaust was a state-sponsored persecution that murdered over six million Jews by the Nazis. When the Nazis came to power in January of 1933, they believed that the Jewish community was an "alien threat to the so-called German racial community." Maria Nowak Bozek was one of the German eyewitnesses during the Holocaust and she helped save her best friend, Helena Goldstein, from the Holocaust.

It was the winter of 1942-1943, when Maria found out that her good friend, Helena Goldstein, was in serious trouble. Ever since the Krakow Ghetto was built in March of 1941, Helena was confined to the Ghetto. Helena had already lost her father, who was murdered in the Ghetto and her mother and brother, who were deported and torched in the Ghettos by the Germans. Helena was now 21 years old and was alone in the Ghetto. Maria had a friend who had a Jewish girlfriend in the Ghetto and somehow he managed to get into the Ghetto so Maria asked him to check on Helena and see how she was doing. When the boy returned from the Ghetto, he told Maria that Helena was in very bad shape, mentally and physically, because after the second deportation Helena's mother and brother were taken. Helena had an older brother that was living in the Ghetto but he lived with his wife and he didn't live with Helena. So Helena was living pretty much alone. Maria soon found out that Helena worked outside of the Ghetto and Helena could leave it. And this was very good. So then Maria decided to get Kennkarte (or identification paper). Maria only was able to get one Kennkarte at the black market and she needed as many papers as she could get to prove that Helena was not Jewish. So then Maria brought a whole empty one. Maria asked her friend with the Jewish girlfriend if he could go to the Ghetto and take pictures of Helena. Maria made Helena's papers and changed Helena's name to Maria Bozek because Maria was Polish and the Germans would think that Helena was Polish too. Maria said that there was no problem of where Helena would live. Maria said that Helena could live with them but there were too many railroad workers around and there was very high chance that some of them would tell. Helena also had a lot of German and Polish friends and she also knew a lot of people and there was a very high chance that they would tell, too. It was winter and Jews were not allowed to wear fur on their coats, so the first thing that Maria did when Helena came out of the Ghetto was put a fur necklace on Helena's neck so that people wouldn't think that she was Jewish.

Maria knew that Helena couldn't stay in Krakow because Krakow was too small to have two people with the same identity. Maria knew two Jewish friends that were living in Warsaw with false papers too. So Maria wrote to them to ask them if Helena could come live with them. One of the friends came to get Helena from Krakow so that Helena could go live with them. Helena got a job as a housekeeper but soon after she found out that the people she worked for were part of the Polish Underground Home Army. Just before the Warsaw Uprising, the Polish Underground Home Army had to run away because the Germans were getting very close to this house. Helena had to change her identity once again. Helena had to get a false marriage name so she named herself Maria Szymczak but Helena never saw her supposed husband. Helena also had no job so she had to go to the German unemployment office where she was sent to Hirschberg, Germany to go work in forced labor. From then until January of 1945, Maria and Helena had no contact and Maria was still very concerned about Helena and how she was doing. Then Maria received a letter from Helena that was under the name of Maria Szymczak. This assured Maria that Helena was doing well and was working in the laundry. So then Maria decided to send Helena some things. Maria asked her mother to cook some food for Helena and Maria sent Helena a her new green dress that wasn't easy to buy but she still sent the dress. So then Maria sent this package but then soon after the Russian Offensive started and Maria was afraid that the package would be destroyed in the bombings.

Maria and Helena had no contact until April but then Helena came to Krakow wearing Maria's green dress. With the Germans defeated, Helena elected to stay in Krakow with her one remaining brother and his wife. They managed to get the back part of the apartment they lived in before the war. Helena chose to give up the name Maria and go back to Helena but she chose to stick with the last name Szymczak.

When researching for my essay, I learned that many non-Jewish families tried to help save many Jewish families. They risked their own life to help save someone else's life. Maria Nowak Bozek was one of these people. The impact Maria Nowak Bozek had on my life was that she showed me that you should stick up for a person. She helped her best friend, Helena Goldstein, get out of the Ghetto and go someplace safe. Never again should an event like this happen to any person because of their race, mental or physical disability, or how they look. The Holocaust was a state-sponsored persecution that murdered over six million Jews by the Nazis. Never again should an event like this happen to anybody anywhere.

Work Cited

"Maria Nowak Z D. Bożek." Maria Nowak Z D. Bożek | Krakowscy Sprawiedliwi. N.p., n.d. Web. 13 Dec. 2016

Tammeus, Bill, and Rabbi Jacques Cukierkorn. "They Were Just People." Google Books. University of Missouri Press Columbia and London, n.d. Web. 13 Dec. 2016.

"Introduction to the Holocaust." United States Holocaust Memorial Museum. United States Holocaust Memorial Museum, n.d. Web. 13 Dec. 2016.

Józef Balwierz

Jedd Mauch

Earlier in history, during World War II, starting in January 30, 1933, and lasting until May 8, 1945, was the Holocaust. The word "Holocaust" comes from Greek words "holos," meaning whole, and "kaustos," meaning burned and was originally used to describe a sacrificial offer burned on an altar. Beginning in 1945, the word took on a new and more horrible name, one that described a massive murder of over six million Jews and many more that were killed due to the German Nazi regime. To the anti-Semitic German Nazi leader Adolf Hitler, Jews, and other races that were not German or allies with them, were an inferior race to their purity and community. Jews were taken to a Ghetto that was dirty and full of diseases. There was very little food and people were dying from starvation every day. However, the Jews tried to live a normal life, though everything had changed for them. After years of Nazi ruling in Germany, during which Jews were constantly persecuted, Hitler's "final solution" was to kill all of the remaining Jews by bringing them to either concentration camps or extermination camps where they would work until they died from starvation, sheer exhaustion, spreading illnesses, and poisonous gasses. People that have lived through the Holocaust, and truly know what it was like to destroy mankind, hope it never again happens, ever.

Józef Balwierz was born on January 1, 1919. He saw the horrible Holocaust and helped many of Jews escape the terrible German Nazi Ghettos, concentration camps, and extermination camps. Before the war started, Józef Balwierz worked at a factory that the Liebeskind family owned in Lwów. Later, when the war reached them in 1941, Shmuel Liebeskind, his wife Zofia and their two daughters, Rita and Irena, were taken into a Ghetto. That year, Shmuel was killed. Later, in 1942, Zofia, Rita, and Irena were able to escape from the horrific and deadly Ghetto. They made their way to Kraków, where they made contact with Balwierz and he immediately reached out to the remaining family, and helped them by feeding them and helping them in any way he could. Balwierz also helped Rita and Irena's cousin Elka Bardach (later Idel), who had managed to escape Lwów and had boarded a train to Kraków. Elka Bardach disembarked from her train a stop earlier knowing that there was a German stop at the end of the line, and the punishment for escaping the Ghettos was death. Elka then found her way to Józef's house where he instantly helped and aided her like he did for Zofia, Rita, and Irena. Later, after staying at Balwierz house for about three weeks, she found a job as a housekeeper in Kraków with a German family. The situation worsened and the Liebeskinds and Balwierz were forced to move to Austria and work there. They made it fine without anything big happening but Zofia, Rita, Irena, and Balwierz fought through the hard times and managed to make it to the end of the war. After the war ended, Balwierz married Irena Liebeskinds and together they moved to Poland. When he was interviewed, he explained that what he had done to save three young women was just merely his human duty; he did not expect nor want any reward for what he had done. There is no written data of when Balwierz died.

After completing this essay, I now realized how awful and cruel the Holocaust was. I learned that hatred does not solve problems; it only can ruin you and your surroundings. Learning about Józef Balwierz had a great impact on my life; it changed me completely. I now know that the Holocaust was a horrifying incident that should never happen to mankind and should never happen again. It was a terrible thing because of all the lost innocent lives and all the lives lost that were trying to save the innocent. It should never happen again because we should be able to respect one another and realize that we are very much alike. It affected me completely because I know that I completed this essay and it affected me by showing me how to deal with problems and to respect people regardless of their background, races, culture and religions. Respecting people more often can show that you do really care about your society and yourself. Saying that a race is an inferior to your race is just showing everyone that you have no respect for anyone and you won't gain any values to yourself. We can start being more kind and caring to one another and showing that you respect others to make sure that this never happens again.

I understand that the Holocaust was an important piece of history and we must keep reminding ourselves not to repeat and continue to pass it on to the next generation in order to never forget. For many years ordinary Germans struggled with the Holocaust's impact, as survivors and the families of victims sought compensation and return of wealth and property confiscated during the Nazis undertaking. Beginning in 1953, the German government made payments to the Jewish people as a way of acknowledging the German people's responsibility for the crimes committed in their name.

Works Cited

EasyBib. Chegg, n.d. Web. 10 Dec. 2016.

History.com Staff. "The Holocaust." History.com. A&E Television Networks, 2009. Web. 10 Dec. 2016.

"Introduction to the Holocaust." U.S Holocaust Memorial Museum. U.S Holocaust Memorial Museum, n.d. Web. 10 Dec. 2016.

"Józef Balwierz." Yad Vashem. Yad Vashem, n.d. Web. 10 Dec. 2016.

Marks, Bernard. "Never Again Holocaust." Albiani Middle School, Elk Grove. 2016. Lecture.

Wojan, Megan. "Intro to The Holocaust." Albiani Middle School, Elk Grove. Lecture.

Camerado Springs Middle School, Cameron Park, CA

Levi Cambridge
Assistant Principal

Levi Cambridge a graduate of California State University Sacramento where he received a Master's degree in Educational Leadership. He taught in the classroom for 13 years at both elementary and secondary levels. He is currently an assistant principal at Camerado Springs Middle School.

Susanna Fong

I have been teaching 8th grade for over twelve years. The past eight have been at Camerado Springs Middle School where we have the absolute best kids around! Being able to teach about the Holocaust is one of the most important units I teach each year.

The Zookeeper's Secret

Alyssa Fong

The Holocaust was an age where some people lost their humanity, and that brought terror to others. The Holocaust, which was from 1933-1945, was a tragic age in our world where over six million people were killed due to their religion and "differences" by Adolf Hitler and the Nazis. Although many bad people come to mind when you hear the word Holocaust, many heroes showed their true colors, and they were beautiful and wonderful. These are the people who often get overlooked for everything that they did during the Holocaust. These people are the real heroes. These people helped those being prosecuted, by rescuing them, feeding them, and keeping them hidden for as long as they could manage. While there were hundreds of heroes that were brought to life during the Holocaust, I'd like to focus on Antonina and Jan Zibinski.

Antonina and Jan Zabinski lived in Poland in 1931, where they owned a zoo. Antonina Zabinski is a woman who I deeply admire and hope to become like one day. She was born in Russia in the year of 1908. She moved to Poland in 1931 where she married her husband, Jan. Jan was an inspiring man who was born in April 8, 1897, in Poland where he grew up. Jan also was a part of the Polish Underground Resistance which tried to prevent bombings, helped Jews escape, and got rid of the Nazis. Together, Antonina and Jan had built up a beautiful life with until World War II. Parts of their zoo, which is called the Warsaw Zoo, were bombed during the war and many animals died. Through all the chaos they somehow managed to find enough courage to help others.

As the war developed, so did a ghetto in Warsaw in which a lot of Jan and Antonina's Jewish friends were living. Jan and Antonina started to help their friends in the Ghetto the best they could. I think the most important thing they helped their friends with was giving them hope that things would get better. When the Ghetto continued to worsen, Jan and Antonina started to hide Jews in the empty cages of the animals that were either killed or deported during the War. They also hid Jews in their own house, knowing the risk they were taking. They helped hide and give hope to over 300 Jews. For the next few years they continued to this in secrecy and helped save so many innocent lives.

When the zoo was first bombed things were a little difficult because a Nazi officer, Lutz Heck, had been a former zoo director and had a taste for animals. Jan and Antonina were able to convince the Nazis to keep the zoo going by saying that it was the best location for a pig farm, and for vegetables to provide the soldiers with food. Growing the vegetables also allowed Jan and Antonina to help support and feed the Jews without looking suspicious. Also, all the work that went into keeping a secret this big took a lot of effort on Jan, Antonina and their son, Rhys. While Jan took care of dealing with the Nazis, Antonina and her son Rhys did a lot of work behind the scenes. For instance Antonina had to be careful about how much food was brought into the house so that the Nazis officers wouldn't be suspicious. Also she often invited large number of family to stay with them to make the "extra" people walking around seem normal and not suspicious. While also worrying about the soldiers who were stationed in parts of the zoo Antonina still had to take care of her son, the hidden Jews, and the animals that still remained in the zoo. Even while she was pregnant with her second child, Antonina made sure everything was organized and in order. How she was able to manage all of these things while keeping the world's biggest secret on her back, will be forever amazing and show off her great zeal. Antonina and Jan's son also helped out around the house and occasionally would help with taking care of the Jews. To be a boy as young as Rhys and to be put in this situation had to take a lot of bravery and courage from him.

While Rhys may not have understood the full gravity of the situation he was brave through it all and is a hero too. All this to say that the Zabinski family were wonderful people, inside and out, and were true heroes of our world. When put in the same situation as they were, one can only hope to show enough bravery, courage, compassion, and strength as the Zabinski family once did. The Holocaust was a tragedy that once faced our great world. Somehow, when humans lost their humanity and were doing unspeakable things there were some people who showed compassion and their true colors. Those people are the true heroes, and people who we should aspire to be like every day.

Works cited

"Jan and Antonina Zabinski." Yadvashem, The World Holocaust Rememberence Center, www.bing.com/cr?IG=B87F7CC0319A4201A2897D9EC18BD4B2&CID=217C513BD1826FB736345B0BD0B36ED9&rd=1&h=8NuMZxpRO3g6oThzktn2zcKZc-m7icc8gi7w0EU6_zw&v=1&r=http%3a%2f%2fyad-ashem.org.il%2frighteous%2fstories%2fzabinski&p=DevEx,5057.1. Accessed 15 Feb. 2017.

Morrison, Lucy. "Antonina Zabinski." Prezi.com, 28 Aug. 2014, prezi.com/yil5zv8mrjy9/antonina-zabinski/. Accessed 20 Feb. 2017

"Jan Żabiński." geni_family_tree, 11 Dec. 2014, www.geni.com/people/Jan-%C5%BBabi%C5%84ski/6000000007311313731. Accessed 20 Feb. 2017

Gomez, Alanna. "Jan and Antonia Zabinski: The Zookeepers." Canadian Centre for Bio-Ethical Reform, www.endthekilling.ca/blog/2013/01/18/jan-and-antonia-zabinski-zookeepers. Accessed 20 Feb. 2017.

History.com Staff. "The Holocaust." History.com, A&E Television Networks, 2009, www.history.com/topics/world-war-ii/the-holocaust. Accessed 20 Feb. 2017.

Maximilian Kolbe

Bryson Zufelt

St. Maximilian was born Raymund Kolbe on January 8, 1894, in the Kingdom of Poland, which was part of the Russian Empire at that time. When he was twelve years old he had a vision of Mary, the mother of Christ, after which he was convinced he would become a priest and then a martyr. Soon after he and his brother joined the

Conventual Franciscans and was given the religious name of Maximilian. At 21 years of age Maximilian earned a doctorate in philosophy. He would then go on to earn a doctorate in theology at age 28. He helped to restore the Militia Immaculata, a missionary group, because he wanted to convert sinners and the people who were enemies of the church, and to "fight for Mary" who he had strong affection for. He was nicknamed the Apostle of Consecration of Mary. In 1918, after being named a priest he pressed on promoting Mary throughout all of Poland. He set up monasteries all over in Poland and Japan, he created a magazine, opened a seminary class, and even established a radio station to broadcast his religious views. To this day the monasteries in Japan still stand and are a symbol of all the great things that Maximilian did. Sadly, due to health issues that plagued him most of his adult life, Maximilian had to return back to Poland and remain there.

Everything changed in Kolbe's life in 1939 when the Third Reich invaded Poland. Maximilian opened the doors to his monasteries and hid 2,000 Jewish refugees from all around. He was one of the few priests who stayed on at the monastery. He set up a temporary hospital to assist the sick and wounded because other hospitals would not take them. Kolbe was captured when his town surrendered and sent to jail, but he was released 3 days later. Eventually, the German Nazis found out about Kolbe's actions and arrested him in 1941. This brave priest was shipped off to Auschwitz, one of the most well known concentration camps. A prisoner escaped this infamous camp during Kolbe's first year being in captivity. The Nazis were not very fond of this act. The guards decided to punish ten random and innocent men by sending them to the famous Block 13. Block 13 was the designated for prisoners of the penal company, where they were completely isolated from other prisoners. They often received the hardest workloads and had to perform them at twice the speed. Assignments in Block 13 lasted from one month to one year, and the prisoners were often beaten severely. One of the men that was chosen to go to Block 13 was Francis Gajowniczek. When the deputy camp director came to take the men away Gajowniczek begged for his life. When the man mentioned his wife and children Kolbe stepped forward and offered the deputy camp director to take him instead of Francis Gajowniczek. And to everyone's surprise the deputy camp director agreed to take the priest Maximilian.

Maximilian was sent to the torture block, but despite his circumstances the priest didn't despair. Instead, he led the other men in prayers and in songs he had sung at his church. Three weeks after the 12 men had been sent into the block for their deaths, Francis was the only man left alive in Block 13. Wanting to finish with his duties, the executioner injected Father Kolbe with a syringe full of carbolic acid. While his body was burned, Kolbe's story of being a hero and a lifesaver would live on and be told for decades. Gajowniczek survived the war and lived until 1995, but up until his death he would tell many other people about the man who saved his life so that he could live and see his wife and children again. The Franciscan priest was canonized in 1982 and was described by the Pope John Paul II as the great "Patron Saint of our Difficult Century."

Maximilian Kolbe was a great and respected man in Poland. He spent his life serving others as a priest, giving them asylum during the war, and protecting a man's life by taking his place for execution. It was the saving of another that made him want to save this innocent man from dying. There were so many people during WWII who were afraid of the Jews and scared to help them. To give up one's life for another person is heroic in itself, but especially during this time when so few were willing to support other's not of their own faith. With so many tragic stories it is heart-warming to hear of such sacrifice from one man. Kolbe's death was still a tragedy, as were all the executions during that time, but there is no doubt that he was a selfless man who gave his life so another could have the chance to be reunited with his family.

"Works Cited"

http://auschwitz.org/en/history/punishments-and-executions/the-penal-company
"St. Maximilian Kolbe," http://www.catholic.org/saints/saint.php?saint_id=370
http://www.jewishvirtuallibrary.org/maximilian-kolbe

"Maximilian Kolbe Biography." http://www.biographyonline.net/spiritual/maximilian-kolbe.html

Irena Sendler: A Polish Hero

Cora Minch

Irena Sendler was a social worker in Warsaw Poland who saved nearly 2,500 Jewish children and 500 adults during World War II. She saved them in a very peculiar way, by giving them new identities and burying their real ones in jars. Mrs. Sendler found a way into the Warsaw concentration camp and was able to help smuggle out 2,500 children some in burlap sacks. Irena was 29 years old when she started saving lives and burying identities in jars. She never considered herself a hero but the rest of the world does. Yad Vashem, who called her one of the righteous gentiles, recognized her as one of the non-Jewish people who risked her life to save the lives of the Jewish people. At the World Holocaust Remembrance Memorial in Israel, "on October 19, 1965, Yad Vashem recognized Irena Sendler as Righteous Among the Nations. The tree planted in her honor stands at the entrance to the Avenue of the Righteous Among the Nations." She did a lot at such a young age which is truly inspiring.

Irena Sendler was born February 15, 1910, in Otwock, Poland with no siblings. Irena's father died in 1917 of typhus. Irena was married in 1932, taking the Sendler name as she was born as Irena Krzyżanowska. Mr. and Mrs. Sendler had two children, Adam and Janka. Her son Adam passed away in 1999. her daughter and granddaughter, whose name is Agniesa, still live in Poland. Mrs. Sendler died in 2008 of natural causes when she was 98 years old. She was a Catholic and stood at only 4'11" and was described as an energetic person and lively spirit.

She helped to organize the underground Polish organization, Zegota, in December 1942 and ran its children's division. Because of her background as a social worker she was able to get into the camp easier than most. "Irena and the 10 who went with her into the Ghetto, used many, many methods to smuggle children out. There were five main means of escape:

1 – Using an ambulance a child could be taken out hidden under the stretcher. 2 – Escape through the courthouse. 3 – A child could be taken out using the sewer pipes or other secret underground passages. 4 – A trolley could carry out children hiding in a sack, in a trunk, a suitcase or something similar. 5 – If a child could pretend to be sick or was actually very ill, it could be legally removed using the ambulance." She buried jars with the children's real name and new name and address written on tissue paper. After the war ended she dug up the jars with the children's new names and addresses and worked with an organization that helped Jewish families reunite.

Irena Sendler didn't only save children. She also saved 500 adults saving a total of 3,000 people. She saved that many people by hiding them and carrying them out in boxes, coffins, suitcases, ambulances and sacks. What she did was incredibly dangerous, very hard, and terrifying. She must have been very brave and strong to carry out those people from the Ghetto. In the process of saving all those people she was captured by angry Nazis. She was in a lot of trouble from not only saving Jewish but for her disloyalty to Hitler. She was tortured and interrogated by the Nazis trying to find out more about the underground network. She never told them anything. However, because of all she had done for society, people were willing to save her. She was supposed to be executed but was saved at the last moment, by a group of people who distracted and possibly bribed the guards and helped her escape. They were referred to as the "hero's who saved a hero," but we do not know the names of the people.

Irena got in trouble many times over her lifespan including in high school and college. She got in trouble for helping her Jewish friends. She always had a can do spirit and attitude and loved helping people. After she was saved from being captured she went into hiding with the children. She still helped out with the children even after she was placed into hiding until after the war ended.

In her adult lifetime she won many awards, such as the Commander's Cross of the Order of Polonia Restituta in 1996 and the Commander's Cross with Star of the Order of Polonia Restituta, 2001, Order of the Smile 2007. Pope John Paul II sent her a personal letter for her work. Irena was nominated for a Nobel peace prize in 2008 before she died. Irena Sendler was relatively unknown until some high school girls doing a history project found her story and started the Life in a Jar project that raised money for survivors and awareness of the Holocaust. The girls asked Irena how she found the courage. "My parents taught me," Irena wrote back, "that if a man is drowning, it is irrelevant what is his religion or nationality. One must help him."

She did so many things with her life. I feel people should know how much she helped the world. I didn't know who she was until I started this essay. There are many other heroes who saved lives that we might never know about but I am glad I got to learn so much about hers. She was an amazing person who did a lot of remarkable things with her life. I am glad I got to find out more about her life and am inspired to do more in my community. That is why I choose to honor Irena with this essay.

Works cited

Buzzfeed, 2016 https://www.buzzfeed.com/polandinusa/7-polish-heros-the-world-should-know-of-on-the-75t-utuk Chabad, 2016, http://www.chabad.org/theJewishWoman/article_cdo/aid/939081/jewish/Irena-Sendler.htm

Don Carina, 2016, http://doncarina.com/HeroinesWWII.html

History's heros, http://historysheroes.e2bn.org/hero/minitimeline/4332

Irena Sendler, http://www.irenasendler.org/the-irena-sendler-family-cast/janka-zgrzembska-irena-sendlers-daughter/

Irena Sendler, Facts about Irena, http://www.irenasendler.org/facts-about-irena/

Life in a Jar, Jack Mayer, 2011

Lowel Milken Center, https://lowellmilkencenter.org/irena-sendler/

The Famous People, http://www.thefamouspeople.com/profiles/irena-sendler-6152.php

Yad Vashem, The World Holocaust Remembrance Center, http://www.yadvashem.org/yv/en/exhibitions/righteous-women/sendler.asp

A TRUE AMERICAN HERO

Hank Robertson

The holocaust was a terrible event. Hitler thought only certain people should live. Many, many people were tragically killed. There were also many heroes. My personal favorite is Varian Fry. Many people call him the American Schindler. Schindler saved a thousand people by out smarting Hitler. Fry was a journalist who ran a rescue network. This is one of the reasons he is famous. In this process he saved about 3,000 people. He was born in October 15, 1907, and died September 13, 1967. Fry got married in June, 1931, to Eileen Avery. He graduated in 1926. His full name is Varian Mockery Fry.

Fry also helped raise money for anti-Nazi campaigns. Fry also had small groups of people that would hide people from Nazis. Among the people, he helped were Oscar Goldberg, Jean Arp, Hannah Arent, and Giuseppe Garetto. Because of his brave actions, Varian got a street named after him. Fry saved people such as 200 scientists, artists, writers, and doctors. It was risky business setting up contacts with the French resistance, Corsican mob, and hired forgers. The next part I added because it was an inspiring quote by Fry himself. "Memory is a passion no less powerful or persuasive than love. What does it mean to remember? It is to live in more than one world to prevent the past from fading and to call up the future to illuminate it." Here is one more quote from Fry: "I remember what I had seen in Germany. I knew what would happen to the refugees if the Gestapo got hold of them... it was my duty to help them... Friends warned me of the danger. They said I was a fool to go I might never come back alive."

Varian was 32 and American when he travelled to France. He always had money and a list of refugees in his pocket. When he got to France he figured he underestimated his mission. He stayed there for 13 months. When Hitler's armies moved toward Paris, refugees fled south. In New York the news of France was alarming. Members of the emergency committee worked hard. They asked help from the first lady Eleanor Roosevelt.

Varian Fry was an editor and writer in New York City. He was not a likely candidate for this mission. He could speak many languages; he was familiar with politics in France. While he was there he stayed at a Hotel Plendide, it was gross, dirty, and noisy. And when news spread the refugees fled to Marseilles. Even though some were fortunate enough to secure visas for entry into other countries by time a set of papers was done, the chances of the papers being updated was unlikely. Eventually in December, 1940, French police searched and Fry and his colleagues were caught and placed on a prison boat at a harbor. Soon after, Fry's passport expired. Just like most of the greats Varian did not get recognized until after death. I had a lot of learning experience during my research in the holocaust research unit at school. I even had once in a life time opportunity. I got to meet a real survivor of the holocausts. His name was Mr. Marks. He was a great person to meet. He was very informative about actual events. This was my firsthand source at school. It was one of my favorite parts of the year. I had a lot of fun learning about Fry. He was a hero in my book. He risked his life many times. He saved a lot of people and he didn't want money or fame he just wanted to help. And he believed everyone should get help. He is not the only one that deserves credit. He also had many friends that helped him. They also risked their lives. Both Fry and his friends were great people in this process of saving lives. Fry has been honored in many ways. Somebody even made a movie about him.

I learned what the real definition of hero was in this process. Hero- a person who is admired or idealized for courage, outstanding achievements. He really defines the word hero. Some people have actually published. His works can be found in books and online. I highly encourage you to find some of his quotes. They are highly inspirational. It was an amazing experience to learn about. It was very interesting to learn about all these people from the Holocaust. It was also cool to learn about what all these people did. It was fun to learn the history of people and how they sacrificed themselves. It was interesting to learn how people got themselves out of this situation. I hope you go research your hero who ever that might be. You should learn and teach so we can all pass these stories on. Please go research a history hero and learn.

Sources

Holocaust-trc.org/varian
Almondseed.com
Varianfry.dk
Varianfry.com

John Damski: A Holocaust Hero

Hanna Briggs (Winner)

John Damski was born sometime in 1914, though his actual birth date is not known. He spent his early childhood in Germany with two brothers and one sister, but moved to Poland after World War I ended, from where his parents were originally. At the time of the move from Germany to Poland, John was only five years old. By the time World War II started, John was serving in the Polish army. It was because of this that he was taken as a prisoner when Germany invaded.

He escaped before the Germans could take him to a camp or a holding cell. Soon after, John and some of his friends tried to move to France, but they would have to pass through Hungary in order to do so. It was near the Hungarian border, in early December of 1939, that John and his friends were caught by the German police and taken to a jail near Sanok. John and around 45 other prisoners were held in a single cell that was much too small. About six months later, in early June of the next year, John heard some trucks roll up to the prison. The trucks were then packed full of prisoners and they drove away. The same trucks kept coming back and each time they loaded up more prisoners. It wasn't long before John figured out that each time a truck took prisoners out, they would kill the prisoners. Luckily, John wasn't taken.

A little later, the remaining prisoners (those who weren't taken on the trucks) were sent to Auschwitz, a German labor camp. Strangely, John wasn't taken with them. A German soldier then came up to him and said that something was wrong; he didn't have any record of John. The soldier then started to ask him questions. John lied, said he was German, and that he was arrested at a local railroad station. The soldier believed him, only because he spoke fluent German. It wasn't until August 9, that John was released from prison.

John then went to Zamosc, a tiny town in Poland, to meet up with his brother. There he got a job as an electrician to help build a nearby airfield. It was while he had that job that John first helped Jewish prisoners. He recruited several Jewish prisoners from a local labor camp to help him with the airfield. He arranged for them to sleep in a storage place instead of in the labor camp, though they later got kicked out because a German man didn't want to sleep in the same building as Jews. One of the Jews, a man named Feigenbaum, even became a sort of friend to John.

Along with being a friend of Feigenbaum, John became liked by his boss, Enderlein. Enderlein told John about the Nazis' plan to invade Russia, then Italy, and finally Japan. After his meeting with John, Enderlein told him that he needed more electricians. John decided to help more Jews, and this time went to the Warsaw Ghetto. When the Jews he already hired heard about him going to the Ghetto, they asked to go with him because most of them had relatives there. John agreed, and they left for the Ghetto with two German air force men. Somewhere on the road, the driver lost control of the car, and the truck they were in rolled over three times. Many of the Jews were injured, yet they could not go to the hospital because of their religion. So, a nearby colonel lent his car to John and the Jews to continue on to the Ghetto while the soldiers stayed back with the truck.

John stayed in the Ghetto for five days, and collected materials for the air force base while the other Jews he brought with him met up with their families. As John was leaving, he felt as if it was taking too long to load up the truck, and when he went to ask if everyone was ready to go, he discovered that there were ten more Jews in the back of the truck trying to sneak out. He decided that he would try to get the Jews out of the Ghetto, so he told the driver to continue on. At the gate, a German soldier stopped them, but, luckily, didn't notice any of the Jews in the back of the truck.

After they were a distance away from the Ghetto, John let the Jews who were not with him in the first place out of the truck. He bribed the drivers to keep quiet, and gave the Jews some money so that they would not go hungry.

While he lived in Zamosc, John and his brother lived in an apartment building, where John met his soon-to-be wife, Sara. When John told his story at an interview, he told the interviewer, "From the first moment I heard her voice, I fell in love." However, Sara was there illegally, and one day, the German police, or Gestapo, came for her. John had moved beneath a window to see what was going on in her apartment, when Sara jumped right into his lap. This was their first meeting, but it was not a romantic or happy one. They both immediately hid from the police in a nearby cemetery until around 10 at night.

After that, Sara moved from place to place, with John acting as communication between her and her mother. John then arranged for a meeting to take place in Warsaw where he would get both Sara and her mother, Helen, Aryan identification papers. John knew that doing that would help to keep them safe, at least for a little while. After they got the papers, Sara became Christine, and Helen became Zofia. Christine posed as John's wife, while Zofia was John's aunt. After John helped Christine and Zofia, there was a terrible day in which the Germans came and rounded up a bunch of Jews. They killed about 100 of them before having the surviving Jews load up the bodies. The Jews then had to sit on top of the corpses before being transported, most likely to a nearby Ghetto. After that, many people came to John to help them get fake papers.

John Damski did many great things during the Holocaust, and a lot of them have not been mentioned here. He is truly a hero and, like many other heroes of the Holocaust, deserves to be more well-known. He will always be remembered by those whose lives he saved, and by those who were influenced by his story. Sadly, John has passed away. He had an, "inner sense of satisfaction for what I did," stated by himself in an interview on May 14, 1988. John was later awarded with the Righteous Among the Nations Award in 1989. In conclusion, John Damski was a great man who risked his own life to help others, and will always be remembered as a hero.

Works Cited

"Holocaust Survivors: John & Christine Damski." World History Project. Web. 11 Jan. 2017. <https://worldhistoryproject.org/1914/holocaust-survivors-john-christine-damski>

"John Damski Story, Part 1." John Damski Story, Part 1. Web. 11 Jan. 2017. <www2.humboldt.edu/rescuers/book/damski/johndstory1.html>.

Roraback, Dick."A Con Man Who Became War Hero." Los Angeles Times. Los Angeles Times, 24 Sept. 1989. Web. 11 Jan. 2017.<articles.latimes.com/1989-09-24/news/vw-28_1_con-men>.

"What's New." What's New. Web. 26 Jan. 2017.<www2.humboldt.edu/rescuers/book/whatsnew.html>.

Heroes in the Holocaust- Irena Sendler

Hayden Grevelding

January, 1933: the worst killing to innocent people happened. Over 1.1 million kids died and millions of others. People were murdered, beat to death, tortured, starved, put in gas chambers and died from diseases. But those who survived helped others. Irena Sendler, a survivor of the Holocaust was born on February 5, 1910 in Warsaw, Poland. Irena and her family then moved to Otwock in Poland, about 15 miles southeast of Warsaw. Her real name was Irena Krzyzanowska. Her father was Stanislaw Krzyzanowska who was a physician and was married to his wife Janina. Irena's father was a doctor and was the first Polish Socialist. He taught Irena to love and respect others regardless of their religion or what they look like. Her father worked with many patients, mainly poor Jews with typhus. Typhus had broken out and killed many people including one of the only doctors in Otwock. The only one left was Irena's father. After seeing many patients with typhus, Irena's father eventually got it and passed away in February, 1917. She was an only child and grew to be an amazing hero.

There are many reasons why I think she is a hero. Not only did she help people but she survived the Holocaust and I think if you survive a Holocaust you are a very encouraging person, like you, Mr. Marks. Listening to your speech was amazing. Getting to listen to how you survived was amazing and I am very thankful to have had you come in and speak for us. It was amazing because not too many people that survived the Holocaust are alive today.

Irena Sendler was an amazing person. She saved kids from camps. She was a Jewish sympathizer since childhood. She started out by offering Jews food and shelter. She had been helping people from the Warsaw Ghetto. In 1940, the Ghetto was erected and she could no longer help Jews. This area was as big as New York Central Park and had over 450,000 people inside. Once she could finally get in she began getting the orphan children. There were five main methods to get children. The first one was to use an ambulance. Kids would go under the stretcher and then in the ambulance. The second way was to go through the courthouse. The third way was that children could go through sewer pipes to a secret underground passage. The fourth way was to use a trolley; they would put the children in sack, trunk or something similar to a suitcase. The fifth way was to pretend to be sick or to be actually sick. They could be legally removed using the ambulance. A Polish worker had helped Irena get into the Ghetto. He was part of the Contagious Disease Department, and he was also a member of Zegota. He had made over 3,000 fake documents to let Irena into the Ghetto. Once the kids were in safety with Irena, Irena's mother would help the children. Sendler and her friends made thousands of false documents to help Jewish families prior to joining the resistance group. Upon her appointment as head of Zegota's newly formed children department, she organized the smuggling of 2,500 children out of Warsaw Ghetto and had them placed in Polish families, orphanages and convents. She gave each child a new identity and carefully recorded their names and placements so that they could be returned to surviving relatives after the war.

Irena Sendler was arrested on October 20, 1943. She was beaten, tortured, and sentenced to death in a Gestapo death camp in 1943. She was put in notorious Piawiak prison where she was questioned. During the questioning she had her legs and feet fractured from being tortured. The interrogator was a young German who was very stylish. He wanted the names of the Zegota leaders, addresses, and the names of other people involved. She had given him false information. She was then given a death sentence. She was supposed to be shot but Zegota had bribed the German executioner who helped her escape. The next day there were posters everywhere saying she had been shot and killed. She then went into hiding and resumed her work for Jewish children for the remainder of the war. After the war was over she dug up the bottles, and then she tried to find living homes for some of the kids. In 2003, she received Poland's highest civilian decoration, the Order of the White Eagle. She was an amazing hero saving up to 2,500 children lives, and finding them new families. I think she should be recognized more for what she did, and she should be taught to kids on what she did and how she was a big influence on not only kids but me showing that you can succeed no mater how dangerous or hard it is. We need to help people even if you know you will fail, but you still have to try.

Sources

www.Shalomshow.com/holocuast_heroes.htmwww.irenasendler.org/facts-about-irena/.htm

www.chabad.org/theJewishWoman/article_cdo/aid/939081/.../Irena-Sendler.htm www.yadvashem.org/righteous

Heroes of Poland 1939-1945

Ivana Morales

From the years 1939-1945, a war went on. It is known as World War II. Many lost their lives, rights, and hope, as well as their reasons for living, and wanting to go on with their miserable lives. If it weren't for the heroes that made them selves present during this time, who knows what would have happened. The countries that participated in the war were either allies with Germany or against them. The countries that were against Germany, Italy, and Japan were the U.S, China, Britain, France, Australia, Canada, New Zealand, and the Soviet Union. Poland was one of the countries that was a part of the Soviet Union, and participated in World War II.

The country of Poland served as very helpful during the World War II. While the world was in chaos, this country supplied multiple heroes that helped lead to the end of Hitler's tyranny. The war for this country began on September 1, 1939; within the first week more than 20,000 soldiers were captured by their enemy. There were many heroes, but some of the most famous one include, Jan Karski, Witold Pilecki, Henryk Slawik, and Irena Sendler.

Jan Karski, also known as "Humanity's Hero," tried his best to prevent and end the Holocaust all together. Karski was a professor and well-educated in the areas of geography and languages. These skills proved useful for the Soviet Union, and he became their prisoner. After his capture he was taken to what is now commonly known as Ukraine. He then escaped and joined Poland's underground movement. He continued to help Poland's movement, but was captured yet again. This time it was by the Gestapo. Karski continued to travel. Locations he visited were the Warsaw Ghetto, London, finally Washington D.C. While in Washington he conversed with the president, which at the time was Franklin D. Roosevelt, trying to make things better for all of those who were suffering back in Europe. Safe in America he tried to help others affected deeply by the war that was going on in the other side of the world. Even after the war Karski continued to try to help people whose lives were different due to the toll that the war took. He was rewarded with highest Polish civic decoration, as well as having honorary citizenship in the country of Israel.

Mr. Witold Pilecki was another young hero who helped his country in its time of need. Pilecki was a part of the Polish Calvary and then later volunteered to be put into Auschwitz to gather information then report back to the Polish Resistance. During the time spent in the death camp, he organized a resistance movement in the year 1941. He then informed Nazi Germany and all of its allies of the camps cruelties. Nearly two years later he escaped the concentration camp, just as he was ordered to do. Pilecki continued to work for the resistance until his execution in 1948. He was 47 years old at the time of his death.

Another one of the countless Polish heroes is Henryk Slawik. This Polish politician helped thousands of asylum seekers. It didn't matter if they were being persecuted against or not, they could find help in him. Slawik helped defend Poland in the year of 1939; he then began to lead the Citizen's committee to Aid Polish Refugees. This man also helped form an orphanage for Jewish children, without the public knowing. When assisting the refugees, he would supply them with false documentation. In the year 1944, Henryk was arrested, and then tortured to his death at Methuen concentration camp. He ended up saving and helping about 30,000 Poles and 5,000 Jewish Poles in his lifetime.

Irena Sendler was one of the only women who was recognized for her heroism during World War II. She was a part of the Polish underground resistance, similarly to Witold Pilecki. She worked as a nurse as well as a vigorous organizer for Zegota. Zegota was created by Poland's government. She started a motion to help Jewish children escape. She was arrested and interrogated by Nazi soldiers, but never gave up information. One year before her death in 2008, Irena was nominated as a candidate for the Noble Peace Prize. This brave woman ended up living a long and eventful life until May 12, 2008.

There are countless heroes from the Second World War, from all of the countries that participated in it. Whether the country was small or large, or in between, they all contributed something, for example how many heroes Poland supplied. Even though there are numerous more Polish heroes, ones that really stand out are, Jan Karski, Witold Pilecki, Henryk Slawik, and last but certainly not least, Irena Sendler.

Works Cited

"Jan Karski" United States Holocaust Memorial Museum. United States Holocaust Memorial Museum, n.d Web. 21 Feb. 2017.

PolandinUSA "7 Polish Heroes The World Should Know Of On The 75th Anniversary of WWII". Buzzfeed. Poland USA Community Brand Publisher, 31 Aug. 2014. Web. 21 Feb. 2017.

"Poland Searches for Remains of WW2 Hero" Spiegel Online. N.P., n.d. Web 18, 2017

"The Righteous Among Nations." Yad Vashem- Request Rejected. N.p.,n.d Web. 21 Feb. 2017.

"Witold Pilecki." Wikipedia. Wikipedia Foundation, 21 Feb. 2017

Heroes of Poland: Irena Sendler

Jason Bach

A 29-year-old social worker named Irena Sendler was employed by the Welfare Department of the Warsaw municipality. She, and many others, continued to take care of a great number of poor and dispossessed people in the city, even after the German occupation. In November 1940, Irena took advantage of her job to help the Jews. But, it made it almost impossible once the Ghetto was sealed off. Almost 400,000 people had been taken to a small area in the Ghetto. In the crowded Ghetto, there were poor hygienic conditions. Also, the lack of food and medical supplies resulted in epidemics, and very high death rates. Yet,

Irena, at great personal danger, still tried to help the dying Jews. She took time to obtain a permit from the Warsaw Epidemic Control Department so she could legally get into the Ghetto and "inspect" the sanitary conditions. Once inside the Ghetto she found contact with Jewish people to help smuggle them out of the Ghetto. When trying to smuggle them out she brought the Jews to the Aryan side and helped set up hiding places for them. In fall of 1942, the Council of Aid of Jews was created and Sendler was the main activist. After it was created, 280,000 Jews were deported from Warsaw to Treblinka. Most of the Jews in Warsaw were there by the end of the year when it began to function. What happened played a crucial role in a rescue of a large number which survived massive deportations. This organization took care of such things as seeking hiding places and paying for the upkeep and medical care. Four months after the Warsaw Ghetto was destroyed in September, 1943, Sendler was appointed director of Zegota's Department for the Care of the Jewish Children. When Sendler was underground she had a different name. Her name underground was "Jolanta" and she exploited her contacts with orphanages and institutes for abandoned children to send them there. When the situation became dire for the Ghetto's inhabitants, Sendler went beyond rescuing orphans. She began asking parents to let her try to get their children to safety. There was no guarantee for any child's survival but she would still tell the parents that their children had a chance. Now Sendler kept very detailed records and lists of the children she helped. She kept the information buried in a jar. Sendler had a plan; her plan was that she would reunite the children with the parents after the war ended. But, when she went to return the children most of the parents had died. Many of the children were sent to the Rodzina Marii Orphanage in Warsaw and to the Religious institutions run by nuns in nearby Chotomow and in Turkowice, near Lublin. The exact number of children saved by Sendler and her partners is unknown. What is known is, she personally saved around 400 lives but all together around 2,500 people. On October 20, 1943, Sendler was arrested. She managed to stash away incriminating evidence. When she was arrested, she was sent to the infamous Pawiak prison. There they tortured her to try and get the names of her associates. She refused and was sentenced to death. Luckily for her, her fellow activists managed to bribe the officials to release her. When they tortured her, they broke her legs and feet. After that day, she was never able to walk again without crutches. She did not learn after a close call to death, and it did not deter her from continuing her underground activity. After her release in February, 1944, Sendler continued her underground activities, even though she knew the authorities were keeping an eye on her. The danger forced her to go into hiding. One of the most tragic things was she was in so much danger that after her mother died she couldn't even make it to her funeral. After the war ended she got engaged into her first marriage. That marriage led to a divorce. Then she got married again to Stefan Zgrzembski and had three children. The daughter was Janka, and her two sons were Adam and Andrzej, who tragically died in infancy. After the death of her husband, Zgrzembski, she got remarried to her first husband Mieczyslaw Sendler. After a while they once again ended in divorce. After everything was over, in 1965, Yad Vashem, Israel's Holocaust memorial organization, caught attention to Irena Sendler. They named Irena as "Righteous Among the Nations" for her work and job saving Jewish Children. In 2003, Poland honored Irena with one of Poland's awards, its "Order of the

White Eagle." Sendler was nominated for a Nobel Peace Prize in 2008, but sadly did not win. In April, 2009, The Audrey Hepburn Foundation posthumously awarded Irena Sendler the 2009 Humanitarian Award. Surprisingly, Sendler died May 12, 2008, in Warsaw, Poland, at the age of 96. Everyone who has recognized Irena Sendler was sad. She had changed just a little bit of the world, and that was just enough to make a difference.

Work Cited

Yadvashem.org/RIGHTEOUS among the NATIONS

Heroes of Poland

Jocelyn Foos

When most people talk about the Holocaust they only think of the negative situations. They grieve for all the innocent people that were killed or they think about how horrible Hitler and the Nazis were. However, there are quite a few things for which to be grateful, such as, all the courageous people who risked their lives to save and protect as many victims as they possibly could. Over 50,000 Jews were hidden by other people who were against Hitler. Although many abhorrent things happened, there are many memorable heroes who salvaged a great number of people.

One of the many people who helped the victims of the Holocaust was Irena Sendler. She was born in 1910, and died in 2008. Sendler was a 29 year old Polish woman who was a nurse and also head of children's section of the Polish Council to Aid Jews. She took advantage of her job so that she could smuggle Jewish children and prevent them from going to any camps. However, this became quite difficult when close to 400,000 people had been forced into a Ghetto. Irena risked her life to try and obtain a permit that allowed her to enter the Ghetto. Once she had gotten it she helped smuggle Jewish children out of the Ghetto and kept them in a secret hiding place until she found non-Jewish families to adopt them. Sendler was arrested on October 20, 1943. She had been able to keep the address of the hidden Jews a secret. The police sentenced her to death, but an "underground activist" bribed them into letting her get released. Even after Sendler was almost sent to her death, she still continued hiding and helping as many Jews as she possibly could. In the end, Irena save around 2,500 Jewish children.

Secondly, there was a woman named Karolina Juszczykowska. Karolina was born in 1898, and she died in 1945. She lived in Poland, as well, during the time of WWII. Karol was a single mother to her daughter and had just moved from Germany. She had met two boys on the street, Janek and Paul, who had offered her money for a shelter. She only had a chance to hide them for about six weeks. Her neighbors had been suspicious and told some officials. The Secret State Police came and immediately shot the two Jews. Karolina's daughter was sent to work on farm. Karolina was sent to prison and waited for trial. She was found guilty and sentenced to her death. Although Karolina was not able to keep the

Jews safe for as long as she wanted, she still managed to keep them away from being put into any sort of Ghetto.

Another hero who helped Poland was Witold Pilecki. Witold was born in 1901, and died in 1948. He willingly volunteered to be captured by the Nazis so that he could gather intelligence for the Allies. He was captured and from September, 1940, until April, 1943, he had organized an underground resistance network within Auschwitz. He was able to send messages to outside allies. Some of his documents are considered the first detailed records of the Holocaust.

Finally, a man named Oscar Schindler, who was actually a German and a Nazi, was a hero. He was born in 1908, and died in 1974. Schindler worked for his father in a machinery company. Later, he worked for the German Intelligence and then joined the Nazi party. He would gather information for the Nazis. He was looked at as a selfish and rich man and looked for more of the finer things in life, such as money and goods. However, during the war he employed over 1,000 polish Jews to work for him in a factory. Oscar was still hard on the Jews but he saved them and gave them jobs. He saved them from going to concentration camps and getting executed. Schindler used to bribe SS officials to prevent execution of his workers. By 1945, he had spent most of his fortune on bribes and purchases for his workers. In 1993, Steven Spielberg made a movie about Oscar and it was called "Schindler's List". Schindler was named "Righteous Among the Nation" by the Israelis and buried in Jerusalem. He was the only member of the Nazis to be honored this way.

So many more heroes helped rescue people during the time of World War II. Irena, Karolina, Witold, and Oscar were just some of the many who helped save a number of Polish people. They risked everything and stood up for people that no one else would. Although a lot of horrid things happened, these people, who helped many in the holocaust, should be remembered as amazing Heroes.

Works cited

"Women of Valor". Irena Sendler - Stories of Women Who Rescued Jews During the Holocaust - Righteous Among the Nations - Yad Vashem. N.p., n.d. Web. 27 Jan. 2017.

Google. N.p., n.d. Web. 29 Jan. 2017.

"Irena Sendler". Irena Sendler. N.p., n.d. Web. 29 Jan. 2017

The Power of People

Kaitlyn Yi

During the time of 1939-1945, heroes of Poland, and the Holocaust, helped many Jews, Jehovah's Witnesses, homosexuals, dissenting clergy, Communists, Socialists, and other political enemies. Sadly, many people had died during this time, and although that is true, many people also did survive because of people that helped the victims go into hiding. About six million Jews had died in the Holocaust, but in Europe altogether nine million five hundred thousand Jews had been killed sadly. Such people as Irena Sendler, Julian Bilecki, Hugh O'Flaherty, Georg Ferdinand Duckwitz, and finally Sophia Kritikou all helped many people. All of these people had helped innocent people escape from the horrible Adolf Hitler, and his army of the Nazi Party.

Irena Sendler was an amazing, strong social worker. At the age of 29, she saved approximately 2,500 Jewish children from 1942-1943, during World War II. As a Zegota activist Sendler helped smuggle children out of the Ghetto. A Zegota activist stands for the Council for Aid to Jews. She used her job as a social worker to help out many Jews in the Ghetto. Later she was arrested on October 20, 1943, and was also sentenced to death, but some activists had bribed officials for her release. Knowing that the Nazi people were watching did not stop her from helping more people, but before doing so, she went into hiding because of the threats that she could face. During this time, she morosely had missed her own mother's funeral. Sadly at the age of 98, she passed away on May 12, 2008, being remembered as the woman that helped, and saved people, and later was recognized as Righteous Among the Nations.

As a young teenage boy, Julian Bilecki and his family took in 23 Jews. At first the people had made bunkers but had almost been found by a passerby in the woods. Scared for their lives, they moved into another manmade bunker. When it was winter and it snowed, Bilecki as a young boy had to go and make sure that the people were okay. Not being able to make any foot marks on the snow, he dangerously had to swing from tree to tree. He was brave for what he had done, for if he were caught, he was putting everyone in the manmade bunkers at risk, and at risk of their lives and his. In 1992, Bilecki, and seven others received an honorable award for helping the Jews during the Holocaust.

Unlike Julian Bilecki, there was an Irish priest by the name of Hugh O'Flaherty. Bravely being a priest, he saved 4000 Jews and allied soldiers. There was a group called Vatican, which helped him from being arrested by the Nazis. Being a priest and having the protection from the Vatican gave him the chance to save about 4000 escapees. Dangerously, he was almost assassinated but gladly survived, alongside the Catholic Church. Most Jews that he had saved were in Rome. Later in 1963, he had sadly passed away.

Georg Ferdinand Duckwitz was part of the German Nazi Party. Many people know that the Nazi's never showed sympathy to Jews. Except knowing that he was risking his life, he went to Sweden to convince the Swedish Prime Minister, Per Albin Hansson, to let the Danish Jews escape to Sweden. After letting Hans Hedtoft, a Danish politician, know about the transportation, after about two months, they had finally boarded 6000 Jews to Sweden in boats. After he had returned to his Nazi duties and never spoke the truth about what he had done even though it could cost him, his job or even possibly worse. But surprisingly he went back to his job as West Germany's ambassador to Denmark. Sadly in 1973, he passed away, but in the end he saved 99% of Denmark's population of Jews.

This last person I am going to talk about is, Sophia Kritikou. She was single mother that helped hide Jews near Athens, and roughly she had her own difficulties. She had to deal with not even knowing that the family that she was helping was Jewish, but also instead of kicking the family out she kept them safe. If someone found out that she was housing Jews, she could be killed. Her hidden family, the Kritikoy's, was kept safe in Sophia's home until the war was over. Although she was a poor woman, she was a hard worker. Later, as years went by, she died at the age of 100, and was recognized as Righteous Among the Nations, on August 23, 1998.

In the end, these amazing, strong, and brave people all helped the Jews in their own way. Even though they were risking their own lives, they hadn't thought twice what could've happened, because they knew what was happening in the Holocaust, was very wrong. Writing about this topic has really opened my eyes to what happened in this time period. Many people did sacrifice their lives for other people, and reading that not just men, but also women risked their lives was an eye opener to other people too, including me.

Works Cited

Blumberg, Antonia. "The Holocaust's Forgotten Victims: The 5 Million Non-Jewish People Killed By The Nazis." The Huffington Post. TheHuffingtonPost.com, 27 Jan. 2015. Web. 27 Feb. 2017.

"Julian Bilecki, A Holocaust Hero." Julian Bilecki, A Holocaust Hero. N.p., n.d. Web. 15 Feb. 2017.

"10 People Who Saved Jews During World War Two." Listverse. N.p., 14 June 2014. Web. 25 Feb. 2017.

""Women of Valor"." Irena Sendler - Stories of Women Who Rescued Jews During the Holocaust - Righteous Among the Nations - Yad Vashem. N.p., n.d. Web. 12 Feb. 2017.

""Women of Valor"." Sofia Kritikou (Kritikoy) - Stories of Women Who Rescued Jews During the Holocaust - Righteous Among the Nations - Yad Vashem. N.p., n.d. Web. 27 Feb. 2017.

"Zegota: Council to Aid the Jews." Zegota: Council to Aid the Jews. N.p., n.d. Web. 12 Feb. 2017.

A Confidential Hero

Paige Kaufman (Winner)

The Holocaust was a truly horrific event in which many people of the Jewish faith were killed by the Nazis. Within all these terrible events, involving terrible people, there were some great events with great people. These stories include heroes. Quite a few of these heroes who helped jews during the holocaust were in Poland.

One of these heroes was Irena Sendler. Unlike the heroes we think of today--with animated super powers--this young lady did not have the power to fly, yet she still did some incredibly heroic deeds. Sendler was born in 1910 and was 29 years old when World War II started. She knew that what was happening to the Jewish people was wrong, and she decided to do something about it. Sendler was employed by the Welfare Department of Poland's capital, Warsaw. This organization was helping families in need, just as a welfare department would today. Helping the Jewish people who lived in bad conditions became her goal. Sendler said, "You see a man drowning, you must try to save him even if you cannot swim." She set a goal to do what was right, even if it was going to be hard.

A ghetto was a place where the Nazi's confined the Jews into a closed off section of town. In 1940, the largest Ghetto was sealed off. This just so happened to be in Warsaw. The main causes of death in the Ghetto were from disease and starvation. Five-thousand people were dying per month. Of course, Sendler found a way to help. Using her job with the Welfare Department, Sendler was able to convince the local government to give her clearance to enter the Ghetto. While she was supposed to be looking at the sanitary conditions, Sendler was helping the Jews escape the Ghetto, and finding them hiding spaces. This woman was starting to save lives.

Irena Sendler joined the Council for Aid to Jews, which was known as Zegota. This underground organization helped Jews get to safety. As a prime member of this organization, Sendler focused on helping children. Having the difficult job of administrating the parting of parents and children she was able to smuggle out a lot of children. She hid children in items ranging from body bags to potato sacks. Sendler became extremely creative. "I sent most of the children to religious establishments. I knew I could count on the Sisters," said Sendler. After helping each child, she kept a record of them--including their real names and fake identities--even though they only knew her by her code name, Jolanta. Irena Sendler kept these records buried underneath her neighbor's apple trees. She was making a positive difference by helping the Jewish people in need.

On April 19, 1943, the Warsaw Ghetto was destroyed after new deportation plans for the Polish Jews were announced. Refusing to show up for their new deportation, the people went into hiding. Therefore, the Nazis decided to set the Warsaw Ghetto on fire, forcing the Jews to come out of hiding. After the destruction, Irena Sendler became director of the Department for the Care of Jewish Children for Zegota.

Shortly after--October 20, 1943--Irena Sendler's luck had run out. The Nazis became aware of what she was doing. They soon tortured her, trying to make her tell where the children she helped were located. The Nazi soldiers could not get her to talk, so she was sentenced to death. Sendler was sent to Pawiak Prison where she was supposed to be executed. Unexpectedly, her fellow members of Zegota bribed one of the Nazis, enabling her to escape her execution. When the Nazis began to look for her again, she went into hiding herself. However, Sendler managed to survive until the end of the war. This long awaited triumph was good news to many.

Irena Sendler dug up the jars with the records of the children that she helped--an amazing 2,500--once the war had come to an end. Even though most of the children's families were murdered during the Holocaust at the terrible death camps, Sendler tried to reunite as many families as she could. She truly took her good deeds as far as they could go.

Predictably, Irena received many different awards. These many notable acknowledgments included Poland's highest award, the Order of White Eagle (2003). Irena would not have received all the recognition that she has today without the help of four high school students. These young women wrote a play called "Life in a Jar". Making her story widely known, this play is about the amazing things Irena Sendler did during the

Holocaust. Irena Sendler lived an extraordinary life. She died in 2008 at the age of ninety-eight.

The Holocaust is an event that forced people to choose to follow along with the bad or to stand up for what is right. Although many people did the first, some exceptional people did the latter. Irena Sendler was one of Poland's amazing heroes throughout the years 1939-1945. Her story, along with others, should be well known. We should learn not only about the evil of the Holocaust, but about the great heroes that came from it.

Bibliography:

1)""Women of Valor"" Irena Sendler - Stories of Women Who Rescued Jews During the Holocaust - Righteous Among the Nations - Yad Vashem. N.p., n.d. Web. 26 Dec. 2016. <http://www.yadvashem.org/yv/en/exhibitions/righteous-women/sendler.asp>.

2)"Ghettos in Poland." United States Holocaust Memorial Museum. United States Holocaust Memorial Museum, n.d. Web. 26 Dec. 2016. <https://www.ushmm.org/outreach/en/article.php?ModuleId=10007706>.

3)Mayer, Jack. Life in a Jar: The Irena Sendler Project. Middlebury, VT: Long Trail, 2011. Print.

4)"Irena Sendler." Irena Sendler | Jewish Virtual Library. N.p., n.d. Web. 26 Dec. 2016. <http://www.jewishvirtuallibrary.org/jsource/biography/irenasendler.html>.

5)"Jewish Resistance:Konrad Żegota Committee." The Żegota | Jewish Virtual Library. N.p., n.d. Web. 26 Dec. 2016. <http://www.jewishvirtuallibrary.org/jsource/Holocaust/Zegota.html>.

Never Forgotten

Samantha Bacon (Winner)

Jan Karski was an incredible and courageous man who went through hostile and menacing times in order to be known as the hero he is today. This astounding man's full name was Jan Kozielewski. He was born on April 24, 1914 in Lodz, Poland. Karski was born into a Catholic family and he remained Catholic his whole life. He grew up around many Jews and other cultures. He was a man that always had a sense of right and wrong. Because of this, he became known as a hero of the Holocaust time period. Jan Karski risked his life numerous times in order to try and save the innocent victims of this terrible event in history known as the Holocaust.

Jan Karski was a research officer and a young Polish diplomat. He fought in the defense of his home country before he was taken prisoner for the first time on a Nazi prison train when the Nazis took control of Poland in 1939. He was not going to have his life end there without putting up a fight. He jumped off of the train in the middle of the night and began to fight with the Polish underground after walking many miles. One of the many things he did to help the Polish underground army was carry messages to England and France. This was a life-risking task and soon he was taken prisoner. His life almost ended in the hands of the Nazis.

This hero went through many hardships while held captive by the Nazis. He was brutally beaten and tortured. Furthermore, almost all of his teeth were knocked out. This was a way for the Nazis to get him to tell the names of his colleagues helping him. Not one name left his mouth. It had gotten to a point where he was terrified that he would not be able to take any more beating or torturing, so he tried to kill himself. After failing at this, he was saved by resistance fighters who knew how courageous and meaningful this man was. After doing so, 15 of them were executed. Right after he escaped, Karski planned a trip to England where he met with Jewish leaders. Here, he confirmed that he would visit the Warsaw Ghetto to see exactly what was happening there under the Nazi control. He reported back to the Allies and what he saw would haunt him forever. His eyes witnessed screaming children, people dying in the streets, and children too weak to move. He demanded that actions should be taken to stop the Holocaust.

Jan Karski made a risky plan to stop the Holocaust. He was smuggled into the Warsaw Ghetto again and the Izbica transit camp. He needed to discover firsthand accounts about the plight of European Jews under Nazi rule. Next, he traveled west. There, he met with British Foreign Secretary, Anthony Eden, President Franklin D. Roosevelt, and others. Karski showed them the plan to exterminate the European Jewry and begged for allied action to help him stop the Holocaust. However, a problem arose. The Nazis discovered his true identity, so he had to stay in the United States. If he returned to Poland, he would have been executed. Jan had to make plans in order to help Poland.

Karski knew that the Communists of Poland would take over the Polish government. He had to make the government of Poland free. He got support from national journalists to help the Polish government's exile. Karski refused to return back to Communist Poland, so instead he earned a PhD at Georgetown University. He also promoted Polish freedom in Washington and became a professor at Georgetown University where he helped even more lives of people.

The nightmares of the Holocaust would always remind Jan Karski of this terrifying event, so he worked non-stop for Polish-Jewish understanding. Not only that, he also honored the remembrance of all of the innocent people who died under Nazi rule. He received the highest Polish civic and military decorations from his home country, Poland. He also became known by many people as an honored citizen. He was recognized by his courage by numerous countries. Not only this, but he also was made an honored citizen of the State of Israel and is celebrated on Israel's Avenue of the Righteous. Jan Karski wrote several books about the things he endured in this time period. One of the books was called The Secret of Senate. One of his quotes in this book was, "The Nazis did it because they could. The Allies denied it because they did nothing about it." This tells just how powerful and persuading the Nazis were to millions of people. After the amazing actions that he took, a year was chosen in order to remember his heroic and helpful acts during the Holocaust and World War II. The year that was chosen was 2014. It was chosen by the Polish Sejm because that was the centennial, or 100 year period after his birth. He died on July 13, 2000, at 86 years old. After his death, Karski, along with his courageous actions, continue to live on. Jan Karski is a man that should never be forgotten and continuously recognized as a hero of history.

Works Cited

"Jan Karski." United States Holocaust Memorial Museum. United States Holocaust Memorial Museum, n.d. Web. https://www.ushmm.org/wlc/en/article.php?ModuleId=10008152. Accessed 29 December 2016.

"Jan Karski Institute." Jan Karski Institute. N.p., n.d. Web. 29 December 2016. http://jankarskiinstituteus.org/.

Jones, Nigel. "Story of a Secret State by Jan Karski: Review." The Telegraph. Telegraph Media Group, n.d. Web. 29 December 2016. http://www.telegraph.o.uk/culture/8560682/Story-of-a-Secret-State-by-Jan-Karski-review.html.

The Holocaust

Spencer Ward

The Holocaust was a devastating event for Jewish people in the years 1933 to 1945. January of 1933, was when Adolf Hitler came to power and immediately started targeting Jewish people. One of the first things Adolf Hitler did was open the first Concentration Camp to Dachau in March of 1933, which gave him absolute power. Surrounding the concentration camp high walls and barbed wire fences. Adolf Hitler's first start of power came with Jews limited rights to marry with other religions, soon to be known as the start of the Nuremberg Acts. After a couple of years, more and more Jewish people were arrested and taken from their homes until more serious effects started happening in 1938.

In 1938, Adolf Hitler put up orders to have Jews arrested. With his orders 30,000 Jewish people were arrested and had their homes destroyed. After going to jail the Jewish people would be sent to concentration camps, mainly Bergen-Belsen. The Nazis main killing interest became children because they thought the fewer children the less developing Jews in later years. After targeting many Jewish, the Nazis started to invade Poland starting World War II, occupying half of Poland. The Nazis took away Polish Jews in Poland and sent them to concentration camps. Hitler started attacking everyone including Jews, gypsies, homosexuals, Soviets, Jehovah's Witnesses, Poles, physically and mentally disabled, and Slavs. Adolf Hitler started to check Germans for the characteristics and if they were one of those then they would be chosen for gas chambers and would be gassed with others in the concentration camps. Hitler thought disabled people to be useless as over 245,000 people who died were handicapped. The trouble of bringing Poles over from Poland was a lot of work so they opened Auschwitz Concentration Camp to have less work of transporting people from Poland. Throughout 1940 Hitler expanded the German empire by conquering Denmark, Norway, the Netherlands, Belgium, Luxembourg, and France. They then with a couple of allying countries attacked the Soviet Union and Hitler ordered the armies to kill any of the Soviet Jews. After conquering the Soviet Union the Germans killed over 500,000 Jews. Jews that were not captured yet were declared to wear a yellow star so they would be easy targets starting another period in 1941.

In 1941, the Germans started using Zyklon B in the Gas Chambers to burn the bodies and found more and more hidden Jews who had their yellow stars. The German Nazis went back to the Soviet Union and buried 33,000 Soviet Jews. Going back to Poland Hitler wanted to kill off the weak people including the sick, the old, the weak, and the young. Those taken were sent to the Belzec Concentration Camp. If they survived Belzec they were sent to one of the five biggest killing centers, Chelmno, Sobibor, Treblinka, Majdanek, and the largest of them all Auschwitz. Most of the sick, young, old, and weak were sent during the summer and fall of 1942 with the deaths at 300,000 people. The Nazis were starting to get some negative feedback on the camps when their "secret" camps were being discovered by people who were watching them from outside the walls and they would complain about what they were seeing including the rough work, the death marches, and them wearing striped pajamas. The eyewitnesses were also complaining about the camps being mass slaughterhouses. In the biggest camp Auschwitz there was in 1943 over 2 million deaths. The Nazis would continue to be unresponsive and would keep killing more people.

The Nazis started limiting the gas chambers to only killing Jews but it wasn't just Jews dying. Other people would die from starvation, diseases, or the brutal death walks in freezing weather conditions and only underwear and for girls, bras. If people lived from those then they most likely died from hypothermia. But most who were healthy, strong, and good workers stayed and lived and worked.

The Soviet offense started fighting back again and started the beginning of the end for Germany. But the Nazis just kept sending Jews to Auschwitz and started killing 12,000 Jews a day. Not long after though, the last gassing in Auschwitz, they are ordered to evacuate January 19, 1945. Auschwitz was then liberated by the Russians on January 27, 1945. When all the camps were evacuated Hitler blamed everyone but himself and then April 30, 1945, Adolf Hitler committed suicide at the age of 56.

In the end of what Adolf Hitler did there were about 11 million total deaths in the Holocaust with six million deaths being Jews. Second to Jews was Soviets with three million deaths, followed by Poles with about 1.8 million deaths, and then Serbians with 312,000, and disabled people with 250,000 deaths. But after the people who survived were out most of them found it extremely difficult to return to their own homes with missing family members. After some of the internal scars were healed, families were given individual checks to repair some things torn down in their homes by the Germans. In my opinion the Holocaust was one of the worst things to happen in our world's history.

Works Cited

https://www.factretriever.com/holocaust-facts
http://www.history.com/topics/world-war-ii/the-holocaust

The Men and Women Who Saved Countless Lives

Trent Moyer

There was a king or a Maharaja in Poland during World War II (WWII) who saved countless lives. This man had saved the lives of 640 Jewish women and children. While the Nazis were tearing Poland apart, the Maharaja was putting it back together. He was on a British ship when he heard about all of the refugees. He then tried to persuade the captain to let them go. However, the captain refused. The Maharaja then became frustrated by the non-tolerance of the Captain so he ordered the ship to dock back at Rosi Port in his province. When the Jews got off the boat, they were taken to tented areas where they could stay. The Maharaja built the camps near his summer palace, which was 25 kilometers from the capital city of Jamnagar. This man is an inspiration to many till this day.

Another person who saved the lives of many Jewish children is Irena Sendler. Irena Sendler was a Polish nurse and the head of the children's section of Zegota. Zegota was a Polish council to aid Jews. The council was active from 1942 to 1945. Irena Sendler was assisted by two dozen of other Zegota employees. It was reported that she smuggled about 2,500 Jewish children out of the Warsaw Ghetto. She saved more than any other person during the Holocaust. The Germans found out about her secret and was arrested by the undercover German police. She was then tortured and sentenced to death but, she managed to avoid execution and survived the war. Later in life she was awarded the Order of the White Eagle, which is Poland's highest honor. She recently died at the age of 98 in May, 2008.

There was another woman by the name of Wanda Krahelska Filipowicz who was the leading figure in Warsaw's resistance to Jewish persecution by the Nazis. She was a well-connected wife of a former ambassador to Washington. She had connections with the military and political leadership which helped her support the Poland Jewish population during the war. Previous to helping the Jews, she used her influence to persuade the Polish government in exile, which included the members of the Delegatura and its military counterpart, the AK. This was significant as it supported the establishment of a central government to help Poland's Jews, and to get significant funding. She also sheltered Jews personally in her home during the German occupation. Before World War I and II, she attempted to assassinate the Russian governor. She then went into hiding for many years until WWII. She later died at the age of 82 in 1968.

Wanda Krahelska Filipowicz created the Home Army, which was the dominant Polish resistance movement. Within the next two years it absorbed most other Polish underground forces. It was the armed wing of what became the Polish Underground State. By 1944, it had between 200,000 and 600,000 troops. It then became one of Polish's largest resistance movements. The Home Army's main objective was to take over and sabotage German supplies. They also sabotaged many German transports. They had fought many full-scale battles with the Germans. One of the main operations was Operation Tempest which had aimed to take over German and Soviet occupied cities and areas in Poland. Since the Home Army was taking back Poland land from the Soviets, conflict grew between the Home Army and Soviet Russia. Following the end of the war in 1945, the Home Army was disbanded with many other underground resistances.

During the war there was a Polish Underground State. The Polish Underground State is where the Polish military would harbor saved Jews. It was like a safe haven for the military and civilians. The final elements to the Underground State were created in the final days of the German invasion of Poland, which began in 1939. The Underground State was a place where you could have an education, cultural and social services. Although it was well organized, it was not supported by communists. The nationalists also disapproved of the Underground State. Then the Soviets created a copycat army which was to capture the Polish Underground State. When captured, members of the Underground State were prosecuted as alleged traitors and executed. By doing this it was impossible to negotiate with the Soviets. Hundreds of thousands of people were directly involved with the Underground State. They were quietly supported by millions of Polish citizens. To avoid a civil war with the Soviets, they dissolved in the first half of 1945.

Before and during the Polish Underground State there was the Union of Armed struggle (ZWZ). The ZWZ was directed from Paris by a General named Kazimierz Sosnkowski who, after Poland's defeat, escaped to France via Hungary. Due to simple problems, the control of his organization was very limited. He came together with his former staff and created the idea of Polish units. After the fall of France, he partnered with his Colonel and put they put together their own government which gave him authority of the Polish Government. He then had the power of the military to occupy the country. He was later arrested under German occupation. He died at the age of 83 in October, 1969. All of these men and women saved Jewish lives for the people of Poland because they saw them as friends and family. We should honor these heroes every day, knowing there are people willing to sacrifice their lives for others.

Works Cited
https://en.wikipedia.org/wiki/Wanda_Krahelska-Filipowicz,

https://en.wikipedia.org/wiki/Individuals_and_groups_assisting_Jews_during_the_Holocaust#Poland

http://www.thebetterindia.com/52118/maharaja-digvijaysinhji-ranjitsinhji-jadeja-nawanagar-ww2-little-poland-in-india/

https://en.wikipedia.org/wiki/Home_Army

https://en.wikipedia.org/wiki/Operation_Tempest

https://en.wikipedia.org/wiki/Union_of_Armed_Struggle

Congregation B'nai Israel, Sacramento, CA

Denise Crevin is currently the Education Administrator, Congregation B'nai Israel. After graduating from UCLA with a degree in Communication Studies, Denise received a Masters degree in Broadcast and Electronic Communication Arts from San Francisco State University. She worked as a writer for CNN Headline News in Atlanta, did PR for Marriott Hotels during the 1996 Olympics in Atlanta and then returned to the Bay Area to run a business - Service Impressions - with her husband, Dan. She is the proud mom to Ava (age 8) and Max (age 6), and enjoys volunteering for a variety of organizations including the PTO at their school, Hadassah, Girl Scouts and her college sorority, Alpha Epsilon Phi. As the daughter of a Holocaust survivor, she is glad to help review essays for the Eleanor J Marks Holocaust Essay Contest and ensure that future generations never forget.

Joe Gruen works and lives in Sacramento, CA. He is a a full-time accounting student at American River College and works part time teaching Hebrew and Judaica at B'nai Israel Congregation.

Erica Cassman is a California State credentialed teacher. She taught at the elementary school level for ten years in Los Angeles before starting her family and moving to Sacramento. She is currently staying at home with her 3 year old daughter Lilah and 1 year old son Gavin. Since moving to Northern California Erica has become an active member in the Jewish community. Erica's educational background includes a Bachelor of Arts in Liberal Studies with a Concentration in Art and a Master's degree in Educational Administration, both from California State University, Northridge.

The Forgotten Hero

Aiden Moseley

Irena Sendler (Sendlerowa) was born on February 15th, 1910 in Otwock, Poland, a city 15 miles east of Warsaw. Irena had lots of kindness in her heart and strength from family. Irena's great grandfather led a rebellion against the Czars. She was greatly influenced by her father who wasn't just a Polish physician, but also one of the first members of the Polish Socialist Party also known as the PSP. His fellow doctors refused to treat the Jewish victims of typhus but he did. Sadly, about a week before Irena's seventh birthday, he contracted typhus from his Jewish patients and passed away. But the leaders of the Jewish community paid it forward by helping pay for Irena's college. She studied literature at Warsaw University and, like father like daughter, joined the PSP. She got herself expelled by protesting against the ghetto-bench system.

In the late 1930s, Irena moved to Warsaw and began working for the municipal Warsaw Social Welfare Department. Not far after Germany invaded the defenseless city, beating the Jewish citizens. After that terrible invasion, Warsaw was turned into a Ghetto full of 450,000 Jewish people. She couldn't waltz in and help the oppressed anymore because of the isolation. As Senior Administrator of a group that provided for orphans, the elderly, and the poor, Irena offered clothes, medicine, and money for the Jews. This was very illegal so Irena posed as a nurse to get inside the Ghetto. Intelligently, she had worked to get issued a pass from the Epidemic Control Department and worked the Germans paranoia of germs against them. She saw the worst in people that day. Irena Sendler quoted, "People can be only divided into good or bad; their race, religion, nationality don't matter." She engaged in even more courageous activities by illegally making false documents for escaped Jews. This allowed Jews to leave without the Nazis having a clue as to what was happening. She registered them under fictitious Christian names and diagnosed them with infectious diseases so the Germans wouldn't search for them. For four years, she continued to work, live, and succeed. But she didn't think that she was good enough. She became depressed because 5,000 people were dying each month, not from torture or murder, but by disease and starvation. In the fall of 1942, Irena was offered something that she couldn't turn down. Irena's close friends Zofia and Wanda founded Zegota, the Council for Aid to Jews in Occupied Poland. Zegota was a branch of the Polish underground resistance movement. Irena was asked to lead the Children's Department. Irena later stated, "I lost no time in reflecting [on the danger] knowing that I and my heart had to be there, had to be a part of the rescue."

The Children's Division of Zegota was dedicated to saving the children of the Ghetto. The first step of the process was getting her nickname, Jolanta. She had already planned her main routes, the still-standing abandoned courthouse on the edge of the ghetto and a church where the kids had to learn Catholic prayers to survive. Following that, the kids would leave through the front door with the gathering which was protected by vigilant Nazi soldiers. She rescued the children, sometimes at rates of 25 children per trip. She would hide under the ruse of stopping the spread of disease. She began her work with orphans, but later met with parents to tell them that their kids must be taken. All she heard was questions, asking about the Jewish parent's kids, asking if they were guaranteed to live. If they stayed, they would die. Irena made it clear to families that they would see their kids again after the war. Until the end of her life, she heard the screams, tears, and trembles of kids leaving their parents in her dreams. She kept a list of names so that families could be reunited. As a young mother, she understood the hardships of giving away your children for their safety, especially knowing that if they were caught, the consequences would be dire. Small children were harder to save because they could not be saved through the buildings. They had to be carried in gunny sacks, carts, coffins, and even toolboxes. Intelligently, she sometimes had a dog with her to avoid detection; she would get the dog to bark loud. This made the Nazi dogs bark along with hers.

When she was on the other side, the Piotrowski family, her best family friends, would feed and prepare the kids for whatever journey they would take. Her best friend Maria Kukulska housed many kids for the remainder of the war. Other children were given new identities and lived in orphanages and convents where they could make new friends. Irena had another problem. To get them back to their parents, Sendler had to code the children's original and new names. Their only true identities and ways to reunite with their families lied in jars hidden beneath an apple tree. One day she had hoped to use those names, inform the 2,500 growing kids of their past. Unfortunately, the Nazis became aware of Irena's activities and it changed her life. On October 20, 1943, Irena Sendler was arrested for multiple counts of saving the Jewish kids. She was imprisoned at the infamous Pawiak Prison in which she was tortured by the Gestapo. They broke her arms and legs but they could never break her spirit. She powered through the pain and only she knew the names of the families sheltering the Jewish families. She is said to have saved 2,500 children, but by remaining silent about everything, she saved millions. She was sentenced to death but at the last second Zegota members bribed the Germans to halt the execution and help her escape. She read posters saying that she had been shot when in fact she had lived to see them. But that was well known by the Gestapo who would stop at nothing to find her until the war ended. She remained hidden just like the kids that she saved. Luckily for her, the war came to a conclusion on September 2, 1945.

After the war, Irena dug the jars up from beneath the apple trees. She tracked down 2,500 children and reunited them with their Jewish relatives. Unfortunately, most of the kids lost their families during the Holocaust in Nazi death camps, especially the Treblinka death camp. Only one percent of the 450,000 Jews from the Warsaw Ghetto survived the war. She was unknown and unappreciated by many except for the survivors. She kept in touch with the children for years. In 1947, she divorced her first husband. She had a baby with her second husband, but the baby died at infancy. Her second husband died not long after. She lost her oldest son to a heart failure. She fell into depression and refused to be called a hero even though she was known as the "Female Schindler". She said, "Heroes do extraordinary things. What I did was not an extraordinary thing. It was normal." Her life ended with regret, claiming that she could have done more. "I could have done more," she said. "This regret will follow me to my death."

Irena Sendler was one of the most incredible women in the world. All 24 women and the one man who helped Irena took tremendous risks, but only Irena entered the Ghetto every day for 18 months. She saved thousands with nothing but a doctor's mask, and her intelligence, which spread as wide as her heart. She has constantly been honored by Jewish organizations around the world, even after death. She accorded the title of "Righteous Among the Nations" by the "Yad Vashem" organization in Jerusalem and in 1991, she was made an honorary citizen of Israel. (JVL) In Warsaw, she was given the most incredible award, the Order of the White Eagle. Her work and willingness to speak up saved thousands of lives. Her courage during torture proved her dedication to the cause.

Although she was unknown for very long, she was incredibly happy when she heard about the Life in a Jar project. Four students created a History Day project that began on one website, and spread to hundreds of thousands. In hearing about the project, Irena was very surprised and very interested. So Irena decided to write a letter to the thoughtful students. She wrote, "My emotion is being shadowed by the fact that no one from the circle of my faithful coworkers, who constantly risked their lives, could live long enough to enjoy all the honors that now are falling upon me.... I can't find the words to thank you, my dear girls.... Before the day you have written the play "Life in a Jar" — nobody in my own country and in the whole world cared about my person and my work during the war ..." She became happy and won many awards. She won the Tikkun Olam award for fixing the world. In 2006, 2007, and 2008, Irena was nominated for the Noble Peace prize, but she never won. But she still smiled and became the oldest receiver of the Order of the Smile award which was given by children which made it her favorite award along with the Right Among the Nations award. She even received a letter from the pope. She always smiled near the end of her life, but never forgot her horrible memories from the earth-shaking war. She was honored by the Polish Senate, American Congress, and governments around the world. Her last words to the students were, "You have changed Poland, you have changed the United States, you have changed the world. I love you very, very much." Irena Sendler peacefully passed away on May 12, 2008 at the age of 98.

Work Cited

Kroll, Chana. "Irena Sendler - Rescuer of the Children of Warsaw." Rescuer of the Children of Warsaw - Dealing with Challenge, Chabad-Lubavitch Media Center, 2017, www.chabad.org/theJewishWoman/article_cdo/aid/939081/jewish/Irena-Sendler.htm.

"Irena Sendler." 2017. The Famous People website. Jan 17 2017 //www.thefamouspeople.com/profiles/irena-sendler-6152.php.

Levine, Jason. "Irena Sendler." Irena Sendler | Jewish Virtual Library, American-Israeli Cooperative Enterprise, 2017, www.jewishvirtuallibrary.org/jsource/biography /irenasendler.html.

Life In A Jar. "Facts about Irena." Life in a Jar, Word Press, www.irenasendler.org/ facts-about-   irena/

"You see a man drowning; you must try to save him even if you cannot swim."

Irena Sendler's Act

Elayna Weber

I chose to write about Irena Sendler because she helped a lot of kids escape death and live a successful life. As a B'nai mitzvah student, I connected my Torah portion, Lech L'cha, to Irena Sendler's story. Lech L'cha is about going forth and doing incredible things. Irena Sendler did just that! She was a very selfless and brave woman who, as a health worker, courageously smuggled 2,500 babies and children out of the Warsaw Ghetto and away from death camps in 1942 and 1943.

Irena Sendler was born in 1910 in Otwock, in central Poland, 15 miles away from Warsaw. Her father was a huge influence; he was one of the first Polish Socialists and a physician. Her mother, a social worker, was also a great influence for young Irena. Her father showed acts of kindness to the Jewish patients who his co-workers didn't bother to treat. Eventually in 1917, he died of typhus spread from the ill patients.

In 1939, Irena Sendler served as a Senior Administrator in the Warsaw Social Welfare Department, where she managed the canteens in every district of the city. The canteens provided meals, financial aid, and other services for elderly, orphans, and homeless. Irena convinced the canteens to also provide clothing, money, and medicine for Jews that couldn't receive help elsewhere. Because she was so shocked that the Nazis moved hundreds of Jews into the sealed off Warsaw Ghetto, she decided to join Zegota, the Council for Aid to Jews. She obtained permits from the Warsaw medical department to inspect sanitary conditions. She was also named head of the children's section of Zegota and decided to help save Jewish children within the Warsaw Ghetto. Irena contemplated that there were many risks that were involved in trying to save the children, but she decided to do it anyway. This was one of the many examples of Irena's bravery and selflessness toward others.

Irena and her small group of social workers managed to smuggle 2,500 children and babies from Warsaw. Some were squeezed in body bags or buried inside loads of goods. A mechanic hid a baby in his toolbox and other children were smuggled in potato sacks and in coffins. Identities were changed from Jewish to Christian through a church in the Ghetto. She also hid them in ambulances and wheeled them through the sewer pipes and other underground paths on trolleys in suitcases or boxes. A few of the children went through the old courtyard that led to areas with no Jews.

The parents of the children were worried sick with fear. They asked, "Can you guarantee they will live?" Irena said that they would definitely die if they stayed. Irena has recalled, "In my dreams, I still hear the cries when they left their parents." Irena was successful with the assistance of the church. "I knew I could count on the Sisters."

The kids were given false names and were placed with new families, orphanages, and convents to keep them safe. She kept the children's true identities written on cigarette paper in jars buried across the street from the German barracks under a neighbor's apple tree. She hoped that someday, she will be able to locate the children and inform them of their past. Eventually, after the war, she dug up the jars and used the notes to track down all 2,500 children she had rescued. Irena hoped to reunite the adopted citizens with their scattered family members across Europe, but sadly, most of their families were gone because of the Nazi death camps.

The Nazis eventually became aware of Sendler's actions. The Gestapo arrested her on October 20, 1943. They imprisoned and tortured her by breaking her legs and feet, ultimately sentencing her to death in the Pawiak Prison. Despite these tragedies, no one could darken her spirit! Irena was able to stash away the evidence, such as the coded addresses of the children in Zegota's care and a large amount of money to pay those who helped the Jews. Though she was the only one who bore the knowledge of the children's true identities, Irena withstood the torture, refusing to deceive her associates and the Jewish children in hiding. Luckily the underground activists were able to bribe the officials to let her go. They released her by the roadside and knocked her unconscious, only later to be rescued by Zegota activists.

Irena did not think of herself as a hero. "I could have done more," she said. "This regret will follow me to my death." She was awarded the Order of White Eagle in November 2003 for her noble services. Unfortunately, she passed away on May 12, 2008 at the age of 98.

This courageous woman was one of the most active and dedicated workers in helping Jews during the Nazi occupation in Poland. She saved the lives of 2,500 children and has influenced generations of Jewish people through the teachings of the Torah—Love Thy Neighbor as Thyself. This Torah teaching implies to treat others the way you want to be treated no matter what their gender, religion, or interests are. She showed and acted upon this all throughout Poland's time of distress and uncertainty. Irena Sendler influenced me as a young Jewish girl by realizing that you can make a difference in the world and help people in need no matter what the costs. I connected her story to my upcoming Bat Mitzvah Torah portion, Lech L'cha that implies: Go forth in the world and do great things. Irena Sendler went forth, took action, and saved the children in the Warsaw Ghetto, inspiring all of us to make the world a better place, especially in difficult times.

References:

1. www.yadvashem.org/yv/en/exhibitions/righteous-women/sendler.asp; "Women of Valor", Irena Sendler, 2017 Yad Vashem. The World Holocaust Remembrance Center.

2. www.jewishvirtuallibrary.org/irena-sendler; Irena Sendler (1910-2008), American-Israeli Cooperative Enterprise, 2017

3. www.theguardian.com/world/2007/mar/15/secondworldwar.poland; 2017 Guardian News and Media Limited or its affiliated companies.

4. https://en.wikipedia.org/wiki/Irena_Sendler; Wikipedia page modified on March 5, 2017.

Henryk Slawik

Harris R. Prunier (Winner)

 The person I chose to write about is Henryk Slawik. He was a Polish man who helped over 30,000 Polish refugees in Hungary during WWII. That is almost 30 times the amount of people in my school. About 5,000 of these people who were helped by Mr. Slawik were Jews. That is almost the size of my town in Massachusetts. Mr. Slawik was able to do this by providing Jewish people with fake documents hiding the fact that they were Jewish and making them look like they were Christians. He also created an orphanage and boarding school for Jewish children and made it look like a Catholic orphanage and school, even having the children visited by Catholic Church officials and attending services at the local church. He did this to help them so they would not die in the war.

He was born on July 16, 1894 in Timmendorf, Poland, into a poor Polish family where there were five children. His mother sent him to an academic secondary school which must be like our high school. After graduation Slawik left his hometown for Pszczyna where he was drafted into the army during WWII.

Even though Slawik was Polish, he did most of his work in Hungary because Germany defeated Poland in September, 1939, and then occupied the country. He was a member of the Polish army and after the occupation he and his men were ordered to retreat to the border with Hungary. Then he crossed the border into Hungary. It must have been a very difficult and confusing time for Slawik. Thousands of other Polish people also crossed into Hungary and settled there after the Nazi invasion of Poland. This relocation included many Jewish people. They settled there because Hungary was still relatively safe. The Nazi's were liquidating the Polish Ghettos where the Jewish people had lived in Poland. Eventually, the Nazis invaded Hungary. It must have been a very scary time to move around and try to avoid this Nazi danger. Fear was probably everywhere.

When Slawik realized the Nazi's invaded Hungary, he made all the students and teachers at the school attend regular services at the local church. This was to make the school have a more Polish and Christian image. After the Nazis took over Hungary in March, 1944, Slawik went underground and ordered as many of the refugees that were under his command to leave Hungary. They were all able to escape and leave Hungary. The children from the orphanage were also able to escape. It is impossible to imagine how difficult it was for these children. Slawik must have been very brave to help these people when his own life was in such danger.

Slawik was arrested by the Germans on March 19, 1944. Slawik was brutally tortured, but he still did not tell on his Hungarian colleagues who had helped him save so many of the Polish Jewish people. Slawik was then sent to a concentration camp called Gusen. There he was hanged with some of his fellow colleagues on August 23, 1944. No one knows where he was buried. What horrible people the Nazis were. Did they have any morals at all? How could they hate so many people? Didn't they see the good in people? How could they kill so any people the way they did?

Many years after his death, he was awarded the title of Righteous Among the Nations by Yad Vashem Commemorative Authority. This was January 26, 1977. Henryk Slawik is remembered as one of the Holocaust Rescuers. He is also remembered as a Polish "Raoul Wallenberg," a man who saved over a thousand people in 1944 by also giving them false documents. He is consistently referred to as a hero because he saved so many children. If you saved even one person you would be considered a hero. Slawik saved thousands of people and it is really impossible to imagine this.

Yad Vashem is the Holocaust Museum in Israel that wanted to honor all the people in the world who stood up and rescued or saved Jews during the war. Many people are honored there and considered to be "Righteous Among all the Nations" for the heroic work that they did. The website is amazing in how it honors all of these people who did so many things to help people that they did not know and people who were hated by some. It is important to study heroes like Henryk Slawik so that you can understand the good things that people can really do in this world. It is very hard to really understand exactly how many people Slawik saved. When so many people were being killed Henryk Slawik saved so many other lives.

Works Cited

Yadvashem.org?Righteos by Country/Poland

Jan Karski

Hudson Prunier

I chose to write my essay about Jan Karski, a member of the Polish underground during WWII. His real name was Jan Kozielewski but he shortened it to Karski. Karski took a great risk: he told the British and US governments about the destruction of the Warsaw Ghetto and the Holocaust of the Polish Jews. He did this in 1942 and 1943 at a time when many Jewish people could have been saved if only the US and British governments would have listened to him and then would have taken action. Unfortunately those governments did not do anything about it. Many more people would be alive today if Karski was believed and not disregarded. Karski could have been one of the greatest heroes of all time because the war might have ended sooner

And many more lives saved.

Jan Karski was born in Lodz, Poland, on April 24, 1914. He was a Catholic and his mother showed him how to be tolerant of other people. In 1935, he finished his studies in demography at the Lwow University and got into government work. With the war, Karski joined the Polish underground also called the Home Army. Because of his photographic memory he became a courier between the Polish government and the Polish underground.

In 1939, he was on a Nazi train but fought his way back to the Polish Underground. The Nazis captured him and tortured him.

In 1942, he was ordered to go to the West and inform them about the situation of Polish occupation. Karski met with Jewish leaders and gave reports on the war situation. When he went to talk with the two Jewish leaders he was asked to spread the word of their plight, that they and their people would be destroyed. He was smuggled into the Warsaw Ghetto and then into a camp and he saw the destruction and horror. He witnessed so many awful situations that he wanted to go to the leaders of the free world in the West and tell them about the situation. He saw extremely weak people who were dying in the streets. People were screaming and he was trying to tell of what he saw. He was smuggled into one of the death camps and saw how life was so bad for the people in the death camps and he needed to get the message out to the people.

In 1942, he went to London and met with Winston Churchill and told him about the situation with the Jewish people. He also met with many other people to spread the word. He then traveled to America and met with President Roosevelt who asked how the horses in Poland were and never asked about the Jews. Some people in the government did not even believe what he said. He stayed in Washington DC where he was after the war appointed professor at Georgetown University. There he became committed to preserving and defining the memories of Holocaust survivors. Even though he didn't save individual Jews themselves he risked his life to tell the world of the situation of the Jews. He was awarded honorary citizenship in Israel and was nominated for the Nobel Prize. He won many other medals and published reports and books.

In 1982, he was listed in Yad Vashem in Israel as Righteous Among Nations for his good deeds during the Holocaust. Yad Vashem is the museum in Israel which lists all people who rescued or saved Jewish people during the Holocaust. Karski was also recognized by the UN General Assembly for his work. Of course if people had really listened to him from the beginning, history would be very different. Persuading people to believe things that he saw that were horrible was a difficult job. Important people did not want to believe what he was saying.

On July 13, 2000, in Washington DC, Jan Karski died and was buried there next to his wife. They had no children together. In 2012, President Obama awarded Jan Karski the Presidential Medal of Freedom which is the highest honor in America. For some reason his family was not invited to the ceremony. In honor of his important life, a play was made about him. Hopefully he will be remembered forever for his righteous acts. Few people have had the opportunity to meet such important people as did Karski who tried to warn the world of the evils that he witnessed. If only he was believed then the world would be much different because there would have been so many more Jewish people and so people would not have lost their relatives. Luckily Yad Vashem keeps the memories of these important people alive today.

McCaffrey Middle School, Galt, CA

Ron Rammer

My name is Ron Rammer and I am proud to be principal of McCaffrey Middle School in Galt, California. Our students have learned about the atrocities of the Nazi regime through readings and class discussions. Many 8th graders made the journey to Washington DC and were able to experience the Holocaust Museum. The knowledge they gained from this experience along with the firsthand accounts of Holocaust survivor Bernard Marks at a school assembly has forever impacted their view of what some humans are capable of. Hopefully this piece of their education will motivate them to always stand up for what they know is right.

Mrs. Leann Salamy

Mrs. Leann Salamy is an 8th grade Language Arts Teacher at McCaffrey Middle School in Galt, CA. She majored in Liberal Studies with a minor in English. She attended Holy Names College and California State University of Sacramento. She has studied and taught about the Holocaust since teaching at the middle school level. Ryv Taylor who wrote the story on the Holocaust is a fabulous student with a bright future ahead of her. She is a gifted writer and artist.

Ari Colondres, M.A.
Reading and Literacy Leadership Specialist
"Receive the children in reverence, educate them in love, and send them forth in freedom," Rudolf Steiner.

The Rosolinska Family

Ashlin McCormick

The Holocaust was a very traumatic and horrible event over in Europe on January 30th, 1933 to May 8th, 1945. Nazis and some Germans thought that Jews should be treated different since they have different beliefs compared to theirs.

This essay is going to explain what it was like for some people that tried helping Jews get away from the Nazis. People should care about all of the righteous Polish gentiles because they helped save millions of Jews that would've lost their life to a disbelief in varieties of people and their personal beliefs. The family that is going to be mentioned is the Rosolinska family for helping out 3 Jews. There are other people in this story who are known as in the family but isn't biological to them who also put part into helping Jews.

Roman Talikowski had helped Zdzislaw and Irena escape the ghetto they were in. Zdzislaw and Irena had a daughter named Joanna, which Roman also helped smuggle her out. Roman had arranged Zdzislaw a work permit and a place for Irena and Joanna to stay, a house that belongs to Maria Kaczyńska. Maria Kaczyńska was already helping hide two woman Jews, those names are unknown. One day, the Nazis demanded a search of Maria's home. They killed Irena and one of the unknown women but not Joanna or Maria herself. When Zdzisław arrived at Maria's home, he took Joanna and brought her to Irena's sister, Alicja and her husband, Mieczysław Dortheimer, who were hiding with false papers in Tarnów.

Zdzislaw joined them as well continuing to hide Jews. He arranged a job for Mieczysław in Suchedniow after the ghetto in Tarnow was liquidated. Joanna lived with Alicja and Mieczysław in Suchedniow until they were arrested. There are different stories about how Joanna was released in January of 1944, but they don't know which story is true. Joanna chose to live with one of the nuns, Sister Kornelia Jankowska, until she died at the end of the war. After the war, Joanna was brought out of Poland, went to Germany, and was adopted by Mieczysław & Alicja who immigrated with her to Australia in 1948. On July 9, 2013, Yad Vashem recognized Maria Kaczyńska, Roman Talikowski, and Sister Kornelia Jankowska as Righteous Among the Nations.

Once again, mentioning the Rosolinska family, had helped save not as many as others but enough to make a difference in the tragic event. Learning that people had saved Jews really had an effect on me because the Holocaust was all about killing people who were different from the Nazis and some Germans. After researching the Holocaust and putting myself in those people's shoes, I realized they were being hurt and attacked for just being different people. Today is similar to back then because if someone is a different race, people will bully him or her for being different. Every single person living on this earth is exactly the same, just are unique in their own way.

Mieczysław Fogg

Autumn Hillard

A righteous gentile that deserves appreciation is a man that goes by Mieczyslaw Fogg (born Mieczyslaw Fogiel). Mieczyslaw was a Polish singer and artist that hid a Jewish family in his apartment until World War 2 ended. Mieczyslaw Fogg should be known as a righteous gentile because of the courage and kindness he had during the Holocaust.

The Holocaust was a very exhausting, laborious time in which Jews were sent to dirty, crowded places called "the Ghettos" where they had to perform hard labor. In the Ghettos, food was such a low supply that some people starved, while others would steal food so that them and their families wouldn't starve. Disease was also said to be rampant at the time. By the time 1942 rolled around, 1,500,000 Jews were said to be killed. This evidence shows just how hard life was for Jews.

Although times were hard, certain civilians still risked themselves to help Jews. Mieczyslaw Fogg was one of many people that did tasks for the benefits of Jews. Mieczyslaw Fogg was kind enough to allow a Jewish family to hide out in his apartment until the end of World War 2. He was also nice enough to start performing concerts in the very few cafes available to Poles under German occupation. Mieczyslaw also gave countless concerts both on barricades, hospitals, and bomb shelters beneath the city. This evidence shows how Mieczyslaw saved some Jews, and how he was kind enough to perform to Poles under German occupation.

After the war, Mieczyslaw continued to pursue his singing career and decided to open his own cafe. Mieczyslaw opened his first cafe after the war in 1945 and it was located in the ruins of Warsaw (his "hometown"). The cafe was nationalized by the new communist authorities of Poland, and was later closed. Fogg opened another cafe in 1951. During his time in between the openings of cafes' Fogg continued giving hundreds of concerts in all parts of Poland. Mieczysław later started his own private music record firm called ," Fogg Records". Fogg was chosen as the most popular Polish singer, for the second time, in 1958 by the Polish Radio audience. This evidence shows what Mieczyslaw pursued after the war.

Because of Mieczyslaw's courage and kindness during the Holocaust, he deserves to be known as a righteous gentile. I learned that the Holocaust was a very hard time and that even though it was hard, certain people were still righteous and brave enough to help Jews. After reading my essay, I think people should definitely pay more attention to the righteous gentiles of the Holocaust because of the positive impact they had.

Works Cited

Colondres, Ari R. "English 8." 26 Jan. 2017, Galt, McCaffrey Middle School, Holocaust Gallery Walk.

"Mieczysław Fogg." Wikipedia. Wikimedia Foundation, 20 Feb. 2017. Web. 25 Feb. 2017,

https://en.wikipedia.org/wiki/Mieczys%C5%82aw_Fogg

Yad Vashem. "Names of Righteous by Country." Names of Righteous by Country, The Holocaust Martyrs' and Heroes' Remembrance Authority, 2017, www.yadvashem.org/righteous/statistics. Accessed 23 Feb. 2017.

Edward Chacza

Cruz Melgoza

Out of several people who were righteous during WWll, one of the many people was Edward Chacza. Edward is considered a righteous hero because he smuggled fugitives out of the sealed ghetto. I chose Edward Chacza because not only did he put his life on the line to save these people, but he also put his family at risk, and if you ask me, that takes a lot of gut to risk losing your family.

The Holocaust was a sad event that took place in 1933 to 1945. The Holocaust started after the Nazi Party was elected. Adolf Hitler, who was leader of the Nazis, was the reason as to why the Holocaust began. The Holocaust was mainly about getting rid of Jews, but it also struck Gypsies, the disabled, and Slavic people (Poles, Russians, and many others.)During the Holocaust, about six millions Jews were killed, not even counting the other groups that they were after. Many of their own people died because they helped Jews. WWII was ended after the United States decided to lend a hand, and they were just in time too. The "Final Solution would have ended the Jewish population". The "Final Solution" was sending Jews into concentration camps where they would then be killed. The Holocaust was a really sad event.

Edward Chacza was born in 1918. He grew up in Baranowicze in the Nowogródek district, and he worked as a miner. His nationality was Poland, and his religion was Roman Catholic. He lived and worked like a regular person, but when the time came for him to be righteous, he was a hero. He could have lived normally with no worries, but instead he decided to fight and help those in need. He helped as many Jews as possible from the beginning of 1942 to his arrest in November 1943. Even after the liquidation of the Baranowicze ghetto, Chacza continued to liaise between partisan groups whose members included those he had saved. This shows how much he was appreciated..

Edward saved Jews by smuggling fugitives out of the sealed ghetto and accompanied them to the nearby forests of Belorussia, where local Jewish partisan units, and where they were supplied with several rifles and ammunition absorbed them. Jewish fugitives knew his address as a refuge where they received food, medical care and temporary shelter. Edward Chacza was motivated solely by love for his fellow men and humanitarian considerations. Edward Chacza wanted nothing in return for all he did for people. Being appreciated and thanked by the people he helped was enough for. The exact number of Jews who Edward Chacza saved is not known to this day. Most of them immigrated to Israel after the war, and even invited him to visit once they had learned his postwar address. On 24th March 1964, Yad Vashem Recognized Edward Chacza as Righteous Among the Nations.

In Conclusion, I chose Edward Chazca because not only did he put his life on the line to save people that he didn't even know, but he also risked his family's lives too. After completing this research assignment, I have learned that anybody could be righteous by doing good/generous deeds for people other than yourself and your family. After reading this essay, people should always do well when ever possible so that this part of history will not repeat itself.

Work Cited

Colondres, Ari R. "English 8." 26 Jan. 2017, Galt, McCaffrey Middle School, Holocaust Gallery Walk.

Yad Vashem. "Names of Righteous by Country." Names of Righteous by Country, The Holocaust Martyrs' and Heroes' Remembrance Authority, 2017, www.yadvashem.org/righteous/statistics. Accessed 23 Feb. 2017.

Yad Vashem. "The Righteous Among The Nations."The Righteous Among The Nations,The World Holocaust Remembrance Center,2017. http://db.yadvashem.org/righteous/family.html?language=en&itemId=4014275. Accessed 20 Feb.2017.

Yad Vashem. "The Righteous Among The Nations."The Righteous Among The Nations,The World Holocaust Remembrance Center,2017. http://db.yadvashem.org/righteous/righteousName.html?language=en&itemId=4014275. Accessed 20 Feb.2017.

Google Books. "Facing Death: Confronting Mortality in the Holocaust and Ourselves"Facing Death: Confronting Mortality in the Holocaust and Ourselves,2016. https://books.google.com/books?id=Jop6DQAAQBAJ&pg=PA63&lpg=PA63&dq=edward+chacza&source=bl&ots=6pVXsOXes5&sig=flVDNoHBHeTl--4oyKPbeZQmnwA&hl=en&sa=X&ved=0ahUKEwi967_rw6TSAhVI12MKHTwAC40Q6AEIPDAK#v=onepage&q=edward%20chacza&f=false. Accessed 20 Feb.2017.

Boleslaw Dabrowski

Devin Alford

I will be discussing a righteous person who wanted to help out during the Holocaust. I

found some information about one person who wanted to help out. This person risked his life to save one hundred Jews for a short period of time. The righteous person is named Boleslaw Dabrowski, who was just a farmer when groups of Jews asked for help, in which he agreed.

The Holocaust, referred to the Hebrews as the Shoah, was a horrible genocide when 6 million European Jews were killed by Adolf Hitler and Nazi Germany. It was started when Adolf Hitler had Nazi Germany build Concentration Camps to put the Jews in to make them work. Boleslaw Dabrowski was born on 16 July, 1902. He was born into a Roman-Catholic family and remained that religion until his death on 31 January 1943.

Bolesław was a farmer living in the village of Starościn, Poland with his wife and 3 young children. A Jew named Frank Blaichman convinced approximately one hundred Jews to find a place to hide. They found Dabrowski's farm and asked to stay. Boleslaw agreed and hid them in bunkers on his farm. Blaichman could only stay for one night, however, due to the lack of space. On Blaichman's way leaving the farm the next day, he heard gunshots behind him. Those gunshots were coming from Dabrowski's farm, when Polish, German, and Hebrew police had infiltrated his farm, and killed all one hundred Jews. The police took Dabrowski into custody, leaving his wife and kids behind. They later shot and killed him in a forest on the way to the police station.

The Holocaust was absolutely horrifying, not only for Europe, but for the rest of the world, too. There were many people that risked their lives to help during the Holocaust, but I personally selected Boleslaw Dabrowski for his courage and the fact that even though he knew he could die, he still wanted to help the Jews, as he didn't feel it was right.

Works Cited

Colondres, Ari R. "English 8." 26 Jan. 2017, Galt, McCaffrey Middle School, Holocaust Gallery Walk.

"Digital Collections." Digital Collections - Yad Vashem. Web. 24 Feb. 2017.

"Polscy Sprawiedliwi." Polscy Sprawiedliwi. Web. 24 Feb. 2017.

Yad Vashem. "Names of Righteous by Country." Names of Righteous by Country, The Holocaust Martyrs' and Heroes' Remembrance Authority, 2017, www.yadvashem.org/righteous/statistics. Accessed 23 Feb. 2017.

Henryk Slawik

Emily Brianne Evans

It was September 1, 1939 when Poland was invaded by Nazi Germany. Sixteen days later, the country would be invaded by the Soviet Union as well. While the two forces occupied Poland, an approximate 5.7 million Poles died, including 3 million Jews. During this period of time however, many Poles generously lent a helping hand to fellow prosecuted Jewish citizens. One such example was Henryk Slawik, a Polish man credited with selflessly helping over 30,000 individuals, 5,000 of them holding Jewish beliefs.

January 30, 1933 was the unofficial beginning of the Holocaust. During this dark period in time, many Jews faced discrimination. They were seen as less than human by many, and were inhumanly killed as a result. An estimated five to six million innocent Jews in total died during this time. Although dark, this is a very important time in history that should always be remembered. If forgotten, history may repeat itself with a new holocaust targeting a new group of people.

Henry Slawik was born in what was known then as Timmendorf on July 16, 1894. He was brought up as one of five children in a Polish silesian family. During his childhood, he was sent to an academic secondary school by his mother. After graduating, he left his hometown for Pszczyna. While living in the new area, Slawik was drafted into World War I. Once World War I came to an end, Slawik pursued a career in journalism. After just a year of working for Gazeta Robotnicza, Sławik became promoted to editor-in-chief.

Slawik performed many notable acts during the Holocaust. While in Budapest, he provided counterfeit documentation for Polish refugees. During this time, Slawik established an orphanage as well. However, unknown to the authorities, Jewish orphans were being housed in the orphanage. When Hungary was invaded and captured by Nazis during March 1944, Slawik helped many refugees evacuate the country. He is credited with helping over 30,000 Poles, 5,000 of them being Jewish. Without his generosity during the Holocaust, the Poles that he saved might have not survived.

It is apparent that Slawik was a very selfless, and generous man who did not hesitate to help others. He gave others something that was very scarce during the time; hope. It is essential to not forget to show each other simple acts of kindness. Simple acts of kindness may be more important than many make them out to be.

Works Cited

Colondres, Ari R. "English 8." 26 Jan. 2017, Galt, McCaffrey Middle School, Holocaust Gallery Walk.

Yad Vashem. "Names of Righteous by Country." Names of Righteous by Country, The Holocaust Martyrs' and Heroes' Remembrance Authority, 2017, www.yadvashem.org/righteous/statistics. Accessed 23 Feb. 2017.

https://en.wikipedia.org/wiki/Henryk_S%C5%82awik
http://db.yadvashem.org/righteous/family.html?language=en&itemId=4017525
https://www.facebook.com/YourRootsInPoland/posts/1196913256985451

Brave Souls

Fernanda Sanchez

During the Holocaust there were a lot of brave souls that helped out the Jewish. Poland had the highest number of citizens that helped out and the place that had organizations to support Jews that were going against the Germans. Helping Jews took a lot of courage because the put their life and, if they had one, family's life in risk. Getting caught hiding Jews or helping out in anyway would end up in torture and death. There were many Polish heroes named in the "Righteous among the Nations" but there are some of them that stood out.

Irena Gut was a polish nurse who aided Jews that were persecuted by the Nazi army. She was one of 5 girls in her family who lived in a small village in Poland. When her family moved to Radom she enrolled to study nursing. When Germany invaded Poland she joined a Polish army unit and went into hiding in a forest. She got arrested while she was praying and got taken to a factory to work, where she fell ill. Her life changed after she witnessed a

Nazi soldier kill an infant. Gut worked as a housekeeper in a villa and she used the villa cellar as a hiding spot for 12 Jews. When the owner found out that there were Jews hiding there he made Gut become his wife to avoid punishment. The owner was a 70 year old German soldier. Later, her husband left with the Germans and Irene found William Opdyke in a camp she worked at and soon got married.

Henry Iwanski is known for making one of the most daring acts in helping the Warsaw Ghetto uprising. Iwanski had been promoted to captain in the Polish army before World War 2 started. His family was dedicated to helping Jews so they smuggled in weapons and ammunition to the ghettos by carts and tunnels. He also started and supported strikes against the Germans and Nazis.

Alfreda and Boleslaw Pietraszek were a married Polish couple who sheltered families that in total were 18 people. Alfreda spoke 4 languages including German and this helped her very much when Nazi soldiers wanted to search her property. The couple lived in a barn in Ceranow where they hid the Jewish families in their barn, basements, and in pig pens. They relied on the neighbors and other inhabitants to help give them resources for food and necessities. During the whole time no one betrayed them and no one except a baby died. After the war had ended, the couple had to leave the village after being accused of over a dozen robberies and assaults.

Irena Adamowicz was a scout leader and a resistance worker during World War 2. She was a religious Catholic and leader of the Polish scout movement. During the Nazi invasion of Poland, Irena delivered messages underground to different ghettos in different distant cities. She also supported Jewish in the ghettos. Before the invasion of Poland she had close contact with the Jewish Zionist movement and was able to create a strong connection in transporting communication between the ghettos. In 1942, she made a dangerous trip across Poland and Lithuania to make contact with clandestine organizations in the Warsaw ghettos. Because of her various trips she earned the nickname "The Pioneering Gentile". After World War 2 ended she remained in close contact with the holocaust survivors she had worked with underground.

Ferdynand Arczynski was one of the founding members of an underground organization called Zegota, which helped aid Jews during the holocaust. His job was to find Jews and provide food and shelter for them. Ferdynand was head of the "Legalization Department" that produced many fake ID's, work cards, and other forged documents to over 40,000 Jews. He also provided aid for Jews in the concentration camps.

Anna Borkowska also known as Sister Bertranda was a Polish Dominican nun who served in her monastery near Wilno, Poland (now Vilnius, Lithuania). During World War 2 she sheltered 17 young Jewish activists from Nazi persecutions. When the Germans took over Vilnius the killing of the Jewish started immediately. Mother Bertranda wanted to save all the Jewish population and seeked help from the Vilnius Catholic leadership but they rejected her offer in fear of church property getting destroyed and Christians getting killed for helping Jews. After this Mother Bertranda took the 17 activists and hid them in the grounds of her monastery. Soon after she left to give her service in Jewish ghettos. She helped smuggle weapons and hand grenades to Jewish resistance fighters. The uprising was crushed and Mother Bertranda was caught by the German's and sent to a labor camp.

In the end, there were many brave souls in Poland that helped the Jews during the tough times of the holocaust. From sheltering Jews in their homes to supporting organizations, these courageous people risked a lot. Being fully aware of the consequences, several Polish people still went ahead of continuing their task of supporting Jews in going against Germans. Many Jewish owe their lives to these people.

Cited Works

http://www.telegraph.co.uk/education/3313193/Irene-Gut-Opdyke.html
http://www.yadvashem.org/odot_pdf/Microsoft%20Word%20-%205717.pdf
https://en.wikipedia.org/wiki/Henryk_Iwa%C5%84ski
https://alchetron.com/Henryk-Iwanski-1329012-W
http://db.yadvashem.org/righteous/family.html?language=en&itemId=4013722
https://en.wikipedia.org/wiki/Anna_Borkowska_(Sister_Bertranda)
https://en.wikipedia.org/wiki/Alfreda_and_Boles%C5%82aw_Pietraszek
https://en.wikipedia.org/wiki/Irene_Gut_Opdyke
http://www.yadvashem.org/odot_pdf/Microsoft%20Word%20-%205717.pdf
https://en.wikipedia.org/wiki/Irena_Adamowicz

Jozef Marchwinski

Hannah Freitas

Have you ever thought about the people who have risked their lives to save Jewish people during the Holocaust despite the fact that they themselves are not? Well, they're called righteous gentiles and they deserve much more recognition than they get. Jozef Marchwinski is a perfect example of a righteous gentile for he has gone even as far enough as defying his comrades to take care of an entire family of Jews.

The word Holocaust originates from the Greeks, meaning "sacrifice by fire". In 1933, the Nazis rose to power because they considered themselves racially superior compared to the Jews, who they thought were beneath them and a so called "alien threat" to the community. In total the Nazis were the cause of murder and persecution of 6 million Jewish people. Gypsies, the disabled, and a part of the Slavic peoples were also targeted due to this belief of "racial inferiority". Over 200,000 patients living in institutions alone died as a result. As Nazi authoritarianism branched across Europe, the killing continued. Starvation, disease, neglect, and maltreatment were the cause of death for 2 to 3 million Soviet prisoners of war. The Nazis also deported millions of Soviet and Polish people to Germany or Poland for the use of forced labor where they then would die due to the horrible living conditions. During the youth of this tyranny, concentration camps were created by the National Socialist Government to force their ideals the Jews that were kept there. Other means of keeping the Jewish population monitored were created such as ghettos, transit camps, and forced-labor camps during the war. These ghettos and extermination camps were used for the purpose of murdering Jews, often by specialized gassing chambers. After the invasion of the Soviet Union in June on the year of 1941, mobile killing units and militarized battalions comprised of Order Police officials cross behind German lines in order to mass murder operations aimed at Jews, Soviet state party officials, and the Roma. These units altogether killed more than a million Jewish women, men, and children. These crimes devastated Jewish communities everywhere in Europe, and completely destroyed hundreds of the Jewish communities who once occupied eastern Europe.

Just 23 years before the start of the era of the Holocaust, Jozef Marchwinski was born. He was born in Lodz, Poland and was a partisan company commander. A partisan is a person who is a part of an abnormal military force which was formed in order to oppose an area by a certain foreign power which was in this case, the Nazis. His immediate family was Franciszek Marchwinski, which was his dad, and Helena Marchwinski, who was his mom. He also got married to a woman named Esther Marchwinski and had children. He died in Copenhagen on the year of 1982, living a long life of about 72 years. His burial still remains unknown.

Jozef marchwinski has truly earned the right to be considered as a righteous gentile since he has saved an entire group of jewish fugitives, even going against his comrades to do so. During the summer on the year of 1942, the Nazis eliminated the Jewish people living in the towns known as Nieswiez and Mir, in the district called Nowogrodek. There was very little people that actually managed to escape and those who did were aimlessly wandering throughout the countryside in the hopes of evading the police that sought after those who remained. Since the fugitives were fearing the anti-Semitism of the partisans in the area, they were pleasantly surprised to find Jozef Marchwinski, who instead chose to care for them rather than discard them along with his comrades. He offered them to enlist in his company, which was met with such a strong disagreement from the partisans in his company that they had even threatened their lives. Even though Marchwinski himself was discriminated against, he still included the Jews in operation against the enemy and continued to look over them. His decision was met with aggravation of his anti-Semitic opponents who grew suspicious that he was Jewish as well. They decided to transfer Marchwinski along with the Jews he had taken in to a company of only Jewish partisans, which was under the control of commander Tuvya Bielski. However, he did not stay under that commander for long, as he was soon promoted to the rank of deputy brigade commander in recognition of his talent and bravery. Eventually, after the war was over, he moved to an area with new Polish borders where he continued to oppose the anti-Semitic acts of the Polish authorities. He was forced to move to Denmark because of this after a couple of years. In 1970 Marchwinski was invited to go to Israel by his former subordinates and was honored with a hero's welcome.

To conclude, Jozef Marchwinski was a truly inspiring righteous gentile who deserves much more recognition for many reasons. He was a selfless person who saved people who he barely knew, knowing it was an extremely big risk. I have learned many important lessons while researching him, one being that no matter race, religion, or background, everyone is created equal.

Works Cited

Colondres, Ari R. "English 8." 26 Jan. 2017, Galt, McCaffrey Middle School, Holocaust Gallery Walk.

"Introduction to the Holocaust." United States Holocaust Memorial Museum. United States Holocaust Memorial Museum. Web. 25 Feb. 2017.

"Jewish Partisans." Wikipedia. Wikimedia Foundation, 29 Jan. 2017. Web. 25 Feb. 2017.

"Jozef Marchwinski." Geni_family_tree. 07 Nov. 2014. Web. 25 Feb. 2017.

Yad Vashem. "Names of Righteous by Country." Names of Righteous by Country, The Holocaust Martyrs' and Heroes' Remembrance Authority, 2017, www.yadvashem.org/righteous/statistics. Accessed 23 Feb. 2017.

Maria Andzelm

Jaelyn Farris

I will be writing about how the holocaust affected us and someone that was a hero during that time, named Maria Andzelm. I will also be talking about why the holocaust started, how Maria Andzelm helped Jews, who she helped, her past, why the holocaust started, how it ended, who was there, and how Maria Andzelm helped. Maria Andzelm is important because she helped Jews live and not be in ghettos or killed. she saved people. It is important to read this so you can get insight on how a hero at a young age made it into the concrete of hero.

The holocaust is a very bad time in history but it should make us think about how separating people based off of something such as religion is not right. Many people died because of this. Over 11 million people killed during the Holocaust, six million were Polish citizens. Three million were Polish Jews and another three million were Polish Christians. They started out slow. This is important to the essay because it shows how one person can help in a time of need.

Maria Andzelm was born on an unknown date. Her whole family was already very poor before the holocaust. She lived on a farm in Janowiec. When she was 15 everything changed. Her best friend was deported. That when she desired to help the Jews and knew that Hitler was bad. She didn't have a job before the holocaust. She was only a kid. Also, one link stated that "Maria Andzelm Kershenbaum received the Yad Vashem Medal and Certificate of Honor in November 1994 and was designated as one of the "Righteous Among the Nations" by the Israeli government (the distinction is awarded to a non-Jewish person who risked his or her life, freedom, and safety to save Jews from the threat of deportation or death)." This shows she was a hero because she did something great even though she could have major consequences.

Maria Andzelm saved 2 Jewish men by hiding them and giving away her freedom and risking her life for them. "Maria Andzelm Kershenbaum received the Yad Vashem Medal and Certificate of Honor in November 1994 and was designated as one of the "Righteous Among the Nations" by the Israeli government (the distinction is awarded to a non-Jewish person who risked his or her life, freedom, and safety to save Jews from the threat of deportation or death)." I believe she discovered this medal because she shows you even in a time of war and hate there was still love and hope. Maria saved these Jews because she knew what was right. She gave the Jews food and water. Sometimes she would give them things to read, like a book. Towards the end of the war there was an attack. Maria and her friend hid in caller for two days. Then someone came and told her dad was shot and killed for saving Jews.

A righteous person that stands out to me is Maria Andzelm because she saved Jews that were in danger from Hitler and the Nazis because of their religion and she was willing to give up her freedom and live for them. She did something that meant something to her even when some many people saw what she did as a bad thing. Also, how she stayed strong even though she lost people and things that meant a lot to her. I learned that I should do good all the time, even when some people disagree with me or if there are consequences to my actions and that anyone can do go even if they are just 15 from her. I believe this essay shows that people should think about their actions and how they affect people. Also, to do what you think is right.

Works Cited

Chief/Monmouth, Jill Huber NJJN Bureau. "NJ Jewish News | A 'righteous' Choice to Help Others Survive." NJ Jewish News | A 'righteous' Choice to Help Others Survive. Web. 24 Feb. 2017.

Colondres, Ari R. "English 8." 26 Jan. 2017, Galt, McCaffrey Middle School, Holocaust Gallery Walk.

Gettman, Shad. "Heroes of the Holocaust; Maria Andzelm." Prezi.com. 13 Jan. 2014. Web. 24 Feb. 2017.

"Maria Anzelm." Heroes of the Holocaust. Web. 24 Feb. 2017.

Yad Vashem. "Names of Righteous by Country." Names of Righteous by Country, The Holocaust Martyrs' and Heroes' Remembrance Authority, 2017, www.yadvashem.org/righteous/statistics. Accessed 23 Feb. 2017.

Maria Andzlem

Janiece Lucas

Starting from 1933 the Holocaust was a rough moment for all people but it was especially hard on the Jews. When the Nazis gained power over Germany they targeted Jews because they didn't like their religion. The Nazis targeted Jewish people harshly, controlling them and forcing them into labor or suffering. Concentration camps, ghettos, and other establishments were put into place by Hitler and his Nazi's. Maria Andzelm is a very admirable person because even though if the Nazi's knew you were hiding Jews they would be arrested, beaten and probably killed. She still helped hide Jews however because it was the right thing to do.

About 6,000,000 Jews were put in Concentration camps, labor camps, and Ghettos. This all started because Hitler believed that all Germany's problems were caused by Jews and many people followed his ideas due to his high political stance as president. His solution was to banish Jews from this society. On buses, trains, and park benches Jews had to set on seats marked for them. In other ways, they were heavily set apart from other members of society, standing out and being judged heavily.

In 1942 Germans soldiers began to round up the Jews in Janowiec, Poland. Some Jews were killed on the spot, some were betrayed by their neighbors and others just outright disappeared. Maria Andzelm was 15 years old when her dad brought in two Jews to hide. She was scared because she didn't want her family to get caught. She was also a farmer, Maria and her family was very poor.

When Maria was a child, her best friend got deported. After that, she felt she needed to start saving Jews because they don't deserve to get deported or put in concentration camps. Later, her dad hid two Jews in their home to prevent them from being treated in that way. In order to hide the Jews so the Nazi's couldn't see them, they dug a little box underground beneath a barn pen where the cows stayed so they can be out of sight. What scared her was that they had to feed them and take them out for air time to time.

Maria Andlem was a Righteous Gentile because even though if the Nazi's knew you were hiding Jews they would be arrested, beaten and probably killed she still did in honor of her best friend. Maria is a very strong and brave person I am glad we learned about the Holocaust because I would not have learned about what people did to save Jewish lives. Learning about people who survived the Holocaust is very interesting people should learn more about Hitler and the Nazi's.

Works Cited

Colondres, Ari R. "English 8." 26 Jan. 2017, Galt, McCaffrey Middle School, Holocaust GalleryWalk.

Yad Vashem. "Names of Righteous by Country." Names of Righteous by Country, The Holocaust Martyrs' and Heroes' Remembrance Authority, 2017, www.yadvashem.org/righteous/statistics. Accessed 23 Feb. 2017.

Chief/Monmouth, Jill Huber NJJN Bureau. "NJ Jewish News | A righteous Choice to Help Others Survive." NJ Jewish News | A righteous Choice to Help Others Survive. Web. 24 Feb. 2017.

Gettman, Shad. "Heroes of the Holocaust; Maria Andzelm." Prezi.com. 13 Jan. 2014. Web. 25 Feb. 2017.

"Introduction to the Holocaust." United States Holocaust Memorial Museum. United States Holocaust Memorial Museum. Web. 25 Feb. 2017.

"Maria Anzelm." Heroes of the Holocaust. Web. 25 Feb. 2017.

Zullo, Allan, and Rachel. "Rachel's Review of Heroes of the Holocaust: True Stories of Rescues by Teens." Goodreads. Web. 25 Feb. 2017.

Irena Adamowicz

Jasmine Truong Him (Winner)

Irena Adamowicz was recognized as one of the righteous among the nations by Yad Vashem on the 14th of January 1985. Adamowicz was a member of the underground home army. She provided aid for people in the ghettos, lifting their spirits and giving moral support. She also delivered messages to the ghettos in different cities. Irena Adamowicz delivered messages notifying the underground leaders of the annihilation of the Jews.

The Holocaust, took place between the 30th of January 1933 to the 8th of May 1945. It was a time in history in which mass genocide and murder occurred, targeting Jews under the control of a malevolent leader, Adolf Hitler. He was a ruthless dictator. Hitler served in the German army during World War I . He believed the Jews were to blame for the country's defeat and Germany's loss of status and wealth. Hitler was designated as chancellor of Germany on the 20th of January 1933. He viewed himself as the supreme ruler of Germany. Under his rule, discrimination against people because of their race, religion, and sexual orientation became more widespread. Shops would have "No Jews Allowed" signs, and children would be segregated into separate schools based on their race and religion. Tens of thousands of Polish Jews were forced out of their homes into the ghettos by German police in September of 1939. The ghettos were captive city-states with widespread hunger and poverty. The ghettos were a temporary method of isolating Jews from society. Jews, Soviet prisoners of war, Jehovah's witnesses, homosexuals, gypsies, people with disabilities, blacks, and other minorities were alienated, discriminated against, and excluded from society. Those viewed as least useful would have their possessions confiscated and be transported from the ghettos to concentration camps first to be gassed: the weak, old, and very young. Mass gassing first occurred at the Camp of Belzec. The largest of all the five mass killing centers was Auschwitz-Birkenau where more than 2 million people were murdered. Over six million Jewish people that were sent to concentration camps were executed. Throughout the holocaust, there were many cruel medical experiments forced upon people, such as freezing young children, injecting unhealthy amounts of testosterone into men in order to "cure" homosexuality, changing people's eye colors by injecting chemicals into their eyes, and placing them in gas chambers (only Jews were killed in gas chambers). The death rate at concentration camps was extremely high and the majority of the inmates in them would be worked to death. The inmates had to live off of small pieces of bread and watered down soup. Though they were extremely physically undernourished and tortured, the people in concentration camps were still forced to hard labor in cruel conditions.

Irena Adamowicz was born in Warsaw, Poland to a Catholic family on the 11th of May 1910. As a graduate of the University of Warsaw, Adamowicz held a degree in social work. Adamowicz inspected the homes of children, and she continued this occupation during World War II. Because of her profession, Adamowicz was enabled to visit the Warsaw Ghetto. She was also a Polish-born scout leader, coordinating its activities and providing counseling as a Senior Girl Scout. Adamowicz was a resistance worker, and she took part in the educational and social work activities of the Ha-Shomer ha-Tsa'ir Jewish Zionist Youth Movement in the 1930's.

Adamowicz carried out many missions for the Jewish underground organizations in the Warsaw, Bialystok, Vilna, Kovno, and Siauliai ghettos. The ghettos were an area isolated from society; they were filthy, filled with disease and sickness, and were overpopulated. Irena also provided shelter to her Jewish friends in need.

As a member of the underground home army, Irena delivered a numerous number of messages between the different ghettos disguised as a German nun. Providing aid for the Jewish in the ghettos, Irena also uplifted the confidence of the Jews that were incarcerated. Irena Adamowicz met with the underground leaders surreptitiously to pass on information. She set out for the Vilna ghetto to inform the underground leaders on the mass destruction of Jews. With a great amount of struggle and difficulty, Irena successfully arrived and entered the sealed ghetto, Vilna. After this perilous mission, Adamowicz delivered the news to the Jews of Kaunas and Siauliai so they could form their own resistance armies in Lithuania. Although in mortal danger, Irena Adamowicz fulfilled the missions because she believed it was her duty in life.

Risking her life, Irena Adamowicz aided in delivering messages between the different ghettos. She informed the leaders of the Jewish underground about the mass destruction of Jews. After the war, Adamowicz remained in Poland and stayed in close contact with the members of the Zionist pioneering youth movements who survived. Tragically, Irena Adamowicz passed away on the 12th of August.

The Holocaust was a horrific event that is of great significance today and should not be forgotten. The thought of the death of many innocent children, people, and families reoccurring is horrendous. Irena Adamowicz was a part of the solution, a hero throughout one of the most tragic parts of our history, the Holocaust. She remained strong, courageous, and lion-hearted, a savior for the many people she rescued from possibly deadly fates. Irena Adamowicz was honored with the title of righteous among the nations by Yad Vashem because of her selflessness and bravery during World War II. Irena Adamowicz: a courageous woman with a heart filled with the love for others and a light in the dark when it was needed most.

Works Cited

Colondres, Ari R. "English 8." 26 Jan. 2017, Galt, McCaffrey Middle School, Holocaust Gallery Walk.

Yad Vashem. "Names of Righteous by Country." Names of Righteous by Country, The Holocaust Martyrs' and Heroes' Remembrance Authority, 2017, www.yadvashem.org/righteous/statistics. Accessed 23 Feb. 2017.

> https://en.wikipedia.org/wiki/Irena_Adamowicz
> http://db.yadvashem.org/righteous/family.html?language=en&itemId=4013667
> http://www.yadvashem.org/odot_pdf/Microsoft%20Word%20-%205717.pdf
> https://en.wikipedia.org/wiki/The_Holocaust
> http://www.history.com/topics/world-war-ii/the-holocaust

Agnieszka Kaniut (Kansy)

Jimena Morales

 Agnieszka Kaniut (Kansy) was a hero to a Jewish families and helped their children from the harsh labor of the concentration camp. I will describe how the Kaniut family risked her lives to save others and even manage not to get caught in the worst times. I picked Agnieszka because she respected their religion and was brave enough to take care of them. Agnieszka was a very kind and loving person that took the risk to save lives and brave enough to risk hers and her families.

I learned that the Holocaust was a very tragic war that started from January 30, 1933 to May 8, 1945, many people not just Jews died because the German leader didn't like a group of people. The camps where Jews, Gypsies, Poles, and other Slavs, and people with physical or mental disabilities were put in, were treated very badly. They didn't have a full meal, worked for hours in the hot burning sun, and slept in very crowded rooms that were infected with fleas.

Also children and women were killed because they couldn't help work in the camps. This is important because we live in a very difficult time where everyone is being discriminated because of his or her race, religion, and because they aren't a "normal" person because they have a disability. The children that weren't killed because they change their birth certificate would worked hard everyday and would have the same hard work like older people. Also if people learn about the Holocaust and know the story of an individual that went through it, then maybe they will understand and work to be in peace.

Agnieszka Kaniut would go into the Ghetto and snuck out little girls in a garbage bag. She was a maiden, acquaintances to Lea and Abraham Spiegel from Chorzów and took two of her daughters Ester and Zipora. When the Ghetto was getting worse Lea and Abraham were forced to leave daily for labor, and would leave their daughters. They knew that Germans were in the lookout for Jewish children, at first they would hide under their beds and in the cupboards but the danger grew to an unbearable level. They smuggled them out of the Ghetto in garbage and then from there Kaniut would take the girls to safety. These matters because at first Kaniut agreed to take one of the girls but Lea insisted for her to take both because she didn't want to leave one behind, and then in the end Kaniut took both.

Lea's daughters grew up in different environments because Ester had to move with Kaniut brother's wife, Maria Kansy because her sister was sick and Kaniut couldn't be seen with two girls. Zipora was later moved with a Paszyn family that were of German origin so Kaniut didn't tell them Zipora was Jewish. Mrs.Paszyn became suspicious because when bathing Zipora she had "goose skin" which she claimed was a typical Jewish phenomenon. Mrs. Paszyn didn't tell the Germans but told Zipora not to tell anyone who she was.

Ester wasn't that lucky because Maria's daughter was dating a German, and he started to become suspicious because Ester didn't go to school. Kaniut then moved her to a peasant's family who didn't know she was Jewish, she was made to work hard, was treated brutally and often be beaten by the husband. Ester was sometimes taking by Maria to visit Zipora who was now with Kaniut again.

Kaniut took care of both girls in the end when the Red Army neared Chorozów, she hid them until liberation in January 1945. After liberation Lea Spiegel returned from the camps but her husband didn't because he had been murdered, she searched for the girls and found them. Ester and Zipora didn't recognize the thin and sickly woman and at first refused to go with her. The Paszyns wished to keep Zipora but the courts rule said she has to return her to her mother. The girls and her mother tried to rebuild their lives in Chorzów but the Polish neighbors made it difficult so they left for Germany and later to Israel.

After the holocaust Agnieszka Kaniut was recognized in 27/12/2011 with Maria Kansy and was put on the Wall of Honor in Warsaw, Poland. Once she was rescued she was rescued from Chorzów, Katowice in hiding she later died in 1980. We should care because we need to recognize and be thankful for what so many righteous people did to save lives.

In conclusion Agnieszka Kaniut saved many the girls' lives and took them back to their family and also risked her live to save another person's life. The Holocaust will always be remembered because of the so many righteous people and the stories the Jews went through. Overall I learned that many righteous people saved Jews and that there are still loving and caring people in the world. People should change the way they see others and to not discriminate people because of their religion or race because we can still go through something like the Holocaust again.

Works Cited

Colondres, Ari R. "English 8." 26 Jan. 2017, Galt, McCaffrey Middle School, Holocaust Gallery Walk.

"Digital Collections." Digital Collections - Yad Vashem. Web. 24 Feb. 2017.

Yad Vashem. "Names of Righteous by Country." Names of Righteous by Country, The Holocaust Martyrs' and Heroes' Remembrance Authority, 2017, www.yadvashem.org/righteous/statistics. Accessed 23 Feb. 2017.

Maria Andzelm

Jonah Garcia

 There were many righteous gentiles that helped others during the holocaust but one question that many people are asking is, why did they? Many people in our current society question why those righteous gentiles did what they did but some of them have shared their reasons. One righteous gentile is Maria Andzelm, she is an inspiration to all of our society and if we acted more like her then the world would truly be a better place.

The Holocaust was a dark time in the world's history, whenever we look back at it we should always remember to never recreate such horrid events. The war killed around 11 million people in all but if we were to focus on the Jews themselves then you would know that nearly half of those deaths were Jews. The holocaust caused almost every major country of that time to go to war and wherever the holocaust was mentioned a chill was sent up everyone's spine. The fear alone that was caused by this war was monumental. This war has left deep scars on many people's souls, but scars can heal and thanks to many righteous gentiles some people can now heal instead of having to be buried with many others.

Maria Andzelm became popular after the holocaust for what she did but what was she before this terrifying event? Maria Andzelm was a simple farmer's girl who lived in Janowiec, Poland. Her father was Stefan Andzelm and her mother was Stefan Andzelm. She had two brothers. Her life shows that you don't need to be something important in order to do something important

Maria and her family one day decided to hide two Jews, Israel Szwarcwort and Moses Kershenbaum, by building a box under their house where the Jews could live. They were able to hide the Jews for two years until they were caught. However, while they were hiding the Jews something quite extraordinary happened. Despite the war, destruction, and fear that they were constantly living in Maria fell in love with one of the men that was living with her. Maria fell in love with Moses Kershenbaum and in the end, they truly had a happy ending. They might not have helped that many people but Maria's family still helped.

Maria Andzelm may have only helped two Jews but at least she contributed to a good cause. I learned that sometimes something simple can evolve into something bigger than expected. Now that they have read my essay they should try to be more altruistic.

Works Cited

Colondres, Ari R. "English 8." 26 Jan. 2017, Galt, McCaffrey Middle School, Holocaust Gallery Walk.

Chief/Monmouth, Jill Huber NJJN Bureau. "NJ Jewish News | A 'righteous' Choice to Help Others Survive." NJ Jewish News | A 'righteous' Choice to Help Others Survive. Web. 24 Feb. 2017.

Gettman, Shad. "Heroes of the Holocaust; Maria Andzelm." Prezi.com. 13 Jan. 2014. Web. 24 Feb. 2017.

Yad Vashem. "Names of Righteous by Country." Names of Righteous by Country, The Holocaust Martyrs' and Heroes' Remembrance Authority, 2017, www.yadvashem.org/righteous/statistics. Accessed 23 Feb. 2017.

"Maria Anzelm." Heroes of the Holocaust. Web. 24 Feb. 2017.

Julianna Bartoszkiewicz

Julianna D'Ottavio

During the time of the Holocaust, Jews were constantly being abused. Because people of this religion were to be punished, saving the life of a Jew could get one into serious trouble, if they were caught. Julianna Bartoszkiewicz, in particular, helped a family from the horrific abuse that took place during the Holocaust. Bartoszkiewicz rescued Mrs. Sredni's daughter, Esther, because of her love for Mrs. Sredni. She later welcomed Esther's husband into her household as well. Because Julianna Bartoszkiewicz put her life on the line to save the Jews, she sets an example; to do good and help those in need, instead of watching people around us suffer.

The Holocaust was a drastic period in history that caused many people to suffer and die. Hitler wanted to take over, and he was willing to destroy anything in his path. During the Holocaust, people were brutally punished for their beliefs. Hitler wanted to gain maximum control over those who did not already agree with him. As part of his plan to take over, he prepared a variety of ways to kill Jewish women, men, and children. People were hung in the streets, and if they stole food, they could have lost a hand. The Jews were sent to concentration camps, where they were forced to work hard, and survive off a pernicious diet, consisting of bread and water, with occasional vegetables. His objective here, was to make these people suffer to death. It is important to have knowledge on this spiteful topic, in order to ensure something like this does not happen to the world again.

Bartoszkiewicz was determined to help save a Holocaust victim, but she also had a family of her own. Before she began rescuing people, she was living with her husband and 3 children. She may have felt sympathy for those who needed to be rescued because she had a family of her own. Her maiden name was Kucnerowicz, and she was born on May 21, 1909. She had discovered that Esther was in danger, because she was a friend with Esther's mother (Mrs. Sredni).

Because of her relationship with Mrs. Sredni, Julianna Bartoszkiewicz was determined to help. Esther had been placed in a ghetto, which was a segregated and unsanitary location for Jews to live. Mrs. Sredni hoped her daughter could escape the dreadful place. In order to sneak out, Esther fled to the public bath, prior to being rescued to come and live with Bartoszkiewicz and her children, in January 1943. A month passed by, and Julianna Bartoszkiewicz decided to move to Warsaw with her children and Esther. She signed a Volksliste to prove her "German racial background" (db.yadvashem.org). Esther's husband, Abe (whom she'd married August 16, 1942), wrote to her, asking her permission to stay with her in Warsaw. Julianna Bartoszkiewicz delightfully agreed, and later welcomed Abe into her household as well. The Jews lived with the Bartoszkiewicz family until the "Warsaw uprising of 1944". In order to pay for all of them to eat, Julianna Bartoszkiewicz traded in older furniture, as well as her son's newspapers.

At one point, when the house was being searched for the Jews, her two guests considered jumping from the window so Bartoszkiewicz would not be punished for saving them. But she stopped them from doing so, worried for their survival. She managed to escape the city with her kids, Esther, and Abe. Esther and Abe Waldman ended up living in Lodz, while the Bartoszkiewicz family stayed in Leszno. The Waldmans visited Julianna Bartoszkiewicz and her family once more in 1996.

Julianna Bartoszkiewicz had the courage and determination to take two struggling Jews under her wing, which sends a positive message to others. Being educated on the Holocaust shows what victims had to go through. Despite the dreadful events going on around them, rescuers such as Julianna Bartoszkiewicz still remained helpful and righteous. After learning about the Holocaust and individuals who saved the lives of victims, we should be inspired to be aware of history repeating itself, help those around us who are struggling, and take advantage of having a voice.

Works Cited

Colondres, Ari R. "English 8." 26 Jan. 2017, Galt, McCaffrey Middle School, Holocaust Gallery Walk.

Yad Vashem. "Names of Righteous by Country." Names of Righteous by Country, The Holocaust Martyrs' and Heroes' Remembrance Authority, 2017, www.yadvashem.org/righteous/statistics. Accessed 23 Feb. 2017.

Yad Vashem. "The Righteous Among The Nations". The Righteous Among The Nations. Julianna Bartoszkiewicz, 2017,
http://db.yadvashem.org/righteous/righteousName.html?language=en&itemId=4065252. Accessed 14 Feb. 2017.

Natalia Abramowicz

Lizbeth Zavala

The Holocaust began on January 30, 1933, many Jewish people were killed. There was many non-Jewish people who helped the Jews escape the Nazis, they were known as a righteous gentiles. Natalia Abramowicz was one of those people, she helped Jews from Poland. She would hide the Jews in her attic for about 9 month ,until it was safe to come out. You might wonder why it all started, well the Nazis believed that getting rid of the Jews was justified. They were affecting the lives of the Germans, they would blame them for all the social and economic problems in Germany. So, many people wanted to exterminate all Jews and Germany supported the Nazis and their racist ideas.

Auschwitz-Birkenau was the largest and deadliest of the 20,000 concentration camps established by the Germans during World War II. The concentration camps were made to exterminate the Jewish people. Auschwitz-Birkenau the place where the Nazis would torture the Jews to death or would keep them captive. The Jews would be at the concentration camps for a long period of time until the Nazis have decide to kill them. The Jews were very lucky that people tried to help them escape because without their help Jews would not be able to escape the Nazis. Natalia Abramowicz was not the only one who helped in her family, they would help save Jews, too. Natalia Abramowicz's parents are unknown but her family was Evangelical Protestants.

As a child, many of Natalia Abramowicz's' rights were taken away, the Jews could not do many things. Some of the things they could not do were stay out after 8pm in public. They also could not run a business, and if they did run a business the would be fired. Jewish children could not go to the same school with the non-Jewish kids. So they were separated to go to two different schools. If they did not follow the given rules, the Jews would either be killed or beaten. After the holocaust had ended, about 11 million people in total died, and about 6 million of those victims were Jewish. There were also about 1 million children killed during the holocaust.

The word holocaust is a Greek word for " holokauston", which refers to sacrifice by fire. Some of the righteous Gentiles were killed because they were caught helping the Jews. Natalia Abramowicz was spotted helping the Jews escape in 1979. She was beaten badly and later on died on January 1, 1979. Many Jews were killed because their religion was different than others ,and for standing up for what they believe in. The holocaust is a very important event to us in the United States because we now have freedom of religion. To have in mind how many people died just for being different.

The word holocaust is a Greek word for " holokauston", which refers to "sacrifice by fire". "Sacrifice by fire" means that the Nazis' persecution and planned slaughter of the Jewish people. Over 200,000 people are estimated to have been holocaust perpetrators. No one had any respect for the Jews. If Natalia Abramowicz and other righteous Gentiles didn't help save Jew, there would have been more people dead. There were people who do try to make a difference and help save the Jews escape the Nazis.

I like to sometimes think about how the world would be if something in the past that affected the world would have happened differently. Like the holocaust, the Nazis going after the Jews for being a different religion. That has impacted the United States because now we have freedom of religion.so everyone that died during the holocaust were heroes and a big help to the United States. They helped people realize that being different isn't bad and doesn't mean you have to kill someone, because of it.

I chose to write about Natalia Abramowicz, she used a method of hiding to save the Jews. I learned that the Abramowicz family had a tree in their honor because they all help save many Jews. People should respect everyone because many children died during the holocaust. They were killed when they arrive at a killing center or killed immediately after birth. Even though people tried to help not everyone was saved, lots of people died during the holocaust. The holocaust is something that no one should ever forget about, in honor of all those who died.

Works Cited

Colondres, Ari R. "English 8." 26 Jan. 2017, Galt, McCaffrey Middle School, Holocaust Gallery Walk.

http://www.sixmillioncrucifixions.com/Auschwitz-Birkenau.html

Yad Vashem. "Names of Righteous by Country." Names of Righteous by Country, The Holocaust Martyrs' and Heroes' Remembrance Authority, 2017, www.yadvashem.org/righteous/statistics. Accessed 23 Feb. 2017.

Helena Kurek/Sara Blam

Madison Blank

The Holocaust is a part of history that will never be erased or forgotten. All too many people suffered under the rule of genocide and the unjust will of a nation. Under the will, so many people did what they could for the protection of individuals they never knew, all because that would be one more person saved from death. However, by saving them, consequences would be heavy. Orders would be given and with short discussions whole families would be dying, or more camps would be built. The woman I picked continued to keep people she barely knew under her care and protection in circumstances that could have easily been against her. Helena Kurek, who lived with her mother and stepfather, and held out open arms to people that needed it most. She hid Jewish men and women in her home that weren't found even with the on property investigation by Nazi police, and went to the extremes to ensure lives could be saved on her own time. Pushing her own struggles aside, she kept doing the right thing, even if it meant disregarding the law.

There is a lot to learn and take in from the events in the Holocaust. We should recognize exactly how much power our leaders have and what their decisions can do to impact the lives of not only one nation, but potentially the whole world, as well. Adolf Hitler went to prison and wrote about his awful thoughts, found in Mein Kampf. Despite so, he became a strong political candidate, and gained presidency of Germany in 1934. Even before he used his position as a dictatorship, he eliminated all rivaling political ideologies and groups, soon abolishing the office of president yet keeping all the powers. Considering all Hitler did next with no hesitation, we should bare in mind that his executive decisions were final, just how decisions that can be made in our government today are final. Having a leader that silences the voice of the people he serves cannot happen anymore, we should be aware of our rights and use them to the extent we feel comfortable with regarding voicing our opinions. With his power, Hitler controlled the nation and broke out in war over Europe. He segregated citizens by religion and put those he didn't agree with through torture, famine, and death. His ideas were so unreasonable and discriminatory, yet with his power he put millions of Jewish people through suffering for years with nobody stopping him. He was greedy for power and wanted to unite a falsely lead nation of united and unjust countries under hate and discrimination.

Helena survived through the Holocaust, the life she carried on from that point is much calmer compared to all she did prior. She married one of the men she snuck out of a concentration camp by the oil refinery right beside it, the one she worked at. His name was Mozes Blam, and she moved with him to Israel in 1948, it is also said that she converted to Judaism. She changed her name to Sara during their marriage, which is all that has been recorded of what her life was like after the Holocaust. Helena Kurek still proceeded to go on with her life after everything she lived through and did. She didn't quit after peace was found, and she kept moving on.

Helena Kurek rushed to be available aid once Eastern Galicia was overtaken by the Germans, and continued to help them till the end of the war. She opened up to her Jewish acquaintances immediately once Galicia was inhabited and hid them during the Aktionen, while ghettos were being enforced into their area. More people started to hear about what help Helena and her family was giving out, unfortunately, word got out to Ukrainian nationalists; leading to the murder of her stepfather. That did not stop her, and she continued to give out help. At a forced-labor camp, she snuck out and also hid multiple Jews. The police had their assumptions of Kurek and her mother hiding people in their home, and searched along with interrogating the two women forcefully. They were beaten and arrested. Luckily, nobody was found in the home by the police. The seven people that were in hiding did flee, and in the summer of 1944 were safe. Helena Kurek should be thanked for all the work she did during the Holocaust to protect and defend the Jewish people attacked by hate. She could have easily looked away from the violence and refuse to give protection, but she kept defending those that came to her from the beginning to the end of the war. By not only hiding, but also sneaking out Jewish people from their controlled and brutal environment, she could have faced horrible consequences but decided to take such a chance.

Helena Kurek went to great lengths to save the lives of so many people, despite the risks of having her life in danger during the process. She was a brave woman who did things some of us wouldn't dare to do. While working on this essay, it put into perspective exactly how many people were willing to go out of their way to help a minority with so much pressure and judgment upon them. It really made me think about how lucky we are today, to not be in the middle of such a violent and aggressive time like that. People followed through with faith and compassion alone, and that is powerful, to live through the odds and go on with trust and beliefs. Though the numbers are only a few by now, you can see and meet people who were alive during the Holocaust and understand the struggles they lived through. There are opportunities you have currently that won't be around for your future family. You can understand what circumstances they lived under and how they managed to keep their hope through days passing. There were no promises of a tomorrow, they could only hope. Show respect for things they had to go through that you wouldn't put on yourself or any other person, learn that what they lived through is still impacting our lives today. Diversity is accepted more than it used to be, and just dozens of years ago it wasn't. Be grateful of the life you have currently, despite its downfalls, there can always be worse.

Works Cited

"Adolf." Hitler's Rise to Power. Web. 24 Feb. 2017.

Colondres, Ari R. "English 8." 26 Jan. 2017, Galt, McCaffrey Middle School, Holocaust Gallery Walk.

Yad Vashem. "Names of Righteous by Country." Names of Righteous by Country, The Holocaust Martyrs' and Heroes' Remembrance Authority, 2017, www.yadvashem.org/righteous/statistics. Accessed 23 Feb. 2017.

Marchlewicz Bronislaw

Madison Ligaya Felix

Marchlewicz Bronislaw, was a Polish gentile that risked his life to save Jewish people during the holocaust. He risked his life and title as resistance officer, and during World War II risked his title as a member of the Polish police. He saved many people during the Holocaust and earned the "Medal of Righteous Among Nations." He truly is a brave person, and people today should be lucky that they never have to deal with this type of pressure and stress, like it was during the Holocaust.

In 1949, he was arrested for participating in fascist political life in Poland, in the years 1927-1937. So basically, he was arrested for trying to help save people that had not done anything wrong, but Germans thought that because those people were Jewish, they didn't deserve to have the same respect and rights as common men. In 2004, Bronislaw was awarded the medal of the Righteous among the Nations awarded by the Institute in Jerusalem Yad Vashem.

People should care about this because, they don't think about what it would be like if they were part of the holocaust. They don't have to think about if they would risk their life to save other people that have been suffering. Sadly, Marchlewicz had to make their decisions and chose to risk his life and title to help save Jews.

Before the war Marchlewicz Bronislaw was the director of the police station in Otwock before the war of 1937 and during World War II as a member of the Polish police. At the same time, active in the resistance movement as an officer of the Polish National Team Independent, Security Corps and Army. After the war, he was arrested for participating in fascist political life in Poland in the years 1927-1937.

During World War II, he was also a member of the anti-Nazi resistance movement and had saved plenty of people during the holocaust. Bronisław Marchlewicz had helped Maria Borowiecki when she was a young orphan when someone brought her to a police station which Bronislaw was heading. He gave her to his neighbor who hid her unit priest, who issued her with a fake baptism certificate under the a name of Halina Brioza. He also helped her older cousin Hanna Kamińska-Goldfeld whom she later reunited with to give Bronslaw Marchlewicz the "Metal of Righteous Among Nations." He also ordered the release of a group of captured Jews that were captured in a rai. He was informed of every baby that was left on the doorstep of the police station and had a deal that his wife would take care of every one of the babies as if they were her own.

Bronislaw Marchlewicz was a part of the Holocaust as a Polish gentile that risked his life to save Jews. He was also a righteous gentile that served during WWII, and helped save Jews during the Holocaust. He saved many people and helped reunite two family members after the Holocaust was over and they in return rewarded him with the "Metal of Righteous Among Nations." This essay helped learn about him and how he risked his title as resistance officer, and as a Polish Police, to help save people.

Works Cited

"Bronisław Marchlewicz." Wikipedia. Wikimedia Foundation, 18 Jan. 2017. Web. 24 Feb. 2017.

Colondres, Ari R. "English 8." 26 Jan. 2017, Galt, McCaffrey Middle School, Holocaust Gallery Walk.

Kurek Ewa. "Jewish children in Monasteries" "Marchlewicz Bronislaw." Story of Rescue - Marchlewicz Bronislaw | Polscy Sprawiedliwi. Web. 24 Feb. 2017.

Yad Vashem. "Names of Righteous by Country." Names of Righteous by Country, The Holocaust Martyrs' and Heroes' Remembrance Authority, 2017, www.yadvashem.org/righteous/statistics. Accessed 23 Feb. 2017.

Adamowicz, Irena

Makynna Snow

There were certain people that risked their lives to rescue people. There were a lot of people that risked their lives to rescue people, but one person I thought really risked their life was Adamowicz, Irena. My evidence works because Adamowicz, Irena saved a lot of people and she really risked her life to save so much people. Irena did not care if she would die in the process, she only wanted to save the poor innocent lives that Hitler and the Nazis were turning into horrible ones. Adamowicz, Irena was a very caring and loving person and she wanted to at least try to save as much people as she could.

The Holocaust was not a good thing at all because Hitler made the Jews lives horrible. Hitler captured over 6 million Jews and made their lives so bad. Each Jew was a part of the Holocaust for about 2 years that's how long the Holocaust went on. My evidence is good because it shows how the Jews lives were ruined by Hitler and their lives were ruined forever after the Holocaust because they had all of those images still in their head. Many Jews didn't even make it out of the Holocaust alive. If the Jews did make it out of the Holocaust alive, they still had so many bad memories and bad images in their head so their life would never be the same.

Irena was born on May 11, 1910. Her job was that she was a Resistance worker and a Polish-born Scout leader during World War II. Irena's childhood was good. She was born in Warsaw, to a Polish noble family and held a degree in social work from the University of Warsaw before World War II. Irena did not have kids, so she would want to save as many children as she could because she did not want their parents to be without them. Since Irena never had children she did not know what it felt like to have kids. She always wanted one so she knew it must have felt really good to have one and how much their parents loved them, so she wanted to save all of them. Irena was a very truthful person so when she said she was going to do something or made a promise about something she would always try to go through with it. If Irena promised people she would save their children's lives she would try and do anything in her power to keep that promise. She would give the children some of her food and she would go without eating sometimes so that the kids would get more food. She would try and do everything in her power to save all the children's lives even if she didn't know them.

Irena saved a lot of Jews. Some of them she had reasons for like she knew them and some of them she didn't know and she just wanted to be nice and save the children. Adamowicz, Irena was in the Holocaust for a very long time. She knew what life was like during that time and it was not fun. She wanted to save as much people as she could even if it meant she had to risk her life in the process as well. She made many life threatening decisions to save other people and even young children. My evidence is valid because she really had to put her life on the line and she did not care if she died in the process, she just wanted and needed to save the lives of the other innocent people. She also did not care if they were old or young she just wanted to save them from the Holocaust. Irena really liked helping and saving other people's lives. She was a very kind person as well and all of her wonderful and righteous traits helped her to save all of the people that she did save. Even if she couldn't save some people's lives it would hurt her that's how much she cared about saving the innocents people's lives. Adamowicz, Irena was a very good person and she cared about everyone's lives not only hers.

There were a lot of people that had horrible lives in the Holocaust for many years. I learned that the Holocaust was a not a very good thing at all. The Holocaust was not good because Hitler made their lives suck if the Jews were involved in it. Hitler and the Nazis made all the Jews lives horrible if they were in the Holocaust and even if they weren't. If the Jews weren't in the Holocaust they could have had family members that he took away and that would have been just as hard for them. The Holocaust was a very big and important part of people's lives because it made their lives miserable. Irena tried as hard as she could to save as many lives of innocent people as she could and she tried her best.

Works Cited

Colondres, Ari R. "English 8." 26 Jan. 2017, Galt, McCaffrey Middle School, Holocaust Gallery Walk.

"Irena Adamowicz." Wikipedia. Wikimedia Foundation, 05 Feb. 2017. Web. 25 Feb. 2017.

Yad Vashem. "Names of Righteous by Country." Names of Righteous by Country, The Holocaust Martyrs' and Heroes' Remembrance Authority, 2017, www.yadvashem.org/righteous/statistics. Accessed 23 Feb. 2017.

Zofia Bania

Michelle Abarca (Winner)

For my Righteousness Gentile Essay I am writing about Zofia Bania, a Polish woman who helped save the lives of a Jewish couple. Zofia Bania was a Polish woman buying basic goods from a small shop owned by Frania and Israel Rubinek who were a Jewish couple. Without knowing, Zofia became a part of a dangerous, life saving situation during the time of the Holocausts. She became a Righteous Gentile.

Zofia was born in 1907 and was just a poor farmer in the village from Wolch when she met Frania and Israel. Zofia would often go and buy basic goods from their small shop in Pinczow Poland. Often times when Zofia was unable to pay, Frania would give her food and other items on credit. The two women got to know each other and became good friends.

When Frania and Israel heard about the fate other Jews were facing when they were sent to concentration camps, Israel decided to build a bunker underneath their store, and hide there until the Germans were gone rounding Jews up. Although, when the Germans were gone, Frania and Israel weren't able to leave to a farther country. Frania was expecting a baby soon in 8 months. So they went to a nearby town instead.

Later on, the couple heard Zofia was looking for them, so they decided to return to Pinczow. With the help of a trusted Polish man, and hidden in a wagon, they finally arrived and visited Zofia. The couple stayed with Zofia and her family in her one room house.

When Frania and Israel first arrived to Zofia's house, Frania immediately thought, "I'm going to survive through the war here." The first few weeks though, Zofia's husband Ludwig was not exactly on board with Frania and Israel staying with them in his home. Frania and Israel had to be very nice or bribe Ludwig to help keep the couple a secret from the community knowing they were hiding in his house. Even though Ludwig, Zofia's husband was not fully on board, the whole family, along with their six-year-old son Maniek helped to keep the couple a secret from the Germans.

Zofia and their family had to do several tactics to keep the couple a secret. Her husband bought a dog that barked every time someone approached the home. This gave them a signal to signal the family to keep quiet and hide. They moved their son's bed to cover the underneath cellar to hide the family in the cellar. There was a close call when Israel was sick, hiding in the cellar while the Germans were in Zofia's house, Maniek had to pretend that he was sick to cover up Israel's coughing coming from the cellar. Zofia and her family were determined to help the Jewish couple at all cost.

All in all, Zofia and her family helped the Jewish escape their terrible fate of ending in concentration camps like all other Jews did. Zofia and her family faced risks for hiding the couple, but they were determined to help because Frania was her friend. Someone who had helped her in times when she had no money to pay for her goods. Even though Zofia and her family had to go through all that danger, they made a difference in someone's life, influenced others around them, and today we still look back at these days of the Holocaust.

Works Cited

Colondres, Ari R. "English 8." 26 Jan. 2017, Galt, McCaffrey Middle School, Holocaust Gallery Walk.

Yad Vashem. "Names of Righteous by Country." Names of Righteous by Country, The Holocaust Martyrs' and Heroes' Remembrance Authority, 2017, www.yadvashem.org/righteous/statistics. Accessed 23 Feb. 2017.

Maria Adamkowska

Miriam Valerio Osuna

I will be writing about Maria Adamkowska and how she helped Jews during the Holocaust. She let Jews live with her and all of them survived except for the one that died in hiding from sickness , but other than that no one else died meaning she did her job well . She did the right thing knowing she could die if things didn't go as planned. I picked Maria Adamkowska because she was a good woman who helped Jews by hiding them, giving them shelter, food, and water . In total she helped 5 Jews, not many people were willing to endanger their lives to help at least one Jew while Maria saved 5 Jews. She risked her life , as not many accomplished but few did by helping the Jews . Many people knew that the Jews didn't really do anything bad , actually they knew they didn't do anything bad at all that they were just trying to have a good life and help their families ,but most of the non-Jews were too scared for their own families to help anyone.

I learned that many people that were not Jews helped Jews knowing that they could get into serious consequences if they go caught. . There were many righteous people during the Holocaust and they are very important because without them even more Jews would've died. I learned that the Holocaust was basically that the Germans were being racist against Jews and that the Holocaust can happen any day , even today cause there are many people out there who are racist and don't like the fact of change or difference. People like Maria Adamkowska are heroes of the Holocaust . Maria saved 4 people seems like nothing at the time but looking at it now she saved them and generations to come . Without her kindness of the heart people wouldn't be here today, many family's owe their life to her .Maria is not the only one who saved Jews though a bunch of people did and yes some got caught and killed but it still matters that they tried.

Maria's birth date is unknown , she was a Roman Catholic ,and she was a teacher during the war .Roman Catholics believe in resurrection of the body and Jesus, I'm guessing that was one reason Maria helped Jews because she believed in Jesus who also sacrificed himself to help others. Since she wasn't a Jew she didn't get taken and she could help Jews from getting taken or at least attempt to. Also it was a known fact that Maria's profession was teaching, since she worked with kids she probably felt that if she could to save Jews she should, so that the future kids that were coming would be safe from all the fighting and killing of the Holocaust. Also since she was only a teacher meaning nothing big or important the Germans didn't really pay attention to her so she could hide Jews and no one noticed.

She hid and arranged shelters for Jews . The Jews that survived because of her are evidence that she was a righteous person .Also the fact that she put herself in harm's way knowing she could get punished or even worse killed along with the Jews she helped show her righteousness . I think the reason she saved these Jews was that she knew that what the Germans were doing was wrong ,so she helped who she could. I think you should care about my evidence because there weren't a lot of people who were like Maria that put their life on the line and did what Maria did. People who were unselfish, kind, caring, and very noble. So it important that we recognize the people who did , this woman was very lucky to not get caught and the Jews she helped were even luckier cause if she wouldn't have helped them they would have died, been put in concentration camps , or they would have to be hiding all by themselves where no one could help them .

Maria Adamkowska was a good woman who risked her life to save Jews , she would hide the Jews so that the Germans wouldn't capture them . I learned that in a state of crisis there will always be heroes there to help. Even though they won't be superheroes with superpowers they are heroes that have powers that come from their heart. We all have heroes , and Maria Adamkowska was and forever will be a hero to all the lives she helped by having kindness in her heart. I think we should all just be happy we have people who are glad to help anyone and everyone they can .We have to step aside and thank all these "heroes" we have .The Holocaust was a really bad point in history but it brought out some good in people so remember to always see the bright side of things.

Works Cited

Colondres, Ari R. "English 8." 26 Jan. 2017, Galt, McCaffrey Middle School, Holocaust Gallery Walk.

Yad Vashem. "Names of Righteous by Country." Names of Righteous by Country, The Holocaust Martyrs' and Heroes' Remembrance Authority, 2017, www.yadvashem.org/righteous/statistics. Accessed 23 Feb. 2017.

http://db.yadvashem.org/righteous/family.html?language=en&itemId=4013666

http://db.yadvashem.org/righteous/righteousName.html?language=en&itemId=4013666

Sarah Blam

Montserrat Pintor Paramo

Sarah Blam, also known as Helena Kurek, was a huge righteous hero in the Holocaust because of her bravery and willing ability to help people no matter their race or beliefs. She helped many Jews escape from camps and let them stay in her house for shelter and a home, which is very important in my point of view. Because of her, many lives were saved. This essay is an opportunity for me and many other people to learn about the Holocaust terror and the bravery of people, like Sarah, who helped Jews live a longer life and landed them a helping hand when it was needed the most.

On 1941, a genocide called The Holocaust began. This event took place in Europe and Germany where many Jews were harshly killed because of their race or beliefs. This included six million European Jews, which was two thirds of the entire Jewish population including 1.5 million children. The Jews were taken to concentration camps and gas chambers where they were forcefully separated from their families. The thing that got to me the most though, was that the Nazi doctors would do experiments with children making their eye color change and they even froze kids till death. I ask myself, how could a human's heart be so dark and heartless with no feeling for the victim at all. At the concentration camps, they were forced to work and march until it was their turn to get killed by being gassed to death. The camps also made the Jews wear the same striped uniform so they could easily identify their victims. They were barely fed, there only food being watered down soup and a piece of bread while living in a horrible environment, which was a dusty land field fenced all around. Many tried to hide before the Nazi came for them, but not all of them had the success of not ever being found. Some were discovered years later and taken to the camps being treated worse. If they tried to escape, they instantly were murdered. No human being has the right to live such a horrible experience no matter how bad they are. This event is very important because it can still happen again.

Sarah Blam was born in Eastern Galicia where she lived with her mother and stepfather. She had always been a happy and giving young girl, which her mother loved about her. She began later on in her life working in a local oil refinery, which was located right next to a forced- labor camp of Jews. This gave her an opportunity to help Jews escape from the camp and come hide at her house. After many years of this, the Ukrainian nationalists killed her father on September 1943. This didn't bring her down though; she kept going even when they suspected of her. She married a Jew who hid in her house for many years named Moshe after World War ll .

Sarah saved the Jews who were brought to the camp next to her job because she couldn't stand seeing the harsh things the soldiers did to them. She had the wise idea then to carry on the word that she would give her home as a refuge to all the Jews who needed it. She also helped the Jews in the camp by her job escape and took them to her home for shelter. There she fed them, washed them , and clothed them with nothing in return but to see families reunite. She was a very brave person for doing this because she didn't let any person down no matter what. She kept on her promise even when the police suspected of her, but had no evidence to accuse her. This is a great example of a hero who helped anyone in need.

Sarah Blam was a huge example of a righteous person because of her ability to help those in need. Overall, I learned that you don't have to have a cape or superpowers to be a hero, you just need to be able to help anyone in need from the bottom of your heart. Sarah didn't need anything in order for her to save lives and be a hero but the confidence and ability to want to help someone out. Everyone can be a hero even if you just stop someone from being bullied to saving the world. Nothing is too small for being an objective for you to be a hero. Everyone should be able to be treated the same and be able to help someone out EVERYDAY from now on. I know that from this day forward I will look at the word and myself differently since researching Sarah Blam and learning about the Holocaust. I will see the Holocaust as an insult to humanity. I will now also wake up now every day being thankful for life and for what I have because someone out there in the world is really suffering and fighting to survive when I am living a wonderful life people would give anything to have.

Works Cited

Colondres, Ari R. "English 8." 26 Jan. 2017, Galt, McCaffrey Middle School, Holocaust Gallery Walk.

"Digital Collections." Digital Collections - Yad Vashem. Web. 24 Feb. 2017.

"Main Page." Wikipedia. Wikimedia Foundation, 23 Feb. 2017. Web. 24 Feb. 2017.

Yad Vashem. "Names of Righteous by Country." Names of Righteous by Country, The Holocaust Martyrs' and Heroes' Remembrance Authority, 2017, www.yadvashem.org/righteous/statistics. Accessed 23 Feb. 2017.

Unearthing the Jar

Myracle P. Franco (Winner)

There are those who consider themselves as heroes. There are those who earned the title. Irena Sendler, a Polish nurse, humanitarian, and social worker rightfully earns the title- hero. She was courageous, inspirational, and displayed noble qualities. She risked her life to save thousands of Jewish children in Poland. Irena's experiences and character influences her heroic actions. Her determination and perseverance helps her through all challenges.

Irena Sendler's early life was her foundation that would influence her decisions later in life. Irena Sendler (Krzyżanowski) was born to Dr. Stanisław Krzyżanowski and Janina Krzyżanowska on February 15, 1910 in Otwock, Poland. She grew up in Otwock, which was fifteen miles southeast of a Jewish community in Warsaw. She was an only child. Around the age of seven, her father died of typus and Jewish community leaders offered to help her mother with Irena's education. Her mother declined the offer. This is an example of her early exposure to charity and community. This is pivotal to her development because she learned early in life the value of sharing.

Irena's parents had an exceptional influence on their daughter. Stanisław Krzyżanowski, her father, was a doctor who mainly treated less fortunate Jews. Irena's father made an extreme impact on his daughter because he saved lives. Later on, she took that example and inspiration, and applied it to her life. She went on to save thousands of Jewish children during the Holocaust. The following quote is important because it shows her respect and honor for her father. It also shows that she learned so much from him. His influence inspired her great works later on in life. She was willing to sacrifice her safety for the greater good, and for this reason, she is a hero.

"I was taught by my father that when someone is drowning, you don't just ask if they can swim, you just jump in and help." –Irena Sendler

Irena's education is important to her character development. She studied Polish literature and joined a Polish Socialist party at Warsaw University. She did not agree with the ghetto-bench system that was present at some of the pre-war Polish universities. The ghetto-bench system was a form of segregation in the seating of students at the universities. As an outcome of her public protest, she was suspended from the University of Warsaw for about three years. This is an example of her determination and her courage. She is goal oriented and firm in her values. She expressed her beliefs with no hesitation.

In addition, soon after her education she wanted to settle down and have a family. She started a family with her first husband, Mieczysław Sendler in 1931, but later divorced. She then married a Jewish friend, Stefan Zgrzembski, from her university years. She had three children with him. In 1959, she divorced Zgrzembski, and remarried her first husband, Mieczysław Sendler.

Irena is one true hero. The meaning of "hero" is a person admired for courage, outstanding achievement, and noble qualities. Although Irena Sendler did remarkable things, she remained humble about her achievements. The following quote is important because it shows her simple view of herself. Her sacrifices are big in the eyes of the people. But, she remains humble throughout her life.

"Heroes do extraordinary things. What I did was not extraordinary, it was normal." – Irena Sendler

Irena served the Polish Underground in a German-occupied Warsaw, and was head of the children's section of Żegota. Żegota was a Holocaust-era cryptonym or code name for the council to aid Jews in Poland. As an employee of the Social Welfare Department, she obtained a permit to enter the Warsaw Ghetto. During her visits, she wore a Star of David as a sign of solidarity with the Jewish people.

One achievement that truly stands out during the time of World War II, is when Irena and ten co-workers helped smuggle 2,500 Jewish children out of the Warsaw Ghetto. She helped care for them, provided false identities for them, and gave them shelter. As a Polish Catholic, she taught the children prayers, since their false identities identified them Catholic instead of Jewish. The children only knew her by her code name, Jolanta.

Ms. Sendler and her co-workers smuggled the children out by using an ambulance and a stretcher. Other times the children were smuggled through a courthouse. Children also escaped through sewer pipes and other secret passages. Sometimes trolleys carried the children out in sacks, trunks, and suitcases. Mothers feared so much for their children, that they made the choice to give their children to Ms. Sendler in order to protect them. It was difficult to have those goodbyes. Irena's job was very tough. She made sacrifices and overcame the challenges.

Ms. Sendler and her co-workers comforted the children in anyway that they could. Some of the children who were smuggled out stayed hidden by the Catholic nuns. Sometimes Ms. Sendler would also escort the children herself to reassure them. Ms. Sendler and her co-workers kept the names of the children in jars, and the jars were carefully hidden from sight.

Unfortunately, Ms. Sendler was caught, tortured, and sentenced to death. She managed to evade execution by persuading the guards to spare her life. Also other women were with her in the prison cell. When she was too weak, the women would help her up and secretly aid her torture wounds. Sadly, these women were later murdered by a firing squad. It was a miracle she survived. Her amazing courage helped her persevere. Thankfully, the children she saved saw the light of day.

Later on, Irena Sendler acknowledged the exceptional people who helped her save many lives. She remained humble, because saving the innocent lives was the right thing to do during the events of the Holocaust. The following quote is important because she recognizes the value of life and her strong belief in children. She wanted them to have a chance to experience life and make a change in this world. That is why she worked so hard to save them.

"Every child saved with my help and the help of all the wonderful secret messengers, who today are no longer living, is the justification of my existence on this earth, and not a title to glory." –Irena Sendler

Ms. Sendler inspiring story was sadly not known for nearly sixty years. Until, a teacher from Uniontown High School in Uniontown, KA showed his students an article on Irena Sendler for their National History Day competition project. At that moment, Ms. Sendler's story was unearthed.

Later on in life, Irena was awarded various awards. She won Poland's highest honor, the Order of the White Eagle. Another award was the Jan Karski award for Valor and Courage. The ceremony for this event was held on October 23, 2003 in Washington, D.C. Ms. Sendler was also sent a personal letter from Pope John Paul II, which praised her wartime effort. A book by Norman Conard, was written about her journey during the Holocaust called, Life in a Jar. In 2007, she was nominated for the Noble Piece Prize and received, the Order of the Smile award. Which at that time, Ms. Sendler was the oldest recipient of the award. She died on May 12, 2008 at the age of 98. She also has various street signs and plaques in her name. Ms. Sendler has a headstone on her grave in her honor in Warsaw Powąski Cemetery.

Irena Sendler did not consider herself as a hero. As she once said, "We are not heroes. I continue to have qualms of conscience that I did so little." With her courage to save others, inspiration, and noble qualities; Irena Sendler classifies as a hero. Imagine, as she dropped numerous names in the simple, jar. She would go on and later, unearth it. Through this simple act, she was securing the possibility of a future for these young children. She gave them a chance at life; a chance to begin their own journey.

There is much to learn from this remarkable human. It was an interesting journey learning about her past and how it to came to influence her actions in the future. Her traits of strength and unselfishness at this difficult time in history are very moving. We can only aspire to be as inspirational as Irena Sandler, someday. I have learned a lot from this humble hero and will take her lessons and values to heart. I am grateful for her hard work, sacrifices, and contributions to the community.

Sources:

https://en.wikipedia.org/wiki/Irena_Sendler
http://www.irenasendler.org/
www.jewishvirtuallibrary.org
https://en.wikipedia.org/wiki/Stanis%C5%82aw_Krzy%C5%BCanowski
http://www.yadvashem.org/
http://www.chabad.org/
https://www.kshs.org/p/kansas-history-day-holocaust-and-life-in-a-jar/14874/
https://www.youtube.com/watch?v=HA6kvHRcPGU&app=desktop

Jan Karski

Natalie McConnell

 To define a hero is difficult. In the dictionary a hero is any person admired for courage and nobility. But, it is up to the individual to define what a hero is from their point of view. Jan Karski is a hero for many reasons, he tried to find ways to help stop the holocaust, he was very courageous, intelligent, and he lived to tell the tale.

The Holocaust was a very hard time in history. Over 6 million Jews died, and Over 11 million people in general were killed. Many Jews were forced into concentration camps where they were forced to work with only 500-600 calories to eat each day. There are very few survivors from the holocaust that are still alive today. Jan Karski is one of the very few survivors.

Jan Karski was born in 1914, in Lodz Poland. He was the youngest of eight children. His father died when he was young, so he always had great respect for his mother. Through school, Karski was a good student. He excelled most at history, poetry, and literature. Karski finished school in 1931, but his mother did not want him to go into the military, so instead he went to college. He majored in diplomatic science and law, and received his master's degree in 1935. After graduating, Karski found a job in the League of Nations. He became the secretary of the Department of Immigration, and the secretary of personnel in the Foreign Ministry.

Karski is most known for his daring mission to try and stop the holocaust. He was smuggled into the Warsaw Ghetto as well as into the Izbica transit camp to gather first hand accounts about the plight of European Jews under Nazis rule. He also pleaded with Anthony Eden, the British foreign secretary and President Franklin D. Roosevelt for allied action to stop the holocaust. In September 1939 Jan Karski joined the Polish army, but he was captured and taken to a detention camp in what now is Ukraine. Luckily Karski was able to escape from the detention camp. After he escaped Jan Karski joined the Polish underground army. In late 1940 while on a mission to gather information about how Jews were treated in ghettos, he was captured by the Gestapo and brutally tortured. Fearing that under duress he might reveal secrets, Karski slashed his wrists, but was sent to a hospital from which the underground helped him escape.

Jan Karski remained in the United States after conveying the news about how Jews were treated in concentration camps to Franklin D. Roosevelt. He earned a PhD from Georgetown University's School of Foreign Service. Karski refused to return to Poland after the war, so he spent the remainder of his life in Washington promoting Polish freedom and serving for many decades as a professor at Georgetown. In conclusion, Jan Karski made a huge impact on how Jews were treated during the Holocaust.

Works Cited
Colondres, Ari R. "English 8." 26 Jan. 2017, Galt, McCaffrey Middle School, Holocaust Gallery Walk.

"Jan Karski." United States Holocaust Memorial Museum. United States Holocaust Memorial Museum. Web. 24 Feb. 2017.

"Jan Karski." Wikipedia. Wikimedia Foundation, 17 Feb. 2017. Web. 24 Feb. 2017.

Yad Vashem. "Names of Righteous by Country." Names of Righteous by Country, The Holocaust Martyrs' and Heroes' Remembrance Authority, 2017, www.yadvashem.org/righteous/statistics . Accessed 23 Feb. 2017.

"Jan Karski." United States Holocaust Memorial Museum. United States Holocaust Memorial Museum. Web. 24 Feb. 2017.

Krystyna Danko

Mattingly

Krystyna Danko was a polish gentile who rescued many people from death's grasp. She sacrificed many things to help keep the Kokoszko family alive. Without her, people would have not been able to escape the Otwock Ghetto, meaning she saved people from an almost sure death when they would have been shipped to a concentration camp. She was a phenomenal person, which was proven by her actions. She was a true righteous person who demonstrated a great example of what should all recognize. She was also a courageous person who diminished her fear to save desperate people.

The Holocaust was a large genocide committed by Adolf Hitler and his Nazis. It was a state-sponsored persecution of Jews and many other religions in which about 6 million Jews were murdered. In 1933, Adolf Hitler was elected and became chancellor of Germany. He had many followers and even had a political party named the Nazis. They believed that they were the superior race and felt like many other groups or races, were inferior to Germany and it's community. So, Adolf Hitler mainly targeted and persecuted Jews by sending them to communities that were cut off from the world, called ghettos. Hitler and his Nazis created over 1,000 ghettos in hope to isolate the Jews from the German Society. The ghettos were not safe and didn't provide much food, water or shelter. Ghettos were surrounded by fencing and barbed wire and they were located in the poorer areas of communities. Some ghettos were only around for a couple of days, others could still be functioning over the course of multiple years. Jews were forced to wear armbands, with the Star of David on it inside the ghettos. The armbands would signify to the Nazis who were Jews. Because the armbands told Nazis who were Jews, the Nazis were able to treat the Jews the worst. The ghettos also made people slave away, doing hard labor to build buildings for the Nazis. Then after a few years of Jews having been forced in the ghettos, the Jews were then sent to concentration camps. Hitler sent these people to the concentration camps to exterminate the rest of the Jews, along with many other cultures, races, and people he felt had mental stability issues. The camps were ran by the Nazi's. The Concentration camps were his attempt to what he called "The Final Solution". These camps, however, were torturous places meant for killing and murder. Sbicjasbdi

Krystyna Danko was born on the 9th day of July 1917 in Otwock Poland. She grew up as an orphan with a rough childhood. At a young age, Krystyna befriended the Kokoszko family. Several years prior to the beginning of World War ll, Krystyna Danko formed a strong friendship with the oldest daughter of the Kokoszko family, Lusia. They attended the same high school, and were classmates. She stayed with the Kokoszko family and stayed with them for quite a bit of time. She discovered warmth and was comfortable in the Kokoszko family home. Because of the Kokoszko family allowing Krystyna to stay with them, Krystyna felt that she needed to repay the Kokoszko family. She didn't repay them with money, however, she repaid them by saving all of their lives. She was very committed and loyal to the Kokoszko family.

In 1942, the Kokoszko family was sent to the Otwock Ghetto. Krystyna was not though, because she was a gentile and not a Jew. Krystyna Danko then endangered herself by helping the Kokoszko family escape the Nazi's and the Otwock Ghetto. Krystyna helped to hide the Kokoszkos. She hid the mother, father, and Lusia in an location in a nearby village. Also, she sent the youngest daughter on a train to a Warsaw orphanage. She registered the youngest daughter in the orphanage as an assumed name. She delivered money (of her own), news, and food to the Kokoszko family to keep them aware. She didn't ask for anything in return from helping the Kokoszko family either. She even stated that helping others was her main moral obligation as a human being. Krystyna Danko was a very caring person who risks, endangered, and nearly jeopardized her own life by caring for others and wanting them to be alive and healthy.

Krystyna Danko was an honorable person that set an amazing example to all people. I learned while writing this essay that an ordinary person can do many extraordinary things, by living with a caring example. Krystyna demonstrated this by caring for the Kokoszko family when they were in times of need. I also learned that no matter how old you are, you can still make a difference or impact on not just one, but many people. I think that more people should think about the purpose of being righteous and why it is such a great thing. They should also look at the righteous people, then see what they can do better to be more like them. They also should make decisions like Krystyna Danko did, and devote their time and effort to make sure that other people are healthy and safe. Krystyna Danko was a spectacular person who was brave, caring, and mainly righteous.

Works Cited

Colondres, Ari R. "English 8." 26 Jan. 2017, Galt, McCaffrey Middle School, Holocaust Gallery Walk.

Yad Vashem. "Names of Righteous by Country." Names of Righteous by Country, The Holocaust Martyrs' and Heroes' Remembrance Authority, 2017, www.yadvashem.org/righteous/statistics. Accessed 23 Feb. 2017.

Jozef Marchwinski

Rusty Cooley

 There are people who risked their own lives, to rescue others, such as Jozef Marchwinski.

Jozef Marchwinski saved many people who were innocent that got taken to extermination camps because of their who they were. Jozef was born in Lodz Poland. He had a large family, his daughter's names were; Enoch, William, Pearl, Rose, and Sophia Marchwinski. Jozef's Wife was Frances Marchwinski. Before the holocaust, also known as the Shoah, started the family lived their normal life. The Holocaust started on January 30, 1933.

Everybody was okay until there were German soldiers invading Poland. When Jews saw the soldiers, people were scrambling to get away and not get caught. The people that did get caught were taken to extermination camps. When Jews were in the extermination camps, they were forced to work and were abused. A lot of people that refused or didn't do their work anymore were put in gas chambers. After the people died in the gas chambers, other Jews had to take the bodies out and bury them. A total of about 6 million Jews died during the holocaust, causing a depression for all of the families.

Jozef Marchwinski is a very righteous person because, he saves many people during the holocaust. He risked his own life to save other people that he probably did not know. There were a lot of Jews that helped each other during the holocaust. Jozef did not have to go back and save people, he could have said that the people were on their own, but he felt that he needed to go in and help. People that were righteous during the holocaust, were probably greatly appreciated by all of the people that they saved.

While Jews were in extermination camps, they were treated very badly, only some of the Jews got mattresses to sleep on, while the rest had to sleep without one. Before Jews enter the camps, they had to check in and get a tattoo number on their arm to identify them. The first use of a gas chamber for mass murder was on November 13, 1939. Hitler ruled for the first use of the gas chamber for mass murder.

One thing that I learned is that about 6 million Jews, died because of people having bad feelings about Jews. Another thing that I learned was that young children were mainly targeted by Nazis. A third thing that I learned was that in September, 1941, 33,000 Jews were murdered in just two days. Finally, more than half of the victims of the holocaust were women.

People that were like Jozef Marchwinski, during the holocaust, were very righteous, risking their own life just to go and save other people that needed help.

Works Cited

Colondres, Ari R. "English 8." 26 Jan. 2017, Galt, McCaffrey Middle School, Holocaust Gallery Walk.

"Frances Marchwinski." Ancestry. Web. 24 Feb. 2017.

"Jozef Marchwinski." Geni_family_tree. 07 Nov. 2014. Web. 24 Feb. 2017.

"Why Did the Holocaust Start?" Why Did the Holocaust Start? Web. 25 Feb. 2017.

Yad Vashem. "Names of Righteous by Country." Names of Righteous by Country, The Holocaust Martyrs' and Heroes' Remembrance Authority, 2017, www.yadvashem.org/righteous/statistics. Accessed 23 Feb. 2017.

"91 Interesting Facts about the Holocaust." FactRetriever.com. Web. 25 Feb. 2017.

Rudolf Stefan Weigl

Sebastian Mcarthur

Righteous Gentiles helped saved people during the holocaust and risked their lives to do something they thought was the right thing to do, save people. I will be writing about the holocaust and people who made a difference. The holocaust started because of Hitler's reign as the leader of Germany and officially started the deportation that started the holocaust in January 30th 1933. Some Germans known as Righteous Gentiles harbored Jews and hid them from Nazi Patrols. Weigl Stefan Rudolf was one of many Righteous Gentiles was an inventor during the beginning of world war 2 and was renown because he created the first effective vaccine against epidemic typhus and he also harbored Jews.

The Holocaust was the systematic, bureaucratic, state-sponsored persecution and murder of six million Jews by the Nazi regime and its collaborators. Holocaust is a word of Greek origin meaning "sacrifice by fire." The Nazis, who came to power in Germany in January 1933, believed that Germans were "racially superior" and that the Jews, deemed "inferior," were an alien threat to the so-called German racial community. It is important to remember the holocaust because it could happen again.

Weigl, Rudolf was born on September 2, 1883 in Prerov, Czech Republic. Weigl was an Austrian of German ethnicity, born in Prerau, Moravia, when it was part of the Austrian part of the Austro-Hungarian Empire. When he was a child, his father died in a bicycle accident. His mother, Elisabeth Kroesel, married a Polish secondary-school teacher, Józef Trojnar, and they raised Weigl in Jaslo, Poland. Later the family moved to Lviv where in 1907 Weigl graduated from the biology department at the University of Jan Kazimierz, where he had been a pupil of Professors Benedykt Dybowski (1833–1930) and J. Nusbaum–Hilarowicz (1859–1917). After graduating, Weigl became Nusbaum's assistant and in 1913 completed his habilitacja in the department of comparative zoology and anatomy. During the Holocaust, he harbored Jews, thereby risking execution by the Germans. His vaccines were also smuggled into the Lwow Ghetto and the Warsaw ghetto, saving countless additional Jewish lives.

Even though righteous gentiles risked their lives to save people it was the right thing to do in times where people lost their hope in humanity and went off of their will to survive.

Works Cited

Colondres, Ari R. "English 8." 26 Jan. 2017, Galt, McCaffrey Middle School, Holocaust Gallery Walk.

"Professor Dr Rudolf Weigl (1883-1957) and the Activity of His Typhus Institute in Lvov between 1939 and 1944." Archiwum Historii I Filozofii Medycyny. U.S. National Library of Medicine. Web. 24 Feb. 2017.

"Rudolf Weigl." Wikipedia. Wikimedia Foundation, 10 Feb. 2017. Web. 24 Feb. 2017.

"Waclaw Szybalski: The Genius of Rudolf Stefan Weigl (1883-1957), a Lvovian Microbe Hunter and Breeder - In Memoriam." Waclaw Szybalski: The Genius of Rudolf Stefan Weigl (1883-1957), a Lvovian Microbe Hunter and Breeder - In Memoriam. Web. 24 Feb. 2017.

Yad Vashem. "Names of Righteous by Country." Names of Righteous by Country, The Holocaust Martyrs' and Heroes' Remembrance Authority, 2017, www.yadvashem.org/righteous/statistics. Accessed 23 Feb. 2017.

The Mikolajkow Family

Valeria Cuevas

The Holocaust was a tragic genocide of Jews, killing of Undesirables, and killing of those who helped the Jews. About six million Jewish people were killed during the atrocious years of the reign of Hitler. There are many known virtuous heroes that had a hand in preserving the lives of Jews during the dreadful Holocaust, but there are withal many that are not as known as they deserve to be. Among the many Polish heroes was the Mikolajkow Family, a family of four who risked everything to save lives the of innocent fellow civilians with no other reason than altruism.

Aleksander Mikolajkow's profession was as a doctor and he was a father and husband to this righteous family. His date of birth is unknown but it is known that he was murdered on January 01, 1945. This man was finally recognized on January 29,1980 for risking and losing his life to save Jews. His wife Leokadia's profession was as a physician and she was the leading female figure in the Mikolajkow family. Leokadia was born in 1906 and the date of her death is unknown, though it is known that she died a victim of bombardment and warfare actions. She, like her husband, was recognized by Yad Vashem on the date of January 29, 1980. Their oldest son, Leszek, was born in the year 1933. Leszek survived long after the Holocaust but his date and cause of death is unknown. The younger of the two brothers was Andrzej Mikolajkow who was born in the year 1937. He, like his brother, survived the Holocaust and died on an unknown date some time after. Both brothers were later recognized for their actions on June 29, 1989 in Warsaw, Poland.

Aleksander was a doctor in an insurance firm during the beginning of the German occupation in Debica. After a ghetto in their town had been established, he employed a young man who went by the name Efraim Reich. Young Efraim's family was soon thrown into the ghettos themselves. Once this information was acquired by Leokadia and

Aleksander they decided that they would try to help the family in anyway possible upon Efraim's request. They began by providing the Reichs with medication and food for nourishment. Despite the dangers the children would face, Leokadia and Aleksander soon after sent Andrzej and Leszek to get packages they had arranged into the ghetto for the Reich family. Two times in 1942, once in spring and once in fall, the ghetto had been due for liquidation action. Each time the Mikolajkows got word, the Reichs had been snuck out of the ghetto and kept hidden in the two hiding places that had been prepared beforehand. Once the liquidation action ended, the Reichs decided that since they didn't want to keep the Mikolajkows in more danger than necessary they would return to the ghetto. The third time, in the late December of 1942, the Germans called for the final liquidation action. The Mikolajkows helped sneak out the ten members of the Reich family for the last time. Upon the ten were Efraim's parents, brother, two sisters, brother-in-law, uncle, aunt, and their two daughters.

After the successful liberation from the ghettos, the Mikolajkows cared for and kept the ten Jews in hiding at their house on 248 Kosciuszki Street. Eventually, the Polish family took it upon themselves to take two other Jews under their wing. Those two Jews identities are unknown to this day. All thirteen Jews stayed hidden in the Mikolajkow house from around December of 1942 to late August of 1944. Just days before liberation by the Red Army, Aleksander lost his life when he was shot dead. His son Lezek was the first to come upon Aleksander's dead body, running off and bringing Leokadia to the gruesome scene. It is still unknown whether Aleksander had been killed by Soviets or Nazis but it is known that who ever shot him killed more people than just Aleksander. Upon leaving Poland, many of the thirteen left to find a home in the United States. No matter how much time had passed, they never forgot the family who risked everything for them and asked for nothing in return. In 1960, Efraim Reich published a short, sincere epitaph that said, "I remember the anniversary of his death every year. I believe in life after death, and I believe that Dr. Mikolajkow is one of the greats there. If there are still people like him around, the world will have to become a better place at last."

During the infamous Holocaust there were many unsung heroes, like the Mikolajkows, who are not recognized as they deserve to be after doing everything in their power to save the lives of people. It is people like the Mikolajkows that we should learn from, for their altruism is something we should all want to see more of. Just as Efraim Reich stated, this world would be a much better place if we all thought like Dr. Mikolajkow. These Polish heroes are examples of people who are willing to do the right thing, expecting nothing in return, even if it means risking their lives to save people they have never met.

Works Cited

Colondres, Ari R. "English 8." 26 Jan. 2017, Galt, McCaffrey Middle School, Holocaust Gallery Walk.

"Dembitz, Poland (Addendum)." Dembitz, Poland (Addendum). Web. 24 Feb. 2017.

Yad Vashem. "Names of Righteous by Country." Names of Righteous by Country, The Holocaust Martyrs' and Heroes' Remembrance Authority, 2017, www.yadvashem.org/righteous/statistics. Accessed 23 Feb. 2017.

Helena Kurek (Sara Helena Blam)

Veronica Garcia

Imagine a period where you had to go into camps and put to work or else you would be killed because of where you came from. Imagine yourself not being able to live a normal life like the others because of your religion, where you cannot do anything or go anywhere, where the rest of the people can go or else you would be beaten and killed. Imagine that you were judged by the way you think and believe in something. Well that's exactly what happened to the Jews. The Holocaust was a scary event in history for the Jews. The Holocaust started in 1933 and ended in 1945. There were many people that were taken to camps during the Holocaust. There were people that wanted to make a difference by helping the people that were in the camps. Helena Kurek (Sara Helena Blam) was one of the persons that helped many Jews escape from the camps and she hid them from the police. She put her life in danger to help others, knowing that if she got caught she would get killed by the police or the Nazis.

During the Holocaust, many people got their lives taken by trying to help others. After the Holocaust ended, about 6,000,000 to 11,000,000 people died because of the Holocaust. The Holocaust is where about 6,000,000 Jews were killed by Adolf Hitler Nazi Germany. Over 200,000 people are estimated to have been Holocaust perpetrators. After 1939, there were concentration, labor, extermination, prisoner-of- war, and transit camps. Some camps increasingly became places where Jews were either killed or made to work as slave laborers, undernourished and tortured. During the Holocaust, Jews were not allowed after 8 p.m. in public or else they would get killed or beaten. Jewish kids had to go to a different school than the other kids. The Jews were not allowed to run a business and if a Jew was a worker at a business, they must get fired. About 1.5 million children were killed and represent two- thirds of the nine million Jews in Europe.

The term "Holocaust," is originally from the Greek word "holokauston" which stands for "sacrifice by fire," which refers to the Nazi's persecution and planned slaughter of the Jewish people. The Holocaust is important because people's lives were taken for being from a different religion and believing in what they want. People from a different religion like the Jews and others were treated badly, no one had respect for them because they were different and not the same as the others This affects the people in present day because now people have the right to believe in what they want.

Helena (Sara) was one of the persons that has helped Jewish people. Helena Kurek (Sara Blam) lived with her mother and stepfather. Sara was born on 1915. She lived in Borysław near Drohobycz, in the former Lwów Province. She worked at a local oil refinery. Her stepfather named Jozef Kurek worked in the refinery. The place where she worked in was for making gasoline. It was located next to one of the camps. This helped Sara and her family to sneak out Jews from the camps.

This is how Sara helped the Jews. Some Jews came to her home and she rushed to look for a place for them to hide. If she didn't help some of the Jews, some Jews might have gotten killed by the Nazis. Her stepfather and Helena put their lives in danger by trying to save them from the Nazis. In September 1943, people in the area where Helena and the Jews were located at, snitched on Helena, causing her stepfather to be killed. Her mother and she were arrested and beaten by the police. The police then later let them go because the police didn't have proof that they had the Jews hiding and because neither of them admitted to the police that they were hiding the Jews. When the police didn't find the Jews, seven Jews who Sara saved succeeded to escape and go to the forest, but then the Red Army liberated them in the summer of 1944.

One of the Jews that Helena helped escape, name Moshe Blam owes his life to Helena. After the war, Moshe ask Helena to marry him. On 1948 they got married, then moved to Israel. When they arrived in Israel, Helena changed her name to Sara Helena Blam. Sara then converted into Judaism. On 1944 Sara Blam was recognized as one of the Righteous Among the Nations.

Helena Kurek (Sara Helena Blam) is known as the Righteous Among the Nations. She helped many Jews escape from being killed by the Nazis. Overall, the Holocaust is a very important event in history. During that period of time, the government didn't give the people the rights we have in present day. The people back then didn't have the right to believe in what we now believe in. People from a different race would be killed or beaten because no one liked them and the government didn't respect the decisions of the Jews or from where they came from.

Works Cited

"Blam Helena Sara." Story of Rescue - Blam Helena Sara | Polscy Sprawiedliwi. Web. 24 Feb. 2017.

Colondres, Ari R. "English 8." 26 Jan. 2017, Galt, McCaffrey Middle School, Holocaust Gallery Walk.

Digital Collections." Digital Collections - Yad Vashem. Web. 24 Feb. 2017

Jennifer Rosenberg 20th Century History Expert. "33 Facts You Should Know About the Holocaust." About.com Education. 09 May 2016. Web. 24 Feb. 2017.

"The Holocaust." Wikipedia. Wikimedia Foundation, 24 Feb. 2017. Web. 24 Feb. 2017.

Yad Vashem. "Names of Righteous by Country." Names of Righteous by Country, The Holocaust Martyrs' and Heroes' Remembrance Authority, 2017, www.yadvashem.org/righteous/statistics. Accessed 23 Feb. 2017.

Yad Vashem - Request Rejected. Web. 24 Feb. 2017

Dr. Miron Lisikiewicz

William Isaiah Farren

Dr. Miron Lisikiewicz is a righteous person for several reasons. First, he saved two Jewish nurses Rena Dworecki and Sala Friedman. I picked Dr. Miron Lisikiewicz who was catholic, he helped save two important Jewish nurses. You should care about this since it showed that people who were not even Jewish helped the Jews who were hiding and suffering. We also, should not forget the Holocaust for several reasons.

First of all, the Holocaust unofficially began on January 30, 1933, and ended on May 8, 1945. The Holocaust's beginning is often linked to when Adolph Hitler became Chancellor of Germany. As a result of the Holocaust, 6 million Jews would die at the hands of Nazi oppressors by the war's end. We should care about this, since 6 million people dyeing in a period of time less than 20 years should be a thing we care about so we do not repeat history. If we do not know what happened then we might make the same mistake the Nazis did.

On the other hand, Dr Miron Lisikiewicz saved two Jewish nurses for several reasons. The Jewish nurses were in a cemetery and one of his assistants escorted them after they hid for hours in between the trees until the community dispersed. You should care, since the people that he saved may have changed some people's lives and since he saved them they could live their life to the fullest. Dr. Miron Lisikiewicz got a ceremony after death. Dr. Miron Lisikiewicz got a tree burial for being righteous. This is important since he was important that they gave him a tree burial, which few people got. He also got a document from William Bein of the American Joint Distribution committee on July 7. I picked Dr. Miron Lisikiewicz who was Catholic, he helped save two important Jewish nurses.

In conclusion, you should care about this since it showed that people who were not even Jewish helped the Jews who were hiding and suffering. That all the people who saved Jews were truly righteous. Make sure to remember how many people died in the holocaust to make sure they do not repeat history. The holocaust unofficially began on January 30, 1933, and ended on May 8, 1945. The Holocaust's beginning is often linked to when Adolph Hitler became Chancellor of Germany. As a result of the Holocaust, 6 million Jews would die at the hands of Nazi oppressors by the war's end. We should care about this, since 6 million people dyeing in a period of time less than 20 years should be a thing we care about so we do not repeat history. If we do not know what happened then we might make the same mistake the Nazis did.

Works Cited

Colondres, Ari R. "English 8." 26 Jan. 2017, Galt, McCaffrey Middle School, Holocaust Gallery Walk.

http://search.archives.jdc.org/multimedia/Documents/W_4549/W_4549_337/W_4549_337_0457.pdf

Yad Vashem. "Names of Righteous by Country." Names of Righteous by Country, The Holocaust Martyrs' and Heroes' Remembrance Authority, 2017, www.yadvashem.org/righteous/statistics. Accessed 23 Feb. 2017.

Maria Belszan

Yahaira Ramirez

Maria Belszan should be more known for the things she went through and the people she was able to save. Maria Belszan had a rough middle-aged life and helped 2 Jewish people survive the war in Poland. Her involvement in the Holocaust and her struggles made her become braver. She was able to gain trust from others by helping and being kind to them. Maria Belszan saved a husband and wife, who were young, during the war. The husband wanted to seek a better life for his wife and himself, so he suggested the only way to survive the war was to be swallowed up in the Christian population. Maria suggested that he could go with her to her hometown, so if he needed her help she would help him and even try to save him. The husband went to Władimir Wołyński, Włodzimierz, Wołyń, Poland to seek help to find a job. Maria got fake documents for the husband and wife, which turned them Christians, and the husband got more opportunities to get a job. Even though her life, as well as others, were at risk she still decided to help and save at least two people.

Maria Belszan was born in February 2,1895. Her profession was to be a housewife. She was a middle-aged woman who was from Władimir Wołyński, Włodzimierz, Wołyń, Poland. Maria Belszan was a devout Catholic, the wife of a Polish soldier, who had been exiled to Siberia. Maria Belszan liked to travel, so she was planning to go back to her hometown. She met a man and his wife ,who were Jewish, and helped them get fake documents which turned them into Christians. The husband and wife were doctors, but with the Holocaust happening, the husband needed a new job. The husband and wife got fired or quit their jobs as doctors because of their religion and they were treated very bad. The husband stayed in a Polish family and met there a relative of the housewife, Maria Belszan. Maria decided to help him get a new job since the other one had been taken away. While they had been searching for a new job, he wanted to be a doctor, but the opportunities were low since they already knew or believed he was a Jew. Maria already knew that they were Jewish, but she still had the courage to help them and she trusted them for the things that they were doing. The plan they all created was a big of a risk which could of caused them to get kicked out of their place or even death for all of them.

Maria Belszan's achievement was about how she saved the two Jewish people. She saved Stanisław Wiczyk and Barbara Wiczyk when she went back to her hometown in Poland. She noticed two people in Poland who wanted documents to turn into Christians. The first instant she saw Stanisław, she demonstrated to help him in his new locality. She already knew they were Jewish, but she still decided to help them survive. She helped him get a new job even though people didn't accept him because his forged document probably didn't look like the actual one or they knew he was Jewish. When the husband asked her why she is helping him, she said that her religion commanded her to help people in need without reference. She was able to represent him as a relative which opened doors for his wife to get to him. She had the courage to face the danger that came with helping the two Jewish people get the forged documents. Later on Maria provided the wife with a forged identity document, and created around them a circle of loyal, influenced people, who were able to protect them from the suspicions that abounded. Maria Belszan helped save Jewish people because she saw them suffering and they had many tragedies occurring to them. She wanted to save the couple because her religion actually refers to helping others in need.

In conclusion, Maria Belszan should be more known for the things she did. Even through the dangers she had to go through, she still decided to help others, keep going with her life, and she started accomplishing new things. Maria Belszan was recognized on July 19, 2001 by Yad Vashem as a Righteous Among the Nations. Maria was a survivor of the Holocaust as well as the two people she had saved. Maria was rescued and was hiding at Władimir Wołyński, Włodzimierz, Wołyń, Poland. Belszan had a ceremony organized by Israeli Diplomatic Delegation. Maria's death was in March 30, 1980, which she lived up to be about 95 years old. Maria was 38 years old when the Holocaust began and she was 50 when the Holocaust had ended. Maria got a spot in the Wall of Honor located at the Ellis Island. The Holocaust changed Maria Belszans's life as it probably changed many others life by leaving either good, bad, or okay memories. The Holocaust proved how cruel people are against humanity and that they will do anything to gain or have all the power.

Works Cited

Maria Belszan was recognized on July 19, 2001 by yadvashem as a Righteous Among the Nations.

Rolling Hills Middle School, El Dorado, CA

Kristin Cheatham has worked in the Buckeye Union School District for the past 8 years. She has taught 8th grade Language Arts for the past 5 years. Her favorite unit to teach is the Holocaust unit. The students really have a strong emotional connection to the unit, and it is the most meaningful.

The Heroes of Poland

Aaron Hoversten

Imagine losing your identity and not knowing what your real name is, but only knowing who you truly are because your name was left on a slip of paper buried in the ground for many years. This was how it was for the 2,500 Jewish children Irena Sendler saved from the Nazis in Poland during World War II.

Irena was born in Otwock Poland on February 15, 1910. Her father was a doctor and tried to cure people that other doctors would not go and see, like Jews, who had typhus disease. He ended up getting the disease from one of his patients and died. Irena's father died when she was only nine years old, but left an impact on Irena's life that would help her stand up to the Nazis in her later years. Irena was only in her 20's when World War II started and she began her journey to try and save as many people as she could from the Ghettos of Warsaw in Poland. During the war, she was caught by the Gestapo, tortured and sentenced to death but she escaped. After the war, she went on to live until she was 98. She died on May 12, 2008. Although she was caught and nearly killed, she still managed to save many people from death and keep a record of who they were.

The story of a Polish woman who saved 2500 children from certain death is intriguing and many people wonder how she managed to get children out of the Ghetto and give them a new life. To get children out of the Ghettos, she first had to get into the Ghetto. She did this by using a fake nurse registration to get through the Nazi checkpoints. Using this pass, she smuggled medicine and money to the Jews to try and help them survive. Once, she was in the Ghettos she persuaded families to give her their children so she could smuggle the children out of the Ghettos. She smuggled children across the Ghetto border by hiding them in ambulances and claiming they had a disease. Also, she hid children in suitcases she brought with her, garbage cans, coffins, and toolboxes. Sometimes, she would ask children she had snuck out, if they knew any ways other people could get out. This is how she learned that some of the people tried to get out through small holes in the wall, or through the sewers. After she got children out of the Ghettos, she had to find a place for them to live. "It was easier to escape the ghetto than to survive the Aryan side. The rescue of a child required at least the help of at least ten people (on the outside)", she said. (Irena Sendler 1) She usually gave them fake ID's with fake registrations and gave them to willing polish families, or church groups. Before she gave them away though, she taught the older children tricks that would help them survive against Nazi SS officers. She taught them how to speak Polish and certain Catholic songs to prevent questioning officers from killing them. Irena managed to save over 2,500 children from the Nazis by doing this. Even with all the dangers involved with saving Jews, Irena said, "No one ever refused to take a child from me." (Irena Sendler 1) Overall, what Irena did for these people is very heroic, even though it nearly got her killed.

Although smuggling children from the Ghettos was extremely dangerous if one was caught, Irena never questioned her work. However, "On October 20, 1943 she was arrested and imprisoned by the Gestapo." (Irena Sendler 2) Irena managed to survive this encounter.

She was taken by the Gestapo into interrogation because the Gestapo was suspicious about her activities. During her time getting tortured, the Gestapo broke both of her legs and arms. Despite the torture, she never gave in and never revealed to the police who was helping her. "...she withstood the torture and she refused to betray any of her associates or the children in hiding." (Irena Sendler, The Economist 1) They later sentenced her to death, but her friends bribed a German officer and he helped her escape the execution. After she escaped, she returned to her friends and continued saving people under a fake identity. Although Irena was nearly killed, she showed remarkable courage to continue her mission and throughout it all never quit and never gave in to the Nazis.

Throughout the war, Irena showed great determination and intelligence in how she saved people. For example, to keep her identity hidden, "All the couriers in her network had code names like she did. The children only knew her by her code name Jolanta." (Mazzeo 166) This way if the children were discovered they could not reveal who it was that had helped them. The smartest thing she did was keep records of everybody she saved, so that after the war they could be reunited with their families. Irena did this by getting the children's actual identity and birth certificates and writing them down on thin slips of paper. She also wrote down the fake identities of the children on the same piece of paper. Most of the people that helped her smuggle children were against this idea because it made the operation a lot more dangerous and risky. At one of the meetings between Irena and her friend, the Gestapo came and almost found the papers of the names of the children. Her friend hid them in her clothes and the Gestapo never found them. After this happened, Irena decided to bury jars with the paper slips in her friend's garden to avoid the Gestapo from finding them. "In all, the jars contained the names of 2,500 children." (Irena Sendler 2) Ultimately, Irena showed great courage in making the decision to keep records of the children, even though it made her life more risky.

After the war, her courage was recognized by many people and she was given many awards and blessings. One award she got was the order of the white eagle; the highest award Poland can give. "In 1965 she was recognized by Yad Vashem, Israel's Holocaust authority, as a Righteous Gentile..." (Woo 2) Additionally, Irena was given the Jan Karski prize for her courage and heart during the war and she received an Apostolic Blessing from Pope John Paul II. The Pope wrote to her, "Please accept my sincere congratulations and expressions of respect for your exceptionally courageous activities..." (Message from the Pope 1). Although she has been given many awards, Irena was always very humble. Even though she saved more than 2,500 people, in one of her last interviews she said, "I continue to have qualms of conscience that I did so little." (Soares 1). Irena never took credit for her accomplishments, always acknowledging those that helped her. "...I did only what was my duty as a human being. (Please) allow me to receive this award also on behalf of my trusted colleagues who are no longer with us, but I want to keep alive the memory of these many honorable people who risked their lives to save our Jewish brothers..." (Address by Irena Sendler 1). Additionally she said, "Every child saved with my help is the justification of my existence on this Earth, and not a title to glory." (Woo 2). In 2007 she was nominated for the Nobel Peace Prize but ultimately the award was given to Al Gore that year.

In all, Irena was a courageous woman who was determined to stand up to the Nazis and save as many people as she could. Elzbieta Ficowska, one of the children she smuggled from certain death in the Ghetto summed up Irena's courage. "The survival instinct is to save ourselves, but she saved others." (Soares 2) The legacy of the 2500 children saved by Irena Sandler must now number in the tens of thousands. Sadly Irena's life accomplishments, her love for all human beings, and her lessons of courage are not honored by all. In 2010 Irena's gravestone was vandalized with graffiti in the words, "Jews out". (Lipman 1) In the end, Irena showed remarkable courage and should be honored worldwide.

Works Cited

Cukavac, Tyrus. "The courageous Heart of Irena Sendler." Junior Scholastic 23 Nov. 2015: 8-11. Print.

ConVistaAlMar.com.ar. "Irena Sendler." The International Raoul Wallenberg Foundation. Web. 7 Feb. 2017. <http://www.raoulwallenberg.net/saviors/polish/irena-sendler-409/>.

"Irena Sendler." The Economist. The Economist Newspaper, 22 May 2008. Web. 7 Feb. 2017. <http://www.economist.com/node/11402658>.

Lipman, Jennifer . "Grave of Warsaw Ghetto heroine vandalised." The International Raoul Wallenberg Foundation. N.p., 19 July 2010. Web. 7 Feb. 2017.

<http://www.raoulwallenberg.net/highlights/grave-warsaw-ghetto-heroine/>.

Mazzeo, Tilar J., and Mary Cronk Farrell. Irena's Children . Young Reader Edition ed. New York: Margaret K. McElderry , 2016. Print.

Warszawa, Grupa MAK http://www.grupamak.pl. "Address by Irena Sendler." The Association of "Children of the Holocaust" in Poland. N.p., 4 Dec. 2003. Web. 7 Feb. 2017.

Warszawa, Grupa MAK http://www.grupamak.pl. "Message from the Pope to Irena Sedler." The Association of "Children of the Holocaust" in Poland. N.p., 8 Nov. 2004. Web. 19 Feb. 2017. <http://www.dzieciholocaustu.org.pl/szab51.php?s=en_wysz.php&slowa=irena%2Bsendler&szukaj=search>.

Warszawa, Grupa MAK http://www.grupamak.pl. "The Association of "Children of the Holocaust" in Poland." The Association of "Children of the Holocaust" in Poland. N.p., 8 Nov. 2004. Web. 19 Feb. 2017. <http://www.dzieciholocaustu.org.pl/szab51.php?s=en_wysz.php&slowa=irena%2Bsendler&szukaj=search>.

Woo, Elaine. "Irena Sendler, 98; member of resistance saved lives of 2,500 Polish Jews." The International Raoul Wallenberg Foundation. N.p., 12 May 2008. Web. 7 Feb. 2017.

Polish Heroes

Adam Hurst

A hero isn't always just someone who battles "bad guys" or fights crime. This image has become stereotypical in today's society. A hero is someone who goes out of their way to help others for the greater good, and Jan Karski surpasses this definition. Jan Karski was a Polish hero during and after the Holocaust and World War II. Karski was a Polish spy, an officer, an author, a prisoner of war, and--most importantly--a hero. During the Holocaust, millions of innocent people, including Poles, were murdered by Nazi Germany. With their idea of becoming the superior race, many Germans discriminated, persecuted, and exterminated other races. Karski was born Jan Kozielewski on April 24, 1914 in Łódź, Poland. Despite enduring countless hardships, Karski was able to stand in the way of the Nazis and help others--leaving a large impact in the world with his selflessness. His hardships, reports, and selfless actions define him as a hero.

Jan Karski was one of the first people to give an eyewitness account of the Holocaust to Allied leaders. His documented struggles opened the world's eyes to the Holocaust. After studying law and diplomacy, Karski served many diplomatic posts in Switzerland, Germany, and Britain from 1936 to 1938. Jan Karski was also originally a reserve officer, or backup police officer. However, when war erupted and Germany invaded Poland on September 1, 1939, he enlisted in the Polish army and became a second Lieutenant for reconnaissance. Despite a nonaggression agreement between the Soviet Union and Germany, the Soviets invaded Poland too. The invasion took place on September 17, 1939. Thousands of policemen, citizens, and officers were herded like cattle and sent to detention camps. Karski was one of them. He managed to escape two months later and joined the Underground Polish Army, a resistance movement against Nazi Germany. Karski soon changed his last name to keep hidden. With his knowledge of geography and foreign languages, he became a courier, spying and gaining insight on Nazi Germany. He then communicated information to the Polish resistance movement and the former Polish government. Karski repeatedly crossed enemy lines and on one mission, was captured by the secret German police, the Gestapo. He was brutally tortured for information. Rather than reveal his secrets, Karski tried to commit suicide by slitting his wrists. To keep him from dying, the Gestapo rushed Karski to a hospital. There, a team from the underground movement secretly helped Jan Karski escape. In spite of the obstacles that stood in Jan Karski's way, he continued to report on Nazi Germany. In August of 1942, Karski disguised himself as a Jew and covertly entered the Warsaw Ghetto via a tunnel. He witnessed the horrors of the suffering Jews in the concentration camp ravaged by disease and starvation. In addition to the lack of food and medical supplies in the concentration camp, young Nazis killed Jews for sport. Karski also disguised himself as a Ukrainian militiaman, sneaking into the Izbica camp where he saw Jews carelessly thrown onto trains. Remaining stationary on the tracks, some rail cars were overloaded and the masses suffocated or starved. The remaining trains transported the Jews to gas chambers located throughout Germany. Jan Karski risked his life to gather information on the unnoticed mass murder of Jews.

Continuing with his reconnaissance, Karski distributed his findings to the Allied nations. The underground movement's reports were compiled onto microfilm and put inside a hollowed-out door key. In November 1942, Jan Karski traveled to London to give his account to senior British authorities. He warned of the mass murder of European Jews by Nazi Germany. His plea for action, however, was seen as unrealistic and unimportant. In July 1943, Karski traveled west to the United States. In Washington D.C., Jan Karski met with President Franklin D. Roosevelt. His warnings did not receive much concern as well. The Allied governments were focused on the military defeat of Germany instead. Karski also met with Supreme court justice Felix Frankfurter, yet he too disregarded Karski's account. Jan Karski's mission had failed. However, John Pehle, the head of the War Refugee Board, a federal agency that helped surviving Jews settle, gave Karski some positive news. Mr. Pehle stated that Roosevelt had created the board because of his talks with Mr. Karski. The United States' policy of disregarding the mass murder of Jews turned to immediate action. The president also gave twelve million dollars to the underground movement. While Jan Karski planned on going back to Warsaw, his superiors advised him not to as the Germans knew and recognized Karski, making it unsafe for return. When the war ended, Poland was free of Germans. The Yalta agreement, however, gave Poland to the Soviet Union. Jan Karski decided not to return because of his hatred of communism. Karski's reports likely saved thousands and maybe even millions of lives, preventing Nazi Germany from taking further action.

Jan Karski stood up for what was right, disregarded his personal concerns for the concerns of others, and sacrificed his life for the millions of lives of Jews. Therefore, he was and still is a hero--Humanity's Hero. Joining the Polish army revealed Karski's heroic nature as he risked his life for the country he loved. Despite being taken prisoner and then escaping, Jan Karski joined the Underground Polish Army where he risked his life again working as a spy. His selfless attitude and courage makes him a true hero. Karski's selflessness is also revealed when he slashes his wrists to avoid giving away information-- which would have likely made Nazi Germany kill more Jews. To witness the grave situation of the Jews, Karski snuck into the Warsaw ghetto and Izbica camp. He didn't focus on the fact that he could be caught, killed, or tortured, but on the fact that innocent Jews were dying and he needed to save them. Although his warnings were not heeded in the beginning, they eventually got out to the world, preventing mass casualties. While Jan Karski was a hero during the Holocaust, he continued to be one after World War II and his death. His legacy still lives on to this day. When people hear of Jan Karski's story, they can learn from his experiences and do the right thing when the situation arises. For example, a child could stand up to a bully or voters could stand up to a governmental change. After not being able to return to Poland near the end of World War II, Karski remained in Washington, promoting Polish freedom and writing to magazines about what was happening to Jews in Europe. Karski earned a PhD at Georgetown University's School of Foreign Service and taught there as a professor for forty years. He continued to spread the word and teach the world of the hardships the Jews had to bare. Jan Karski wrote about his story in his books: Story of a Secret State and The Great Powers and Poland, 1919-1945. Jan Karski also participated in many speaking tours in Canada and the United States. Karski was awarded numerous awards for his bravery and service. He received the highest Polish civic and military decorations and was made an honorary citizen in both Israel and Łódź, Poland. Yad Vashem rewarded Jan Karski the distinction "Righteous Among the Nations" and in 2002, a monument was erected at Georgetown University. He also received honorary doctorates from Georgetown University, Baltimore Hebrew College of America, Warsaw University, Marie Curie--Sklodowska university, and Łódź University. Poland awarded him two high honors: Order of White Eagle and Virtuti Militari. Karski can be described as a hero for his selfless attitude and bravery, leading to his many contributions.

Jan Karski demonstrated heroism by tirelessly helping others when his life was in jeopardy. He helped others not for the fame, money, or rewards, but for the greater good. By joining the Polish army and volunteering to go inside a ghetto to report on the mass murder and persecution of Jews, he exhibited bravery. Furthermore, he selflessly and purposely withheld secrets from the Germans by trying to commit suicide while being tortured. Karski died on July 13, 2000 at age 86. Nevertheless, His perseverance through hardships, reports on the killing of Jews, and heroic actions shook the world. Jan Karski showed true heroism as a Pole after selflessly risking his life for others in spite of the hardships he endured, leaving a lasting impact on the world to this day.

Works Cited

Bulow, Louis. "Jan Karski." Jan Karski, auschwitz.dk/rescuers/id2.htm. Accessed 23 Feb. 2017.

"1991, Jan Karski." Wallenberg Legacy University of Michigan, wallenberg.umich.edu/medal-recipients/1991-jan-karski/. Accessed 23 Feb. 2017.

Kaufman, Michael T. "Jan Karski Dies at 86; Warned West About Holocaust." The New York Times, The New York Times, 14 July 2000, www.nytimes.com/2000/07/15/world/jan-karski-dies-at-86-warned-west-about-holocaust.html. Accessed 23 Feb. 2017.

"Jan Karski." Jan Karski, www.jewishvirtuallibrary.org/jan-karski. Accessed 23 Feb. 2017.

"Upcoming Events." Jan Karski's Life · Jan Karski Educational Foundation, www.jankarski.net/en/about-jan-karski/jan-karski-life.html. Accessed 23 Feb. 2017.

"Oral History Interview with Jan Karski." United States Holocaust Memorial Museum, United States Holocaust Memorial Museum, collections.ushmm.org/search/catalog/irn506527. Accessed 23 Feb. 2017.

"Jan Karski." United States Holocaust Memorial Museum, United States Holocaust Memorial Museum, www.ushmm.org/wlc/en/article.php?ModuleId=10008152. Accessed 23 Feb. 2017.

"Alerting the World: Jan Karski." United States Holocaust Memorial Museum, United States Holocaust Memorial Museum, www.ushmm.org/information/exhibitions/online-exhibitions/special-focus/jan-karski. Accessed 23 Feb. 2017.

HEROES OF POLAND

Adrian Tongthaworn

 What makes a person a hero? Most people think of superheroes or police when they think of heroes, but there are very different characteristics that make someone a hero. During the Holocaust many people had hard times making a living if Hitler didn't like them. For example, Adolf Hitler didn't like Jews so most Jews ended up dying in concentration camps and in other torturous ways. Although there were a lot of mean and bad people at the time there were also a lot of people that were good and considered heroes. Raoul Wallenberg and Chiune (Sempo) Sugihara were commended for the many lives they saved.

Raoul Wallenberg was a Swedish Diplomat who was born on August 4, 1912 in Stockholm, Sweden. He studied in the United States in the 1930's and built a business career in Sweden. In June 1944 Raoul Wallenberg traveled to Hungary after being recruited by the United States War Refugee Board (WRB). After being recruited he was given the status of a diplomat by the Swedish legations and his job was to save, assist, and maintain the lives of Hungarian Jews as they were being hunted down by Adolf Hitler and the Nazis. Assigned as first secretary in Hungary, he led one of the most extensive and successful rescue missions during the Holocaust. His work with the WRB saved thousands of Hungarian Jews from being deported. Raoul Wallenberg was forced to help Hungarian Jews not only because of his job but because the Sztojay government was prepared to not only continue the war but also to deport Hungarian Jews to German occupied places of Poland. The result of the Sztojay government was the rounding up of Hungarian Jews and the transfer of Hungarian Jews to German custody. With authorization from the Swedish government Wallenberg began distributing certificates of protection issued by the Swedish government to help protect Hungarian Jews from being deported and to help others from being exiled in concentration camps. He also used WRB and Swedish funds to construct hospitals, nurseries, soup kitchens, and safe houses to help the Hungarian Jews. Unfortunately the ghetto reserves were only for Jews and their families holding certificates of protection from a neutral country. Overall, the acts Raoul Wallenberg achieved made him the hero he was and the hero he still is as remembered today in the U.S Holocaust Memorial Museum.

Wallenberg wasn't the only hero but Chiune Sugihara was also a hero in many ways. He was born on January 1, 1900. He was educated at the Harbin Gakuin, Japan's training center for experts on the Soviet Union. Since Sugihara was very talented and fluent in Russian, the Japanese sent him to the Lithuanian capital, Kovno, in November 1939. He was sent here to provide Japan with information about the movement of the Soviet and German troops in the Baltic region. Sugihara also exchanged information with members of the Polish underground in Lithuania and issued them visas for transit through Japan in 1940. He recognized that while officials were engulfed in war the most likely escape for the refugees in Lithuania was an eastern route through the Soviet Union to Japan. In the summer of 1940 when refugees came to him with fake visas he granted them a 10 day visa allowing them to get out of Japan and into other surrounding places. Before closing his business of helping refugees he even gave visas to refugees who didn't even have any travel papers. After Sugihara broke the law and issued over 1800 visas he received a letter telling him not to grant visas to people that didn't have any travel papers or money to travel with. After issuing visas to refugees, Sugihara admitted to breaking the law and granting visas to people who didn't complete the travel documents and in response Tokyo allowed all visas already issued be allowed and honored. In 1944 the Soviets arrested Sugihara along with other diplomats from enemy nations. He and his family were held in fairly benign conditions for the next 3 years. After 3 years of being held captive Sugihara returned back to Japan and the Foreign Ministry retired him with a small pension. Overall Sugihara was a good man and a hero because he helped a lot of refugees escape to live their lives even though it costed him his job.

During these tragic times few rose up to help for the better good and to fight the bad. Although they stood up and fought against the evil in the world they were punished. Overall, the heroes of the Holocaust include Mr. Wellenberg and Mr. Sugihara. These people should be honored for what they have done for the people that didn't have a voice in what happens to them. Some people think that heroes have to be strong and have powers, but a hero is just someone that helps others who can't help themselves.

Bibliography

Chiune Sugihara. Chiune Sugihara. Retrieved February 21, 2017, from http://www.jewishvirtuallibrary.org/chiune-sugihara

History.com Staff. (2010). Raoul Wallenberg. History.com. A&E Television Networks. Retrieved February 21, 2017, from http://www.history.com/topics/wallenberg-raoul

Raoul Wallenberg. Raoul Wallenberg. Retrieved February 21, 2017, from http://www.jewishvirtuallibrary.org/raoul-wallenberg-3

Heroes of Poland

Andrew Chin

There is a large amount of well-known Polish people who stood up against the immoral Nazi party, however there was one person in particular who stood out for his heroism and courageousness, and that was Jan Karski. Karski was a very intelligent and gallant person who attended university, joined the Polish army, and joined underground movement when World War II broke out. He was a very determined person who put his life on the line numerous times as he greatly contributed to help stop the holocaust. After World War II, Karski taught people all over the world about the holocaust and his experiences during that time, and was also awarded many prestigious rewards for his contribution during the holocaust. Jan Karski was a very honorable man who displayed his courage while trying to make a difference during World War II and by educating people around the world about the holocaust.

Jan Kozielewski was born on April 24, 1914 in Lodz, Poland. He was named Jan (John) because he was born on St. John's day, and because it was a Polish pre-war custom to name infants after saints. He and his family were Roman Catholics who grew up in a neighborhood that was populated mainly by Jewish people. He had very close relationships with Jewish people, as most of his friends at the time were Jews. Karski was a very bright child who was successful in school as a child and attended college at the age of 17. He attended the University of Lwow and received his master's degree in Law and Diplomatic Science in 1935. He then traveled around Europe, working at several different diplomatic posts in Romania, Switzerland, Great Britain, and Germany from 1936 to1938.

In 1839, when the outbreak of World War II occurred he immediately joined the Polish army. However shortly after joining he was captured by the Red Army (Soviets) and was sent to detention camp in modern day Ukraine. Within a few months at camp, he was able to escape and make it back to Poland, where he then joined the Polish underground movement. He was a very valuable asset, as he had excellent geographical skills and was able to understand and speak numerous languages. He was used a courier and was ordered to convey secret information between the resistance and Poland. He frequently crossed the enemy lines to send messages from one place to another. In the late 1940's, Karski was caught sending messages by the Gestapo. He was taken hostage and was brutally tortured by the Gestapo. He was afraid that he might jeopardize the Polish plans by revealing their secrets, so he slashed his wrists but was luckily sent to a hospital where the underground was able help him escape. In 1942, before Karski's was about to leave for his last mission as a courier, the underground snuck Karski in and out of the Warsaw ghetto, where he was able to see first-hand, the torture and suffering that the Jews were having to endure. After spending time in the Warsaw ghetto he was able to acquire a disguise that allowed him to sneak him into a concentration camp in Eastern Poland, where he witnessed mass murder. He as one of the first people to witness and report the life of the people in a concentration camp. He witnessed the Jews being starved and saw them being transported to the Belzec killing center. After sneaking out of the Warsaw Ghetto, he was sent to London where he reported he findings to the Polish government and senior British authorities which included Minister Anthony Eden. In 1943, he traveled to Washington D.C., where he met with President Franklin D. Roosevelt to explain Germany's plan to murder Jews. Karski's reports were treated with disbelief as the Allied powers were focusing on the decline of Germany's army.

After being treated with disbelief, Karski felt deterred decided to stay in the United States. He earned his PhD in Foreign Service at Georgetown University. After receiving his education, he still decided to stay in the states, as he did not want to live in communism (Poland was communist). He taught students about Eastern European Affairs, comparative government, and international affairs at Georgetown as a professor for forty years. Karski went on many lecture tours around the world and also testified before congress several times on topics about Eastern Europe. Throughout his lifetime, Karski was presented with honorary decorates from Georgetown University, Oregon State University, Marie Curie-Sklodowska University, Baltimore Hebrew College, Hebrew College of America, Warsaw University, and Lodz University. In 1975, he was named an honorary citizen of Israel and had a tree planted for him at Yad Vashem's Valley of Righteous Among the Nations and had received the highest Polish military decorations. Karski died in Washington D.C. on July 2000, and had monument created for him at the University of Georgetown in 2002. Karski lived his life honoring the fallen Jews who died to Nazism. In 2012, Karski had been rewarded by Barrack Obama with the nation's highest civilian honor, the Presidential Medal of Freedom.

Jan Karski is a very honorable man most known for his contributions during World War II and also for educating people around the World about the holocaust. He was very bright as a child and was able to attend university. After the war broke out, Karski immediately joined the Polish army, and later joins the underground movement to help and stop the holocaust. After the war ended, Karski decided to try and teach people around the world about the holocaust and his experiences during that time. Throughout his lifetime, he had been awarded numerous prestigious awards for his heroic and courageous actions during the war, most notably being named an honorary citizen of Israel by Yad Vashem. All in all, Jan Karski was a very courageous man who contributed greatly in trying to end the holocaust and by teaching people around the world about the tragic event.

Work Cited

Smith, James. Jan Karski. https://www.ushmm.org/wlc/en/article.php?ModuleId =10008152 United States Holocaust Memorial Museum, 2014.

Johnson, Chandler. Jan Karski. https://www.jewishvirtuallibrary.org/jan-karski JTA, 2011.

Kaufman, Michael. Jan Karski Dies at 86; Warned West About Holocaust. http://www.nytimes.com/2000/07/15/world/jan-karski-dies-at-86-warned-west-about-holocaust.html New York Times, 2000.

The Heroes of Poland

Bailey Hofacre

During one of the most terrible times in world history or known as the Holocaust, there were many unsung heroes that saved people at the liability of their own lives. Although, many people believe that most of the heroes and saviors to Jews and other races were men it was actually mainly women. One of these brave young women was a polish spy named Krystyna Skarbek or also known as Christine Grandville. Krystyna was one of Winston Churchill's most trusted and favorite spies, because she was good at getting crucial information and details. This helped out the Allied Forces and many other big rebel groups against Hitler. She risked her life to save countless others and loved the thrill of danger. In this essay it will tell about the peril she went through in her exploits and one her biggest plots.

Krystyna was a thrill seeker, she hiked and skied through harsh mountain ranges and enjoyed it. She loved the adrenaline rush that it gave her. One of her many perilous journeys that she went through is when she crossed the Tatra mountain ranges multiple times with high-risk refugees to save them. Krystyna would lead these refugee's through the rough and cold mountains to Hungary since it was a neutral country in which they would be safe in. She did this about 6 times and for the greater part of the time when trekking through the mountains it was in the -20's to the -30's. Another one of her many plans is when she passed details to London about Hitler's plans for the invasion of Russia almost minute by minute. She also warned them about the Nazi's plans for Barbossa. One of her more nail-biting coups is when she was caught and interrogated. But, she was smart and bit her tongue until it bleed. Krystyna did this and lied about having tuberculosis so that they would free her for fear of getting the disease. She still got away with it even after they took an xray of her lungs. Krystyna got away with this because she used to be a mechanic and back then the machinery wasn't that good so people would always be getting hurt, one day she got wounded by the machinery, so then after her lungs healed they still had scars on them. This lead to her getting away once again with her life in a very dangerous situation. Some of her adventures were almost straight out of a blockbuster spy movie. She had many different journeys and one of these is when she had to ski out of the country. Krystyna had to ski over and throughout the mountains to the neutral country of Hungary where she had to open up new courier lines for Winston Churchill. Even though these stories seem very daring one of her more scary stories is when she encountered 2 german guards on the border. They told her to put her hands in the air which she complied to but when she raised up both of her arms it revealed 2 grenades. With the pins withdrawn, she threatened to drop them on the ground. After she said this the german soldiers got so scared for their lives that they high-tailed it out of there. And once again she got out a tense, life-threatening situation. Overall, she lead many different adventurous feats that to the normal person would scare but to her was the thrill of being a spy and she enjoyed it.

Although, Krystyna had many diverse exploits one of her biggest coups ever was during the year 1944. Her friends had just been caught by the Nazi's. It was her one british bosses, Francis Cammaert, and one of the highest top-ranking SOE agents had fallen for a trap. The nazis set up an execution for her friends and were know awaiting death. But, then she showed up. Krystyna was incredibly smart, she began to sing softly a song that her friend Francis would know which was "Frankie and Johnny". She located them by following Francis's singing of the song, which lead her to the cells they were kept in. Krystyna had to free them but how? She had just thought of a plan. Krystyna walked up to the Military Officer nearby. They began to talk, she lied to him and claimed that she was a british agent and General Montgomery's niece. She told the guard that she had been sent to free the prisoners. But, the guards didn't think about it until she lied and said that there was an invasion coming from the Allied Forces and that it was but only hours away and if the officers were caught that they would be killed or that there would be terrible consequences for them not releasing the captives. So, the military officer freed her friends it also helped that she was a very pretty and the guard thought that he could trust her but he thought wrong. The plan had worked. Krystyna had just walked out of there with her friends by her side and life was good in that small short period of time.

In conclusion, Krystyna Skarbek was one of the best polish spies and a hero. In the holocaust it would bring out the real you. It would either bring out a bad,mean,cruel person or a good, compassionate, heroic person who would risk their lives to save people. She was one of the few good and brave people who would on the daily risk her mortality to save others. Krystyna would lead risky coups and many other adventures during the war. Many times during her exploits she would almost get caught but she was quick-minded which let her get out of situations many times without having a hair on her head harmed.But, throughout the war she was a hero and was saving other people even at the expense of her own life.

Berthold Beitz and Else.

Cade Silva

 The Holocaust was one of the most devastating events that occurred in history. Millions of lives were taken because of one thing, religion. There were also other groups that were killed simply because they were blamed for things that had made Germans seem like a complete fool. This event left people hopeless. Person after person were killed. Propaganda was displayed for anyone who had the chance to see it. These commercials were all lies. It had nothing to do with the gas chamber and actual death camps that the Jews were eventually gonna be shipped of too. They had been told lies their whole lives and when they finally woke up and realized they truth it was too late, they were on there way to a suffocating death. The Nazis were a very powerful group of people who were controlled by Hitler. Hitler took power of the government in 1933 and became abnormally famous and highly respected. While in power he established concentration camps, also known as death camps. This is why his reign was so different than any other of our country's leaders, instead of benefiting the people, he killed the people who he believed were bad, such as the Jews and other groups. But there were some Jews who were lucky enough to survive this event. For example one Jew who was lucky enough to survive was Else Beitz. Else was blessed with the gift of living. She nor did anyone else who was in the camps had a chance or even a believe of living. Her survival was pure luck. She was born on June 11, 1920 and died several years ago at the age of 94 on September 14 2014. During World War 2 Else saved many Jews from the Nazi's concentration camps. Else was married to a man named, Berthold Beitz. Together they save the lives of many Jews. During the Holocaust the the victims were starved. This is why Else and her husband were heroes. They surpassed all the Nazi guards and snuck food into the camps for the Jews to eat. This was important because it gave the Jews the thought and the hope of living. All day they would work and be fed only little amounts of bread and water. After a hard day of work

they would receive this extra food from Else and he husband knowing they had someone who believed they were good people who deserved to live. Not only were they suppliers, they were protectors and hiders. For the Jews who weren't already found and sent to the death camps, they may have been hiding in Else's and Berthold's home. Without the littlest bit of hesitation, the Beitz were willing to take anyone into their home to keep from another life being taken from the monstrous Nazis. Both of these heroic acts, had great risks, that Else and Berthold both knew. This risk was that if they were to be caught sneaking food, or to be caught hiding Jews, they would personally be taken to the concentration camps along with the Jews they were helping and they would be burnt to death or suffocated. These weren't the only things that this family did. After seeing the ongoing destruction of the population, Mr. Berthold realized he had to do something else, that was bigger. As the manager of an oil refinery, Berthold Beitz was capable of punishing Jews by having them shipped to himself on a big train. When the Jews got there they were supposed to work for Berthold until basically they were useless, or dead. But Berthold had tricked the Nazis. After requesting for Jews from the SS, he would have them shipped to him. But instead of making them work he allowed them to run away and be free. Freeing all these Jews was very unsuspicious since he woulv'e just told the government that they ran off, or died and then new trains would arrive to his plantation and he would do it all over again. Without these caring people thousands of more lives would have been taken. Else Beitz and her husband were thankfully smart enough to see the truth in Hitler's rule. After this couple became known, Berthold Beitz was honored as Righteous Among the Nations by Yad Vashem. Later Else also received this same esteem in 2006. This couple was recognized by the Central Council of Jews in Germany with the Leo Baeck Prize in 1999.

Works

https://www.washingtonpost.com/world/europe/berthold-beitz-german-industrialist-who-rescued-jews-during-world-war-ii-dies-at-99/2013/08/01/88d621f8-f9f8-11e2-9bde-7ddaa186b751_story.html?utm_term=.be16ef9e1094

http://db.yadvashem.org/righteous/family.html?language=en&itemId=4013862

Heroes of Poland During the Holocaust

Caden Giaudrone

During World War II, Germans considered themselves superior to Jews and Poles, along with other people of differing views. When Adolf Hitler and the Nazis took control of Poland in 1939, Poles were treated brutally. The Gestapo (German Police) and Nazi soldiers shot and killed tens of thousands of Poles. When the Nazi Party came to power, two million Polish Jews came under Hitler's control. Millions more Jews were controlled by the Nazis when Germany invaded the Soviet Union in July 1941. The way for the German to control all of the Jews, was simple to the Nazis. Their answer was to put Jews into ghettos. Ghettos were concentration camps where men worked hard labor. Most men and women died in concentration camps from gas chambers where they were locked in and then sprinkled with poison. Gas chambers were widely used at concentration camps because they were an easy way to kill large amounts of people.

Bernie Marks came to our school and told his story. When he was eleven years old, he and his family were taken from their home in Lodz, Poland and put into a concentration camp. Of the two hundred family members that made the trip from Lodz to Auschwitz, only five survived. Immediately after their arrival at Auschwitz, men were separated from the children. How did Bernie get into the group of men? His father changed his birthdate, which is 1932, to 1927 to make him 5 years older. This was especially important because the children were killed in gas chambers, while women were sent to Dachau. Bernie and his father were also sent there, to ultimately be liberated, but his mother and cousins were killed in a gas chamber upon their arrival. Had Bernie's father not changed his birthdate, he would not have even made it past the first day at Auschwitz. Why did women have to be transported to Dachau? There were no women at Auschwitz until the end of the war. Auschwitz was perhaps the worst of the concentration camps, but the largest ghetto was Warsaw, which housed more than 500,000 people.

In Poland, there were many heroes, but the main hero was Henryk Slawik. Henryk Slawik was a Polish politician during World War II. He was also a social worker and an activist who helped save 30,000 Polish refugees and 5,000 Jews during World War II. A man who escaped the subcamp of KL Plaszow worked his way from the mountains to the city of Budapest. There he met Slawik who was the leader of the Polish Civic Committee for Relief for Refugees, and also a Polish Socialist Party activist. The two men co-operated and went on many life-saving journeys. Perhaps the largest achievement was the asylum that was built in Budapest. The asylum housed up to 100 Jewish boys, who were then sent abroad undercover. Another man who saved many people was Witold Pilecki.

Witold Pilecki was a Polish army captain, who snuck into Auschwitz to see what was really happening. He snuck into the camp and stayed there for two and a half years, while sneaking out word of the execution and how it was being done. In the early years of the war, Poland was in chaos. It was controlled half by Germany and half by the Soviet Union. Pilecki was assigned to carry rocks in wheelbarrows as his job. While he did this, he was also doing research and smuggling information out of the camp with prisoners who escaped. Pilecki is a true hero because he risked his life inside of Auschwitz and also tried to plan a mass escape. A third man who is a Polish hero is Jan Karski.

Jan Karski was a Roman Catholic who was taken prisoner by the Soviet Union. He was put into a detention camp, which he escaped. He then joined the Polish underground movement and was useful with his knowledge of geography and foreign languages. In the mid 1940s, he was captured by the Gestapo and was brutally tortured. For fear of giving away secrets, he slashed his wrists, which led him to be sent to a hospital. The Polish underground movement helped him escape from this. In 1942, Karski volunteered himself to sneak in and out of the Warsaw ghettos where he saw for himself the starving and killing of Jews. He then went to London to tell of his findings to the Polish and British governments. He is a true hero because he risked his own life for others.

During World War II, Nazis viewed themselves as superior to many people of differing views, including Poles and Jews. Bernie Marks was a Jewish Pole, who endured five and a half years of unthinkable hardships and tormenting subjecting upon him by the Nazis. They treated the Poles like slaves, while a few men risked their lives to save hundreds of thousands of people. These men were Henryk Sławik, Witold Pilecki and Jan Karski. Their heroism put them at risk of brutal torture or even being put to death, but their cause was far greater than themselves. Would you have risked your life like these men?

Bibliography

"Jan Karski." United States Holocaust Memorial Museum, United States Holocaust Memorial Museum, www.ushmm.org/wlc/en/article.php?ModuleId=10008152. Accessed 22 Feb. 2017.

"Righteousness Among the Nations." Yad Vashem - Request Rejected, db.yadvashem.org/righteous/family.html?language=en&itemId=4017525. Accessed 22 Feb. 2017.

Staff, NPR. "Meet The Man Who Sneaked Into Auschwitz." NPR, NPR, 18 Sept. 2010, www.npr.org/templates/story/story.php?storyId=129956107. Accessed 22 Feb. 2017.

Polish Heros

Chase Johnson

From 1941 to 1945 Europe saw the mass murder of six million Jews and millions of other people directed by German Nazi party leader Adolf Hitler. This destruction is often referred to as the Holocaust, which Google defines as "the destruction or slaughter on a mass scale, especially caused by fire or nuclear war." At this time Poland had a large Jewish population. Because of this, Poland is where both the most Jews were killed and the most Jews were saved. Many people attempted to hide and protect Jews from the horrors of the holocaust. There are many people that lived in Poland who qualify as heroes for what they accomplished. They helped save the lives of thousands of Jews from the Holocaust.

One key Polish holocaust heroes was Albert Goering. He was the little brother of Hermann Goering, second in command of Nazi Germany. However, unlike his older brother, Albert hated the Nazi party with every fiber of his being. He did not support the Nazis treatment of Jews. He held a high ranking position in weapons manufacturing. He often turned a blind eye to sabotage and people stealing weapons. He even donated large amounts of money to anti-Nazi rebels. He was arrested many times but his brother got him out of jail every time. He sent a letter telling a death camp to release Josef Charvát, a doctor and resistance fighter. The commandant had two men named Charvát in the camp and, to be on the safe side, released them both. As a result, a communist leader named Charvát was also freed. Albert was very easy going and he was a hero for the lives he saved.

Another key Polish holocaust hero was Oskar Schindler. In October 1944, after the SS transferred the Emalia Jews to Plaszow, Schindler sought and obtained authorization to relocate his plant to Brünnlitz (Brnenec) in Moravia, and reopen it exclusively as an armaments factory. One of his assistants drew several versions of a list of up to 1,200 Jewish prisoners needed to work in the new factory. These lists came to be known collectively as "Schindler's List." Schindler met the specifications required by the SS to classify Brünnlitz as a subcamp of Gross-Rosen concentration camp and thereby facilitated the survival of around 800 Jewish men whom the SS deported from Plaszow via Gross-Rosen to Brünnlitz and between 300 and 400 Jewish women from Plaszow via Auschwitz. This is why Oskar Schindler was a hero.

Henryk Slawik was a Polish politician who saved thousands of Jews. Slawik wound up in Hungary as one of the over 100,000 Poles who had crossed the border to hide from the Nazis in Hungary. Hungary was considered a stop on the way to France, where Polish troops were being gathered. Hungary, formerly allied with the Third Reich, strove to implement an independent policy unofficially supporting Poles. Along the line, someone suggested that Slawik become the leader of the Polish-Hungarian Civic Committee for Relief to Refugees. Slawik quickly obtained the full powers from the Polish Government in Exile, thus becoming one of the official representatives of the Polish state in Budapest. At least one in every ten refugees was a Polish Jew. These are some reasons why Henryk Slawik was a hero.

Another hero of the Holocaust was Witold Pilecki. He was a Polish soldier during the Second Polish Republic and the founder of the Secret Polish Army. The Secret Polish Army was a resistance group in German-occupied Poland, and he was also a member of the underground Home Army. He was the author of Witold's Report, the first Allied intelligence report on Auschwitz concentration camp and the Holocaust. He volunteered for a Polish resistance operation to get imprisoned in the Auschwitz death camp in order to gather intelligence and escape. While in the camp, he organized a resistance movement and informed the Western Allies of Nazi Germany's Auschwitz atrocities. He also took part in the Warsaw Uprising in August 1944. He was executed after a show trial in 1948. As a result of his efforts he is considered as "one of the greatest wartime heroes".

Anton Sukhinski was another person who helped hide Jews. Sukhinski was considered the "local weirdo" and people constantly made fun of him. But when the Nazis rolled into Poland, Sukhinski was the only man in town that would help runaway Jews. He offered protection to a 16 year old girl, hiding her in his basement. Next, he offered protection to the Zeigers, a family he knew from before the war. Eventually, his neighbors discovered that he was harboring Jews, and they started blackmailing him for silence. One of the people Sukhinski was hiding shot the neighbor that was blackmailing him. Fearing that the gunshots would attract the Nazis, they tried to run away but they were forced back to Sukhinski's home when they couldn't find anywhere else to hide. Sukhinski, never fearing for his own safety, dug a hole for them in his basement and hid them there. They spent the next nine months in the little hole, unable to move, while Sukhinski brought them whatever he could scavenge. When the Nazis were finally driven out of Poland, Sukhinski's survivors could barely walk, but they were alive. Sukhinski was eventually honored as Righteous Among Nations.

During December 1941 Japan attacked Pearl Harbor and Hitler announced that Germany would join in the war on the U.S. This caused President Roosevelt to divert 90% of military power towards Germany. In World War II both America and England joined together and attacked Germany from one side while Russia attacked from the other side, ultimately causing Germany's demise and surrender in 1945. As a result of the lost war an end was brought to the holocaust through a gradual freeing of concentration camps. Those still imprisoned were released, although many never lived to see that day. One-third of the World's Jewish community had perished.

There are many heroes of the the holocaust, but no nation has as many as Poland. Poland was the most harshly treated by the Nazis, but it was also the country with the highest number of Jews saved.

"10 Little Known Heroes of the Holocaust." Toptenz.net. N.p., 11 Aug. 2014. Web. 11 Feb. 2017.

"Witold Pilecki." Witold Pilecki. N.p., n.d. Web. 11 Feb. 2017.

Hero of the Holocaust." Hero of the Holocaust -- Isurvived.org. N.p., n.d. Web. 11 Feb. 2017.

"Oskar Schindler." United States Holocaust Memorial Museum. United States Holocaust Memorial Museum, n.d. Web. 11 Feb. 2017.

Surkes, Stuart Winer and Sue, Raphael Ahren, Times Of Israel Staff, Gabe Friedman, Shoshanna Solomon, Judah Ari Gross, Ricky Ben-David, Times of Israel Staff and AFP, and Gavin Rabinowitz. "Top Israeli Honor Eludes Goering's Brother, Who Heroically Saved Jews." The Times of Israel. N.p., 25 Jan. 2016. Web. 11 Feb. 2017.

Heroes of Poland

Gaurav Turaga

 Irena Sendler was born on 1910 in Otwock, Poland. Irena's father was a doctor who treated primarily Jewish people. Irena Sendler was part of The Council of Aid to Jews during the war. During her time in college, Irena Sendler was suspended for 3 years for sitting at a Jewish only table in her college. During the war, Irena and her Colleagues managed to save over 2,500 Jewish children.

Irena and her colleagues saved over 2,500 Jews during the war. Irena managed to get into the concentration camp legally and then convince parents who had kids to let the kid go with her. Irena got into the camp as a doctor. When asked why Irena did what she did, she replied "My parents taught me," Irena wrote back, "that if a man is drowning, it is irrelevant what is his religion or nationality. One must help him." In conclusion, Irena Sendler saved over 2,500 jews by getting into a concentration camp legally.

During the war, Irena sendler was captured by the Gestapo and was brutally beaten. The nazi's brutally beat her because they hoped that she would reveal the location of The Council of Aid to Jews. During Irena's trial, She was sentenced to death. The secret organization managed to bribe a guard that marked Irena as dead before she was executed. Although Irena escaped, She wouldn't be able to walk again due to her injuries suffered by the Gestapo. In conclusion, Irena Sendler was brutally beaten by the Nazis

Overall, Irena Sendler was a Hero of Poland due to her many accomplishments. Her accomplishments include saving over 2,500 Jewish children, and potentially saving more by not revealing the location of the secret organization.

Jan Karski was a polish diplomat. Jan grew up in a diverse neighborhood that had many Jewish families. Jan Karski is from a Roman Catholic family. Jan was born in Lodz, Poland. He received a master's degree in Law and Diplomatic science. During the war, Jan was first a officer in the Polish Army and then worked as a courier for the Polish Resistance.

Jan Karski was a hero from Poland because he notified Allied leaders of the holocaust. He served as a courier for the Polish Resistance. He smuggled himself into a camp to get information from Polish leaders in the camp and then repeat it to allied leaders. During the war Karski was captured 2 times. The first time was by a Soviet Army. Karski managed to escape. The next time, he was captured by the Gestapo. He was tortured there but managed not to reveal information before getting smuggled out. One of his most important missions was to notify Allied leaders of the holocaust. When Karski arrived in London, many Allied leaders denied it our claimed it wasn't real because they feared they would have to take the 1 million refugees from the camps at the time. Finally, A relocation center was set up in North Africa. After the war, Jan Karski received a PhD and become a professor at the University of Georgetown. Jan died on July 13, 2000. Overall, it is safe to say that Jan Karski was a Hero from Poland.

In conclusion, Jan was a Polish diplomat. Jan was from a Roman Catholic family where he received a master's degree in Law and Diplomatic science. Jan served as an officer for the polish army. When the polish army was defeated, he became a courier for the polish resistance.

Henryk Slawik was a politician from Poland Henryk was born in 1894. He was drafted to join the army during World War 1. Henryk joined the polish army during ww2. He is credited with saving more than 30,000 polish refugees including over 5,000 Jews. Slawik was captured and sent to a POW (prisoner of war) camp. All in All, Henryk Slawik saved over 30,000 polish refugees.

Henryk Slawik

Henryk Slawik was a hero from Poland because he saved over 30,000 Polish refugees.

Henryk was brought to Budapest and was allowed to create the Citizens Community for Help for Polish Refugees. He found jobs for many POW. Once Hungary started segregating jews, Slawik started giving out false documents that proved someone to be Polish and Roman Catholic. Once Germany took over Hungary, Slawik went underground and help Jews escape. Sadly, Henryk was captured by Germany and was brutally tortured.

Fortunately, Henryk didn't reveal the location of his colleagues who were helping him. Henryk was then sent to a concentration camp and died there. All in All, Henryk Slawik was a hero from poland because he saved over 30,000 refugees.

In conclusion, Henryk Slawik was a hero of Poland because he helped over 30,000 refugees. Henryk was also a hero because he was captured and brutally tortured and didn't reveal the location of his colleagues. Henryk eventually died in a concentration camp.

Works Cited

"Irena Sendler: WWII Rescuer and Hero By Peter K. Gessner." Irena Sendler: WWII Rescuer and Hero. Web. 06 Feb. 2017. http://info-poland.buffalo.edu/classroom/sendler/

"Irena Sendler: In the Name of Their Mothers." PBS. PBS. Web. 06 Feb. 2017. http://www.chabad.org/theJewishWoman/article_cdo/aid/939081/jewish/Irena-Sendler.htm

https://www.jewishvirtuallibrary.org/jan-karski

http://religiousreader.org/jan-karski-the-catholic-spy-who-warned-about-the-holocaust-in-1942/

https://www.pw.edu.pl/engpw/Research/Business-Innovations-Technology-BIT-of-WUT/Jozef-Kosacki-an-engineer-at-the-fronts-of-WWII

http://db.yadvashem.org/righteous/family.html?language=en&itemId=9076665

http://nowahistoria.interia.pl/polska-walczaca/news-henryk-slawik-piekna-przemilczana-postac,nId,1537146

Heroes of Poland

Jaden DeFazio

 There were several amazing heroes of Poland during the Holocaust and World War II. Many people risked their lives to try to help save others from the Natzis. These people played very big roles in helping Jews live and putting an end to the Holocaust and World War II. Many lives were saved by these very heroic people. Out of the many Polish heroes, I wrote about of few that I found interesting.

First off, Jan Karski was a very big hero for the Jews during the Holocaust. Jan Karski was born on April 24, 1914. During the outbreak of World War II in 1939, Karski became a prisoner of war for the red army. Two months later, Karski escaped from the red army. He returned to Poland and joined the Underground Polish Army. Karski was smuggled into Warsaw Ghetto- the largest Jewish ghetto- to be a witness of awful conditions of the Jews and reveal it to the outside world. After looking through Warsaw Ghetto, Karski put on a disguise and went on a very risky trip to a Natzi concentration camp. He witnesses a mass murder there. When Karski left the camp, he knew it was crucial that he let someone know about the exterminations. His goal was to stop the Holocaust. After his request, a meeting was set up with President Franklin D. Roosevelt in which Karski told him about the mass murder of the

Jews. Many leaders and officials were informed about the killing of the Jews. Although Karski didn't complete his goal of ending the holocaust, he played a very important role by spreading the word of the Jews being killed.

Not many people knew much about the concentration camps in the early years of World War II. A Polish army captain named Witold Pilecki had a plan to gain more information on the camps. Many people thought the concentration camps such as Auschwitz were just POW camps rather than a places meant for killing. Pilecki went to Warsaw where they were rounding up Jews to be sent off into the camps. Pilecki was taken to camp with all of the Jews All of his hair was shaved and he was sprinkled in cold water. Pilecki wore the number 4859- which he could tell was a small number compared to some people in the following years who were in the 15,000s. He was assigned to painful work such as carrying rocks in wheelbarrows. What most mattered to Pilecki was gaining information on the camps. He used the method of sending messages out with people who would escape the camps. He would write messages about the brutality of the camps and how people were being killed and burned in gas chambers. It was so terrible many people didn't believe it. For the next two and a half years, Pilecki kept on building up his reports on the camp and sending them to London. After three years in the camp, Pilecki thought it was too dangerous to stay in that camp any longer. He managed to get a job near the back of the camp which very unsecured. Pilecki and a few other sneaked out during the night. It was very risky and they were almost caught. Pilecki was now seen as a hero who played a very important role for his side during the Holocaust and World War II.

Another hero of Poland during World War II was a woman named Karolina Juszczykowska. She didn't have a big impact on the holocaust as a whole, but this lady was very brave and still heroic. Karolina Juszczykowska was a woman who helped out two young men who were Jewish. They offered her 300 Zloty- the basic Polish currency- per week which she was in desperate need of, so she accepted. Juszczykowska was taking a huge risk here because she wasn't supposed to be helping out the Jews during World War II, but she said she didn't care about politics. The two men would sleep on the floor and they would get locked in during the day when Juszczykowska went to work. Six weeks after the guys started staying with Juszczykowska, they were caught. Juszczykowska was arrested and the police found out what was happening. Juszczykowska was also later given a death sentence for her action, although many people thought that this was a poor decision. Despite her death, Juszczykowska was seen as a true hero and a brave woman.

Henryk Slawik was another Polish hero during the holocaust. When Poland was defeated in September of 1939, thousands on Poles were sent over to Hungary in a city called Budapest. Jews were also being sent into the ghettos of Budapest. Henryk Slawik and many other Poles were arrested for crossing the border and were kept of prisoners of the war. That was when Slawik was introduced to József Antall, the guy who was responsible for the Polish refugees. Slawik convinced Atall to help make a committee for the Poles. The two guys teamed up and created the Citizens Committee for help for Polish Refugees. Slawik was very devoted to his work and did not discriminate against the Jews. Slawik worked together with Atall and the head of the Polish Red Cross in Hungary to forge christian documents for the Jews. All the Jews in the refugee camps were located by the group. Out of the thousands of

Jews in the refugee camp many were spared. For example, in July 1943, a group of 76 children between the ages three and nineteen were gathered by the Committee and taken to Vac- a city about 30 kilometers away. The Polish committee proclaimed an official boarding school there for the kids. When the war was over, a few of the kids from Vac returned to Poland but many of them resettled in the United States and Israel. Out of the thousands of Jewish refugees that were saved that was just one example. The Citizens Committee for the Polish Refugees remained strong throughout the war and Henryk Slawik was recognized as a true hero.

Those were just a few of the many Polish heroes during the Holocaust and World War II. Without any Polish heroes the Holocaust might've been a lot worse for the Jews. It is important for people to have the courage to stand up for what is right.

Work Cited

"Jan Karski" https://www.jewishvirtuallibrary.org/jan-karski

NPR Staff, "Meet the man who sneaked into Auschwitz" NPR http://www.npr.org/templates/story/story.php?storyId=129956107 September 18, 2010

"Karolina Juszczykowska - Stories of Women Who Rescued Jews During the Holocaust" http://www.yadvashem.org/yv/en/exhibitions/righteous-women/juszczykowska.asp

"The Righteous Among The Nations" http://db.yadvashem.org/righteous/family.html?language=en&itemId=4017525

The Heroes of Poland

James Burgos

Though some heroes of the Holocaust are recognized many aren't remembered. People from different nations risked their lives to fight for what was right. People of different professions whether it be soldiers or common people helped those in the concentration camps. A nation full of Holocaust heroes at the time was Poland. Many Polish, men and women alike, did anything they could to help those confined in the camps.

Jan Karski was a Polish soldier who, when captured by the Soviets, escaped and joined the underground Polish movement. He was used as messenger, crossing enemy lines to give information to the allies. During his mission in Poland, he was sent to Warsaw, the capital of Poland, and he saw the terrible things the Nazis were doing to people there. After seeing this horrible images, he disguised himself to sneak into a concentration camp. He was met with mass killings and murders of people. He witnessed the terrible conditions the Jews and other ethnic groups were put under. Jan Karski went down as one of the first people to know about what happened inside the concentration camps, and one of the first to tell the allied powers about it. He moved to the United States where he spent the rest of his life teaching and educating people about the remembrance of the Holocaust. He died in 2000 in Washington D.C.

Like Karski, another Polish soldier Witold Pilecki was sent behind enemy lines to investigate a concentration camp. Witold Pilecki, like Karski, was also part of the underground resistance in Poland. The underground resistance had wanted to know what was happening in a camp known as Auschwitz. They believed at the time that it was a POW (prisoner of war) camp. Pilecki volunteered himself to go and investigate. He found much more than they had expected, and he spent the next 3 years in Auschwitz undercover delivering secret messages while delivering laundry into the town. Like Karski, he was one of the first people to tell the allies about what was happening inside a concentration camp. But unlike Karski he was in the most devastating and destructive camp, Auschwitz. Very few people know of his story because after the war, he was captured by the Soviets, and was shot only a short time after the war had ended. He has been known as hero for telling the allies of the horrors in one of the most notorious concentration camps during the war.

Irena Sendler was a nurse for the underground resistance during the war. Her efforts in helping the Jews started as soon as Germany invaded Poland. She began to give food and shelter to Jews. When Warsaw was formed into a ghetto about a year later in 1940, she helped by saving Jewish orphans from the Nazis. As a nurse, she could go into Warsaw and smuggle children out in her ambulance. After smuggling them out, she would set up hiding places for them to stay. Sources say she helped save around 2500 Jewish children in Warsaw. Almost all of the orphans' parents were killed in a concentration camp called Treblinka, and without her, they would have died also. In 1943, she was captured by the Nazis, and tortured. She was told to give the names of the orphans she managed to smuggle but she wouldn't say a word. She was sentenced to death, and she would have been killed but underground activists bribed the Nazis to let her go. She had managed to escape death, and in 1944 she was released. She would survive until the end of the war and live until 2008.

Though most of these heroes were a part of the Polish underground resistance, others were normal common people. In Zborow, a man named Anton Sukhinski lived alone and was seen as a loner in the town. But when the war broke out, he took in 7 Jews into his home and they hid there from 1943 until the end of the war. Sukhinski dug a hole in his cellar where the Jews stayed after people became suspicious there were Jews living with him. He would give them what little food he had and they barely survived. For 9 months the Jews would stay in that hole, unable to move. When let out they thought they had been caught, but it was just Anton telling them the war was over. Since he was known as the loner of the town, he was able to hide the 7 Jews without being caught. Sukhinski would be later recognized as "Righteous Among the Nations" by Yad Vashem in 1974, and passed away in 2006.

After Poland was taken by Germany 1939, thousands of Poles tried moving to Hungary, and a Polish activist named Henryk Slawik would help immensely. With help from other Polish leaders, Slawik helped forge Christian documents for all Jewish immigrants moving into Hungary, and put them in refugee camps. Slawik at one point gathered 76 orphans and put together a boarding school for them in safe place away from the capital in Vac. When the Nazis invaded Hungary, Slawik made the school seem more Christian so the children would be spared. But in 1944, he was captured and tortured by the Nazis in concentration camp. Through his brutal beatings he would still not give up one name of any of the Polish Jews the immigrated to Hungary. Eventually, he was killed in the Mauthausen concentration camp some time in 1944. Because of his actions, he was recognized as "Righteous Among the Nations" like Anton Sukhinski.

Though all of these people may have never known of each other or what they had done, they all put their lives on the line to help others. Their selflessness and actions saved thousands of people from death.

Works Cited

""Women of Valor"" Irena Sendler - Stories of Women Who Rescued Jews During the Holocaust - Righteous Among the Nations - Yad Vashem. Web. 20 Feb. 2017.

"Anton Sukhinski." Anton Sukhinski. Web. 20 Feb. 2017.

"Jan Karski." Jan Karski. Web. 19 Feb. 2017.

Staff, NPR. "Meet The Man Who Sneaked Into Auschwitz." NPR. NPR, 18 Sept. 2010. Web. 19 Feb. 2017.

Heroes of Poland

Kate Fujiwara

Have you ever faced a life or death situation? A situation where your religion or belief is held against you and you are harmed or even killed because of it? During World War two, the fight between America, Great Britain, and France against the axis powers Japan, Italy and Nazi Germany, over 10,000,000 people died because of their beliefs or their religion. Many different countries contributed to this war. Poland being one of them. Poland was one of the greatest contributors in saving the lives of the Jews in Germany.

Poland is located in the continent of Europe and neighbors with many countries including Germany on its western side, and Belarus on its eastern side. During the time of the holocaust, Belarus was part of Nazi germany and Poland was the centerpiece between them. According to the article The Truth About Poland and the Holocaust by Abraham Foxman, Jewish concentration camps were mostly located in Poland because most Jews lived there during this time period. So since most of the Jews were in Poland, Poland was considered the first country to be aggressively overtaken by Nazi invaders. In taking in consideration of this, Poland's political point of view saw this and the imprisoning of the Jews as an act of despotism. This point of view from a political standpoint creates disputes between the thoughts and actions of different countries.

Although the Jewish concentration camps that were located in Poland were in German territory, under German control, Polish leaders figured that they should take a stand in ending the bitter treating towards Jews and other people imprisoned because of their religious standpoint and the fact that the Nazis were slowly but surely taking over their home country. After a while, Jews started fleeing towards Poland with a thought that they might have a better chance at escaping imprisonment by the Nazis. In regards to this, Nazi Germany had an even better reason to invade Poland even further in search of the Jewish refugees. The attacks the began to occur against Poland created friction between the two countries and Poland decided to do something about it.

Poland began to establish a bigger more organized army that could defend poland and everyone in it. Over time polish leaders came up with different tactics that would help solve the Nazi problems. Some of these tactics according to the article Democracy Dies in Darkness by The Washington Post, included invasions, protests, and secret deportation of Jews from Germany mostly by a sea route, which means a journey by ship. As time passed the Nazis grew even more furious by the advancing of Jewish refugees into Poland, and on the authority of the article German Invasion of Poland, Jewish Refugees, around right after the Nazis seized into eastern Poland, which was where most of the Jewish refugees were hiding out, around 300,000 Jewish refugees had been captured by the germans, and a little after this, german police had captured hundreds to thousands of more Jews who had escaped to Poland. In view of the fact that the Nazis were continuing to trap the Jews in spite of that the Polish were continuing to fight against them to stop it, some Polish leaders started to conflict even more with the war.

Since Polish leaders were so determined in defeating Hitler and his Nazi party, Poland would still not back down from the war. As more and more Jews were captured, and the more Poland was taken over, the Polish became more enraged. Knowing this,

Hitler planned an attack on the eastern and western sides of Poland. Hitler chose to form the attack this way because he figured that all the chaos happening, if he sent a group to one of the directions, then Polish soldiers may be of less quantity on the other side. In this case, Hitler was right. As claimed by the article German invasion of Poland, Poland did not survive the Nazi attack for long and Poland was taken over by Nazi Germany. In spite of Poland's efforts during the war, most Jews were taken hostage by Nazi Germany.

Poland is still known today as one of the greatest contributors towards freeing the Jews. Polish leaders came up with tactics to help support their fight against Nazi Germany. Overall even though in spite their efforts, Poland was unable to make it the whole way but they still did leave a great impact on the holocaust. So whenever the statement "Heroes of Poland comes , you could figure that there were a few people who made the greatest impact, but in this case Poland itself was a hero. Poland wasn't a hero because it lost the fight, it was a hero because it fought for others when they could have backed off even though they were not Jews and they were not completely targeted on the capture list. In conclusion, if you have even been in a life or death situation, one where your religion or belief can determine your fate, you can refer back to the impact that Poland had on the Holocaust.

Work Cited

Foxman, Abraham. "The Truth about Poland and the Holocaust." MSNBC. NBCUniversal News Group, 21 Apr. 2015. Web. 23 Feb. 2017.

"German Invasion of Poland: Jewish Refugees, 1939." United States Holocaust Memorial Museum. United States Holocaust Memorial Museum, n.d. Web. 23 Feb. 2017.

"Where Is Poland?" WorldAtlas. N.p., 02 Oct. 2015. Web. 23 Feb. 2017.

An Underground Hero

Lauren Buckmaster (Winner)

"The world is a dangerous place to live: not because of the people who are evil, but because of the people who don't do anything about it" -Albert Einstein. When most people hear the word Holocaust they think of a horrible time in history. It was a time that was so unimaginably terrifying that many of us cannot begin to truly grasp the horror of the events that occurred. For millions of people, however, the Holocaust was more than just a story in history books. Those who lived during that time experienced a suffering that was incomprehensible. Due to the fact that many of the Holocaust survivors are still alive today, we have an opportunity to hear first hand stories of pain, torture, and abuse. We also have the honor of hearing amazing stories of survival, thanks to the unnoticed heroes who put their lives on the line to save others from death. One of these heroes was Leopold Socha.

Leopold Socha was a young Catholic man who lived in a extremely poor neighborhood in Poland with his wife and daughter. Although he was a convicted criminal, he was also deeply horrified by the German hatred for the Jewish people and wanted to help out. He also was in need of money and knew that the Jewish people would pay him quick money. At that time, however, it was very dangerous to help hide people from the German army. Leopold had a wife and daughter to protect as well, so he knew he needed to be careful if he wanted to help the Jewish people. Leopold worked in the sewer canals in his town. In 1943 he took a group of 21 Jewish people into the sewers to hide them. He decided that he would take a risk to earn money and help them hide from the German Army.

There were a lot of risks with helping the Jewish people during the Holocaust. One of the biggest risks was being caught. A flyer issued by the German police in 1942 stated "not only Jews who have left their designated residential area will be punished with death, but the same penalty applies to anyone who knowingly provides refuge (a hiding place) to such Jews." Socha was fully aware of these risks when he started aiding the jews in the sewer. It was also a finial risk for Socha and his family because he need to use his own money to continue aiding the Jews. Hubpages quotes "Jews had no source of income. It made no difference to the Sochas and Wroblewskis, they provided for the needs of the Jews from their own pockets" Even though Socha was a poor man he started to feel sympathy and still by essential needs for the jews with his own money. Helping out jewish people was a very dangerous job.

Leopold Socha went through thick and thin with the 21 Jews in the sewer. Socha brought essential items to them and helped preserve their faith. David lee Preston quotes in an interview with CNN "The sewer workers brought them food, washed their clothes, moved them when their safety was in danger and visited them every day except Sunday." Socha made it his top priority to keep these Jews safe and help them out to the best of his capability. As previously stated, he started aiding the Jews in the sewer to earn money. After their money ran out, he continued to help them out of the kindness on his heart. It was a very emotional time for the Socha family. One of the most difficult times for Socha was having to witness eleven of them die. David lee Preston also quotes "Some decided to leave as the ordeal wore on and were killed above ground, and one older woman died of natural causes. A baby was born and had to be suffocated lest its cries give away the group. My mother was among 10 who survived the entire 14 months." Seeing people many die was very hard for Socha but he was able to stay strong and and even dug some of their graves. Leopold Socha had to go through many challenges with the people in the sewer but he got through it.

In 1945 the war ended and the remaining 10 survivors saw the sunshine for the first time in 14 months. The survivors called Socha their angel and knew they could not have made it through without him. Unfortunately, Leopold Socha's life came to an end soon after the war ended. Less than a year later he was riding bicycles with his daughter and a huge truck swerved and almost hit her. As he pushed his daughter out of the way, the truck struck and killed him. As for the people in the sewer, they went on to live a normal life. Their unforgettable story was recently written in a book called The Girl in the Green Sweater. A movie titled In Darkness was made based on that book. One of the girls that Socha saved in the sewer, Krystyna Chiger, is still alive today. She vividly remembers Socha as a true hero and recognizes that he is the reason she is here today. "My mother used to say that he was an angel that was sent by God to save us...he selflessly helped a group of Jews when so many collaborated in their destruction." -Chiger

Works Cited

United States Holocaust Memorial Museum. United States Holocaust Memorial Museum. Web. 22 Feb. 2017.

CNN. Cable News Network. Web. 22 Feb. 2017.

"'These Were Terrible Times': The True Story behind In Darkness." Film Blog. Guardian News and Media, 23 Mar. 2012. Web. 22 Feb. 2017.

"Angels in the Dark." Aishcom. Web. 22 Feb. 2017.

"The Chiger Family." The Chiger Family. Web. 22 Feb. 2017.

"Leopold Socha." ActsofCourage - Leopold Socha. Web. 22 Feb. 2017.

Weill, Asher. "New Honors for the Polish Sewer Worker Who Saved Jews from the Nazis." Haaretz.com. 23 Nov. 2014. Web. 22 Feb. 2017.

YadVashem. "Rescued by Righteous Among the Nations: Testimony of Kristina Keren (Krystyna Chirowski)." YouTube. YouTube, 01 Mar. 2011. Web. 22 Feb. 2017.

Rlbert00. "Heroes of the Holocaust: Leopold Socha and Stefan Wroblewski." HubPages. HubPages, 30 Nov. 2014. Web. 22 Feb. 2017.

Irena Sendler: Brave and Courageous

Lauren Rodenberg (Winner)ian

Irena Sendler was a remarkable hero. She went up against the Nazis and put her life in danger to rescue innocent children in the ghetto. This is the story of an amazing woman and how she was able to rescue so many Jews. Irena's courageous acts during World War II, her childhood experiences, and her public recognition all tell an amazing story of an amazing woman.

Irena Sendler was a hero for many reasons. She was a big part of Zegota. Zegota was an underground Polish group that helped Jews. Sendler worked in the children's area. Before she was a part of Zegota, she made over 3,000 fake documents to help the Jews. Irena visited the Warsaw ghetto and carried in food, medicine, and clothes. She and her friend went undercover as Jews to smuggle people out of the ghettos. The ways children snuck out were creative. Some went out in suitcases, ambulances, and even a toolbox. Also, some went out through the courthouse or sewers. She gave them all new Christian names and sent them out with other families or orphanages. But, Irena was smart. She wrote down all the names of the kids she saved and put them in jars. Then, she buried the jars under an apple tree, hoping that the kids could be reunited with their parents one day. Sendler had a brave soul to do all of those good deeds because that just made her a target of the Nazis. Unfortunately, the Nazis finally found her and took her to prison on October 20, 1943. They came looking for the list of names Irena had. Before they came in, Irena had thrown it to her friend, who hid it inside her underwear. The Nazis searched through the entire house, until giving up and taking Irena to the Pawiak prison. There, they tortured Sendler so much that she broke her feet and legs, but the courageous woman would not give in. Sadly, Irena was sentenced to death. But, one of her guardian angels from the Zegota bribed the guard to delay the execution, so Irena was able to escape. Without a doubt, Irena Sendler was a fearless hero during the Nazi regime.

Before the war, Irena Sendler lived a fairly simple life. Her original name is Irena Krzyżanowska. Sendler was born on February 15, 1910 in Warsaw, Poland. Irena actually was raised in Otwock, Poland. She was an only child. Her family was Roman Catholic. Her father was a doctor and most of his patients were Jews. He taught her many things. She was taught to respect people for who they are. Irena mentioned a saying from him, "I was taught that if you see a person drowning, you must jump into the water to save them, whether you can swim or not." This is where Irena developed her caring personality. Her father unfortunately died in 1917 from the typhus disease that he caught from his patients. Later, Irena went to Warsaw college. But her fiery personality got her in trouble and kicked out for three years. Irena Sendler's childhood and her father's teaching her to become a caring and selfless human being prepared her for her courageous acts during World War II .

Irena Sendler has a breathtaking legacy. Right after the war, Irena immediately started searching for the families of the kids whose names were in the jars she buried. Unfortunately, most of their parents were put in the Treblinka camp. It was a death camp that Irena had saved their kids from. Irena was very humble because she wanted no credit for her actions and insisted she was not a hero. Later, Irena said, " We who were rescuing children are not some kind of heroes. That term irritates me greatly. The opposite is true-- I continue to have qualms of conscience that I did so little. I could have done more. This regret will follow me to my death." Sendler is honored as a Righteous Gentile by Yad Vashem, which is a Jewish organization devoted to honoring those who helped Jews during the Holocaust. In the year 2000, some high school students created a play for National History Day called "Life in a Jar" about Irena's experiences during the horrific war. The play has been all over Europe and the United States. Elzbieta Ficowska was five months old when Irena rescued her. One frightening night, Irena snuck Elzbieta out of the Warsaw ghetto in a carpenter's box. Elzbieta still travels around telling people about the Holocaust and Irena's legacy. There is also a biography about Irena Sendler. Back then when the play first came out, there was only one website about Irena. Now there are over 500,000 websites about her and her remarkable work during the war. In 2003, Sendler was awarded Poland's highest award - The Order of the White Eagle. With her second husband, she had two boys and a girl. But, one of the boys died as a toddler and the other son died in 1999. Irena died peacefully on May 12, 2008. She was 98 years old. Irena Sendler's legacy will continue to live on in plays, books, and websites.

Irena Sendler was a hero in Poland during the Holocaust. Her actions during that terrible time, how she was raised, and her legacy tell her full story. Irena saved many innocent children and she had a tender heart. Those she rescued will always remember Irena Sendler as their gentle hero. They are her legacy.

Works Cited

"Facts about Irena." Life in a Jar. N.p., n.d. Web. 22 Feb. 2017.

"Irena Sendler." Irena Sendler. N.p., n.d. Web. 22 Feb. 2017. < http://www.auschwitz.dk/sendler.htm >.

"Irena Sendler." Irena Sendler. N.p., n.d. Web. 22 Feb. 2017. < http://www.jewishvirtuallibrary.org/irena-sendler >.

Heroes of Poland

Logan Milano

If I told you someone volunteered for Auschwitz would you believe me? From all of the horrible things you've heard about Auschwitz, you would think that they were either insane or incredibly brave. During World War II, one stout-hearted man by the name of Witold Pilecki was purposely imprisoned at Auschwitz and stayed for three long years. Incredibly, he did this to spill the secrets of the death camp to the public.

World War II was a rough time period to grow up in. World War II started because Nazi leader Adolf Hitler attacked Poland. WWII was between the axis powers and allied powers. This was a very difficult time for Poland. East Poland had been annexed by the Soviet Union while the western half was taken by Nazi Germany. The Polish managed to establish secret networks under Germany that were called the Underground State and the Home Army. As if the war wasn't bad enough, the Holocaust began. Hitler had plans to commit genocide against the Jews along with other classes of people he deemed "flawed". It was tough for bystanders in this time too because they had to decide whether to risk their own lives to help the targets or to sit and watch them be massacred. There were a lot of things to deal with in these tough times.

From the moment Pilecki was born, he was destined to be a soldier. Witold Pilecki was born on May 13, 1901 in Karelia, Russia. His family moved to Wilno where he joined the secret ZHP Scouts organization. He joined the Polish self defense units in 1910 where he disarmed retreating German troops and helped collect weapons. In 1920, Pilecki joined the regular Polish Army where he became a cavalry officer. The Poles were eager to assist in the decline of German rule so they helped the allied powers in the war. The Poles didn't know what was happening in concentration camps and didn't think they needed to find out, but Pilecki was onto the Nazis and called for a mission to infiltrate the Nazi camps. Pilecki's background definitely contributed to his later success in the challenges he faced.

Sneaking into Auschwitz wasn't easy. First, Pilecki's commanders didn't want to sign off on the seemingly wasteful mission at first; they didn't think anything important would be found. Second, he didn't know exactly how he would get into the camp. Luckily he figured out that he could enter a street round-up of Poles in Warsaw, which he did on Sept. 19, 1940. He was sent to Auschwitz and took the alias Tomasz Serafinski. Once he got in, he realized the tough part was just beginning. The Nazis shaved Pilecki's head bald and tattooed the number 4859 on him. He was fed very little and got hit in the head with a metal rod taking out two of his teeth. Auschwitz was even worse than he had anticipated.

Meanwhile, Pilecki learned all of the secret information and needed to find a way to tell people while in prison. He had two main ways of smuggling out the secrets. First, he helped prisoners escape and sent them to tell specific people about Auschwitz. Second, he wrote messages on dirty laundry. Part of the work at Auschwitz was to do laundry. The laundry had to be done in the nearest town so the Nazis made the Jews do that too. Pilecki would write secrets on dirty laundry and have the Jews that delivered the laundry secretly drop Pilecki's laundry with messages along the way to the town. An officer from The Underground Poland Army would pick them up and deliver Pilecki's messages from there. When people in the underground Polish army first read his messages they thought it was exaggeration. In horror, the Polish read of the gas chambers, ovens, injections and other terrible things of the camp and spread the word. They began vigorously planning to stop the concentration camps but there wasn't much that they could do. Even though the people couldn't do anything about the camps, it revealed how terrible Hitler truly was and most likely influenced more people to join in the fight against the Nazis.

It took Pilecki three years but he finally felt he had enough information and was ready to escape. Pilecki had a job as a baker. He had noticed a weak door with little security.

Pilecki decided the time had come. He and a few other inmates gathered around the door and then took off. Pilecki says he remembers hearing gunshots from behind and luckily no one was hit. It took a lot of courage but Pilecki escaped with not only his life but the secrets of Auschwitz and other prisoners.

Witold Pilecki's actions were dangerous and he knew it, but he did it anyway because at heart, Pilecki is a true hero. He volunteered to go to Auschwitz to try to help the world. It took courage and bravery to not only volunteer, but come up with the mission of infiltrating a Nazi death camp. He went on this seemingly suicide mission to find out about what is really happening in the Nazi camps, which was vital information. When he escaped Auschwitz he took prisoners with him. Most people would have stayed safe and just left. Pilecki however took other prisoners with him even though it was risky and ended up saving their lives in addition to his own. Pilecki's courageous work should not go untold, for he was a genuine savior.

Witold Pilecki had a lasting impression on the world. Pilecki's discoveries were helpful to winning the war. The information of Auschwitz built up even more hatred towards Hitler and the Nazi party. It also most likely influenced more countries to join in on the fight against Nazi Germany. The Polish had always overlooked the Nazi camps. Nobody ever thought the camps were anything special until Pilecki opened their eyes to the horrors within. If not for Pilecki, people wouldn't have known about the camps until after the war and more people would've died. Pilecki's effect on the war was substantial.

In total, Witold Pilecki has vanquished some of the most arduous tasks; all with the intent of making the world a better place. If you were to tell me that Witold Pilecki is not a hero, then I don't have the slightest idea what is.

Works Cited

Macherez, Félix "Witold Pilecki Was the First to Report on the Horrors Taking Place in the Nazi Concentration Camp." Vice. , 8 Apr. 2014. Web. 17 Feb. 2017. < https://www.vice.com/en_us/article/witold-pilecki-the-auschwitz-volunteer-interview >

Unknown "Biography - Witold Pilecki" Rotamaster Unknown 17 Feb. 2017. < http://www.en.pilecki.ipn.gov.pl/rpe/biography/8193,Rotamaster-Witold-Pilecki.html >

Netanyahu, Benjamin "Witold Pilecki." Jewish Virtual Library. N.p., n.d. Web. 19 Feb. 2017. < http://www.jewishvirtuallibrary.org/witold-pilecki >

Staff, NPR. "Meet The Man Who Sneaked Into Auschwitz." NPR, 18 Sept. 2010. Web. 20 Feb. 2017. < http://www.npr.org/templates/story/story.php?storyId=129956107 >

Snyder, Timothy. "'Were We All People?'." The New York Times. 23 June 2012. Web. 22 Feb. 2017. < http://www.nytimes.com/2012/06/24/books/review/the-auschwitz-volunteer-by-witold-pilecki.html >

Heros of Poland

Lydia Taylor

"How wonderful it is that nobody need wait a single moment before starting to improve the world", - Anne Frank. During the Holocaust many Jews were massacred, and a few people tried to save the Jews' lives, but if they were caught they would suffer the same fate. Despite the consequences, over six thousand Polish people heroically tried to help the Jews in the area. In Poland many people helped the Jews, four of them were Józef Biesaga, Janina Radlińska, Marek Arczynski, and Alina Stalkowska.

Jozef Biesaga was the father of the Biesaga, who hid different Nassan family members throughout the war in Smardzowice, Poland, a small village twenty kilometers from Krakow, Poland. First, in June 1941 they hid Dora Nassan along with her child for about three months. Though it was the beginning of the war, in Poland Jews were already hiding, and the consequence of hiding them was great. Later on David Nassan decided to move his wife and child from hiding into the forest, but on the way they were caught by the Nazis in a cemetery in Skala, and only David survived. He went back to the Biesaga, and even though it was dangerous, Jozef hid him in their barn. Once again, Jozef risked him and his families life to protect a Jew.

The Biesaga family protected David for the rest of the war and occasional helped Dora's brother. Until the end of the war David would live in the barn, only coming out to do farm work at night, and every day a family member would bring him food; David would come to the house every fortnight to bathe and talk. Jozef never was caught sheltering David. Jozef would cautiously make his sons check the neighborhood, before David would do farmwork. Jozef also helped Samuel Zelinger, Dora's brother. He occasionally showed up at their house, and was given food and bed. After the war ended David Nassan left for Israel and died about 1958. Ultimately, Jozef's kindness saved David from death during the holocaust.

Janina Radlinska was a doctor who protected Jews in Warsaw, Poland many different ways. First, she did plastic surgery on Jews who wanted a new identity to help them hide during World War Two. She risked her life fifteen times by helping Jewish people hide their identity. She used plastic surgery to remove any common Semitic features. This helped Jews hide in plain sight from the Nazis. Second, she gave medical attention to Jews in hiding. Despite the danger of being caught and killed, she still operated on several Jews including a girl named Krol. In the end, Janina helped many Jews by medically assisting them.

Along with helping people medically, Janina saved two children and one adult from a deadly ghetto where Jews were forced to live. First, a friend of Janina, Dr Halina Szenicer-Rotstein, had two kids in the ghetto, and Janina helped them escape.

Afterward she hid them in a deceased soldiers orphanage where they survived the war. The plan was risky, but Janina managed to pull it off successfully. Next, from 1943 until fall of the uprising of Warsaw she hid Czesława Frendler in her apartment. She had to help rescue Czeslawa from the ghetto, but both of them survived and they left Warsaw together.

Czeslawa emigrated to the United States in 1946. Overall, Janina Radlinska rescued many Jews in many ways.

Alina Stalkowska lived in Warszawa, Poland supplied food and shelter for eight people during the Holocaust. First, she sheltered Michael Breskin, Hanna Breskin, Galecka Cwilling, Galecki Cwilling, Mosze Warth, Binjamin Tykociński, Rachel Tykociński, and Irena Golebiewska. It was very difficult to survive while sheltering eight people at once, but it would be harder to stay quiet and avoid being captured. It would require a lot of patience. She also provided food for all of them. During World War Two, and with such limited food she still managed obtain enough food for herself and the eight people she hid through World War Two . Ultimately, Alina saved eight Jewish people by sheltering and supplying them through the war.

Marek Arczynski was a member of the board of Zegota, he worked in Krakow, Poland to help Jewish people in many ways. Zegota is the council of aid for Jews, and Marek acted as their treasurer. Also, he was a representative of the Underground Democratic Party and worked in the " Legalization Department". At this department he labored to create forged licenses, such as work permits, identity cards, and marriage certificates, and sent them to Jews in hiding. Lastly, he acted as coordinator of the organization's branches in Krakow to its headquarters in Warsaw. Through his dedicated service many Jews owe their lives to him.

In conclusion Józef Biesaga, Janina Radlińska, Marek Arczynski, and Alina Stalkowska helped Jews in Poland survive the holocaust. Jozef protected mainly David Nassan by giving him food and shelter during the war. Janina Radlinska was a doctor who treated Jews medically and helped some escape the ghetto. Alina Stalkowska sheltered eight Jews during the war. Lastly, Marek worked at a organization to protect Jews. All of these people decided to try to help even if they risked their lives in the process, instead of turning away because the Nazis weren't targeting them.

Works Cited

Russell, Tony, et al. "MLA Formatting and Style Guide." The Purdue OWL. Purdue U Writing Lab, 27 Jan. 2017. https://owl.english.purdue.edu/owl/resource/747/05/

Arter, Urszula, "Story of Rescue- Biesaga Jozef." Polish Righteous. Polin. Aug. 2010. https://sprawiedliwi.org.pl/en/stories-of-rescue/story-rescue-biesaga-jozef-0

Ciesielska, Maria. Jackl, Klara , " Story of Rescue- Radlinska Janina Natalie." Polish Righteous. Polin. Aug. 2014. https://sprawiedliwi.org.pl/en/stories-of-rescue/story-rescue-radlinska-janina-natalia

"Stalkowska Alina" Yad Vashem. The Righteous Among the Nations. 2017. http://db.yadvashem.org/righteous/righteousName.html?language=en&itemId=4017622

Arczynski, "Rescue Story" Yad Vashem. The Righteous Among the Nations. 2017. http://db.yadvashem.org/righteous/family.html?language=en&itemId=4013722

The Heroes of Poland

Max Fields

Six million? What does that represent? Is it the number of people who watched the Super Bowl? No. Is it the amount of people that live in the United States? No. It represents the number of Jewish people who had their lives taken away from them during the Holocaust. Over 3 million people live in Los Angeles. Over 6 million died in the Holocaust. That's twice the number of people that live in one of the largest cities in the U.S. The things that happened during this time of hatred were awful, horrible things, but many people tried to make things right for those who were not. Irena Sendler, a Catholic social worker, Adolf Avraham Berman, an editor, and Maximilian Kolbe, a Franciscan friar. These names may be nothing to many people, but they should never be forgotten. These people tried to make things right in times of corruption and evil. These people are heroes to all Jewish people whose lives were forgotten by the evil people who did these things to them. These heroes are the heroes of Poland.

Irena Sendler was a Polish Catholic social worker who helped children escape from the Warsaw Ghetto in Poland. Irena, as being a social worker, was granted access to the ghetto by being part of the Epidemic Control Department. She gave children false identities, and delivered them to non-Jewish families that were willing to accept them into their families. Children stowed away in body bags, potato sacks, coffins, food trucks, and any other way they could get out. The names and identities of each individual child was stored in a jar that was buried in the yard of one of her neighbors. There was a total of 2,500 names. However, on October 20th, 1943, Irena was arrested by the Gestapo. They tortured her, but her spirit was as tough as nails, and she never gave up. She was sentenced to death, but the Zegota, a Jew aiding organization, bribed a Nazi soldier to stop the execution, so she escaped. Subsequently, Irena dug up the jars consisting of 2,500 names, and tracked down people all over Europe to reunite them with their families. Irena Sendler, a Holocaust hero, helped 2,500 innocent escape the horror that lay ahead for them. Because of her acts of constant heroism and bravery, Irena Sendler is an obvious hero for those who needed one in times of distress.

During the Holocaust, many Jews went into hiding. One way that many Jews hid was by surviving underground. Adolf Avraham Berman, a Polish editor, helped these many Jews by contributing funds to help them remain alive and well. With his many titles: director of CENTOS (Federation of Associations for the Care of Orphans), secretary to the presidium of Zegota, and representative of the Jewish National Committee, Berman was able to aid the Jews in their survival and able to keep their identity hidden. Berman was eventually arrested by the Germans for his help with the Jews, but he paid the ransom, and got out. After, he took part in the uprising at the Warsaw Ghetto, in Poland. Subsequently, he migrated to Israel, where he could practice his belief of a communistic world in the communist party of Israel. Adolf Avraham Berman was able to share his knowledge about the Holocaust and his part in it through his books called: The Underground Period --

published in 1971-- and The Place Where Fate Brought Me: With the Jews of Warsaw -- published in 1977. All in all, Adolf Avraham Berman was a very heroic figure during the fight for justice of Jews everywhere.

Maximilian Kolbe, a Franciscan friar, was taken into the Holocaust by the Nazis. Kolbe became a priest in 1919. He was also diagnosed with Tuberculosis. At the opening of the second world war, Kolbe was abducted, and deported to Auschwitz, the most notorious Nazi death camp. There were many families that died together during the Holocaust, a very depressing fact. But, there were also family members that watched as their loved ones were murdered at the hands of the Nazis. Maximilian Kolbe of Poland, however, would not have it. On August 14th, 1971, three people escaped Auschwitz, a nearly impossible task. Instead of spend countless days trying to search for the refugees, the officers chose ten people at random to be starved to death in an underground chamber. One of these men was named Franciszek Gajowniczek, a husband and father. Maximilian Kolbe confronted an officer and stated,"I am a Catholic priest from Poland, I would like to take his place, because he has a wife and children." With this, the officer accepted his offer, and Kolbe was lethally injected. Gajowniczek would live to the day Auschwitz was liberated, and forever thank Kolbe. Because of his overwhelming acts of bravery to help others, Maximilian Kolbe is a Holocaust hero.

The Holocaust was likely the most horrific event that the world has ever witnessed. Millions of people died. However, there were people who risked their lives to save others when the time came. Irena Sendler, Adolf Avraham Berman, and Maximilian Kolbe where three of those people who contributed to the protection of Jews all over Europe. They are part of the reason in which the death toll stayed where it was, and did not increase. The Holocaust was probably the most evil moment in world history, but that doesn't mean that there wasn't a handful of people who played a part in saving others.

Works Cited

"Holocaust Heroes." Holocaust Heroes. N.p., n.d. Web. 21 Feb. 2017.

"Heroes of the Holocaust - The Courageous Fighters against Hitler's Nazi Regime Genealogy Project." Geni_family_tree. N.p., n.d. Web. 21 Feb. 2017.

"Irena Sendler." Irena Sendler. N.p., n.d. Web. 21 Feb. 2017.

"Berman, Adolf Abraham." YIVO | Berman, Adolf Abraham. N.p., n.d. Web. 21 Feb. 2017.

"Maximilian Kolbe Biography | ." Biography Online. N.p., n.d. Web. 21 Feb. 2017.

Heroes of Poland: 1939-1945: Irena Sendler

Neha Hariharan

On February 15, 1910, a future nurse, and savior was born. Obviously, no one knew this, but Irena Krzyżanowska saved over 2,500 Jewish children and babies. Irena was supported and inspired by many people, but her father inspired her most of all. During her childhood, "She was greatly influenced by his selfless service to the patients, most of whom were Jewish and poor..." (thefamouspeople.com) Her father was a physician, who helped people that others refused to treat for fear of catching a disease. In addition, both her parents were part of the Polish Socialist Party, which had a key role against communists. Bravery and compassion ran in her family's blood, as Irena's great grandfather led a rebellion against the Czars. Eventually, Stanisław Krzyżanowski, her father, died after catching Typhus from the poor and unhealthy Jews. Her father once said, "If you see someone drowning, you must jump in and try to save them, even if you don't know how to swim." Irena grew up learning and living by his beliefs. After his death, the Jewish community leaders offered their support for Irena and her mother. Using this, Irena studied Polish literature at Warsaw University. Since Irena was so compassionate about people, she outwardly opposed the ghetto-bench system. This caused her to be suspended from the school for three years. Clearly, Irena was a strong, stubborn, and determined woman who went on to help many Holocaust victims.

In 1939, the Germans invaded Poland, and with that came the Nazis, who terrorized the citizens. The Jews, feeling the most of the wrath were scared and in danger. At the time, Irena, now Irena Sendler, was Senior Administrator in the Warsaw Social Welfare Department, which means she, like her father, helped and cared for the poor. Not only was she the Senior Administrator, she, "... was in charge of the Children's Division of Żegota, a Polish underground group to assist Jewish people." (Biography.com) She clearly saw the pain and torture that was being inflicted by the Nazis in the ghettos, and decided to stop it. At first, she was sneaking in food, clothing and other necessities, but she soon realized that this was only prolonging their lives, not saving them. After joining Żegota, she started actually saving lives, but only the children, as that was the most she could do. To do this, she and other followed a plan. Since she was a nurse and a social worker, she was allowed entrance into the Warsaw ghetto to examine the people for diseases. Using this as an excuse, she got into the ghetto, and left with children. The article, Irena Sendler Biography, by biography.com explains how and what Irena did to safely transport the Jewish kids, "Some were carried out in caskets or potato sacks; others left in ambulances or snuck out through underground tunnels. Still others entered the Jewish side of a Catholic church that straddled the ghetto boundary and left on the other side with new identities. Sendler then helped place the children at convents or with non-Jewish families." To keep the kids safe from inquisition and questioning, Sendler created over 3,000 fake identity papers. Sendler and some of the other Żegota, also called the Council to Aid Jews, put their lives at risk regularly to save and shelter those Jewish children. To protect the kids' real identities, she wrote all their real information down, and buried it. Later on, the information was found, and even thought most of the kids' relatives were gone, some still found their remaining family. All of their hard work paid off because in the end they saved over 2,500 lives. But still, Irena was still not pleased, she says, "I only did what was normal. I could have done more." In reality, she saved many more lives than even the most famous of Holocaust heroes.

As previously stated, Irena grew up watching and learning from her father. He was a very compassionate and loving man, who deeply cared about the people. While growing up, her father was someone that she was deeply influenced by, so his beliefs and goals were then passed on to her. At the age of seven, Irena lost him, but he lived on in her heart. So when WWII began, and she saw the horrible things that were happening, and she couldn't resist the need to help the victims. At the age of almost thirty, she took the new and frightening situation head on. "When the war started, all of Poland was drowning in a sea of blood. But most of all, it affected the Jewish nation. And within that nation, it was the children who suffered most. That's why we needed to give our hearts to them," Irena Sendler stated on ABC news. This shows that she was willing to risk her life to save the Jewish children, who were experiencing so much pain, physically and mentally. Her father's beliefs and ways made Irena who she was, and that is why she did what she did.

Irena Sendler was a kind and compassionate woman who saved over 2,500 lives. Until very late in her life, she was not very known. Today, she has won the following: 2007 - Order of the Smile, 1996 - Commander's Cross of the Order of Polonia Restituta, and the higher award; 2001 -Commander's Cross with Star of the Order of Polonia Restituta. Some of her lesser known awards are: 2009: the Humanitarian

of the Year award from The Sister Rose Thering Endowment, and the Audrey Hepburn Humanitarian Award. Also, she was recognized by Yad Vashem as one of the Polish Righteous among the Nations in 1965, and in addition, a tree was planted in her honor at the entrance to the Avenue of the Righteous. On top of all these awards, she was also nominated for the Nobel Prize. Other than awards, there was a play that was made in her honor, which depicted her life in a mere ten minutes. Now, it is performed around the world, and it was made by a group of high-schooler girls. Unquestionably Irena Sendler was a very important person in the dark times of WWII. She was not only honored by awards and plays, but a long life, and a lot of love. Sendler lived until she was ninety-eight, which is almost a century! Her life spanned out from 1910-2008, which after the war, was spent confined in a wheelchair. Still, love poured into her life, many of the survivors of WWII that she saved came to thank her. Irena is someone that I chose to acknowledge because even though she isn't widely known, she saved so many lives. To me, even saving one life is a feat in itself, and Irena saved 2,500 souls, and still thought that she didn't save enough! Mahatma Gandhi once said, "You must be the change you wish to see in the world," and Irena definitely made a change.

During the Holocaust, over six million people died in the hands of the heartless Nazis. But through it all there were many heroes, for there cannot be evil without good, cruel without nice, sad without happy, or even dark without light. Irena Sendler was one of these heroes who saved so many lives, and stood bravely in the face of death.

Works Cited

"The Courageous Story of Irena Sendler." Life in a Jar. Web. 20 Feb. 2017.

"Early Childhood - Irena Sendler." Early Childhood - Irena Sendler. Web. 20 Feb. 2017.

"Irena Sendler." Biography.com. A&E Networks Television, 21 Mar. 2016. Web. 20 Feb. 2017.

"Who Is Irena Sendler? Everything You Need to Know." Childhood, Life Achievements & Timeline. Web. 20 Feb. 2017.

yadvashem,org/RIGHHTEOUS OF THE NATIONS/

Heroes of Poland: Irena Sendler

Nikki Spies

Who was there to save the children who were starving and slowly dying in the Warsaw Ghetto? A remarkable woman named Irena Sendler was saving those who could not save themselves. Irena Sendler is a historical figure who saved a myriad of children from dying in these ghettos by smuggling them out. If it wasn't for her, more than 2,000 Jewish children would not be able to tell their story.

Irena Sendler was born in Poland in 1910, and was born into a happy family of just her and her parents. Growing up, her father was a doctor and taught Irena that helping people is the only way to live. Irena remembers her father saying, "If you see someone drowning you must try to rescue them, even if you cannot swim." Unfortunately, Irena's father died of disease and her and her mother moved to Warsaw. As Irena grew into a young women, she always kept her father's words of kindness in her head which gave her the bravery of what she would do in years to come. Irena Sendler was a Roman Catholic, a religion that would keep her safe from being put into a ghetto. Her first step into becoming a Polish hero, was refusing to stop eating with her Jewish friends. The school she went to started separating the Jews from the other kids, making them eat at different tables. Irena refused to move to a different table, which led to her being expelled. Though this may not have saved anyone's life, this was her first step into becoming a fighter.

Irena Sendler started in the Warsaw health department, which gave her access to the Warsaw Ghetto. Irena did not work alone, she was part of the Zegota organization, a place which helped Jews escape and survive from the ghettos. Irena was depended on for helping thousands of children escape from the Warsaw Ghetto, and even more importantly, without being caught. Irena couldn't sneak the children out the same way every time, there were a variety of ways, some used more often than others. Babies were snuck out in boxes and toddlers in coffins. For younger children, Irena brought a dog with her, when a child started crying, Irena would hit the dog which caused it to bark and cover up the child's cries. Older children would be taught a few Catholic prayers so they could be smuggled out through the church. Irena said that the hardest part was not sneaking out the children, but convincing the parents to let her do so. Irena tried to convince the parents that it may give the children a life that they could never have in the ghetto, she sometimes failed but was determined to come back the next day and try to convince them again. Irena said the scariest part of it all was when she came back the next day, and they were gone, nowhere to be found.

Irena was one of the most famous Zegota members because of her names in a jar method. After smuggling a child out of the ghetto, she would bring them over to the Piotrowski's house, where they would get a change of clothing and some food before transforming into a new person. The Piotrowski's were good friends of Irena, and Zegota members themselves. They would lend their house over to the Jewish children just smuggled out of the Ghetto and more importantly, lend their tree over to Irena. Irena kept track of every child's name that she smuggled out of the ghetto, and keep it in jar buried under that tree. This way, after the war she may be able to locate some of the Jewish children's family members, though many decided to stay with their new adopted families.

Irena was expelled from school, snuck Jewish children out of ghettos, and put her life on the line every day, could jail really stop her? Irena Sendler was arrested October 20, 1943. Irena recalls the German soldiers marching up the stairs, ready to shove her into a small jail cell and threaten her until she would give up the Zegota secrets, fortunately she did not. As the soldiers barged through her door she threw a package out the window to one of the Zegota members with a list of the most recent children smuggled out. She was brought to Pawiak prison where they tortured her and broke both of her legs. Still not giving up the secrets of Zegota, they sentenced her to death. Irena could have died there, her memory and her life being erased forever, but that was never going to stop her. Zegota bribed a German soldier into letting her go. She was thrown into the forest where she stayed until a Zegota member found her. Irena's face was plastered all over the city, reporting she was dead. She recalls all this happening saying, "I read the posters myself." Irena wasn't just a hero, but a survivor.

Years later, Irena got married and had two children. She was given many awards and a student play was written about her called Life in a Jar. She lived until she was 98 and died May 12, 2008 in a Warsaw nursing home. Her memory lives on through the children she saved and through the play Life in a Jar that talks about her struggles and her heroic life.

Irena Sendler was a Polish hero that saved thousands of children and risked her life every day. For everyday she lived, and every step she made, she lived by her father's words "If you see someone drowning you must try to rescue them, even if you cannot swim."

Work Cited:

"The Courageous Story of Irena Sendler." Life in a Jar. N.p., n.d. Web. 07 Feb. 2017.

""Women of Valor"." Irena Sendler - Stories of Women Who Rescued Jews During the Holocaust - Righteous Among the Nations - Yad Vashem. N.p., n.d. Web. 07 Feb. 2017.

Kroll, Chana. "Irena Sendler - Rescuer of the Children of Warsaw." Rescuer of the Children of Warsaw - Dealing with Challenge. N.p., n.d. Web. 07 Feb. 2017.

"Meet Unsung Hero Irena Sendler." Lowell Milken Center for Unsung Heroes. N.p., 11 June 2014. Web. 09 Feb. 2017.

"Irena Sendlerowa Survivors Stories Www.HolocaustResearchProject.org." Irena Sendlerowa Survivors Stories Www.HolocaustResearchProject.org. N.p., n.d. Web. 09 Feb. 2017.

"Zegota Www.HolocaustResearchProject.org." Zegota Www.HolocaustResearch Project.org. N.p., 2013. Web. 09 Feb. 2017.

"Sendler, Irena." The Jewish Foundation for the Righteous. N.p., n.d. Web. 18 Feb. 2017.

"Irena Sendlerowa." Irena Sendlerowa - Timeline - History's HEROES from E2BN. N.p., n.d. Web. 18 Feb. 2017.

Pendlebury for the Daily Mail, Richard. "The 'female Schindler' Who Saved 2,500 Jewish Children but Died Wishing She'd Rescued More." Daily Mail Online. Associated Newspapers, 22 May 2008. Web. 18 Feb. 2017

"Sharing StoriesInspiring Change." Irena Sendler Saves Jewish Children from the Warsaw Ghetto. | Jewish Women's Archive. N.p., n.d. Web. 18 Feb. 2017.

Heroes of Poland

Ryan Enney

There were few survivors of the holocaust, some of them were heroes, some were witnesses, but everyone united to survive. There were heroes outside and inside the camps. Heroes on the inside helped aid and keep everyone serine while the heroes on the outside could provide food and defend against the Nazi's. There were many heroes from various nations but some of most influential were from Poland. In this essay those heroes of Poland are identified.

One of these heroes was a man called Kolbe, Saint of Auschwitz. He was a catholic priest at the time whose real name was Maximilian Kolbe. He was born in Poland and lived to serve god. Maximillian was taken to Auschwitz, a death camp, in May of 1941 with four others. There he was tortured and beat up by camp employees, he would have died if not for his companions who dragged his frail body away. Despite of this cruelty he still believed in god for all his life. He was so passionate of this that other victims noticed including Rudolph Diem who said,"I can say with certainty that during my four years in Auschwitz, I never saw such a sublime example of the love of God and one's neighbor". This man saying this about Kolbe shows how he affected other people and how he made sure that god's wisdom could still shine through the discriminance. Kolbe made the hard times more bearable for inmates. Other people wanted him around, they would go to his bed at night and ask for forgiveness. In a way Kolbe was a hero for the subconscious. He gave people hope and was like a father figure. He was said to have not cried out when tortured, but to pray for his tormentor's forgiveness. Although he was a hero he did not make it through the holocaust giving his life so that another could hold his for longer. For those reasons Maximilian Kolbe will go down as a Polish hero.

There were still many other things that people could do to help the Jews outside of the camps. One of the people that did these things was Irena Sendler. She was born in Poland and by the time the war started she was 29 years old and worked in Warsaw. She worked in the Welfare Department of the Warsaw municipality, which meant she was already assisting others. After the Jewish ghetto was blocked off it made it extremely difficult for her to help the jews. She still prevailed and tried to find a way to help. Since she could not get into the ghetto she got a permit to inspect the cleanliness of the ghettos from her work so she could get in. Once she was inside she conspired with the jewish leaders to help save some people. Sendler then could smuggle Jews out of the ghettos and transport them to other cities or help them find hiding. She was also a main contributor of The Council of Aid of Jews which helped rescue Jews and provided resources to the Jews. After, in September of 1943 she was given the job of director of Zegota's Department for the Care of Jewish Children. She sent many orphans and kids to orphanages and church groups so they could get away. She did end up being arrested and sentenced to a death penalty. Her friends bargained the penalty off so she continued to help Jews. She eventually had to into hiding to not be caught and continued helping others. Irene Sendler was a hero of Poland because of her gratitude and courtesy towards the Jews and other minorities.

Another Polish woman that helped Jews survive during the holocaust was Karolina Juszczykowska. She did not help as many Jews as the previous two heroes but she did what she could. What she did was house two Jews during the holocaust. She kept them in her cellar and they were not discovered for 6 weeks. When the police raided her house she made it seem as she was very innocent and testified for her innocence. She said that the only reason she did it was because she was in need of money but the Jews were on the run so they probably didn't have that much money. Instead she probably kept them out of the goodness of her heart. When she was tried in court three judges did not approve of her death penalty and tried to get it revoked, but bitterly got turned down and she was then executed on January 9, 1945. Even though she only tried to help Jews she is still courageous and gave her life trying so in that way she is hero.

One more hero that helped during World War II was Anna Stupnicka. Anna shouldn't be the only one recognized though because her mother helped and stayed with Anna for most of the holocaust. They did many things to help people back then. They started by bringing food and provisions to the Warsaw ghettos. After they were done giving food they were approached by a man that begged for them to take his daughter to be safe, so they did. They took her back to their home and kept her there and took care of her. They were never caught and that girl is still alive today. They gave her a fake name and a whole new identity of Anna's cousin. These actions of bringing food to the ghettos and also housing a Jew makes Anna and her mother heroes of Poland.

Finally, two more heroes of Poland are Manko and Maryna Swierszczak. These two heroes used an interesting way of helping out Jews. Mr. Swierszczyk had a friendship from when he was a boy with two brothers called the Rozens. The Rozens were Jewish and when the holocaust started they went to their old friend and asked for help. The Swierszczaks decided to help them by taking advantage of their resources. Since Manko worked at a cemetery they all dug a bunker in the cemetery where they stayed. After the bunker was made they added four other Jews that Manko saved. This lasted for a while until the neighbors tattled on Mr. Swierszczyk. They noticed that he had been buying an abundance of food that he shouldn't need. The police cleared his house but didn't find anything so they arrested him out of suspicion. He was tortured to make him confess but he never broke. After he was released they moved the Jews to a different location and they were never found. Helping his friends and some strangers no matter their religion makes them heroes.

In this essay multiple heroes were talked about and acknowledged. Hopefully now they can be realized as some of the greatest heroes in the holocaust no matter how large or tney their generous feat was.

Works Cited

"Kolbe, The Saint from Auschwitz." Kolbe, The Saint from Auschwitz. N.p., n.d. Web. 22 Feb. 2017.

""Women of Valor"." Irena Sendler - Stories of Women Who Rescued Jews During the Holocaust - Righteous Among the Nations - Yad Vashem. N.p., n.d. Web. 22 Feb. 2017.

""Women of Valor"." Karolina Juszczykowska - Stories of Women Who Rescued Jews During the Holocaust - Righteous Among the Nations - Yad Vashem. N.p., n.d. Web. 22 Feb. 2017.

"Stupnicka, Anna." The Jewish Foundation for the Righteous. N.p., n.d. Web. 22 Feb. 2017.

"Manko and Maryna Swierszczak, Michal and Genowefa Dukiewicz." Manko and Maryna Swierszczak, Michal and Genowefa Dukiewicz. N.p., n.d. Web. 22 Feb. 2017.

Heroes of Poland: Those who stood up

Vaibhav Turaga

The Holocaust was a deadly event that killed six million Jews. While the Nazis started killing Jews, many people ignored it. The punishment for helping Jews was death. Still, many people from Poland, and other parts of Europe helped the Jewish people. Karolina Juszczykowska, Władysław Kowalski, and Irena Sendler were among the many Polish people who saved Jews.

Karolina Juszczykowska was born in Budków, Poland, in 1898. She lived with her parents in Poland until she was 13. Then, she moved to Mecklenburg, Germany, and lived there for five years. Juszczykowska later moved back to Budków and then on to Tomaszow, Poland. Karolina Juszczykowska was a single mother with one child. Juszczykowska had many jobs during the war including a road constructer, laundress, and a maid. She met 2 boys who were willing to pay her 300 zloty per week for food and shelter. She agreed to house them. Six weeks later, they were found by the Gestapo. On July 23, 1944, the Gestapo raided Juszczykowska house. The two Jews she was sheltering were shot instantly. Juszczykowska was arrested. It is possible that one of their neighbors betrayed Juszczykowska and alerted the Nazis. The Nazis put Juszczykowska on trial at a Piotrków Sondergericht, a court the models the German judicial system. She was sentenced to death at the court. However, three judges requested her to be pardoned. According to Yad Vashem, The judges said "We recommend pardoning the accused who was sentenced to death, because her hiding the Jews was not motivated by her wish to prevent their deportation or to profit from it. The accused is in a difficult financial situation and succumbed to the temptation to improve her life." Despite the judge's requests, Juszczykowska was sent to Frengesheim Prison in Frankfurt am Main, Germany. She was executed the next day. This may have been because 300 zloty per week would not have been enough to feed two people, which shows that she wanted to help the Jewish people. Karolina Juszczykowska was recognized as Righteous among Nations on May 17th, 2011.

Władysław Kowalski was born in 1896 in Kiev, Ukraine. He went to school in St. Petersburg. During World War I, he joined the Polish Brigade and fought for Poland's independence. At the end of World War I, he joined the Polish Army and reached the rank of Colonel, before retiring in 1935. After his retirement, he joined a dutch electronics company called Philips. His job took him to Warsaw, Poland. When Germany invaded Poland in 1939, Kowalski was called back into the army. He was given command of the brigade defending Warsaw. When it seemed Warsaw was impossible to defend, he was ordered to surrender. He refused his commander's orders and continued fighting. Even when Warsaw was captured, Kowalski did not stop fighting. However, he was later captured and sent to a German prisoner of war camp. Because Kowalski worked for Philips, a dutch company (Neutral in the war), he was paroled. The first Jew that Kowalski rescued was a 17 year old boy named Borel Bruno. Wladyslaw Kowalski took the boy home, found him a fake passport, and got him a job in Philips. Next year, a lawyer asked for his help. He took him home as well. Kowalski continued to save more Jews. Because he was a worker at Philips, he was able to enter and exit the Warsaw ghetto whenever he needed. Kowalski smuggled in weapons and medicine to the underground resistance. His help contributed to the Warsaw Ghetto Uprising. After the war, he said "I do not consider myself a hero, for I was only fulfilling my human obligations toward the prosecuted and the suffering." He was named Righteous Among Nations in 1963. When he was 63, he moved to Israel. He lived a normal life and worked at a grocery store. Before his death, he asked to be buried along with the Jewish people. Despite the Jewish community having mixed feelings, his request was granted. He died in a fire at Gedera Nursing Home.

Irena Sendler was born in 1910, 15 miles southwest of Warsaw, Poland, in a place called Otwock. She was greatly inspired by her father, who was one of the first polish Socialist. Her father mainly treated the poor. When Germany invaded Poland in 1939, Irena was a senior administrator in the Warsaw Social Welfare Department. The department operated canteens throughout Warsaw to provide food, water, and financial help to the poor, orphaned, and elderly. Additionally, because of Sendler, they started providing food, money, and clothing to Jews. Irena Sendler then joined Zegota, the council for aid to the Jews. She organized the polish underground movement. Sendler managed to get a pass from Warsaw's Epidemic Control Department. This allowed her to enter and exit the ghetto freely. She visited the ghetto daily, bringing food, medicine, and clothing to the Jews along with her. Then, Sendler decided to help save Jewish children. She managed to recruit one person from each of the ten departments of Warsaw's Social Welfare Department. Using their help, she gave out hundreds of forged documents. Irena Sendler began smuggling children out in an ambulance. During the war, she smuggled over 2,500 children out of the Warsaw Ghetto. In the Ghetto, there was a church that had one entrance from the ghetto, and another from the city of Warsaw. Many people say, "She brought the children in as Jews, and out as Christians." That is exactly what she did. Once the children had been brought out of the Ghetto, she sent many of the children to religious establishment. Sendler gave each child a new identity. However, she kept the true identity of every child in jars buried under her neighbor's apple tree. She hoped to find each child when the war ended. Unfortunately for Sendler, the Nazis found out about what she was doing. On October 20th, 1943, Irena Sendler was arrested. She was sent to Pawiak Prison. The Nazis tortured her, and even broke her feet and legs. However, no one could get her to reveal information about her colleagues or the children she rescued. She was ordered to be executed. Luckily, members of the Zegota bribed a Gestapo agent. The execution was stopped, but Sendler was sent back to prison. She escaped prison, but Nazis continued to look for her until the war was over. Irena Sendler was recognized as Righteous Among Many by the State of Israel, and Righteous Among Nations by Yad Vashem. She became an Honorary Citizen of Israel in 1991. She also won the 2003 Jan Karski Award for Valor and Courage. Sendler was also honored by the Polish Senate and the United States Congress. In addition to these awards, she was a 2007 Nobel Peace Prize candidate. Irena Sendler died the next year, on May 12th, 2008, at the age of 98.

Irena Sendler, Władysław Kowalski, and Karolina Juszczykowska showed immense bravery when it came to saving Jews. They stood up when the Nazis were killing the

Jewish people and everyone was sitting back and watching. These selfless acts helped save the lives of thousands of Jews across Europe.

Works Cited

"The Righteous Among the Nations" Yad Vashem. Web. 21 Feb. 2017.

""Women of Valor"" Karolina Juszczykowska - Stories of Women Who Rescued Jews During the Holocaust - Righteous Among the Nations - Yad Vashem. Web. 21 Feb. 2017.

"1945: Karolina Juszczykowska, Who Couldn't Say No." ExecutedToday.com. 09 Jan. 2015. Web. 21 Feb. 2017.

Aderet, Ofer. "Mystery Surrounds Righteous Gentile Who Saved Dozens of Jews." Haaretz.com. 20 Apr. 2012. Web. 21 Feb. 2017.

Bartrop, Paul R. Resisting the Holocaust: Upstanders, Partisans, and Survivors. Santa Barbara, CA: ABC-CLIO, An Imprint of ABC-CLIO, LLC, 2016. Print.

"Irena Sendler." Irena Sendler. Web. 21 Feb. 2017.

Kuttler, Hillel. "Seeking Kin: Kibbutz Searches for Descendants of Holocaust Hero Buried in Its Cemetery." Jewish Telegraphic Agency. 15 Dec. 2015. Web. 21 Feb. 2017.

Paldiel, Mordecai. The Path of the Righteous: Gentile Rescuers of Jews during the Holocaust. Hoboken, NJ: Ktav, 1993. Print.

Saint James School, Davis, CA

Kathryn Baggarly

Kathryn has been an educator for 25 years, both in public and Catholic schools. She has been at St. James School in Davis, California for seven years, where she is the St. James Eighth Grade teacher and Junior High English/Language Arts teacher. Kathryn has been teaching about the Holocaust since arriving at St. James. She is a member of CVEN and the online education community of Facing History and Ourselves. Her students are deeply touched by what they learn about the Holocaust and are honored to be able to give voice to the unsung heroes of the Holocaust. She and her students are indebted to Mr. Bernard Marks and his tireless efforts to make sure we never forget.

Michele Banister

Michele has been an educator for 25 years, both in public and Catholic schools. She is the Writing and Reading Resource teacher at St. James School in Davis, California. Along with her colleague Kathryn Baggarly Michele has assisted the Junior High students with their Holocaust essays. She looks forward to many years of participation in the Eleanor J. Marks Holocaust Essay Contest.

The Amazing Untold Stories of Zofia Bednarska and Janina Zilow

Alondra Landin

The Holocaust begun in January of 1933 impacted many peoples' lives during Hitler's reign of terror. Many families lost their loved ones. Almost seven million Jews and non-Jews lost their lives. Many people were brave and courageous. Two courageous heroes were Zofia Bednarska and Janina Zilow.

Manny Jews and non-Jews were exterminated beginning on January 30, 1933 as Hitler's reign as Chancellor began in Germany. Over six million innocent Jews were killed. Children and parents were separated from each other. Many were terrified and shocked. Five million guiltless non-Jews were killed. Hitler was in reign for 12 years. Many, many Jews were made fun of because of who they were. During this reign there were many steps implemented against the jews . On April 1, 1933, Jewish businesses were boycotted. On April 7, lawyers were disbarred. On April, 22 doctors were banned from practice, and on April 25, all children were banned from schools. They did not get to learn for a really long time. The ghettos and camps led to extermination camps.

During the Holocaust many heroes' stories were unsung. One unsung hero was Zofia Bednarska. Zofia's birthdate and death date were not found. On October of 1942, a family was warned by a Polish acquaintance. Filip Gottfried, a professional dentist, hid his wife, Ita and five year old daughter, Ruth. His wife and daughter hid in the attic of their home frightened and fearful that the Germans would find them. They had adopted Felicja Widerhorn after her parents perished during an Aktionen, an event where they banished the Jews to concentration camps. One of Filip's patients , Zofia Bednarska, a teacher, helped them hide in her home. She lived in a one room apartment and hid them in a bunker underneath the kitchen floor. Zofia was very nice enough to take the family in, even though the dangers of being caught were high. Even though the Gottfried family did not have a lot of money Zofia supported them. She worked in a storeroom of a German soup kitchen. After all those hard days working there Zofia was able to maintain food and supplies for the family. The Gottfrieds had moved to a nearby village where they lived with a Ukrainian farmer for a short period of time. He had family problems and the issues became very intense. The family had to return again to Zofia where they were kept until June of 1944. The family of four left the apartment, as well as Zofia, after her home had been damaged by bombs that the Germans dropped. They all hid in the forests and in the fields frightened that they would get caught. After the war, the family migrated to Israel. They continued to stay in touch with Zofia who had assisted them whenever they needed help. On May 27, 1981, Yad Vashem recognized Zofia Bednarska as Righteous Among the Nations.

As we all know, there are many different kinds of heroes' stories being told right now. I wanted to make this into a two hero essay. So, another hero's story that has been unsung is Janina Zilow. Her birthdate and death date were not said in the information. Janina was a survivor of the war. She helped a family who were looking for a hiding spot. This family was the Trilling family. Liliana Ruth was born in 1929 in Lodz, Poland and was the third child out of seven. She was the daughter of Anatole and Raissa, a Polish-speaking couple who owned a small factory. Liliana attended the Jewish Gymnasium for a year. The family attempted to flee. After the attempt, they ended up in a large Ghetto in Warsaw with Raissa's sister Rosa Trilling and her three year old daughter Elizabeth. Both Rosa and Elizabeth arrived from Lwow after Elizabeth's father Roman, had been arrested by the Soviets for being a 'ca pitalist' and unfortunately died in prison. They were both devastated when they heard that news. Anatole suggested to Rosa that she should obtain the help of Elizabeth's former nanny, Janina Zilow. In the summer of 1942, the family moved into the small ghetto. Elizabeth was sent to work in a factory. Not long after Janina appeared to them, Elizabeth and Lily were taken away from their parents and never saw them again. They were murdered in Treblinka. Escaping from the ghetto was not as smooth as they had planned it to be. They were approached by a hostile group of young Poles. They managed to get to Lwow. Janina started working and Lili took care of the household and Elizabeth. After a short period of time, a Jewish little girl called Anitka came into the family. Sooner than later, Anitka was captured and murdered. Anitka's death affected Janina a lot, so she decided to move away. She then managed to get Lily working papers. Her Jewish looks were a danger to her, so she then joined a group of Armenian workers with whom she could blend in. Lily was working in the town on Lage from November of 1943 until almost the end of the war. Her Polish workers were about to betray her. She then fled into the forest and luckily survived. Lily migrated to England and in 1947, she was off to the United States. In the meantime Janina and Elizabeth were hiding in Lubilin. After the war, Janina was insistent on fulfilling her promise to Elizabeth's mother to take her to her family in Los Angeles. Unfortunately, Janina Zilow died in 1957 at the age of 56. In honor of Janina, Elizabeth named her daughter Nina after her rescuer's name. She then mentioned Janina as her 'wartime mother'. On September 2, 2007, Yad Vashem recognized Janina Zilow as Righteous Among the Nations.

We know during the Holocaust many lives were taken from many many families. All sad, mad, and frightened. Hitler's reign was overwhelming to many people. There are many ways we can help prevent another Holocaust from happening again. One way we can help is by being brave and courageous. If not, many innocent lives will be taken away from families. We can learn from what happened in the last Holocaust and try to fight the people who are hurting other families. If we want to prevent another Holocaust from happening we need to fight as a team and together we will conquer. I know I cannot do much, but what I can do is to love others the same way as I love myself.

Bibliography

Zofia Bednarska and Janina Zilow; Date of visit: 9 January 2017
http://db.yadvashem.org/righteous/search.html?language=en
http://yadvashem.org/

The Holocaust

Darian Lopez

The Holocaust was a very sad and tragic time during the twentieth century. There were many people who were killed during the Holocaust, but one of the few who helped the Jews was a gentleman by the name of Jan Benisz.

Jan Benisz was born on the 26 of April in the year 1891. Also, he was a father of two kids Lech and Mieczyslaw who aided Jews but were later shot and killed by the Germans on October, 19, 1943. He would gather up additional food stamps and collect lunch for both Jews and Polish guerillas. He was expelled from Katowice. He was also awarded with the highest amount of food resources for the poor people. He and a group of other people also tried to make the Germans into putting more food onto the cards. Jan moved underground where he helped many families, and also helped organize transportation for Jewish females.

In conclusion, Jan Benisz was one of the few helpers to save many of the Jews from being killed or starve to death due to the Germans poorly feeding them and mistreating them.

Another gentleman who helped during the Holocaust was a man by the name of Julian Ambroziewicz. He was born on the 12th of February 1899 and died on the 7th of November 1989. His family was well known for their four story residential building that had two courtyards. Also, they had a large guesthouse in the health spa town of Kaczy Dol. He was a very wealthy man, but he and his family later found themselves in the ghetto. Before the war he was working at a German cloth producing workshop that produced sweaters and warm socks. He and his wife Anna lived in a house near the factory. He was given a pass to be able to leave the ghetto with his wife Anna. Then later, people from the underground spread the word that all people who worked at German workshops and all jews would be moved to a liquidation camp or an extermination camp. One of his fellow friends named Jozef Rozenowaj, who worked at the K.Kulwiec junior high school, asked about creating a hiding place for one of his friends. They designed four hiding places for their friends. The hiding places had two purposes: for equipment storage for the home army and for an escape route from the ghetto. They stayed at an unfinished and unusable as a hiding place. His wife was very ill at this time and was later diagnosed with advanced cancer. A few days later sadly she passed away. He left the apartment on the 7th of september and jumped onto a train with Jews headed to a German camp. They somehow managed to escape and go to the nearest village. He moved back into another apartment. They finally left to the apartment and travelled to New York. Finally Julian was awarded with the title of Righteous Among the Nations, He later died in 1989.

http://www.yadvashem.org/yv/pdf-drupal/poland.pdf

https://sprawiedliwi.org.pl/en/stories-of-rescue/story-rescue-ambroziewicz-julian

http://www.sztetl.org.pl/pl/article/gorlice/13,miejsca-martyrologii/27364,getto-w-gorlicach/?action=viewtable&page=2

John Damski

David Studer

In 1933 the people of Germany elected Hitler into office. Later in 1933 Hitler started to make concentration camps for the Jewish citizens. Many Polish people decided to help their Jewish neighbors. One of these individuals was John Damski.

John Damski was born in Germany in 1914 and moved to Poland to raise himself, his sister, and his two other brothers. On December 9th, 1939 John and two of his friends got caught at the border of France and were then deported to the Gestapo. He and his friends were lined up naked and shouted at with racial slurs. He was later put on a truck and loaded away with other prisoners to a prison camp. On August 9th he was released only weighting 97 pounds. He moved to Zamosc with his brother to find work and get away from the war. In Zamosc every day Damski digged ditches. A few days later John went to the Warsaw ghetto to get electricians. In Zamosc, John and his brother rented a two story room. When the Germans told Jews that they had to wear a Star of David John knew that the Germans were going to make fools of them so he did not wear it until they made him. During his time in Gestapo he saw many people who got killed the sick, the handicapped. After Damski got out the of Gestapo and went to Czestochowa he decided to split up with his wife Christine to have a better chance of staying alive. He quit his job at Zamosc and for half a year they lived there and commuted to Christina's mother. John started to put Christina on a train because there was a chance Polos were coming into Czestochowa but he stayed behind to work. He got a job exclusively selling fruits, and vegetables to German. He also got divorced and received false papers to say that he never was married to Christina. Christina and John kept moving from town to town and finally got to a place called Ozarow where they began selling fruits and vegetables. The business got off the ground and employed 190 people and sold 400,000n vegetables. John knew a lot about agriculture because he worked at that exclusive shop which sold fruits, and vegetables to the Germans. He had all the supplies he needed like trucks supplied from the Germans. He used these vehicles to load fruit and vegetables on trains to ship them pretty much anywhere he needed. In January, 1945 the Russians entered Ozarow, and that was the happiest moment for John and his wife that meant they could no longer have to live a lie, he would live his life as a Jew.

The Holocaust was a horrible act. Nobody should die because of what religion they believe in. Overall, Hitler was a crazy man who would not stop no matter what was in his way. His actions ended up killing millions of innocent Jews. Throughout John Damski's life he supplied many Jews with food and vegetables, and he also helped people sneak out of the ghetto for his electrician jobs. He was a caring guy who would give his life up for people around him.

http://www2.humboldt.edu/rescuers/book/damski/johndstory1.html
http://www.yadvashem.org/

Unsung Tale of a Hero

Dominic Rodriguez

The Holocaust. A terrible time in human history. The world was at a loss of innocence, bombs rained down on cities, monuments, and synagogues. Families were separated, children cried holding onto the few possessions and family members they had left. Jews sent off to Nazi death camps. One cruel man bent on a perfect race and world domination oversaw this terrible new world: Adolf Hitler. But this is not the story of Hitler, no, it is the unsung tale of a family of brave heroes who risked their lives, and freedom, to save those persecuted by Hitler. This is the tale of Jozef and Janina Abramowicz and their adopted daughter Rella Glowinska.

Jozef Abramowicz was born in 1907 and his lovely wife Jenina Abramowicz was born into the world in the year 1907 also. After getting married the couple settled down in the town of Warsaw, Poland. Later in 1942, the Abramowiczes adopted a small child from a family whom they had known before the war. Rella Glowinska was three when she was adopted by the Abramowiczes, and later on in her life, she would change her name to Relli Robinson. With her parents killed at such a young age, one would think that a small child such as herself would have been torn apart by this, but young Rella stayed strong and aided her adopted family's fight against the Nazis.

Mr. Abramowicz owned and operated a small workshop in Warsaw, Poland. When the Gestapo came and established the Warsaw ghetto, imprisoning the Abramowiczs' Jewish friends, Mr. Jozef Abramowicz visited his dear, but ill fated friends. One of those friends by the name of Aleksander Malec, managed to evade the patrols and escape that God forsaken ghetto. Malec had a plan to stay with some friends who lived out on the Arjin side of Warsaw while the Gestapo searched for the escaped fugitive. Mrs. Janina Abramowicz offered to help with food and shelter in her husband's workshop. Malec politely refused and continued on his journey. Several months further into the terrible war, Malec returned to the Abramowiczs this time in need of their help. For an amount of time Malec stayed close by at a friend of the Abramowicz family and over time began to visit the workshop ever so frequently and eventually was appointed to a position as bookkeeper and cashier. It was a good life for Malec for the time being until one traitorous neighbor informed the Gestapo that the Abramowiczes were harboring a Jew. The Gestapo arrived later and asked who the owner of the workshop was. Mr. Abramowicz answered that he was the sole owner of the workshop. The Gestapo asked if Aleksander Malec worked in his workshop. Once again the answer was yes. When the Gestapo asked where, Abramowicz said that he was out to lunch, and keeping self-control, took them to a restaurant a couple miles away and when the Gestapo came up empty handed, they questioned Abramowicz, but left him alone after a few hours. Mr. Abramowicz contacted Malec and set up a new shelter for him. Below his workshop was a beer distillery that had been put out of use when this terrible war started. Mr. Abramowicz and Malec dug a secret escape route from the old distillery to the new shelter that Malec was to go to. Only ten people were told, but in light of the recent Warsaw Uprising, 50 people showed up. Another refugee who the Abramowiczes saved was mentioned earlier, Rella Glowinska. Young Rella had her childhood torn apart by the war, with adopted parents (the Abramowiczes) and a ravaged, war torn, and prejudiced world going on outside her bedroom window, Rella was sent away when her parents were taken to a concentration camp in 1942. Adopted by the Abramowicz family they raised her as their own child, Rella even attended a local kindergarten in Warsaw. One day while Rella was having a playdate at her friend's house she returned to see her adopted mother gagged and bound on the floor while the Gestapo raged and questioned Rella about her identity. Rella used the identity given to her should she ever find herself in trouble, Halina Abramowicz. After that snafus her parents decided it would be best for her to leave Warsaw. Mrs. Abramowicz and Rella left to the area of Lublin, where her friends had a farm. Along the way the mother-daughter pair went with the Red Army. Unable to reach their destination, Rella was left with a peasant family. Later in 1950, Mrs. Abramowicz returned for Rella. Later Rella's relatives took her to Jerusalem.

Mr. and Mrs. Abramowicz made a great contribution to humans during the war. Their quick thinking and smart actions kept many Jews safe from execution and inspired others to do the same. These people were lights in the dark of the world, a saving grace to those who were persecuted. Mr. Jozef Abramowicz and Mrs. Abramowicz's story has been in the dark for too long and with this article hopefully people will remember them and keep them in their hearts as true world heroes.

Works Cited

http://db.yadvashem.org/righteous/family.html?language=en&itemId=4037409 1/08-2/21

Abramowicz FAMILY Author unkown

Irena Sendlerowa helps stop the Holocaust

Emma Lyons

The Holocaust was a tragic and horrible time in human history. Shockingly, six million Jews and five million non-Jews were killed between the years of 1933 - 1945. History has told how the Germans invaded many countries including Poland, Netherlands, France, Yugoslavia, Norway, Belgium, Denmark, and Western Poland. Many people tried to stop the Germans. Some of the countries that added aid against the Germans and fought for peace were: Great Britain, Canada, Belgium, United States, Denmark, New Zealand, Poland, South Africa, and Yugoslavia. The Germans' allies were Japan, Italy, Hungary and Romania.

The Nazis wanted to control and slaughter the Jews because they thought that the Jewish race was inferior. The leader of this horrible event was Adolph Hitler, and he was responsible for empowering the German soldiers to go into towns and kill Jewish people.

Interestingly, Germans targeted the Jewish citizens. Why ? The Germans thought the Jewish people were inferior because the Jews were thought as the "killers of Christ," and the Jewish race was becoming more powerful and populated and was seen as a threat to the Germans. Also, the Jewish people were mostly in charge of the banking systems in Europe and this made the Germans feel like they could not trust the Jewish people. Germany was struggling because of the First World War, and the country's leaders wanted to get more money for themselves. So they decided to make a plan to turn people against the Jewish people because they controlled the money. The Nazi Party made camps to detain Jewish prisoners. At first, the six camps or relocation sites created by the Germans were built to help retrain and educate the Jewish people to do other stuff. However, the camps quickly became deathtraps for the people. The people who were sent there were the Jews and punishable people who had done wrong in their community. In addition, anyone who did not agree with the Germans or their way of thinking were imprison. During this time, the Germans made Jewish people leave their families and homes and travel to these camps. Many families were separated and never saw their loved ones again. At the camps, the people were separated by size and health. The children were sent away from their parents and the boys were sent to work in fields and camps. Many people were tortured and made to take medicine to make them sick. The Jews became human ginea pigs for disturbing medical experiments. This tragic time in history lasted twelve years and ended in a war between the peacemakers and the Germans and their allies. When the long war was over and many had died, there was peace back in our world between the two sides. However, the Jewish people lost all their homes and things and never got them back. The Germans stole paintings and jewelry from the Jewish people. They even lived in their homes. At the end of the war, people tried to give the stolen stuff back to the Jewish people, but many survivors lost everything and everyone.

During the time of the Holocaust many Polish people helped their Polish neighbors and friends. One of them was Irena Sendlerowa who was a 29 year old Polish Catholic woman. Irena Sendlerowa was a Polish social worker. She was part of a secret organization that was named Zegota. Irena hid Polish-Jewish children to protect them against the Nazis who were invading their land. She worked in the Warsaw Health Department as a nurse. She was allowed in the ghetto because of her nursing background and worked undercover hiding and saving over 2,500 children. Irena hid them in ambulances, sewer pipes, underground passages, suitcases, and took them to old courtyards to keep them away from danger.

Irena grew up in Otwock, Poland. Her mother's name was Janina and her father's name was Stanislaw. Irena was the only child of Stanislaw. Her father was close to Irena. He inspired her. Her father was a doctor and sadly died in 1917 from a disease while trying to help patients that other doctors would not help. Until 1939, it was her mother and Irena living together until the Nazis invaded Poland. Sadly, Irena was captured and tortured. Her feet and legs were broken. She never gave any information away about the children she helped, and she was the only one who knew where they were hidden. After the war, she worked hard to reconnect the separated families. The Holocaust was a truly horrible and ugly experience, but there were hidden angles like Irena who helped to heal the hurt.

Since we know how awful the Holocaust was, we should work hard to not allow this type of thing to happen again in our world. First, we need to be aware of history and how the Holocaust started. Many small steps and choices led up to the experience we call the Holocaust. Then, we need to watch what is around us and make sure we are protected. We need to make sure laws are fair and right and that the people who break them or threaten to break them are punished. Our country needs to not allow for these things to happen again by having a strong military and police system that works. We need to educate people about the bad and help them protect the good. Finally, if someone does something bad or hurts our country, they need to leave or go to jail. If Hitler went to jail or was made to leave, then maybe the Holocaust would not have happened. If we, as a country, work together, we can make the Holocaust never happen again!

Bibliography

Kate Connely, February 15,2017 , Im no hero, says the woman who saved 2500 children http://www.theguardian.com/world/2007/mar/15/secondworldwar.poland

Life in a Jar, irenasendler, February 6, 2017, http://www.irenasendler.org/facts-about-

Women of Valor, February 6,2017

Women who rescued Jews during Holocaust irena/http://www.yadvashem.org/yv/en/exhibitions/righteous-women/sendler.asp

Heroes of the Holocaust

Ensley Barbosa

The Holocaust was a terrible time that took place from 1941 to 1945. In this time, Adolf Hitler and the Nazi party put Jews in concentration camps and killed more than six million of them. In Poland, many people did great deeds of bravery to save their Jewish neighbors. One such example was the Job Family.

Hania Sturm, her mother, Briendla Sturm, and her father, Berl Sturm were taken to the Debica Ghetto in around 1942. Her mother was killed a few months after they arrived at the camp, so it was just Hania and her father. They tried to leave, but could not find anywhere to go, so they returned. When she was thirteen, Hania and her father escaped from the Debica ghetto again. This time they left and offered to pay a shoemaker to let them stay and hide. The shoemaker agreed and kept them in his home until his wife heard the Germans would be coming, looking for hiding Jews. They kicked them out and Hania and her father wandered the streets looking for somewhere else to hide. They heard that there was another Ghetto in Tarnow, so they headed that way.

On the way, the Sturms went from door to door asking for food, help, or shelter. Everyone turned them down and some even threatened to call the Gestapo (Nazi police). A few times, they were robbed and blackmailed. Not only was there the fact that nobody offered Hania and her father shelter, they also had to deal with the weather. It was very cold and sometimes rained. They probably wandered for several weeks before they found shelter. They were cold, freezing, and starving when they ran into a girl in the streets. She was a 16 year old peasant girl named Stefania Job who, after seeing they were Jewish, offered to help them. She took them to meet her father Jozef Job, who welcomed them into their home. They were introduced to her mother, Wiktoria, and her siblings, Edward and Izabela.

At first to hide Hania and her father, the Jobs would put them in the cellar, but when friends came to visit, they would hide behind a large stone oven and use logs to cover them. They felt that hiding the Sturms in the cellar was too risky and they had a chance of being seen when company was over, so they moved them up to the attic of an unfinished building on their farm. The conditions outside were terrible. There was rain and snow and with the building not being finished, it did not always block out these harsh elements. Hania and her father suffered from the cold, but still chose to stay there and hide.

Later, the Germans were recruiting people to come to Germany and work in agriculture or in factories. Stefania was chosen by the Germans, but her father went in her place. Stefania's brother was also chosen to go to Germany, leaving her and her mother to look after the farms. Though she had to keep the farm, Stefania still attended to the Sturm's needs. In the last years of the Holocaust, Hania, her father, and the Jobs faced a new danger. The retreating German army created a military camp in the Jobs' village, and all its inhabitants evacuated. Stefania cried and went to tell the Sturms about the announcement. She told the Sturms, "I'll tell you why I cried so hard; it was because of you that I cried so hard. Not because I have to leave the village, I'm not the only one who has to leave; there are so many people living in the village and they all have to leave. Besides, I have places to go ...We lived through so much together and it's not so long before the war will be over, and now we have to part. The reason I cried is because I am very worried about what will happen to you." (Yad Vashem). I included this quote to show that in their time with the Jobs, they had become close and cared for each other like family. It shows that Wiktoria thought of them as family and was fearful of what would happen to the Sturms when they were forced to leave their home. Maybe she even thought they would be taken back to a concentration camp, or even killed for escaping the ghetto.

Stefania and her sister arranged an underground shelter near the forest for the Sturms. Hania and her father stayed in the shelter until they were found by some Germans who helped them escape and hid them in their horse stable. They woke one morning and found that the area had been liberated by the Red Army. Hania and her father went back to Debico with the remaining survivors. Jozef came back to see that they were alright and was relieved to see the Sturms among the other survivors. They sent Hania on a train to France along with the other children of the survivors so they could be treated and taken care of while the parents stayed and tried to help with all they could. This is the story of one of many heroes of the holocaust.

Works Cited

"Yad Vashem, The World Holocaust Remembrance Center-The Righteous Among The Nations, 1980"

Witold Fomenko: Little Things Make a Huge Difference

Erin Ayotte

"Carry each other's burdens, and this way you will fulfill the law of Christ" (Galatians 6:2). During Hitler's reign of terror many people showed great courage all over the world. One of them was Witold Fomenko from Lutsk, Poland. Witold Fomenko grew up with Jewish friends and neighbors and admired them. He saw what the Nazis started to do to the Jews in Germany and Poland. He immediately started to help. Witold Fomenko showed that it does not matter what the risks are, but how one responds to them that is important.

Witold Fomenko grew up in Poland. As a young boy in the town of Lutsk, he was influenced by many Jews even though he was a Catholic boy. During his childhood he had many positive interactions with Jews and their culture. He was inspired to be just as hardworking as they were. When he got older he became a music teacher and a barber. He was open with many of his customers and students who were Jewish. Before 1933 when Hitler came to power in Germany, many Jews lived peacefully in almost every country in Europe. Many of the Jews lived in Eastern Europe, including Poland, the Soviet Union, Hungary, and Romania. The majority of them spoke their own language, Yiddish. They lived as farmers, tailors, seamstresses, factory hands, accountants, doctors, teachers, and small business owners. When they were not working, they spent their free time going to the movies, reading books, and spending time with their family. In the 1930s when the Nazis started slowly coming to power, their lives were changed forever.

Witold Fomenko watched from Poland as changes happened in Germany. Hitler assured the Germans that the Jews were the problem in their society. At the time, most of the Germans believed him. With many unemployed German citizens during the Great Depression this situation provided Hitler a political opportunity, so he ran for the President of Germany. Hitler lost the Presidential election in 1932, but his wish was granted when he was appointed Chancellor on the 30th of January 1933. At first Hitler started to change hundreds of laws to restrict the Jews from doing anything. In April of 1933, he made even more laws restricting Jew from going to certain schools and universities, and then taking away their jobs as doctors and as members of legal professions. With no doctors, no one could be cared for, and with no lawyers no one could stop Hitler. In September 1939, the Nazis invaded Poland and the Soviet Union. It was marked as the beginning of World War II in Germany. After years of fighting, the Red Army was able to get rid of the Nazi invaders from across Poland. About 21.4% of Poland's population died between 1939 and 1945. Witold Fomenko watched these events with great concern.

Witold Fomenko knew that this was wrong. He would not stand for the cruel treatment given to these many innocent Jews whose lives were being ruined for no reason. When the Germans began invading Lutsk in 1941 and started setting up ghettos, he instantly started to help his neighboring Jews. He secretly started to bring firewood, food, and the limited medicines he could find to the Jews in the ghettos. When he brought the Jews food and supplies, he would sing to them and tell corny jokes to try to cheer them up. Right before the liquidation in the ghettos, he started forging identification papers he made for them. One day Fomenko went to the ghetto to bring supplies for the Jews. That day he was captured and tortured for helping the Jews, then the Nazis forced him to tell tell them his name. Luckily, the city's military commander happened to be one of Fomenko's customers at his barber shop. The Military commander saw nothing wrong in Fomenko, so he released him. Even After the camp's liquidation, he still continued to help the imprisoned Jews in a new labor camp in Lutsk. After about a year the camp was destroyed in 1942. When the Jews were free he helped the Jews who had nowhere to go, and began to hide them in Christian homes around the city. In 1945, when the war was over, he met a Jewish woman he rescued and together they moved to Israel.

"God is not unjust; he will not forget your work and the love you have shown him as you have helped his people and continued to help them" (Hebrews 6:10). Witold grew up influenced by Jews, who inspired him throughout his life time. He saw what the Nazis did to them and knew it was not right. He helped many Jews in the ghetto, but he did not do extraordinary things to save them. He did something much bigger, by doing small thing after small thing, with love and without thought of himself. Witold Fomenko showed the world that it does not matter that one does not have to do something giant to make a giant difference.

Bibliography:

Soah Resources Center - Fomenko, Witold Yad Vashem, 15, January 2017
http://www.yadvashem.org/odot_pdf/Microsoft%20Word%20-%206624.pdf
Biography.com Editors The Biography.com website Bio., 17, January 2017
http://www.biography.com/people/adolf-hitler-9340144#synopsis
Jewish Life In Europe Before the Holocaust, Ushmm 15, January 2017
https://www.ushmm.org/outreach/en/article.php?ModuleId=10007689
Invasion Of Poland Wikipedia 5, February 2017
https://en.wikipedia.org/wiki/Invasion_of_Poland

The Holocaust and Irena Adamowicz story

Gabriella DeMarais

The Holocaust was a tragic time in human history. Almost seven million individuals, Jews and non-Jews alike were slaughtered. Many people showed great courage and fortitude during Hitler's reign of terror. One of these individuals was Irena Adamowicz.

The Holocaust was an abysmal time period in history. It started on January 30, 1933 and ended on May 8, 1945. It all started with the boycott of Jewish businesses. Then, lawyers and doctors were disbarred and banned from their practice. After, the Jews were banned from all schools. Finally, the horror began. Jews were moved into ghettos with gates and guards surrounding it. There were three types of ghettos, closed ghettos, open ghettos, and destruction ghettos. The ghettos were a horrible place to live. They had limited connection to the world outside of the ghettos. Closed ghettos were tremendously crowed and very unsanitary. Most ghettos were closed ghettos. Open ghettos didn't have walls or fences but, they had restrictions on leaving or entering. Open ghettos were in Poland and the Soviet Unions, which were German-occupied. Destruction ghettos were firmly sealed off and only lasted two – six weeks before the Germans destroyed them. The Jews inside the destruction ghettos would be deported or killed by German officials. Ghetto police were given orders from the German authorities. If they didn't follow through with the orders they would be killed. The Jews were forced to wear armbands or identifying badges in the ghettos. The majority of the ghettos were killed by disease, starvation, or shot. From the ghettos, they were moved into the concentration camps. Some people were kept there or killed. Many times, Nazi soldiers would murder Jewish people before they even made it to a camp. They would put children and their mothers in cars with no air and let carbon dioxide kill them. The Nazis would keep the strongest and put them to work until they died. Hitler, also, lied used propaganda to lie to the German people and the world at large. The Nazis would take photos of the concentration camps, but they would make it look like the camps were more of a safe haven to the Jews.

On July, 6 1941, mobile killing units, called einsatzgruppen, shot nearly 3,000 Jews at the Seven Fort. People that were sick concentration camps would be burned or shot to death.

On October 1, 1943, the Jews in Denmark were rescued. Things started looking up for the Jews. In August, 1944, Allied forces invade southern France and Paris gets liberated. On January 25, - January 27, 1945, the Death march happened. The Death March was the march of concentration camp prisoners to different concentration camps. The Death March had three purposes, SS authorities didn't want prisoners, that were alive, to fall into enemy hands and tell their stories to Allied and Soviet liberators, the SS thought they needed prisoners to keep the production of weapons wherever, and whenever possible, and some SS leaders believed unreasonably that they could use Jewish prisoners as hostages to haggle for an unconnected peace in the west that would promise the survival of the Nazi rule. On April 30, 1945, Hitler committed suicide! This made Germany lose its hope and they surrendered to the Soviets on May 9, 1945. That act ended the Holocaust.

There were many sung and unsung heroes during the Holocaust. One of those unsung heroes was Irena Adamowicz. She was born on May 11, 1910 in the Russian Empire. She was born into a noble Polish family. Irena was raised a catholic and went to college at Warsaw University. She held a degree as a social worker. During her time as a social worker, Irena befriended a Jewish woman and she participated in educational activities. Before the war, Irena was a leader of a Polish scout group, called the Polish Scouts, in Warsaw. She was interested in the Zionist organization and Hashomer Hatzair.

Irena died on August 12, 1963. Irena Adamowicz held a very important role in helping the Jews throughout the Holocaust. Irena did many things that helped and saved many people and the Allied Forces. Irena risked her life by carrying out Jewish underground organization missions in the ghettos. She carried important messages from different ghettos. She helped establish contact between the Jewish underground organizations and the Home Army (Polish military). She armed the resistance. Everything that she did boosted the morale of the Jewish people. After the war, Adamowicz maintained her relationship with the remnants of the Zionist pioneering youth movements in Poland who were preparing Jews to immigrate to Israel. She also kept in contact with her friends in the movements. In 1958, Adamowicz came to Israel for an extended visit as the guest of the Ha Kibbutz Ha Artzi movement. On January 4, 1985 she was recognized as one of the Righteous Among Nations by Yadveshem.

There are many unsung heroes throughout Holocaust history. Some helped tremendously, others did small things that helped many people. There were many resistance members that helped the destruction of the Holocaust. These people showed great fortitude and endurance during this time.

Bibliography
1. Yadveshem, Irena Adamowicz, Righteous Among Nations, 1/12/17, http://db.yadvashem.org/righteous/family.html?language=en&itemId=4013667
2. Wikipedia, Irena Adamowicz, Wikipedia, 2/7/17 https://en.wikipedia.org/wiki/Irena_Adamowicz
3. Holocaust Encyclopedia, Ghettos, Holocaust Encyclopedia, 2/15/17 https://www.ushmm.org/wlc/en/article.php?ModuleId=10005059 \
4. Holocaust Encyclopedia, Death March, Holocaust Encyclopedia, 2/15/17 https://www.ushmm.org/wlc/en/article.php?ModuleId=10005162

Krystyna Adolph's Story

Heather Breckner

It all started with a man named Adolph Hitler who was elected as the representative for the Nazis. Hitler then proceeded to "cleanse the races", meaning death for all who did not meet the requirements of having light skin, blue eyes and blonde hair and also being Christian. This fatal idea soon became a reality and the Holocaust started, wiping out millions of people both Jews and non-Jews. Almost seven million individuals, both Jews and non-Jews, were brutally slaughtered in this horrid massacre. Many people showed great courage and fortitude in the Holocaust, despite this happening during Hitler's reign of terror. One of these people was Krystyna Adolph.

Krystyna Adolph was a middle aged woman who lived in Vilna, and was a teacher at a local school known as Czartoryski High School. There she met Jewish twin sisters Monika and Lidia Glushin who were students in her class. By the time the war broke out, Krystyna had been widowed, and was left with her small farm in Ignalino and her daughter. The Germans arrived in Vilna in 1941, searching for all Jews. Krystyna sent a message to the twins saying they could take shelter at her place if they were to be in any danger. Soon a ghetto was set up in Vilna, and the sisters fled to Krystyna's house for protection. The sisters then spent the next three years at the farm helping Krystyna doing housework, chores, and tending to the livestock in trade for food, water, shelter, clothing and protection. The sisters were seen to strangers as nothing more than long distance relatives, but the only people who knew the sisters' real identities were Krystyna's daughter and her late husband. Krystyna provided the twins and their mother with false identification papers through her sister in law. The twins survived the Holocaust, and later moved to Israel, and for many years after Krystyna and the sisters kept in contact with each other.

The Holocaust was a horrible point in history, so it is important to be aware of national problems. Discrimination of religions is a huge problem to this day, which is half of what the Holocaust was. Discrimination is such a horrible problem to this day, not only making people feel bad about themselves, but also their race, and the past. Discrimination of Muslims or people from Arabia is a big problem now because of the Islamic terrorists attacking people and other countries. The terrorist attacks are giving the Muslim and Arabic people a bad image, making it easier to find a reason to pick on them or make claims of violence on them. Another subject of great political importance is the idea of one race being more superior than the other. Hitler believed the "truly perfect race" was of being a tall person with lighter skin, blue eyes and blonde hair. Today the race of African Americans believe that they are being discriminated by other races, but Caucasians being the main offender to them. Another problem is the problem of human trafficking through foreign countries into others. Slavery was not really part of the Holocaust, but the Jews were treated poorly, many times like slaves.

Although the world has many problems, that does not mean we cannot do anything to fix them or solve them. There are also many campaigns and organizations that are against discrimination of all kinds from race to religion, or just protecting those who are more vulnerable to such things that we are. One place that helps with discrimination of all kinds like being bullied for your gender or sexuality is the Human Rights Campaign, showing that everyone is equal and you must be treated with respect because they are human too. Another organization is the International Rescue Committee, helping refugees who need our help with getting homes, jobs, clothes, food, water, and their life back on track. This helps the refugees fleeing from their country, or just those around who need our help, and is truly a blessing in more ways you can imagine. Organizations and committees like these help people feel more confident about themselves, give them a new purpose in life, help them survive by themselves, or just give them a helping hand in their recovery.

The Holocaust was all started by a cruel and powerful Nazi leader named Adolph Hitler. Hitler started the idea of a "cleanse of the races" by wiping out all of those who were not Aryan: those who did not have light skin, blue eyes and blonde hair were to be eradicated from Germany and its surrounding areas. Almost seven million people were brutally murdered by the Nazis, wiping out a nation's worth of people. Many times we are told "History tends to repeat itself." To this day we can learn from our mistakes, and see the signs and take action before anything bad ever happens.

Yad Vashem, 02/01/2017, http://db.yadvashem.org/righteous/righteousName.html?language=en&itemId=4013669

Holocaust Essay

Ian Falkenstrom (Winner)

 In history, many horrible events have occurred. These events are important to understand, so they do not happen again in the future. Horrifying events are usually caused by people who have prejudices against certain groups. These negative feelings can lead to discrimination. One group of people, who experienced extreme discrimination and mass extermination, was the Jews in the Holocaust. To gain a better understanding of the Holocaust, this essay will focus on three major points: the Holocaust in its most basic form, a brief account of a Polish hero, and ideas about how another Holocaust can be prevented.

To understand the Holocaust in its most basic form, it is necessary to realize that it was a period of extreme persecution towards Jewish people by the Nazi ruler, Adolf Hitler. It lasted from the early 1930's to the late 1940's. The main reason that the Holocaust occurred was because the Nazis hated Jews. The Nazis blamed the Jews for many of their country's problems. They also saw the Jews as a threat to their society because of their socioeconomic status. The Nazis started the events leading to the Holocaust slowly, but then they escalated them. First, the Nazis began taking away Jewish rights and wealth. Wood states, "The Nazis introduced many laws to discriminate against Jews and deprive them of their rights" (Gluck-Wood, 50). This quote shows that Jewish rights were taken away, and these laws eventually led to Jews being stripped of their wealth and banned from all schools. Next, the Nazis began to round up Jews in Europe and put them into concentration camps. In these concentration camps, Jews were forced to work long hours without pay. For example, Martin Gilbert says, "The Jewish prisoners worked in special detachments and received the hardest tasks. Many Jews were also beaten and starved to death" (Gilbert, 57). In addition, Angela Wood states, "Suffering and hardship in the Ghettos was a deliberate approach taken by the Nazis. The starvation was so bad that the Nazis could lure people into being deported with a promise of something to eat" (Wood, 62). These quotes illustrate how cruelly Jews were treated in the ghettos and the concentration camps. Fortunately, some Jewish heroes started an underground resistance that helped many Jews escape. With an understanding of the Holocaust in its most basic form, it is possible to appreciate its heroes.

Many great heroes arose during the Holocaust. People do not have to do things in a recognized way to be a hero. Sometimes, it's the brave, humble, unrecognized things people do that are heroic accomplishments. Joseph Campbell says, "A hero is someone who has given his or her life to something greater than oneself" (brainyquote.com). This quote shows that heroic deeds can be as simple as giving your time and effort to something that does not benefit you. One person who did this was a Polish man named Adam Czternastek. Adam Czternastek saved some concentration camp survivors. This is not generally known, but it is still heroic. Nothing is more valuable than a human life, and Adam saved more than one. Adam Czternastek was a victim of the Holocaust himself, and he assisted in the underground resistance against the Nazis. During his time in the resistance, Adam smuggled two Jewish women to Slovakia, and he took care of his friend's daughter, Nuna. Nuna was a Holocaust survivor from a concentration camp in Janowski. She escaped to a ghetto in Kurowice with her family before she was entrusted to Adam. Adam gave Nuna a decent lifestyle and an education until his death. The reason Adam Czternatek is a hero is because he helped two Jewish women escape, and he helped a Jewish family by taking care of their daughter. Adam Czternastek was one of many great heroes that helped the victims of the Holocaust. Along with the help from great heroes, society in general is responsible for preventing another Holocaust.

In order to prevent another Holocaust, many precautionary steps can be taken. First, schools can improve history classes to give the next generation a better understanding of the past. Winston Churchill said it best when he described how the events of WWII were allowed to grow without opposition: "When the situation was manageable it was neglected, and now that it is thoroughly out of hand we apply too late the remedies which then might have effected a cure" (nationalchurchillmuseum.org). Second, new millennials can improve their character, so they do not become selfish or destructive. People, who are taught that they should have everything, will always look for someone to blame for what they do not have. Finally, parents can stop being so preoccupied with monetary concerns and take the time needed to work on their child's character. Teaching children that good character is as important as academic or business success will teach them to stand up for what is right, not for what is materially beneficial. It is clear that steps such as improved history classes, better character development, and more parental involvement should be taken in order to prevent another Holocaust.

In summary, the Holocaust was a horrifying time in history that lead to the extermination of many Jewish people from the early 1930's to the late 1940's. It was mainly due to people's willingness to follow Adolf Hitler and the Nazis. While many horrible events occurred, some heroes, such as Adam Czternastek, managed to escape and save others. To help prevent another Holocaust, many precautionary steps can be taken such as improved history classes, better character development, and more parental involvement. Even though the Holocaust was an extremely evil time in history, it taught people to value human life more and to be aware of the devastating effects of prejudice and discrimination. This is a very important lesson to learn, so that people will have more respect for each other, treat each other more humanely, and live peacefully together.

Works Cited

"Czternastek FAMILY." Yad Vashem. The World Holocaust Remembrance Center, n.d. Web. 2 Feb. 2017.

Gilbert, Martin. The Holocaust: A History of the Jews of Europe during the Second World War. New York: H. Holt, 1987. 11+. Print.

"Joseph Campbell Quotes." BrainyQuote. Xplore, n.d. Web. 2 Feb. 2017.

Wiesenthal, Simon. The Holocaust FAQ: 36 Questions and Answers on the Holocaust, 1933-1945. Los Angeles: Center - Museum of Tolerance, 1994. Print.

"Winston Churchill's Speeches." National Churchill Museum | Sir Winston Churchill's Speeches. National Churchill Museum, n.d. Web. 2 Feb. 2017.

Wood, Angela Gluck. Holocaust: The Events and Their Impact on Real People. New York, NY: DK, 2007. N. page. Print.

Holocaust Heroes

James Blaize Benson

The Holocaust was a horrific time in history. During the tragic event known as the Holocaust many people suffered and even more died. About 6 million Jews died and 5 million other people died, too. Some people went to concentration camps to be slave labor. Some went to death camps to be killed. But, the labor and the killing did not all happen right away. When the Nazi party was elected in 1933 they promised to end the depression they were in. When Hitler was elected Chancellor everything started to go downhill. Soon, Jews could not work in a business or own business. They could not be doctors, lawyers, or teachers. Hitler saw the Jews as a threat. Then the Nazis decided to create Ghettos. 400,000 Jews crowded into a 1.3 square mile perimeter. People had no money, poor housing, and very little food. Jews could not leave without permission and were gated in like animals. Many died from hunger or illness. Jews were also sent off to concentration camps and death camps. Soon, Allied forces such as the Red Army came together to save all the people suffering in the Holocaust. One person who showed courage and saved several lives was Stefan Konopka.

In January 1943, Konopka, A supervisor of public building repairs that were damaged early in the war helped Krotowski (or Krajewski Antoni according to his forged documents) hide. Konopka let Krotowski stay in his apartment and Konopka treated him like family. Konopka looked after him and obtain forged documents for him. They, in 1944, all the residents of Warsaw, poland were driven out. Konopka decided to take Krotowski with him to a village near Sochaczew and they pretended to be relatives even though Krotowski looked Jewish. Their plan did not work. They were both arrested and sent to Praszkow concentration camp, They then escaped from the concentration camp and looked for a hiding place. They waited in the Hiding place until the Red Army, the Russian Soviet army air force and ground, liberated the area.

Furthermore, during the Holocaust, Konopka saved many lives of 300 Jewish fugitives and more. He helped them hide with Krajewski Antoni. Later, he went on to provide the Retchman family, who was wealthy, with work permissions. After, he tried to save the lives of Lipszyc Ludwik and his son. They were in the concentration camp, Lublin. Ludwik refused to leave the camp even though Konopka already had arranged and illegal transfer to Warsaw with Ludwik's family. Another person whom he tried to save was Jerzy Cwibak. Konopka let Cwibak stay in Konopka's apartment in Warsaw until the uprising on August 1st, 1944. Konopka also helped Irean Leszczynska deliver a baby.

Stefan Konopka saved many lives during the Holocaust. He saved so many and still did not expect anything in return. He risked his life for others. Konopka worried about the lives of others more than his own. His is one of the many great life savers during the Holocaust and he should never be forgotten.

Baran Boleslaw, a very amazing human being who was recognized for saving the lives of Jewish people at the time of the Holocaust. He mainly supplied them with Aryan documents or otherwise known as ration cards. Baran worked as a clerk in the municipality. A local actor, Mrozewski Zdzislaw from the Contemporary Theatre in Kraków, wanted help and went to Baran asking him if he could get forged Kennkarte documents for his Jewish girlfriend, who was a singer named Jozefa. Kennkarte documents were used to tell the identity of a person during 1938 and could be obtained through a police precinct. Baran had no doubt that he could fulfil their request for the documents they needed to survive; however, if he was caught in the process he and his family would be in great danger. He would go on to risk his life for others whom he barely even knew. Baran's reputation soon spread and other people appealed to him for help. Another actor heard about how Baran helped Mrozewski Zdzislaw and his girlfriend. Singer Wernicz, from Bagatela and Juliusz Slowacki Theatres, asked Baran to help her to find forged papers. Baran agreed to help her and once again another life was saved by Baran Boleslaw.

Baran Boleslaw did very courageous deeds for other people and did not expect any recompense in return. Therefore, Baran is a very incredible human and should be recognized for the amazing things he did.

The Holocaust was a very tragic time and we, as a whole, should do anything we can to prevent another one. A way we can prevent another Holocaust is by being generous to other people, no matter what color skin they have or what religion they are. No matter what gender or what size. We are all humans and none of us are pieces of trash to be used and thrown away right after. We are all equal in a world that everyone shares. If everybody does their part in caring about others and treating them equally, we can prevent another horrible event like the Holocaust. It all starts with helping someone in trouble or picking someone up after a bad day. Even just trying to make someone laugh could help our society become better. No matter what happens, if we just all keep calm and try to keep the bad things from getting to us, we could become the greatest thing to ever happen to the world.

WORKS CITED

Baran Family Yad Vashem January 26, 2017
http://db.yadvashem.org/righteous/family.html?language=en&itemId=4013800

Konopka, Stefan Yad Vashem January 26, 2017
http://db.yadvashem.org/righteous/family.html?language=en&itemId=4015719

A Tragic Period of Time

Janie Ming

January 30, 1933 started a disruptive and horrific time in history. An estimated six million Jews were killed. There were six death camps in Poland where many people were murdered. The camps were places of great deprivation. Prisoners were tortured, beaten, starved, and killed. If prisoners survived the camps, freedom sometimes brought its own dangers. Ironically, some Holocaust survivors died from chocolate and candy overdoses within their first week of freedom. During this time of tragedy many people and families showed great courage and pride in fighting off Hitler's wrong doings. One such man who took matter into his own hands was Michal Zytkieewicz.

Michal Zytkieewicz was a painter and a building contractor. Michal lived in Czestochowa, Poland before the war. However, during the war, he lived in Warsaw and the village of Dwikozy, in the Country of Sandomierz. Irena, his wife, was a Jew. In May 1943, an old friend of Irena's family, Nina Boniowka, approached Irena after escaping from the Warsaw ghetto. Irena handed Nina over to her husband who took her to his home in Dwikozy and secured Aryan papers for her under the name of Stanislawa Wisniewska. Nina hid there for three months, but, after she was betrayed, she had to leave. She returned to Warsaw and then Michal took her to the village of Burakow Maly, near Warsaw, where he bought a house that had been partially burnt in September 1939. He invested a lot of effort and money into rebuilding the house. He even installed camouflaged hideouts. He carried out the work with the help of one trusted man, Mieczyslaw Szaszkiewicz, and in the final phases of work, he was also assisted by two Jews who later hid in the house along with Nina. Michal also hid Feliks Brodzki in Dwikozy from the time he left Lwow in December 1941 until he left for the Czestochowa ghetto in April 1942.

Feliks found shelter with Michal a second time, as well; this time in more dramatic circumstances, in October 1942. Feliks had jumped off a train heading for Treblinka near Warsaw. His dress immediately aroused suspicion and he had bruises all over his body. He had no money or documents. Fortunately, Feliks found Michal, who hid him in his apartment until May 1943. Feliks would have died were it not for Michal's help. In Burakow Maly, a few other Jews apart from Irena and Feliks found shelter with Michal. They were Nina Boniowka, Izabella Boniowka Brodzka, and Leon Rappaport. They were all hidden from June 1943, and in February 1944, Henryk Boniowka joined them. When Michal returned to Dwikozy, Halina and Mieczyslaw Szaszkiewicz, who pretended to be the house's sole inhabitants, took care of the charges. However, Michal often visited them and brought them food. Some of the hidden Jews paid for the food, but those who had no money did not and still received food.

In August 1944, when the Warsaw Uprising broke out, the residents of Burakow Maly were deported. Among them was Nina who, thanks to the papers that Michal arranged for her, found shelter as a Pole in another village where she awaited the liberation. After the liberation, Nina returned to Warsaw to thank Michal, who was then sick with tuberculosis and was living in a sanatorium. He died before she had a chance to meet him. Of the six people that Michal hid, five survived the war.

Finally, May 8, 1945, the suffering of all people was done with. The Allied Forces liberated prisoners from the camps and Germany surrendered. An estimated six millions Jews were killed. About one third of all Jewish people alive at the time of the Holocaust were murdered. Along with all the Jews being killed, five million non Jews were killed too. Even though the odds of having another Holocaust are slim, anything is possible. So together we must join hands and know that criticizing someone's race and religion is very wrong. People who do not learn from history are bound to repeat it. Hopefully, one day we can all live in peace and harmony without caring about someone's race or religion. By, doing this, we can honor those who died, as well as the unsung heroes of the Holocaust who tried to help the persecuted Jews.

Bibliography
1. "The Holocaust: 36 Questions and Answers". Simon Wiesenthal Center - Museum of Tolerance Library and Archives: Educational Kit.Publishing date unknown.
2. Righteous Among Nations - Michal Zytkieewicz Yad Vashem-The World Holocaust Remembrance Center January 9, 2017 www.yadvashem.org

The Unsung Heroes of the Holocaust

John Seiler

8 October 1939 at Piotrków Trybunalski, the first ghetto was opened. All Jewish residents around the area were forcefully moved there. Their homes were given to other non-Jewish people. Their businesses met the same fate. Later, the first "Action" happened: Jewish ghetto residents were forcefully moved to Extermination (concentration) camps such as Auschwitz and Chelmno. The death toll for Jews, Jehovah's Witnesses, homosexuals, disabled people, and Roma, was in the millions. Although, the Holocaust was a time of terror, there were people along the way who helped the Jews plight...

In the fall of 1939, Germany invaded Poland. The Polish army was destroyed in a matter of weeks. In 1941, a ghetto was established in Krakow for non-Jewish citizens of that area. Four pharmacies with non-Jewish owners were there; the Nazi government offered them all new places to move to. All of them did but one. That pharmacy was run by Tadeusz Pankiewicz. He gave out medicine to ghetto residents for free. That man was one of the thousands of the under credited, "unsung" heroes of the Holocaust. These are just a few of their stories. Many of which are widely unknown by the population of the world.

After The Soviets annexed Lvov, a woman named Maria Charaszkiewicz, while donning a Star of David arm band, smuggled food in and gave it to the needy in the Warsaw ghetto. After 1941 and the capture of Lvov by the German forces, she returned to her native town to help some of her old Jewish friends. At massive risk, she, along with a Ukrainian friend, managed to save the two daughters of her friends, Janek and Cesia Lewin, by providing them with "Aryan" documents and hiding them outside the city. She also found the parents a hiding place in Warsaw, giving them fake IDs. During one of the many large scale actions put forward by the German government. In the Lvov ghetto, Maria smuggled a dentist out of the ghetto named Kamila Landau. After obtaining Aryan documents, she brought her to her sister's house. Kamila remained there until a neighbor of the sister became suspicious. Then Maria brought Kamila back to Lvov where they were until the area was liberated by the Soviets in 1944.

In July of 1942, the annihilation of the Jewish population in Molczadz left very few survivors. One of those survivors was named Jerachmiel Bronicki. His whole family was killed. While wandering through a field, he met another refugee named Szmaja. (Szmaja has no known last name) The two went to the nearby village of Sorgowicki. There they traveled to the Władysław Sorgowicki's farm. Wladyslaw was an old acquaintance of Bronicki's father. The Sorgowicki family dug a small bunker under their pig stye where the two Jews lived. The other and daughters were their main caretakers; therefore making Yad Vashem recognize the women as heroes in 1995. The Wladyslaw family remained there until the area's liberation by the Red Army. Bronicki and Szmaja joined the Red Army and eventually Bronicki immigrated to Israel, but, Szmaja was never heard of again. In 1995, Yad Vashem accepted the mother and daughters as Righteous Among the Nations.

Another case in Lvov, 1941 concerns the Gruenbaums family. Karolina Zaluska lived with her husband and daughter Lidia. Near them lived a Jewish family, the Gruenbaums. The two families had a rather good relationship, so in 1941 after the German invasion, helped hide the Gruenbaums in a distant apartment by putting a Ukrainian worker of Mr. Grunbaum's name on the lease. In the summer of 1942, there was an action in the Lvov ghetto and the Jews were transported to concentration camps. One of the daughters, sixteen-year-old Gizela Grunbaum, escaped and managed to reach Karolina who gave her shelter. Karolina also hid other Jews in her apartment: Donia and Grzegorz Wiernik. At the same time, the apartment rented under Marynia Kulik's name served as a hiding place for Gizela Nuss, Anita Teitelbaum, Landsberg, and Gizela's uncle Herman Fuchs. Karolina helped all of these fugitives and took care of their needs and safety. Karolina sewed clothes for those she was hiding and also to sell. Lidia brought food to the apartment, since it was thought as a schoolgirl, she would attract the least attention delivering packages. All those hidden by the Zaluskis survived the war. Afterwards, the Wierniks left Lwow with the Zaluskis, and, after a while, they passed away in Wroclaw. Herman Fuchs also passed away. All the children would later leave for Israel. The Zaluska family did this without any form of reward. These heroes deserve to have their stories told to the public

Still, thousands, if not millions of those who praised their leaders because of their beliefs. When the Nazis came into power, the country was poor and crushed by the Versailles Treaty carved a new a machine like a hammer and chisel on granite. If we were to ensure that something like this will never happen again, the best way may be to give a country something to hope for. Otherwise, hopeless people with bleak futures in their perspectives will create things like Nazi Regimes. Karl Marx or the founder of Communism, said that "Religion is the opium of the masses." (I do not endorse or condone Communism, this quote just matches) Religion is based on hope. If you are going to stop another Reich, you need people to have hope. (Also, don't take their money, countries will kill over that too.)

Bibliography:

Information From Yad Vashem http://www.yadVashem.org/

United States Holocaust Memorial Museum

https://www.ushmm.org/wlc/en/article.php?ModuleId=10005059

Zofia Majeska: An Unsung Hero

Katherine Fio

The Holocaust was a devastating and life changing time in the human history. Simply saying that "people had died" is a great understatement since over six million Jews were murdered at the hands of the Germans. They had been killed simply because of their religion. During this time, Hitler, the new joined Chancellor of Germany, had a very particular taste in the people that he ruled over. Because of his tactics, many feared to stop the unbearable abuse he laid upon the poor Jews. However, there were many fearless people who let no such fear stop them. They all showed courage and strength during Hitler's reign. They risked their lives for the greater good, failing to cooperate with Hitler's rules. They are the ones who are known as heroes. They are the ones who were brave enough to stand up for what they knew was right. One of those fearless people was Zofia Majewska.

On January 30, 1933, President Hidenburg appointed Adolph Hitler as the new Chancellor of Germany. This marked the start of the dreaded Holocaust. Hitler had many warped ideas of making a perfect race, and he decided that Jews would not be part of it. It all started on March 20, 1933. Ghettos were made near the outposts of the Poland towns, and soon after that, Hitler established the first concentration camp on the outskirts of Munich. Not only that, but soon after, the German Parliament granted Hitler dictatorial powers on March 24. Jewish businesses began being boycotted on April 1. Lawyers were disbarred, doctors were banned from practice, and children were banned from schools simply because they were Jewish. The Jews continuously lost more and more of their rights. From there, the ghettos, concentration camps, and extermination camps began. Many lives were lost while others suffered. Through all of this, many valiant people attempted to rescue and help stop the Jews' suffering.

In December of 1942, Zofia Majewska rescued the six member Wajsbard family from the Warsaw ghetto and hid them in her own home in Mniszew. The family was safe for only a few days before they were captured and taken to the Treblinka extermination camp where they would soon be killed. One of the sons in the family, Chaim David who was twenty years old, managed to escape and with all the strength he had left he made it to the Vistula River. Thinking that he had escaped his pursuers, he boarded a vessel that would take him across the river to what he thought was safety. However, when he reached the other side of the river, he was captured once again by a German ambush. The Germans threw him into the river and shot at him. Their shots luckily missed him, and on the verge of complete exhaustion, he swam back to shore and then lost consciousness. When he finally had woken up, Zofia was by his side ready to rescue him once again. She created a mat made of reeds and dragged him through the freezing snow to her home. She hid him in a pit behind her home until the liberation in August 1944. During that time, she kept him safe and met all of his needs. He was given food and water, clothing, and straw matting that he would be able to sleep on. Since it would be so taxing to do all of this on her own, she was assisted by her niece Lucyna Majewska. They both risked everything to keep Chaim David safe, seeking no material reward. He was kept safe and hidden throughout the entire war thanks to the two valiant women. Chaim and Lucyna became very close to each other and when the war was finally over, he married Lucyna and adopted the family name of Majeska. He became Henryk Majewksa and stayed grateful to Zofia his whole life, taking care of her devotedly until her death on January 1, 1967.

The Holocaust was a tragic time in history, and it is important that people are aware that it happened. Many people would rather deny it and hide from the terrifying truth that discrimination is still a huge problem in our world today. Many people are ridiculed and discriminated against because of their race, the color of their skin, their religion, and so many other things. A horrifying fact is that because of how much judgment people pass on others, there could very well be another holocaust against a different group of people. If people could try to accept everyone for who they are, maybe there would not be so much of a threat.

One thing that can give us hope is the brave people in the world that have enough courage to stand up for the less fortunate. To not only say that something is wrong, but do something about it and attempt to stop it from going on. It is brave people like Zofia Majewska who should be remembered as heroes and be role models to us all. They are the people who matter. They are the ones who make our world just a little bit better.

Yad Vashem - The World Holocaust Remembrance Center
http://www.yadvashem.org/ February 1, 2017

The History Place Holocaust Timeline http://www.historyplace.com/worldwar2/holocaust/timeline.html February 7, 2017

The Charuk Family Heroes

Libby Slater

The Holocaust was one of the greatest human tragedies of all time as eleven million people were killed under the Nazi power. Included in the eleven million killed were six-million Jews, five-million non-Jews and over one million children, all innocents. How could so many good, innocent people have gotten exterminated? Why would someone, a government, want to kill this many people? The answer was for power.

The time period of the Holocaust was twelve very long years between January 30, 1933, when Adolf Hitler came into power as the Chancellor of Germany, and ended finally on May 8, 1945, when the Nazis were defeated by the Allied Powers in World War Two. Twelve whole years! From the beginning of Hitler's regime, at best, people quickly lost most basic rights and freedoms and at the worst, the Nazis under Adolf Hitler killed many innocent people because of differing religious or social beliefs. Although the Jews were the largest target of the Holocaust, they were not the only group targeted, other religions and disabled persons were also persecuted.

Once Hitler took power, the first step the Nazis took was boycotting the Jewish businesses and then Jewish lawyers were disbarred. On April 4, 1933 all Jewish doctors were banned from practice and three days later all Jewish children were outlawed from every school in Poland. Even after all of these horrible steps to torture the Jews, the Nazis went on, sending the Jews to death camps and ghettos. But the worst of all of these things were that most of the Jewish community was exterminated. Women and children were told that they were going to take showers, but they were really put in gas chambers and murdered.

There were six death camps all of which were in Poland. So many of the Polish people, Jews or not, were affected by the Holocaust. The purpose of the death camps was to have the Jews work so hard and feed them very little until they died. The camp was meant to kill you and if you did not die naturally then they would basically just exterminate you. Again, although the Jewish people were the main targets of this extermination, many non-Jews were exterminated as well. Adolf Hitler had an idea of a "perfect race". To be considered into Hitler's "perfect race" you had to be blonde haired, blue eyed and tall. In Hitler's eyes, if you did not fit those categories you were to be exterminated. In a way Hitler's "perfect race" was very ironic, because Hitler did not even fit his own idea of a perfect race. Adolf Hitler was brown haired, brown eyed and very short. Adolf Hitler thought that to take over the world the race had to be pure. The Holocaust had many different stages, but every single one ended in the death of many innocent persons!

"Every moment counts, every second matters" -Elie Wiesel (Holocaust survivor) The Charuk family of four, Jan and Rozaila and their two children, represented these words in the quote. The Charuk family lived in the town of Lechowka. The family used their house as a type of safe house to help Jewish families. For almost four years, the Petcher family stayed with the Charuk family, while they were only supposed to stay with the family for two weeks. The family had a hiding place in the barn. When two other fugitives showed up, the Charuks could not deny them help. The Charuk family was very poor and had very little, but being the devout Catholics that they were they helped the struggling Jews out of the goodness of their hearts. The Charuks were even attacked themselves a few times for hiding the fugitives. Whenever the Nazis would try to bust the Charuks they could never find any evidence because the Jews would always be hiding, along with the Charuk children, in the field or in the barn. The children had made holes in the attic of the barn and would hide in there until they knew it was safe to come out. The Charuks went through many, many hard times in order save the Jewish fugitives. The Charuks put up with torture from the Germans! They were strangled with pillows and bitten by the Germans! There were also some shootings in the Charuks house. The Charuks were a godsend for the Jewish fugitives. Just imagine if the Charuks had not been there to help the fugitives, they would have been caught and killed right away. After the war the Petchers slowly migrated to Israel, but still kept in touch with the Charuk family.

The Holocaust was truly a horrible act. For the few people who did get help from people whether it be Catholics, or Protestants, or people who were truly kind, the Holocaust did not end in death, but in survival. The people who were saved were very lucky to find such great people with a heart that gives them the grace to help out the people who were truly in need of shelter and food. The Petchers and the two Jewish fugitives had to have been the luckiest. To have a family who would take you in for almost four years was truly a gift. The Charuks were such amazing heroes and should be recognized for their faith in God that everything would turn out right and their ability to put others before themselves. There were many heroes of the Holocaust and everyone should be so grateful that despite the evil that was going on there were people who were doing God's work.

WORKS CITED

Unknown author Charuk Family Yad vashem January 20http://db.yadvashem.org/righteous/family.html?language=en&itemId=4034480

Antoni Tomczak

Logan J. Hirsig

The Holocaust was a tragic time in our human history. Almost seven million Jews and non-Jews, lost their lives. Many people showed courage, determination, and the will to help others stay alive even though you may not. One person who risked their lives to save other people was Antoni Tomczak.

The Holocaust started on Jan. 30, 1933 and ended on May. 9, 1945 on what people call V - E Day. It started when the new chancellor Adolf Hitler was appointed into office by President Hindenburg. The Germans were systematically murdering Jews in the most tragic and deadly genocide ever. Hitler hated the Jews leading up to the Holocaust because he believed that the Jewish financiers (elite, ruling class of Jews) were responsible for sending the world into its First World War, causing the deaths of over 100,000 German soldiers. Adolf Hitler wanted a master race that had blonde hair and blue eyes and that were tall and intelligent.

Antoni Tomczak was a teacher and was active in the Polish Home Army underground. From there he was able to obtain forged "Aryan" papers for the boys. He also organized for them to be tutored by other Polish teachers who could be trusted with the great secret. Antoni also was a go between for Seweryn and his mother and small brother who were hiding elsewhere, and for whom he also obtained forged "Aryan" identity papers. Antoni further provided money, apparently from underground sources, to the Procheras for keeping the boys each month. The Procheras made it clear though that they would keep the boys even without this source of funding. When the boys indicated their eagerness to join the AK underground, Antoni helped them, but not before warning them of the anti-Semitism they were liable to find in its ranks.

The holocaust ended 10 days after Adolf Hitler committed suicide on April 30, 1945. On May 7th 1945 Germany surrendered to the western allies and on May 9th 1945 Germany surrendered to the Soviets. I think that there are many ways that we can prevent another holocaust from happening. One way is to prevent conditions from existing in countries where they feel they need to take matters into their own hands and elect a ruler to solve problems. Germany went into a severe depression in the 1920s which allowed. This gave Hitler the opportunity to rise to power. Since Germany had little experience in its history with a democratic government, Hitler was able to seize power relatively easily.

To conclude the holocaust was a very sad and tragic time in our human history in which over 6 million Jews and non-Jews were murdered in the most catastrophic and life changing event we have had.

Bibliography

yadvashem.org The Righteous Among the Nations1/16/17
http://db.yadvashem.org/righteous/family.html?language=en&itemId=4149911
Introduction to the Holocaust Encyclopedia1/27/17
https://www.ushmm.org/wlc/en/article.php?ModuleId=10005143

Witold Maczak

Lukas Crawford

The Holocaust was a tragic time in human history. Almost seven million individuals, lost their lives during the treacherous reign of Adolf Hitler. Many people showed amazing courage and fortitude during this time of catastrophic genocide. One of these courageous individuals was Witold Maczak.

The Holocaust was a time where the Chancellor of Germany,

Adolf Hitler, started to begin the worst genocide the world has ever seen. The time period of this horrible event started January 30, 1933. At the start, new laws were passed to boycott Jewish businesses, disbarring Jewish lawyers, banning Jewish doctors from their practice, and forbidding all Jewish children from their schools. Throughout this dreadful affair six million Jews were killed and five million non- Jews were also killed. The Jews were put into ghettos where they were locked in and only consumed about 600 calories a day and were tortured. Some were put on trains to death and labor camps to be put to work or die a gruesome death. Then others were exterminated in their homes when resisting the laws. There were a few people in this time period who helped others survive the treacherous reign of Hitler.

Witold Maczak was a marvelous person who was a hero in the Holocaust helping others to survive. He did this with no profit or earnings; it was done through the love and courage of his heart. Maczak was a male Christian from Poland whose occupation was that of a farmer. He provided false evidence and arranged shelter and a place to hide for a family of Jews who were being sent to Belzec death camp before Witold intervened. He first became involved after one day when he found two women concealed in a haystack in a farmyard of a Ukrainian farmer. The two Jewish women hidden in the haystack were Sela Katz and Hanna Grunwald who escaped the Lubaczow ghetto and found shelter with Koziejs, a farmer. They received Aryan papers, allowing them to transfer over to nearby Jaroslaw. Then from Jaroslaw, they took a train west where they found Witold who sheltered them and gave them food. After about a week, Annie Wertman escaped the Lubaczow ghetto and came to the house of Maczak and asked for refuge. He let her enter his home and later led Wertman to the train station to get her of out Poland. While on the train she encountered the Polish police and was beaten severely and was jailed in Krakow ghetto, yet she survived. With time, Maczak's house became an address for runaways seeking aid, where he could provide for them without receiving anything for his actions. The last group of people who Witold saved were David and Szija Blieberg. They were able to escape from the Lubaczow ghetto, then ran to the forest where they hid. Huge, abandoned farming towers and buildings were looming above them when their friend and ex-neighbor came to save them. They were brought to Witold and he was able to transport them safely to a train to get out of Poland. Clearly, Witold Maczak was one of the untold heroes of the Holocaust. He is an inspiration and saved many families from the cruel, harsh time of the Holocaust.

The Holocaust was an appalling time of human existence and should never be repeated. A few people are working to prevent future genocides occurring all over the world. There are several ways to eliminate these atrocious events. One, we need to help our fellow countries realize that they do not need to turn to a dictatorship if they need help or to solve problems. A dictator receives too much power from his country and has too much ability to cause destruction and death. Another way to avert crisis is to stand up to the country that is mistreating its people or violating the terms of its treaties. Not much was done when the Nuremberg Laws were passed, denying basic rights to Jewish people. Finally, it is very important for survivors to share their stories and to take pictures of what it was like in these times of trouble. This way future generations will have significant sources of information of what really happened. There are some people who deny the existence of the Holocaust, but if these stories are shared and preserved everyone will get a first hand look at what it was really like during this experience. Even after the Holocaust occurred there have been other mass murders like in Bosnia, Rwanda and Yugoslavia. Clearly, the world needs to work to prevent these unnecessary killings.

The Holocaust was a calamitous event in history where millions of people were cruelly murdered under the monstrous reign of Hitler. Many people showed amazing acts of courage, grit and fearlessness that helped many others survive this time. One of these people was Witold Maczak, and he was an untold hero of the Holocaust.

Bibliography

Unknown The Righteous Among the Nations Yadvashem https://yadvashem.org

Krystyna Adolph

Madeleine Smith

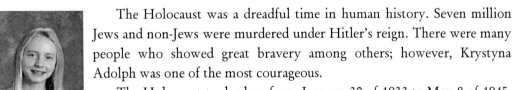

The Holocaust was a dreadful time in human history. Seven million Jews and non-Jews were murdered under Hitler's reign. There were many people who showed great bravery among others; however, Krystyna Adolph was one of the most courageous.

The Holocaust took place from January 30 of 1933 to May 8 of 1945. An enormous amount of Jews were killed, almost six million Jews total. Not only six million Jews were killed, but 5,000,000 non-Jews were killed. There were so many terrible ways these people were murdered. Most of them were sent to death camp and there were six camps in Poland. The Jews there were forced to work on farms, repair roads and clear forests, and toil in industrial and armaments plants. Almost all of the Jews were starved as they had no food or water for long periods during their time at the camps. More than half a million Jews alone were killed in the camps. New Daily life at the camps was unbelievably horrific. Each morning the prisoners had to stand completely still for almost an hour every day. The guards did not care if it was raining or snowing; they forced to Jews to do it. The food the Jews received were extremely inadequated and barely sustained life. As little as a cup of watery vegetable soup and half a piece of bread made up a typical daily meal. There was a list of chores and instructions to do in the morning; some demands were sent to individual prisoners.

The ghettos were composed of Jews who were stripped of their homes and businesses and forced to live in terrible conditions with little food. The Jews could only take a few personal things from their home to the ghetto. The ghettos were extremely crowded and starvation and disease increased with many people becoming seriously ill. Death was common. Many Jews risked lives for higher valves, such as education of children. Some children wrote and drew in order to document the fear and dread that descended among the Jews' communities. Others would read books and do music and theater to distract them from their horrible reality. The young had so little to eat that many risked their lives to smuggle food.

So many Jews died and suffered during the Holocaust.Only About ten percent of the Polish Jewry population survived the Holocaust; surprisingly more of Jews survived.. In Italy and France about twenty-five percent of the Jews perished.

Yet during this time of great tragedy, many individuals showed great courage by helping their Jewish friends and neighbors one hero who should be remembered is Krstyna Adolph. Krystyna Adolph was a Catholic and she taught at the Czartoryski High School in Vilna. Two of the Jewish students she rescued were in her class. They were sisters named Monika and Lidia Gluskin. Krystyna supported herself and her young daughter on their small farm in Ignalino. Krystyna Adolph sent a special messenger to the Gluskin sisters. She offered to shelter them because they were in danger. Monika and Lidia spent the next three years with Krystyna at the farm. The two sisters helped Krystyna Adolph at the farm feeding the animals, taking care of housework, chopping firewood, and tending the vegetable garden. To keep them safe, Krystyna introduced them to her neighbors as relatives who had fled from forced labor. The only people who knew their true identities were the father and the sister of Krystyna. Krystyna Adolph was fully aware that she was risking her life by sheltering the Jews even though the Germans burned down a house right next to hers because they found Jews hiding in there. She also helped the twins' mother by keeping false identity papers with her which kept the mother alive in the ghettos. After the war, the Gluskin sisters settled in Israel and stayed in touch with Krystyna Adolph for many years. On May 14, 1984 Krystyna Adolph was recognized as a Righteous Among the Nations by Yad Vashem.

Although the Holocaust was a horrific and dreadful part of history it is something we should reflect on, and learn from, so that it is not repeated in the future. The Holocaust happened because groups, individuals, and nations made choices that were not smart. We must learn to embrace each other's differences and be tolerant of other's beliefs. It is important that we educate people about different cultures and that we encourage everyone to peacefully interact with one another. It is important to believe what you want to believe and to not follow one person. So many Jews were unequally treated during the Holocaust We must take part and not let this happen again. Hopefully, we as people can maintain peace with everyone. The mistakes that we made in the past should not reflect on the future. Treating one another equally is an important part of life and we should never treat anyone different from who we are.

Unknown "Adolph Krystyna" Yad Vashem January 21
http://db.yadvashem.org/righteous/family.html?language=en&itemId=4013669

Natalia Abramowicz

Maria Aldrete-Witten (Winner)

On January 30, 1933, a very tragic event happened in human history. Adolf Hitler came into power as the Chancellor of Germany. Even though the people of Germany did not realize it at the time, the appointment of Hitler as Germany's Chancellor began a very dark period in Germany's history. Unfortunately, not long after Adolf Hitler was appointed the Holocaust began. The reason why the Holocaust began was because Hitler was so afraid of the Jews because he thought they were smart and held the best jobs such as doctors and lawyers and that they were becoming too powerful. He also told the Germans that the Jews were responsible for Germany's problems and blamed the Jews for the loss of World War I and the economic crisis in Germany. The Holocaust lasted from 1933 to 1945. That is 13 years of death camps and gas chambers. Over six million Jews were killed, and more than five million non-Jews were killed during this time. In the first year of the Holocaust, Hitler banned Jews from all schools, doctors from their practice, lawyers were disbarred, and Jewish businesses boycotted. The Holocaust was very terrifying for the Jews and those who befriended them, which is why I feel that one person in particular should be recognized for her great bravery and hospitality in hiding a Jewish family: Natalia Abramowicz.

Natalia Abramowicz was born on October 2, 1897 and died on January 1, 1979. Natalia Abramowicz was Catholic and her nationality was Polish. Before the war began Natalia knew a Jewish man named Michael Steinlauf. Then when the war started, Michael and his family were interned in the local ghetto. Ghettos were created by the Germans to separate the Jews from everyone else. It was a way to control the Jews by keeping them in enclosed neighborhoods and the living conditions were very bad, full of hunger and disease. Natalia tried to help Michael and his family and would visit them every once-in-awhile and give them food. As soon as the Germans started to take the Jews from the ghetto and transport them to death camps, Michael escaped with his family and they became so called "fugitives". Natalia offered Michael and his family protection by offering them a place to stay and she kept them safe by hiding them in her attic for nine months. Natalia Abramowicz risked her life by keeping Michael and his family in her home.

When the Germans started to search homes for Jews in hiding, Natalia and Michael decided that it would be best for Michael to stay behind at Natalia's, but his family should go to another hideout in Czestochowa where a man had offered them sanctuary. A friend named Weronika Kalek was asked to take them by train to their new safe haven. Sadly, when they arrived, they found out that they had been betrayed by the man who had offered them safety. They were met at this new hiding place by Gestapo agents, also known as the secret police in Germany. The Gestapo was made up of a large network of spies and informants creating great fear in Germany since the Gestapo operated independently of the other police and could pretty much do whatever they wished regarding arresting and killing people. The Gestapo agents ended up killing the entire group, including Weronika Kalek.

After the Gestapo agents murdered Michael's family in Czestochowa, the Gestapo also raided Natalia's apartment and arrested her. Michael and the other fugitives hiding there managed to escape before the Gestapo agents could find them in Natalia's apartment, but she was not so lucky. It is not known where Michael and the other fugitives hid during the rest of the war; however, we know that Michael and his brother-in-law survived the war and later they moved to Australia.

Following Natalia's arrest, she was deported and sent to Ravensbrueck, a German concentration camp for women in Northern Germany, until the war was over. It was the only concentration camp built especially for women and thousands of women were executed at Ravensbrueck. Between 1939 and 1945 more than 100,000 women passed through Ravensbrueck as prisoners. Most were Polish and a great many of them were Jewish. Only 15,000 of the prisoners at Ravensbrueck survived until liberation. Natalia Abramowicz was one of them. While she was still alive, Natalia Abramowicz was recognized as Righteous Among the Nations on July 8,1969 by Yad Vashem. This honor is bestowed by Israel on non-Jews who risked their lives during the Holocaust to save Jews.

Natalia Abramowicz also has a Tree of Honor in her name. I feel that she was recognized as a Righteous Among the Nations because of her bravery in hiding Michael and his family in spite of great personal danger. (Natalia's story is like those of many other non-Jews living in Germany and Poland who were incredibly brave and had strong character that inspired them to help people being persecuted by a terrible dictator. Even though discovery of harboring fugitive Jews usually meant death or deportation to concentration camps for those brave enough to risk everything to help others in danger many individuals still risked their lives to help.) Natalia Abramowicz was the one that stood out to me out of the courageous group of souls.

Bibliography

"The Righteous Among Nations." Yad Vashem. Copyright 2017 Web 20 Feb. 2017
http://db.yadvashem.org/righteous/righteousName.html?language=en&itemId=4013659
"Adolf Hitler." About Education. Copyright 2017 Web 20 Feb. 2017
http://history1900s.about.com/cs/hitleradolf/p/hitler.htm
"Gestapo." Wikipedia. 10 Feb. 2017 Web 20 Feb. 2017
https://en.wikipedia.org/wiki/Gestapo
The Gestapo is Born." The History Place. Copyright 2001 Web 20 Feb 2017
http://www.historyplace.com/worldwar2/triumph/tr-gestapo.htm
"GHETTOS." Holocaust Encyclopedia United States Holocaust Memorial Museum n.d. 20 Feb 2017
https://www.ushmm.org/wlc/en/article.php?ModuleId=10005059
"Ravensbruk Concentration Camp." Wikipedia 15 Feb. 2017 Web 20 Feb. 2017
https://en.wikipedia.org/wiki/Ravensbr%C3%BCck_concentration_camp
"Righteous Among the Nations." Wikipedia 14 Feb. 2017 Web 20 Feb. 2017
https://en.wikipedia.org/wiki/Righteous_Among_the_Nations

Krystyna Danko

Matteo Espinosa

The Holocaust was a very fearsome time. Not only did six million Jewish people die during the Holocaust, but five million non-Jews died. There were a lot of courageous men and women who stood up to the Nazis and Hitler. These people did many things to help the Jewish people. They formed underground stations were they would help the injured, cure the sick, feed the hungry, and give them shelter. They did different things to help the Jewish people as well. Some people helped individual Jewish families live with them, feed them and heal them. Many of these heroes are not known. One of these brave unsung heroes is Krystyna Danko.

After World War I Germany was in a very bad economic depression. People were losing their jobs, there were many more street fights, people were greatly fearing Communism and there were extreme Nationalists. Germany had lost many members of the country and was less than one percent of the total population at the time. The Germans were looking for a leader to get them out of this depression. On January 30th 1933, the Nazi party was elected to choose the leader of Germany. They chose Adolf Hitler to be the leader.

The first thing that Adolf Hitler did that showed that he wanted to get rid of the Jews was on April 1, when Hitler demanded Germans to boycott the Jewish shops and businesses. Then only six days later on April 7th he passed a new law restricting the Jews from holding civil service, universities, and state positions. On April 26th he established the Gestapo or a German police that patrolled the cities of Germany. After creating the Gestapo he publicly burned the books of Jews, political dissidents, and others not approved by the state.

Even before Hitler was chosen to be the leader of Germany in January 1933 the first Germanic concentration camp was built. It was called Dachau. One of the worst concentration camps was Auschwitz. It was located in Poland. It was active from April 1940 to January 1945. This camp was a death camp as well as a labor camp. Another terrible death camp was Belzec which also was located in Poland. The camp was active from March 1942 to June 1943. There were many more camps that Jews were forced to work at and where they were killed for believing in a religion.

Hitler was quiet for a year, then, in August 2nd 1934 he proclaimed himself Fuhrer und Reichskanzler (Leader and Reich Chancellor). This action made it so all armed German forces must swear allegiance to him. He did not do anything for about another year. On May 31, 1935 he restricted any Jews from serving in the German army and military, then in September 15th he made a huge change: Hitler took away the citizenship from the Jewish people, so they were not German. After taking the citizenship away from the Jews, Hitler forbade Jewish doctors from practicing medicine in German institutions.

On March 13th 1938, Hitler made all of the Jews living in Germany give up their land to the Germans. At this point, a lot of people were realizing that Jews were getting heavily persecuted and were making places for people to emigrate and put Jews into hiding. On

November 12th, all Jewish children were kicked out of the German schools. The Germans started making plans to exterminate the Jews in all of Europe on January 20th. They started exterminating the Jews on March 17, 1938 and killed 600,000 Jews by the end of 1942. The German people opened many more concentration camps and death camps.

This was all before World War II even started. World War II started on September 1st 1939 when Germany invaded Poland. By the end of 1940 Germany was invading countries on a regular basis. On May 7th 1940, Germany sent out attacks and invaded the Netherlands, Belgium, Luxembourg, and France. A few months later on August 8th, Britain and Germany began to battle. Many other countries took sides and made enemies with Germany which ultimately led to the defeat of the Nazis.

On July 9th 1917, an unsung hero was born. Krystyna Danko was a Polish orphan. Krystyna grew up in a small town named Otwock. As she grew up she formed a close relationship with a woman who was the eldest daughter of a Jewish family, the Kokoszgos. She spent most of her time with the Kokoszgo family. Danko felt obligated to help the family stay safe. She hid the mother, father, and sister in a secret location nearby in a village. Danko sent the smaller sister to a Polish orphanage in Warsaw. The city of Warsaw later became a huge concentration camp containing over 500,000 people; not only people who were Jewish, but others that Hitler disliked. Knowing where they were she sent messages from the parents and older sister to the youngest sister. All of the Kokoszgos survived after the Holocaust was over because of Krystyna Danko.

There are many more unsung heroes who have done very dangerous and treacherous tasks for people that they might not even know, and they are still not famous! These people are the true heroes of the Holocaust. They risked their life to save people. These heroes need to be recognized for what they did.

Bibliography:

Krystyna Danko Poland. www.yadvashem.org/righteous/stories/danko unknown author. Publishing date unknown.

"The Holocaust : 36 Questions and Answers." Simon Wiesenthal Center-Museum of Tolerance LIbrary and Archives: Educational Kit. Publishing date unknown.

The Holocaust

Ricky Reinl

The Holocaust was a bad time in our history but there were many people doing things to end it including Leopolda Kuropieska and Stanislaw Szostak.

The Holocaust happened between January 30, 1933 through May 8, 1945. During that time, six million Jews were killed and five million non-Jews were killed. There were six death camps and all of them were in Poland. On April 1, 1933 Jewish businesses were boycotted. Later, lawyers were disbarred. Then, doctors were banned from their practice, and Jews were banned from schools. After that, Jews were forced into ghettos for a while. Then, they were put into concentration camps where they would later die.

During 1942, a six year old boy had to flee his home in Warsaw, Poland with his father and brother. Unfortunately, the boy looked very Jewish and they could not find a safe place to rest. Then they met Leopolda Kuropieska. Leopolda was a mother of two and her husband was taken by the Germans. Leopolda decided to give the boy shelter in her home without payment. She made sure the child would not go outside of her home. There was a hole in the wall of the closet that the boy hid in whenever there was a knock at the door. Leopolda cared for the boy like he was her own child. The boy's father visited from time to time, but he stayed in other places Although Leopolda was a Catholic, she never tried to change his religion. The boy's sister also stayed with Leopolda for a temporary period of time. Leopolda also took care of the boy's brother, and two young Jewish women. Eventually, the authorities were alerted about the residents and all of them except the boy was arrested. A large bribe was paid to release them but all of them left. The boy moved in with his father in Warsaw until the Uprising. Then they left for home.

During 1917, Stanislaw Szostak graduated high school and decided to enroll in the army as an officer. Stanislaw was involved in an unsuccessful mutiny,

he was imprisoned in Petrograd. After his release, he negotiated with the Polish military and he joined the "junkers" company of the First Knights Legion of the First Polish Corps. Then, he spent most of his time with the officer in the First Corps until June 6, 1918. During the beginning of his tour, he took part in capturing Fort Bobrujsk which was occupied by Bolshevik troops. After the closing of the First Corps, he was sent to study at the Politechnika Warzawska. He eventually chose to stop studying and join the Bialystok Rifle Regiment of the 1st Lithuanian-Belarusian Division which was commanded by General Jan Rzadkowski.

First as a private he commanding a section, subsequently as a corporal in charge of a platoon. During the Polish-Soviet war of 1919 he fought on the Lithuanian-Belarusian Front in the regimental technical support company and remained with them until May 20 1920. From May 25 to August 18 1920 he was an officer at Infantry Officers School in Warsaw. After completing the course he was sent to serve with the reserve battalion of the 56 Wielkopolski Infantry Regiment as a commander. On December 15 1920 Stanislaw Szostak was promoted to the second lieutenant rank. On May 3 1922 he was verified as a lieutenant with seniority from June 1 1919 in the corps of Infantry Officers. In June of that year he was promoted to adjutant of the Second Battalion of 56th Wielkopolski Infantry Regiment. Early in 1924 Lieutenant Szostak joined the Central Tank School of the First Tank Regiment, which was supplied with French tanks, and from August 1925 he commanded a squad of the Seventh Tank Company. From 1928 to 1931 he commanded 6th, 7th, and then 4th squads of tanks. On March 19 1928 he was promoted to the rank of a captain. From June 1931 to April 1938 he took up training responsibilities. First, from June 1931 to April 1934 he lectured at the Training Center of Tanks and Armored Cars in Warsaw. Later, during the time between 1935 and 1938 he was the head of the Training Department at the headquarters of the Armored Corps attached to the Ministry of Military

Affairs in Warsaw. On March 19 1937 he was promoted to the rank of major in the Corps of armoured Officers. From April 1938 Major Szostak was a deputy commander of the Seventh Armoured Battalion in Grodno . Which was right before the invasion of Poland by Germany, in August 1939 Major Szostak became the commander of the mobilised 32nd Reconnaissance Armored Unit consisting of 3 squadrons with 13 TKS tankettes and 8 type 34-II armored cars took part in the battles of Grajewo and Szczuczyn. The unit covered the withdrawal of the Podlaska Cavalry Brigade. On September 12 he took part in the battle for Kita. By 16 September he lost all his armour but fought the invading Soviets in Grodno and organised defence of the town of Giby. On September 24, with the remainder of his men Major Szostak crossed the Lithuanian border and was interned. Until July 1940 he was in the internment camps of Calvary, Kurszany and Fort V. After the invasion of Lithuania by the Soviet Union he was transferred to Kozielsk II, and later to the camp. He was released to the signature to the Sikorski-majski Pact of July 30, and on August 25 he joined the Polish Army that was being organised in the Soviet Union.

The holocaust was a bad time in our history but because of it we can learn ways to prevent another one from happening or stop a holocaust.

http://db.yadvashem.org/righteous/family.html?language=en&itemId=4015929
author unknown, Kuropieska Family, yad vashem, 1/10/17
https://en.wikipedia.org/wiki/Stanis%C5%82aw_Szostak author unknown, Stanislaw Szostak, wikipedia, 2/15/17

Zofia Jeżewska

Riley McEvilly

During the late 1920's and early 1930's Germany was experiencing a life threatening economic crisis. This terrible crisis, known as the Holocaust, was caused by Germany's defeat against Europe during World War I, from which Germany never recovered. The start of the Holocaust began on the Thirtieth of January, 1933 when President Hindenburg appointed Adolf Hitler, a former general of the Nazi party, to become the Chancellor of Germany. The Nazis had believed that the German population were made to dominate the world and that they needed to cleanse the population. Therefore the Nazis began to persecute the Jews. In the month of April 1933, Jewish businessmen were boycotted, lawyers were disbarred, Jewish doctors were banned from their practice, and even the young Jewish children were banned from their schools under Hitler's strict orders. Adolf Hitler targeted the young children in particular, for he knew that if the Jewish children were to survive the Holocaust, that they would grow to bring a new generation of Jews into the world. Although most of the entire German population did not agree with the persecution of Jews, many followed Hitler and supported the unforgivable things being done to all the Jews. Most Germans had been terrified of the harsh punishments that they would face if they had rebelled against the Nazis, yet some had the courage to take a stand for what they thought in their heart was the right thing to do. The Germans had done what they knew was right, and they knew of the consequences they would face if they had been caught. By late 1944 and early 1945, about ninety percent of the population in Poland alone had been killed due to their religion, appearance, and sexuality of men, women and children. The Holocaust took more than three million Polish Jews lives in Poland alone under Hitler's rule. The millions of people who were disabled, and political rivals to Hitler were also murdered. The Holocaust lasted for twelve years, until May Eighth, 1945 when the collapse of the Nazi party had started to crumble. The downfall of the Holocaust began as soon as the Americans and other Allies of the Jews started to liberate the German cities. When Auschwitz was liberated, more uprisings began. Over one million Jewish women and children were murdered at Auschwitz, which was the most deaths that had ever been recorded in a single place. The liberation not only gained power for the Jews and their allies, but it also took power from the Nazi Party. Yet, there were some who resisted accepting Hitler's new rules, and abusive ways; one of those people was Zofia Jeżewska.

Zofia Jeżewska was born on the Fifteenth of June, 1911 in Warsaw, Poland. She was a twenty one year old Roman Catholic who at the time lived in Warsaw when President Hindenburg appointed Hitler to become the new Chancellor of Germany. During the war, Zofia ran her own seamstress business, working for the Nazi Party as a translator, and working on a journal which was her wish to become a published journalist. As a young woman she had many friends, friend in particular was Hanna Pilichowska, a Jewish woman and Zofia's age. Hanna Pilichowska had a seven year old Jewish niece Ella Blasbalg who at the time was living with Hanna after Ella had been abandoned by her own family. Hanna was taking care of Ella on her own, but Hannah had quickly came to realized that it was no longer safe to live alone with Ella, this especially when one of the many ghettos had appeared in the town where they lived. When the Ghetto of Warsaw was finally established, on the First of September 1939, Zofia had opened her home to Hanna and Ella. They kept undercover, the two young women ran a seamstress business together in hiding of the other Germans. However, the women faced several obstacles during their time together under one roof. One particular obstacle that the women had faced, was when a few German soldiers were quartered in Zofia's home. This situation not only brought out danger to Hanna and Ella, but to Zofia and her only son Krzysztof, as well. Yet Zofia kept a strong head and the friends were able to overcome that potential danger.

The two families continued to live together until the Nineteenth of April, 1943, when the act of the Jewish resistance started the Warsaw Ghetto Uprising. The Warsaw Ghetto Uprising lasted for five long weeks. On the Nineteenth, Zofia and her son Krzysztof were separated from Hanna and Ella. Although there are no specific details on how they were able to escape from Warsaw, it is known that Hanna and Ella spent the rest of the time during the war in a village by the name of Końska.

After the war ended Hanna went to live in Australia. Ella; however, went on to live in Israel. Ella never was able to see Zofia again. Hanna; on the other hand, several years later, contacted Zofia. Zofia eventually went to Australia to visit Hanna and the two continued to see each other frequently. By the time they had first reunited formally, Zofia had become a famous human rights advocate and a Polish journalist that had published the book called Choplin which she had been working on during the Holocaust. Zofia Jeżewska died on the First of January, 1995, at the age of eighty three.

While Adolf Hitler was in power, many Polish citizens persevered and showed great compassion, courage, consideration, and fortitude, such as Zofia Jeżewska. Yad Vashem recognized Zofia on July Twenty Eighth 2008. Although Zofia was unable to receive the award, her son Krzysztof received the commendation on behalf of his mother. She was commemorated on the Wall of Honor in 2008. There were many young men and women who helped in the Holocaust. Zofia Jeżewska was one of the few who took everybody's life, Jew or Semite into thought. Zofia Jeżewska saved two lives during the Holocaust, Hanna Pilichowska and Ella Blasbalg. The fact that Zofia was willing to put not only herself in danger, but also her son, to save Hanna and Ella, showed great empathy, mercy, and true friendship.

Bibliography Info for Holocaust:

"The holocaust: 36 Questions and Answers" Simon Wiesenthal Center-Museum of Tolerance library and Archives: Educational kit, Publishing date is unknown

"Jeżewska Faamily" Visited on January 9, 2017
http://db.yadvashem.org/righteous/family.html?language=en&itemId=7057495

"The Collapse of Nazi Germany" Visited on January 18, 2017
http://www.holocaust.cz/enhistory/final-solution/general-2/the-collapse-of-nazi-germany/

"91 Important Facts about the Holocaust" By Karin Lehnardt, Published August 19, 2016 Visited on January 19, 2017
https://www.factretriever.com/holocaust-facts

Janusz and Janina Durko

Ryland Dewar

The Holocaust was a horrible time in history. This time period started on January 30, 1953 after Adolf Hitler was elected, and lasted till May 8, 1945. During this massacre, so many people died, including more than six million Jews. Along with all the Jews, more than 500,000 non-Jews also died.

The Holocaust was a tragic time in human history. Almost seven million individuals, Jews and non- Jews, lost their lives in between January 30, 1922 to May 8, 1945. Many people showed great courage and fortitude during Hitler's reign of terror. Two of these great people were Janusz and Janina Durko.

It all started once a law was passed for Jewish businesses to be boycotted on April 1, 1933. A week later, Jewish lawyers were disbanded from their work. Then, Jewish doctors were banned from their practice. On April 22, 1933 Jewish children were forbidden from all schools. Soon after, ghettos, death camps, and extermination camps were created.

People were shipped on trains to death camps. At death camps, people had to work intensively and then died a gruesome death. In Poland, there were six death camps and many extermination camps. Often other people would die in their house resisting the laws. There were only few people in that this time period who helped others during this tragic time in history.

During this horrible time, there were many people who helped to free and protect Jews. Janusz and Janina Durko were marvelous people who helped many ways during the Holocaust. They did not do it for money, but for the love of everyone. Janusz Durko was born on February 23, 1915 in Poland. He and his wife Janina were both Roman Catholic. Janusz Durko worked as an historian and as a secretary and member of the board of an urban architecture workshop in Warsaw, Poland. The Durkos soon became good friends with many Jews. Although they knew they were Jewish, they kept their knowledge to themselves and made it a point of warning their Jewish friends during particular times of danger. In the fall of 1942, the Durko's moved from their old apartment. When they vacated their apartment, they left it and all of their furniture in it to be used as a shelter for persecuted Jews, especially for people who escaped from the ghettos. Numerous fugitives from the ghetto spent a least a little bit of time in the Durkos' apartments. If a neighbor threaten of being denounced by a fellow neighbor, the Durkos would seek out another hiding place for the fugitive, such as another apartment, the offices of the SPB, or an specially-prepared garage on Senatorska Street. Mrs. Durko, Janina, helped to find employment for many. Until the outbreak Uprising in Warsaw in 1944, more than twenty Jews could be found using the apartments as shelter. This included Jakub Hersz Szapiro, Leon Rytowski, Aleksander Węgierko, and a family consisting of a woman named Irena and her young son. After the war, the remaining people who survived moved out of Poland, but later testified how the Durko's helped them and risked their lives to save many. Out of all the people who sought shelter in the Durko's apartments, Jausz remembered all of them. When someone who sheltered with them did not survive, Mr. Durko felt the deaths of all of them as if they were deaths of his own family. The Durkos survived and Mr. Durko later became the director of the Historical Museum of Warsaw from the years 1951 until 2003. The Durkos received over thirty Polish and foreign orders for their merits in the field of culture. Although many Jews and other non Jews did not survive the Holocaust, Jausz and Janina Durko luckily lived.

There are many ways we can prevent another Holocaust from happening. The leaders of all our nations must take a stand of acceptance and tolerance of all people. The leaders of all our nations must not be biased or sho prejudice against any religious nationally or group. If a country begins to single out a particular group of people because of their ethnic or religious background, they are crossing a line that is dangerously close to what happened in Germany during World War II. If the Leaders of our Nation's follow this, we should not have another Holocaust.

Bibliography

Unknown The Righteous among the nations Yadvashem https://yadvashem.org

Kj Janusz durko Sprawiedliwi https://sprawiedliwi.org

The Graczyk Family

Samantha Rodriguez

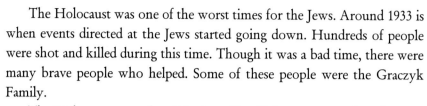

The Holocaust was one of the worst times for the Jews. Around 1933 is when events directed at the Jews started going down. Hundreds of people were shot and killed during this time. Though it was a bad time, there were many brave people who helped. Some of these people were the Graczyk Family.

The Holocaust was a horrible time. The Holocaust was when the Jews were being persecuted. During this time, about 6 million Jews were killed. The worst thing of all is that there were not only Jews getting persecuted, there were a lot more individuals, as well. 5,000,000 non-Jews were also killed. There were six death camps all around Poland. The Holocaust was not done just like that; it took steps for it to happen. The first step happened on April 1,1933 when a Jewish businesses were boycotted. It was when Hitler was elected. The second step happened on April 7,1933 when the Jewish lawyers were disbarred. The third event happened on April 22,1933 when Jewish doctors were banned from practice. The last step happened on April 25,1933 when all Jewish students were banned from all schools. One good thing that occurred was that there were many great heroes who helped stop the Nazis. One family that helped with this was the Graczyk Family.

The Graczyk family helped many people. One member of the family was Stanisław Graczyk. Stanislaw was a farmer from Kaldlbowo. On September 16, 1943 he was arrested because the Nazis found him hiding two Jews in his house: Klin whose last name is unknown and Simcha Frost whose real name was Symcha Frost. He knew both of them since they were good friends from World War I. When they were found they were all arrested even though they were armed. On November 18, 1943 Graczyk was murdered in the jail he was in. People said that it was due to a heart attack.

The next unsung hero is Władysław Rutkowski, Władysław was also a framer from Chloewy. Rutkowski was arrested on October 15, 1943. He was arrested because he was hiding and he was assisting the same two Jews as Stanislaw. He was sent to the Matthausen Concentration Camp where he later died on January 10, 1944 of an "intestinal infection". The third family member was Wladyslaw Mucha. He was a farmer from Dlutowo. He was charged the same and because of the same two Jews. The two Jews were armed again. Rutowski was sent to a concentration camp. Later he was executed there. The fourth member of the Graczyk family were Stefan Dubracki and his wife Marianna Durbracka. They owned a farm in Soboklęszcz. On September 16, 1943 they were arrested. They were arrested because they were charged of participating in an attack together with two aforesaid Jews. They were also arrested for hiding and assisting other Jews. They were both sent to the Stutthof Concentration Camp where they later were executed by hanging on November 21, 1943. The fifth family member was Wladyslaw Szybowski. He was a farmer from Topolnica or Pultusk Country. On January 6, 1944 he was arrested on the charge of hiding and assisting three Jews over the summer and for possessing a gun. The Jews were two men and a woman. Apparently, he was executed in the prison in Posen or Poznarn on May 30, 1944. The sixth member was Wincenty Chludziński who was a farmer from Lazenki. On December 11, 1943 his family was arrested for hiding and employing the Jewish boy named Josef Zaziczki, also known as Józef, Chiel he who from Warsaw a on his farm over two years. He was sent to the Stutthof concentration camp where he died of a heart attack on May 4, 1944. The seventh person was Kazimierz Baniak who was a farmer from Sadowiec or Plonsk County. On December 23, 1943 he was arrested on the charge of also hiding and employing on his farm for two years the same Jewish boy. He was sent to Stutthof Concentration Camp with an order not to be released until the end of the war. His ultimate fate is unknown. The Jewish boy was apparently murdered in Treblinka. The eighth member was Antoni Biernacki, a farmer from Rozdzialy. He was arrested on November 14, 1943 on the charge of hiding a Jewish boy. He was sent to the Gross-Rosen Concentration Camp where he was murdered on March 16, 1944. The ninth member was Stanislawa Olewnik, a farm woman from Krzemien or Makow County. On October 7, 1943 she was arrested on the charge of hiding a Jewish family. The family was Rachela(Ruchla) Mlawska (nee:Frost) and her children Henia Mlawska, Hania Mlawska, and Abraham Mlawska. Stanislawa was sent to Auschwitz where she was later murdered on April 21, 1944. The tenth and last member was Tadeusz Gawlinski. He was a farmer from Rydzyn or Strzegowo Commune. He was arrested in early December 1944 on the charge of hiding a Jewish couple. When they were caught he tried to escape with his sister, but he was shot to death while evading arrest. On June 6, 2005 Yad Vashem recognized all family members as Righteous Among Nations.

The Holocaust was one of the worst time for the Jews. Hundreds of people were shot and killed during this time. Though it was a bad time, there were many brave people who helped. Some of these people were the Graczyk family. They tried and tried even though they got caught. They were great people who sacrificed to save their Jewish friends and neighbors.

Bibliography

"The Holocaust:36 Questions and Answers". Simon Wiesenthal Center-Museum of Tolerance Library and Archives: Educational Kit. Publishing date unknown. January 26, 2017

"The Righteous Among the Nations" Graczyk Family January 26, 2017 http://db.yadvashem.org/righteous/family.html?language=en&itemId=4435361

Roman Talikowski in the Holocaust

Santiago Chang (Winner)

The Holocaust was a terrible part of history that will never be forgotten. The mere idea of this ever happening is unfathomable. The thought of someone trying to exterminate an entire race is unimaginable. The Holocaust ranged from Jan 30, 1933 to May 8, 1945 and caused over six million Jewish fatalities. Five million non-Jewish deaths were also recorded. The Nazi's had six death camps in Poland. Many people showed great fortitude during Hitler's reign of terror. There were hundreds of heroes during the Holocaust, and many of these people need to be acknowledged. One of these brave and courageous people was Roman Talikowski.

The Holocaust was a horrifying event that still brings terror to people's ears when said. During the Holocaust, Hitler and his party attempted to eradicate all the Jews in Europe. It started with the election of Hitler's party, the Nazis. They began on April 1, 1933 by boycotting Jewish businesses. Three days later, all Jewish lawyers were disbarred. On April 22, doctors who were Jewish were banned from their practice. After another three days, all Jewish children were no longer permitted to go to school. Following those steps, Jews were sent to ghettos and death camps to be killed. Over two third of the nine million Jews residing in Germany were killed and one and a half of them were children. One of the people who tried to hinder this process was Roman Talikowski.

Roman Talikowski was one of the brave heroes during the Holocaust. He was born on February 15, 1900 and died on January 23, 1976. Talikowski was in Warszawa during the Holocaust and managed to save multiple people. He was a Catholic man living in Poland at the time. Talikowski, a glove store owner at the time, had smuggled food and other goods into the ghetto for Irena Przygoda's parents. Irena Przygoda was the wife of Zdzislaw Przygoda, an engineer. He also helped to sneak Zdzislaw Przygoda and Irena Przygoda out of the ghetto they were in. After the escape, Talikowski became great friends with them. He helped sneak out Joanna-Joasia, the daughter of Zdzislaw and Irena, as well. He granted Zdzislaw a job at a Polish contracting firm and arranged a place for the Przygodas to live in. There were also two women and the owner of the shelter, Maria Kaczyńska. Unfortunately, German soldier conducted a search of the house on May 22, 1943. They murdered Irena and another woman, but left Joanna-Joasia and Kaczyńska unscathed. Later that day, Zdzislaw came home to see Joanna-Joasia holding her mom's clothes, which contained hidden jewels from the ghetto. Zdzislaw then took Joanna-Joasia to Irena's sister's house. He joined the Underground and managed a factory in Radom. Zdzislaw also helped by hiding Jews under the floor of one of his warehouses. After the war, Joanna-Joasia left Poland to go to Germany and was later adopted by Mieczysław and Alicja Dortheimer. They immigrated to Australia in 1948. Irena was buried next to the other woman who was killed. Then, on July 9, 2013, Yad Vashem recognized Roman Talikowski and the other heroes associated with him as Righteous Among the Nations. He was also honored at a Canberra ceremony for saving Jews. Roman Talikowski was one of the courageous survivors and heroes of the Holocaust.

The Holocaust should have never happened. Thankfully, there are ways humanity can prevent this. First of all, everyone needs to be united in order to ensure peace. People need to pay more attention to the past in order for the Holocaust to never occur again. If people do not learn from their mistakes, then we are bound to repeat the same horrific events. New generations need to be taught to be more tolerant of other people who differ from them in religious and political views. Another way we can help prevent the Holocaust is by making certain that people are more open-minded about race, ethnicity, and other things. People should not judge others by relying on their looks or if they are poor or rich. People should also pay more attention to who they elect as their leader. Hitler was chosen as the leader because no one payed attention to whom they were electing. One way to help decrease the chances of another Holocaust is to encourage people to stick to their moral codes and do the right thing. Though the Holocaust was an unforgettable part of the past, these ways can help give this world a more positive and more open world.

In conclusion, Roman Talikowski was one of the amazing people who helped to spread good during the Holocaust. Roman Talikowski harbored Jews to protect their lives and also smuggled food for them. Thankfully, Yad Vashem worked to spread this hero's story. Finally, the future of this world can be saved from another Holocaust by working together and learning from the past. Humanity cannot allow themselves to be defined from history. Together, they can have a brighter future. Although no one can change the series of events known as the Holocaust, the new generations can still affect what happens the next day.

Bibliography

"The Holocaust : 36 Questions and Answers". Simon Wiesenthal Center-Museum of Tolerance Library and Archives : Educational Kit Publishing Date Unknown.

Yad Vashem. Visited on February 17, 2017. http://yadvashem.org

Janina Siwiec

Savannah Rosenbach

It has been sixty-three years since the Holocaust ended. Many lives have been taken and those who were spared have been filled with pain and sorrow. In the end, there was barely any Jews left to save from their suffering. But who were the heroes in the story? Who was there to protect those who suffered? I will tell the story of one family of heroes who saved a child's life. But before we skip through the pages of this story let's start at the beginning. It all started with a dangerous man who had great influence.

On January 30, 1933, Adolf Hitler, leader of the Nazi Party was named Chancellor of Germany. After the Nazis had taken advantage of the restless people in Germany, they started to set up vicious campaigns against their opponents, the Jews. Their government, which the Nazis had believed was weak and the Jews whom they believed had given them illness and misfortune were the targets. Hitler made sure that nothing would go in his way in order to destroy them. The Nazis started with the newspaper announcing that the Jews were nothing but a nuisance, a bother, and killers of Jesus. Jews were blamed for the fault of their ancestors who nailed Jesus to a cross and had left him to die. Soon after, millions of propaganda were delivered weekly. When Hitler had become Chancellor, he called for new elections trying to gain full control of the Reichstag, the German Parliament, for the Nazis. The Nazis used this opportunity to terrorize other parties, arrest their leaders, and ban their political meetings. On February 27, 1933 the Reichstag building was burned by a Dutchman named Marinus van der Lubbe. Marinus had sworn that he did this alone. Although many believed that it was the Nazis' doing, they managed to blame the Communists, giving themselves even more votes. When the elections were held on March 5, the Nazis had won a majority of votes in the government. The Nazis swiftly moved to strengthen their power into a dictatorship and developed strong police and military forces. On February 8, their police force Gestapo, was allowed freedom to arrest anyone. The Nazis were so powerful they easily uncovered their enemies and kept them under surveillance. They had Jews terrorized, beaten, and sent to one of their concentration camps. Dachau, a camp built for political prisoners had eventually turned into a concentration camp for Jews. By the end of 1934 Hitler was in absolute control of Germany. People hid in fear, afraid that they would end up becoming Hitler's next victim. Though when there is fear and darkness there is also hope and light. Heroes rose up and saved many lives and one of those heroes was the Bachul Family.

In October 1942, there was an attempt on hiding a Jewish child outside of the Ghetto. Miriam and Maks Glaser had realized that the next transport was due to take the Jews in Krakow Ghetto to the extermination camps, they knew survival would not be possible for their child Sarah. They began to look for a place for the girl on the Aryan side. They contacted a woman named Antonina Siwiec to help. Antonina was a business contact in the previous war times. Miriam took her eighteen month old daughter out of the Ghetto in a bag hoping that no one would notice them. Not long after twenty-five year old Janina Siwiec, granddaughter of Antonina, took the child to her family in Bystra. Both Miriam and Janina entered the station separately so they would not attract attention. They walked past a few railway workers when one of them pointed out that the child that Janina was carrying was a Jew. Janina told them to hush, used a handbag as act of self-defense and left them in silence. The workers decided that there was no need to put the woman and child in harm's way and moved on. Miriam and Janina then left in separate carriages to Bystra with the child. Janina's parents Ludwika and Stanislaw, and her sisters Maria and Anna welcomed the child with open arms. The little girl went everywhere with them and would even play with the other children. Sarah was fitting in perfectly. When the war was coming close to an end, Mariam was being transported from Auschwitz to camp in Bunchenwald for liberation. Afterwards, Miriam came to Bystra to take back Sarah. In the end, both the woman and child were safe.

To save the Jews many of our Heroes had sacrificed so much to save them from the Nazis. They would even sacrifice their lives for them. On May 8, 1945 the holocaust officially ended and the Jews had finally found peace.

Hidden Heroes: Maria Andzelm

Sofia Schumaker

Many are blind to the wars being fought around us every day, some for freedom, even for ways of life many of us would never understand. Many of those people not just fought, but sacrificed their lives for the fate of others. The catastrophe begun in 1933 was much the same. Many people did not look twice at the fake pictures being displayed of the starving and beaten Jews. The Germans had made it seem like they were all happy in the conditions they showed in the propaganda. Most pictures were of the Jews at outside markets, smiling and enjoying themselves with fine clothing. The Germans not only did this, but even went out of their way to spread propaganda, such as placing fake trees in the background of non-existent markets, to cover up the abuse they had brought upon the Jews. They wanted to cover up the truth, the truth that many would seethe at. If a Jew even thought to eat a vegetable or one of the meats shown in the picture, his or her hand would be sliced or cut off. Many German cities reacted too late, leaving more than five thousand Jews to die at the hands of the Nazis. However, there were a few who broke through their restrictions and helped all. They were the ones who realized the great mistakes the others around them were making and did something about it. Maria Andzelm, a young, hardworking German girl, may have been small, but was one of the few who made a difference.

On the Eleventh of November, 1918, most Germans were filled with defeat and humiliation after the loss of World War One. This desperation led up to President Hindenburg, Germany's second President, calling forth Adolph Hitler, the leader of the Nazi party as Chancellor of Germany. Hitler had established several ghettos around Polish cities for defenseless Jews everywhere to be forced into. Hitler had planned to set them on their way to the extermination camps from the ghettos they were in. Most Germans were shocked after learning of what was happening to the Jews. Many were at a loss of at what to do, did nothing by pure fear of the consequences they would be faced with if they had been caught helping Jews. Those people did not include Maria Andzelm, a German, non-wealthy, and kind hearted farmer girl, a girl who let no such fear stop her.

Maria Andzelm lived on the outskirts of Janawief, Poland. She had never been wealthy woman. She would spend days and nights with her father in the field to make enough money at the local market for food for the rest of the family. Maria was just a normal girl. Then the year 1933 passed by. She had never expected how much her life would change in one year alone. At the start of January, Maria was confused as many others were by Hitler becoming Chancellor of Germany. Why was her best friend leaving? Why were there people running in the streets late at night, screaming? Yet sometimes, there would never even be a sound? Things were changing drastically for Maria and her family. Not only that, but her young age made everything the more terrifying. She learned with the rest about the ghettos, including the extermination camps, as well as why her Jewish friend had left. She discovered that she had been deported. The difference between Maria's families from the rest was that they wanted to do something about it. However they did not just "want", they did. A few months later, Maria's father came home with two Jewish people. Maria had taken a great liking to Moses, one of the Jews that had been close to her age. The family hid the Jews in the basement of the house, where they had dug another hole within the basement for the Jews to hide. The kind family brought them food, including snacks, from none other than Maria. Maria went to visit them frequently throughout the day, and brought them books to read to entertain them while hiding. This went on for almost two years, and the kind family had never been caught. As the days passed, Maria and Moses became closer and closer. One late evening, Maria and Moses were huddled in the ground space they had dug. Maria's mother was staying at a friend's house so they were alone. No one had expected the blast from above. All Maria could hear was the yelling. Yet by pure fear, Maria, Moses, and the other stayed huddled inside of the bunker until the blasts ended. Maria later walked upstairs to find the house she had lived in most of her life, destroyed. She found her father dead on the ground. Her father had died, protecting the Jews. Then she knew, someone had told about what they were doing.

After, the war passed and left with a blink of an eye. Maria, still struggled over the death of her father, meanwhile growing into the fine young woman she was meant to be. She later fell in love with Moses, and the couple moved to the United States a few years later, leaving the place of many deaths behind. They ended up having two children and living until reaching an old age.

Many had died, and others suffered a great deal. Tragically, many did nothing to prevent this from happening. Maria's story did not quite play out like that. Unlike the others, Maria had taken a defense in what she knew in her heart was right. Maria's family had risked their own lives for the two Jews. Sadly, in the end, Maria's father had done exactly that. Her father ended up dying protecting the two Jews the kind German family had become so close with. In conclusion, many were too frightened to help, no one will know their stories because they had done nothing. However, the ones who took defense during these helpless times are the ones we know about today. Those are the ones who became true heroes.

Biography

Heroes of the Holocaust February 10, 2017
http://4holocaustheroes.weebly.com/maria-anzelm.html
Heroes of the Holocaust; Maria Andzelm February 12, 2017
https://prezi.com/bpowrawpmcmv/heroes-of-the-holocaust-maria-andzelm/
yadvashem.org/RIGHTEOUS of the NATIONS

Wilhelm Tarnawski

Taylor Marks

The Holocaust was a tragic time in the human history. Almost seven million individuals, Jews and non-Jews, were murdered. The Holocaust was the time when Adolf Hitler started the worst genocide in world history. This horrible event started on January 30, 1933. At the start, new Laws were passed called Nuremberg laws. These laws prevented Jewish people from having any kind of official workplace and also prevented them from marrying any Aryan people. People were encouraged to boycott Jewish business.

Soon, the Nazis formed separate concentration camps where the Jews were forced to work under terrible conditions causing many to die from hunger and disease. They also made Ghettos where the Jew would stay until they were sent to the extermination camps and eventually killed in the gas chambers. Most of these ghettos and extermination camps were located in Poland. Six million Jews were horrifically killed during the Holocaust; one million children, two million women and three million men. Five million non-Jews were also killed. These poor people only consumed about 600 calories a day and were tortured every day. There were many people who escaped, but most were put into ghettos and extermination camps and many more were hidden and saved.

Many people showed great courage and fortitude during this reign of terror. One of these was Wilhelm Tarnawski. Born in 1911 Wilhelm grew up in the small town of Galicia in Poland. From 1942-1944 Wilhelm hid seventeen of his wife's relatives. Fearlessly, he hid seventeen of his wife's relatives in his home. While Wilhelm and his wife lived on the ground floor apartment, he hid his relatives in the attic and in a bunker in the cellar. Sometimes Wilhelm had to hide his wife because she too was Jewish. Wilhelm later immigrated with his wife to Israel. After the war was over, Wilhelm's relatives immigrated to Israel and the United States. Wilhelm was, in his wife's own words, "a modest man, capable of making sacrifices for the good of other people, regardless of the beliefs or origins."

There are ways we can prevent a Holocaust from ever happening again. Leaders of our nations must take a stand of tolerance and acceptance of all people. Leaders of nations must not be biased, or show prejudice against any religious group or nationality. If a country begins to single out a particular group because of their religion or ethnic background, they are crossing a line that is dangerously close to what happened in Germany during World War II.

The Holocaust was a calamitous event in human history where millions of people were cruelly murdered and tortured under the monstrous reign of Adolf Hitler. Many people showed amazing acts of courage, grit and fearlessness that helped many others survive this time. One of these people was Wilhelm Tarnawski, and he was unsung hero of the Holocaust.

Bibliography
Unknown The Righteous Among the Nations Yadvashem https://yadvashem

The Banasiewicz Family

Yasmene Christofori-Munir

The Holocaust was a time marked with hatred, mass murder, war, and terrible loss and destruction. It took place during the rule of Hitler's Nazi regime, 1933 – 1945, and especially during the years of WWII, 1939 - 1945. During these years, over eleven million lives were lost, six million of which were the lives of completely innocent Jewish people.

The catastrophe started with mistrust and then open hostility toward Jewish people in Europe from the time Hitler took office in 1933, and culminated with mass murder of Jewish people in concentration camps. In order to "exterminate" Jews, the Nazis constructed six death camps in Poland: Auschwitz-Birkenau, Belzec, Chelmno, Majdanek, Sobbior, and Treblinka.

The death camps were used to kill six million Jewish people and about five million non-Jewish people. The latter included political enemies of the Nazi regime, mentally disabled people, homosexual people, and people of other ethnicities that the Nazis considered unworthy.

During the years of the Nazi regime, many people all over Europe lived in fear of being hunted down, arrested, and murdered. Most people succumbed to fear and tried their best to avoid any interaction or confrontation with Nazi officers.

Only very few people found the courage to stand up to and oppose the Nazi regime. Fewer yet had the courage and bravery to take action in order to help and protect the oppressed and the persecuted. Franciszek and Magdalena Banasiewicz, their son, Tadeusz, and their daughter, were among those brave people: heroes of the Holocaust, "Righteous Among the Nations".

The Holocaust began with the election of the Nazi party in 1933. Once Adolf Hitler came into power as chancellor, he began carrying out his sinister, cruel, and insane plans.

A few months after the election, Jews began to face immense difficulties. The Nazis called for the boycott of Jewish businesses, they disbarred Jewish lawyers, and banned Jewish doctors from practice. Later on, all Jewish children were banned from schools.

However, this was just the beginning of the terrors that would beset the Jewish people under Hitler's dictatorship and absolute control. Jewish people were arrested, their possessions were confiscated, and they were transported to concentration camps where they had to work as slave laborers. They faced unspeakable abuse, starvation, and overall absolutely inhumane conditions.

In this atmosphere of deadly fear and mortal danger, Franciszek and Magdalena Banasiewicz and their children, Maria and Tadeusz, risked their lives to help Jewish people.

The Banasiewicz family lived in Poland which was under Nazi occupation. They were farmers in the town of Orzechowce, in the Przemysl district. In July 1942, Nazis gathered most Jewish workers in the neighboring shtetl of Mackowice. A shtetl was a small Jewish village or town in Eastern Europe.

Salomon Erenfreund and Junek Frenkiel, two Jewish workers who were able to escape the massacre, fled through the fields and forests with the assistance of local peasants. They were joined by Tadeusz Banasiewicz, who was also escaping. Tadeusz had been in a labor camp in Germany and was on his way back home, traveling in secret and hiding, like Solomon and Junek. They were all taken in by Tadeusz's parents.

Shortly after, the ghetto of nearby Przemysl was liquidated. A ghetto in Poland was the part of a town were Jewish people lived.

People who fled from the Przemysl ghetto also came to the Banasiewicz family for help. The Banasiewicz family hid the Jewish refugees in a hideout that had been dug out in their granary.

The Banasiewicz family saved at least fifteen Jewish people throughout the entirety of the Nazi occupation: Salomon Erenfreund's brother Izaak and his wife Janina, their cousin Jakub

Nassan, and his wife Eugenia were among them. So were Macel Tiech, Feiga Weidenbaum and Edmund Orner, Fela Schattner, Samuel Reinharz, Izaak and Berta Reinharz, and Jozef and Lotka Weindlinger.

The bravery of the Banasiewicz family was amazing and admirable. When a neighbor of theirs, Michal Kruk, was found out to be hiding Jewish refugees as well, he and the Jewish refugees in hiding on his farm were shot. Nevertheless, even in the face of this horror and terrible danger, the Banasiewicz family persisted. Even when Nazi soldiers came to search the Banasiewicz family's house, the family did not falter. Fortunately, the hiding place in the granary was not found.

The Jewish refugees who were sheltered by the Banasiewicz family survived until their liberation in July of 1944. Several of the survivors that had stayed there kept in contact with the Banasiewicz family after the war, as a continued gesture of thanks to their saviors. They owed their lives to the nobility and bravery of the Banasiewicz family.

On July 17, 1991, Yad Vashem recognized Franciszek and Magdalene Banasiewicz, their son, Tadeusz, and their daughter Maria Jurek-Banasiewicz as Righteous Among the Nations.

May those who are put in similar positions today learn from their heroism and from the heroism of the Jewish people, so they, too, can be strong and brave in difficult situations, and when injustice and brutality and murder are committed against innocent people, may they also take action to protect those who are discriminated against.

Bibliography

"The Holocaust: 36 Questions and Answers". Simon Wiesenthal Center – Museum of Tolerance Library and Archives: Educational Kit.

Publishing date unknown.

"Banasiewicz FAMILY." Yadvashem.org. 9 January 2017

http://db.yadvashem.org/righteous/family.html?language=en&itemId=4044825

"Shtetl." New Oxford American Dictionary. 2010.

Shalom School

Shalom School's 6th grade team is made up of Ms. Miri Levine, Ms. Frannie Magnani, Ms. Ruthi Ofek, and Ms. Heather Judy. Together they have over 50 years combined experience teaching at Shalom School and are very proud of their students' participation in the annual Holocaust Essay Contest.

The Devastation and the Rescue

Anna Maagdenberg (Winner)

Holocaust is a Greek word which means sacrifice by means of fire. This word now refers to the brutal murder of six million Jews and other minorities, including the disabled, Slavic people, Jehovah Witnesses, gypsies, as well as other groups of minorities. There was a problem, the Nazis were taking over Poland, and threatening Jewish children, women, and men. Irena Sendler decided to help those threatened. Irena Sendler was born on February 10th, 1910. She was a Polish nurse, a Roman Catholic, and human rights activist. She was deeply inspired by her father, a doctor, who treated many Jewish patients and wanted to help people no matter their race or religion. Irena's father was one of the first socialists. Irena Sendler, a Polish gentile risked her life to save Jews and has been recognized as Righteous among the Nations.

When the Germans invaded Poland and started sending Jewish children impetuously into concentration camps, Irena Sendler decided that she could not stand for this; she had to take action, she needed to rescue these innocent children. In 1942, she joined Zegota, an underground organization whose goal was to rescue young Jewish children from the Warsaw Ghetto. One reason she may have wanted to help save Jewish children, is because two of her children died from health problems. One of them died of heart failure, the other died in infancy. Ghettos were usually in the most rundown, shabby part of the city. There was a 10 foot wall surrounding the ghetto, fenced with barbed wire and protected by guards. Rather than dispersing the Jews in the Warsaw Ghetto, around six to seven people shared a room. They were given one tenth of their normal daily caloric intake, essentially starvation. Five thousand people died within a month from disease and starvation.

One incident in the Ghetto was when one of the Zegota members drugged a baby, so the baby would not cry, then put the baby into a tool box, and saved the baby. Eventually, the Nazis found out about Irena Sendler's actions and how she had been saving the Jews from the Warsaw Ghetto. They decided to send her to the Pawiak Prison (a prison for Jews, and prisoners of war), where she was sentenced to death. Luckily, she was rescued from execution by one of the Zegota Members. Although she was saved, bulletins were hanging all over Poland; the Germans were searching for her. Even though it was hard, she persisted to continue her rescues of the Jewish children. Irena Sendler's parents taught her that "if a man is drowning, you must save him, whether you can swim or not." Irena Sendler mentions in her documentary, "In the name of their mothers, that when she saw the children in the ghetto, and then returned, she did not see the same person before, they either were dead or had been sent to a death camp such as Treblinka".

After the war, Irena Sendler ended up staying in Poland, where she received an honorary citizen of Israel award, and the highest award of Poland, the Jan Tarski Award. She even got a letter from Pope John Paul the second. In the end, Irena Sendler saved 2,500 Jewish children, and created 3,000 fake documents for Jewish families. Not only did Irena save 2,500 Jewish children, she also fed them and gave them vaccines against typhoid. After the war, many of the Jewish children who she saved were not united with their biological parents, but were adopted by generous Polish parents.

The lesson learned from my Polish hero is to do what is right for people of all color and religion no matter the cost. For example if a person is drowning in a river and there is a really rough current and you can sink you do it no matter the costs or the religion or perhaps the color of the skin. Although this was a bad part of history, it is still a big part of history and very important to today's world, and it is important to educate everyone about this, and prevent another situation like World War two to happen again. If more people stood up to the horrible, disastrous, regime, this could prevent these problems from happening another time. Irena Sendler inspired me to alter myself and try to become like her. One way I could do this is to be more courageous, no matter the cost, and to respect people for who they are. I think this quote form the Quran represents Irena Sendler "if anyone has killed a person, it would be as if he killed the whole mankind; if anyone saved a life, it would be as if he saved the whole mankind."

Rena Sendler, an inspiring person, who was tortured by the Nazi's and put her life in danger to save the Jews in the Warsaw Ghetto. She has been awarded the title as Righteous among the Nations. Irena Sendler is a heroic, bold person, who faced many challenges during World war two, such as being wanted by the Nazi's, being in the Pawiak prison, and being scared of her life. She is a one of a kind person and makes people want to be like her in many ways, and sand up for their rights.

Work Cited

http://www.imdb.com/title/tt1622549/

https://www.ushmm.org/outreach/en/article.php?ModuleId=10007706

http://www.telegraph.co.uk/news/obituaries/1950450/Irena-Sendler.html

http://www.hitlerschildren.com/article/1482-the-heroism-of-irena-sendler

http://www.yadvashem.org/holocaust/about/ghettos/warsaw

http://www.jewishvirtuallibrary.org/irena-sendler

http://www.chabad.org/theJewishWoman/article_cdo/aid/939081/jewish/Irena-Sendler.htm

http://www.aish.com/ho/p/Irenas_Children.html

http://www.irenasendler.org/facts-about-irena/

http://www.holocaustresearchproject.org/revolt/zegota.html

https://en.wikipedia.org/wiki/Irena_Sendler

Maria Saves the Day

Edena Ichel

Righteous Among the Nations is a term that Israel uses to honor non-Jews who risked their lives to save other people during the Holocaust. Before Maria Kotarba started saving other people during the Holocaust, she led a simple life. Maria was born on September 4, 1907 in Oblazy Ryterskie, Poland. She was Catholic and from a poor family. Maria had been working on a farm since early childhood. The word holocaust comes from the Greek words "holo", meaning whole, and "kaustos", meaning burned. It now refers to the murder of six million Jews and nearly six million other minorities by the Nazis. During the Holocaust, Maria Kotarba, a Polish Gentile, risked her life to save Jews and has been recognized as Righteous Among the Nations.

Following the Nazi invasion of Poland in September 1939 and witnessing the extermination of her Jewish neighbors by the Nazis, Maria pledged to aid any Jew she could. Shortly after, Maria became a courier in the Polish Resistance. The couriers were called Kashariyot and were young women who traveled on illegal missions for the Polish Resistance during the Holocaust. They used fake papers to conceal their identities and smuggled secret documents, weapons, and supplies in and out of the ghettos. The Kashariyot were seen as fearless heroes who did death-defying jobs. Although being a courier was hard, it was not as difficult as some of Maria's other challenges.

One of her most important challenges was taking care of her good friend, Lena. After being a courier in the Polish Resistance, Maria was arrested and sent to Auschwitz, where she met Lena. Auschwitz was a Nazi concentration camp during World War II. It operated from 1940 to 1945. During the first several months, Auschwitz's rooms had neither beds nor any other furniture. The rooms were so cramped, that the prisoners had to sleep on their side in three rows. At Auschwitz, Maria gave medicine to the prison doctors by joining a group of prisoners and going to the infirmary, so the doctors could treat ill prisoners. Maria took care of Lena as much and as often as she could. She arranged for Lena to do easier work at the camps and took care of her when she was sick. In January of 1945, Maria and Lena were both evacuated to Ravensbruck, a German concentration camp for women located near the town Ravensbruck. One day, Maria found Lena dying in the snow and carried her back to the barracks, where she fed her. After they were both liberated on May 2, 1945, Maria protected Lena from sexual assaults by the soldiers. Maria was tortured and beat, but she never gave up.

After liberation, Maria returned to her home in Poland. She never returned to the health she had before the Holocaust. She died of cancer in Owczary, Poland on December 30, 1956. Lena had tried to find Maria but soon learned that she had died. Lena attempted to get Maria recognized as one of the Righteous Among the Nations by Yad Vashem in Jerusalem, but failed. Eight years later, James Foucar successfully resubmitted her testimony, which was approved by Yad Vashem on December 8, 2005.

A few of my family members were in the Holocaust, such as my aunt's parents, my great grandma, and my great grandma's siblings. My aunt's parents were Monek Zlochover and Celina Zlochover. They were born in Poland and survived the Holocaust by immigrating to America. After the Holocaust, they both died. Monek died in Israel, while Celina died in Texas. My great grandma's name was Edna. She also survived the Holocaust by immigrating to Newark, New Jersey in the 1920's. There, she married a man named Frank while her six or seven siblings stayed in Poland. They stayed there because they did not want to move, which got them killed later on in the Holocaust. Learning about the Holocaust has affected me because now I think differently when anyone needs help. I know that even if I help a little bit, it makes a big difference. In my future, I will know not to rely only on what people say, but to rely on my own opinion and other facts. I learned in the Holocaust, Germans made up a lot of propaganda and lied about what they were doing to the Jews and other innocent people. If I know that a certain group of people by race or religion is in need of help, I must help them. It is not right and not fair to think you are better than anyone else.

During the Holocaust, Maria Kotarba, a Polish Gentile, risked her life to save Jews and has been recognized as Righteous Among the Nations. From witnessing the extermination of just one family, Maria did so much to help all the other Jews by protesting against the Nazis, sneaking supplies to prisoners, and more. She faced many challenges throughout her life and took them on along with taking care of Lena. In the end, she got through the Holocaust and returned home, but died not so long after from sickness. Maria Kotarba, along with many other Polish Gentiles, is a hero to the Jews, other students, and I because she has inspired us to be good people and do good deeds.

Works Cited

"Maria Kotarba." Wikipedia. Wikimedia Foundation, 04 Feb. 2017. Web. 20 Dec. 2016. < https://en.wikipedia.org/wiki/Maria_Kotarba >.

"Kotarba FAMILY." Yad Vashem - Request Rejected. N.p., n.d. Web. 11 Jan. 2017. < http://db.yadvashem.org/righteous/family.html?language=en&itemeld=4438290 >.

Hidden In Silence

Esti Shapiro

Do you ever feel like you want to change something, but you're too small? Or maybe you want to change something, but you're afraid that no one will listen to you. It does not matter how big or small you are. It does not matter how frightened you are. If you believe in what you are doing, and what you are doing is good, you will succeed. Stefania Podgorska was born in 1925, and her sister Helena Podgorska was born in 1935. They lived in Przemysl, Poland, with a Catholic family. They had a father, mother, brother, and each other. Stefania worked in a grocery store owned by a Jewish family whose name was

Diamants. In 1938, Helena and Stefania Podgorski's father died of sickness. When the sisters came face to face with decisions during the Holocaust, they went the right way, helping others. The word holocaust comes from the Greek words "holos," meaning whole, and "kaustos," meaning burned. The word now refers to the horrible murder of six million innocent Jews and nearly six million innocent other minorities by the Nazis. During the Holocaust, Helena Podgorska and Stefania Podgorska, Polish Gentiles, risked their lives to save thirteen Jews, and in 1979, were recognized as Righteous Among the Nations.

In 1939, the Nazis invaded Przemysl, Poland and took all the Jews, including the Diamants, hostage. Helena and Stefania's mother and brother were taken away to do forced labor for the Germans. The two sisters then lived alone in an apartment rented by Stefania, who took a job as a machine tool operator. Life was hard, but the sisters managed to get along. In 1942, Max Diamant, the son of Stefania's former boss, arrived back in Przemysl, Poland with his cousin and brother. They had escaped from a train going to a concentration camp where they would be put to death in a way they did not know. Max pleaded and begged to stay in their house, for they had nowhere else to go. Helena and Stefania were frightened but let them stay and hide in their house. This was when the sisters didn't think about themselves, all they thought about was others.

Once the sisters said yes, Max was very thankful, but he still wanted to save more of his family and their friends. Stefania and Helena agreed to let him contact his family. To accommodate the refugees that would be coming, Stefania and Helena bought a cottage with an attic. First the Podgorski sisters moved in along with Max and his cousin. Then came Dr. Shylenger with his daughter, the dentist with his son, and the dentist's friend, a widow with her son. Then came the dentist's nephew and wife. Next was Max's younger brother, Henek and his wife, and the last person to come was a Jewish mailman. After a few weeks, they were without money and food. Everyone in the cottage was starving so Stefania started to knit sweaters and take orders from friends and people in town. She would trade clothes for food, and if she needed to, she would buy the food on the black market, the illegal market. Stefania and Helena managed to make enough money to keep them and the thirteen Jews alive.

In early 1944, a German officer entered the apartment telling the girls that they must vacate the place in two hours. The thirteen Jewish fugitives begged the girls to flee because they thought they were going to die, but Stefania and Helena, after praying to the black Madonna, the blessed virgin Mary depicted with dark skin, said no. The German officer then reappeared telling the girls that he had found a different place for the two German nurses he was trying to find accommodations for to stay. The 13 Jews and the two sisters were very relieved. On July 27th, 1944, the Soviet Union entered Przemysl and all the Jews living alone in the cottage, though emaciated, weak, and tired, were freed. Max, who took the name Josef Burzminski, proposed to Stefania who took the name Fusia. Fusia said yes and the two of them moved to America where Joseph became a dentist. Back in Poland, Helena Podgorska married a physician in Wroclaw and in 1979 the sisters were honored by Yad Vashem in Jerusalem as Righteous Among the Nations. In 1996, a movie was made by Richard A. Colla called Hidden in Silence honoring the sisters.

The lesson the Podgorski sisters taught me is that learning about the past and its flaws helps me understand how the Holocaust happened and how to make sure it doesn't happen again. Helena and Stefania taught me to stand up for what is right and to remember, equality for all. Right now, some of our country's leaders see the world differently than I see it. I see it as a place for all, while they see it as a place for the better. I believe that if all world leaders will read the many stories about the Holocaust, they would see what happens when you separate people by their ethnicity, skin, religion, or class. Knowing that Polish people risked their lives to save others of a different religion makes me wonder why everyone in the world right now can't be that way. I will try to be like Helena and Stefania by helping all people who are hurt or bullied and by sticking to what is right. I will not go against someone just because the majority is going against them, and I will not go against people based off of their ethnicity, color, or religion. Lastly, I will try to show people what happens when we go against each other and I will show them how to prevent it. I believe that if we all work together, the world will become an even better place.

During the Holocaust, the Podgorski sisters put thirteen Jew's lives before their own.. Stefania Podgorska and Helena Podgorska risked their own lives to save those thirteen Jews. The sisters lived alone in a small apartment with just each other, moved to a cottage they could barely afford just to accommodate the Jews, and nearly starved trying to keep them alive. The Podgorski sisters inspire me to stand up for what is right and to help the needy. Next time somebody is doing something wrong, let those two women inspire you to try to lead them in the right direction. The Podgorska sisters put others before themselves, and for this reason, are honored as Righteous Among the Nations.

Works cited

Kennedy, Michael, |J. "Sisters Reunited With Jews They Saved From Nazis : World War II: Unlikely Protectors Were Youngsters When They Hid 13 People in a Cramped Polish Apartment." Los Angeles Times. Los Angeles Times, 10 Jan. 1995. Web. 24 Feb. 2017.

http://articles.latimes.com/1995-01-10/news/mn-18462_1_world-war-ii

Wikipedia. "Podgórski Sisters." Wikipedia. Wikimedia Foundation, 21 Feb. 2017. Web. 24 Feb. 2017.

https://en.wikipedia.org/wiki/Podg%C3%B3rski_sisters

Though it was Risky, it was Done

Eva Channah Freedman

The word holocaust comes from the Greek word "holo," meaning whole, and "kaustos," meaning burned. It now refers to the murder of six million Jews and nearly six million other minorities by the Nazis. On September 1, 1939, a group of German soldiers called Nazis invaded Poland. It took 18 days for the Nazis to completely take over Poland. These Nazis killed more than two million Jews just in Poland itself. There were a group of people called the Aryan. These people were perfect to Adolf Hitler, the leader of the Nazi Party, also the Chancellor of Germany, and a dictator who wanted power. The Aryan weren't handicapped, Jewish, or disabled. They had perfect figures, blue eyes, and blond hair. However, there were people who wanted to help and make a difference, like Zofia Kossak-Szczucka. Zofia was born on August 10, 1889, in a small town called Kosman Lublin Voivodeship. Zofia was the granddaughter of a well-known Polish painter named Juliusz. She was homeschooled most of her life, and, when she was ready, she decided to study literature and painting in the Academy of Fine Arts in Warsaw from 1912-1913. During her first marriage, she lived in Ukraine and survived the bloody Peasant Rebellion and Bolshevik Invasion. The Bolshevik invasion was when the Bolshevik Democratic Party invaded Ukraine. She decided to follow in the path of literature and writing. She wrote many famous books, including Bez Oreza and Conflagration, which she based on her experience during the Bolshevik Invasion. She was Catholic, and wrote a lot for the Catholic press and underground organizations, such as Polska żyje, and Odrodzenia Polski. During the Holocaust, Zofia Kossak-Szczucka, a Polish Gentile, risked her life to save Jews and has been recognized as Righteous Among the Nations.

Mid-summer of 1942, the German Nazis issued a call, deporting all Polish Jews to Warsaw, to live in the Warsaw Ghetto. A ghetto was a penurious part of a city where Jews were forced to reside and surrender in an enclosed area, with walls 6ft high and barbwire on the top. When the ghetto was first announced, Zofia knew she had to do something. Zofia published a leaflet entitled "Protest," to show people what was going on inside of the ghettos. 5,000 copies of the leaflet were printed and sold. In the leaflet she wrote, "All will perish... poor and rich, old, woman, men, youngsters, infants, Catholics dying in the name of Jesus and Mary together with the Jews. Their only guilt is that they were born into the Jewish nation condemned to extermination by Hitler." She wanted to describe the awful graphic conditions that were going on within the walls of the ghetto. Zofia also wrote, "England is silent, so is America, even the influential international Jewry, so sensitive in its reaction to any transgression against the people, is silent, Poland is silent." By Zofia writing this, she wanted to tell the other countries and people that by them not saying anything, they were basically convicting the murder because they were not trying to help or stop the tragedy that was going on.

Zofia co-founded many of underground organizations, and Catholic organizations. During 1939-1941, Zofia co-edited an underground news press called Polska zyje (Poland

Lives), and a Catholic organization called Front Rebirth of Poland. Zofia also edited a paper called Prawda which means The Truth. Even though the German secret police for the Nazi party, called the Gestapo, were looking for her, she boldly exposed herself to help and save the Jews. The Gestapo were the secret police for the Nazi Party. The head of the Gestapo was Heinrich Himmler, who was also the leader of the Nazi police. Zofia decided that she wanted to physically help the Jews, not just by the words of her mouth. She co-founded the Provisional Committee to Aid Jews, which was then called the Council to Aid Jews. They had to codename it Zegota, which meant listen, so they couldn't be found. The purpose of Zegota was to save the Jews by hiding them and feeding them. Zofia knew she could have gotten caught and tortured and then killed, but by doing all of this, it shows how much Zofia wanted to save people.

Unfortunately, in 1943 Zofia was caught and arrested. She was sent to Pawiak Prison and then was sent to Auschwitz, and was held in the concentration camp. Auschwitz was one of the worst and biggest concentration camps. It was located south of Poland, and killed more than 1.1 million Jews, just in Auschwitz. Zofia wasn't in the part of Auschwitz called Birkenau, where the Jews were exterminated. By the efforts of the people in the underground, Zofia was released and went back to Warsaw. At the end of the Holocaust, more than 6 million Jews had died from disease, starvation, and torture. In 1944, Zofia was a part of the Warsaw uprising. The Warsaw uprising was an operation were the Polish Army tried to get Poland back from Germany, but failed. In June 1945, the Polish Minister of Interior, Jacob Berman, who was Jewish, called Zofia in to talk to her. Berman told Zofia that the government disliked her, and for her own protection she should leave. Zofia did leave, but she returned to Poland in 1957. The Polish currency put out a coin with Zofia and two other Righteous Among The Nation heroes on their faces to show their appreciation. Zofia Kossak-Szczucka was named one of Righteous Among the Nations by Yad Vashem, in 1985.

One of many lessons I learned from my Polish hero is, don't be afraid to speak up or do something even if no one else is doing it. If it can make a difference in someone's life, then do it. This lesson is important in today's world because it could change lives just by saying something that has not been said before. Always have the courage to do something, or say something, because you never know whose life you could be saving like Zofia did when she decided to co-found a Jewish organization even though she knew it was risky. If you think something is wrong, protest and show people that if you work together we can make a difference. I really want to try to be more like Zofia by speaking up. For example, I'm against aquariums. I could post something on social media telling people how the animals are living, and being treated, like Zofia did in her leaflet. I could also protest, even though it is risky. If you truly believe in something, or want to change something, speak up. Even if you are scared, embarrassed, or afraid you never know what could happen if. If no one says anything, then nothing can be done.

"Dobre serce i dusza," means a good heart and a good soul in Polish. During the Holocaust, Zofia Kossak-Szczucka, a Polish Gentile, risked her life to save Jews and has been recognized as Righteous Among the Nations. Zofia co-founded a lot of organizations to save the lives of others. From this she risked her life, and thought about other people and what they were going through, before she fought of herself. Zofia, not just helped Jews, She helped a lot of others to, and survived the Holocaust. I will always remember Zofia and all the courage, and bravery she had, and I will never forget what she did to help.

Work Cited

Wikipedia. "Zofia Kossak-Szczucka." Wikipedia. Wikimedia Foundation, 31 Aug. 2016. Web. 20 Dec. 2016.

Jensen, Joyce. "Keepers of the Flame." The International Raoul Wallenberg Foundation. The International Raoul Wallenberg Foundation, 1999. Web. 25 Jan. 2017.f

Making His Mark

Ezekiel Zeff

 One man with one vision can do many things. Henryk Slawik was born on July 16, 1894. After graduation, he went to Pszczyna and was drafted into the army during World War I. He then joined the Polish Socialist Party. He became Editor-in-Chief for the Gazeta Robotnicza newspaper company in Germany, and then became the president of the Worker's Youth Association. He was married to Jadwiga Purzycka in 1928. He then became the president of the Polish Journalists of Siselia and Zaglebia. Sawik was already active before World War II. The word holocaust comes from the Greek words "holo," meaning whole, and "kaustos," meaning burned. It now refers to the murder of six million Jews and nearly six million other minorities by the Nazis. During the Holocaust, Henryk Slawik, a Polish gentile, risked his life to save Jews and has been recognized as "Righteous Among the Nations." Henryk Slawik meant business, but was his high spirit enough to mean business during the Holocaust?

Henryk's unselfish decision to help would cost him big time. Slawik knew what was going on. He knew that having a different religion, skin color, or gender wasn't an excuse to treat people horribly by torturing them. Slawik acted fast. In 1939, he joined the Polish mobile police Battalion attached to the Krakow Army. He and his brigade defended the mountain passes leading to Slovakia. On September 15th 1939, Slawik and his men retreated to the newly-established border with Hungary. On September 17th, after the Soviet Union joined the war against Poland, Slawik tried crossing the border but was caught and sent to a prisoner-of-war camp. In Silesia, Germany, his name appeared on the Nazi German list of enemies of the state. Even though Slawik was captured, this would only be half of the dangers he would face next.

The challenges Henryk faced only made him stronger. Every "Righteous Among the Nations" had to face challenges. Many of these challenges included eluding capture, staying hidden, and getting materials. How would he avoid capture from his enemies? How would he stay hidden to avoid the Nazis? How would he get the materials to keep the refugees healthy? The greatest challenge was keeping alive his family, friends, and anyone who knew him. Slawik was soon freed from captivity because he spoke fluent German and he could help in Budapest to create a Citizen's Committee to help Polish refugees. After the Hungarian government issued racial decrees and separated Jews and Poles, Slawik issued fake passports to confirm refugees of their Polish roots and Roman Catholic faith and to keep their identities hidden. He also created an orphanage for Jewish children. To disguise the orphans true nature, the children were visited by Catholic Church authorities. After the Nazis took over Hungary, Slawik went underground to help refugees escape. Everyone including the children from the orphanage were evacuated. Slawik was arrested on March 19, 1944. Henryk's end would only be the beginning.

Slawik was taken to Mauthausen-Gusen concentration camp in upper Austria. There were about 24,000 prisoners at the camp which operated from 1939 to 1945. Slawik was brutally tortured and weak, but he didn't inform anything about him or his colleagues. He was then moved to Mauthausen concentration camp. Since he didn't inform anything there, Slawik was hanged on August 23, 1944. His burial place remains unknown. It is estimated that Henryk Slawik saved 30,000 Polish refugees including 5,000 Jews, with help, of course. He was awarded "Righteous Among the Nations" on January 23, 1977 by Yad Vashem.

The lesson that my Polish hero taught me is to never give up. Persevere in your dream and push yourself to the limits. This lesson is important in today's world because sometimes people can be scared to come out of their shell. For example, imagine if Martin Luther King Jr. didn't decide to speak out against the difference of blacks and whites. There would be much more violence today. Not only have a couple people pushed the limits, everyone does. Think about it. Your teacher pushed herself to be able to teach. You push yourself to be a better student. Athletes, scientists, coaches, architects all challenge themselves to be better. Everyone can push themselves to make the world we live in a better place. I will try to emulate my Polish hero by being a better me. I could give more tzedakah, or plant trees, or become a better student. Being a better me would make the world better.

In the end, Henryk Slawik was a hero. He did what was best for the world before what was best for himself. His story may not be the most famous, but I'll always remember Henryk every time I hear about the Holocaust. He could've chosen to leave with his family to a different country, but he knew what was more important. Henryk Slawik made his mark.

Works Cited

"Henryk Sławik." Wikipedia. Wikimedia Foundation, 17 Feb. 2017. Web. 20 Dec. 2016.

"Gusen Concentration Camp (Austria)." Gusen Concentration Camp (Austria). N.p., n.d. Web. 15 Feb. 2017.

A story of Strength, Perseverance and Courage

John Maagdenberg

Who is Jan Karski? Born in 1914, Jan Karski was a brilliant person who helped solve the woes of Jews in the Holocaust. He was a brilliant man who risked his life to save his friends and the world. He saved lots of Jews by talking to different nations about the Holocaust, and he persuaded the West to let in Jews as refugees. His long term goal was to end the Holocaust. During the Holocaust, Jan Karski risked his life to be recognized as righteous among the Nations in the Holocaust.

When Jan karski found out about the dire situation of Jews in Poland he initiated a plan of action. He went to different European countries so they would inform people who lived in the German occupied territories to let them know what was going on and have other countries except the Jews as refugees. He went to various countries and was brutally tortured because the Nazis wanted to extract information from him. In addition, he traveled to Britain, France, the U.S and other countries in search of assistance in his cause. He risked his life by traveling in and out of Poland repeatedly. Lastly he went to Britain and talked with Anthony Elden to convince him to take in more refugees.

Another one of his challenges was witnessing what was going on in the Warsaw ghetto. Jan disguised himself as a Jew so he could go into the Warsaw ghetto as a Ukrainian soldier in order to go into the death camps to interpret the situation. He was severely tortured by the Nazis and they took out most of his teeth. He even made a suicide attempt but refused to tell the Nazis anything.

He tried to stop the Holocaust and met with other countries such as Britain to report the situation so they could accept more refugees. He helped by meeting with various world leaders and talked with them about the situation. He met with President Roosevelt and the U.S Supreme Court informing them about the Holocaust. He even wrote a book about all his memories in a 400 page document titled 'The Story of a Secret State'. People praised the book calling it, "a purely good story, a personal story." It sold over 400,000 copies. He did all this to warn the "final solution" to the Allies.

Jan said that he saw Jews being hauled away and eaten alive. People called him heroic in every way, an amazing Polish patriot. People said that everyone around the world should read his story. He was an amazing heroic activist. "In a world where heroism is so overused in politics, sports, and entertainment it has been useless. Karski did both,' said David Harras. We should follow Jan's footsteps by being courageous and always trying to do what is right in the world even when it's difficult. Karski stayed in the U.S. because he would be prosecuted if he came back to Poland. He worked at Georgetown University and was a professor for 40 years in Eastern European affairs.

He also had an interview and talked about why Roosevelt did not help the Jews. He didn't know and didn't ask the President how he felt about the Jews. All I am is the messenger, he said and that America and Britain must have thought it was hard to take in refugees because they didn't do it. Germany thought it was easy to torture Jews because they did it. Jan Karski also wrote a book called The Terrible Secret in one of his class. The book was saying three main topics . One was when did the information come to the people. Two was how was the information sent to the people.the third was how did people handle the news.The book also said how the holocaust was not a secret after all and people were just too shocked by the news to believe that the news was true. They also stated that nothing was done to prevent the holocaust. He died of unspecified heart and kidney disease at Georgetown University Hospital. Jan Karski was a Polish Gentile who risked his life to save Jews and is recognized as Righteous Among the Nations. He was an amazing heroic patriot who had a photographic memory and did everything in his power to stop the Holocaust. He met with various world leaders to try to inform them about the Holocaust in order to end it. He went to the camp in Poland in order to look at the situation to report it to the Allies. He did a lot of things and went to a lot of places to help the Jews. This matters because it shows how people can be so generous and kind and risk their lives for other people that they don't even know. This relates to me because I always research the news and think about how I can help in the real world. The world has a lot of heroes who dedicate their lives to humanity. They did it using speech, strength, perseverance, intelligence; Jan Karski did all of those.

Works Cited

https://en.wikipedia.org/wiki/Jan_Karski

"1991, Jan Karski." Wallenberg Legacy, University of Michigan. N.p., n.d. Web. 18 Feb. 2017.

User, Super. "Inside Israel - August 2016." Chosen People Ministries - Jan Karski: The Man Who Tried to Stop the Holocaust. N.p., n.d. Web. 28 Feb. 2017.

In the Darkness

Maddox Garland

To be recognized by Yad Vashem, you would have had to saved a Jew's life during the Holocaust. Leopold Socha was born on August 28, 1909. He lived in the poor city of Lwow, Poland and worked as the chief sewage inspector and undercover burglar. Lwow had the third largest Jewish population in the Third Reich of 100,000 Jews. The word holocaust comes from the Greek words "holo," meaning whole, and "kaustos," meaning burned. It now refers to the murder of six million Jews and nearly six million minorities by the Nazis. Those minorities included Ethnic Poles, Serbs, the disabled, Romani, Gypsies, Freemasons, Slovenes, homosexuals, and Jehovah's Witnesses. During the Holocaust, Leopold Socha, a Polish Gentile, risked his life to save Jews and has been recognized by Righteous Among the Nations.

Leopold Socha, horrified by what the Germans were doing to the Jews and other minorities, befriended 20 Jews in a nearby ghetto. He was disheartened that the Jews were expelled from schools and kicked out of jobs. The Jews had strict curfews and weren't allowed into certain parts of cities. Jews had restrictions on restaurants and stores and got only a ration of food. For breakfast the Jews got an imitation coffee or herbal tea. For lunch they were given a litre of watery soup and if they were lucky they also found a piece of turnip or a potato peel. And for dinner they were given a piece of black bread weighing 300 grams and a sausage, margarine, marmalade, or cheese. Jews were banned from public transportation and were forced to wear a Jewish star that said "JUDE," meaning Jew in German. Jews were put into forced labor and extermination (concentration) camps such as Auschwitz Birkenau. Auschwitz Birkenau was the largest concentration camp in the Third Reich, Nazi Germany. It contained fortified walls, lots of barbed wire, barracks, gas chambers, and cremation ovens. These items are just a few things that show the genocide the Nazis pulled off. According to investigations 1.5 million people, the majority of them Jews, died at Auschwitz Birkenau. Their cause of death was usually systematic starvation, torture, or murder. When Leopold befriended the Jews, he realized he would need some help. A helper he got was his wife Magdalena. He also got help from one of his co-workers Stefan Wroblewski. With help from his wife and the Wrobleski family he hid the Jews he befriended in the sewers. Leopold hid them away from the nearby Peltew River that would sweep up and kill anyone who got too close.

Though there were many challenges in hiding Jews, Leopold overcame them. The Jews that were rescued tried to pay off their fare, but eventually ran out of money. Leopold was generous enough to pay out of his own pocket for food and clean water. Leopold brought them clothes and every night before bed washed dirty ones. In Leopold's spare time he played with the children to keep them occupied. To be a child in hiding you would have had to be very quiet and if not you would have been found and killed by the SS. The SS or Schutzsaffel was an organization under the control of Adolf Hitler and the Nazi Party. The SS, Adolf Hitler, and the Nazi Party were responsible for the murder of 5.5 to 6 million Jews. He brought the Jews a prayer book he found in the nearby ghetto. On Sabbath, he brought them candles and on Passover brought them a bag of potatoes.

Due to the inhumane conditions of a sewer, only 10 of the 20 survived. Midway through the journey, a woman gave birth to a baby but sadly had to smother it due to the noise it was making. The day the Germans were defeated in Stalingrad was the day Lwow was liberated and the survivors celebrated. Leopold Socha died on May 12, 1946 when riding his bike with his daughter. His daughter was almost run over by a Soviet Military truck but he knocked her out of the way and was crushed instead. On May 23, 1978, Leopold and his wife were recognized by Yad Vashem. In 1981 the Wrobleski family was also recognized by Yad Vashem. In 2011, Polish director Agniezka Holland made the movie In Darkness based on the stories of Leopold Socha. The movie was awarded Polish Academy Award for best actor (Robert Wieckiewicz), Polish Academy Award for best supporting actor (Kinga Preis), and Polish Academy Award for best Cinematography (Jolanta Dylewska).

The lesson that my Polish hero taught me is that if there's a bully, you need to stand for what's right. You don't have to listen to someone even if they're bigger, stronger, and have other people to back them up. Leopold taught me that you have to be the one to start the resistance. This lesson is important now because we cannot let it happen again. We now know that if someone or something is in trouble, pointing someone out is not the answer. Even if you are in a time of distress or pain, it is not right to point out the minorities. An example includes when our country's leader signed the executive order blocking Muslims from the seven countries of Libya, Iraq, Syria, Iran, Sudan, Somalia, and Yemen. It is called the Muslim ban because the majority of the residents in those countries are Muslim. Leopold taught me that you can be an angel and still hide in the dark.

Leopold Socha was a brave man who risked his life in order to save people who had a reason to live. Leopold could have easily turned over the Jews he rescued by decided to save them. With help from friends and family he did all he could to help protect those 20 Jews. He gave them food and water, clothes, and items to keep their religion and beliefs alive. Leopold's actions during the Holocaust matter because we now know that there are people who are willing to do the right thing even if there is a reward for doing the wrong thing.

Bibliography

https://en.wikipedia.org/wiki/Schutzstaffel

https://www.ushmm.org/wlc/en/article.php?ModuleId=10005189

http://whc.unesco.org/en/list/31

A Holocaust Story

Mia Brogan

Have you ever felt like a hero? Well, Anna Borkowska was. Anna Borkowska was born in Poland and raised there. Anna was a nun. She lived from 1900 to 1988 in Wilno, Poland. Before Anna started saving Jews she was one of the sister nuns. When she started saving Jews she got to the mother nun and, by the time World War II ended, Anna had become the head nun during the Holocaust. The word holocaust comes from the Greek words "holos," meaning whole, and "kaustos," meaning burned. It now refers to the murder of six million Jews and nearly six million other minorities by the Nazis. Anna Borkowska, a Polish gentile, risked her life to save Jews and has been recognized as Righteous Among the Nations.

Anna wanted to save Jews lives because of her religious beliefs. Her job was to help others. Back then, the nuns would help other human beings. The other nuns of Anna's church did not help the Jews because they thought that they were going to get into trouble. The nuns believed in God, not having kids, or getting married. Back then they helped lots of people. When Anna saw the Jews and her town getting taken away to labor camp or to concentration camp or being killed, Anna thought that she should save them and hid them in the monastery.

The Catholic leadership wouldn't help her because they didn't want to be killed or their church to be destroyed. Some of the nuns objected to hiding Jews with her. Anna hid

17 Jews in the monastery. One of them was Abba Kovner. Abba Kovner is a boy who Anna saved. Anna volunteered her services in the ghetto. The ghettos for the Jews were to segregate Jews from the Germans and, as Hitler said, the perfect humans. Families either stayed there for two weeks or for two years or longer if they had not died. People died either from starvation or getting shot in the ghettos. Most of the time people slept on the streets. She helped getting the supplies for the Jews underground. The supplies Anna brought were food, water, and blankets for sleeping.

Anna was caught and arrested and sent to a labor camp. The labor camp Anna went to was Perwejnisszki. When Anna was in the labor camp, she met a lot of Jewish people, but the sad thing was after she met them they all died. Anna was in labor camp for five months. After leaving the labor camp Anna went back to her church but is was closed. At the labor camp the officers did not treat Anna well. For food, they gave her half of a sandwich. The clothes that Anna wore were the ones she came in. The shelter Anna stayed in was a small room. In 1984, Anna was nominated Righteous Among the Nations by Abba Kovner, one of the boys Anna saved. Abba was just 12 when Anna saved him and later they became friends.

The lesson I learned from Anna is that you should always help people and that just because you are against something you should not blame it on someone. This is a lesson because we don't want the Holocaust to happen again. For example, I am a Jew, and some of my friends are not Jewish. They should not come up to me and say, Oh, you are a Jew so I am going to ruin your life. Hitler said, Oh, look I have someone to blame for why my life is so bad. Hitler was not a nice man. My hero Anna Borkowska saved Jews. One day I would want to be like Anna Borkowska because she was a lifesaver. I also want to be like her because she was against Hitler and I am against the Holocaust happening again.

This essay is about a woman Anna Borkowska. Anna saved Jews. some of the main point are that she saved Jews and she got nominated for Righteous Among the Nations. This essay is special because we should remember these people because they helped us and if Anna did not do this we would not be alive. This essay relates to the world right now because America has a new president and some people are worried that the Holocaust is going to happen again.

Works cited

Wikipedia. "Anna Borkowska (Sister Bertranda)." Wikipedia. Wikimedia Foundation, 8 June 2016. Web. 20

Dechttps://www.holocaustcenter.org/page.aspx?pid=514. 2016.

Astonishing Adamowicz

Rachel Violet Ichel

A righteous gentile is someone who has helped others whole-heartedly by finding their inner strength and kindness in order to change someone's life for the better. Jozef Adamowicz was born in Krajsk, Poland, around 1880. He was a close friend of Dr. Julian Aleksandrowicz, a famous Polish-Jewish Scholar on Leukemia. The word holocaust comes from the Greek words "holos," meaning whole, and "kaustos," meaning burned. It now refers to the murder of six million Jews and nearly six million other minorities by the Nazis. During the Holocaust, Jozef Adamowicz, a Polish Gentile, risked his life to help a Jewish family and has been recognized as "Righteous Among the Nations" for doing so.

When the Germans invaded Poland on September 1st, 1939, Adolf Hitler, Nazi leader, claimed that this was a preventive action to protect him and his party from the country. He said this so no one would suspect his plan and that he wanted to get rid of any enemy. Two days later, Germany declared war on Poland, which started World War II in Europe. To Hitler, the subjugation of Poland would deliver living space for his people. According to his plan, the strong, beautiful, racially superior, and Aryan Germans would colonize the territory and the native Slavs would be enslaved. The expansion had begun in 1938 with the occupation of Austria and then continued with Sudetenland. This also happened to Czechoslovakia in 1939. These two intrusions had been accomplished without using violence with the major powers, such as the United States, Great Britain, China, and the Soviet Union. Hitler hoped that his invasion of Poland would be tolerated. Meanwhile, Alexandrowicz fought in the 72nd Infantry Regiment against him.

Subsequently, he was imprisoned by the Nazis in the Krakow Ghetto. The Krakow Ghetto was one of five major, metropolitan Jewish ghettos created by Nazi Germany in the new General Government territory or German zone of occupation. It was sealed off with a high wall constructed around it, and four gates guarded by soldiers. The German authorities rigorously rationed food in Poland and decreed that the ghetto Jews might survive on as little as 100 grams of bread per day and 200 grams of sugar or fat per month. The ghetto was overcrowded as at least four families shared one tiny flat or apartment. In order to help Aleksandrowicz, Jozef delivered him packages.

In 1943, at the age of 60, Jozef Adamowicz came every day for a number of weeks to the gate of the prison where the doctor's own father worked and passed onto him packages of clothing, newspapers, and food for his family. These packages were very useful, as the living conditions there were very harsh, cramped, and dangerous. The food kept the family alive, and their clothes were all torn and dirty. The clothes given were clean and gave coverage to their bodies. Newspapers in the prison were rare. The Jews were not provided with outside information about Nazi Germany in Poland. The Alexandrowicz family was extremely grateful for these newspapers and got a sense of what Poland, aside from the cramped ghetto, was like. Sadly, Jozef Adamowicz was caught by the Krakow Jewish Ghetto police for delivering these packages. Punishment came with this new discovery.

Because of the help he provided, Jozef was clubbed nearly to death. He was beaten so badly that afterwards he died. Alexandrowicz escaped the Krakow Ghetto later, the same year. For all his kindness and generosity, Jozef has received the title of "Righteous Among the Nations." This honor was given by Yad Vashem in Jerusalem. His close family received this in 1992 as well. The award is veritably given to non-Jews. It's earned by risking one's life to save Jews in the Holocaust. This story is truly astounding. I feel that saving others is brave, compassionate, and kind; all forces stronger than hate. I also have some family members who experienced the pain of this time.

My aunt's father was a Holocaust survivor. It makes me feel strong to know that I had a family member in the war, who got put through all the torture, but still survived. He was taken to the concentration camps but escaped them. People in the world who help others do make a difference. It seems like a horror story, reading about the Holocaust. I know it's real though and is part of Jewish history. Learning about it in school is hard, especially since the main parts we hear about are death, Nazis, and concentration camps. But every once in awhile, there is light that peeks through the darkness, meaning the brave helpers that save people.

In conclusion, Jozef Adamowicz is someone who did an abundance of good for the Aleksandrowicz family. Without him, the family would be dead, or at the least, starving and in pain. He was appreciated so very much for everything he did and was compassionate enough to help people in need. All the people who helped in the Holocaust matter because, without them, other people wouldn't be able to see that sometimes doing the right thing can be scary, but it's perfectly okay to give it a chance anyway.

Works Cited

Preiss, Lea. "Ghettos." YIVO | Ghettos: Life in Ghettos. N.p., n.d. Web. 16 Feb. 2017.

"Józef Adamowicz." Wikipedia. Wikimedia Foundation, 06 Feb. 2017. Web. 24 Feb. 2017.

"Adolph Hitler." HistoryNet. N.p., n.d. Web. 22 Feb. 2017. <http://www.historynet.com/adolph-hitler>.

Sontheimer, Michael. "Germany's WWII Occupation of Poland: 'When We Finish, Nobody Is Left Alive' - SPIEGEL ONLINE - International." SPIEGEL ONLINE. SPIEGEL ONLINE, 27 May 2011. Web. 22 Feb. 2017.

"Germans Invade Poland." History.com. A&E Television Networks, n.d. Web. 15 Feb. 2017.

He Took Some Risks, But He Did It

Sarah Becker (Winner)

To become "Righteous Among the Nations" you must do something that will help or benefit someone greatly. Tadeusz Pankiewicz did that by hiding Jews in his pharmacy and turning the pharmacy into a meeting place for the ghettos Intelligentsia. Tadeusz Pankiewicz was born on November 21, 1908 in Samber, Poland, and was a Polish Roman Catholic. He was a student at the Jagiellonian University which was located in Krakow. In 1933, he took over the "Under the Eagle" Pharmacy which was founded by his father, Jozef, in 1910. The word holocaust comes from the Greek words "holo," meaning whole, and "kaustos," meaning burned. It now refers to the murder of six million Jews and nearly six million other minorities by the Nazis. During the Holocaust, Tadeusz Pankiewicz, a Polish Gentile, risked his life to save Jews and has been recognized as "Righteous among the Nations."

Tadeusz Pankiewicz first decided to help the Jews when the Nazi soldiers asked him if he wanted his pharmacy relocated. Since he was not a Jew, the Nazi soldiers offered he continue his business off the ghetto grounds, but instead of moving he decided that he wanted to help the Jews and fight against the Nazi soldiers. Tadeusz Pankiewicz persuaded the soldiers into letting him continue operating the pharmacy inside the ghetto grounds. If he had moved his pharmacy, the Jews would not have had much help. With his pharmacy in the ghetto, he was able to help and hide the Jews from the Nazi soldiers. He gave the Jews medications for keeping them from getting sick, hair dyes for disguising their identities, and tranquilizers which were given to scared children during the Gestapo raids. The Gestapo was the Germans secret police force during the Nazi government. The Gestapo was organized in 1933 and was known for its cruel techniques and procedures. Tadeusz Pankiewicz turned his pharmacy into a place for the ghetto's Intelligentsia to gather and have meetings. The Intelligentsia were the ghetto's educated people. They would talk about how they would offer food and information to the Jews. The pharmacy also became a gathering place for the underground activity. His only challenge now was to keep all of this a secret from the Nazi soldiers.

It was going to be a challenge for Tadeusz Pankiewicz to keep all of his the secrets of from the Nazi soldiers, but he had an advantage because he was not a Jew, so the soldiers did not suspect anything. During an Aktionen, the Germans had out in the ghetto, Tadeusz Pankiewicz hid Dr. Abraham Mirowski along with Irena Cinowicz in his pharmacy. Dr. Abraham Mirowski and Irena Cinowicz were Jews who had been taken to the ghetto. Irena Cinowicz was trapped in the ghetto and escaped from a group of Jews who were being taken from the ghetto during an Aktion. Tadeusz Pankiewicz hid her behind the counter and covered her with his own body. Irena already knew Tadeusz Pankiewicz from purchasing medications for her sick mother. Pankiewicz did not allow Irena to pay for the medications and she later realized that she was not the only one to receive medications without paying. Tadeusz Pankiewicz's motivation to save the Jews was his love for the Jews and humanity as well as his patriotic principles. Many of the people whom he helped owe their lives to him. Dr. Abraham Mirowski and Irena Cinowicz later went back to Israel after the war and told of Tadeusz Pankiewicz's actions to save the Jews in the Krakow ghetto.

It was a smart idea for Tadeusz Pankiewicz to start helping the Jews in the Krakow ghetto because he helped and saved many lives, and he was going to be rewarded for doing the right thing. On February 10, 1983, Tadeusz Pankiewicz was recognized by Yad Vashem as Righteous Among the Nations. He was awarded this because he helped and saved the Jews during the Holocaust. I think that Tadeusz Pankiewicz did a magnificent job helping and saving the Jews and the fact he was not caught makes it even better. Tadeusz Pankiewicz died 10 years after he was awarded "Righteous Among the Nations" because of kidney failure in 1993. He is buried in Krakow Rakowicki Cemetery.

The lesson that Tadeusz Pankiewicz taught me is that I should not be worrying about only myself all the time. I should start caring about other people more. I need to look around and try to help the others who are in need. Sometimes helping others may also mean putting myself at risk. If I can become a better person by helping other people, then I am willing to put myself at risk. Tadeusz Pankiewicz also reinforced my belief that everyone is the same no matter what you believe, what you look like, or what ethnicity you belong to. These two lessons that Tadeusz Pankiewicz taught me are important today because it is the right thing to help others who may be hurting. Supporting one another will most of the time lead to a good outcome. This is also important today because our current president is not being respectful to some people in our country even though they have not done anything wrong. We all need to remember that we are all equal no matter what we believe or what we look like. I will try to emulate my Polish hero by helping other people through their hard times. I promise to assist anyone who is in need of help.

A Polish Gentile, named Tadeusz Pankiwicz risked his life to save Jews during the Holocaust and has been recognized as "Righteous among the Nations." Tadeusz Pankiewicz hid Jews in his pharmacy and also turned his pharmacy into a meeting place for the ghettos Intelligentsia. In his pharmacy he offered many products to help all the Jews. He saved many people including Irena Cinowicz and Dr. Abraham Mirowski. He put himself at risk and did as much as he was able to without getting caught. Tadeusz Pankiewicz taught me a very important lesson and how to be a better person. Tadeusz is a very significant person because of standing of standing up for what he believed for and what was not right.

Works Cited

Wikipedia. "Tadeusz Pankiewicz." Wikipedia. Wikimedia Foundation, 16 Oct. 2016w2. Web. 20 Dec. 2016.

American-Israeli Cooperative Enterprise. "Tadeusz Pankiewicz." Tadeusz Pankiewicz. N.p., 12 Nov. 1993. Web. 20 Dec. 2016.

Yad Vashem. The World Holocaust Remembrance Center. "Pankiewicz Family." Yad Vashem - Request Rejected. Yad Vashem, 2017. Web. 20 Dec. 2016.

Sutter Middle School

Jody Cooperman- I have been teaching 8th grade English and U.S. history at Sutter Middle School for teen years. My commitment to teaching about the Holocaust came as a result of poorly it was done in our anthology book. I have been on a quest to learn more ever since. Currently a fellow for the Central Valley Holocaust Educators Network and U.C. Davis. Have studied at the United States Holocaust Memorial Museum, Museum of Tolarance and USC's Shoah Foundation. The underlying theme throughout my teaching is "What You Do Matters." I challenge my students to go deeper in their thinking during study.

Henryk Sławik: A Holocaust Hero

Aaron Asoo

On September 1, 1939, Polish men were standing on guard for the oncoming German soldiers with nervous looks on their faces. While the army stayed back, thousands of Polish citizens ran for their lives, hoping to find sanctuary in another country. Suddenly, with 2,000 tanks and 1,000 planes, the Germans crossed into Poland armed and ready to kill. The Germans quickly swept through the small Polish army. The Polish army was too weak to fight back and retreated. After many shellings, bombings, and deaths, Poland surrendered to the Germans. They captured Warsaw, Poland, and started to abduct people left and right, and sent them to internment camps such as Auschwitz, Treblinka and Sobibór. Most of the Jews were sought out and killed. About 6 million people died in Poland. These deaths included Jews, people who were resisting in any sort of way, and just ordinary people. Within two days, Poland's allies, Britain and France, declared war upon Germany. With the uprising of the Nazis, most Poles fled to the safety of Hungary, or other countries that would allow them stay. One of the heroes who were trying to save other fellow Poles and Jews was Henryk Sławik.

Henryk Sławik was known to many as a hero. He was a politician who was born in 1894, in Szeroka (present day Jastrzębie-Zdrój), Poland. He attended an academic school and then was drafted into the army during World War I after he graduated. When the war was over, he was released in 1918 and was sent to Warsaw for more training. When World War II began, he rejoined the army to protect Poland once again. He and his battalion were stationed at the 2nd Mountain Brigade, which lead right to Sylvania. On September 20th, Sławik and his battalion were ordered to retreat to the border of Hungary, but when they were near the border, Nazi troops arrested them, and sent them to a camp that held prisoners of war (PoW). In the camp, Sławik met Jozef Antall, a man who was in the Hungarian Ministry of Internal Affairs. Since Sławik was able to speak German, both men were able to leave the camp to go to Budapest to establish the "Citizen's Committee for Help for Polish Refugees". While in Budapest, Sławik helped smuggle Polish Jews to Yugoslav partisans, created jobs for the PoWs, and established schools and orphanages. One of the schools that he established was the School for Children of Polish Officers. Since the school was full of Jewish orphans and children between the ages of three and nineteen, Sławik had to disguise the school from suspicious onlookers. To do so, he had everyone at the school attend church, and had church officials come to the school to "teach" the students. With this image of a Polish and Catholic school, it did not draw any attention to Nazis whatsoever. During the time that Sławik was in Budapest, he also secretly manufactured fake passports for the Jews in need of one. He disguised the passports and papers to look as if the owner was Christian and not Jewish. In early March, 1944, the Germans had finally reached Hungary, and invaded it. Knowing that the Germans were well on their way, Sławik ordered all of the Jewish children, orphans, and adults underground, where they evacuated Hungary. On March 19, 1944, Henryk Sławik was arrested again by the Germans. They brutally tortured him, demanding he tell them where the rest of the refugees and his colleagues went off to, but Sławik never told them where they were headed. Providing no use to them, the Nazis threw Slawik in the Mauthausen internment camp. In the camp, Sławik was most likely forced to mine in the Weiner Graben stone quarry. A couple months later, Sławik died in the camp by being hanged.

Henryk Sławik was an ordinary Polish politician with a normal life with a wife and children, but when his country and the world needed a hero to save thousands of lives, he and many others stood together to save countless lives against the Nazis. Sławik risked his life as well as his family's life to do what was right. He helped save the Jews from execution, and inevitably got himself hung in the face of honor. Henryk Sławik was officially declared as "Righteous Among the Nations" on January 26, 1977.

While researching for this essay, it taught me a lot about the Holocaust and what it means to resist, whether it be to save a life or hundred lives. There were many people who believed in the Holocaust, many who disagreed, and a few people who were in the Holocaust that are still alive today who educate the younger generation about their experiences. Many events have happened in history, not all are positive, but it's up to the older generations to pass down the knowledge to the youth of today. We can share with the next generations and learn from past mistakes so that we will not reenact the negative events that happened such as segregation. Unfortunately, the youth of today are not as educated about the past and make the same offensive judgment on others such as equal rights among genders, ages, and intelligence. Luckily, however, there are still people who have learned from the past and want to save the world from war, segregation, and violence. Each person has the opportunity to change the world. They can become a hero and save the world, just like how Henryk Sławik saved the lives of people and changed lives forever.

Work Cited

"Facebook." Henryk Sławik. Facebook, 23 Mar. 2016. Web. 26 Feb. 2017.

"Invasion of Poland, Fall 1939." United States Holocaust Memorial Museum. United States Holocaust Memorial Museum, n.d. Web. 25 Feb. 2017.

"The Rightious Among The Nations." Yad Vashem. Yad Vashem, n.d. Web. 26 Feb. 2017.

How One Man Changed a Whole Family's World; the Story of Jozef Balwierz

Aaron Meylink

During World War II, a lot of madness happened, but there are people who saved lives in many ways. Some helped people escape from concentration camps, while others kept people under safety in their attic or basement. No matter what it was, they helped. One of these people who helped was Jozef Balwierz. Balwierz was born on January 1, 1919, in

Poland. Jozef was one of many who helped families escape the terrible things that were being done to Jewish people. He helped the Liebeskind family more than anyone. He used to work for the family at a factory before they were taken to the Ghettos. On August 6, 2007, Balwierz was recognized as a Righteous Among the Nations.

The start of one of the most devastating wars in history was on September 1, 1939. This war was known as World War II. The war involved 45 countries all fighting for one thing, to stop the Germans. At the time, the Nazi part of Germany was planning to take over the world and make it a dictatorship. The leader of the Nazis was Adolf Hitler, a tyrant. With that, he wanted world domination. As the war was beginning, Hitler and the Nazis declared Britain their biggest enemy. By the end of the war, 73 million people had died, and more that 67% of those who died were civilians. One of the biggest reasons that so many civilians died was the mass killings of Jewish people by the Nazis. They made concentration camps and more just to hurt these people. He did this because he hated the Jews, but the reason that he hated Jewish people was that he believed that the Jewish people had started World War I which had killed more than 100,000 German soldiers. He also thought that the Jews had stabbed the Germans in the back and so did a lot of others. Because of this thinking, Hitler was allowed to get away with the killing of all the Jewish people. In all, more than 11 million people were killed just from the Holocaust. The war ended on May 8, 1945, when the Germans surrendered. About a week later, Adolf Hitler committed suicide, officially ending the German terror over the Jewish people.

When the war reached Lwow, the Liesbeskind family was taken to the Ghetto and the father, Shmuel, was killed later in 1941. In 1942, the rest of the family escaped the Ghetto, and Balwierz offered shelter and did everything he could to help them in any way possible. Jozef acted as a father figure for the kids. He also helped two girls by the names of Elka Bardoch and Irena Liesbeskind board a train to Krakow. They got off the train a stop early to avoid the security check at their original destination. Irena later found a job as a housekeeper in Krakow with a German family. When the situation worsened in Lwow, Jozef moved with the Lisbeskinds to Austria. In 1943, Jozef went to see Irena in Vienna and got employed at a workshop of crude oil industry in Dobermannsdorf. When the war was over, Balwierz married Irena Liebeskind and they returned to Poland, before moving to Sao Paulo, Brazil later on in 1958. Jozef is still living according to all records I could find. All in all, Jozef Balwierz is a brilliant man that did everything in his power to save the Liebeskind family and others.

World War II was one of the worst wars in history according to the number of civilians who lost their lives. It is the most in any war ever. This was because of the concentration camps and more where Jewish people and others of different religions were put. In Poland alone, between 5,620,000 and 5,820,000 people were killed. This is one of the most of any country that was in the war. In fact, the only country that had more was the Soviet Union and they had approximately 10 million civilians who were killed because of military activity and crimes. To show how bad the numbers were where Balwierz lived, over 200,000 Jews lived in Lwow and over half of them were refugees from Poland. Four thousand of these Jews were killed in July of 1941, because of influence from the Germans. By August of 1942, 65,000 Jews had been moved from Lwow and killed. Now imagine this across the whole country. I don't even understand how anybody survived this. It is truly devastating to hear about what people did to each other. This is just one person who didn't like the Jewish and inflicted it on people he didn't even know. Overall, this war changed the lives of many and is still changing lives today.

With all this being said, it is for certain that Jozef Balwierz helped. He basically saved the Liebeskind family from being killed. He did whatever he could to help them, and he was happy doing it. It is honestly just amazing to think that something like this happened, but why did it happen is the real question. I guess the world will never really know.

Works Cited

"Lvov." United States Holocaust Memorial Museum. N.p., n.d. Web. 21 Feb. 2017.

"The Righteous Among The Nations." Yad Vashem. N.p., n.d. Web. 26 Feb. 2017.

Roda, Sara. "Balwierz Jozef." Story of Rescue - Balwierz Jozef | Polscy Sprawiedliwi. N.p., Apr. 2014. Web. 26 Feb. 2017.

"Jozefa Stalkowska and the Future of Holocaust Memory"

Alyssa Shimizu

Before World War II, Warsaw, capital of Poland, was a major center of Jewish life and culture in Poland and more than 350,000 constituted about 30% of the city's population. Once the German invaded on September 1,1939, Warsaw suffered from heavy air and bomb attacks. The German then entered Warsaw on September 29 and took over. Not long later on October 12, 1940, the Germans commanded the establishment of a ghetto and had all Jewish residents to move in a designated area. They were sealed off from the city by German authorities and were enclosed by a 10-foot-high, barbed wire wall to keep them shut. The population grew once more and more Jews moved in from nearby towns and the ghetto contained over 400,000 Jews. German forced the Jews to live in an area of 1.3 square miles and that averaged about 7.2 persons per room. The overcrowding and unsanitary conditions were unbearable. Living with no plumbing and having human waste and garbage fill the streets, many caught deadly, contagious diseases that spread easily. Residents also lived in starvation and hunger. Germany only let their starved residents purchase small amounts of food. Some had money or valuables to trade for food, but most had to beg or steal to survive. Especially during the winters, the heating was scarce and many lacked clothing to wear. People weakening from both hunger and exposure became easy victims for diseases and illness. Tens to thousands died in the ghetto and some even killed themselves from escaping their hopeless and awful lives. Although many residents died from illness, starvation, etc. in Warsaw, some escaped and saved their's and others' lives. One person in particular was Jozefa Stalkowska. Jozefa was a hero who not only saved herself and her daughters, but many other families who were in need of hiding and survival.

Jozefa Stalkowska was one of the many Holocaust survivors and heroes who sacrificed her life to save and help others. A hero was defined as someone who was admired or idealized for courage, outstanding qualities, and noble qualities. Jozefa, similarly, was the one who put others above herself and rescued those in need. She unselfishly shared her five-room apartment with those in need of survival, she regularly brought dairy products like butter and cheese to residents still living in the ghetto, she baked homemade bread and meals, she supplied goods, and she voluntarily kept families hidden. She kept them hidden behind the curtain, downstairs, the cellar, etc. Jozefa tried her best to help Jews as much as she could. Jozefa never denied anyone's assistance and she did it simply out of humanitarian feelings. She helped many other Jews who managed to leave the ghetto and let them settle in. She was sympathetic and caring towards people who ever needed help. Jozefa treated everyone like they were family and took great care of them. Jozefa knew the families had no material of resources or shelter and she took it upon herself to make them feel welcomed and cared for. Her daughter, Alina, knew she was hiding Jews and she tried to help her mom in every way. One of the many acts Alina helped the families with was she would escort Zofia Breskin and Mrs. Galeka to Sunday church services and taught them prayers. During her journey of survival with her daughters, her bravery and kind actions led her to rescue the following, Zofia and Hanna Breskin, Zofia and her husband Jan Galecki, Binjamin Tykocinski, Rachel Tykocinska, Dorota Warth, Mosze and Mieczyslaw Warth, Irena Golebiewska, etc. Many benefited from Jozefa's assistance and she will always be remembered as a long time Holocaust survivor, but also as a remarkable, courageous hero.

Jozefa grew up to be remembered as one of the many Holocaust survivors in Poland and she saved over 5 families who were in need of help. She kept the families and her two daughters inside her five-room apartment she rented in Warsaw, she supplied them with goods and meals, and hid them from the outside world to survive. Jozefa was unselfish and helped as many Jews as she could who escaped the ghetto. Even if this meant risking her life and her daughters' life to survive, she knew that helping and aiding other Jews was the right thing to do. Life in the ghetto were unsanitary and there were horrible living conditions. From having human waste and garbage thrown in the streets to deadly, contagious diseases spread throughout the ghetto, their lives were slowly dying by the minute. Most couldn't stand the conditions in Warsaw. The over crowd ness and weather conditions were unbearable and many lived in starvation and hunger. Although, some escaped and came to Jozefa for material resources and shelter. Those escapers were in need of survival and Jozefa wanted to save them. Some families lived with Jozefa for a few years and felt right at home and welcomed. Jozefa's assistance benefited many families and Jozefa will always be remembered as a hero in their hearts. During the course of the Holocaust, over 6,000 Jews survived in Poland and escaped the power of the Germans. Jozefa was one of the many 6,620 Jews who survived and who helped others. Jozefa Stalkowska unselfishly rescued and put aside her needs for others. Defined as a hero by those who were assisted by her, she was a remarkable person who showed a great amount of courage and kindness. One person who we will never be forgotten for her brave and selfless act and is a great influential role model.

Bibliography

"Name of Righteous Country." Yad Vashem. The Holocaust Martyrs' and Heroes' Remembrance Authority, n.d. Web. 26 Feb.2017

United States Holocaust Memorial Museum," Life in the Ghettos." Holocaust Encyclopedia. www.ushmm.org/wlc/en/article.php? ModuleId=10005143. Accessed on 26 Feb. 2017

United States Holocaust Memorial Museum, " Warsaw." Holocaust Encyclopedia. www.ushmm.org/wlc/en/article.php? ModuleId=10005143. Accessed on 26 Feb. 2017

United States Holocaust Memorial Museum," Introduction to the Holocaust. " Holocaust Encyclopedia. www.ushmm.org/wlc/en/article.php? ModuleId=10005143. Accessed on 26 Feb. 2017

Gertruda Babilinska

Andrew Louie

Born North of Poland near Danzig with five sisters and two brothers, Gertruda Babilinska was a nanny who worked and took care of a Jewish family named Stolowitzky for fifteen years. The Stolowitzky family had a daughter and a son. Suddenly, one day the father was taken to Auschwitz, and an unexpected journey for Gertruda began. With complications to come, Gertruda persevered even though it was hard to raise a boy by herself and to raise a boy to become Jewish in the time of World War II.

Working and taking care of the family was one thing, but moving with a mother and son to one city after another is a huge commitment. This was a commitment that Gertruda took. She didn't mind the commitment because she cared about taking care of the family of two. When the father was sent to Auschwitz and the daughter died, the mother knew she and Mickey, her son, had to move. The mother had heard Warsaw was better, so Mrs. Stolowitzky, Mickey and the nanny moved to Warsaw. Then she heard that the Vilna Ghetto was better, so then they moved once again, to Vilna Ghetto. Once there, Gertruda Babilinska rented an apartment. The people that lived in Vilna Ghetto weren't very happy with their presence because they had a prejudice against people who were Jewish. One day, Mrs. Stolowitzky made Gertruda promise that if anything were to happen to her that she would take care of Mickey and that is exactly what she intended to do.

Soon after, Mrs. Stolowitzky became very sick and died. It was now time for Gertruda to keep her promise and take care of the child and raise him Jewish. One time, Mickey became really sick and the only doctor Gertruda knew was a German doctor. Gertruda lied to him and said that she was his older sister but he didn't believe her. After a few visits to this doctor, Mickey got better. When it came time to pay the doctor, he said, "You have made me feel like a man" and refused to take any money from Gertruda.

After the war had ended, Gertruda knew they had to go to Israel to raise Mickey to become Jewish. They boarded a ship named Exodus, which was manned by the British, to carry them to Israel. As soon as the ship docked, they went to find Mrs. Stolowitzky's relatives. Before Mrs. Stolowitzky died, she assured Gertruda that her relatives would help them. Gertruda soon realized this was not so. The relatives provided Gertruda with a small, cramped room with no water or toilet. In addition to the small room, the relatives only paid for a half of a year of school. They told Gertruda that they wanted to adopt Mickey and send her back to Poland. Gertruda refused to break her promise to Mrs. Stolowitzky or to let the relatives adopt Mickey, so the relatives decided that Gertruda needed to start paying rent for the small room and pay for Mickey's schooling.

One day Mickey came home crying and said, "You are my mother. I don't want them for parents." Gertruda soon began working as a maid to pay for the tiny room she rented from the relatives and for Mickey's education. In the end, Gertruda accomplished and kept the promise that she made to Mickey's mother.

Mickey, now called Michael by friends, had worked for a touring company in Israel and then moved to Miami in 1975. He currently lives in New York. Gertruda Babilinska has since past, but will forever be remembered by Michael. He has also shared his story with schools and even in a book called Gertruda's Oath. Even though many who have read it say Michael's the hero, he says that the book's actual hero is Gertruda, not him. He says that his story is just about "a love story between a Christian woman and a Jewish son." Without her, he would not have been around and this is why he considers her to be his mother.

Gertruda really kept her promise to Mickey's mother even though there were many times when she could have given up, she didn't. She persevered and did everything in her power to care for and protect Mickey. She made sure he went to the doctor when he needed to, helped him get to Israel and worked as a maid so he could go to school and so she could still be his mother.

I learned from Gertruda that it's important to keep promises and to treat others as you would like to be treated. This was shown in this story when she was always taking such good care of Mickey and making sure he had everything that he needed. This has opened my eyes and made me realize what positive things that can happen if you treat your neighbor as yourself and what great outcomes are possible. I have also realized what perseverance can accomplish. With perseverance you can accomplish anything you want, just like how Gertruda persevered and accomplished her goal in life.

Bibliography

P.B.S and K.V.I.E. "Rescuers: Gertruda Babilinska – Shtetl – FRONTLINE." PBS. Public Broadcasting Service, 2014. Web. 26 Feb. 2017.

Ggarrison@al.com, Greg Garrison |. "Catholic Nanny Saved Jewish Boy from the Holocaust: Students Hear the Story First-hand." AL.com. Alabama Media Group, 08 Apr. 2013. Web. 27 Feb. 2017.

You Don't Need Money to be a Hero

Anna Kilmer

Kids screaming for their parents, people crying and suffering, this is what happened during the Holocaust from 1933 to 1945. There was an organization of people called Nazi's lead by Adolf Hitler that believed Jews were below them, and considered Germans "racially superior". Adolf Hitler was one of the most famous and ruthless leaders in history. He took control of the German government in 1933; he began making concentration camps to kill Jewish people. The organization captured Jews, of all genders and ages, homosexuals, and the mentally ill. The Nazis never stopped torturing and killing innocent people until their Allies defeat them. The people that were captured could not escape, but the few that did survive had to start their life over and grieve over all of their family members dying. There are thousands of people that the people of Poland were to thank for saving many Jews.

A couple, Israel and Franciszka (Frania) Rubinek, got married in 1941 in the town, Pińczów. They opened a small store that sold items for farmers. One of their many customers was Zofia Bania; she was a poor farmer from a small town not far from Pińczów called Włochy. The couple would give her food and other things for free because she could not afford it. After many times of Zofia visiting the store, her and Franciszka became friends. After Israel and Franciszka heard about what the Germans were doing to Jews, they asked Zofia if they could hide in her home, but she said she had to think about it. When they heard no answer from her, Israel decided to start building a bunker under their store. In October 1942, Nazis began coming to their town and taking Jews to send to concentration camps. The couple hid in their bunker until the troops left, and they left to a town near them. They were trying to head to Russia, but their trip was stalled because Frania was eight-months pregnant. When they heard the news that Zofia Bania was looking for them, they hired a man to take the couple to her house in a wagon. Zofia was married to Ludwig, her husband, and had Maniek, her six-year-old son; they lived in a packed, one room home. When the Rubineks arrived to her home, Zofia welcomed them with a smile on her face, but her husband was stubborn and didn't want them in his house. She thought it was "her duty to save them" even though Ludwig wasn't happy about them staying. Frania and Israel argued about them staying at their home because they believed he would deceive them. This is only the beginning on how Zofia is a hero to the Jewish couple. Israel let them stay in the barn attached to their home, and in December of 1942 Frania went in labor. Mrs. Bania did all she could to help during her painful labor which tragically ended in the baby dying during birth. After she became very sick for three months, the family let them stay in the main home during their hiding. Their home was on the outside of Włochy which made it safe, but in case her husband bought a guard dog which would bark if anyone came near the home. During the end of the war German soldiers broke into Zofia and Israel's home and demanded that they would spend the night in their home. The couple hid in their bunker where they store their potatoes. Israel had a severe cough because he was sick, so the family was afraid the soldiers would be able to hear him coughing from the bunker. In order for Frania and Israel to stay hidden Maniek, the six-year-old son, pretended to be extremely ill. He pretending to cry and cough all night while laying over the entrance of the bunker, so the Germans wouldn't notice it. This act of kindness shows the Bania family would do anything to help people in need even though their lives were at risk. Finally, in January of 1945 the couple was liberated and moved to Canada to start their lives over. This is just one breathtaking story on how just a few people can save the lives of friends even though they are at risk.

Heroes during World War II were much different than what we think of when we think of heroes now. Many people during this time period think of a hero as a superhero or someone that helps someone. Back in the 1900's heroes risk their life just to save a person or many people. People held groups of people in their home just to save them from being taken by the Germans. The big question during that time was, what would you do to save your neighbor? Would you let someone close to you be taken and killed because of their beliefs?

Bibliography:

"Introduction to the Holocaust." United States Holocaust Memorial Museum. United States Holocaust Memorial Museum, n.d. Web. 27 Feb. 2017.

"The Righteous Among The Nations." Yadvashem.org. N.p., n.d. Web. 26 Feb. 2017.

Krystyna Adolph: A Hero With an Unfortunate Last Name

Annabelle Thalken

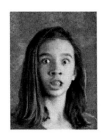

What do you think of when you hear the name Adolph? Does the name strike fear in your heart? Does it make you think of the well-known, feared and hated Adolf Hitler? While that Adolf may be better known, there was another Adolph who acted nothing like this one. Her name was Krystyna Adolph. Although she may have been less popular, she was loved not hated. She was a lifesaver not a murderer. Krystyna helped save people's lives in Poland during the Holocaust and because of her actions, she was named righteous.

The Holocaust was an awful time for everyone who lived in Germany and territory taken by the Germans. When Hitler took power in 1941, the European Jews were his primary target. He had children killed. He had elderly people killed. And he had the disabled killed. Middle-aged Jewish men and women were sent to go and work in factories. By the end of Hitler's reign of terror, between six million and 11 million people had been killed.

Before the Holocaust had started, Krystyna Adolph was a teacher at Czartoryski High School in Vilna, Poland. There were two Jewish students in her class when the war had begun, Monika and Lidia Gluskin. When the Germans occupied Vilna, Krystyna sent out a message to the Gluskin sisters, letting them know that she was willing to give them shelter at her family farm in Ignalino, despite the dangers of housing Jewish people at this time. The sisters took Krystyna up on her offer when the Vilna Ghettos were established.

Vilna was an awful place at this time. The Germans had taken over Vilna in August 1941 and had officially established the first Vilna Ghetto in July of 1941. By then more than 3,500 Jewish people had been killed by a mobile German killing squad and the Lithuania Auxiliary at Ponary. Ponary was the woods in Vilna where thousands of Jewish and other people were killed. In Ghetto number one, men and women were forced to work in factories. And by September 1941 a second Ghetto was established in Vilna. This second Ghetto did not last very long. In October of 1941 Ghetto number two was destroyed along with everyone living there. By the end of 1941, less than a year after the Germans took over, more than 40,000 Jewish people had been killed at in Vilna.

The sisters were glad to get the chance to leave Vilna and go to Ignalino. When the sisters got to Adolph's farm they were introduced to the neighbors as relatives who fled because of forced labor. For the next three years the twins helped on the farm by helping around the house, doing chores, taking care of the animals, cleaning, and chopping firewood. Only very few people knew the twin's real identities. These people included Krystyna, her late husband, her husband's sister and her husband's father. Krystyna knew the risks when she decided to house the sisters. Krystyna's Mother-in-law was a big help and had an important role when it came to protecting the sisters. She was able to get fake birth certificates to prove that the sisters were not Jewish. This was very crucial because if anyone found out the twins were Jewish, Krystyna, her family and the twins would all be killed. Despite the challenges, Krystyna and the twins were never caught. The twins went on to live their lives outside of Poland. And Krystyna Adolph was named Righteous in 1984 for her acts of bravery when it came to risking her life to help others. Krystyna is now honored today with a tree and a memorial plaque to let others now of her actions.

Through my extensive research on not only Krystyna Adolph, I have learned so much about the Holocaust. The Jewish people were treated so poorly during this time. Not only did 40,000 Jews die in Vilna the first year the Germans took over, people around them turned their backs on the Jewish Community. People were living in fear and too afraid to help anyone because they did not want to get caught and die. It was very clear who the bystanders and up-standers were at this time. Bystanders watched while millions of innocent people were killed because they were afraid of loosing their own lives. Up-standers risked everything, their lives, their families and their homes just to try and save others. Despite the consequences up-standers still continued to help those in need. Whether it was by offering shelter, like Krystyna Adolph, helping prisoners escape, getting fake birth certificates or even by delivering food and medicine to the Ghettos. Thanks to Krystyna, multiple lives were saved. Through my research on the Holocaust I have found that it is much easier to live in fear than to risk your own life for others, but those who do risk there lives get noticed. They go on to be remembered as great. They go on and are remembered as Righteous.

Work Cited

"Vilna." United States Holocaust Memorial Museum. United States Holocaust Memorial Museum, n.d. Web. 28 Feb. 2017. < https://www.ushmm.org/wlc/en/article.php?ModuleId=10005173 >.

"POLAND." Blackfriars 25.292 (1944): 241-43. Yadvashem. Web. 28 Feb. 2017.

Krystyna Adolph

Ciarra Nesbit

There were various people who saved and helped Jews during such a cruel war although lots of people who were involved either the holocaust weren't musically Jewish, they were innocent people who risked their lives and everything they owned to protect and save their peers. One of these brace people was Krystyna Adolph, a teacher at Czatoryski High school in Vilna. She was a widowed wife and lived on a small farm with fields, fee animals, and a garden.

Once the war began and Germans invaded in 1941, Krystyna had a messenger go out and give some of her fellow students named Monika and Lidia that she taught at her school and were in her class and said they could come stay with her until the war ended. The twin Gluskin sisters took the opportunity and accepted the offer. She opened up her home to the kids and their family. Krystyna was perfectly aware with the risk she was taking by sheltering her students, Germans has just burned down an entire house with the family inside once they discovered Jewish people living inside and hiding in the house, but Krystyna still didn't care even if her life was at state. Not only did she just let the family live there, she helped the mother fake legal documents to show they weren't Jews and saved their lives. Later on after the war the family moved out and thanked Krystyna for everything she did and they wouldn't have lived without her. Krystyna and her sister help provided the girls with false identity papers once she decided to leave the ghetto which was established in 1941, she survived on the Aryan side. Once Monika and Lidia moved away once they were save they came back to thank her and offer her goods and if she ever needed help with anything ever to call them and they would come back to help, but Krystyna didn't take the offer, she souly did this just out of the understanding and kindness of her heart.

She risked everything she had and was careless to where she did everything possible to be affective in a positive way to save these group of people that were threatened to possibly be killed and tortured and if it wasn't for people like her, even more than the what was originally done would've been worse. During such a difficult and life changing moment in history many people didn't put others who were actually affected from the situation first and did all they possibly could or even just a tiny small thing to try and help out because nothing would happen to them. Lots of people never realized how bad it was for the Jews and even when they did they just sat back watched and let it happen instead of actually

463

going out and to help and protect others from getting hurt, losing their families, losing homes and so much more. But, the people who did help were considered heroes because they took a step forward and put themselves in a position that could've possibly got them killed themselves. These heroes were willing to give up anything and everything they saved families and gave them a chance to live whether than let them just die, they gave them a home, food, and an opportunity to live past this war saying "I'm a survivor" which millions of people did not have the chance to do. As well, these people have the chance to share their stories and experience going through such a rough patch in their lives and during this time in their country, which could help prevent from such a thing happening again. From people like Krystyna Adolph and hundreds of other heroes, they gave others a chance and gave the will to do anything to help people and that's something not very many people have the guts or even have the willingness to help others in these types of ways and because of these people it makes our world just a little bit better. The Gluskin sisters were probably just and terrified as everyone else who didn't live were. Scared of walking outside and getting taken from their families and possibly never seeing them again, cruel heartless people just watching them suffer and putting them through pain, not knowing if they'll actually ever live again. All thoughts people had during these times but because Krystyna just like other gave them a possible chance live and a drive mentally to help others and not let them live in fear was such a beautiful act and everyone can learn from people like her. Some may say the actions people decided to do and take on during this ugly inhuman war were cowardly and dumb but most people on earth didn't and still to this day in 2017 don't have the guts to do anything and risk their lives and possibly suffer along with these people even if they weren't the people attacked, even if they weren't a figure out to get they still opted to help and serve these people because they knew what was right from wrong, based off of what the Germans were doing to Jews, it was over all nasty just because they weren't the same religion or race or whatever it may have been you should've never treated another person so cruel as if they were some type of nasty animal living outside in the dirt. As if they were lower or lesser than others just because of what the believed in, all because of opinions. The people who did see what was right from wrong were the people who helped and made such a difference from saving and helping out others and because of these people they helped others service what couldn't have been possible with out them. Krystyna, She had a take on this time period and will never be a forgotten heroic figure in our lifetime.

Works Cited

Yadvashem.org/Righteous/Poland

The Life of Piotr Budnik

Cole Hanna

A hero is a person who is admired for courage, outstanding achievements, or noble qualities. An example of a hero during World War II is a man named Piotr Budnik. Piotr Budnik was a Polish Roman Catholic who was born in 1916. He was a farmer who grew up in a cottage with his elderly parents in the village of Kaczanowka (Tarnopol district, modern-day Ternopil, Ukraine). As the Germans began to occupy Kaczanowka, many of the local jews including Piotr's neighbors and long-time friends, the Hellraichs, were sent to the Tarnopol ghetto. In 1942, the Germans began liquidating the ghetto and deporting the remaining Jews to the Belzec dealth camp. Piotr remembered his long-time friends and decided to risk his life by going into the ghetto in order to save the three Hellraich children (Adela, Ester, and Zeev). Budnik's courageous act of saving the Hellraich children from the Tarnopol ghetto is one of the many reasons why he is now remembered as a hero of World War II.

In addition to risking his life to save the Hellraich children from the ghetto, Piotr also housed them in the outhouse of his farm. Not only was Piotr hiding the Hellraich children from the Germans, he was also hiding them from the knowledge of his own family. He sold extra produce from his farm to help provide for the three children. Piotr was constantly trying to find different hiding spots for the kids and made sure that they always had enough food and water. After two of the kids contracted typhus and the risk of discovery increased, Piotr dug a bunker in a distant field and transferred them there to keep them safe. Even when he himself had contracted typhus, he would continue to bring them food during the night because he knew that they were his responsibility. This routine of finding new hiding spots almost every other day and providing food for the children carried on for at least eighteen months. It was an enormous feat for Piotr Budnik to rescue and single-handedly care for the Hellraichs while keeping it secret from both the Germans and his own family.

During World War II, the Nazis created hundreds of ghettos which were sections of a city in which all Jews were required to live. The Hellraichs, Piotr's neighbors, were sent to the Tarnopol Ghetto. The Tarnopol Ghetto was a Jewish World War II ghetto that was first created in 1941 in the city of Tarnopol (now Ternopil, Ukraine). In Tarnopol, Jews made up forty-four percent of the city's population which made it the largest Jewish community in the area. In July 1941, a few days after the German army conquered the city of Tarnopol, about 2,000 Jews were killed. Two months later in September of 1941, the Germans announced that they were creating a designated Jewish ghetto in Tarnopol around the Old Square and the Market Square Minor. Twelve to thirteen thousand Jews were soon put into the ghetto and were given minimal food and lived under very harsh rules, including receiving the death penalty for leaving the ghetto illegally. The conditions of the ghettos were appalling. They were filthy, extremely overcrowded and had poor sanitation. Disease spread quickly through the ghettos. Those who did not die from disease, often starved to death due to the short supply of food. In the winter of 1941-1942, the ghetto's condition became so bad and the mortality rate was so high that the Judenrat (an administrative agency imposed by Nazi Germany during World War II) had to begin burying corpses in mass graves for sanitation concerns. In August of 1942, around 3,000-4,000 Jews were gathered and put into cattle cars for two days without water. While this was going on, another cattle train arrived with Jews from two other ghettos. The two trains were connected and sent to Belzec death camp, where a total of 6,700 Jews would be exterminated. On November 10, 1942 another 2,500 Jews from the Tarnopol Ghetto were put onto trains and sent to extermination camps in Belzec. The population of the Tarnopol ghetto decreased by a significant amount and was later partly turned into a labour camp. Although many terrible things went on in this ghetto, it brought out the good in many Polish people who lived in Tarnopol. Many of these people risked their lives to save the lives of others. Their motivation was solely because it was the humane thing to do and could not understand how a civilized person could harm or kill another person. Piotr Budnik is a shining example of one of these people.

There are many things that define a hero, including noble qualities, important achievements, and courageous acts. Piotr and all of the other rescuers performed many brave acts motivated solely for the purpose of helping these people and standing up for what they believed was right. Piotr risked his life by entering the Tarnopol Ghetto to rescue his neighbors, the Hellraichs. He prepared multiple hiding places to keep them safe and to avoid their persecution from the German army. In addition, he provided daily care for them under very difficult circumstances. Piotr Budnik's courageous acts are why he is now known as a hero of World War II.

Work Cited

."Righteous Database." Yadvashem.org. Web. 27 Feb. 2017.
"Tarnopol Ghetto" revolvy.com. Web. 26 February.2017.

Dr. Jan Brzeski: A Brave Man

Dylan Delucchi

Imagine living in a place where you barely have enough space to lay down. A place where you are wondering if you will ever eat again, or you are wondering how long you have until you are shipped somewhere else. Well, that place is the ghettos in Poland and all throughout the world during the second world war from 1940 to 1945. During that time Adolf Hitler, the German dictator, was trying to conquer the world. To do that, according to him, was to kill all of the Jews just because he did not like them. He was probably the most evil man to ever live, he would do anything to gain world dominance. He had a plan called the "Final Solution," it was to destroy all of the ghettos that held the innocent Jews to get to his final goal, being dictator of the world. Thousands of Jewish "ghettos" were formed to segregate the Jews from the rest of society. They were formed by the Nazis, but not kept up very well because they were all usually unsanitary and because of that, full of disease. They housed usually thousands at a time in a very small portion of land. Sometimes they were forced to do labor, but that was up to the council, who chose what the Jews did every day. They were set up for no certain amount of time because at any time the Nazi's could have ordered to destroy the whole camp or ship people off to killing centers. But when the ghettos did get destroyed, there were, of course, some still left, hiding not wanting to be found and killed. These few people were hurt and hungry and it was up to people, like Dr. Jan Brzeski to aid and feed them.

Jan Brzeski was a doctor and resident of Brzesko, in the Tarnow district, during the Holocaust. He was born in 1904. Dr. Jan was one of many people who risked everything, their families and lives, to help the Jewish. He provided medical assistance to the Jews who hid near him after his local ghetto got destroyed. He was known to answer and visit all calls for help, even if it meant he had to walk very far distance in the dead of night to not be caught. Because he was doing it illegally, Dr. Jan Brzeski had to perform most medical procedures in unsanitary places like cellars, pits, and other places where the Jewish families were hiding. He helped a mother give birth, aided some battling pneumonia, and helped a small boy and his mother in hiding. He also helped persecuted Jews to help make up for his anti-jewish actions before the war. Brzeski had been arrested countless times and interrogated. Dr. Jan Brzeski was a brave man who put others' lives before his to help the Jews during World War II. His story really stood out to me because of the way he helped and what he went through. Dr. Brzeski had to walk sometimes a couple miles at night to aid the hiding Jews. It is amazing how he had enough courage to stand up and I hope I would be as brave as him if something ever happened to me or my family. I look up to Jan Brzeski because of his brave actions as a Holocaust rebel.

This has helped me a lot to realize how much I have taken for granted in my life, I had not put my life into perspective. The Jewish people during World War II were tortured and kept in hostile locations. The Nazi's treated them like they were not even human. It was up to other people to risk their lives to help them, something that many people now would never even think of doing. The people like Jan Brzeski were one of the bravest people ever. Putting others lives over theirs. This also makes me think, would I ever do that? Of course anyone would say they would, but you can risk getting put in jail, or even worse, get shot. Would that make people like me be scared to or would we be brave enough to help out. I try not to ever think that my life is unfair or not right because I know that I do not have any sort of problem anywhere close to what the Jewish people had to go through every day. They had to worry if they would eat again, or even live to the next day. Their lives at the time were full of fear and I have not ever come close to having to worry about such things. Adolf Hitler was a terrible man with too much power he had, the Holocaust was a terrible time to be in for all races and religions. He killed too many innocent people, and it could have been even worse if it were not for the thousands and thousands of people who risked their lives just to save 1 or 2 people. The Holocaust was full of terrible people, but the stories of brave and persistent people seem to outshine them all.

Works Cited

"Learn About the Holocaust." United States Holocaust Memorial Museum. United States Holocaust Memorial Museum, n.d. Web. 23 Feb. 2017

"Names of Righteous by Country." Yadvashem. N.p., n.d. Web. 23 Feb. 2017.

Holocaust Survivor and her Story

Emily Brezinski

World War II began in 1939 and ended in 1945, it involved most countries and caused a lot of conflict between people with lots of power. The holocaust lasted from 1941 through 1945 and there were around 11 million deaths of mainly Jews but also people of other races. A third of the Jewish population were murdered and Adolf Hitler is responsible for that. Hitler, born in 1889 was a German politician who is the commander of the Nazi party. He started the holocaust because according to him Jews were "socially undesirable" and the main cause for most of the world's problems. However, during the holocaust some were lucky to find a very kind person to provide them with food or a home and keep them out of trouble for the longest time possible. Antonina Bak is one of those people who helped keep some boys out of trouble and keep them alive in a safer environment than a concentration camp.

Antonina Bak, born March 31, 1909 in Poland. She was one of many generous souls to live through the war and be able to help people who weren't as lucky. Her and her husband Adam Bak found 3 people and helped them during the time of the war. Their names are Yehuda Iwler, Herman Zvi Iwler and Israel Iwler. They supplied them with the essentials they needed to get through the war alive. They supported that family in Jurowce, Poland which is a village in the administrative district of Gmina Wasilkow. Before the war began, the 3 brothers lived in a village near Sanok and were forced into the Sanok ghetto after the German occupation. The ghetto was then liquidated in 1942 and the brothers were selected for a work camp in Zaslaw. The Herman and Israel were sent to a camp in 1942 after being captured by the German and worked there for a while until they found a very sneaky way to get out and work for a farmer with Yehuda. One of the brothers, Yehuda fled to Jurowce to work at a farm and escape the harsh conditions of a concentration camp. The other 2, found a way out and resorted to hiding with Yehuda. Antonina, a woman who lived by the farm, would sneak the boys bread and other essentials to help them out while they were working for the farmer and couldn't come out from hiding. She received nothing in return but was insanely thanked for her kind efforts. The farmer under which the boys worked paid them occasionally and they were able to send Antonina some money for her kind efforts towards keeping them safe after the war was over.

After about 2 years, the Iwler brothers were liberated by the Red Army and taken to safety after the war ended. Yehuda, Herman, and Israel all kept in touch with Antonina and made an effort to keep sending her money and thank her for helping them get through those tough 2 years hidden out in a camouflaged cave fighting for their life. Antonina brought them at least 8-10 loaves of bread a week, carried them through any type of weather and snuck them into their hideout. That shows a huge sign of courage and that she is an extremely thoughtful person because if she was caught by a Nazi, not only would she be killed, but the 3 brothers and the farmer would be murdered as well. Also if they were caught, there would be a chance that other people could be caught too because they certainly weren't the only family helping protect and shelter innocent people from the Nazis. Luckily, no one was caught and the boys lived to escape the war and find another life somewhere healthier and happier.

She has inspired me greatly and she shows helping people during tough times makes the world a better place and should make you feel good about saving other lives. Learning about this has impacted my life because there are some people, in this case the Nazis, who want to cause pain and suffering among one group of people and then there are the others, people like Antonina and Adam who try to get people out of that by doing something as simple as bringing innocent Jews some bread. Some people sat around and felt pity while others chose to try and help and bring people out of this horrible time by providing food or a hideout until the war was over. The holocaust was a horrible time in history and with the help of her and thousands of others, they could help to make times just a little better for some people. Antonina was recognized for her actions by Yadvashem in 1990 as Righteous Among the Nations and hopefully will never be forgotten for saving the lives of 3 young boys trying to escape war and live their life. Hopefully this will inspire people to take the high road in tough situations like these.

WORKS CITED

"The Righteous Among the Nations." Yadvashem. N.p., n.d. Web.

"The Holocaust." Wikipedia. Wikimedia Foundation, 25 Feb. 2017. Web. 27 Feb. 2017.

United States Holocaust Memorial Museum. United States Holocaust Memorial Museum, n.d. Web. 27 Feb. 2017.

A Nanny Who Kept Her Promise

Ethan Firth

 A nanny named Gertruda Bablinska was taking care of a family named Stolowicki during the 1930's in Germany--little would they know all of their lives would be turned upside down. Gertruda was born in 1902 and was the oldest of eight children. Her father was worked at the local post office and her mother was a very helpful person to everybody in town. Gertruda's job was as a nanny for the Stolowicki family for 15 years. The family was raising two children; a daughter and son. Mr. Stolowicki was staying in France and the daughter died so there were only two family members left, mother and son. Gertruda was offered another job to work in Palestine, but she felt obligated to the

Stolowicki family and wanted to care for them. In 1939, Germany attacked Poland during World War II. Other people working for the Stolowicki's turned their backs on them, based on their religion but Gertruda didn't leave because of the Stolowicki's were Jewish. When the Stolowicki's were leaving to escape Germany, Lidia took her son Michael with them and by their side was Gertruda. They went to Vilna because they heard a rumor of an easy escape from Germany during the war. Lidia Stolowicki was scared for her life the entire time and the life of her son the entire time so Gertruda took charge of the kids and the mother to keep them safe.

When the family finally made it to Vilna, many of the other Jewish refugees were there as well in Vilna. Lidia wasn't able to take the harsh conditions much longer in Vilna because of her husband's passing. Then in 1941, Lidia died of a stroke because earlier when she heard the news of her husband dying, her heart was broken. Before her death, Lidia asked Gertruda to take Michael back to the Land of Israel where other family members were living. Then two months later Germany attacked the Soviet Union then a lot of the Jewish people started to die due after the bombing. During this whole thing, Gertruda Bablinska was staying in a small room, afraid for her life. Gertruda started to make fake birth certificates for her pretend nephews so they wouldn't get caught. She was making money to support herself by writing weekly petitions to the authorities on the happenings in Germany. In return she got eggs and poultry products to eat to survive. The Jewish people were in great danger because the Germans were doing surprise checks in some of the houses to find some people and take them to Warsaw to the ghetto, a place where all the Jewish people were collected before being sent to camps. Out of their window they could can see the ghettos, afraid what was going to happen next.

The ghetto that Gertruda was close to was the Warsaw ghetto, which was the largest one in the country. This camp lasted from April 19 to May 16, 1943. These "ghetto" camps were basically used for deporting Jews to Nazi camps or large killing areas. The ghettos usually had harsh conditions that the Jewish people had to live through like lack of food, no sanitation and limited healthcare. The German governor Gerd von Rundstedt created the ghettos. Almost half a million Jews were forced to live together in the camp, many of them losing their lives there in the camp.

Later on Gertruda saw the Jews getting rounded up to be imprisoned into the camps. When Michael was ill, Gertruda tried to avoid a non Jewish doctor just in case if the doctor reported them to the Nazi's. She kept her promise to Lidia that she was going to take her son back to Israel to be with his relatives. When Michael, the son of Lidia asked Gertruda to stay because he felt comfortable and protected with but, she said no because she had to help other people out.

For this paragraph I will be talking about the Holocaust is a word that was created to describe and this word means a destruction or slaughter on a massive scale, especially caused by fire or nuclear war. During the Holocaust in WW II, the Nazi's killed indiscriminately, including mostly looked for children because they wanted them dead because they didn't want another generation of Jewish people alive. Targeting the young accomplished this goal. So as I said they targeted children. Over 11 million people died in the Holocaust but 6 million killed were innocent children, one third of the population. Examples of the torture and killing was that the Nazi's gathered many Jews together, made them dig a big hole, shot them, and put them in a hole. Some and were buried alive as well as put in gas chambers, where countless people lost their lives. There were four very large camps Auschwitz, Birkenau, Monowitz, and Warsaw and one million died in Auschwitz alone. Prisoners went to these camps by cattle wagons with no water, Food, toilet, and ventilation causing many deaths. When they finally got to camp they were usually put in the harshest conditions. In 1933 the population of the Jewish race was about 9.5 million and then in the 1950's in Europe it was about 3.5 million people. This was a shameful part of world history that killed so many innocent people just because of their due to race and religion. It scares me to think about the future of the United States. To me this is like current day because Trump is segregating a certain race back to their country if they don't have authorization. So this is some facts, and a lady that kept her promise.

Bibliography

Ushmm.org
https://www.factretriever.com/holocaust-facts
www.yadvashem.org/righteous/stories/babilinska
www.pbs.org/wgbh/pages/frontline/shtetl/righteous/gertruda.html
https://en.wikipedia.org/wiki/Warsaw_Ghetto
https://www.merriam-webster.com/dictionary/holocaust

Resist to Exist

Ethan Pham

Genocide: the deliberate killing of a large group of people, especially those of a particular ethnic group or nation. On January 30, 1933, the Germans began their campaign to rid the world of every Jewish man, woman, and child. In this process, not only did they almost exterminate an entire religion, but also kill millions of Soviets, Serbians, and non-Jewish Polish civilians. In this time of terror, fear, and hatred, very few had the courage to risk themselves in an attempt to save the lives of their friends, neighbors, and acquaintances. Every smallest action resulted in one more life being spared. A prime example of one of these heroes is Helena Byszewska, a non-Jewish Polish civilian who risked her life to help her close friends escape the mass genocide.

Before the holocaust and Hitler's reign of terror, the Byszewska's had a steady business partnership with the Lew's (a Jewish family), which eventually evolved into a tight friendship. During the holocaust, Krystyna Lew and her family were held captive at the Warsaw ghetto. When they managed to escaped, they immediately reached out to the Byszewskas for aid and were granted safe areas to live. Helena also created a joint fund for their family, which gave them around 150 zlotys per month. Eventually, the janitor of the household became suspicious that the visitors were Jewish, so Helena developed an idea to transfer them to a convent where they could live for the rest of the war. She continued to teach them the religion of Christianity to ensure their safety, she sent them to a convent, where they remained for the rest of the war. Without the assistance from Helena and her family, The Lews were condemned to either death, or living in fear for the rest of their lives.

This example is derived from the Warsaw Ghetto, which has a unique backstory of its own. On April 19, 1943, the Warsaw ghetto uprising began after German troops and police entered the ghetto to deport its inhabitants. The officials killed or deported 300,000 Jews, transferred 265,000 Jews to the Treblinka death camp, and only granted permission to stay to 35,000 people. Outraged by Germany's actions, several underground organizations worked together to resist against the destruction of the Ghetto. Combined, these organizations had around 750 volunteers who were willing to fight. Their first attack on German forces was an ambush on a deportation of Jews from the Warsaw ghetto. With mostly homemade pistons, grenades, and rifles, the Jewish fighters liberated the prisoners. This first victory inspired the remainders of the Warsaw population to rebel too. They began to create bunkers and homemade weapons, and prepare for an uprising because they knew that they were soon going to be deported. When SS and police units entered the ghetto on April 29, 1943, the streets were deserted. Nearly all of the civilians of the ghetto had gone into hiding places or bunkers. One of the organization's commander, Mordecai Anielewicz, lead the Jewish fighters in the Warsaw ghetto uprising. Fighters surprised the Germans on the first day of fighting, forcing the German forces to retreat outside the ghetto wall. On the third day of the uprising, German police forces began burning the ghetto to the ground to force the remaining Jews out of hiding. Jewish resistance fighters made reckless attacks from their bunkers, but the Germans had power in numbers and equipment. The German forces killed Anielewicz in an attack on the command bunker on 18 Mila Street, which they captured on May 8. Although the organized military resistance was in rubble, small groups hid and fought the Germans for over a month. An estimated 7,000 Jews were killed during the battles and 631 bunkers were destroyed. The Warsaw uprising was the most symbolic rebellion in the holocaust because it inspired other rebellions such as the ones in Treblinka and Sobibor.

All of this was just a small contribution to the resistance that was spread all throughout Poland. According to Scholar Norman Davies, "the protests in Poland were more fierce than anywhere in Europe." 1.9 million polish civilians, who weren't Jewish, were killed from German violence. Also, the largest underground organizations in all of Europe were located in Poland. Their way of transportation was through the sewers, so they held their guns above their heads to protect them from getting wet. The fighters' ages were incredibly diverse, ranging from young boys to grandfathers. To stay hidden, they often stole the uniforms of Nazis to blend in or wore regular street clothes, to look as non jewish civilians. One of their primary ways to identify their allies was to have always have a red or white armband on their right hand. Whenever they were informed of an intruder, they were instructed to move their armband from the right to left arm and to shoot anyone that still has the armband on the right arm.

The holocaust was truly a test of character for all races and religions to see who had the courage and strength to stand up to injustice and risk themselves to save others. Although we cannot go back in time to save the 6+ million people who lost their lives, we can respect and honor them, and make sure that an event such as that never occurs again.

"Works Cited"

Smith, John. "Warsaw Ghetto Uprising." United States Holocaust Memorial Museum. United States Holocaust Memorial Museum, 10 Jan. 2001. Web. 27 Feb. 2017.

Valentine, Yolanda. "Polish Resistance." United States Holocaust Memorial Museum. United States Holocaust Memorial Museum, 23 June 2004. Web. 27 Feb. 2017.

Length, Tyler. ""Irek" Was His Code Name. But Most People Knew Him as Tadeusz Borowski." Underground Resistance During Holocaust. Scholastic, 2 Nov. 2009. Web. 27 Feb. 2017.

Wladyslaw Bartoszewski: Poland Hero

Evan Fukuhara

Wladyslaw Bartoszewski, a Polish man who helped many Jews, was born on February 19, 1922 in Warsaw, Poland. At the age of 17, Bartoszewski witnessed Germany attacking Warsaw in 1939. This attack made many residents defend Warsaw. The defense got Wladyslaw arrested and sent to Auschwitz in September 19, 1940. One year later he was released but this isn't the last time he'll be in prison.

Auschwitz was a concentration camp for Jews that the Nazis set up. This camp as well as other camps treated Jews horribly. Over a million Jews got killed in Auschwitz. This was the largest camp ever established by the Nazis with three smaller camps that used the Jews for forced labor. The first smaller camp was Auschwitz I, which was the main camp. The Schutzstaffel authorities (the troops Hitler used) forced the Jews to expand the camp. Within one year of their labor, the camp expanded about 15.44 square miles. This excess space was reserved for the use of the camp. Auschwitz I was made only for three reasons. The first one was to imprison alleged enemies of the Nazis. The second reason was to provide forced laborers to the Schutzstaffel for construction purposes. The last reason was to kill targeted groups that the troops decided on in order to provide the security of Nazi Germany. In addition to this, the camp had gas chambers and crematoriums. The Nazis then created the second camp which was known as Auschwitz II. This camp included sections for men and women. They also incorporated a family camp. Just like other concentration camps, Auschwitz II had killing centers which at the time was important for Germany. The camp was patrolled by Schutzstaffel troops and guard dogs. It also had electric barbed-wire fences. The final camp was Auschwitz III, which was established in October 1942. The prisoners had to work at a synthetic rubber works place, located in a small village. This camp also had a Labor Education Camp that was for non-

Jewish prisoners that were believed to have challenged German-imposed labor disciplines. All in all Auschwitz was a brutal concentration camp that was responsible for over a million deaths and harsh living conditions.

After Bartoszewski's imprisonment at Auschwitz, he did a lot of good things that helped numerous Jews. He played leading roles with the polish resistance as well as Zegota. Zegota was an underground organization in Poland that was meant to aid Jews. This organization lasted for a few years, starting from 1942 and ending in 1945. This organization was a continuation of another organization called Provisional Committee to Aid Jews, which later shut down due to political and financial problems. Zegota helped save over 4,000 Jews by providing food, medical care, money, and fake identities. In addition to playing leading roles with Zegota he played leading roles with the Polish Resistance. The Polish Resistance was Poland's response to the German occupation. The Poles started one of the largest underground movements in Europe. This movement had more than 300 widely supported groups such as political and military groups. Even though the military got the defeated, the Polish government never surrendered. This resistance group set up many underground courts with hopes of collaborating with other resistance groups. Wladyslaw worked for the freedom of the Jews. He also participated in the Warsaw uprising which was a World War II operation. Before the operation, the Germans deported or killed about 300,000 Jews so in response several Jewish underground organizations created an armed self-defense group known as the Jewish Combat Organization. After that the Schutzstaffel chief demanded a liquidation of Warsaw. When the troops came to Warsaw they saw that everyone went into hiding with only the Jewish Combat Organization out. The first day the Jews won but then on the third day the troops gathered police units to help fight the Jews. The Germans won the battle.

After the war Bartoszewski spoke out against Communism which got him thrown into jail again. While he was in jail he wrote many important historical books about the Germans in Poland and the Jews' fates. After the fall of Communism, Wladyslaw served as Poland's foreign minister twice. In later years, he was part of the International Auschwitz Council as an advisory body to the Polish prime minister. Bartoszewski was also a leader of the Polish-Jewish reconciliation which earned him great respect all over the world. In 2013 Wladyslaw Bartoszewski was given the Elie Wiesel Award. Finally he died on April 24, 2015 in Warsaw, Poland at the age of 93.

After doing this essay I learned a lot of new things. One new thing I learned about was the Warsaw Uprising which was super interesting to read about. I honestly think that it's impressive to see how the Jews rebelled against the Nazis. Another interesting thing I learned about was Zegota. This was really fun to learn about because I liked seeing how other people helped the Jews during World War II. Most importantly I really like my person and how compassionate he wass to the Jews. In conclusion this was a really fun essay to do, learning more about the Holocaust and seeing what people do.

Work Cited

https://www.jewishvirtuallibrary.org/the-379-egota

https://jfr.org/rescuer-stories/bartoszewski-wladyslaw

https://www.ushmm.org/information/press/in-memoriam/wladyslaw-bartoszewski

https://ushmm.org/learn/students/learning-materials-and-resources/poles-victims-of-the-nazi-era/polish-resistance-and-conclusions

https://www.ushmm.org/wlc/en/article.php?ModuleId=10005069

https://www.ushmm.org/wlc/en/article.php?ModuleId=10005189

https://www.ushmm.org/wlc/mobile/en/article.php?ModuleId=10005188

Heroes of Poland: Jerzy Duracz

Geoffrey Miyao

The Holocaust was a tough time for every one of the Jewish religion during World War II. Although many people sought help, few courageous people stepped up and helped other people. One of the many heroic individuals was named Jerzy Theodor Duracz. Jerzy Duracz was born on August 9, 1921 in Warsaw, Masovian Voivodeship, Poland. Warsaw, the capitol of Poland, was the second largest Jewish community before the war in the world. During the war, he was a part of the People's Guard (GL-Gwardia Ludowa), an underground armed organization. Throughout the conflict, he did things that nobody would ever dare to do. Jerzy helped carry out combat operations with Niuta Tajtelbaum that would sabotage the Germans, he aided people outside of the Warsaw ghetto, and helped fugitives on the Aryan side of the city. He was never in one place though. He was in Srodborow, Lublin, and Warsaw in Poland, and Amsdorf camp in Germany. Duracz was also in Warszawa, Poland and in the ghetto, where he did most of his rescues. In Poland, the ghetto was established in order to set the Jews away the rest of the other people. It required all Jewish citizens to move into the area so it could be sealed off from the rest of Warsaw. Nobody could go it or out without special requests because it was enclosed in a wall that was 10 feet high and topped with barbed wire. As the war progressed, the population of Jewish people in the ghetto slowly increased until it was over 400,000 total people. Because there were so many people and the ghetto was about 1.3 miles, about 7 people had to live together in the same room. Many people inside the walls of the Warsaw ghetto died because of starvation, exposure, or deadly illnesses or diseases. During the time span from 1940-1942, about 83,000 Jewish people died of starvation and disease. Also, nearly 265,000 Jews were deported to Treblinka from Warsaw and 35,000 were killed in the ghetto.

Jerzy Duracz contributed his time and efforts into helping the Jewish people. Being a part of the People's Guard was very accommodating towards his contributions. During his job, Jerzy could sneak outside of the walls of the Warsaw ghetto to look for people that were in need of saving. Although it was dangerous, it paid off. He was also able to meet and communicate with Jewish activists and in doing so; Duracz was able to become friends with them. Since he knew them, they were able to tell him if they knew anyone that needed help surviving or hiding away from the Germans. For him, the more people he was able to become friends with, the better. In April, he was involved in a destruction of a machine gun post that was firing at the Warsaw ghetto. This act not only showed bravery, it showed the Germans that some of the Jewish community was not afraid to get their hands dirty.

Besides plotting to destroy plans of the Germans, Jerzy Duracz also help people survive outside of the Warsaw ghetto. He helped and rescued about 17 people in total. Two of them were brothers named Natan and Israel Maczkowski. He encountered the two brothers outside of the walls of the ghetto during April. He convinced them to go with him instead of turning themselves in to the German troops. From there, he moved them to an apartment, where three other people, Jehuda Feldwurm and her two young daughters, were already staying, to help keep them safe. Since the Germans had padlocked every apartment outside of the ghetto to make sure nobody goes in, Jerzy put one on to make it seem like there was not anyone inside. Not only did he provide them with shelter, he also gave them food, money, provided forged documents, and updated them with what was going on in the world. His commitment was remarkably strong towards helping others. Duracz slept with the five people that he kept inside of the apartment just to make them feel better, and to get to know how they felt and see things through their perspective. His dedication is so strong that when he got shot in the leg, he came crawling back to get them what they needed. Although somebody found out that there were people being kept inside of the apartment room, it did not discourage him at all. He figured out a way to get the brothers a job as Jewish guerrilla fighters stationed at a close by forest of Parczew (Lublin viovodeship). Jerzy Duracz was determined to help other people, no matter what the cost was for him.

Jerzy Duracz was committed to creating better lives for others that were in need of assistance. From destroying deadly machine gun posts to hiding others in a secret apartment room, he was always there to lend a helping hand to anyone in need. After the war ended, he married a Jewish underground activist by the name of Ania Bailer. They migrated to Israel in 1971, where Jerzy received a hero's welcome by everyone that he saved during the war. Jerzy Teodor Duracz was a lifesaver in many different ways.

Works Cited:

Yad Vashem – The Righteous Among The Nations. N.p., n.d. Web. 26 Feb. 2017.

Yad Vashem –The Righteous Among The Nations. N.p., n.d. Web. 26 Feb. 2017.

"Duracz Jerzy."Story of Rescue - Duracz Jerzy | Polscy Sprawiedliwi. N.p., n.d. Web. 26 Feb. 2017.

"Jerzy Teodor Duracz."Geni_family_tree. N.p., 04 Nov. 2014. Web. 26 Feb. 2017.

"Warsaw."United States Holocaust Memorial Museum. United States Holocaust Memorial Museum, n.d. Web. 26 Feb. 2017.

Jerzy Poziminski

Godebo Chapman

Albert Einstein once said, "The world will not be destroyed by those who are evil, but by those who watch them without doing anything." Einstein meant that those who do nothing to prevent evil are helping the problem. Nothing can be changed without sacrifice. Jerzy Pozimiski was one of these heroes who put others' needs before his own -- even while he was a prisoner in Auschwitz. He risked his life to help, heal and encourage those struggling to survive in that prison camp. Despite the brokenness of the world during the Holocaust, Jerzy and other heroes like him stepped up and risked their lives to save others.

From 1939-1945, war and hatred were on full display across the whole world – but so were acts of bravery. Many people were killed, many joined the battle and many became heroes. This war began when 1.5 million German troops surrounded Poland's 1,750-mile. At the same time, the German air force, called Luftwaffe, along with German U-boats, attacked the Polish air field and naval forces. The leader of the Nazis, Adolf Hitler, claimed that this invasion was a defensive action, but Germany had already shown its willingness to pursue mass destruction for the sake of land in Sudetenland (1938) and Czechoslovakia (1939). Now, Britain and France declared war on Germany, beginning World War II. Hitler's plan was to conquer Poland and build a dominant Aryan race there. At a time of chaos, destruction and bigotry, the world needed heroes who would fight for others using peace and love. Jerzy Pozimiski was one of these heroes.

Jerzy, a Polish Jew, was arrested by the Nazis in April 1940 and arrived at the Auschwitz concentration camp two months later. Auschwitz consisted of three different camps: Auschwitz, the original camp; Birkenau, the concentration and extermination camp; and Monowitz, the labor camp. Jerzy was placed at Monowitz and given a job of providing food to the Nazi soldiers. Through this job, he was able to move to different parts of the camp and interact with the other prisoners, helping them as he noticed their needs. He helped those struggling to survive by distributing food, clothing, and medicine purchased with his own money. He boosted the spirits of many prisoners with his encouraging attitude. As he provided medicines to ill people, he saved many lives. He even helped families escape, risking his life in the process. When other laborers at Monowitz were assigned especially brutal or laborious jobs, Jerzy helped them with those jobs. Even though a prisoner himself, Jerzy acted bravely during this hard time and did all he could do to help the people imprisoned with him.

Many people testified later on about Jerzy's courage. One person was 16-year-old Jacob Maestro, a prisoner who benefited from Jerzy's aid. When Jacob was deported to Auschwitz from the ghetto in Thessaloniki, Jerzy made Jacob his assistant, and through Jacob he helped other prisoners. Jerzy and Jacob worked together to find the needs of the prisoners in Auschwitz and help make their lives better. A group of woman also recounted Jerzy's courage, having been given roles from Jerzy to help each of their families as well as other prisoners in Auschwitz. Both the women and Jacob were thankful of the heroism Jerzy showed towards them.

Recently, John Freund, a Holocaust survivor, came to our classroom to share his testimony. I was very surprised when I later realized that John Freund and Jerzy Pozimiski lived very similar lives. John Freund talked to our class about his childhood and family, his experience in a concentration camp, and how he rebuilt his life after the holocaust. "Life was very good when I was a child," he began. "I went to school and during my free time I would swim, skate and play with other Jewish kids in my hometown...When the Germans occupied our own country we were excluded from public school, all entertainment and swimming and skating were very restricted." Both Jerzy and John lost the comfort of their families and homes and were taken to the horrible concentration camp Auschwitz. They labored with their families and were heartbroken to see each member die right in front of them. They both escaped from this nightmare eventually but the haunting memories and wounds that were dealt to them by the Nazi stayed with them the rest of their lives. In the end John Freund's life gave me a glimpse of what life was like for Jerzy

Heroes such as Jerzy Posimiski and John Freund teach me a lot about fighting for those in need and risking your life to keep others alive. Also, the amazing experience I had of listening to and meeting a Holocaust survivor gave me a little glimpse of what the victims went through. I've learned how important it is to continue learning and sharing the Holocaust with others so they, too, can see the importance of it. Albert Einstein was right: destruction does not come from the evil ones but from those who chose not to stand up and be a hero. Jerzy Posimiski is a hero, because he chose to stand up and fight for others.

Work Cited

"Yad Vashem - Request Rejected." Yad Vashem - Request Rejected. N.p., n.d. Web. 28 Feb. 2017.

Www.auschwitz.org. "AUSCHWITZ-BIRKENAU." Polski. N.p., n.d. Web. 28 Feb. 2017.

"Germans Invade Poland." History.com. A&E Television Networks, n.d. Web. 28 Feb. 2017.

Pelagia Vogelgesang

Grace Hammond

The Holocaust, the persecution and extermination of over 6 million Jewish people in Europe by the Nazis under the leadership of Adolph Hitler, was a shocking and horrific event in the 20th century. Despite so much evil, there were righteous people who came to the aid of the Jews. Many of these honorable people happened to be strangers to the Jews but nevertheless came to their aid by sheltering and hiding them from the Nazi army. These heroes who helped the Jews to escape the Nazis put their own lives on the line because if they were caught they knew they would be executed. One such hero was

Pelagia Vogelgesang, a Polish Catholic woman and teacher who one day heard the sound of a crying child outside her window.

It is inconceivable to many people that millions of adult Jews could be rounded up and murdered in the concentration camps but it is even more unimaginable that Hitler would victimize Jewish children. Tragically, that is what happened. The German army believed most of the children were useless and just more mouths to feed. In the concentration camps, a child over the age of 12 had a better chance of surviving for a while but only because he or she might be used for medical experiments or forced to do labor. Some children endured the camps by being hidden by the Jewish prisoners. However, most children were murdered right after birth or sent to "killing centers." In general, killing centers were used for effective mass murder. These centers usually used poison gas, shooting, or asphyxiation. Almost 2,700,000 Jews were executed in this way. Lusia Farbiarz, a young Polish Jewish girl, was one of the fortunate children who was saved from this horrible fate. She and her mother lived in the Jewish Węgrow ghetto in Poland. While the Germans rounded up the Jews in their ghetto, Lusia's mother was so desperate to save her daughter from the Nazis that she left Lusia outside the home of a stranger. Fortunately for Lusia, it was the home of Pelagia Vogelgesang.

On May 1, 1943, Pelagia heard the sound of crying outside her window. She recalled, "...a kid's weeping could be heard wafting from the wall... at once I guessed that a mother had abandoned her child." Lusia was brought in to the house by Pelagia's niece and immediately came to the young child's assistance. Several weeks later, a Jewish man named Chaim Farbiarz, appeared at her door, asking for some bread. He described his relation to Lusia, explaining that her parents were murdered, and that he was the girl's uncle. Chaim would visit Pelagia's home almost every night to receive food and drinks. Eventually, neighbors in the area started getting suspicious of Chaim's visits. Pelaiga then started leaving the food outside the house for Chaim to pick up in secret. Lusia lived with the Vogelgesangs until after the war. Pelagia had Lusia attend school after the war ended since she was able to speak and recite a few rhymes. Lusia's other uncle, Henryk Farbiarz, came back from the Soviet Union in 1946. Eventually, Pelagia tried to prepare the girl emotionally before reluctantly giving her over to the uncle. After Lusia left Pelagia's home and care, she wrote, "Lusia knew very well that I wasn't her mother, but she was well aware of the fact that I saved her life and have the right to love her."

At the same time she was caring for Lusia, a miller named Klejn (first name unknown) who had also lived in Węgrow, showed up with his young child at the Vogelgesang's door. They were both weak and sick. The man and his child stayed in bed for a week until they were well again and then left. Pelagia knew that if she were caught housing Jews, it would not end well for her or them. It was common practice by the Nazis to inflict severe punishment towards anyone who was aiding Jewish people. Doing so was considered a capital offense in which the death penalty would be imposed. Therefore, it was extremely risky but courageous for the Vogelgesangs to take in the Jewish people who found themselves at their door.

In conclusion, the Holocaust was a shameful and tragic event in our modern history. Today there are still Holocaust survivors and those who aided them during the war who are willing to share their painful stories so that younger generations can learn from them. Our society has recognized those courageous people like Pelagia Vogelgesang who were brave and kind hearted enough to help the Jewish people to survive the war. At the age of 89, and two years before her death, Yad Vashem honored Pelagia Vogelgesang on March 2, 1984, as "Righteous Among the Nations" for her bravery. She and many others selflessly put themselves in danger and their righteous actions are a stark contrast to the evil that took over the Nazis. Even if it was simply feeding and housing a Jew for one night, these were courageous acts and made a difference in the lives of many who suffered.

The Holocaust is one of those significant historical events that really makes one think about good and evil and how they co-exist in the world. Personally, while learning about the horrors of the Holocaust, I hold on to hope that there are more righteous people than evil people in the world. By recognizing the heroic actions of people like Pelagia Vogelgesang, it helps to shine a light on the goodness in the world. Hopefully it inspires individuals and countries to come together and stand up for what is right and speak out against what is evil.

Works Cited

"Vogelgesang Family." Righteous Among the Nations, Yad Vashem the World Holocaust Remembrance Center, http://db.yadvashem.org/righteous/righteousName.html?language=en&itemId=4018098

Aleksiun, Natalia. "Story of Recuse— Pelagia Vogelgesang." Polin Museum of the History of Polish Jews, November 2015, https://sprawiedliwi.org.pl/en/stories-of-rescue/story-rescue-vogelgesang-pelagia

"Children During the Holocaust." Holocaust Encyclopedia, United States Holocaust Memorial Museum, https://www.ushmm.org/wlc/en/article.php?ModuleId=10005142

"Death Penalty for Aiding Jews." Timeline of Events, United States Holocaust Memorial Museum, https://www.ushmm.org/learn/timeline-of-events/1942-1945/german-poster-announces-death-penalty-for-aiding-jews

"Killing Centers: An Overview." Holocaust Encyclopedia, United States Holocaust Memorial Museum, https://www.ushmm.org/wlc/en/article.php?ModuleId=10005145

Natalia Abramowicz

Halle Short

World War II was the deadliest, most widespread war in history. Together, there were more than 50 million military and civilian deaths. It started when Adolf Hitler invaded Poland in 1939 and continued until 1945, six years later. In the midst of all this disaster, an even bigger catastrophe sprang up. The Holocaust lasted from 1941 to the end of the war in 1945, and was the biggest mass murder ever. About six million

European Jews were killed, including 1. 5 million children. It didn't matter if they practiced the religion faithfully, or if they were barely related to someone who happened to be Jewish, in Hitler's eyes, a Jew was a Jew, and they had to be killed. Anyone who helped a Jewish person or family escape or hide was punished too. The Nazi-Germans put the Jews in concentration camps, which were camps where Jewish people of all ages and backgrounds would be kept and tortured until they were killed. Sometimes they were put in gas chambers. However, sometimes the Nazi-Germans kept people alive to send postcards home and act like they are in a good place. The concentration camps were located throughout all of German-occupied Europe, as well as within Nazi-Germany and all territories controlled by its allies. Because of this, many Jews went into hiding in hopes of not being found and surviving the war, and many others offered to help.

Before the war, Weronika Kalek was a domestic worker who was employed by a Jewish man named Michael Steinlauf of Radomsko. Radomsko was a town in in the Lodz district, a part of the country Poland. Michael Steinlauf was a husband and a father. During the war, his family, which included his wife Malka Steinlauf, and their two children: nine-year-old Bajla-Sura Steinlauf and four-year-old Kalman Steinlauf, were forced to move to the local ghetto. Because she was a kind, brave person who deeply cared about the family, Weronika Kalek visited them and brought them food and supplies while they lived in the ghetto. Ghettos were marked off sections of towns where concentration camps were often located. The Nazi-Germans forced Jewish people into these ghetto areas to control the Jewish population if they didn't have enough room for all of them in the concentration camps. When the Nazi-Germans started clearing out the ghetto by sending the Jewish people living there to concentration camps or killing them, Michael Steinlauf, his wife, his two kids, his sister, and his brother-in-law escaped to the home of Nataila Abramowicz. Natalia Abramowicz was a non-Jewish woman in her mid-40s. She was born on February 10, 1887 in Poland and died on January 1, 1979 after living a long and courageous life that she dedicated to helping others. She owned the house she lived in and hid the Steinlauf family in with her brother after their parents died. Her and her family have always been friendly towards everybody. Although the Abramowicz family were Evangelical Protestants, they had always been close with those of other backgrounds. Natalia Abramowicz's brother-in-law had a company specializing in bentwood items, which he owned in partnership with two Jews. Nine years after the Steinlauf family came to live with Natalia, the Nazi-Germans began searching for Jews in hiding. Mrs. Steinlauf agreed to take the children and move with Michael's sister to another hideout in Czestochowa in fear of being caught and taken to a concentration camp. Michael and his brother-in-law stayed behind to help Natalia but planned to join the rest of the group later. However, the man who claimed he was going to house them in Czestochowa betrayed them. As a result, the entire group which included Mrs. Steinlauf, her two kids, and Weronika Kalek, who kindly guided them there, were murdered. After they were captured and killed, Nazi- Germans then raided Natalia's house and, although Michael Steinlauf and his brother-in-law escaped to Australia, Natalia was arrested for illegally housing Jews and was moved to Ravensbrück, which was a German concentration camp for women, until the end of the war.

I believe that the holocaust and the people who helped those in need have most definitely made an impact on present life today. Because people like Natalia Abramowicz so kindly and willingly helped Jews that were in need, they knew that there was some hope for human kind. If no one ever offered to help, there probably wouldn't be any Jews anymore, and if there were, then they would be treated horribly.

On July 8, 1969, Yad Vashem recognized Natalia Abramowicz as a Righteous Person because of her complete bravery and selflessness during the war. To be a hero means to risk something of yours, in her case life, to help other people without anything in it for you, and that's exactly what she did. In researching this topic, I have learned much more about what people did to others because they are a little bit different, and the sacrifices people made to help. I learned what it means to be a hero, and how one small act of kindness can make a huge impact on others.

Works Cited

"The Righteous Among The Nations." Yad Vashem. The World Holocaust Remembrance Center, 2017. Web. 05 Mar. 2017.

Aleksiun, Natalia, Dr. "Abramowicz Natalia." Story of Rescue - Abramowicz Natalia | Polscy Sprawiedliwi. Association of the Jewish Historical Institute of Poland, Jan. 2015. Web. 05 Mar. 2017.

"Introduction to the Holocaust." United States Holocaust Memorial Museum. United States Holocaust Memorial Museum, n.d. Web. 05 Mar. 2017.

Hidden in the Forest

Haydn DeBencik

Throughout life there are times when people are challenged with two different paths to take: one to the point of acting righteously and one to the point of acting out of fear. During World War II and the time of the Nazis, this was incredibly true. People were called upon to stand at a fork in the road and decide whether to help their neighbors and friends or just turn the other way. The choice was not an easy one. Standing up could mean the loss of your own life or risk the safety of your family.

This history begins in a little town of Międzyrzec, a small town in Poland that had a large Jewish community. When World War II came, it was taken over by the German Army. There were so many ways that people were treated poorly but one way was through the establishment of six separate slave-labor camps that were set up by the Nazis for about 2,000 local Jews. The Gestapo was the name given to the Nazi-German police. This police force was created by Hermann Goring in 1933. Its main purpose was to hunt out people who created threats to Nazi Germany. To the Germans, this meant the Jews. The commander of the Gestapo was Heinrich Himmler.

Abromowicz Franciszka lived in Miedzyrezc, Podlaski or Poland. During World War II she took the brave act of hiding a Jew by the name of Sender Deszel in her cellar. Sender Deszel was a Jewish townsman. Sender would have been put to death if the Gestapo found him. And the same would be the case for Abromowicz. One of Abromowicz' neighbors found out about Sender and threatened to report Abromowicz and Sender to the Gestapo. Abromowicz decided it was best to hide Sender in a nearby forest. Abromowicz risked her security and brought Sender food and drink every day until the war was over. She was a true hero for her bravery.

There isn't very much reported about the relationship between Abromowicz and Sender and why she decided to help him. Could it have been just out of the goodness of her heart? Could she truly just be a person who took the path of righteousness instead of being consumed by her fear? There are many people in Poland whom have been recognized for their assistance with helping Jewish people. They could have helped because of their past relationship. There is history between the Jews and the Polish rebels in Midezyrezc, Polaski during the Revolution of 1905. Polish people resisted German occupation and many organizations were involved with helping the Jews.

What Abromowicz did was important because while many helped there were also many who were not brave enough to do what she did. She did not ask for anything of Sender in return. There were no expectations. She simply did it as an act of human kindness. Anyone could have done what she did but many did not.

Today there are so many things in the news that remind me of this situation. People who dislike the direction of our government must be brave to stand up and express their concerns. The President's ban on travel for people coming from certain Muslim countries is exactly one of those things that comes to mind when thinking about protesting government actions. Today, many people are worried about terrorism, but to say that all the terrorists are coming from seven specific Muslim countries only creates antagonism towards people from those countries. This feels just like what happened with the Jews in Nazi Germany and Poland. People in the United States are being challenged to look past their fear and stand up for what is right. Just like Ambromowicz had to be brave and decide that she was going to help Sender in surviving against the Nazis, we need to be brave to support our Muslim friends. Many Muslims have been wrongly banned from the United States just like the Jews were wrongly persecuted.

I am inspired by Abromowicz and the others like her whom have stood for what is right. I hope that I can be as brave as Abromowicz and face my fears and maybe even risk my own life to do what she did. I hope I will have the strength to try and help protect people who are wrongly persecuted.

PEOPLE WHO MADE A DIFFERENCE

Henry Roe

Jan and Maria Domagala husband, wife lived in Zachwiejow, Padew Narodowa, Poland. They were helpful to all and nice people. And most important of all, they were holocaust survivors. Maria earned her medal in 1988 and they were identified as righteous. They would house people like kids and even two brothers named Jerma and Icek who would sneak out of the work camp they were placed in and they would go to Jan and Maria's place. Jan and Maria knew this family. Jan was also the owner of a farm and he would make food there. Jan and Maria were popular and know by lots of people. They made a difference to a lot of Jews.

The brothers mentioned in the first paragraph, Jerma and Icek were twenty and twenty five. In their family they had a sister and one brother. The sister had been shot by Germans and the other brother had passed away. Jerma and Icek were moved to a camp where they would work all day. They would leave the camp go to Jan and Maria to get food and medicine. They would arrive hungry, thirsty, and even ill. They finally left the country later in their lives and Jerma wrote them a letter to tell them that Icek had died on the way there to the U.S. He also offered to pay for their farm that they owned. He was never heard from again.

Concentration camps were a horrendous place during the holocaust. These camps are where Nazis would place innocent Jews and put them to work and eventually killed them. They would have them work in harsh conditions and lots would die from those harsh conditions. Adolf Hitler built the first concentration camp and many more were built during the war, about 40,000. Gas chambers were created too, which was where the Jews were placed inside the chambers and gas was released and they would all die. This is probably one of the worst creations ever made. This is one of the many ways 6 million Jews were wiped out. There was even a boxer who was put in a prison in Auschwitz and the prisoners were supposed to fight and he fought over 200 fights for two years but the camp was then liberated.

Adolf Hitler, the man behind the madness, the one who killed 6 million Jews, was an evil dictator who eventually killed himself after World War II. In World War 1 a soldier spared the life of a German soldier by the name of Adolf Hitler. Hitler, when he was four, was saved by a priest from drowning. These two events could have potentially stopped the Holocaust. When Hitler was kid he wanted to be a priest, surprisingly. Hitler even had a girl friend named Eva Braun. Hitler gave Britain the chance to take in refugee Jews but they declined the offer. Other countries also declined to take in refugees.

The Holocaust. Was the worst thing to happen to mankind. About 1 million children were killed during the Holocaust and about one third of Jews were killed worldwide. Japan took in a lot of refugees from the Holocaust and shut down the Nazi protests. Even the Leica camera company helped out Jews by hiring them. Today some of the worst things people do regarding the Holocaust is deny it. In some countries the denial of the holocaust is illegal especially in Germany. There was a family who was Muslim who would help Jews, they were saved by Israel and decided to convert to Judaism. Those people were like Jan and Maria Domogala. They would help Jews that were hungry and in need of medicine or warmth.

Starting in 1920 German youth was a way of propaganda. Nazis wanted to teach kids to be like Hitler so everyone else would too, it was called Hitler Youth. By 1933 the Hitler Youth had 50,000 members. By 1936 it skyrocketed into about 5 million members of the Hitler Youth. The age to be in Hitler Youth was between ten and eighteen. The program was also designed to get boys ready for the military. They had to learn how to dig trenches, they would learn how to throw grenades. The boys would learn how to shoot pistols and even how to kill someone with a bayonet. Barbed wire was used as a practice device so the boys could crawl under it. They had to learn how to read maps and how to defend themselves against gas. Lastly they had to learn how to march. Luckily Balder von Shirach shut down the whole program in 1945 near the end of the war.

The Holocaust, one of the biggest acts of genocide of all time. Something unbelievable is how Nazis would kill so many Jews and then just go home at night not feeling anything. How would they go to bed knowing they have ended adults' and children's lives. Some of them would go home to their children and families and just act like they are living a sin free life. This Holocaust destroyed many families emotionally and physically.

If more people had been like Jan and Maria Domogala so many more Jews would've been saved during this hellish time period in our history.

Biography

http://www.factslides.com/s-Holocaust
http://www.historylearningsite.co.uk/nazi-germany/hitler-youth-movement/
https://www.ushmm.org/

A Female Hero of Poland During the Nazi Occupation

Isabel Dixon (Winner)

The Nazi occupation of Poland started in September of 1939 and was the beginning of World War II in Europe. This invasion was met by Polish resistance. Sadly, it was not enough. The Germans and their Soviet allies surrounded Poland on all sides, so the Polish were unable to defend so many fronts. In addition, the Germans sent 2,000 tanks and 1,000 airplanes to shell and bomb the city of Warsaw, which soon surrendered. As a result, Britain and France, because of their Polish alliance, declared war on Germany on September 3, 1939. Although Poland never officially surrendered, Poland was soon under Nazi German and Soviet Union control with the Polish government in exile. Despite their heroic efforts, after only a few weeks, Poland fell to the Nazis. During the many hard years that were to come under Nazi occupation, the Polish people truly demonstrated heroism. Many of these heroes and their heroic actions remain unknown to the world. Yad Vashem, the memorial in Israel for the victims of the Holocaust, also memorializes non-Jewish people who risked their lives to save Jewish people during the Holocaust. The Polish people make up about a quarter of all the people recognized; 6620 people. Among the names listed, is an obscure woman named Zofia

Babinska. This is her story.

Zofia Babinska lived in Warsaw, the capital of Poland. She was a widow with two daughters named Danuta and Krystyna. They ran a bordering house as a way to make money. Under Nazi occupation, the city of Warsaw was broken up into two sides: the side for the Jewish Poles and the other side for the others, the Poles of the Aryan race. The Jewish side was called the Warsaw Ghetto and over 400,000 Jews were forced to live there. The conditions there were horrific. There was a severe shortage of food and people were crowded into homes, typically seven people per room. Due to these conditions, disease soon became wide-spread. The Germans put up poster all around the city to warn the Polish people that anyone who helped the Jews would be executed. Not only would they be killed, but their whole families would be, too. Despite knowing this, tens of thousands of non-Jewish Poles risked their lives to help their Jewish neighbors, including Zofia Babinska and her two daughters.

Zofia Babinska and her two daughters helped in many ways. They believed that saving others, regardless of their religion, was their Christian duty, which they fulfilled without any regard to the mortal danger they placed themselves in or to the financial gains they could have benefited from. Some of their fellow Poles were not as honorable. They used these desperate times to charge Jews exorbitant` prices for their own financial gain. The Babinskas used their boarding house to shelter fugitive Jews or anyone else who needed assistance. As well as offering free shelter, they also helped provide free food and offered financial loans, which they never asked for repayment. These are but a few of the people they saved.

Janina and Julian Wolman, as well as their two children Alina, later known as Pradzynska and Waclaw were saved thanks to their assistance. They also helped a former neighbor, Goldbergowa and her seven-year-old, son. Sadly, they later perished when they returned to the Warsaw Ghetto. Another woman, Hanna Landau, was also sheltered and saved by the Babinskas when they helped her get food while she was in the Warsaw Ghetto and later sheltered her in their boarding house after the liquidation of the Warsaw Ghetto. They gave them loans in the form of money in which they never required payment.

On January 18, 1943, the Germans were met with resistance when they entered the Jewish Ghetto to roundup more Jews for deportation. By this time, it was known that the Nazi's were not relocating Jews to other places, but sending them to death camps for extermination. The first attempt at armed resistance by the Jews had begun. By April, the Warsaw Ghetto Uprising had been squashed. Over 56,000 were killed on the spot or sent to death camps. After the liquidation of the Warsaw Ghetto, the Babinskas work to help Jews did not stop. For example, they took in an elderly Jewish woman named Melania Przepiorkowa who was desperately needed help. None of her prewar friends would assist her because her appearance was too obviously Jewish.

The last bit of information known about the family involves a key event on the timeline of World War II and further demonstrates the personal sacrifices that Zofia endured. Zofia's daughter, Danuta Babinska, was one of the150, 000 to 200,000 civilians killed in the Warsaw

Uprising in August to October 1944. The Warsaw Uprising was a failed attempt by the Home Army to liberate Poland from Nazi occupation. Minimal help was provided by Soviets and Allies, so the attempt failed. The Allies provided supplies sent in by The North African Air Force, the Royal Air Force, the US Army Air Force, and the Soviet Union Air Force. In addition, there was only minimal Soviet help on the ground. The failed resistance resulted in the destruction of an estimated 75% of the buildings in the city and very heavy casualties. Despite her great personal loss, Zofia continued to assist the Jewish people. After Zofia ran out of money, she sold the real estate that was left to her by her late husband and was thus able to continue to help the Jewish people.

Zofia Babinska is the epitome of a true hero. Today we hear the use of the word hero applied so readily to people. This over use of the term has made the word lose the significance it should have. According to Merriam-Webster dictionary, a hero is "one who shows great courage." Zofia Babinska and countless other Poles showed great courage during the Holocaust. They knew that helping their Jewish neighbors would not only jeopardize their lives, but the lives of their entire families. Yet still, they courageously chose to do so. The Avenue of the Righteous at Yad Vashem is a standing reminder for the world's citizens to see what true heroism is. Finally, it should inspire us to do what we can and not just be a bystander to injustice and evil.

Bibliography:

"Righteous Database." Yadvashem. The Holocaust Martyrs' and Heroes' Remembrance Authority, n.d. Web. 27 Feb. 17.

United States Holocaust Memorial Museum. "Invasion of Poland." United States Holocaust Memorial Museum. United States Holocaust Memorial Museum, n.d. Web. 27 Feb. 2017.

Wikipedia. "Warsaw Ghetto." Wikipedia. Wikimedia Foundation, 25 Feb. 2017. Web. 27 Feb. 2017.

Wikipedia. "."Warsaw Uprising." Wikipedia. Wikimedia Foundation, 25 Feb. 2017. Web. 27 Feb. 2017.

The Potato Cellar of Freedom

Isaiah Ortego

September 1, 1939 The Germans started to invade Poland. They went straight to the Polish capitol, Warsaw. The capitol city quickly surrendered on September 28, 1939 only twenty-seven days after being invaded. By October all of western Poland was controlled by the German Nazis. Many ghettos were built including one in Chelm, Poland. Isaac Perec lived in Chelm and owned a small sewing business. He was from a large, successful, Jewish family. Isaac was starting a family of his own, he had a wife named Bela and a daughter named Sara. When the Nazis came to Chelm the Perecs were forced to live in a small apartment within the Chelm ghetto along with Sara's aunt and uncle and their three children. There was never enough food to provide for all the people in that apartment. It was so hard to live off of that once, Bela tried to sell all her belongings for just two bags of flour. She was arrested but only with small charges. In 1941 Isaac heard rumors that the Nazis would start to kill the Jewish men. He escaped to Russia to try and avoid being killed. On his way to Russia a new rumor spread that not only Jewish men would be killed, but the women and children would too. He attempted to come back and save his wife and daughter but was captured and killed by the Nazis on his way. Bela was forced into salve labor and had to leave Sara and her cousins with her sister-in-law. One time the Nazis invaded their home and killed Itta and some of the children. Sara survived with two of her cousins. They would hide under the stairs when the Nazis would come to make it seem like nobody was home.

At the time of the Holocaust there weren't many people who were willing to risk their lives in order to save the people in danger. A hero is someone who decides to do what is right, even if they could get in trouble or in this situation killed. Bela was able to contact a family friend, who was a polish policeman, to help free Sara. His name was Grzegorz Czyzyk. He was able to free Sara and hide her in the grass when her mother was working in the fields or in the factory attic where Bela sometimes worked also. When he found out the people in the ghetto would start to be killed, he decided to take action and hide Bela and Sara in his house. His family didn't agree with his decision. They were scared that they would be killed by the Nazis for hiding Jews and his wife was especially scared to bring them into her home. She was so scared that when Sara's cousins came to ask if they could hide with them too, she sent them away without telling her husband. Isaac hid Sara and Bela in his chicken coop at first. Later, he decided to hide them in his potato cellar. They stayed there for the next two years and Grzegorz brought them water and food every day. On July 22, 1944 Sara was saved by the Soviets at the age of seven and a half. Grzegorz ended up getting cancer and in the last few weeks of his life his wife decided to abandon him. Bela would come out of hiding at night to help Grzegorz and care for him. Bela managed to keep her dear friend alive until two weeks after the war ended. If he were to die just two weeks earlier, Bela and Sara probably would've been found and killed. Seven months later, Bela died from pulmonary embolism in her leg. This story is very interesting because not only did Grzegorz go against what his family said, he was a policeman who was supposed to be turning Jews in and stopping people from saving Jews. He did the exact opposite of what he was supposed to do and decided to help because he knew what was right.

Sara was put into a Jewish orphanage system. She lived with many other Jewish orphans in a children's home in Darmstadt, Germany. There were about fifty children all together living in the same building which was a former castle. Sara got a proper education for the first time along with Hebrew instruction. She was going to move to Israel to live with her uncle from her mother's side of the family along with his wife. October, 1947 Sara moved to Israel at age eleven. She got married and had a daughter there. In 1971 the family moved to the United States where Sara changed her name to Sheila and became a children's nurse.

Works Cited

"POLAND." Blackfriars 25.292 (1944): 241-43. Web.

"Poland in 1945." United States Holocaust Memorial Museum. United States Holocaust Memorial Museum, n.d. Web. 26 Feb. 2017.

"START OVER Sala Perec Rests in Her Baby Carriage in Prewar Chelm." United States Holocaust Memorial Museum. United States Holocaust Memorial Museum, n.d. Web. 26 Feb. 2017.

Yadvashem.org/Righteous 2013

The Story of Irena Sendler

Jacob Eaton

 There were many heroes during World War II, but in specific one person who I thought made one of the bigger differences was a woman named Irena Sendler. Irena Sendler was born on February 12, 1910 in Otwock, Poland. Her father was a physician and her mother stayed at home. Sadly, her father died from typhus when she was only 7 years old. Since her father died so soon her mother had a hard time paying for her school. The Jewish community offered to pay for her school, but Janina (her mother) said no. She studied Polish literature at Warsaw University, but she later got suspended for three years due to protests on the treatment of Jews. During this time, Irena married Mieczysław Sendler in 1931. After this Irena pursued a job as a social worker and began to aid Jews before World War II started. WWII officially started on September 9, 1939. Of course, as the war started many Jews were being sent to the ghetto. The ghetto was a place where a certain group of people were moved into a restricted area and held in isolation. The Warsaw ghetto was a place in Poland that had about 1.3 million people, and of those people 30% were Jewish. It at the time was the second largest city in the world, and the largest Jewish area in all of Poland and Europe.

Irena started working at a zegota which was a code name to an underground organization helping Jews to get away from the ghetto. This was incredibly dangerous because anybody who was involved in saving Jewish people usually were executed along with their family. At this time, Irena was working at a ghetto for children only. She became the main leader of the underground organization in 1943. During this time period, she always wore the Star of David patch to show that she was with the Jewish people. Throughout the time, she was there she rescued a total of approximately 2,500 kids. The kids looked up to Irena, because she was able to save over 400 kids by herself and then directed others involved on what to do. She hid them in many places like orphanages, convents, schools, hospitals, and in private homes. Along with babies she often hid them in suitcases or even packages. Not only did she save them from the ghetto, but she also took more risks by taking the time to find them a safe homes. Along with everything she did, Irena also recorded who and where they were, so after World War II their parents or relatives could find them a lot easier. One day, in the fall of 1943 the gestapo came to her house. The gestapo were the secret police for the Nazi's during WWII. They knew that she had been smuggling a lot of children to safety and they went to arrest her. Luckily though, just when the gestapo arrested her she had given the list of the children (who she rescued) to her friend who hid the list in her bra. Although she was not safe the children would be at least. When they captured her they brutally beat her. In the process the gestapo broke her feet and legs, but she stayed strong and never gave any information up about any of the children she had rescued. She was then sentenced to be executed. The zegota saved Irena's life by bribing the guards moments before her execution.

After this happened, she gave herself a fake name and stayed away from the Nazi's. She surprisingly continued her involvement, helping kids escape from the ghetto. Luckily, she and her co-workers never got caught again by the gestapo. When the Warsaw uprising happened, she was a nurse and she worked at a hospital, so she hid five Jews there. She kept doing her work as a nurse until the Germans left Warsaw. Once the war was over she and her co-workers collected all the info on the children, and gave it to a colleague. Sadly, he found out that almost all of the children's parents had either gone missing or had been killed at Treblinka concentration camp. After the war, Irena was brutally interrogated by the communist secret police. She was in jail from 1948 to 1949. As a result of the interrogation, she gave birth to a premature baby named Andrzej who did not survive. Although she was released she was never recognized as a hero. But in 1965 Yad Vashem gave tribute to her as a Polish righteous among the nations. However, she couldn't travel to Israel to get the award until 1983 because Poland's communist government didn't give her permission to. Later she worked jobs at medical schools and various social programs. She was forced into early retirement for her public declarations for Israel in the Israeli-Arab war in 1967. Sendler spent the rest of her life in Warsaw until 2008 when she passed away from pneumonia. Throughout her life, she had 2 different husbands and a total of 3 children (two of the three dying in their early life). She has made a very positive influence on many people, Jews and non-Jews alike and I myself am inspired by her.

Bibliography

"Irena Sendler." Stories of Women Who Rescued Jews During the Holocaust. Yad Vashem, 2017. Web. 22 Feb. 2017.

"United States Holocaust Memorial Cite." United States Holocaust Memorial Museum. United States Holocaust Memorial Museum, 2017. Web. 22 Feb. 2017.

"Yad Vashem." The Righteous among the Nations. Yad Vashem, 2017. Web. 22 Feb. 2017.

Dr. Henryk Slawik, a True Polish

James Sarracino

Throughout the duration of World War II, many races and religions were unreasonably and savagely targeted by the Nazis of Germany. The Germans had considered this specific group, the innocent residents of Poland, inferior to themselves. In 1939, Poles received horrid treatment by Nazis who invaded their country. Innocent civilians were fired upon, and all surviving males were forced to do laborious tasks for the Germans. Political and religious leaders as well as teachers were assassinated in order to terrorize the citizens of Poland. A year later, Hitler launched AB-Aktion, a plan to eliminate all signs of leadership in their already devastated country. Other inhabitants were then deported to concentration camps such as Auschwitz and Stutthof where they would be tortured and killed. During Germany's "Germanization," a German-made form of the word conquer, of Poland, a two-month long rebellion rose from the ashes by the last existing form of Polish government. The attempt failed and over 200,000 Poles were found dead. Despite the horrid conditions of Poland and the devastation of its people, some lucky survivors assessed the deadly situation and vowed to devote their life to saving other ethnic groups targeted by the Nazis. One noble man, Dr. Henryk Slawik, made the commitment to saving as many Jews as he could from the tyrannical grasp of the Nazis and their efforts to create a perfect race during the tragic event known as the Holocaust.

The righteous Dr. Henryk Slawik was born in Poland on July 16, 1894, 45 years before the start of WWII and the tragedy it caused. As a child, he was raised under Christianity, a trait that would later aide his most prominent accomplishment. Walking along the path of life, he adapted two careers of activism and journalism simultaneously. Being an active member of the Polish socialist party, he truly felt that all should be equal in every way possible. He looked at the conditions of his people and saw that they weren't the only ones in devastation. He noticed the Jews were the prime target of the oppressive Nazis and vowed to do anything in his power to stop them from harming any more undeserving innocents. He greatly succeeded in his efforts to do as much as he could for the victimized Jews. Before his help, Itzak and Mina Brettler took care of over 100 orphans whose ages span from three to nineteen years. Noticing the devotion to their work, the Christian man of many great values made the decision to do these heroes a favor. He, alongside József Antall, started an asylum for the orphans and provided other means of escape for other refugees such as refugee camps in Mohacz and along the Romanian-Yugoslavian border. The children's facility was given a Christian facade and served as an unsuspecting hideout for the children. Slawik appointed a man named Franciek Świder to run the program and hire teachers such as Maria Tomanek and Priest Dr. Pavel Boharčík that pretended to teach Christianity but instead taught Hungarian. During the Nazi invasion on March 19, 1944, every teacher and student attended the local church to eliminate any remaining suspicion. The plan succeeded and the students and teachers were delighted they would live another day. Meanwhile, Slawik, Countess Erzsébet Szapáry, and Jan Kołłataj-Srzednicki forged documents that labelled each and every orphaned student as Christian and Aryan, two groups not targeted by the Nazis. 2 months later, Slawik and Antall's creation become a Polish educational institute that would serve to help many more to come. Three months after his great accomplishment, Dr. Henryk Slawik met with a terrible fate. He was captured by Hungarians and arrested as a prisoner of war. Refusing to give up the locations of hidden refugees, he was inhumanely tortured and left this world on the 25th of August, 1944. His legacy inspired a man named Zvi Zimmerman to publish a book featuring his trials and tribulations in 2004 called I Have Survived, I Remember, I Am a Witness. He is also compared to the Swedish Raoul Wallenberg, another hero with a similar story. In 1944, Wallenberg saved 100,000 Jews in concentration camps from Hitler's "Final Solution" and was arrested the next year. Nevertheless, Slawik went to great lengths to save such a large sum of people and shall be remembered by those who see his amazing effort and success.

Few people today can say that they were born humble and died righteous. This gem of a man, Dr. Henryk Slawik, shall leave an astounding taste in the mouths of those seeking heroes who deserve their title. Every single bit of effort he made to save so many people shall not go unnoticed. The great lengths this hero reached to provide a working system of saving the lives of innocent adults and children are amazing. Not only did he leave his legacy, but his creation itself, the children's facility, left its own imprint on the country of Poland. Those attending this now educational facility must never disrespect what it had done to save hundreds of children from their demise. Dr. Henryk Slawik truly deserves his wonderful title of being righteous among the nations, especially his own.

Works Cited

Schwartz, Terese Pencak. Holocaust Forgotten. Yad Vashem. 2009-2012. January 13, 2017.

United States Holocaust Memorial Museum. United States Holocaust Memorial Museum. n.d. February 22, 2017.

Yad Vashem. The World Holocaust Remembrance Center. 2017. January 13, 2017.

Risks Make Heroes

Jane Gregory

"The council to aid Jews" or "Konrad Żegota Committee," was a secret underground organization in Poland formed to save the Jews during the Holocaust. The Holocaust began in 1933 and was aimed to wipe out the Jews in order for the Germans to create a large and overruling country. The Germans always had a hatred for the Jews, who they believed were an inferior race. The Germans believed Jews and several other groups were responsible for submitting Germans to illness. Zofia Kossak- Szczucka founded Żegota in 1942 as a resistance writer. Kossak-Szczucka was shocked and distraught when she heard about the terrible things that had been happening to the Jews. After targeting the "inferiors", killing hundreds of thousands of people, and the ongoing threats the Germans made for many years, she found a way to help protect the Jews in Poland with her sidekick Ferdynand Marek Arczynski. Żegota was made up of political activists from all over the world and was connected to many camps and ghettos used to reach out for support. The members of Żegota worked together to help provide food, clothes, medical care, and shelter to thousands of Jewish families. Żegota was constantly on the search for new hideouts and refuges to keep it a secret. Many volunteer advocates were willing to take the risk of being caught for others, in order to save them from the Holocaust.

Ferdynand Marek Arczynski was a very important Polish activist during the Holocaust. Ferdynand was born December 8, 1900 in Krakow, Poland. In his early life, he was a veteran of the Silesian Uprising. At the age of 42, he became the Treasurer of Żegota as well as a member of the Polish Democratic party. He worked with both groups from 1942 until 1945, when the Holocaust rescuing configuration closed. While a member of Żegota, Ferdynand was head of the legalization department and communicator of several local branches in Warsaw, Poland. Ferdynand worked his hardest to cover all aspects a savior would by donating many supplies, staying up late to organize papers and spending as many hours as possible comforting and conversing with the Jews. Many Jews owe their lives to Ferdynand because of the risks he took for them and their families. While employed at the Legalization Department, he produced hundreds of fake identities, certificates, and business cards on a daily basis to assist Jews. By doing this, he risked his own safety and saved numerous lives from the Germans. Aside from that, he also aided the Jews at the concentration camps. By talking to them and offering free fake identities, he made the Jews feel welcome and wanted, as they should. Underground, Ferdynand solely dedicated his life to the Jewish countrymen that he helped and knew the best. Ferdynand became close friends with many Jews he met in the camps and underground in Żegota. Ferdynand continued to assist, comfort, hide and cure the Holocaust survivors who came in and left. Two years after World War II ended, Ferdynand Arczynski served as a member of the parliament and worked as a journalist until 1952.

The years 1942 to 1945 were some of the hardest years throughout history that most people tried to avoid. With the sound of gunshots in the air, yelling for help, and the sight of many dead bodies, no Jew - or anyone who opposed Nazi Germany - wanted to step out of the house fearing the risk that they might get shot or be taken into a gas chamber. Ferdynand was one who chose to step outside and be different, make a change in the world that clearly had a bend in it. By taking charge, he inspired many others to volunteer, donate and make a difference in such a bad period in time. He made it clear that by becoming the treasurer of Żegota and a member of the Polish Democratic Party, he was dedicated and ready to make a change in the world. Even as a young adult, Ferdynand acted selflessly as though he was more interested in others wishes and worries than his own. He decided to take on the career of a veteran in the war before he took the big role of a treasurer in Żegota. He helped save hundreds of the six million innocent people that were killed during the Holocaust just by helping them find a place to sleep at night - without having to worry that there is a bomb outside or a group of Nazis standing at their door. Ferdynand was a good example of the saying, "Doing the right thing isn't always the easiest." It's true because he could have chosen to sit inside his house all day and ignore the problem; but instead he choose to face the problem head on to make a change in the world. With no risk there is no hero. He took the risk that many others would not dare to, not even approach, Ferdynand Marek Arczynski is a true hero that dedicated his life to thousands of others that he believed deserved it more than himself. He was one that was recognized under Righteous Among the Nations at Yad Vashem in 1965.

Bibliography

Ushmm.org
Sfi.usc.edu
Sprawiedliwil.org.pl
Db.yadvashem.org
Research.omicsgroup.org
www.history.com

Not All Heroes Wear Capes

Jennifer Goi

When hearing the word "hero", most imagine a person with a cape and super powers. Another thing that comes to mind is modern technology and protecting people from the evil that is trying to take over. Although not all heroes wear capes and have unique power and has the latest gadgets, they all have one thing in common. Heroes came way back during World War II when the oppressed needed them the most. One of these super-beings is Aniela Barylak, a woman from Poland, who helped save and protect a young Jewish girl from the Nazis. From 1941-1951, Aniela hid a Jewish person in her house even though she knew her, her family, and the person she was hiding would be killed if the Nazis found out. This brave savior was recognized as a righteous person by Yad Vashem - The World's Holocaust Remembrance Center on July 16th, 2007 for her bravery and willingness to help the oppressed. Aniela Barylak truly is a hero for protect those in need during this time period.

First of all, a big base of Jewish oppression was set when Adolf Hitler was announced chancellor of the Nazi state in 1933. Nobody was guaranteed basic rights, for he ran a dictatorship. He destroyed an entire republic established during World War I. He continued to create concentration camps for groups who were considered "dangerous" such as homosexuals and Jehovah's Witnesses. He targeted Jews starting by setting 400 orders and regulations that interfered with both public and private lives of German Jews. Germany and its allies started to conquer, and they ended up invading most of Europe. In 1939, the Nazis invaded Poland and started oppressing Jews in that area as well. They took away the Jewish property, made them wear identifying armbands, and forced them to go into restricted and isolated areas called ghettoes, concentration camps, and forced-labor camps. When put into these camps, their fate was often death, for none of these camps were in

494

good shape. People died from starvation and disease from the lack of food and nutrition and the cleanliness of these areas. Nazis also moved Jewish people in gas chambers and held arrest and shooting raids in neighborhoods with people of this decent. They deported millions of people out of Germany and the countries surrounding it. By 1945, over six million Jewish people were killed out of the nine million that stood in 1933.

Aneila Barylak lived in Nadworna, Poland, during World War II. She had a husband named Jan Barylak, a two-year-old named Boleslaw Andrzej, and a baby named Teresa. During 1941, an eight-year-old girl named Jafa Kurz survived a raid the Nazis did in Nadworna where half of the Jewish population in this town was killed. Aneila saw the little child, and as a mother herself, she couldn't leave her behind. She brought Jafa into her home and decided to hide her. Jafa's family was deported from Hungary, Germany, to Kamieniec Podolski, Ukraine. They fled to Nadworna where Aneila and her family lived. When the Nazis did their raid, Jafa was the only one left in her family and was soon saved by Aniela.

Aniela family helped take care of Jafa with the support of her immediate family. They hid her in their house and the young girl was taken care of just as if Aniela was her own mother. However, her in-laws, the Schmidts, were anti-Semitic Volksdeutsche and disapproved Jafa being hid in the house. To prevent the Schmidts from turning in Aniela, the Barylak's made fake documents to show she was from Nardworna, and they called the young girl Sefania. Aniela also baptized the eight-year-old to appease her in-laws, and this helped satisfy them. They still made threats to call the police, but Aniela was able to keep Jafa safe in the house.

After the major part of liberation during this time, the Barylak's and Jafa moved to Wroclaw in 1951 so that the now eighteen-year-old can finish her studies. She soon started a family that includes a husband and children. They decided to move to Israel three years later. Aniela died on April 8, 1974, and before her death, she told her daughter, Teresa, to keep in touch with Jafa to make sure she stayed safe. Aniela truly cared for the eight-year-year-old from beginning to the end.

If Aniela had turned a blind eye towards Jafa, the young child would have been forced into the ghetto established that following winter after the raid. The next summer in 1942, hundreds of the people living in that ghetto were sent to the Belzec death camp. As they arrived and came off the train, the camp workers ordered them to hand over all of their possessions, including clothing, at the reception center. They were forced to run naked through a narrow path. This path connected the reception center to the gas chamber which were labeled "showers" to deceit the Jewish people into continuing through the tunnel. Once all of the people from the train was inside of the gas chamber, they secured the doors shut and filled the room with carbon monoxide. The outside of the buildings and the reception station was bordered with barbed wire fencing and trees so that passerby's won't suspect anything. This way nobody would see hundreds of people die because of the oppression.

Jafa could have easily been an unlucky victim of the horrific gas chamber if Aniela didn't save her like a hero. Without her, the little girl would not have received an education, nor would she have been able to create a family of her own. Aniela's hero-like mindset to save those from evil led to one more success rather than one more person dead. Jafa turned into a woman who escaped from prosecution just because someone had the heroism to save a little girl without a family. Aniela truly was a savior for the eight-year-old girl who received a safe place to live, food, water, and an education.

Overall, Aniela Barylak was an amazing person who took in a little girl she knew nothing about when the Jewish were being oppressed. Even though she knew the risk of being killed if Jafa was found, she still hid her and provided for her until the eight-year-old grew up and moved to Israel with the family she developed. Without her savior, Jafa would have died in a ghetto from starvation or disease or have been gassed in the Belzec death camp. Aniela cared for the young girl since the day she saw her until the day she died. She provided Jafa with everything she wouldn't have had if the hero wasn't there to save her. Aniela truly shows that not all heroes wear capes.

Works Cited

Ideo Sp. Z O.o. - Www.ideo.pl. "The "Righteous among Nations" Have Been Awarded."The "Righteous among Nations" Have Been Awarded | News | Science & Scholarship in Poland. Science and Scholarship in Poland, 21 Oct. 2010. Web. 25 Feb. 2017.

Sotkowitz, David, and Ada Green. "The Shoah in Nadworna." Shoah - Nadworna. Jewish Gen Kehila Links, 2005. Web. 25 Feb. 2017.

United States Holocaust Memorial Museum. "Belzec." United States Holocaust Memorial Museum. United States Holocaust Memorial Museum, n.d. Web. 25 Feb. 2017.

United States Holocaust Memorial Museum. "Ghettos." United States Holocaust Memorial Museum. United States Holocaust Memorial Museum, n.d. Web. 25 Feb. 2017.

United States Holocaust Memorial Musuem. "Timeline of Events." United States Holocaust Memorial Museum. United States Holocaust Memorial Museum, n.d. Web. 25 Feb. 2017.

Yad Vashem. "The Righteous Among Nations." Yad Vashem. Yad Vashem, n.d. Web. 25 Feb. 2017.

Balwierz

Joseph Marques

Józef Balwierz is recognized as a heroic person according to "righteous among the nations" in yadvashem. One of those reasons why he is considered heroic is because of what he did during the time of World War 2, he saw that Liebeskind the family he used to work for before they were taken to the ghetto in 1941, and had managed to escape it a whole year later. Balwierz immediately reached out to the family to care and shelter for them the best he could. While the situation worsened, he went to Austria to go to work with the Liebeskind family. After the war had ended Józef had married the daughter of Shmuel Liebeskind.Irena.

When Józef worked for the Liebeskind's he worked in their brick factory. This factory was owned by Wehrmacht, which was unified armed forces. The ghettos were set up to segregate Jews from the rest of the population. Some ghettos lasted only a week or a day, but some also lasted a couple months or years, so they were meant to be temporary. There were three types of ghettos, opened, closed, and destructive ghettos which all had a different purpose. They also had horrible habitats and living styles. Many people died of disease, starvation, or were killed by soldiers. These places were key parts in the Nazi process of separating, persecuting, and destroying Jews.

He also helped their cousin Elka Bardach who had escaped from Lwów and she wanted to leave so she boarded a train to Krakow. She never actually reached Krakow though she got off in Prokocim. When she got off she went looking for Balwierz. She stayed with him until she could find a job in Krakow. So those are two examples why Józef Balwierz is considered "righteous among the nations".

What is a hero? A hero is a person who is honored for their courage and What makes a person heroic is their actions. Balwierz's actions were very heroic because he thought it was the human duty to do what he did. The greater the risk, the greater the heroism, his risk was that he housed Jews that were looking to be prosecuted by the soldiers. Józef didn't have to house his old employers, but his generosity told him that he had to save these three women Zofia Balwierz, Irena Balwierz, and Rita Balwierz.

Józef didn't only stay in one place he stayed in two different places to be a hideout person which was his rescue mode for the Jews that escaped the ghetto and needed somewhere to stay. The first place he stayed at was Krakow which was in Poland the German armed forces took over this place in 1939. Also during this year, the Germans had required all the Jews and people from Poland to do forced labor which was basically humiliation for everyone because they had to do it off what the soldiers gave them, and most of the tools wasn't the kind they needed to complete a task. They also didn't have correct clothing, treatment, or conditions. Towards the end of that year it was required for Jews to wear a white armband with blue stars of David. In 1942, the year the Liebeskind's escaped the ghetto is when they Germans built a killing center which they called "Belzec".

The next place he stayed was Prokocim. This was also in Poland, in Prokocim they made their Jews wear striped pajamas that were white and blue. There is not much information on Prokocim but Józef housed Elka the girls' cousins because she never secured a job over in Krakow, so when she got off the train she went straight to Józef's house so that she wouldn't be put in a concentration camp or be noticed that she escaped the ghetto that same year.

After he took Irena's hand in marriage after the war, they moved around, first back to their home...Poland then later they moved all the way to South America in the country of Brazil. He was later asked about why he was determined to do those actions during the war, and he said "it was merely my human duty" and he didn't expect any type of reward or praise from anyone, because it was his act of bravery and courage to do what he did.

Józef Balwierz was recognized righteous among the nation according to yadvashem in 2007 because of his hiding technique. This had a lot of connections for me, especially the part were the people in Prokocim wear striped pajamas because of the book I read "The

Boy in Striped Pajamas". The boy Shmuel was in a concentration camp and wore white and blue striped pajamas so the soldiers knew who the Jews and Non-Jews were. He always came and told the other boy how bad they were treated and how the soldiers talked to them, which is connected to the ghettos because they both had horrible habitats and living styles. They both also didn't eat a lot some even died of starvation, to conclude Józef Balwierz was a righteous man according to us and the nations.

Work Cited:

"The Righteous Among The Nations." The Righteous Among The Nations. N.p., n.d. Web. 27 Feb. 2017.

"Prokocim." United States Holocaust Memorial Museum. United States Holocaust Memorial Museum, n.d. Web. 27 Feb. 2017.

"Krakow." United States Holocaust Memorial Museum. United States Holocaust Memorial Museum, n.d. Web. 27 Feb. 2017.

"Lwow Factory." United States Holocaust Memorial Museum. United States Holocaust Memorial Museum, n.d. Web. 27 Feb. 2017.

"Ghettos." United States Holocaust Memorial Museum. United States Holocaust Memorial Museum, n.d. Web. 27 Feb. 2017.

The Act of Seeing

Julia Heckey

"When you first come across it, you look but you don't see, you listen but you don't hear, your mind closes down... They were beyond having a voice," said Rockie Blunt, an infantryman, U.S. Army. Thousands of people are gone now, they are dead. People watched as others got shot, taken, criticized. These people were their neighbors, they would see each other at the grocery store, see them with their kids around town. Now they were getting dragged into camps, where they would die. They would not come back to the town, people would no longer live near them, see them around town, playing with their children. Many people watched this cycle happen, their chin dropped in awe. They stared even, wondering how such a thing could happen. However, did they see?

The act of seeing was for a certain kind. Someone who could be named a hero, someone capable of committing an act that was able to save a life, whether it was now or in the future.

The Jews' chances were very slim. Most were too weak to escape the camps, they had been to close to death. They had smelt it. If they made it out of the camps they were likely to be recognized due to the language barrier and their strong accent, not to mention difference in religious customs and physical appearances. Walking through town would be like a whale swimming with a school of fish. It was for this reason that escaping was so hard. If a Jew was to escape they would then be followed with the struggle of finding a compassionate person willing to house them and give them food and shelter. They would have to find someone who had truly seen what was going on. Someone who had received the rare gift of understanding the present and the future, the before and the after, of the Holocaust. They would have to be willing to risk their life for another person. Someone found guilty for helping a Jew escape or for even housing one could be charged with the death penalty.

In 1939, Poland was taken over in nearly a week. France followed and was attacked on May 10, 1940 causing it to collapse just six weeks later. Two countries with strong and fearless armies had been defeated, demonstrating just how powerful the German army had been. Throughout World War ll not many Jews survived the "Final Solution" which was Nazi Germany's attempt to wipe out Europe's Jewish population. By 1944, nearly half a million Jews had already been taken to Auschwitz. Many of the Jews that had been taken to camps had only heard rumors and whispers of what was happening in the death camps, some didn't believe that such a terrorizing and bone chilling event was becoming their reality. Once they reached Auschwitz some were forced to write postcards to loved ones with messages such as "Arrived safely. I am well." After these messages were written they would most likely be sent to the gas chamber.

Few people were motivated enough to help Jews. Most locals were living in harsh conditions themselves. Those who did have the privilege of helping Jews were most likely inspired by their disagreement with Nazi racism, compassion and thoughtfulness, or by moral goodness. I say "privilege" of helping Jews because it truly is a privilege to me. To be able to reach out to others, to risk your life to save another is inspiring, heroic, and something to admirer.

A hero to me is an individual who understands that someone needs to make a change, that someone need to stand up despite the fact that everyone is sitting down. Someone who doesn't just recognize the problem but knows how to be involved in the act of solving it.

Franciszka Abramowicz was not only able to see that someone was in need of a savior but she was able to be a savior. She took Sender Dyszel into her home that was located in Miedzyrzec Podlaski, she saved him from shootings that were occurring in their town. He hid in her cellar until the neighbors threatened to tell the occupation authorities about him being their. His only option then was to flee to the nearby forest. Franciszka was still kind enough to bring him food until he was able to return to her cellar. Finally, in 1947, Sender was able to leave Poland and go to Argentina.

Looking then seeing, listening then hearing, is the act of a true savior, of a hero. A gift that only some choose to embrace. The strongest, most powerful, meaningful, fulfilling gift out there. It is a present that everyone receives and some choose to open. Everyone was watching the shootings that occurred along the streets of people's home towns. Everyone listened to the gunshots that were guilty of taking people's lives. Yet only some were able to commit the terrorizing act of seeing the sight that was laid down in front of them, only some were able to bring themselves to hear what was happening outside their locked door. But those who did, were able to become heroes. Franciszka Abramowicz was able to save a life after committing a heroic deed.

Work Cited

"Abramowicz Franciszka." Story of Rescue - Abramowicz Franciszka | Polscy Sprawiedliwi. N.p., n.d. Web. 27 Feb. 2017.

"Jewish Population of Europe in 1933: Population Data by Country." United States Holocaust Memorial Museum. United States Holocaust Memorial Museum, n.d. Web. 27 Feb. 2017.

"Rescue." United States Holocaust Memorial Museum. United States Holocaust Memorial Museum, n.d. Web. 27 Feb. 2017.

"Rescue and Resistance." United States Holocaust Memorial Museum. United States Holocaust Memorial Museum, n.d. Web. 27 Feb. 2017.

"Saving Jews: Polish Righteous." Saving Jews: Polish Righteous. N.p., n.d. Web. 27 Feb. 2017.

Holocaust Essay

Kaley Poon

What if one was living in a world of terror? In a place where every move someone made had an effect on one thing or another. Children were taken away from their parents, sobbing and screaming just so that they would able to stay with the ones they love most. Families were separated all for one thing to happen. The Holocaust. The Holocaust was led by a man named Adolf Hitler and he was the one who was in charge of the mass murder of a lot of the population of 6 million Jewish individuals. It took place in the years of 1933 through 1945. There were concentration camps where the Jewish men, women and children were held and kept until they were killed. Others hid in hiding places some could never even imagine. Adolf had the idea that the Jews were an inferior group of people and would take away from the purity and community of the Germans. All of this took place in Poland, Germany during World War II. The group of people who took part in the murder were called Nazis and Adolf Hitler was their leader. This affected many people, but not only Jewish, also people of other races and religions, like Maria Dabrowska.

Maria was born on October 6, 1889 in Russow, Poland. She was a housewife for her husband and they got married in 1911. She was a writer and novelist, also an author of historical dramas. In 1907 through 1914 she studied science, sociology and economics at the University of Lausanne and Brussels. For a little while Maria also lived in London as a scholar at the Association of Cooperatives. She temporarily worked at Polish Ministry of Agriculture, venturing more into newspaper reporting and public life. In 1927 she became more involved in writing about human rights. When Maria would read novels, newspapers and watch plays, she would analyze the psychological consequences of the hardship and life traumas for the everyday citizen. She was a very scholarly woman and enjoyed her educational experiences. Maria was interested in both literature and politics, devoting herself to help those born into poverty. She passed away on May 19, 1965 in Warsaw, Poland. In her time when she was not involved in educational opportunities she was living her life with an innocent Jewish girl who was involved in the suffering and misery of the Holocaust. Maria and her husband were the ones to take her in.

The couple was the keepers of Genia Zeifert. Her family and herself were kept in the ghettos but in 1943 of December she was able to escape. Genia eventually came across the Dabrowska's home that looked inviting. She found a man outside with a dog and they seemed quite friendly. After many rejections of not letting her stay with other families because they already had too many people they were housing for, Maria and her husband welcomed her and let her stay there. In the months off her hiding with them, she was kept behind a double wall in one room where the family usually kept their money, jewelry and all their expensive belongings. They were considered wealthy at the time and were worried they might get robbed, so they thought what better place to hide the young girl. During the night when everything was locked up and the windows were closed, Genia would come out to have dinner with the couple where they socialized and became almost a family of their own. Seven long months later, the Russians arrived and Genia was liberated. When she soon found out that all of her family members had passed away she decided to stay with the people who rescued her, Maria and Marian Dabrowska. She had already built a bond between the couple but it became even stronger, they treated her as if she was a daughter of their own.

Maria Dabrowska was a scholar, writer and a hero. A hero is one who is courageous, bold and tough. Maria knew that when taking this young girl in, they could get caught and the same thing that happened to the Jewish population could happen to them because they were taking this one risk. They knew the consequences but they needed to do something if they thought it was wrong, and they did. In the time Maria was not learning she saved a young girls life. Her and her husband were two ordinary citizens doing their own thing, living their life. But when something big happens like the Holocaust they knew that they needed to do something to help. The couple did not need to take in Genia but when they realized the small impact that they could make, they chose to save and be heroes. They did not regret the decisions they made and Genia loved the couple as if they were her own parents. Maria Dabrowska was considered a savior and one who took part in the Holocaust. Although she only saved one life she still she made a big impact for that one girl, Maria was the one who Genia looked up to, her very own role model.

Works Cited

The Editors of Encyclopædia Britannica. "Maria Dabrowska." Encyclopædia Britannica. Encyclopædia Britannica, Inc., 26 Apr. 2002. Web. 27 Feb. 2017.

Koziol, Paul. "Maria Dąbrowska | Twórca." Culture.pl. N.p., Dec.-Jan. 2009. Web. 27 Feb. 2017.

"The Righteous Among Nations." Yad Vashem - Request Rejected. N.p., n.d. Web. 27 Feb. 2017.

The Life of Hanna Jozefa Grudzinska and Wojciech Grudzinski

Kamania Griffin

When considering what it means to be a hero or someone who stands up for others, there are many things that come to mind. Will you be the person who stands up in the face of danger when it means saving your friend or your neighbor? Will you be a person who turns the other way and pretends that nothing is happening because it doesn't affect you? These were some of the questions that ran through people's minds in Poland during WWII.

"The Holocaust, also referred to as the Shoah, was a genocide in which some six million European Jews were killed by Adolf Hitler's Nazi Germany, and the World War II collaborators with the Nazi (Wikipedia.com).". The Holocaust was a mass murder in which over 6 million European Jews were killed by a Nazi army led by Adolph Hitler. Over 6 million people were killed because Hitler felt that there needed to be an ethnic cleansing of the Jewish faith. When Hitler was trying to dispose of Jewish people he realized that he needed people to help him carry out his plans, so he used propaganda to help enlarge his army to help him. "Propaganda is the dissemination of information to influence or control large groups of people. In totalitarian regimes like Nazi Germany, propaganda plays a significant role in consolidating power in the hands of the controlling party (ushmm)." In 1933, he created a ministry named Reich Ministry of Public Enlightenment and Propaganda (RMVP). This ministry gave him and his companions a strong control over the German culture. One of his heads of the ministry, Joseph Goebbels went out and propagandized people in Nazi ideology. The way the Nazi's felt about things were put into almost every newspaper, radio broadcast, and film. These messages were made to mobilize the German people to support all Nazi military and social efforts, including the deportation of Jews and others to concentration camps. Hitler saw that some people thought this was wrong and were trying to hide the Jews from the Nazis, he proclaimed that anyone trying to hide the Jews or help them will be killed or sent to the concentration camps with the Jews.

Concentration camps are the camps where they sent people to hold them and do work. Although it is also the place where they decided to put Jews in gas chambers or kill them other ways. There were about over 40,000 concentration camps that the nazis and their allies had put into place. A few of them were named Auschwitz, Belzec, and Chelmno. Auschwitz is the most commonly known camp. It was also the largest. Although the Nazis and their allies were very threatening and scary to some people, quite a few people helped saved the lives of many people.

Hanna Jozefa Grudzinska and her son Wojciech were just a couple of those amazing people who decided to put their life and the lives of their family at risk by helping the people being persecuted. They were both recognized by Yad Vashem on March 23, 1971. They lived in Blohie, Blohie, Warszawa. Hanna parented Wojciech on her own . At first she was a little neglecting at the thought of housing 5 Jewish people, but her aunt persuaded her into housing one more family. Hanna was a very caring person. She showed this trait by having her son give some his earnings from his work to the families that they are housing. This shows that she was caring because she was in extreme poverty. Her story shows that any efforts can make big differences in people's circumstances.

"The 20th century taught us how far unbridled evil can and will go when the world fails to confront it. It is time that we heed the lessons of the 20th century and stand up to these murderers. It is time that we end genocide in the 21st century." (Allyson Schwartz) In today's age, people are able to look back at the stories of people in the time of the holocaust and relate the events back to the things happening in today's government. Some examples that might seem

similar to people are the travel ban on certain things countries that President Trump put in order, multiple protest happening for different reasons, the revoking of protection for transgender children, and the plans for a wall to keep out "immigrants" that our president feels are harming the country. Many people are standing up to our government today. People of all ages are speaking their minds and not letting the people who run our country do what they want. I wonder sometimes what if people had done peaceful protest or stood up for what was right during the deportation of Jews if the holocaust would have even went as far as it did or had even taken place. The stories of all the amazing survivors have many lessons that can be taught to us as a country today so that we can make sure horrific events aren't able to occur again. Some people are afraid that the current events show signs of history repeating itself. Although if today's people are able to take, learn, and make anything of the stories like Hanna and Wojciech Grudzinska us as a people will be much stronger and united against things that try to separate the country.

Righteous Saviors: Krystyna Adolph

Kylea Tanner

A hero is someone who risks or sacrifices themselves to help out or save someone or something else. There are countless heroes people that deserve recognition and to be honored for how they helped Jewish people during the Holocaust (the holocaust is when people of the Jewish religion were being killed because of Adolf Hitler), but one that stood out to me is Krystyna Adolf. She was a teacher at Czartoryski High School in Vilna, but she lived on a small farm near Troki and what was considered the Jewish ghetto. Krystyna was already going out of her way to get all the way from her village to Vilna. During these times all teachers were forced to join the Nazi Party. They brainwashed them to follow their policy that shows they are prejudiced against Jews. They were forced to forget about their previous political beliefs, and to make matters worse if they refused to do what they were told they were "retired" from their jobs. Some teachers felt the need to come to school dressed in Nazi uniforms just to show their loyalty. Krystyna Adolf did not let any of this affect her conscience and what she knew was right. So, when the war started she gave an invitation for two Jewish twins, Monika and Lidia Gluskin, to come stay with her at her farm.

Krystyna Adolf helped these girls out in countless ways, but the highlights of her story were giving them a good life, keeping them alive, providing them with fake identities, and saving their mom. She was not like most people who helped by letting Jews live with them, she did not have them trapped in a basement somewhere just feeding them to keep them alive. These two twin girls had a regular life at her house, but since they were there for three years Krystyna did put them to work. They would help her out around the house by taking care of animals, chopping firewood, and help tend the vegetable garden and fields. Because these twins, Monika and Lidia, weren't somewhere locked in a basement, hidden so no one could see them, Krystyna had to introduce them to people with fake identities. She was telling her neighbors that they fled from forced labor. Her sister and mother in laws were the only people that knew the Gluskin sisters real identities. Her sister in law provided Lidia and Monika Gluskin with forged papers, she also provided the twins mother with false identity papers, which were able to get her out of the Jewish ghetto and help her survive. Even though Krystyna was fully aware she was risking her life by sheltering the twins she did not care because if they survived she would know that she was able to help someone instead of being apart of the group of people that say this does not involve me, so I have got nothing to do with it. What made her even more admiring is that a family in a neighboring village was caught sheltering a Jewish family and their house was burned down, even this did not make Krystyna rethink her decision to shelter Monika and Lidia.

Creating forged papers was very common at this time, especially for people who were in a similar situation as Krystyna Adolph and the Gluskin twins were. People would use a black metal October 1944 typewriter to make the papers that were needed, which were papers with a fake identity on it. The persons name, age, and birthday were required to be listed. You may wonder why the people could not tell the difference. This is because there were companies that provided fake stamps that assured that the papers were real. One company in particular that was known for this was a dental company from south France. This stamp was made by Gilbert Leidervarger as a sign of resistance and it was his way of contributing to help the Jewish religion/ people. The stamp from this company only lasted from 1942 to 1944, but it was a great and smart way to help out the Jewish people.

The twins, Monika and Lidia, are very grateful for what Krystyna has done for them. At one of the Holocaust memorials they spoke and voiced that they felt bad because they did not know if there was anything they could do to pay her back or show how thankful they were for her help. This Catholic woman risked her life and safety to do what was right instead of just trying to save herself she did that for herself and a whole other family. Krystyna Adolph used her own connections and resources to help save these two girls. She housed them, gave them fake identities, helped their mother escape the Jewish ghetto, and much more. Not only did she provide for these girls and their mother but every single one of them escaped without being killed by the Nazi. She did not attempt to save this family she did save the family, and that is why we recognize her today as one of the numerous righteous saviors.

Helena Barchanowska

Lilian Valencich

 When harsh times accrue, true character is tested. Those who use any possible power they have to help others is what makes a person heroic. Helena Barchanowska takes risks to help a man in need during this era of suffering, World War II. Her perseverance through these difficult times is what is admired about her. Even today with the hatred spreading towards different groups, it is people like her who show resistance towards ruling tyrants.

Helena Barchanowska's courageousness and kind actions are what make her a Polish hero. Brezing, a small town near Lodz, Poland, was where she was born. Her passion for a career in math lead her to graduate from the University of Warsaw, from the department of mathematics. She continued this profession as a math teacher in the cities of Dabrowa, Górnicza, Gorlice, Gostynin, Sandomierz, Sosnowiec, and Warsaw. During this time, she raised two daughters, Janina in 1929, and Zofia (Inka) earlier in 1926. Before the war, Ludwika Labendzianla and Oskar Gleicher (who were both Jewish) were her closest companions. She would later visit Ludwika in the Warsaw ghetto, which in Europe was the largest Jewish Ghetto. This ghastly place forced Jewish residents in nearby areas to live in a 1.3 square mile, 10 feet high wall-in enclosement. With as much as 7 people per room who were all starving, Helena went to see this pain for her friend. She even later tried to persuade Labendzianka to let her hide him in her home, but he refused. Also in Gorlice, Poland, she was part of a group that was made to help Jewish refugees from the Third Reich. The Third Reich, "Means 'third regime or empire,' the Nazi designation of Germany and its regime from 1933-45," according to A Teacher's Guide to the Holocaust, definitions. The Third Reich era was a time in which Adolf Hitler "ruled" over Germany. Helena was involved to help others against such groups in a committee in the beginning of the war, showing the start of her involvement of aiding Jewish people. During the war, Germans were arresting and mistreating educated Polish people and in 1940 in the spring, one of those people was Helena. She was able to return to Gorlice after being set free and decided that it would be wise to move to a small farm called Mory in Golabki. There she was able to arrange hiding places for Jews and helped get fake documents for them. These times were very difficult and she was able to earn money by teaching classes at Warsaw in secret while maintaining a garden with fresh produce to save money. Helena met a Jewish man named Michal Krynski while part of underground work. Before the war, he was a principal at a Jewish school in Warsaw, but originally he was a chemist, and graduated from the Technological Institute in Petersburg. He luckily was able to escape the Warsaw ghetto but his wife and daughters died there. While he was in the ghetto he was able to organize secret lessons for secondary school students. He was able to stay in Helena's house between 1943 in October and January of 1945 and was able to stay with the fake name of Jan Majewski. He taught physics, chemistry, and English to Helena's daughter in Warsaw with secret classes, despite the risk of being caught. Later it became even more difficult to hid him with the many random house checks that the Germans would conduct. But Helena was able to hide him under the kitchen in the basement. Also, at one point Helena was able to temporarily keep Jews and other fleeing refugees in her house before finding them a better place to hide. With these risks taken by Helena, there is no surprise that she is a Polish hero.

After the war, Krynski was set free from many years of hiding from the Nazis and was able to start his own life. He married Stefania Spincel and adopted Ewa Rayzacher, who was born in 1928 in Lviv, Ukraine. His connection with Helena and her children stayed strong even when he moved to Sopot, Poland, where he continued his previous passion as an educator. His wife, Ewa, and him were both very grateful for her generous act. Barchanowska was recounted by Ewa as, "One of the unsung heroes of the Nazi occupation in Poland who helped save Jews from extermination." Helena was later recognized for her acts of heroism and after she died received the Righteous Among the Nations Title by Yad Vashem Institute in 1993. Her daughters were the ones who asked them saying, "She always said that you need to help the suffering and the weak without expecting any recognition or reward. If she were alive, she would probably say that announcing the service she had rendered to Jews was embarrassing and unacceptable." This modestly shows one of the many aspects of her heroism.

With evil thriving back in Work War II, it is people like Helena Barchanowska who can fight this hatred with compassion and kindness. Her generosity of helping those who are less fortunate not only saved an innocent man's life, but gave hope to others in the future to do the same. She could have looked away and left for a safer situation, but she risked her family's, as well as her life, to save another. Overall, Helena was an incredible woman, who is marked as one of Poland's most treasured heroes in WWII.

Work Cited:
"Story of Resue." Sprawled Kiwi. Nov. 2015. 2015. Https://sprawiedliwi.org.pl/en/stories-of-rescue/storyrescue-barchanowska-helena
"A teacher's guide to the Holocaust." Definition of Ghettos. https://fcit.usf.edu/holocaust/DEFN/ghettos.htm
"A teacher guide to the Holocaust." Definition of Third Reich. http://fcit.usf.edu/holocaust/DEFN/third.htm
"Warsaw."Ushmm.https://www.ushmm.org/wlc/mobile/en/article.php?ModuleId=1 0005069

A Hidden Hero

Lilly Toby

"A hero is someone who steps up when everyone else backs down." There are hundreds of heroes to remember from the holocaust and two of those are Maria Sitko and her daughter Wanda Sitko. There are many unknown heroes that we need to remember. The heroes from Poland risked themselves to help other Jewish fugitives. Maria Sitko and her daughter opened their home to five Jewish refugees and saved them from having to suffer like the millions that did. The Sitkos lived in Sosnowiec, Poland. After the ghetto in the Srodula neighborhood in Sosnowiec was liquidated the Sitkos didn't have running water or indoor conveniences. The Sitkos were very generous and offered all that they could to the five refugees that they housed. They hid the refugees even when the Gestapo searched their home hoping to find hidden Jews. The Sitkos showed extreme courage by helping the five refugees survive this dreadful time.

The year 1933 was the beginning of a horrible time period, the Holocaust. It began when Adolf Hitler was appointed Chancellor of Germany by President Hindenburg. A few months after Hitler was appointed, the first Nazi concentration camp opened in Dachau, a small village near Munich. Auschwitz was the largest concentration camp of its kind and was broken into three smaller camps; a prison camp, an extermination camp and a slave labor camp. It was located 37 miles west of Krakow. Rudolf Hoss built and ran Auschwitz. He was so attached to the camp that he created, that he lived with his wife and four children in a house that was just yards from the crematorium. Prisoners were treated inhumanly at Auschwitz. They were fed 300 grams of black bread and 25 grams of sausage which made them malnourished. They slept in brick barracks with up to ten people in each bed. The only bedding that they had was either straw or paper mattresses. The barracks were originally built to house forty prisoners but 700 were placed in each one. The prisoners slept with their belongings, if any, so that the other inmates wouldn't steal them. To make conditions worse the barracks at Auschwitz were not heated in the winter which made it miserable to even sleep. When Auschwitz first opened the prisoners weren't even allowed to shower themselves because they didn't have access to any water. The prisoners at Auschwitz were treated more like animals than humans by the Nazis. In fact one of the camps functioned as a killing center for a period of time. The mission of Auschwitz was to exterminate the entire population of Jews that entered its walls. Many people were saved from this horrible place but many more were killed.

On January 17, 1945 a death march of over 50,000 prisoners began at Auschwitz. This death march was from Auschwitz to Loslau and was the largest death march out of 59 death marches. So that more prisoners would die, the Nazis made the death marches take place in the dead of winter. In previous death marches not even half of the prisoners that started survived until the end. The Nazis forced the prisoners to walk until they couldn't walk any more. If someone couldn't walk any longer they would shoot them. Thousands of prisoners died during the march due to overexposure, starvation or exhaustion. The death march was very hard to escape since there were always guards watching. It was more likely that a prisoner died then escaping a death march. Two fortunate prisoners named Frymeta Feder and Felicja Feder escaped the nightmare walk. Maria Sitko welcomed the two refugees into her house so that they wouldn't have to struggle out in the open and have to worry about the Nazis. Maria didn't only have room for the two refugees but she housed three more. Leon Weintraub, Jerzy Feder and Nechemia Mandelbaum had escaped from the Warsaw ghetto in 1943 and also made their way to her household. Maria went out of her way to help some of the fugitives that stayed under the kitchen floor in a specially prepared hideout and others stayed in a roomette. These five refugees were hidden at the Sitko' until the liberation in 1945.

Learning about the holocaust has changed my life. Before I had even read anything I had heard rumors about how many millions of people had died. This information stunned me because I didn't think that any human could have so much hatred against one group of people. When I read that 1.1 million people were killed just at Auschwitz I can't even imagine treating other human beings so horribly. The Holocaust was filled with dreadful events that many people, including myself, wish did not occur. Reading about the holocaust has made me more appreciative for my life and what I have. I used to think that the Holocaust wasn't a big deal until I actually learned about it. When I learned what had actually happened it was the worst thing that I had ever heard of. Learning about the holocaust has broadened my knowledge of what humans actually have the gut to do. The holocaust is a time that should never be forgotten. I will never forget what happened during the Holocaust and I hope that a time like 1933-1945 will never happen again. Overall learning about the Holocaust changed my life and how I think.

Bibliography

"Auschwitz-Birkenau: Living Conditions, Labor & Executions." Living Conditions, Labor & Executions at Auschwitz-Birkenau. N.p., n.d. Web. 27 Feb. 2017.

"Auschwitz: The Camp of Death." Holocaust Teacher Resource Center. N.p., n.d. Web. 27 Feb. 2017.

"Introduction to the Holocaust." United States Holocaust Memorial Museum. United States Holocaust Memorial Museum, n.d. Web. 27 Feb. 2017.

Rees, Laurence. "BBC - History - World Wars: Rudolf Höss - Commandant of Auschwitz."BBC News. BBC, n.d. Web. 27 Feb. 2017.

"The History Place - Holocaust Timeline." The History Place - Holocaust Timeline. N.p., n.d. Web. 27 Feb. 2017.

"The Righteous Among the Nations." The Righteous Among the Nations. N.p., n.d. Web. 27 Feb. 2017.

Gertruda Babilinska: A Hero Among Us

Madison Bennett-Wells (Winner)

The Holocaust. A terrible time period where six million Jews were persecuted because the Nazis believed they were "racially inferior" and a threat to the German community. Not only were Jews targeted, but many other groups including Jehovah Witnesses, the disabled, homosexuals, communists, and socialists. "In the year of 1933, around nine million Jewish people were living in Germany, but just twelve years later, two out of three Jews were alive." (ash.com) Jewish people were banned from many activities and were treated horribly by the Nazis. They were put into concentration camps and ghettos to work and then be murdered. When the Holocaust ended in 1945, survivors were put into displaced persons camps until they were re-homed. Adolf Hitler and some of his Nazis committed suicide before they could be captured, but those who didn't were put into jail for life. Some people that knew about the Holocaust did everything they could to help the people on the other side of the gates. They risked everything to do the right thing, and one of the most selfless of them all was Gertruda Babilinska who tried her best to save people from becoming the next to die in a gas chamber.

Gertruda Babilinska was born in 1902 in the city of Starograd, Poland as the oldest child of eight. Her father worked as a post-office worker making just enough money to raise his growing family. At just nineteen years of age, Gertruda started working as a nanny in Poland. The first family she worked for moved away, but Gertruda decided to stay. She then became a nanny for the Stolowicki's, a rich Jewish family who lived in a mansion in Poland. Mr. and Mrs. Stolowicki had a daughter whom Gertruda looked after while her parents were at work. Sadly, the girl died at a young age because she was very ill, so Gertruda decided to stay with the family to take care of Lidia Stolowicki, Mr. Stolowicki's wife, who was grieving after the loss of her child. In the year of 1936, the Stolowicki's had another child, a son named Michael. Gertruda looked after Michael for many years to come, through thick and thin, almost like he was her own son. Gertruda was the Stolowicki's most loyal worker when disaster struck. Mr. Stolowicki was on a job trip in Paris when the Germans attacked Poland and ever since then, he never was able to reunite with his family. Michael's father ended up remarrying a non-Jewish woman who recommended that they move to Italy in order to protect him. Mr. Stolowicki and his new wife were found and sent to Auschwitz. "They immediately put my father in the gas chamber and burned him in the oven," Michael said." (al.com) All of the Stolowicki's workers left the family after the tragedy except for one, Gertruda. When Lidia and Michael decided to move away, she moved with them, knowing they needed all the help they could get. They all fled to Vilna, Poland where thousands of Jews lived. Vilna was a city run by the Soviet Forces until June 22, 1941, when the Germans attacked and took over. The Germans created two ghettos and killed 40,000 Jews in just seven months. Gertruda, Lidia, and Michael stayed in Vilna by renting out a small apartment. In April of 1941, Lidia couldn't handle the harsh conditions and ended up passing away from a stroke.

Michael and Gertruda stayed in Vilna where raids from the Germans were common, so Gertruda received false papers and a baptismal certificate, and adopted Michael to be her son. She cleaned houses for a living and wrote petitions to the authorities for locals in exchange for milk, eggs, dairy products, and poultry. Before Lidia died, she asked Gertruda to keep a promise to bring Michael to the Land of Israel where he could grow up for the rest of his life. Gertruda did just that, and in 1947, they were off on a boat. Michael and Gertruda were sent back when War ships turned the boat around, forcing all Jews to return to Poland. They didn't reach The Land of Israel until 1948 by a boat called the "Exodus". Gertruda realized that her life was going to be completely different from that point on because she was a Catholic woman raising a Jewish boy, but she never stopped taking care of him. Lidia explained that there were relatives of Michael that lived there to take care of them, so Gertruda and Michael went to their house to live. Gertruda had a small bedroom upstairs with no water or toilet, while Michael had a nice bedroom downstairs. She became a maid in Israel to pay for Michael's school and her own room which she lived in for 18 years. When Michael grew older, he got a job arranging tours, and in 1975, the tour company had him move to Miami, Florida. Michael now lives in New York and visits Israel to see Gertruda, who also visits the US to see her son. Gertruda went through thick and thin to raise a Jewish boy as a Catholic woman, but in the end, she ended up saving a young innocent boy who is still alive to this day. "Late in her life, Gertruda went to stay in a nursing home in northern Israel for Christians who saved Jews. There is an alley of 22,000 trees, dedicated to Christians who saved Jews, at Yad Vashem, the Holocaust memorial in Israel. Since 1962, Gertruda's name has been on a plaque on Tree No. 7," Michael said." (al.com)

From the interview that Michael Stolowicki had with children from an Alabama school, I realized that risking your life can change a lot for someone else. Gertruda endangered her life in order to save an innocent kid who would have never been able to tell his story to hundreds of other people if it wasn't for an amazing woman who put herself in danger. I learned that people who are this selfless receive wonderful things in return like when Gertruda Babilinska was recognized as Righteous Among the Nations on June 4th, 1963.

Works Cited

Ggarrison@al.com, Greg Garrison |. "Catholic Nanny Saved Jewish Boy from the Holocaust: Students Hear the Story First-hand." AL.com. N.p., 08 Apr. 2013. Web. 15 Feb. 2017.

History.com Staff. "The Holocaust." History.com. A&E Television Networks, 2009. Web. 01 Feb. 2017.

"Introduction to the Holocaust." United States Holocaust Memorial Museum. United States Holocaust Memorial Museum, n.d. Web. 15 Feb. 2017.

"Righteous Among the Nation." Yad Vashem. N.p., n.d. Web. 17 Feb. 2017.

"Virtual Shtetl - Http://www.sztetl.org.pl/." Flickr. Yahoo!, n.d. Web. 28 Feb. 2017.

A Hero of the Holocaust

Maggie Downs

There are many definitions of a hero. Some heros wear capes, other heros are our mentors, teachers, parents, and some heros risk their lives to save others. When the Holocaust began in 1933, people's characters were put to the test. The Holocaust was a massacre in which about six million European Jewish Citizens were killed by Adolf Hitler's Nazi Germany. Adolf Hitler was a cruel and selfish leader who lead over Germany, promoting ideas that led many to believe the Jews were poisoning our world. Some people hid during this horrible time, turned their backs on the problem, or just ignored it all together, but there were others who wanted to help those who had fallen. Most of those people today are known as the Righteous People Among the Nations. This list of selfless people includes influential individuals such as Oskar Schindler, Irene Sandler, and Jan Karski.

Jan Kozielelwski was born on June 24, 1914 in Łódź, Poland, a city in Central Poland, and raised by a Roman Catholic family where he grew up with six other brothers, Marian Kozielewski, Boguslaw Kozielewski, Edmund Kozielewski, Uzef Kozielewski, Stefan Kozielewski, and Cyjarian Kozielewskiand, one sister, Laura Kozielewska. After Jan finished attending Lviv University, he joined the Polish diplomatic service, but soon after joining the diplomatic service, he joined the Polish army to fight a newly outbroken war that had started in September 1939. Unfortunately, during the war currently known as World War II, Karski was captured by the Red Army, the army of the previous Soviet Union, formed after the revolution of 1917, and sent to a detention camp that was located in what now is known as Ukraine. Karski then escaped from the camp and returned to German-occupied Poland where he joined the anti-nazi resistance.

Karski became a useful messenger for the resistance due to his incredible photographic memory and his understanding of geography and different foreign languages. He carried valuable and secret information between the resistance and the Polish government. Jan Karski continued to work as the courier until late 1940, where he was abducted by the Gestapo and was barbarically tortured. The Gestapo is a secret police league under control of the Nazis. Karski began to worry that during his torture he would give into a moment of weakness and reveal important secrets from the resistance, so he decided to slit his own wrists, hoping that by his death his torturers would not be able to obtain any information that could be used against him. Before Jan was completely successful in taking his own life, he was found in his cell and was immediately sent to a hospital, where he began to make his recovery.

During his recovery in late 1942, the underground (the resistance) managed to smuggle him out of the hospital, and transported Karski in and out of the Warsaw ghetto and a transit camp located in Izbica. In the camp he witnessed first-hand the suffrage that the Jewish people endured under Nazi control. This horrible treatment included many barbaric punishments, such as mass starvation and dehydration, and the gas chambers, a large room that filled with deadly gasses used to kill many people at a time, mostly women and children, elders, or those who were too sick to work. Disgusted by the terrible things he had witnessed, Karski made his way to London, where he delivered a report to the Polish government and senior British authorities. He informed them of what he saw was happening inside the Nazi camps, and warned them of the Nazis plans to slaughter all of the European Jewish citizens. In the July of 1943, Jan Karski made his to Washington and met with Franklin D. Roosevelt, the American President, to deliver the same warning and once again, plead his case to call for action, but his warning was met with the same disbelief. Disheartened, Karski decided to stay in America, where he earned his PhD from Georgetown University's School of Foreign Science after refusing to return to Poland.

Jan Karski, although haunted by the Holocaust, managed to make a life for himself in America. While he was in Washington, Karski promoted Polish freedom and remained a college professor, at Georgetown University. He also got married to a woman named Pola Nirenska, and they had remained married until Pola passed away in 1992. Jan Karski was also recognized as "Righteous Among the Nations" by Yad Vashem, and was awarded Presidential Medal of Freedom, awarded to him in December 2011, and the Wallenberg Medal. He had also written a number of books about his life and experiences, like his books A Secret State, Great Powers & Poland 1919-1945, and Great Powers and Poland, The: from Versailes to Yalta. After a long, eventful life, Jan Karski ended up passing away on July 13, 2000, in Washington D.C.

WORK CITED

"Our Mission." Welcome · Jan Karski Educational Foundation. N.p., 13 Feb. 2017. Web. 27 Feb. 2017.

"The Righteous Among The Nations." The Righteous Among The Nations. N.p., n.d. Web. 27 Feb. 2017.

A Righteous Pole Named Stefan Jagodzinski

Marcus Yamamoto

During the Holocaust, under Adolf Hitler's rule, the Germans persecuted multiple groups of people but the group mainly targeted were the Jews. When the Germans invaded Poland they took control over everything that the Poles owned and made ghettos for Jews specifically to live. The Germans treated everyone poorly because they starved people, overworked them in concentration camps, and made them struggle to stay alive. Over six million Jews died during the Holocaust and millions of other people died as a result of their religion, resisting the German rule and other various reasons. That is the short background of what was happening in Poland during World War II.

Since Stary Korczyn was near Krakow this is some background information on what kind of conditions Stefan Jagodzinski lived near. The first recorded existence of Jews living in Krakow was from the early thirteenth century. In 1931 55,515 Krakow citizens recognized themselves as Jews and the day before the war the amount of Jews living in Krakow was about 56,000 of a 250,000 population. By 1939 the population of Jews in Krakow was about 70,000. Within the first week of September 1939 when the Germans invaded Poland they split the country into three parts with the central third being made into the Generalgouvernement which was divided into four districts: Krakow (Cracow), Warsaw, Radom, and Lublin. Krakow served as the administrative center and after the Germans attacked the Soviet Union in 1941 they added Eastern Galicia to the Generalgouvernement and it added three million to four million people to the population. The head of the Generalgouvernement was Hans Frank, but he could not just do what he wanted because the racial policies were carried out by the ss and the police. The Germans treated Poles horribly, killing 50-100 Poles if a Polish underground killed a German, arresting school staff members, and taking their food and leaving them to starve. In late 1939 Jews were put in ghettos where they were isolated and in 1942 the Jews were beginning to be sent to extermination camps in the Lublin district. By 1944 all ghettos in the Generalgouvernement had been liquidated and by 1945 the Generalgouvernement was completely liberated by Soviet troops. That is the background and history of Krakow, Poland during the Holocaust.

Stefan Jagodzinski was an activist in the polish underground that lived in Stary Korczyn near Krakow and was wanted by the Gestapo. He helped save Dr. Bronislaw Tenenwurzer's son, Emanuel and also his wife and daughter. He mainly helped in saving Emanuel because after the liquidation of the Miechow ghetto Dr. Bronislaw sent his son to a Polish acquaintance. This Polish acquaintance then arranged for Emanuel to stay with Stefan Jagodzinski. As local inhabitants discovered Emanuel being Jewish they fled to a new place. Although they fled to somewhere new rumors had spread about Emanuel so they decided to go to Krakow. Emanuel was smuggled into Hungary and was liberated by the Red Army in 1945. He helped Emanuels mother and sister by giving them aryan documents. Although he tried to help Dr. Bronislaw with forged documents it ended up with him getting caught and shot to death in the Plaszow camp.

Since Stefan helped save Jews using fake documents there must be have been an importance of documents. Documents were very important during the Holocaust because Jews could escape to other countries to escape German persecution. Documents could be the decision between life and death because to pass into a different country you needed a visa, an endorsement and a signature on a passport from a consular official. Even if Jews hadn't gotten permanent residence in another country they were allowed to leave german occupied territory. To get a transit visa Jews had to provide written testimonies from past employers or from well respected people in the community confirming their good behavior and papers listing personal assets so that the country's consulates could determine if they were to be a financial burden. Even if the Jews got a visa they would still require confirmation of German authorities to leave. In 1938 Swiss officials started requiring German and Austrian Jews' passports to be stamped with a J and to be denied access. In 1939 the start of World War II lowered the chance of getting a visa even more because the consulates closed down or reduced staff and immigration policy became even tighter. In 1941 Germany banned all Jewish emigration, but they could still be saved by either forged documents or protective papers from other countries. That is why documents were so important during the Holocaust.

In conclusion the history of the Holocaust is very extensive and very interesting. Some of the events and importances included were the documents and the making of ghettos. The importance of documents is shown when Jews had to show their visa to pass to other countries and when other countries granted them protective papers. Even when they had forged papers it could save them from death. The making of ghettos was an important event because it contributed to the Germans having more control and if they didn't make them they could have wiped out more people than they did. That is why the history of the Holocaust and the people that saved Jews are important.

Works Cited:

United States Holocaust Memorial Museum. "The Holocaust and World War II: Timeline." United States Holocaust Memorial Museum. United States Holocaust Memorial Museum, n.d. Web. 28 Feb. 2017.

Fromowitz, Dan. "Importance of Documents." Importance of Documents : Center for Holocaust & Genocide Studies : University of Minnesota. University Of Minnesota, n.d. Web. 28 Feb. 2017.

United States Holocaust Memorial Museum. "Krakow (Cracow)." United States Holocaust Memorial Museum. United States Holocaust Memorial Museum, n.d. Web. 28 Feb. 2017.

Yad Vashem. Generalgouvernement. Breslau: Hirt, 1941. Yad Vashem. Yad Vashem. Web. 28 Feb. 2017.

Yad Vashem. "Stefan Jagodzinski." Yadvashe. N.p., n.d. Web. 28 Feb. 2017.

United States Holocaust Memorial Museum. "Documenting Numbers of Victims of the Holocaust and Nazi Persecution." United States Holocaust Memorial Museum. United States Holocaust Memorial Museum, n.d. Web. 28 Feb. 2017.

Compassion Within

Mason Oto

Courage alone does not make a hero. So what characteristic do heroes have within them that stands out? The answer is compassion. There are many characteristics of heroes, but the main one is that they all have some type of compassion within them. Doing research on this essay, I found that there were many heroes that helped the Jews during the Holocaust. All of them were from different countries throughout Europe. They knew what the Nazis were doing was not right, and those who had compassion within them helped the Jews and others. I found out that these heroes were just ordinary people ranging from adults to children that helped the Jews in some kind of way. Many of us have not heard of them at all, or even learned about them in school but I was fortunate that I got to learn about them while doing research on this essay. I could not believe how many of these heroes tried to save the Jews during this terrible time when they knew that helping them in any way was against the law and potentially could have them killed, but they still risked their lives. It's what heroes do, right? I learned that the different heroes acted in a variety of ways in their attempt to "save people," including letting them stay in their homes, giving them food, and some of them even helped them escape by making fake IDs just to name a few.

The hero that I chose and wanted to learn more about was Franciszek Antczak. As I was researching, I found that not only did he help the Jews, but his family helped them as well. It was a true family affair. During the occupation of the Nazis in Poland, Franciszek helped harbor two Jewish men, Mojzesz Kuperman and Josek Lewin. The two men had escaped from the Syszogrod Ghetto and needed a place to hide out. They went to Franciszek and asked for help. Franciszek did a heroic act by taking the two men to his sister, Zophia's farm in the nearby village of Nacpolsk. Even though Franciszek and Zophia knew that helping the two Jews would be putting their lives at risk, their compassion towards the two Jews made them want to help them. They knew it was the right thing to do. It's important to recognize that not everyone would make this type of decision. Franciszek and Kazimierz, who was Zophia's oldest son, dug a large hole in the barn where they camouflaged it so that the Mojzesz and Josek could live in there. The hole was so big that its size was almost of an actual room. There they had a couch and their personal belongings that they fled with. Mojzesz and Josek stayed in the hole during the day and only came out in the evening when the family invited them to eat. Franciszek and Zophia did not expect anything from the two men. Since both of them could not work and they wanted to help the Antczak family, they assisted them with anything that they were capable of doing around the house and on the farm. Sometimes they helped the family by illegally slaughtering animals for food. They were very grateful that the Antczak family was doing this heroic act for them that they gave Zophia's daughter, Jadwiga some of their belongings so that she could sell them to get money for the family to buy food.

In March 1944 Mojzesz, went out of hiding during the day to go visit a friend who lived the nearby town of Wyszogrod. On his way home, Mojzesz was followed by a Nazi policeman and captured. He was interrogated and tortured until he eventually revealed to the Nazi where he was hiding. The Nazis then raided Zophia's house and arrested Zophia, Franciszek, Kazimierz, and Josek. They were all captured and tried for helping Jews. Zophia was sentenced to 3 years in Frauenzuchthaus und Sicherungsanstalt, a women's prison camp in Fordon near Bydgoszcz. Kazimierz was sent to prison in Plock and Franciszek was sent to a prison in Plock and then transferred to the Stutthof concentration camp. Zophia survived the women's prison camp and returned home to her family, Kazimierz ended up receiving a death sentence and was shot to death, Franciszek eventually died in the concentration camp because he never returned home, and Josek fled from the Nazis and managed to successfully escape their wrath. He hid until the Holocaust was over, and after the war ended, he moved to the United States. Even though he moved to the United States, he still sent letters to Zophia's family.

Without the help of these compassionate heroes many Jews would have even suffered greater losses and some did. Because of these compassionate heroes from Poland, there were survivors who were able to tell their stories of the Holocaust. These stories are not the ones that are typically taught in schools but the real stories that people went through and experienced. Researching and learning about the Jews made me understand a piece of history. Even though it was a sad part, it made me want to learn more about what people went through and how they survived such a horrible time period. Also, it made me open my eyes that just because people are different we should not treat others in this manner like the Nazis did. With everything going on this world, I hope that leaders of different nations do not make the same mistakes like the Nazis did to the Jews and that they learn from this historical event.

Works Cited

"Ghettos in Poland." United States Holocaust Memorial Museum. United States Holocaust Memorial Museum, n.d. Web. 28 Dec. 2016.
< https://www.ushmm.org/outreach/en/article.php?ModuleId=10007706 >.

"The Righteous Among The Nations." Yad Vashem The World Holocaust Remembrance Center. Yad Vashem, n.d. Web. 20 Dec. 2016.
< http://db.yadvashem.org/righteous/righteousName.html?language=en&itemId=441032 4 >.

"The Szkop Family." Story of Rescue - The Szkop Family | Polscy Sprawiedliwi. Martyna Gradzka-Rejak, Sept. 2015. Web. 28 Dec. 2016.
< https://sprawiedliwi.org.pl/en/stories-of-rescue/story-rescue-szkop-family >.

"The Szkop Family." Yad Vashem The World Holocaust Remembrance Center. Yad Vashem, n.d. Web. 20 Dec. 2016.
< http://db.yadvashem.org/righteous/family.html?language=en&itemId=4410324 >.

Franciszka Abramowicz

Mateo De Hoyos

The Holocaust happened in the 1930's. The Holocaust was a very bad time because the Germans took all the Jewish people to concentration camps, because Hitler wanted to exterminate all Jewish people because he didn't like them. A lot of people tried helping the Jewish people because they didn't think what Hitler was doing was right. Franciscka Abramowitz was a brave person who hid a Jewish person. Risking her life, she was eager to do it because she wanted to save the Jew's lives. Everyday she brought food to the Jewish person that was in the forest she was helping. A lot of people helped save the Jews. Everyone who helped hide them from the Germans was very very brave.

The impact this person had on my life was very heart warming because she risked her life to save a Jewish person. To me I think she is very brave because I would want to do it but I wouldn't want to risk my life like she did. This affected a lot of people because it was very sad that six million Jewish boys and girls died and 4 million survived.

I understand that the Holocaust was a very bad time because the Germans killed millions of Jews all around the world. The Holocaust was a time in the 1930's where Adolf Hitler was killing all the Jews. The impact it had on everybody was very bad, because it was a very bad time when it was happening. The Holocaust was hurting a lot of people around the world including Jews, but it hurt the Germans more than it did to anyone. It hurt them more because they were losing respect from people around the world because what Hitler was doing was very bad. I also understand that the Germans made the Jews shave their heads and were forced to lose their loved ones. I now know that six million Jews died and four million Jews lived.

"NEVER AGAIN." I don't ever want this to happen again because it was a very bad time. If this ever does happen again we don't know who will be attacked and that is very bad. I don't ever want this to happen again because I don't want my family and everyone to get hurt and lose loved ones. I don't think anybody wants this to ever happen again because it will end with World War III. After the Holocaust we fought against the Germans for the Jews because they also didn't think what Hitler was doing was right. "NEVER AGAIN" is what we should be saying everyday we talk about the Holocaust because it was very emotional time for everyone. It is very sad that six million Jews died and the ones who lived were forever changed. I am very sorry for everyone who witnessed that.

You can easily prevent this by not being rude to anyone because just one little screw up could mess up the whole world. If that one little thing can screw up the world imagine what would happen if everybody made one silly mistake. If Hitler didn't do that then none of this would be happening and no Jews would've been harmed and the Germans would be liked a little more.

I love how a lot of people in Poland tried to help the Jewish people trying to hide from the Germans. There are over 6,000 people in Poland who tried to help the Jewish people in Poland. Out of all the people I looked through I took Franciszka Abramowicz's story to write an essay on because it was interesting.

A Hero of the Holocaust

Maya Milliken

Imagine that your parents just got taken away to be murdered. Imagine being in fear twenty four-seven that you will be the next victim. Imagine having to hide in dark small spaces with little to no food just for survival. Imagine relying on a complete stranger to keep you and your family safe. This was a reality for nearly nine million Jews and other non-German races, six million of them not surviving through the war. The Nazis, and their partners, who came in power of Germany in January, 1933, felt that the Germans were the superior race. In 1933, the first concentration camps were established, imprisoning its political opponents, homosexuals, Jehovah's Witnesses, and others seen as "dangerous." Then they began to target any Jewish people and people of disabilities. They were sent to concentration camp complexes to be killed. One of the most well-known camps was called Auschwitz, located in Poland. Auschwitz was the largest camp, it having three main parts. All three of them were used for forced labor by the prisoners, but for a period of time, one of them was used as a killing center. The Nazis used gas chambers to kill a majority of the people and others were killed through mass shootings. Some outsiders turned into heroes and rose above the fear to try to help the victims in any ways they could. These heroes housed families, brought them food, and did anything they could to save innocent people's lives. They knew they were in a time of need and wanted to help. Even though they could not overcome the power of Adolf Hitler and the Nazis, these heroes tried to save who and what was left of their community. These were some of the worst times the world has ever seen. These times are known as the Holocaust.

Maria Frackowiak, a christian, lived in the city of Dubno, Poland with her husband. She worked to save many Jews during the time of need. From 1942-1944 she hid 23 Jewish-fugitives in their small apartment. In 1941, Dranchowa-Malarowa Genia's husband died along with 700 of the first Jews to be killed. At this point her family and Maria were neighbors. Maria then suggested that she and her children move in with her. After this, her house became a hiding place. She housed them until they found a better hiding place. When one family that she had been housing moved to another hiding place, Maria came and brought them food. By doing this she saved and woman and her child. She would have to buy large amounts of food, and to cover that up she would say she was throwing a party for German soldiers. When one of the families that she was hiding was found, she helped them move to another, safe hiding place in a small village. She kept in contact and checked up on them until the end of the war. When the war was done, the fugitives that had survived said Maria was extremely helpful and very selfless. She helped all these different people and families, expecting nothing in return. She even went against her disapproving husband to save the fugitives. This later resulted in a divorce for them. After the war, most of the survivors moved to Israel, and Maria moved to the city of Wroclaw in the Lower Silesia. She became a righteous among the nations on January 9th, 1979 for amazing work and dedication to doing good for others.

Holocaust: "a word of Greek origin meaning "sacrifice by fire"....The Holocaust was the systematic, bureaucratic, state-sponsored persecution and murder of six million Jews by the Nazi regime and its collaborators" (ushmm.org). Six million people died because of these times, but many more suffered. They suffered because of lack of food and water, shelter that was dark and small, and most of all the loss of their families. Kids lost their parents, children lost their siblings, and parents lost their daughters and sons. It was heartbreaking and unbearable for all the victims and families. It feels almost unreal that something so inhumane actually happened in our world. I can't seem to wrap my head around the idea of the Natizs slaughtering six million innocent people. They felt that the Germans were the superior race and wanted a world only filled with their own kind. This is in no way an excuse or reason to kill all the other innocent races and types of people in the world. Luckily there were some extraordinarily brave people, like Maria Frackowiak, who saved the lives of many. She knew she was risking her life but she also knew saving many other lives was worth it. If I was alive at this time, I would have hid anyone I could. I don't think I could have just sat back and let this happen in the world: let it happen to my neighbors, teachers, friends, or anyone I know. I understand the dangers and risks hiding the Jews came with, but to save someone's mother or son or aunt or grandmother is more than worth it.

Works Cited

"The Righteous Among The Nations." The Righteous Among The Nations. N.p., n.d. Web. 21 Feb. 2017.

United States Holocaust Memorial Museum. United States Holocaust Memorial Museum, n.d. Web. 23 Feb. 2017.

Ezio Giorgetti: Rescuer of 38 Jewish Refugees

Melyssa Mendiola

"I am telling the unvarnished truth when I say that Ezio's help, personal sacrifice and devotion saved the whole group, including my family and parents, from death at the hands of the Nazis," Dr. Neumann said. This was one of the many memorable remarks about Ezio Giorgetti that came from one of the rescued refugees. Ezio was an Italian hotel owner who saved 38 refugees with the help of a man named Osman Carugno. Giorgetti was born in 1912, and he died in 1970. The conflict between Germany and Italy was disastrous, and it caused terror and death, as well as people suffering. Although it was hard to get through, Ezio still went his way to do whatever he could to help and support the Jews in any way possible. He built a strong connection with them, and he made them feel loved and well cared for. With strength and guidance, Ezio was not only a man of heart but also, one of the "Righteous among the nations."

Filled with panic, sinking battleships, uncoordinated defense, and death, the aftermath of Italy's armistice was a tragedy. Germany had always been a military ally since 1936. They had numbers up, better quality armor, light weapons, and were well provided with resources. When the Germans attacked, Rome's individual military units and armed citizens were unorganized. They were defeated because of their lack of a plan, so with Field Marshal Kesselring, General Calvi had to sign a surrender of Rome. Operation Axis was the attack of Italy and the disarmament of the Italian troops in Yugoslavia, France, Italy, Greece, and the Aegean. Over one million men were disarmed. Also, many ships headed over to La Spezia to protect the allied operation at Salerno, but they were greeted with a bombing, which resulted in a sinking battleship and over 1,200 deaths. Even through all of this danger, Ezio still managed to keep the Jewish refugees sheltered, protected, and he made them feel safe.

Giorgetti was one who took the responsibility of both, owning hotels, as well as saving 38 refugees in the aftermath of Italy's armistice with the allies. In 1943, he was met by a group of 38 refugees who were asking for his help to find somewhere to hide. He promised to provide a place to stay, Hotel Savoia, for them in exchange for a small fee. Later on, Ezio's financial relationship with the Jews had come to an end, and he no longer charged them for their stay. He was there to shelter and protect them for no cost at all. The refugees were repeatedly moved to different locations to stay. They did this so they could remain safe from the Gestapo (German secret police under Nazi rule). First, they were moved to a smaller hotel on Adriatic. Then, they were moved to an empty farmhouse that was filled with furniture that Giorgetti provided. Next, he took a risk and moved them to another hotel called the Pensione Italia. Lastly, Ezio contacted some friendly villagers, and the refugees ended up being placed in their homes. Giorgetti was being mentally supportive along with emotionally supportive. The Jews highly appreciated his help and care. Josef Konforti, a Jewish refugee, claimed that the group was well provided and thankful for this kindness. They had to share all of their resources. Ezio took many risks to be sure that the refugees were well provided and safe. He went his way and did anything to get them whatever they needed. A man named Osman Carugno helped Ezio with these deeds. In 1964, he was given the title of "Righteous among the Nations" because of all the effort he put into rescuing the group if Jews. Also, a square was named after Osman in Bellaria-Igea Marina. By September 21, 1944, the German troops had left the village, and the Jews were finally declared safe and free. Ezio and Osman's hard work had paid off, and they saved the Jews from the Germans.

Throughout my research, I noticed that I was not only writing about an unforgettable figure, but I was also uncovering the true definition of generosity, devotion, and courage. Ezio Giorgetti provided the Jews a place to stay, food, and emotional support. He made sure that each one of them felt emotionally stable, as well as physically stable throughout their stay. He never let them down or gave up on them, and he treated them with kindness and respect from beginning to end. He moved them from place to place, and the group of Jews ended up staying in friendly villagers' homes. Giorgetti also put his life at risk just to rescue them. He could've just chosen to let them suffer, but he didn't. He wanted to support them and lend them a hand. I chose to write about Ezio because I saw him as a perfect example of someone who puts others before themselves. He was willing to risk both, himself and ownership of his hotels. These inspiring acts of Ezio Giorgetti have explained to many why he is considered one of the "Righteous among the Nations."

Works Cited

"The sad story of the Italian armistice of 8 September 1943." WAR HISTORY ONLINE. 23 September 2016. Web. 24 February 2017.
< http://www.warhistoryonline.com/articles/sad-story-italian-armistice-8-september-1943.html >

Raoul Wallenberg Foundation. "Ezio Giorgetti." The International Raoul Wallenberg Foundation. Web. 24 February 2017.
< http://www.raoulwallenberg.net/saviors/italian/ezio-giorgetti/ >

Committee of the gardens of the righteous worldwide. "Gariwo: the gardens of the Righteous." 23 November 2012. Web. 24 February 2017.
< http://en.gariwo.net/righteous/the-righteous-biographies/holocaust/stories-reported-by-users/the-village-of-pugliano-vecchio-7581.html >

The Kwarciak Family: Holocoaust Heroes

Mia Waki

The Holocaust took place during World War II and is considered to some people one of the most horrifying events in human history. Hitler was the leader of Germany and hated all Jewish people because he thought that they were the ones who caused him to lose World War I. He thought of Jews to be less than human. During the Holocaust when Germany invaded Poland, in the year of 1939, more than two million Jewish people became prisoners to the Germans. After they captured the Jews they forced them to live in certain places marked-off in towns and cities the Nazis called "ghettos". Ghettos were fenced off with barbwire and guarded with high security. There was not much water, food, or medicine available to the prisoners. The Nazis created over one thousand ghettos. A lot of the camps were set up in places that Jews were already being concentrated. Not only the Jews from Poland were captured, but Gypsies and Jews from surrounding regions were taken into the ghettos as well. The Nazis would mark off the oldest most rundown sections in the city and use that location as their camp. Children in the Holocaust were considered especially vulnerable during this time. The Germans killed over 1.5 million children. The fates of the Jewish children's lives could be put into four categories. One being children were killed when they arrived in killing centers. Another being that they were killed after birth or if in institutions. Also, children who were born in the ghettos could survive by being hidden by the prisoners. Finally, children usually over the age of 12 would be kept alive and used for forced labor and medical experiments. One of the thousands of ghettos located in Poland was the Dubno ghetto. Dubno is a city located on the Ikva River. The Dubno ghetto only lasted seven months before liquidated. Within the ghetto, 12,000 men, women, and children lived in small areas. The camp soon became overcrowded, and hunger and sickness struck frequently. The prisoners were treated with not one ounce of respect. Although there were many imprisoned Jews there was multiple survivors. Some people were able to survive by hiding from the Nazi's with non-Jewish families. They would pretend to be part of their family and sometimes hide in hidden rooms or in basements.

One rescuer was the Polish family named Kwarciak. The Kwarciak family consisted of the father, Piotr, the mother, Maria, and their three children, Anatoliusz, Alfred, and Feliks. Together the family saved three families, a total of fifteen Jewish prisoners, from the Dubno ghetto. The Kwarciak family saved the Fisher family, along with their relatives the Shenker family, Półtorak family, and the Schneider family. It all started in the year 1942, when Fisher, the Jew, was working outside the camp and saw Piotr Kwarciak and remembered him from long ago. Turns out, that Kwarciak and Fisher were old time friends before the Holocaust began. Knowing that the Dubno ghetto would soon be liquidated, Piotr Kwarciak offered to hide the Fisher family and their relatives in his private house located on the outskirts of the city if they were in any sort of danger no matter how big the risk may be, he was willing to take it. When the Fisher, Shenker, Półtorak, and Schneider family showed up in the Kwarciak's backyard they hid in a camouflaged shelter made out of bricks based under a pigsty. The room was separated into 5 sections, one for each family, using partitions. Even though the Jewish refugees didn't have much money to give, they paid for the food and cloths they received for as long as they could. Eventually they had to run out of money, and once they did the Kwarciak family didn't out their secret hideaway, but kept housing them as friends and out of pure kindness of humanity. As a consequence for hiding the families, Anatoliusz, Alfred, and Feliks, children of Piotr and Maria, had to give up their social lives to keep the Jewish refugee's hiding more secretive. In 1944, the Kwarciak family left to join the Fisher, Shenker, Póltorak, and Schneider family because the front line was coming close to it's end and the Germans were looking for Polish people to move to Germany to work in forced labor. After twenty-five long days of hiding hungrily and filthily the Red Army freed all the families. Later, the refugees moved to Isreal, and the Kwarciak family moved to the new territory in Poland. Overall, you could easily say that the Fisher, Shenker, Póltorak, and Schneider family owed their lives to Piotr, Maria, Anatoliusz, Alfred, and Feliks Kwarciak for saving them from their death.

After reading and researching the Kwarciak family and the overall Holocaust it has made me realize that the Holocaust is still important to kids, adults and us today. It is important because it reminds us to make sure that the genocide of at least six million people never happens again. Also, that just because you may be different than other people doesn't mean that you are not important. That nobody has the power to wipe out any race of people not matter how inhuman you may think they are.

Work Cited

"Children during the Holocaust." United States Holocaust Memorial Museum. United States Holocaust Memorial Museum, n.d. Web. 27 Feb. 2017.

"Ghettos." United States Holocaust Memorial Museum. United States Holocaust Memorial Museum, n.d. Web. 27 Feb. 2017.

"Names of Righteous by Country." Names of Righteous by Country. Martyrs' and Heroes' Remembrance Authority, n.d. Web. 27 Feb. 2017.

"The Righteous Among The Nations." The Righteous Among The Nations. Yad Vashem, n.d. Web. 27 Feb. 2017.

The Life of Zofia Bania

Miraya Gomez

The Holocaust happened almost a century ago, but it is still a miserable time in history. About 6 million Jews across Europe were murdered and imprisoned for practicing their religion. Adolf Hitler, the commander in chief of the Nazi's was the cause on this, he felt like Jews or people with physical or mental disabilities were a threat to the Germans. He believed that there should be an empire filled with only Germans because the Germans were above everyone else. People who disliked Jews were called anti-Semites. Anti- Semites were another word for racist people, in this case Jews. During these years, many lived in fear, but some were heroes who had the courage to step up for what they believed was fair. By the time Germans arrived in Poland, many of the surrounding countries were under the Nazi control, thus limiting the places people could escape to. Some didn't have a way to flee and had to stay in Poland to hide. Heroes like Zofia Bania did all they could to assist people during this time of war. Although she knew the risk that she might not survive, she still helped those who had nowhere to hide when the Germans came to Poland.

Zofia Bania was a poor farmer who lived in a small town called Pinczow, located in the south east of Poland. She would shop at a basic good store owned by Frania and Israel Rubinek. The Rubinek family and Zofia became friends and sometimes the couple would give Zofia free goods, for she was too poor and could not pay for much. In October 1942, the Nazi's came to Poland, and the city of Pinczow was attacked. That meant Frania and Israel had to flee, but because Frania was pregnant she couldn't flee to Russia like many Jews in Poland did. Therefore, they asked Zofia if they could stay at her house while the Nazi's were invading. Zofia had to think about it; she lived in a small one room house with her husband Ludwig and 6-year-old son and dreaded her and her family would be killed if they helped Jews. The Rubineks meanwhile built a bunker under their store to use as a place to hide. When the Germans came they attempted to flee, but fortunately Zofia ordered a man she trusted to go find her friends and bring them back. The Rubineks stayed at Zofia's house with her family. There they could hide from the Nazi's for a while. Ludwig although was an anti-Semite. Israel noticed this and him and Frania helped around the house to keep Ludwig from kicking them out. For safety Ludwig bought a guard dog who'd bark whenever someone approached their home. One night on December 1945, towards the end of the war, soldiers barged in Zofia's home. Frania and Israel hid in a small cellar as the men searched through the house. The soldiers insisted on staying the night at the house to make sure no one was hiding. Unfortunately, Israel had a terrible cough that night. This put the couple at risk, therefore Zofia's son, Maniek pretended to be sick. He cried and coughed to cover up Israel's noises. Although Maniek was only 6 years old he understood what was happening and felt the need to help the Rubineks. Their plan worked, and the couple stayed at Zofia until January 1945 when the war had ended and the town was freed by the Red Army.

Zofia Bania, like many others helped those in the holocaust find a safe place to live during this tough time. With her willingness and bravery, she was able to help her friends keep safe. Today the United States goes through similar situations. Recently Donald J Trump was elected as the President and many are frightened about his plans towards refugees and Illegal immigrants. Recently Trump made an executive order to ban Muslims from several different countries to come to America. He did this to prevent terrorist attacks. Many argue this is act of racism. Citizens fear he'll gain too much power. In addition, Trump, has made several remarks on keeping Mexicans out of the United States. Similar to what Hitler believed Trump wants a country with only white people. He believes the many immigrants shouldn't live in America and that they should go back to where they came from. People who believe that Donald Trump isn't the right candidate for being the President are protesting against his actions. Like in the Holocaust many believed that what Hitler was doing was unacceptable, so they fought in a war against him and the Nazi's. Many although agreed with Hitler and supported him and that's how he gained power and was able to kill so many innocents. Today many of the citizens of the United States voted for Trump and therefore he became president, but now that he is people are protesting because they strongly believe that he's unfair. From writing g this essay and researching I learned that history repeats itself and us people need to step up when we believe something isn't right. It's important that countries work together and collaborate so situations like these can be prevented. With everything happening today from presidential elections to terrorist attacks it is important students are educated on these factors. In conclusion, the issues on racism that's happening today with President Donald Trump is similar to what Hitler did during the Holocaust, but those who take risks and step up for others like Zofia Bania help make the world a better place.

What Makes A Hero

Natalia Arzbaecher

The word hero is quite subjective; what makes a hero? According to the dictionary, a hero is 'a person who is admired or idealized for courage, outstanding achievements, or noble qualities.' To me, a hero doesn't always have to be loud, or stand out; though if you ask most people they'll say a hero is like Superman. They might say a hero is someone known, someone who stands out in the crowd; but most heroes blend in, they defy authority or negativity quietly. But when someone is quiet, when someone blends in, they never really get credit for the things that they do. So, to me, heroes are those who defy and fight against all odds, just because they know it's right, not for the glory. meaning in this world, which moves so fast, many of those heroes go unnoticed. Those who look see them, but as we are a shallow species, many of us never even look. My hero is Natalia Abramowicz, a woman who helped a Jewish family, not because she had to, but because she knew it was right. Though my reasons for picking her are quite shallow, my name is also Natalia, I found that she was quite an amazing person, somcone who fills the category of hero quite well in my eyes.

Natalia Abramowicz was born on February 10, 1897, and passed away on January 1, 1979. She was a Catholic woman living in Radomsko, Lodz, Poland when Adolf Hitler took power. She lived near the Radomsko ghetto, which soon began to swell in size due to the Nazis sending Jewish families there. One of the Jewish families that was forced to live in the Radomsko ghetto was the Steinlauf family. The Steinlauf family consisted of Michael Steinlauf, his wife, two kids, sister, and brother-in-law. This family was were supplied with food and other necessities by their old housekeeper, Weronika Kalek, but when the Nazis started sending the Jews to the concentration camps, Natalia took the family in so they could hide in her attic. She provided them with everything they needed for nine months. She did this for no other reason than to be a good person, and because it was the right thing to do. When Nazis started looking for Jews in hiding, the Steinlauf family thought it be best if the women and children got sent to a safe house further away so they would have less of a chance of being caught. But sadly, the man running the safe house turned on them, and Gestapo agents were at the house when the family arrived. The agents shot and killed the entire family, and Weronika, who had dropped them off. The agents then came to Natalia's house and she was arrested and sent to the Ravensbruck concentration camp, which was the second largest women's concentration camp. This camp gassed over 5,000 people before it was liberated by Soviet troops in April 1945. By 1945, it housed almost 50,000 prisoners from over thirty different countries. It was very overcrowded, and because of all of the overcrowding a typhus epidemic happened. Natalia was at the camp when the epidemic occurred, but she luckily never got infected. She was finally liberated from the camp in 1945, along with Michael and his brother-in-law. At the end of the war Michael and his brother-in-law moved to Australia, but Natalia remained in Poland. She stayed there until her death at 82 years of age. She ended up getting awarding the title of righteous on August 7, 1969, and she also had a tree planted and dedicated to her.

Natalia Abramowicz was a hero. She was someone who would never been persecuted or sent to a concentration camp, but she stood up for what she knew was right, and she suffered for it. Though she only saved two people, she still is a courageous hero. This is because not everybody can save the whole world, some can only save some of it. Two people may seem insignificant, but in reality, saving just two people can be so impactful to the course of society. The majority of the saviors in the Holocaust only saved a few people, but each one of their contributions helped change the course of humanity. This sends the message that if we get every person helping just a little, no matter how small, we can win a war. Natalia is a hero because she didn't lie down in silence, instead she stood up when she knew she could help. She gave hope to a family, and she fought when most people didn't. She's a hero because she knew what was right, and chose to do it. She's a hero because she knew that helping one family tears down evil at its core. She's a hero because she put her safety, and her life, on the line to preserve goodness. She removed her rose-colored glasses and saw what was happening, and she refused to let it continue. In conclusion Natalia Abramowicz is a hero because she did what so many were afraid to do, she refused to let darkness win.

Bibliography

"Auschwitz." United States Holocaust Memorial Museum. United States Holocaust Memorial Museum, Web. 01 Mar. 2017.

"Radomsko Ghetto." Radomsko Ghetto. Web. 01 Mar. 2017.

Yad Vashem - Request Rejected. Web. 01 Mar. 2017.

Jewish Righteous

Nicholas Takeda

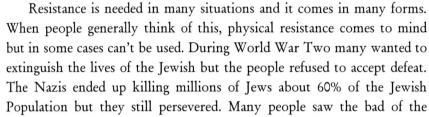

Resistance is needed in many situations and it comes in many forms. When people generally think of this, physical resistance comes to mind but in some cases can't be used. During World War Two many wanted to extinguish the lives of the Jewish but the people refused to accept defeat. The Nazis ended up killing millions of Jews about 60% of the Jewish Population but they still persevered. Many people saw the bad of the Nazis and helped the oppressed. One of these heroes was named Edward Chadzynski. Edward provided many people with forged documents to save their lives. With the help of the resistance many people survived. Some people fought back with words, some fought back with records, but just the fact that they still lived was the ultimate resistance. Chadzynksi worked for Registry Office of Municipal Council where he provided Jews with fake documents to get out of the Warsaw Ghetto. These acts helped the people get out of the ghetto with hope.

After the first world war, Germany was humiliated with its defeat and the economic problems were striking the county hard. Desperate, the people of Germany were attracted to a powerful speaker, Adolf Hitler. At this time in the USA, the stock market was collapsing leading to America calling in its foreign loans. This destroyed Germany leading to its unemployment rate to 6 million. Hitler earned more and more support by the angry workers but other workers turned to communism which scared the wealthy business owners. These owners began to fund the Nazi propaganda. The middle class could not believe the fall of the democratic society and turned to the strong leader. In July 1942 the Nazi party became the largest in Germany. Soon after, the president made Hitler chancellor believing they could control him to gain support. In February 1943, a communist leader was caught burning a government building and soon every communist leader was locked up. With now supreme Nazi representation in the parliament, a law was passed making Hitler with absolute power. He dismisses all other party leaders making Germany a Nazi state. He also sets up new labor organization, courts swearing oath to the Nazi party and the army join the party. Now unable to be removed from power in August 1945, the president of Germany dies. Soon after the European war starts in September 1939. When Nazi Germany, under the leadership of Adolf Hitler, invaded Poland. This was the beginning of World War 2, the bloodiest war of nations. Germany used the blitzkrieg tactics and rapidly overwhelmed the country. The globe was surprised. France and Britain then responded by declaring war on Germany but took little action to do so. Then, in 1940, Germany quickly defeated Denmark, Norway, Belgium, the Netherlands and France. This sent Britain to retreat. Alone, Britain was attacked by Germany however the army failed to conquer. In 1941, the Nazis invaded Russia breaking a treaty, under the code name Barbarossa. Later that year the Japanese attacked pearl harbor dragging the USA into the war. Germany, Italy, and Japan made the axis powers rivaling Britain, Russia, and the US. In 1942 Germany had its final plan, to exterminate all Jewish people. Russia then invaded in the east and captured the German capitol of Berlin. Germany surrendered in May 1945 after Adolf committed suicide. August 6, the Americans dropped their newly made atomic bomb on Hiroshima Japan, killing millions. Only 9 days later the Japanese surrendered. World War Two was finally over.

The Jewish people oppressed during World War 2 owe their freedom to resistance, perseverance, and heroes. One of these saviors was named Edward Chadzynski. Edward worked for the Warsaw registry office and there he helped provide many with fake identities. The number of Jews he helped is unknown but one time he helped an eleven-person family by placing some with his own family members. His effort helped many throughout the years and his resistance was inspiring to many. Not much is known about Chadzynski and his backstory but none can agree with him not being a hero.

Warsaw is capitol of Poland with 1.3 million citizens before World War Two. Warsaw was the Polish center of Jewish culture and life. About 30% of the city's population was Jewish. After the German invasion the city was bombed until its surrender on September 29, 1939. This defeat was only one of many. Two weeks later the Germans decreed the establishment of a Ghetto requiring all the 400,000 Jews living there to move in the designated area. The thousands of Jews were than sealed off from the outside world surrounded by ten-foot-high walls. In the 1.3 square mile area disease and starvation ran through the community. An estimated 83,000 people died there. From July 22 to September 12, 1942, 250,000 Jews were deported to the killing center Treblinka. Coming back a second time with the intent on deportation, the remaining Jews were ready to resist and after a while, the Nazis halted. Finally, in January 19 the Nazi forces appeared outside of the wall intending on liquidating and deporting the rest of the people. The people living there resisted the forces and after one month, the uprising was put down. Only 20,000 people were left in hiding and the rest were dead or soon dead. After World War 2 only 6% of Warsaw population lived.

Resistance is one of the fundamental freedoms many share but not all are brave enough to do so. During World War 2 only a few stood up to the Nazis. One of those people was Edward Chadzynski and he helped the Jews knowing the consequences of doing so. Resistance can be shown through many forms but it can also be shown by helping others. Because of this resistance the Jews were able to persevere through the evil.

Bibliograephy

http://db.yadvashem.org/righteous/family.html?language=en&itemId=4014276

https://sprawiedliwi.org.pl/en/stories-of-rescue/story-rescue-chadzynski-family

http://www.historynet.com/world-war-ii
https://www.ushmm.org/wlc/en/article.php?ModuleId=10005188

Under the Pigsty: Aleksander & Helena Wiejak

Nicholas Tidwell

"We left home with empty hands, without our children or any money, and they saved us - and not for money, since we had nothing. Throughout our stay in the pit I swore to myself that I will lend any help possible to the family that rescued me... Aleksander and Helena loved helping people, and the most sacred value for them was human life... We, who lost four children, regard our saviors' daughters as our own daughters." This was written by Avigdor after the war when he was free as a thank you to the Wiejaks for protecting him, his wife, and his friends from the Nazis in World War II. While the sequel to the "War to end all wars" showed the how low the human race could go, there were many examples of the strength and beauty of the human heart. These people who chose to save the Jews and the other minorities in the Holocaust, the genocide committed by the Nazis in order to remove said minorities from Europe, are honored today with the title of "Righteous Among the Nations." Two of these "righteous" people are Aleksander and Helena Wiejak, a married couple from Konskowola, Poland, near Lublin.

During the German occupation of Poland, which lasted from 1939 to 1945, many Jews and other minorities were forced into hiding in order to escape the reach of the Nazis. Four of the Jews that escaped persecution for the entire war were two married couples, one those couples being Avigdor and Faiga Mandelbaum. These four stayed with Aleksander and Helena Wiejak, who were gentiles, under a pigsty at their farm in Konskowola, Poland. They took care of the four fugitives for the entire war. Earlier in the war, when the Mandelbaums lived in the Koskowola ghetto, they sent their children to the Warsaw ghetto in the hopes that they would be able to survive under the custody of Faiga's brother. Unfortunately, this did not help them as most people in ghettos and in hiding were moved to forced labor camps such as the one in Lublin or extermination camps such as Auschwitz or Treblinka. The Warsaw Ghetto was set up by the Germans in order to separate the Jews from the rest of the "Aryan" population. It was administered by a Judenrat, or Jewish Council, which enforced German policies in the hopes that through cooperation, they could save at least some of the Jews throughout Europe. These Judenrats were composed of mostly local Jewish leaders before the war, such as Rabbis or Jewish businessman. The Mandelbaums, after the Nazis forced all the Jews in Konskowola to move to labor or extermination camps, fled to the Wiejaks' house to escape persecution. This was where they would spend the rest of the war.

Despite the Mandelbaums being under the care of the Wiejaks, they frequently succumbed to bouts of depression and suicidal thoughts. The Mandelbaums were not only dealing with the loss of their children, but also the decimation of their culture at the hands of the Nazis. Avigdor frequently contemplated committing suicide because of this, but Aleksander was always trying to cheer him up. He begged him to not commit suicide. Aleksander did this because he wanted Avigdor, Fajga, and the other married couple to serve as a testament. If they survived, it would show the world that anything can be overcome. Helena always fed the couples the same thing that the Wiejaks would eat. She would make sure to get anything the Mandelbaums or their friends needed. An example of this was when Fajga needed medical care because of her poor health. Helena would always get medicine from a local apothecary. However, their mercy put them in danger. Rumors spread that not only was Aleksander a partisan for Polish independence, but he was housing Jews as well. Both of which happened to be true. Eventually Aleksander went into hiding, but he was found and killed by Nazi soldiers in May of 1944. Ironically, later that year, Poland was liberated, along with the Mandelbaums and the other married couple.

Partisans were people that resisted Nazi rule or the atrocities committed by them. There were many of these groups throughout Soviet Russia, Poland, Slovakia, and other axis-occupied territories. Many of these partisan groups were captured and killed by the Nazis. Some of these partisans were even German officers, such as Colonel Klaus Schenk Graph von Stauffenburg, who led a number of politicians to attempt to assassinate Adolf Hitler. Others, such as Aleksander Wiejak, were people for fought for the independence of their country. There were even politicians or leaders of former countries who led organized resistances, such as Charles de Gaulle from France. In Eastern Europe, some of these partisans formed armies and attempted to retake their lands through force and push out the Germans and their allies. There were wven people who carried out attacks on their own, such as Georg Esler, who planted a bomb where hitler spoke every year, but failed to assassinate Hitler because Hitler left before the bomb was supposed to go off. These partisans helped disrupt the Nazis during the offensives launched by the Allies, lending a hand in the eventual defeat of Hitler and the Nazi regime.

It is easy to realize how much of an affect the inhumanity of the Nazis had on the people subjected to their will. World War II brought some of the evilest people in history to power, but that same tyranny and suffering wrought by the Nazis also brought out the humanity in many others. This heroism was expressed by the "Righteous Among the Nations," a title given to the people who saved Jews during World War II. The Wiejaks were two of these people, and one of them, Aleksander, paid the ultimate price for trying to save the Jews and his Poland motherland. Their story is one of the many stories should be remembered as a testament to why we should prevent something like the Holocaust from ever happening again.

Works Cited

USHMM - https://www.ushmm.org/wlc/en/article.php?ModuleId=10005069

Yad   Vashem   -
http://db.yadvashem.org/righteous/family.html?language=en&itemId=4035414

HEART - http://www.holocaustresearchproject.org/ghettos/judenrat.html

Anna Paszkiewicz

Owen Karlsen

When Adolf Hitler became the prime minister of Germany in 1933 and the country fell under Nazi control, the entire history of the Jewish race was forever changed. For Eugenia Wirszubska, a Polish Jew, the Holocaust meant losing her home and her freedom. However, thanks to Anna Paszkiewicz, she did not lose her life.

During the Holocaust, showing anything but hatred or indifference towards Jews was a crime punishable by death. The Righteous Among the Nations is the name given to the people who were brave enough to lend a helping hand to their fellow human beings. Whether they hid Jews in their homes, provided them with false papers, helped them flee to a safer country, or did any other life-saving deed, they are heroes among men. The Righteous risked their lives, families, homes, freedom, and more by helping people who were largely seen as the common enemy. While this paper only tells the story of Anna Paszkiewicz, a Polish woman who saved the lives of a Jewish woman and her two daughters, there are many more brave citizens like her who have been honored, as well as many whose stories have never been told.

Before her world as she knew it was taken from her, Eugenia Wirszubska lived with her daughters Regina and Ada in Wysokie Litewskie, a town in the Polesie district, an area that stretched across Poland, Belarus, and Ukraine. Germany invaded Poland in 1933, and many Jews fled, though few successfully. Wirszubska and her children were relocated to the Pruzany ghetto. During the time of the Holocaust, ghettos were closed districts that the Germans used to separate Jews from the rest of the population, as well as other Jewish communities. They were usually set up as temporary housing for the Jews until they were transported to camps or killed. Conditions in ghettos were unbearable. They were crowded and dark, breeding grounds for disease. There were often food shortages, causing many to die of starvation. Jews were forced to wear badges or armbands that identified them and perform manual labor for the German Reich. Eugenia, Ada, and Regina remained in the Pruzany ghetto until October 1942, when rumors began to spread that their ghetto would soon be liquidated. "Liquidation" involved everyone in the ghetto being either killed on the spot or sent to a concentration camp—where they were likely die sooner or later. Eugenia knew she had to save herself and her daughters, so she contacted an old friend and hoped for the best.

When Anna Paszkiewicz received a cry for help from her Jewish friend, she made the beyond risky decision to assist them. She knew that the consequences of being caught were severe, as notices were posted all over Eastern Europe that anyone who was found to be sheltering Jews would face not only their own execution, but the execution of their family as well. However, out of the kindness of her heart, Anna planned an escape for the three women and helped them execute it. After they had escaped, she allowed them to live in her apartment and provided them with anything they needed. She asked for nothing in return for her sacrifice, and acted only out of true care and friendship. She came to think if Ada and Regina as her own, and did everything she could to preserve their safety as well as their mother's.

However, the Wirszubska women could not stay in their dear friend's apartment forever. It was only three months before, yet again, they were forced to relocate because of a rumor. Paszkiewicz's neighbors began to spread whispers that there were Jews in the area. And, since whispers only grow louder, the women knew it was time for a new plan. Through the Holocaust, Hitler and the Nazi party were trying to create a "superior race" by eliminating anyone who did not fit a certain set of characteristics. Their ideal world was full of able-bodied and able-minded people of "Aryan" descent. The Aryan race as defined by Hitler was a set of European people typically characterized by their pale skin, blonde hair, and blue eyes. However, some Jews could pass as Aryan with the right forged background. These backgrounds were usually created by forgers, but sometimes government officials created the needed documents. Jews were given new names, identities, religions, and ancestries. Anna managed to acquire fake Aryan papers for Eugenia and her children, which allowed them to start their own new life. They packed up and moved to Narew, a city in the Białystok district. Because of their new identities, they were able to live relatively normal lives there. Eugenia began working and they remained in the city until it was liberated in the summer of 1944.

By 1945, World War II was over in Europe. Hitler was gone, the Nazi party was defeated, and all concentration camps had been emptied. Both Paszkiewicz and the Wirszubskas got happy endings. Anna Paszkiewicz moved to Switzerland and was honored as Righteous Among the Nations by Yad Vashem on December 13, 1998. Eugenia, Ada, and Regina Wirszubska moved to England and lived the rest of their lives as free women. But very few were so lucky. Approximately six million Jews had died by the end of the Holocaust. The world could never quite be the same.

When we look back at the atrocities of the Holocaust, we wonder who we would have been back then had we been given the chance. Could we be Anna Paszkiewicz and risk everything to preserve our humanity? Or would we be one of the millions who stood by and watched as our fellow human beings were slaughtered? The exact answer to that question can never be truly known. However, current events right here in the United States may give us the chance to prove just how dedicated we are to helping our fellow man. Will we stand by our undocumented brothers and sisters? Will we protect the Muslim population? Or will we let the powers that be decide the worth of human beings by their skin color, religion, sexuality, or gender? Only time can tell.

Bibliography

"About the Righteous." About the Righteous. Yad Vashem, n.d. Web. 26 Feb. 2017.

"German Invasion of Poland: Jewish Refugees, 1939." United States Holocaust Memorial Museum. United States Holocaust Memorial Museum, n.d. Web. 26 Feb. 2017.

"Ghettos." United States Holocaust Memorial Museum. United States Holocaust Memorial Museum, n.d. Web. 26 Feb. 2017.

"HISTORY OF THE HOLOCAUST - TIME LINE." The Holocaust History - A People's and Survivor History - Remember.org. Remember.org, n.d. Web. 26 Feb. 2017.

History.com Staff. "The Holocaust." History.com. A&E Television Networks, 2009. Web. 26 Feb. 2017.

History.com Staff. "World War II History." History.com. A&E Television Networks, 2009. Web. 26 Feb. 2017.

"Paszkiewicz, Anna." The Righteous Among The Nations. Yad Vashem, n.d. Web. 26 Feb. 2017.

"Victims of the Nazi Era: Nazi Racial Ideology." United States Holocaust Memorial Museum. United States Holocaust Memorial Museum, n.d. Web. 26 Feb. 2017.

John Damski: a Holocaust Hero

Ronel Dumag

The Holocaust was a tragic event that happened from 1941-1945. Roughly 6 million Jews were murdered by Adolf Hitler and the Nazis. Jews were held in concentration camps and were being killed, numbers at a time. Only few people have escaped, and survived. John Damski is one of those people. He was born in 1914 in Germany. He had two brothers and a sister. He grew up in a small town called Solec-Kujawski. When John was young, he was very athletic. The sports he was good at were track and field and soccer. He was in an organization with Jewish people, called the Polish Falcons. In the group, someone made a statement about Jews, and this caused them to break up. This had affected John very much, for he felt no difference between him and Jews. He had been encountering them throughout his lifetime, some good some bad. In 1935, he was in a training camp with Israelowicz, a state champion going to the Olympics. He said that the U.S. want people to travel, but won't let Jews go, which was the first time John had realized that Jews were being treated differently. The next time he had been with Jews was at a nightclub. He had seen an old pal from school and his girlfriend. They started saying mean things about Jews, which got John upset. He also saw a sign that said "Don't Buy From A Jew" all over in the public. John soon served in the Polish Army during World War II. He served in the Battalion for the Defense of the Seashore on the Baltic coast at Gdynia.

On September 1, 1939, Germans invaded, and John was taken hostage. On the way to the prisoner of war camp, he escaped. They asked him to become a German national, for he was born in Germany and could speak the language very well. He refused. On June 13, he and his friend were captured hostage as prisoners. He was thrown into prison, but he was let out because an official couldn't find any record of him. He survived, but this wasn't the end. He pretended to be German, and he became a savior. He worked with the Polish Underground

532

helping Jews escape the Warsaw ghetto for 6 years. He had been imprisoned 3 times, but he escaped each time.

The Warsaw ghetto was a designated area for Jews to stay during the Holocaust. There were many other ghettos and areas for Jews during the Holocaust, but the Warsaw ghetto was a known one. A wall over 10 feet high enclosed it. The population of the ghetto was approximately 400,000 Jews. They were only allowed to bring the slightest amount of things with them. This was normally clothes and belongings. The Germans limited food supplies in the ghetto, which made it hard to survive. Jewish associations in the ghetto tried their best to give the prisoners what they needed. In the ghetto, many Jews died of starvation. In between 1940-1942, 90,000+ Jews died. On July 21 1942, the Nazis started the 'Gross Aktion Warsaw'. This meant that the Jews from Warsaw ghetto would be transported to the Treblinka death camp and be murdered. Around 300,000 Warsaw ghetto residents died in gas chambers. No one would want to be where the Jews were during this time period.

Many Jews died during the holocaust. Only the luckiest people would survive, and not very many did. John Damski was a very lucky survivor, and continued to give prisoners the freedom that he was given. Jews were treated very harshly, and for no reason at all. All of this research helped me stand up for what I want, and to never give up. John Damski didn't give up, and neither should I. If anything like this ever happens to my friends, family, or me, I will not stop until it is over. I've also learned to become more aware of things and to see things from a different point of view. John Damski was a man who has been caught many times, but he's also escaped many times. If I ever get caught during a 'holocaust', I will be aware and see if I can do anything to help the current situation. Other people survived, and if they can survive and become a hero, so can I. I wouldn't like a holocaust to happen again, so I will do whatever it takes to prevent that from happening.

John Damski was a hero. In my opinion, a hero is someone that takes risks to help out someone or a group of people. John Damski risked his life to save Jews that were going to be killed. He was a great hero that should be remembered by many people and I hope to be similar to him if anything related to another holocaust happens again in the real world. Many other people can help me with this hope and dream, but in general, I hope to prevent a holocaust from happening in the world again, because that would be another very tragic event.

Works Cited:

Roraback, Dick. "A Con Man Who Became War Hero." Los Angeles Times. Los Angeles Times, 24 Sept. 1989. Web. 26 Feb. 2017.

"The Warsaw Ghetto HolocaustResearchProject" The Warsaw Ghetto HolocaustResearchProject H.E.A.R.T., n.d. Web. 27 Feb. 2017.

Glawrence. "Daily Life In The Warsaw Ghetto." Imperial War Museums. N.p., 20 Oct. 2016. Web. 26 Feb. 2017.

"Warsaw Ghetto Uprising." United States Holocaust Memorial Museum. United States Holocaust Memorial Museum, n.d. Web. 26 Feb. 2017.

Damski, John. "John Damski Story, Part 1." John Damski Story. Humboldt University, n.d. Web. 26 Feb. 2017.

Henryk Slawik: Hero of Poland

Sarah Cloninger (Winner)

If someone from the U.S. thinks about the Holocaust and they haven't been taught it, what do you think they'll say? They will most likely say it was a war that involved Germany, Russia or Japan. But did you know that Poland was a pretty big part of the war as well but everyone seems to forget to mention them. Even though they weren't on anyone's side they still fought back to defend their country. Poland was hit hard in September of 1939 when the Nazis invaded them from the west on the first of September. Then later on the seventeenth they were invaded from the east by the Soviet Union. Poland did their best to defend themselves but during that process they lost over 65,000 troops. This invasion didn't stop until October and by then 90% of the Polish Jews were completely wiped out. It was a devastating time for Poland, but they did not give up. Many people started to fight back and form a resistance but the Germans were just too well armed and they had a lot more people. They failed to form the resistance and lost many people in the process. Even though Poland went through a lot in the beginning of World War II many Polish people did not back down. For example, one hero that arose from Poland was a man named Henryk Slawik, who was a Polish politician who saved over 30,000 Polish people and Polish Jews. Slawik was born on July 16, 1894 in Szeroka, Jastrzębie-Zdrój, Poland and was raised along with 4 other siblings. He was sent to an academic secondary school and then left his hometown after graduation. He was drafted into World War I but got released in 1918. He then became a journalist and as very successful as he was the president of the Polish Journalists Association. Henryk Slawik was a hero of Poland and did the thing that most people did not have the courage to do: save and rescue refugees of the war.

Henryk Slawik did the impossible during the war by saving over 30,000 refugees that included children, Jews, and Polish Jews. After the invasion in 1939, the Nazis grew stronger and more powerful so they started to increase the deaths of Jews and concentration camps to put people in. Some people tried to flee and run for their lives, but other people like Slawik decided to stay and rescue people. Following the attack on Poland Henryk joined the Krakow Army and tried to fight back but ultimately failed. When he left the Krakow Army his name appeared on the list for enemies of the state. After the Soviet Union attacked Poland from the east, József Antall who was a member of the Hungarian ministry of internal affairs responsible for the civilian refugees spotted Slawik. Together they went to Budapest and created the Citizen's Committee for Help for Polish Refugees. He organized jobs, displaced people, schools, and orphanages. Also, along with Antall, he organized a system that helped exiled Poles travel to France or the Middle East to join the Polish Army. He saved over 30,000 Jews and Polish refugees by giving most of them false Polish passports with Catholic designation. Unfortunately, all heroes' stories must come to an end and Slawik was killed on March 19, 1944. He was captured and brought to Mauthausen concentration camp. Even though he was brutally tortured, Henryk didn't give up a single name or contact. Slawik was definitely a Polish hero and people even called him the polish Raoul Wallenberg who saved 100,000 people by issuing false documents. This title is very special because only a few heroes, let alone people, get that sort of entitlement. Also, the Australian Society of Polish Jews and their Descendants bestow an annual Henryk Slawik award and katrinashawver.com says that it is "upon an individual or organization that contributes to a greater understanding of the unique and dynamic contribution by the Polish Jewish community to the all-embracing Polish culture and ethos." There are many other organizations that recognize the contributions to Slawik however they are all in Polish and only a few could be translated. Although Henryk Slawik could not live very long to tell is tale he is still considered one of Poland's greatest heroes because he could what most people were afraid to do.

Henryk Slawik was one of the greatest polish heroes for what he did but there are many other examples of people standing up for what they believe in today. For instance, many people do not like our new president because they believe he will not protect this country and they will not just sit around waiting for something to happen. They stand up and fight which created the women's march around the entire United States which consisted of so many people. Also, in my own family my sister is one of the people that I admire because she will not back down if anyone tries to harm anyone she knows. For example my brother was getting bullied by someone a lot bigger than him and was too afraid to fight but my sister on the other hand pushed the kid on the ground and that kid never bullied our family again. I believe that being a hero and standing up for people is a lot harder than just sitting around and watching other people do and the people that really do make a difference deserve recognition which is why I liked writing this paper so much because not only did I learn about Henryk Slawik, I learned more about World War II and what it was like for Poland back then. Slawik saved over 30,000 people and he was only a veteran during WWII and a politician but as you can see he made a huge difference during the war for Poland and he should definitely. I hope that I get a chance to make a difference and not sit back and what other people do it because I want to be more like Henryk Slawik, a hero to all nations.

Works Cited

ConVistaAlMar.com.ar. "Henryk Slawik." The International Raoul Wallenberg Foundation. N.p., n.d. Web. 27 Feb. 2017.

"Dr. Henryk Slawik - a Polish Raoul Wallenberg?" Dr. Slawik - Was He a Polish Raoul Wallenberg? Terese Pencak Schwartz, n.d. Web. 27 Feb. 2017

"Dr. Henryk Slawik." BossierAIM. N.p., 2017. Web. 27 Feb. 2017.

"Henryk Slawik." Yad Vashem - Request Rejected. The World Holocaust Remembrance Center, n.d. Web. 27 Feb. 2017.

"Righteous among the Nations." Yad Vashem. The Holocaust Martyrs' and Heroes' Remembrance, n.d. Web. 27 Feb. 2017.

"Shawver, Katrina. "Henryk Slawik - Polish WWII Hero -." - An American Meets Poland. N.p., 23 Mar. 2015. Web. 27 Feb. 2017.

Stand Up or Stand Down: Natalia Abramowicz

Benjamin Yeargain

"Hero: a person who is admired or idealized for courage, outstanding achievements, or noble qualities." At first thought you may think of a flying crime fighter that saves a damsel in distress. Although this may be true in todays society, during the holocaust, heroes stood up for what they believed was right no matter how big or small the risk was. In October of 1942, the Germans started to liquidate more than 233,000 Jews. At the time Poland was the second largest city in Poland. Germany and most of the world was in the middle of World War II. During this rough time, Natalia Abramowicz took in a family of six and hid them away in her attic for nine months. She risked her safety and security for the well being of other people. Natalia wasn't a crime fighting citizen with super powers, but she saved a family from being separated and killed which demonstrates what true heros

Before the war had started, Weronika Kalek worked as a domestic worker in the Lodz district. After the war had broken out and Nazi Germany was in reign, many Jews including Kalek had lost their jobs and were interned into the ghettos. While his family was in this awful place, Natalia Abramowicz supplied his family with food and water. The conditions in the ghettos weren't so good. There was no sewage system which meant that disease was spread easily. Many people didn't have excess to running water. The food portions were controlled by the German Officers. Many times families would try to smuggle as much food as possible even if it meant death. More than 20 percent of Jews died in the ghettos because of the conditions. They were fortunate that none of the members in their family were killed or caught disease because children everyday became orphaned. Older brothers and sisters had to take care of the family if needed. When the Nazis started to liquidate people, the Kalek family escaped and found shelter in the home of Abramowicz. They stated there for nine months seeking shelter from the killing that was going on. After the Germans started searching houses, it was decided that they would move the family to the house of Michael's sister in Czstochowa. Kalek undertook the arrangement however the man that was going to transfer the family by train betrayed them.

Once they got to the meeting spot, Gestapo agents were there waiting for them. At the time, the Gestapo was one of the most feared polices forces in Europe. Gestapo agents commonly ran their own courts and was commonly the "judge, jury and frequently executioner." Their main purpose was to hunt down anyone that was a threat to Nazi Germany. This may have included Jews, homosexuals, and even disable people. Most of the fear that came from the Gestapo was people talking about how their agents were everywhere. This created an ever lasting fear that you could trust nobody. After the war was over gestapo slowly disappeared and their leader Henrich Müller was never heard of again. The Gestapo Agents ended up killing Weronika and the whole group. They also invaded Abramowicz's apartment and arrested her for housing Jews in her home and was deported to Ravensbruek until she was released when the war ended. The surviving members of the family eventually immigrated to Australia after the war. After the war many Jewish people feared to go back to their homes so they turned to immigration. In 1945 the current president of the United Sates, Harry Truman opened its borders to approximately 28,000 Jews. Many of Germany's western allies set up "refugee centers" for the Jews. Some of these allies included the United States, Great Britain, and France.

Through researching this topic I have learned many things about the holocaust and how it affected many people at the time. People such as Natalia Abramowicz inspire me to stand up for what's right and not to just let people suffer. Just because you are not affected from what is going on doesn't mean that whats going on is alright. Abramowicz could've lived a normal life without pain or suffering, but instead she risked her own well being to save the lives of family. She wasn't the only person during the holocaust that did acts such as this. Many people stood up for what was right, and it astonishes me how human kindness can trump over evil. This just doesn't go for the holocaust either. People in our everyday lives stand up for what's right, whether its saving somebody's live or something as simple as picking up a piece of trash. From superheroes flying in skies, to the people that stand up for what's right, you are surrounded by people who are propelled by the greater good. These types people saved so may lives during the holocaust. Life isn't about standing back and letting people suffer, its about doing your part to make the world a better place.

Works Cited

"The Aftermath of the Holocaust." United States Holocaust Memorial Museum. United States Holocaust Memorial Museum, n.d. Web. 25 Feb. 2017.

"Homework & Online Education Tool for Students." The Holocaust Explained. N.p., n.d. Web. 25 Feb. 2017.

Truman, C. N. "The Gestapo." History Learning Site. N.p., 16 Aug. 2016. Web. 25 Feb. 2017.

Locked Away

Camille St. James

 What is a hero? Is it really about having super powers and a cape, or does the job come with different requirements? Heroes are made every day, even when people least expect it they can become a hero in any shape or form. Putting others needs before yours and being selfless are traits found in heroes all over the world. When the odds were anything but in her favor, one girl still rose to the challenge of being a hero during a time of darkness, hopelessness, and strife. This time is known as the Holocaust. The holocaust was a time when a group of people put a disturbing label on another group of people and found it right to dispose of them. The Nazis believed diversity was wrong and they found it fitting to kill off Jews and anyone from Jewish decent. Although this time seemed to hold no chance of people seeing the light of compassion

again, this event provided a door for people to step up and save what had been lost, humanity.

Stefania Podgorska was born in 1925 in Lipa, Poland (a small town near Przemysl) and into a catholic family. Her childhood was not all that pretty, her mother was sent away to Germany for forced labor and her father died from an illness in 1938. Stefania and her sister, Helena, eventually started to grow up and ended up moving to Przemysl. Stefania worked in a shop owned by a Jewish family, the Diamants, she became very close with the family and that bond never changed even through all the danger that came upon them. In July 1942 the Germans established a ghetto in Przemysl, which the Diamants got forced into. The family and Stefania kept in touch through letters and one day two Diamant brothers, Maksymilian and Henryk, asked the young woman to help them when they got out of the ghetto. In result Stefania and Helena moved out from their apartment, in the middle of the city, and got a house out in the suburbs. A bit before the liquidation of the ghetto the Diamant family managed to escape, along with many others from the ghetto and they all made it safely to the sisters' home. Getting out before the liquidation was crucial, either they would've been sent to Auschwitz or been killed automatically. Thankfully the brothers managed to bring along thirteen people (including themselves): Teodora Zimmerman, Janek Zimmerman, Ms. Zimmerman, Krystyna Jelenska, Mr. Jelenska, Leon Hirsz, Siuniek Hirsz, Krystyna Orlicz-Szylinger, Wladyslaw Orlicz-Szylinger, Danuta Karfiot, and Jan Dorlich. The living conditions weren't ideal with the small attic and thirteen people in one space. While hiding out the Jews couldn't go outside or they could risk being caught and left to face brutal consequences, but they could go into the garden momentarily to stretch or to get fresh air. While her older sister went out and worked during the day Helena would help the Jews any way she could. She would wash their clothes, bring them food, dump the waste, and water to wash themselves. Although she had to keep providing for the Jews Helena had to be careful that neighbors didn't find out that they were hiding Jews in their home. In order to keep the Jews' presence a secret she would have to deliver food and different times throughout the day and go different places.

In the end the two sisters went down in history. All thirteen of the Jews they hid survived the war in that tiny cramped basement. They kept in touch with all the families and Stefania ended up marrying a man named Josef Burzminski, who had jumped off a boxcar that was taking him to a death camp and ended up walking back to Przemsyl, seeking help from Stefania. In 1961 she moved to the United States with Josef and till this day she is in her 90's and living well, unfortunately Mr. Burzminski passed away on July 17, 2003 and he was 88 years old. What fueled these two young women to put their lives in the line to save these Jews? Was it sympathy or was it they felt it was the right thing to do? They knew their lives were in danger yet they carried through. When we are in threating situations we seem to back away from the problem, run, and never look back. It all comes back to the question, what is a hero? These two souls were willing to help these Jews even though they were strangers, wanted, and looked down upon. They looked conflict in the eye and said, "Bring it." In all the holocaust was a timeline of brutality, but a light was much needed for the Jews and their souls. Would we put our lives on the line, would we face injustice when we see it or would we cower away in fear of being judged and ridiculed?

Through these various events I've learned that if you know what's right then do it. It all comes down to our morals in life and what each of us believe. Should we do what's right just because we know it's right or should we do it because we want to make a difference and see where our choices take us. What do you believe?

"Work Citied"

"United States Holocaust Memorial Museum." United States Holocaust Memorial Museum, United States Holocaust Memorial Museum, www.ushmm.org/. Accessed 27 Feb. 2017.

The Holocaust Martyrs' and Heroes' Remembrance Authority. "'Names of Righteous by Country.'" Www.yadvashem.org/. Accessed 27 Feb. 2017.

Hero by the Numbers

Cara Ishisaka

"Hard times don't create heroes. It is during the hard times when the "hero" within us is revealed" once said by Bob Riley. This quote means that any uncommon person rises up and displays uncommonly noble character no matter how difficult the circumstance they are in may be. On January 30, 1993, Adolf Hitler had become appointed by President Hindenburg as the new Chancellor of Germany. With his power, Hitler had led his army of the Nazi to attack Poland in 1939, starting World War II. He had invaded the Jews because he felt that they were evil and weren't as good as themselves. They moved the citizens of Poland into small, overcrowded areas called ghettos. Here, people couldn't escape and if they tried, they would be executed. After making life hard for the Jewish, Hitler and the Nazi decided to kill all. Some ways the Nazi killed the Jews were putting them in concentration camps and making them work till death or holding them hostage in gas chambers. Because of various terminations, up to 6 million people were killed. This mass slaughter was known as the Holocaust. At the same time, families and other Jewish individuals were able to withdraw from the giant massacre with the "voluntary help" of accomplices.

The accomplices of Poland weren't just ordinary people. Instead they showed themselves as giving his or her life to something bigger than oneself. As mentioned before, uncommon comrades rescued families and citizens. From the random acts of compassion and kindness of these helpers, many Jewish were saved from experiencing more pain from the hardship of Hitler. One aide that helped keep people alive was Adela Domanus. Adela was a young adult who lived with her family in Warsaw, the capital of Poland. Her care was selfless and supported those in greatest need financially. In addition, she saved 6 Jews (living in the Warsaw Ghetto) during the Nazi occupation whether they were strangers or close friends. Although she couldn't hide all of her clients at her home (due to the risks of public censure and blackmail), Adela occupied herself with finding hiding places and getting forged/legal documents for them. The dwellings she found were either in another country or different sites in Europe. As for the forged/legal documents, Adela had her guests use new names and backgrounds so that they didn't get executed for their real identity when they moved to their hiding spot. Adela's considerations towards others had quite an impact on her companions' lives.

Warsaw had the largest ghetto in Europe, holding 375,000 Jews just before the war. This huge center had widespread the significance of Jewish Culture and life in Poland. Unfortunately, when the Germans invaded, Warsaw had grieved from the convulsion. On October 12, 1940, all Jewish residents were enclosed in the Warsaw Ghetto. The ghetto was much more complex than it was before. Nazi had put a wall that was about 10 feet tall, finished with barbed wire and sharply guarded to keep anyone from fleeing. Now you're probably wondering, how did these people escape when there was no exits around? Well, between 1941-1943 underground movements developed underneath all Nazi occupations. In other words, the rescuers like Adela, built escape hatches from the ground to release most of the prisoners.

One of the first people that Adela had saved was her son's girlfriend, Stefania Adler. After her son got Stefania out of the ghetto, Adela had received forged documents for the couple. The son and Stefania had married and hid together, while Adela sheltered Stefania's mother, Helena. Prior to her first tuck away, Adela continued to hide more and more members. The next victims she guarded were Klara Szapiro and her 7-year-old daughter, Nina. These two ladies were brought to Adela during the winter of 1942 by Makary Sieradzki (a friend of Adela's from the underground involvement). During their stay, Adela had found "legal" documents for them, but only located a hiding spot for one. Klara had moved to the Saska Kepa district under the name of Helena Kowalska and Nina stayed with Adela covered by the name Janka Kowalska. Meanwhile during the Warsaw Uprising, Adela looked after a lawyer named K. Metta and his wife. He was transported to Sedziszow and the wife was kept at the sister's place. Even though most of these folks were separated from each other or other relatives, Adela had made sure that they all (including herself) stayed in touch.

In conclusion, Adela's service to her country was a tremendous sacrifice. She showed that it not only takes the time and effort, but it takes courage and compassion to complete the mission. Despite the risks/challenges involved, Adela carried through the process. She didn't fight for her country to just save/rebuild a life or because she was forced too. In her own words, Adela wrote, "My heart bled for all the sympathy and sorrow I felt..." From her back story and her words, Adela was just an ordinary person, until she found the strength to persevere and endure! Because of her heroism, many lives were saved and all of the people whom she helped were all thankful for Adela's help and Adela in general. Sadly, Adela had died on January 1, 1968. In honor of her assistance, Yad VaShem inducted her into the "Names of Righteous by Country" list on May 26, 1989.

Works Cited

"Names of Righteous by Country." Names of Righteous by Country, Yad Vashem, www.yadvashem.org/righteous/statistics. Accessed 26 Feb. 2017.

Urynowicz, Dr. Marcin. "Domanus Adela." Story of Rescue - Domanus Adela | Polscy Sprawiedliwi, Oct. 2015, sprawiedliwi.org.pl/en/stories-of-rescue/story-rescue-domanus-adela. Accessed 26 Feb. 2017.

"Warsaw." Religion Past and Present, doi:10.1163/1877-5888_rpp_sim_224066. Accessed 26 Feb. 2017.

"Warsaw." United States Holocaust Memorial Museum, United States Holocaust Memorial Museum, www.ushmm.org/wlc/en/article.php?ModuleId=10005069. Accessed 26 Feb. 2017.

World War II Heroes

Carson Dorais

During World War II, The Nazi's, led by Adolf Hitler, were trying to capture all of the Jews. He believed that the Jews were responsible for their loss in World War 1 and losing 100,000 German troops. Hitler also blamed them for an economic crisis in Germany and was directly responsible for many of Germany's problems. He targeted them as their main enemy and wanted them all killed. Over 6 million Jews were captured by them. Many of Hitler's people stood by him throughout his cruel battle while he decimated most of the Jewish population. The Nazi's took over a city in Poland called Sieniawa and turned it into a ghetto. Hitler's goal was to wipe out the Jews and have world domination. During the Holocaust, Jews were driven out of the city and put into ghettos which several streets were surrounded by a three meter barbed wire fence. The Nazi's one day announced they needed people to work. The two options were to go to a concentration camp in Pelkinic, or be transported by wagon to the gas chambers of the Belzec camp. After they captured Poland, the Nazi's required the Jews to perform unpaid forced labor. The Nazi's made people believe that they needed people to work, but they just wanted them all killed. In August of 1942, the Sieniawa ghetto was liquidated and the people who were still there were executed by the German militia. Some people tried to hide in the cemetery, but were killed and burned immediately. Although many people were captured from the Sieniawa ghetto, many were saved by the courageous efforts by Michal Mazur and Helena Szelewa-Kurasiewicz.

Michal Mazur and Helena Szelewa-Kurasiewicz worked in a forestry in Rudka, Rzeszow district. Michal worked as a carter, and Helena worked in the kitchens. A. Mankowski, an agricultural engineer, was the leader of the forestry and employed Jews from the Sienisawa ghetto. When the war started, the ghetto was liquidated, and Mankowski suggested they hide in the forestry. In an oral history interview, Michal described that there was fear in the atmosphere in his camp and that he and his family would hear gunshots from a mass killing. He also witnessed German forces killing a young Jewish boy. The leader of his village was ordered by the Germans to organize a manhunt to find Jews that were hiding. He and Helena built them shelter under a cattle shed, and Helena brought them leftovers from the kitchen and milk after she milked the cows.

During the winter months, Michal would let people into his room that was next to the cattle shed to warm up by the stove. He kept them updated on the situation in the region by giving them newspapers, and supplying them with clothes and soap. Leizer and Rubin Braten, Michal's neighbors before the war, were in a fit of depression. He talked them out of committing suicide and promised them that they would not be caught by the Nazi's and that he would help them survive the long war. Upon liberation in 1944, Leizer and Rubin joined the Red Army, and after the war, they migrated to the United States, and kept in contact with Michal and Helena. On September 25, 1986, Yad Vashem recognized Michal Mazur and Helena Szelewa- Kurasiewicz as Righteous Among the Nations.

The Nazi's did many terrible things to people and has affected my life and other people's life personally. I do not understand why Adolf Hitler and his army would want to destroy all of the Jews. His terror has brought much fear to the world, so countries will not allow an army to have domination. The fear they brought to people will make the Nazi's much harder to replicate. After learning about what happened in World War II I want to treat all people with the same respect, and not to criticize anyone by their race or gender. Today when people call someone a Nazi, it is a deep insult, implying the absolute worst in human behavior. Many of the world's government have slowly moved away from their racial superiority. This took an enormous amount of sacrifice, pain, and human effort to make that happen. The story of Michal Mazur and Helena Szelewa-Kurasiewicz saving many Jews from the Sieniawa ghetto has motivated me to always help others when they are in need. Their bravery shows me how difficult it was to survive during World War II and that it was very risky to help Jews out because they could have gotten killed if they were caught. The encouragement Michal brought to the people in the shelter who wanted to commit suicide was inspiring to me that he wanted everyone to survive and helped everyone until the end of the war. It made me step in his shoes and realize how challenging it was to push people to endure hiding in a shelter while they risk their lives. Even though World War II has had many terrible things happen to innocent individuals, many people like Michal Mazur and Helena Szelewa-Kurasiewicz were courageous to help out people from Poland and other countries.

Works Cited:

"Forced Labor: An Overview." United States Holocaust Memorial Museum. United States Holocaust Memorial Museum, n.d. Web. 25 Feb. 2017. <https://www.ushmm.org/wlc/en/article.php?ModuleId=10005180>.

"POLAND." Blackfriars 25.292 (1944): 241-43. Web. 20 Feb. 2017.

"Saving Jews: Polish Righteous." Saving Jews: Polish Righteous. N.p., n.d. Web. 22 Feb. 2017. <http://www.savingjews.org/righteous/mv.htm>.

"What Was Adolf Hitler's Rationale for Hating Jews?" What Was Adolf Hitler's Rationale for Hating Jews? - Quora. N.p., n.d. Web. 25 Feb. 2017. <https://www.quora.com/What-was-Adolf-Hitler%E2%80%99s-rationale-for-hating-Jews>.

"World War II." HistoryNet. N.p., n.d. Web. 23 Feb. 2017. <http://www.historynet.com/world-war-ii>.

John Damski - A Hero

Christian Gong

In 1933 one of the world's most devastating events had begun. Millions of innocent people died, adults, elders, and even infants and children. This horrible tragedy is remembered today remembered as the Holocaust. But because of many true heroes, such as John Damski this catastrophe ended in 1945.

John Damski was born in Germany in 1914 and lived in a small town known as Solec-Kujawski with a small population of about 5000 people. He had two brothers and one sister, John himself, exceeded at track and field, and even placed second nationally for the triple jump. belonged to a local organization known as the Polish Falcons which was a gymnastics organization. He later went on to serve in the polish army in 1939.

In the town that John lived in, there happened to be only one Jewish family, the Daumans. In his early years he was on a team with Jacob Dauman and often had him over for Sunday meals. The team, polish falcons soon fell apart because many of the teachers didn't want help Jews. John, even at his young age beleived then that there was no difference between him and Jacob.

John next met a man named Israelwicz, they had met him while training in 1935 for the Olympic Games in Berlin. Israelwicz was the first to fully open John's eyes to all the unfairness towards Jews. When Isarelwicz came across a sign advertising travel to the U.S. he explained to him that he was unable to receive a passport and was treated differently than other people.

His third encounter with a Jew took place in Gdynia in a night club. After meeting an old school friend they decided to have a few drinks when suddenly his friend blurted out, "Take a look! Those are Jews over there! To hell with the Jews!" Embarrassed, he left the club without his old classmate. He thought about his friends out lash and realized all the hatred direct toward Jews. After these experiences John started to realize what was happening to the Jews, segregation.

While serving in the polish army, John Damski was taken prisoner by the Germans on September 1, 1939. While on the way of being transported to a prisoner camp, John was able to escape. He then returned to Gdynia where he managed a job working a power and water company. Soon after he received a paper demanding all Poles to leave town within the next 24 hours. Three months later when John and his two friends tried to get to Hungary and then hopefully to France, German soldiers caught them and took them back to Gestapo. After being forced to strip down completely, sent them to jail at Sanok, the jail that they were in happened to be for professional people such as doctors and lawyers. There were about 345 men in total they were shoved into cell packed with about 45 other men when the cell was only meant to hold 7-8. On June 13 in the early cracks of dawn, he could hear giant trucks back into the prison yard. He soon figured out that they were loading the truck with the prisoners of war and killing them right outside the border. Eventually they had taken all the prisoners except him, John stayed in the jail. A little bit later he would find out that the Germans had no record of him and didn't know why he was there. The next two hours were spent interrogating him asking how he got here, what he was doing in the town, etc. John explain that his mother tongue was German and that he felt that he was German because of his ability to speak German so fluently. John even said phrases in German that impressed his interrogator. He was later released and was told to leave town immediately. John left town on August 9th weighing only 97 pounds. He continued to Lubin to reconnect with his brother Zygmunt, but because he didn't have enough money for train tickets John would board the train without a ticket. He then got on to the next train and the next until he got to Lubin. There, he met his brother, they both agreed that it would be easiest to survive the war by traveling to a small town, about 80 kilometers away.

Even after John's close encounter he wasn't done, John worked with the Polish Underground State to help bring captives to safety. The Polish Underground State was established in early September, 1939. This Underground State included one of the largest military resistance in the world and had many civilian structures including education, culture and social services. The Polish Underground State received tons of support throughout the war. Many heroes such as John Damski were involved with the state and helped hundreds of people hide behind forged documents or escape the horrific Warsaw ghettos.

John lived a courageous life and we will remember him and many others as true heroes; he went on to save many lives and is an inspiration to many.

Bibliography

https://www.ushmm.org/
www2.humboldt.edu/rescuers/book/damski/johndstory1.html
www2.humboldt.edu/rescuers/book/damski/johndstory2.html
http://articles.latimes.com/1989-09-24/news/vw-28_1_con-men
http://teacher.scholastic.com/frank/stories.htm

Wladyslaw Bartoszewski, the Righteous Pole

Benjamin Delfino

 "All people need heroes-men and women who we can admire and from whom can draw inspiration," said Lawrence Weinbaum. Wladyslaw Bartoszewski is one of these heroic figures that people looked up to. Wladyslaw was born in Warsaw, Poland on February 19, 1922. He was one of the 350,000 Jewish people in Warsaw before World War II, which were the largest population in Europe and the second largest in the whole world. The Nazis invaded Warsaw on September 1, 1939 and took the city over on September 29th. They immediately started closing down shops and schools. The Nazis also made all of the 350 thousand Jewish people wear white armbands with a blue Star of David on it. Not long

after that people started to be shipped off to concentration camps around Poland. Wladyslaw Bartoszewski was one of approximately 300 thousand Jews were deported from Warsaw and most of them went to Auschwitz, These poor men, women, and children were forced to travel about half-way across Poland to where they knew they were going to be treated terribly and might even die. The worst part about these camps besides the killing was little the people were fed. On average the prisoner were only gave 1,125 calories a day, but the average amount of calories burned in a day is 1,600 to 2,500. The Nazis finally retreated out of Warsaw in January 1945 by Russians.

Most people who were deported from Warsaw were sent to Auschwitz concentration camp, including Wladyslaw. Another name for Auschwitz is Auschwitz-Birkenau. Its lifespan was from 1940 to January 27, 1945 when Soviet forces seized the compound. Auschwitz was located in southern Poland and was the largest concentration camp ever built. Other than being the largest camp during World War II Auschwitz was famous for how many people they killed during the little time it was running. More than one million people, mostly Jews, lost their lives there. Most of these people lost their lives in gas chambers. If they weren't killed in the gas chambers, they were forced to be slaves and to manual labor for the government. Also, some were even forced to be subjects to very inhuman experiments. When they weren't being forced to do things they were living in terrible conditions. They were living in very cramped spaces. They lived in small barracks where they could be over 700 people in one place. One barrack was built to fit 52 horses, but they actually held hundreds of people. The beds were either wooden or brick. In one building there were hundreds of three-story bunk beds. Another problem about where they lived is that there was no insulation. Also there was no heating and very little airflow throughout the building. To make things worse it was very dirty and smelled awful because there was no restroom for them to use. To make it worse the prisoners were being starved. If a prisoner didn't do manual labor they would get about 1,300 calories a day, but if they did do manual labor then they got about 1,700 calories a day. Since they are working hard and sweating they were burning a lot more calories than what they were given. Because of this they were very malnourished and after a few weeks they started developing what is called the muzulmen state. Many people died because of this. Just when the inmates thought the end was near 60 thousands of them were evacuated from Auschwitz and relocated elsewhere. They did this because the Soviet Union was closing in on them and in January of 1945 Auschwitz was officially closed the suffering there will hopefully never happen again.

Wladyslaw Bartoszewski was a big part of the fight against the communist regime. A part of that is because he was a main figure in an organization called the Zegota. The group in general is responsible for rescuing and saving 40,000 to 50,000 Jewish people. That wasn't all that Wladyslaw Bartoszewski did to fight against the Nazis and become an inspiration to many. One of the things he did was he was outspoken against the communist regime. During that time very few people did that because they knew that it was very dangerous, but Mr. Bartoszewski only cared about fighting for what is right. The other group that he was part of was the Home Army, also known as the defense of Warsaw. This is an underground group that helped in the rebirth of Poland. Being that Wladyslaw was born and raised in Warsaw it is fitting and courageous that he defended it.

Researching about Wladyslaw Bartoszewski really restored faith in humanity for me. I saw that no matter how hard a time could be you need to fight for what is right. Wladyslaw did that in so many ways. He is someone people should learn from and remember forever. He didn't care about what might happen if he fights for what he believes in. He showed a lot of courage while a lot of people did not. People should learn from this so history won't repeat itself especially now considering what is going on in our country. Because of everything Wladyslaw Bartoszewski did and what he went through he is a hero and a role model.

Bibliography

"Auschwitz-Birkenau: Living Conditions, Labor & Executions." Living Conditions, Labor & Executions at Auschwitz-Birkenau. N.p., n.d. Web. 26 Feb. 2017. <http://www.jewishvirtuallibrary.org/living-conditions-labor-and-executions-at-auschwitz-birkenau>.

"Auschwitz-Birkenau." The Liberation of Auschwitz - January 27, 1945. N.p., n.d. Web. 26 Feb. 2017. <https://www.scrapbookpages.com/AuschwitzScrapbook/History/Articles/Liberation.html>.

"Bartoszewski, Wladyslaw." The Jewish Foundation for the Righteous. N.p., n.d. Web. 26 Feb. 2017. <https://jfr.org/rescuer-stories/bartoszewski-wladyslaw/>.

"Clothing." Auschwitz Concentration The Basics The Historical Timeline Http://www.HolocaustResearchProject.org. N.p., n.d. Web. 26 Feb. 2017. <http://www.holocaustresearchproject.org/othercamps/auschwitzbasics.html>.

History.com Staff. "Auschwitz." History.com. A&E Television Networks, 2009. Web. 26 Feb. 2017. <http://www.history.com/topics/world-war-ii/auschwitz>.

"How Many Calories Does the Average Person Burn in a Day?" Reference. N.p., n.d. Web. 26 Feb. 2017. <https://www.reference.com/health/many-calories-average-person-burn-day-9f3ada7f889b9183>.

"The Legend That Was Wladyslaw Bartoszewski." There's a Jewish Story Everywhere. N.p., n.d. Web. 26 Feb. 2017. <http://www.sdjewishworld.com/2015/05/04/wladyslaw-bartoszewski-zl-righteous-among-nations/>.

United States Holocaust Memorial Museum. United States Holocaust Memorial Museum, n.d. Web. 26 Feb. 2017. <https://www.ushmm.org/information/press/in-memoriam/wladyslaw-bartoszewski>.

"Warsaw." United States Holocaust Memorial Museum. United States Holocaust Memorial Museum, n.d. Web. 26 Feb. 2017. <https://www.ushmm.org/wlc/en/article.php?ModuleId=10005069>.

Zofia Bania

Balin Albers

During the Holocaust, there were many points of view toward the Jewish community. Some were innocent bystanders, some believed that this was the right thing to do, and some believed that they would benefit from their neighbor's abandoned property. There was a very small minority of bystanders that resisted against the Germans and the rounding up and murdering of innocent Jews. One of the most common acts of resistance was keeping wanted Jews hidden with them on their property or in their home. Those who wished to do this had to really care because it was a very risky "business". If one of these people were found hiding a Jew in or around their home, the penalty could be as severe as death. There may have been only few who were willing to sacrifice their lives and homes to do what is civil to one another, but every person counted, because a person is a person no matter what their beliefs are.

A hero is someone who has given his or her life to something bigger than oneself", said Joseph Campbell, a famous American mythologist and writer. In many ways, Zofia Bania of Poland easily fits this category of heroism. Zofia Bania, a poor farm owner near the village of Włochy, lives in her tiny one-roomed home with her husband Ludwig and her 6-year-old son Maniek. From time to time, she travelled to the town of Pińczów to buy basic farming goods from a small shop owned and operated by Israel and Franciszka (Frania) Rubinek. Zofia was a poor farmer, so she paid for what she could in money and then used

food and other things and credit. Israel and Frania were married in Pińczów in 1941, while the town was already under German occupation. After overhearing rumors about what has been happening to the Jews elsewhere, Israel decided it would be smart to build a bunker underneath their shop. When the Germans came around and started rounding up the Jews to take them to concentration camps, Israel and Frania hid in the bunker. They couldn't flee to Russia like others who had the opportunity because Frania was eight months pregnant, so Zofia sent a trusted friend to pick up the two and take them to her farm. She had them stay the hay loft of the barn, which was connected to the side of her house. Ludwig was not on board with this plan. Frania and Israel had to pay him for his silence and help. Her house was on the outskirts of Włochy, nearly half a kilometer from the closest neighbor, so it was a good, safe place to hide out. When it was time for the baby to be born in December of 1942, it had to be delivered in the loft with only the assistance of Zofia and Israel. Sadly, the baby died shortly after birth. With Frania's pregnancy out of the picture, they continued to stay with Zofia. Then one night, towards the end of the war, the family guard dog that Ludwig bought as an extra precaution began to bark at something. It was a group of German soldiers, who demanded that they stay the night on Zofia's property for the night. If it weren't for the dog, Israel and Frania would not have been able to sneak from the loft to the cellar used for storing potatoes. Zofia moved Maniek's bed over the entrance, so it could not be seen. If they had been found by the Germans they probably would have been sent to the camps or just killed then and there. Luckily for the couple, Maniek understood the situation, and stayed quiet about the whole thing. Israel had been having a cough recently, so he kept coughing through the night. To cover this up, Maniek began to cough and cry to cover up the sound of Israel's coughing, which ended up saving the couple's lives. Israel and Frania lived with the Zofia, Ludwig and Maniek for a few more years, until the Red Army liberated the area in January of 1945. After World War 2 the Rubineks fled to Canada. Many years later in 1986, the family returned to Poland to visit Zofia with their son Saul, who was a movie director. On August 16, 2011, Yad Vashem recognized Zofia Bania as Righteous Among the Nations, just like many others from Poland.

Heroism during the holocaust was seen in many ways. It could be a simple act of rebellion, such as art or speech, or it can be big and complex, like hiding people in houses and smuggling people out of camps. Heroism is also outlined by the amount of risk involved in rebelling. If there is no risk, then there is no reward. In Ludwig, Maniek, and Zofia Bania's case, the risk was big and the reward was bigger. By taking a leap of faith and letting Frania and Israel into her home, she ended up saving their lives, even if it meant death for everyone if they were caught. Not everyone is recognized as Righteous, but Zofia's open heart and mind ended up getting just that, and she deserved it.

Bibliography

"Zofia Bania." Yad Vashem. N.p., n.d. Web. 27 Feb. 2017.
< http://db.yadvashem.org/righteous/family.html?language=en&itemId=9358834 >.

Maria Kotarba,

Ashley Magley

Maria Kotarba was held in Auschwitz concentration camp from 1943 to 1945.

 Auschwitz was opened in 1940 in Southern Poland. Auschwitz was the largest Nazi concentration camp and held about 1.3 million people from 1940-1945. About 1.1 million people were killed in Auschwitz and only 144 people in Auschwitz escaped successfully without being caught. Before Auschwitz was a concentration camp, it was a detention site for political prisoners. There were 3 parts to Auschwitz two parts held Jewish prisoners that were forced to help build and extend the camp and one part was where most of the Jews were murdered. The first building started being built in 1940. The second building started being made in October 1941 and the third building started being made in October 1942. The very first prisoners were transferred from the Sachsenhausen concentration camp to Auschwitz. In 1945 Maria was transported to Ravensbruck. It was the second largest women's camp with over 50,000 prisoners in 1945. They started building Ravensbruck in November 1938 and it was located 50 miles north of

the city of Berlin. The women prisoners came from 30 different countries, but most of them came from Poland. Only women guards could oversee the prisoners held in the camp.

Maria Kotarba was a Catholic, who was born on September 4, 1907 in Nowy Sacz, Poland. Maria saw her Jewish neighbors being killed and taken away to camps and she wanted to help any Jew possible, so she joined a local armed resistance as a courier. In the resistance her job was to steal clandestine messages, food and medicine. Once she was caught and was arrested she was brought to Auschwitz concentration camp as a political prisoner. In Auschwitz, Maria worked in the garden. One Jew she helped save was named Lena Mankowska, who was born on November 20, 1922 in Warsaw. Maria and Lena met when Lena was taking sick prisoners to the infirmary and Maria pretended to be sick so she could steal medicine and gave it to the prisoner-doctors for sick Jews in the camp. Maria stole medicines so often that eventually she and Lena got to know each other. There were many times when Maria saved Lena's life. There was a time when Lena was supposed to be quarrying gravel. This task would have killed her, but thankfully Maria was able to get her an easier job. Another time Lena had a sickness called typhus and Maria made her soup with some of the vegetables she stole from the SS garden she was forced to tend. Another time she also spotted Lena almost dead in the snow while she was on the death march to Ravensbruck concentration camp and carried her back to give her food and water. Lena thought of Maria as her mother because of all the nurturing she did for her. Maria also cared for Lena's sister in the concentration camp. On January 1945 Maria and Lena were sent to Ravensbruck. Maria found a place for them to stay in the French part of the barracks. Then they were transported to Neustadt-Glewein in February 1945. The Red Army liberated their concentration camp on May 2, 1945 and they were separated from each other when Maria went home to Poland and Lena ended up in Britain. Maria died on December 30, 1956. Lena tried to contact Maria after their separation but it wasn't until 1977 that she found out that she had died. Maria Kotarba was recognized as a Polish hero in September 2005.

World War II started because Germany started to establish some of their countries that they owned before World War I. Britain and France were leading Europe at the time and gave Hitler territory to avoid war. Hitler was the leader of Nazi Germany. Hitler and the German Army invaded Poland in 1939, causing World War II to officially start when Great Britain and France declared war against Germany. In 1941, the Nazis attacked the Soviet Union which broke the non-aggression agreement between the two countries and this attack brought Russia in to the war. Japan and America got into the war when the U.S placed an embargo on Japan. In retaliation Japan bombed Pearl Harbor causing America to declare war on Japan on December 8, 1941. During World War II Germany also invaded Denmark, France, Norway, the Netherlands, and Luxembourg. During the course of World War II Germany also defeated Greece and Yugoslavia. Hitler and the Nazis targeted Jews and Gypsies because he thought they were an "evil race" and he blamed them for losing World War I.

During this study I learned that during World War II millions of people were murdered because the Nazis targeted the Jews. During this time more people should have helped to try to save Jews and stick up for them just like Maria and more Poland heroes did. Everything you do to help makes a difference whether it is big or small. If more people did small helpful things less Jews would have been murdered during this time period. I also learned that it is important for everyone to learn about what happened so history is not repeated and another group of people are targeted.

Work Cited

"Auschwitz." United States Holocaust Memorial Museum. United States Holocaust Memorial Museum, n.d. Web. 28 Feb. 2017.
< https://www.ushmm.org/wlc/en/article.php?ModuleId=10005189 >.
"POLAND." Blackfriars 25.292 (1944): 241-43. Yadvashem. Web. 28 Feb. 2017.
< http://www.yadvashem.org/yv/pdf-drupal/poland.pdf >.

To Hide a Jew

Anthony Garcia

The definition of a hero is "a person noted for courageous acts or nobility of character." "The Holocaust was the systematic, bureaucratic, state-sponsored persecution and murder of six million Jews by the Nazi regime and its collaborators." (USHMM) There were many people in Poland that helped Jews hide after they escaped from a ghetto. Though there were definitely more people that needed to be saved and would do anything to be safe. In a ghetto Nazis (police) would shoot people because they were Jewish, there would be dead bodies on the streets and it was so common that people would just keep walking. You were extremely lucky if you escaped from a ghetto, and it wasn't easy. It took a lot of bravery which would be hard if you were trying to escape with your family. It also took bravery for the people who hid the Jews because they were risking everything that they had for the safety of others lives.

My person's name is Jozef Balwierz and he was one of the people that hid a family in his house after they escaped from a ghetto. He was born in 1919 and his death date is unknown. During the war he lived in Krakow, Poland. He opened his home to the Liebeskind family and he cared for them every way he could. Shmuel Liebeskind owned a factory the Jozef worked at. Shmuel had a wife and two daughters, but when the war arrived to Lwow the Liebeskind family was put in a ghetto. Unfortunately, while they were in the ghetto Shmuel was killed but his wife, Zofia, and two daughters managed to escape from the ghetto. They somehow got a hold of Jozef and then he took them in and aided them. He also helped two women named Irena and Elka Bardach who escaped Lwow and boarded a train to Krakow. She got off the stain a stop before, to avoid the check that awaited her at the end. She then found Jozef's home and stayed there for three weeks until she could secure a job as a housekeeper with a German family in Krakow. When the situation got worse the Liebeskinds and Balwierz went to work in Austria together. After the war Jozef Balwierz married Irena Liebeskind, and they went back to Poland. They later moved to Brazil. When he was asked about his honorable acts during the war he said that it was his "human duty". (Yad Vashem) He didn't act selfish towards any of his acts because he didn't expect or want an award for the Jewish women that he saved.

It's not every day that you think of a hero but when you do, you think of capes and powers or unnatural things but that's what it takes to be a hero. Going back to the beginning a hero takes courage and noble acts, but even more it takes a kind heart. I believe that there are many heroes in the world and there are many that did what Jozef Balwierz did but I thought it amazing what he did for those 4 Jewish women. I know it seems selfish but I would probably be too scared to hide those women because I wouldn't want to be killed. It scares me because I know it wasn't right away but back then Jews were being killed for being Jewish. The crazy thing is everything was organized. They filed every dead body and where it was being sent. Now our president is educated, rich, and many things he says don't sound very smart. Just imagine what he could do especially because he is rich. Now I'm not saying that he will do anything bad but lots of things are possible. Though I can say I am proud to be alive in this period of time because we have passed many tragedies and segregation which is extremely good progress and I don't even know how lucky I am.

I'm sure that anyone who did research on Jozef Balwierz would say he is a hero and that he could represent the definition of it. I'm really glad that I chose him for my project because even though there was only about a half a page of information about, I found very inspiring. Knowing myself I would be too scared to hide basically wanted people in my basement because I would be too afraid of the consequences and I wouldn't want to die. It was a cool experience writing this paper. I for some reason actually wanted to write it. I was not sure if it was just because of the prize money or something else but something drove me to want to write this paper and I did. It really made it easier for me to have a character like Jozef because he was very interesting and I wish I could learn more about him because I didn't know anything about him or his family. Like I didn't know if he had parents and siblings or any friends growing up but that would have been nice to know. This was a great adventure to learn about the Holocaust and the harsh things that people had to go through and I feel horrible but I am just so blessed to live in this time. Thank you for your time and I hope you enjoyed.

Works Cited

"The Righteous Among The Nations." Yad Vashem - Request Rejected, Yad Vashem, db.yadvashem.org/righteous/family.html?language=en&itemId=6231833. Accessed 27 Feb. 2017. /.latest_citation_text

"Introduction to the Holocaust." United States Holocaust Memorial Museum, United States Holocaust Memorial Museum, www.ushmm.org/search/results/?q=what%2Bis%2Bthe%2Bholocaust. Accessed 27 Feb. 2017. /.latest_citation_text

True Heroes in Poland

Clayton Ketcher

World War II was the deadliest conflict of all time, with over 60 million people killed in total. Over 6 million of those 60 million died in the Holocaust, a mass murder of Jews across Europe, most prominently in Germany and Poland. Jews were being hunted and killed by the Germans during this massacre that began as early as 1933. They had two options: running away and trying to escape the massive army of Germany, or hiding in homes of other people. Many people decided to both protest the war and save the lives of Jews by housing them and hiding them from the Germans. Helping Jews during World War II was very risky business. From September 1942 onwards, the death penalty would be issued by the Germans for anyone caught helping out Jews. Despite this, many families still housed Jewish families who were hiding. One of these families were the Ulmas. Jozef and Wiktoria made a living working on their farm, and in addition Jozef photographed and documented much of his family, and their life on the farm. They lived in Markowa, a small village in Southeastern Poland in the county of Lancut. This was a very rural area where other families were hiding Jews. The Ulmas had already seen what would happen if they were hiding Jews; in summer 1942 many Jews were killed in front of their own eyes. However in late 1942 the Ulmas agreed to hide the Szall family along with two other Jews despite what could happen if they did get caught. The story of the Ulmas is ultimately inspiring, and it shows the true heroism it took to hide Jews in the face of death.

The Ulmas agreed to let the Jews hide in their home during late 1942, by which time both Germans and even residents of Poland were trying to find Jews. According to one of the Ulma's neighbors, "[The Jews they were housing] never hid in particular, since all of them were busy helping to run [the] farm." Jozef and Wiktoria hid them for nearly 18 months before the Jews' location was discovered. It is likely that a policeman that had helped them out earlier in their journey tipped off the Germans, and they came to the house of Jozef and Wiktoria Ulma on the night of March 23, 1944. They ambushed the Ulma's home and killed all the Jews they were hiding. After they shot the Jews, they proceeded to execute Jozef and Wiktoria, proceeded by their six children. The day after the Ulmas and the Jews they were housing were murdered, over 20 Jewish corpses were found in the village of Markowa. These people were killed by the people who were housing them out of fear for their own lives, even though some of them had been helping the Jews for over two years. However, others still continued to shelter Jews from the Germans despite the risk of death.In conclusion, the Ulmas were extremely heroic people who decided to protest the Holocaust by helping out Jews at the cost of their own lives.

The Ulmas are a perfect learning example that everyone should aspire to be like. They agreed to hide a Jewish family well knowing the consequences that were coming if they were caught. The reason they helped these people is because they did not approve of what Hitler was doing. In a day and age with so much controversy and uncertainty surrounding nearly everything that we do, it is ever more important for people to stand up for what they believe in. Jozef and Wiktoria Ulma were true heroes because they not only helped to save lives, but they stood up for what they believed was right while doing so. They would not have taken in the Jews if they believed the Holocaust was a good thing; they would have simply turned them in to the police. Likewise today so many people are standing up for what they believe in, such as all the marches that happened nationwide and the protests that are occurring. The reason the Holocaust ended was because of people like Jozef and Wiktoria- these people resisted the Germans and protested by helping out the Jews who were being hunted down. If these people had not helped out, there would be nothing to stop the Germans from essentially wiping out all the Jews in Europe. This is extremely relatable to today because people do not support some things the president is doing, so they are resisting by holding protests and being very vocal about their opinions. In addition I can relate to what the Ulmas did because like everyone, there are things that I disagree with. Once again like other people, I don't just stand around and let something that I don't like just slide past; I take action and try to change it. Overall, the Ulmas were the essence of what a hero is; they showed that even normal people living seemingly "boring" lives can help change the world. In the dark and awful time that was the Holocaust, Jozef and Wiktoria Ulma were truly amazing people that paid the ultimate price- their lives.

Works Cited

Martyrs' and Heroes' Remembrance Authority. "Names of Rightous by Country." Yad Vashem. N.p., n.d. Web. 27 Feb. 2017.

Poray, Anna. "Saving Jews: Polish Righteous." Saving Jews: Polish Righteous. N.p., n.d. Web.

27 Feb. 2017.

A Survivor's Voice

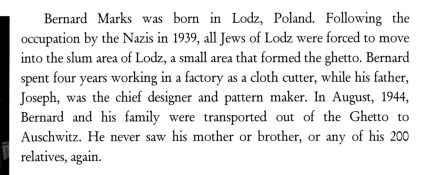

Bernard Marks was born in Lodz, Poland. Following the occupation by the Nazis in 1939, all Jews of Lodz were forced to move into the slum area of Lodz, a small area that formed the ghetto. Bernard spent four years working in a factory as a cloth cutter, while his father, Joseph, was the chief designer and pattern maker. In August, 1944, Bernard and his family were transported out of the Ghetto to Auschwitz. He never saw his mother or brother, or any of his 200 relatives, again.

When he and his father arrived at the selection ramp in Auschwitz, Joseph presented his young son's work permit and Gestapo registration to an S.S. officer to prove that Bernard had been working for the German government in the Ghetto. The officer then permitted Bernard to join his father at the selection ramp; both were assigned to work commandos in the Auschwitz/Birkenau camp. Later, it was learned that his father had been speaking to Dr. Mengele, the infamous doctor who performed hideous medical experiments on twins in Auschwitz.

Soon, Bernard and Joseph were transferred to the Dachau concentration camp and then to one of sub-camps to work as slave laborers building the Weingut II Bunker, an underground factory which was designed to produce Germany's ME262 jet planes. Beginning April, 1945 Bernard contracted Typhoid fever in camp Hurlach. (Kauferig IV)

On April 27, 1945, Bernard and his father were liberated by the U.S. Army 12th Armored Division. Bernard spent the next two years in Bavaria attending high school, trade schools, and university to catch up on studies he had missed during the five years living under the brutal Nazi regime.

Bernard Marks immigrated to Kansas City, Mo., in 1947 where he graduated for the second time from high school. He served in the US Army in Europe and Korea and was awarded the Army's Presidential Unit Citation, the Korean Presidential Citation and two Bronze Stars for bravery. He recently received a special medal from the President of Korea for the work he did with the local population, especially with children in need of medical attention.

Following his military service, Bernard graduated from Finley Engineering College in Kansas City, Mo., with a degree in Electrical/Nuclear Engineering.

In 1954, Bernard moved to Sacramento to work for the Aerojet General Corporation as a senior engineer on the Delta Rocket for the moon landing, Titan I and II ballistic missiles and various other research projects for both military and civilian applications.

Currently, Bernard is semi-retired as an environmental engineer, widowed, with two daughters and four grand children. In 2008, after 66 years of waiting for the right time and the right place, he finally achieved his goal of having a Bar Mitzvah at Congregation B'nai Israel., Sacramento.

Every year, Mr. Marks travels around the world to give presentations about the Holocaust from his first-hand perspective.

Bernie served for many years as President of B'nai Brith David Lubin Lodge, he is also a PP of Central California B'nai Brith District Grand Lodge #4, a recipient of the coveted AKIBA AWRD for community service.

Served in the U.S. Army with SHAEF Hdq. European theater as a translater and witness to the Dachau Trials. Also, served in Korea/Japan in the medical field. Recipient of the special Korean Presidential Medal for the work with children during the conflict. Recipient of many military medals including 2 bronze stars and the U. S. Presidential Unit Citation

Eleanor (Ellie), Bernie's wife of 56 years, passed away on April 15th, 2008. She served as President of B'nai B'rith Women, Sacramento Chapter #15.

Their daughters are active in Temple Beth El Sisterhood in Fresno, California.

Acknowledgments

I hereby wish to truly thank the teachers who encouraged their students to write these essays, the judging committee and proof-readers, editors and anyone else who helped with this project.

Judging Committees

Chief Judge: Nadine Muench

Finance Operation, Leadership for Verizon Corporate

Senior Rabbi Mona Alfi, Congregation B'nai Israel, Sacramento, California

Danise Crevin

Education Administrator Congregation B¹nai Israel Sacramento, California

Margo LaBayne . Has lived in Elk Grove , California for the past 6 years with her husband and two children is working for the Elk Grove Unified School District for the past 3 1/2 years .

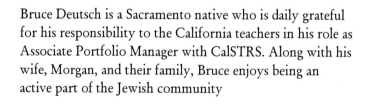

Bruce Deutsch is a Sacramento native who is daily grateful for his responsibility to the California teachers in his role as Associate Portfolio Manager with CalSTRS. Along with his wife, Morgan, and their family, Bruce enjoys being an active part of the Jewish community

Erica is a California State credentialed teacher. She taught at the elementary school level for ten years in Los Angeles before starting her family and moving to Sacramento. She is currently staying at home with her 3 year old daughter Lilah and 1 year old son Gavin. Erica's educational background includes a Bachelor of Arts in Liberal Studies with a Concentration in Art and a Master's degree in Educational Administration, both from California State University, Northridge.

Bina Lefkovic -- Bina Lefkovitz, has worked in various capacities in the youth and community development fields for the past 35 years. Her expertise is in policy, program and partnership development, community planning and youth development. Currently she is part time faculty at CSUS, and consults with organizations on youth engagement strategies.

Brie Bajar has been teaching at B'nai Israel Congregation since 2010, and is a Middle School administrator during the week. She lives in Elk Grove, California with her husband Billy and son Ethan. She enjoys reading, practicing Yoga, and spending time with family and friends

Chuck Rosenberg Retired for five years. Former school psychologist for 26 years

Laura Mahoney, Staff Correspondent for Bloomberg News

Abbie Blackman is a Sacramento native and long-time member of Congregation B'nai Israel. After many years working in politics, she shifted gears to pursue more creative endeavors; teaching art and dabbling in graphic design. She and her husband Andrew, along with their two curious teenage daughters, enjoy movies, sports, theater and a black lab named Ziggy.

Christina Stevenson is an English Instructor at San Francisco Art Institute and Cosumnes River College. She also teaches beginning English to refugee families at Sacramento Food Bank and Family Services. Mostly, however, she spends her time raising two wonderful boys.

Sheila Budman taught grades 6-8 for 20+ years while also working as a writing specialist and presenter for the Area III Writing Project at UC Davis and SJUSD. A voracious reader, theatergoer, writer of light verse and collector of cookbooks, Sheila lives in Fair Oaks with Ken, her husband of 54 years. They have 2 sons, an editor and a musician.

Anita Warmack is a teacher for the Sacramento City Unified School District. She has taught Parent Education Preschool for 30 years, working with young children and their families.

Janet Stites teaches Religion, Performing Arts, and Science at St. Francis Elementary School in Sacramento, California. She has been teaching there for 12 fabulous years.

Rachel Stern is a member of the California Juvenile Parole Board. Prior to this she was staff counsel at the California Department of Corrections and Rehabilitation, working on improving the treatment and conditions of confinement for juvenile criminal offenders in state custody. She, her husband Eric, and their two sons live in Sacramento.

Eric Stern is a budget manager at the California Department of Finance. He previously worked for the Little Hoover Commission, and before that was a newspaper reporter and editor in three states, primarily covering state politics and government. He, his wife Rachel, and their two sons live in Sacramento.

Stephen Prunier of Carmichael, California is a member of Congregation B'nais Israel along with his wife Jody and 3 sons: Hudson, Harris and Holden. He is Group Counsel for Guardian Life Insurance Company.

Jody Schwab Prunier, MSW, JD is a retired Assistant District Attorney from Worcester, MA and trained mediator. She is currently a stay-at-home mother and volunteer at-large in the local community.

Nicholle Collins works for human resources at the DMV. In her spare time she enjoys spending time with her daughter and playing drums.

Nick Collins works for the registration department at DMV. He enjoys playing guitar and spending Ike with his family

Matthew Archer, Professor of Anthropology at Sierra College, Rocklin, CA. Graduate of UCLA and UT-Austin.

Mahala Archer has been an educator for 20 years having worked as a teacher, administrator, consultant and researcher primarily focusing on issues of literacy, curriculum reform, and equity. Mahala graduated with an environmental science degree from UCLA and has a Master's in education from UC Berkeley.

Laurel Rosenhall. Current CAL matters graduate UC Berkley School of Journalism, correspondent Sacramento Bee, correspondent Los Angeles Times.

Susan Orton Attorney, retired

Zlata Arestova Mechanical Engineer, Graphic Designer

Jody Cooperman- I have been teaching 8th grade English and U.S. history at Sutter Middle School for teen years. My commitment to teaching about the Holocaust came as a result of poorly it was done in our anthology book. I have been on a quest to learn more ever since. Currently a fellow for the Central Valley Holocaust Educators Network and U.C. Davis. Have studied at the United States Holocaust Memorial Museum, Museum of Tolarance and USC's Shoah Foundation. The underlying theme throughout my teaching is "What You Do Matters." I challenge my students to go deeper in their thinking during study.

Mandy Greene, Administrator, Congregation B'nai Israel, Sacramento, CA. Now retired.

 Steven Millner, Vice President, US Bank, Rancho Cordova, CA

 Rachel Zerbo, Public Health Educator

 Joel Schwartz, Senior Research Analyst, California State University, Sacramento

 Rachael Horsley -- State Water Resources Control Board, Associate Governmental Program Analyst

 Elaine Hussey has taught about The Holocaust for over ten years. She studied with the Museum of Tolerance in Los Angeles, and received a Fellowship to study at Yad Vashem. She primarily taught middle school children, and more recently has been giving lectures to adult study groups.

 B. Carl Miller – Teacher/Author/Researcher

 John Jackson – Retired teacher, California General Contractor, Music Lover and Member of Congregation B'nai Israel choir and two other choirs.

Jana Stewart is a Jewish artist and mom of three. She is an Autism advocate with a love of Torah, running, and all things Star Trek.

Sara O'Connor. Wife, mother, dog trainer and therapist with hobbies of gardening and golf. BA, MA and some doctoral work. Native Californian with roots in So California and Far No California.

Julie Schiffman. Born in New York City and relocated to San Diego at age 13, Julie Schiffman currently works as an Air Pollution Specialist at the California Air Resources Board in Sacramento. She graduated cum laude with a bachelor's degree in Applied Mathematics from UC San Diego and holds a master's degree in Transportation, Technology, and Policy from UC Davis. Julie and her family are members of Congregation B'nai Israel.

Tami Nelson has been teaching middle school for 14 years. She is also an elected trustee with the Los Rios Community College school board. Tami enjoys traveling with her family, reading, and trying new foods.

Ari Colondres, M.A.

Reading and Literacy Leadership Specialist

Greg Grunwald was born August 5th, 1980. He currently works as a teacher's aid and owns a small business. His grandparents, uncles, great aunts and aunt were holocaust survivors from Berlin, Germany.

Shayna L. Horwitz earned her B.A, in American Studies and B.S. in Human Services from Cal State University, Fullerton in Southern California. She currently is a full-time preschool teacher at Shalom School in Sacramento. She also teaches 3rd grade Hebrew and Religious School on Sundays at Congregation B'nai Israel in Sacramento. She is passionate about spending time with her family, learning new things, and engaging in tikkun olam.

Davita Levin-Robinson. I am originally from Skokie, Illinois and have lived in Sacramento since 2004. In 1995 I received my B.S from University of Wisconsin-Madison and then in 1999 my Master of Social Work from Virginia Commonwealth University. I am quite active in the Jewish Community including being on the Board of Trustees at Congregation B'nai Israel. My husband and I have two children ages 7 and 11 who attend Shalom School.

Brooke Steurer-Lopiccolo is an educator of young minds by day. In her free time you can find her in the garden, reading a book, or having creative adventures with her family.

Maya Colondres: I teach because I believe education is a way to build knowledge, compassion and confidence in our future generations. "Educating the mind without educating the heart is no education at all." ~ Aristotle

Larry Friedman, a retired labor lawyer is a native New Yorker. Among his current projects he is spending time with his new grandson.

I am most appreciative to all the teachers and the judging committee for their dedication and work with the students from the many schools who contributed essays to this volume.

I am also greatly appreciative to the Editors and Translators listed below.

Laura Mahoney, Staff Correspondent for Bloomberg News

Abbie Blackman is a Sacramento native and long-time member of Congregation B'nai Israel. After many years working in politics, she shifted gears to pursue more creative endeavors; teaching art and dabbling in graphic design.

Christina Stevenson is an English Instructor at San Francisco Art Institute and Cosumnes River College. She also teaches beginning English to refugee families at Sacramento Food Bank and Family Services. Mostly, however, she spends her time raising two wonderful boys.

Sheila Budman taught grades 6-8 for 20+ years while also working as a writing specialist and presenter for the Area III Writing Project at UC Davis and SJUSD. Sheila lives in Fair Oaks with Ken, her husband of 54 years. They have 2 sons, an editor and a musician.

Anita Warmack is a teacher for the Sacramento City Unified School District. She has taught Parent Education Preschool for 30 years, working with young children and their families.

Janet Stites teaches Religion, Performing Arts, and Science at St. Francis Elementary School in Sacramento, California. She has been teaching there for 12 fabulous years.

Nina Bochilo – Library Assistant, Sacramento Public Library, Russian Translator

Ken Chau – Library Assistant, Sacramento Public Library/ Chinese Translator

Elise Huggins – Teacher/French Translator

David Ayotte – Librarian/French Translator

Celine Sankar CPA retired -/French translators.

Bernard Marks - Author/Russian, German, French
Translator

I am also greatly appreciative to the proof-readers listed above. And thanks to the
Sacramento Public Library's I Street Press and Gerald Ward who helped assemble and
publish all Volumes of these essays.

Gerald F. Ward, Librarian, Sacramento Public Library,
I Street Press

Former Judges

Jessica Braverman-Birch , Don Burns, Ilene Carroll , Melissa Chapman , Wendy Fischer, Teena-Marie Gordon , Rabbi Shoshanah D. King-Tornberg, Tuula Laine, Shirley Lange, Rabbi Michal Loving, Wendy Miller, Ann Owens, Bonnie Penix, Elissa Provance , Susan Ross, Sara Sault, Frank Severson, Katherine Severson, Tom Tolley, Gary Townsend, Heather Wilde, Leslie Wilde, Laine Josphson, Joel Gruen, Shoshana Steel, Carolyn Brokshire, J. Gordon Dean, Bernie Goldberg, Geoff Rohde, James Scott, Joe Spink, Roxana Puerner